world development report 2007

Development and the Next Generation

world development report 2007

Development and the Next Generation

THE WORLD BANK
Washington, DC

Cover design by Chris Lester of Rock Creek Creative, Inc.

Typesetting by Precision Graphics.

Printed in the United States by Quebecor World USA, Inc.

Cover images by Paul Olaja. Paul is a 19-year-old artist studying at Kyambogo University in Kampala, Uganda. In his paintings, Paul represents the many facets of youth: youth performing as a way to share their rich culture, working hard to survive, and growing into their adult roles. He depicts the central role of women, the tremendous diversity in the world and how young people strive to become a part of it. In his own words "youth need to do something for the world to hold it up."

As a teenager, Paul lost his parents to HIV/AIDS. Art is Paul's passion, and his goal is to use art to share the stories of his homeland and to help other young people in need in Africa.

Softcover
ISBN-10: 0-8213-6541-X
ISBN-13: 978-0-8213-6541-0
ISSN: 0163-5085
eISBN-10: 0-8213-6542-8
eISBN-13: 978-0-8213-6542-7
DOI: 10.1596/978-0-8213-6541-0

Hardcover
ISBN-10: 0-8213-6549-5
ISBN-13: 978-0-8213-6549-6
ISSN: 0163-5085
eISBN-10: 0-8213-6550-9
eISBN-13: 978-0-8213-6550-2
DOI: 10.1596/978-0-8213-6549-6

Contents

Part III   Across transitions and next steps   **187**

Boxes

Figures

Tables

Foreword

The time has never been better to invest in young people living in developing countries—that is the message of this year's *World Development Report*, the twenty-ninth in the series. The number of people worldwide aged 12–24 years has reached 1.3 billion, the largest in history. It is also the healthiest and best educated—a strong base to build on in a world that demands more than basic skills.

Today's youth are tomorrow's workers, entrepreneurs, parents, active citizens, and, indeed, leaders. And, because of falling fertility, they will have fewer children than their parents as they move through adulthood. This in turn may boost growth—by raising the share of the population that is working and by boosting household savings. Rich and poor countries alike need to seize this opportunity before the aging of societies closes it. Doing so will enable them to grow faster and reduce poverty even further.

This Report examines five pivotal phases of life that can help unleash the development of young people's potential with the right government policies: learning, working, staying healthy, forming families, and exercising citizenship. Within each of these transitions, governments need not only to increase investments directly but also to cultivate an environment for young people and their families to invest in themselves. The Report identifies three policy directions for helping youth develop themselves and contribute to society: *expanding opportunities, enhancing capabilities,* and *providing second chances.*

Investing in young people strongly contributes to the Bank's overarching mission of fighting poverty. At the same time, investing in young people is a challenge for governments in all countries, rich and poor. It is my hope that this Report contributes to addressing this challenge by sharing the experiences of countries where young people, supported by good policies and institutions, have been able not only to cope but to flourish—and in the process, contribute to a future of hope and opportunity for all generations.

Paul Wolfowitz
President
World Bank Group

Acknowledgments

This Report has been prepared by a core team led by Emmanuel Y. Jimenez and comprising Jean Fares, Varun Gauri, Mattias K. A. Lundberg, David McKenzie, Mamta Murthi, Cristobal Ridao-Cano, and Nistha Sinha. The team was assisted by Amer Hasan, Sarojini Hirshleifer, Natsuko Kiso, and Annette Richter, all of whom also contributed to drafting parts of the Report, as well as Mehmet Ziya Gorpe, Claudio E. Montenegro, and Victor Sulla. Additional contributions were made by Deon Filmer, Paul Gertler, Elizabeth King, and Peter Orazem. The work was conducted under the general guidance of François Bourguignon and Jean-Louis Sarbib. Extensive and excellent advice (including help in preparing background papers) was received from Jere Behrman, Robert Blum, David Lam, and Cynthia Lloyd, to whom the team is grateful without implication.

Many others inside and outside the World Bank provided inputs and helpful comments (see the bibliographic note). The Development Data Group contributed to the data appendix and was responsible for the Selected World Development Indicators. The team would also like to acknowledge the generous support of a multidonor programmatic trust fund, the Knowledge for Change Program. Additional support was also provided by the Hewlett Foundation and the governments of Denmark, Germany, Japan, Sweden, and the United Kingdom.

The team benefited greatly from a wide range of consultations managed by Maya Brahmam, Stephen Commins, Viviana Mangiaterra, Juan Felipe Sanchez, Gerold Thilo Vollmer, and Kavita Watsa. Consultations included events and workshops held in 26 developing countries and a few developed countries in Europe, North America, and Asia, as well as online discussions of the draft. The team wishes to thank participants in these workshops, videoconferences, and discussions, which included staff in country offices, researchers, government officials, staff of nongovernmental and private sector organizations and, of course, the young people themselves. Particularly noteworthy were the efforts in the three countries "spotlighted" in this Report: Brazil, Sierra Leone, and Vietnam.

Rebecca Sugui served as senior executive assistant to the team, Ofelia Valladolid as program assistant, and Jason Victor as team assistant. Evangeline Santo Domingo served as resource management assistant.

Bruce Ross-Larson was the principal editor. Book design, editing, and production were coordinated by the World Bank's Office of the Publisher under the supervision of Dana Vorisek, Susan Graham, Andrés Meneses, and Randi Park.

Methodological Note

Writing about young people

One of the biggest challenges in writing this Report was that the evidence base was uneven. Data to carry out diagnostic analysis for some topics, such as youth citizenship and migration, were limited. More importantly, there were very few rigorous evaluations of youth programs and policies for any of the transitions and issues covered in the Report. To help address these gaps, the team used consultations and surveys, as described below. It also supported several impact evaluations that were either ongoing or could be concluded within the Report's timeframe.

Listening to young people

In one of the most elaborate and wide-reaching consultations for a *WDR,* over 3,000 young people participated in focus group discussions in 26 developing countries: Argentina, Bangladesh, Brazil, Burkina Faso, China, the Dominican Republic, the Arab Republic of Egypt, Georgia, Ghana, Honduras, India, Kenya, the former Yugoslav Republic of Macedonia, Mexico, Mozambique, Nepal, Nigeria, Papua New Guinea, Peru, the Russian Federation, Sierra Leone, Thailand, Timor Leste, Turkey, Vietnam, and the Republic of Yemen. We consulted youth workers and experts from governments, nongovernmental organizations, partner organizations, and the World Bank to ensure that participants were representative of the youth in their country. From November 2005 to May 2006, these young women and men debated and discussed the Report's five life transitions. The process was undertaken by the country offices, supported strongly by a joint team of the Children and Youth Unit of the Bank's Human Development Network, the External Relations Vice-Presidency (EXT), and the *WDR.* A special effort was made to reach out to young people whose voice is often not heard, such as young women, rural youth, and those living with a disability. The team found the discussions immensely helpful in forming hypotheses, validating quantitative findings, and providing a rich context. Some meetings lasted a few

hours, others three days. In a few, members of the core team for this Report engaged directly; in others, they were sent reports, which are available on our Web site, www.worldbank.org/wdr2007. The team also engaged with representatives of global youth organizations and youth leaders in Europe, Japan, and North America, including members of the Bank's Youth, Development and Peace Network and the Francophonie and the Organización Ibero-Americana de Juventud (OIJ). New media were used for e-discussions and videoconferences with youth leaders from around the globe, as well as for an open youth commentary on the World Bank's Web site.

The quotations in the margins of this Report were taken from the *WDR* youth consultations (see Mangiaterra and Vollmer [2006] and www.worldbank.org/consultations) and the e-discussion connected to the Youth Social Technopreneurship Conference in October 2005. For quotations taken from sources other than these, the source is given in an endnote or below the quotation.

Surveying young people

Several of the issues covered in this Report are not covered by existing developing country surveys. To provide insights on these issues, the Report team added questions to nationally representative audience surveys by InterMedia in late 2005 and early 2006 for Albania, Bangladesh, Ethiopia, Iraq, Malaysia, Romania, and Tajikistan. In addition, rich data on information and communication technology use and political attitudes were obtained from InterMedia's survey databank.

A large new database was constructed from existing country household surveys in 97 developing countries, covering all Bank regions and 21 developed countries. For all developed countries and more than half of the developing countries, at least two survey points per country, covering the 1990s and early 2000s, were used for the cross-country comparisons. These data complemented those from the Demographic and Health Surveys (ORC Macro) and Living Standards Measurement Study surveys.

Abbreviations and Data Notes

Abbreviations

ABC	Abstain-Be faithful-use Condoms	MENA	Middle East and North Africa region
AGETIP	Agence d'Exécution des Travaux d'Intérêt Public	MTV	Music Television
AIDS	Acquired immune deficiency syndrome	NEPAD	New Partnership for Africa's Development
ART	Antiretroviral therapy	NER	Net enrollment rate
ASER	Annual Survey of Education Report (India)	NFHS	National Family Health Survey
AVU	African Virtual University	NGO	Nongovernmental organization
BMI	Body mass index	OECD	Organisation for Economic Co-operation and Development
BRAC	Bangladesh Rural Advancement Committee		
CDC	U.S. Centers for Disease Control and Prevention	ORC	Opinion Research Corporation
CDCA	Centro de Defesa da Criança e do Adolescente	ORT	Oral rehydration therapy
CEDECA	Center of Defense of Children and Adolescents	PETI	Program to Eradicate Child Labor (Brazil)
CEDPA	Center for Development and Population Activities	PIRLS	Progress in International Reading and Literacy Study
CORFO	Corporación de Fomento de la Producción (Chile)	PISA	Program for International Student Assessment
DDR	Disarmament, demobilization, and rehabilitation	PRS	Poverty Reduction Strategy
DHS	Demographic and Health Surveys	PRSP	Poverty Reduction Strategy Paper
DPT	Diptheria, pertussis, tetanus	SACMEQ	Southern and Eastern Africa Consortium for Monitoring Education
ECD	Early childhood development		
EFA	Education for All	Sida	Swedish International Development Agency
EPL	Employment Protection Legislation	SMS	Short Messaging Service
EU	European Union	SPW	Student Partnerships Worldwide
FAO	Food and Agriculture Organization of the United Nations	STD	Sexually transmitted disease
		STI	Sexually transmitted infection
GDP	Gross domestic product	TIMSS	Trends in International Mathematics and Science Study
GNI	Gross national income		
GNP	Gross national product	UCEP	Underprivileged Children's Education Program
HIV	Human Immunodeficiency virus	UNAIDS	Joint United Nations Program on HIV/AIDS
ICL	Income contingent loan	UNDP	United Nations Development Programme
ICT	Information and communication technology	UNESCO	United Nations Education, Scientific, and Cultural Organization
IEC	Information education and communication		
IFPRI	International Food Policy Research Institute	UNHCR	United Nations High Commissioner for Refugees
ILA	Individual learning accounts	UNICEF	United Nations Children's Fund
ILO	International Labour Organization	UNODCCP	United Nations Office for Drug Control and Crime Prevention
IMF	International Monetary Fund		
INCAP	Institute of Nutrition of Central America and Panama	USAID	U.S. Agency for International Development
		WDR	*World Development Report*
IUD	Intrauterine device		
LRA	Lord's Resistance Army	WHO	World Health Organization

Data notes

The countries included in regional and income groupings in this Report are listed in the Classification of Economies table at the end of the Selected World Development Indicators. Income classifications are based on gross national income (GNP) per capita; thresholds for income classifications in this edition may be found in the Introduction to Selected World Development Indicators. Group averages reported in the figures and tables are unweighted averages of the countries in the group, unless noted to the contrary.

The use of the word *countries* to refer to economies implies no judgment by the World Bank about the legal or other status of a territory. The term *developing countries* includes low- and middle-income economies and thus may include economies in transition from central planning, as a matter of convenience. The term *advanced countries* may be used as a matter of convenience to denote high-income economies.

Dollar figures are current U.S. dollars, unless otherwise specified. *Billion* means 1,000 million; *trillion* means 1,000 billion.

Serbia and Montenegro is used in this Report either because the event being discussed occurred prior to the independence of the Republic of Montenegro in June 2006 or because separate data for the Republic of Serbia and the Republic of Montenegro are not available.

Overview

Her performance is riveting. Geórgia, 15, an impoverished street child, failing student, and aspiring actress, moistens the eyes of the international aid officials visiting a halfway house for young girls in Recife, Brazil. She is playing the part of an abused young girl on a makeshift stage, where she dreams about coping with the stresses of her life: the indifference of her family, the difficulty of staying in school, the pressure to sniff glue, the unwelcome advances from men, the part-time work as a housekeeper. Perhaps she finds it easy to play the role because it mirrors her life so closely . . . but she also has plenty of talent.

After the play, as she speaks to the visiting foreigners, the precocious performer reverts to the shy, awkward teenager that she still is. She is thankful for the opportunity to develop her craft in a safe space while also improving her reading, writing, and knowledge about life's practicalities. She is anxious about her future, especially how to get motivated for the boring classes in the public school that she occasionally attends. But for the first time in her young life, she is hopeful.

Across the ocean in Freetown, Sierra Leone, Simeon, 23, is wondering what to do next. For the past 15 years his life had been disrupted by the long civil war. He and his family, living in Koidu, a hotspot of the conflict, had to flee for their lives several times. They were once captured and forced to serve the rebel forces for two years. The impact of such unrelenting exposure to violence is clear when he says that he feels as if he has already died three times: when his father was killed for failing to provide a fighter with enough food, when his mother was raped and later died, and when his sister was forced to return to Koidu as a sex worker.

Still, he wants to restart his life. Working as a volunteer for a nonprofit organization that serves and rehabilitates youths through counseling and education, he feels good to be part of a group and learning again, including how to operate computers. He also wants to bring his sister to Freetown and away from her nightmarish life in Koidu. If only he had a paying job.

Half a world away, Van, 21, a third-year student at one of Hanoi's most prestigious tertiary institutions, is at a friend's house rehearsing Celine Dion songs with her band. A conscientious student, she passed the rigorous entrance examination with the unconditional support of her parents, both professionals. She earns extra money by translating newswires from English to Vietnamese on her home computer—experience she hopes would help her enter the journalism field. Her enthusiasm for playing computer games and surfing the Internet gives her uncommon self-confidence in technology. It also helps that she is in almost constant contact with her friends, thanks to Internet telephony and instant messaging.

Her most immediate concern is that her parents may not let her join her boyfriend on his newly acquired scooter to cruise Hanoi's streets on a busy Saturday night. She knows that they rightly fear for her safety, having heard of several friends who recently had serious motorcycle accidents.

There are many young people like Geórgia, Simeon, and Van—indeed, more of them than at any time in world history. Each is entering an age fraught with risks and laden with opportunities, not just for them but for their families, their societies, their economies. Together, their experience will determine the quality of the next generation of workers, parents, and leaders. Decisions about developing their skills, about starting on the road to financial independence, and about engaging with the broader civic community will have long-lasting effects that have repercussions far beyond them and their families.

Most policy makers know that young people will greatly influence the future of their nations. Trying to help, they face dilemmas. When primary school completion has gone up so dramatically, thanks to public investment, why does illiteracy seem so persistent? Why do large numbers of university graduates go jobless for months or even years, while businesses complain of the lack of skilled workers? Why do young people start smoking, when there are very visible global campaigns to control it? What is to be done with demobilized combatants, still in their late teens, who can barely read but are too old to go to primary school? Tough questions, these, and there are many more. The answers are important for growth and poverty reduction. This *World Development Report* offers a framework and provides examples of policies and programs to address the issues.

Decisions during five youth transitions have the biggest long-term impacts on how human capital is kept safe, developed, and deployed: continuing to learn, starting to work, developing a healthful lifestyle, beginning a family, and exercising citizenship. The report's focus on these transitions defines our choice of whom to include as "the next generation." Because they take place at different times in different societies, the report does not adhere to one defined age range, but it takes 12–24 years as the relevant range to cover the transitions from puberty to economic independence.[1]

Young people and their families make the decisions—but policies and institutions also affect the risks, the opportunities, and ultimately the outcomes. Putting a "youth lens" on these policies, the report presents three strategic directions for reform:

- *Opportunities.* Broaden the opportunities for developing human capital by expanding access to and improving the quality of education and health services; by facilitating the start to a working life; and by giving young people a voice to articulate the kind of assistance they want and a chance to participate in delivering it.
- *Capabilities.* Develop young people's capabilities to choose well among these opportunities by recognizing them as decision-making agents and by helping ensure that their decisions are well informed, adequately resourced, and judicious.
- *Second chances.* Provide an effective system of second chances through targeted programs that give young people the hope and the incentive to catch up from bad luck—or bad choices.

Invest in young people—now

The situation of young people today presents the world with an unprecedented opportunity to accelerate growth and reduce poverty (chapter 1 of the report). First, thanks to the development achievements of past decades, more young people are completing primary school and surviving childhood diseases. However, to succeed in today's competitive global economy, they must be equipped with advanced skills beyond literacy; to stay healthy, they must confront new disease burdens, such as sexually transmitted diseases and obesity. Second, lower fertility rates in many countries mean that today's youths will enter the workforce with fewer nonworking dependents, and thus fewer to support. If they remain unemployed for long periods, though, they could be a drain on the economy.

Building on a stronger base of human capital

Because labor is the main asset of the poor, making it more productive is the best way to reduce poverty. This requires enhancing the opportunities to earn money and developing the human capital to take advantage of those opportunities. Broad-based economic growth is important.[2] So is providing basic education and health care, especially for children—to provide the foundation of basic skills and well-being. Doing both has brought significant progress. Primary school enrollment rates in low-income countries outside China and India rose from 50 percent in 1970 to 88 percent in 2000. Average life expectancy at birth worldwide rose from 51 years to 65 in less than 40 years.[3]

With these advances come new challenges. Further progress requires young people who are more capable and involved. But higher completion rates at primary levels strain the capacity for places in secondary school (figure 1). Almost all Indonesian children attend six years of schooling, and 80 percent of even the poorest complete primary levels. Then, however, enrollments drop dramatically, especially for the poor. Fewer poor Zambian children enroll to begin with, but they, too, fall off at secondary levels. Girls particularly are left behind, just as they were in the expansion of primary education, except in South America, Eastern Europe, and the former Soviet Union.[4] Even more disturbing, the vast numbers spilling out of primary schools have not learned what they should. Standardized tests—not just for science and technology but for the command of basic skills—show that students in developing countries lag far behind those in the Organisation for Economic Co-operation and Development (OECD) countries (chapter 3).

Concerns about the quality and relevance of basic training come just when the demand for advanced skills, such as problem-solving abilities critical for many industries, is increasing. Contrary to what might be expected, the greater availability of skilled and educated workers in a more integrated global economy may not necessarily lead to falling returns to skills. It may actually boost the demand for skills even further by inducing faster skill-intensive technological change.[5] Investment climate surveys show that more than a fifth of all firms in developing countries as diverse as Algeria, Bangladesh, Brazil, China, Estonia, and Zambia rate inadequate skills and education of workers as a major or severe obstacle to their operations.[6] The private returns to secondary and higher education have been rising, especially in countries that have close to universal primary education.

There are also new challenges in health. Having survived the scourges of childhood, young people confront health threats at a very vulnerable time, initiating sexual activity and entering the age of identity-seeking and risk-taking. In 2005, more than half the estimated 5 million people who contracted HIV worldwide were young people between 15 and 24, the majority of them young women and girls (discussed in chapters 1 and 5 of the Report). The economic effect of such devastating diseases can be enormous. In South Africa, HIV/AIDS can reduce GDP growth by as much as a fifth. It is by far the leading cause of death among young people ages 15–29 in Sub-Saharan Africa. In other regions, noncommunicable diseases are now the leading cause of death for young women. Injuries caused by accidents and violence are the leading cause for young men.

> "... even the most low skill jobs ... require secondary school completion, sometimes even university studies—even though there is no need for it. It leaves behind those kids who, for some reason or other, could not finish secondary school."
>
> Young person,
> Buenos Aires, Argentina
> December 2005

Figure 1 High enrollment rates in primary school are followed by significantly lower rates at secondary levels in Indonesia and Zambia

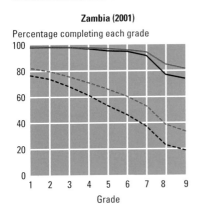

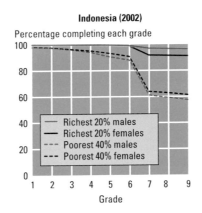

Source: Authors' calculations from Demographic and Health Surveys.
Note: Quintiles are based on an index of assets and housing characteristics.

Addressing these challenges will affect poverty reduction far into the future for at least two reasons. First, the capacity to learn is much greater for the young than for older people, so missed opportunities to acquire skills, good health habits, and the desire to engage in the community and society can be extremely costly to remedy. Second, human capital outcomes of young people affect those of their children. Better educated parents have fewer, healthier, and better educated children. In all developing countries, but especially in the low-income regions of South Asia and Sub-Saharan Africa, immunization rates are higher among families whose mothers have some secondary education. These intergenerational effects lift families out of poverty over the long term.

Seizing the opportunities from a "youth bulge" in the population

The need to address youth issues now is also rooted in demographics—because of the fiscal demands of the sheer number of today's young and their share in the future labor force.

Today, 1.5 billion people are ages 12–24 worldwide, 1.3 billion of them in developing countries, the most ever in history. This number will rise but not by much more, because it is fast approaching a plateau as fertility rates decline, producing a "bulge" in the world's population structure. Perhaps as important as this bulge is the diversity in age structures across the world's countries, due to differences in the timing of the fall in fertility rates. For developed countries, this fertility transition occurred so long ago that the bulge is composed of the middle-aged, the baby boomers. Their immediate challenge is how to ensure adequate and sustainable old age income support.

A few developing countries, especially those in transition in Europe and Central Asia, mirror developed country age patterns. However, in most developing countries, the number of young people is peaking or will peak in the next 10 years. Others, including all of Sub-Saharan Africa, Afghanistan, Iraq, West Bank and Gaza, and the Republic of Yemen, will not hit the peak for 20 years

or more. They have more classically shaped population pyramids with broad bases for the youngest ages, tapering up gradually with age.

These numbers can be a fiscal and economic risk. A recent study estimates the yearly cost per secondary school student in Sub-Saharan Africa to be almost three times that of public cost per pupil in the primary level.[7] Add to that the cost of addressing AIDS and noncommunicable diseases, and financing the fiscal burden, difficult to manage in the best of times, can be a constraint on growth. Moreover, if youth remain unemployed for long periods, as happened when the baby boom occurred in Europe and the United States, this not only wastes human resources—it also risks misaligned expectations and social unrest that could dampen the investment climate and growth.[8]

These large numbers can also be an opportunity. The fertility transition means that many developing countries are in, or will soon enter, a phase when they can expect to see a larger share of people of working age. This expansion of a workforce that has fewer children and elderly to support provides a window of opportunity to spend on other things, such as building human capital.

The window of falling dependency rates can stay open for up to 40 years, depending on the rate of fertility decline. Then aging closes it. The good news is that almost all developing countries are still in this window (figure 2). Of those that entered the window early, some have taken full advantage, and others have not. One study attributes more than 40 percent of the higher growth in East Asia over Latin America in 1965–90 to the faster growth of its working-age population and better policies for trade and human capital development.[9] If countries fail to invest in human capital—which is most profitable for the young—they cannot hope to reap this demographic dividend.

Other poor countries in Sub-Saharan Africa, South Asia, the Middle East and North Africa are about to see the window of opportunity open (figure 2). If they are to follow the Asian economies' growth path, they need policies and institutions that broaden the opportunities for young people to develop their human capital and use it productively in work. Indeed, the overall skills of the labor force, built largely in childhood and youth, strongly affect the climate for investment in firms. And, where enrollment in postprimary education is high, skill shortages, a feature of all developing countries, are lower.

Getting it right today can have huge payoffs for the future because young people, as the next generation of household heads and parents, will have profound impacts on their children.[10] To illustrate, consider Kenya, where AIDS is projected to have very damaging effects on human capital investment because premature parental death weakens the mechanisms for forming it. Reinforcing these effects is the fact that higher expected mortality among young adults in the next generation reduces the family's expected returns to educational investment. Public investment in young people, costly as it may be, is well worth it (box 1).

Investments during youth's five life transitions

The decisions that will affect young people's well-being and society's are those that shape the foundational human capital to be productive workers, family heads, citizens, and community leaders. That is why this report focuses on the transitions that the young undergo in learning, work, health, family, and citizenship. If made well, decisions about these transitions will develop, safeguard, and properly deploy human capital. If made badly, the consequences will be very costly to correct because dropping out of school, prolonged periods of unemployment, or risky health behaviors can leave permanent scars.

Public policy can do much in determining which way things go. As youth undergo each transition, the development of their human capital is hampered, not only by poverty, but also by policy failures that affect their options, especially the failure to provide or finance adequate services when markets do not work.

Figure 2 Opening and closing demographic windows of opportunity

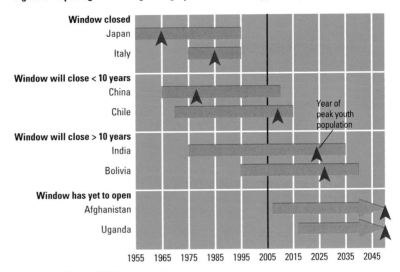

Source: United Nations (2005b), medium variant.
Note: Bars show the range of years for which the dependency ratio—the number of dependents relative to people of working age—is falling.

BOX 1 *Investing in young people pays off big time: Estimating the long-term and interactive effects of human capital investments*

Adapting an overlapping-generations model that was used to estimate the macroeconomic impact of AIDS, researchers have recently applied it to a broader range of investments in human capital in Africa: "By killing mostly young adults, AIDS does more than destroy the human capital embodied in them; it deprives their children of the very things they need to become economically productive adults—their parents' loving care, knowledge, and capacity to finance education."[11]

In a recent paper that explicitly models the effects of secondary education, the AIDS epidemic that shocked Kenya in 1990 is estimated to lower human capital and per capita income so much that it does not recover its 1990 levels until 2030. An education investment—in the form of a 30-year program to subsidize secondary education costing about 0.9 percent of GDP starting in 2000 and rising to 1.8 percent in 2020—

would lead to income per capita that is 7 percent higher than without the intervention, with gains continuing far beyond 2040. The net present value of the benefits, at plausible discount rates, would be between 2.0 and 3.5 times that of costs—a worthwhile investment indeed.

Because of the long-run synergy between postprimary education and the health of young adults, combining this subsidy with direct measures to combat the AIDS epidemic and treat its victims would do better still. A program that combines a lower educational subsidy with measures to combat the epidemic and treat its victims would, for the same amount of money, produce even more dramatic gains. Those gains come not only from saving lives but also from increasing the incentive to invest in education, a result of the reduced mortality.

Source: Bell, Bruhns, and Gersbach (2006).

Learning after primary school age

At the age of 12, more than 85 percent of all children in developing countries are in school, a proportion that declines as they grow older (figure 3). (Figures 3, 4, 6, 7, and 8 are stylized representations of figures from

Figure 3   Youth enrollment rates decline with age

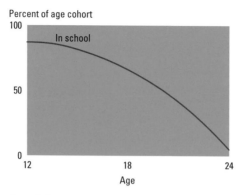

Percent of age cohort

Source: Authors.

chapter 1 that use actual data.) Almost all are out of school by age 24. What they learn early in life lasts a lifetime and is much harder to master if they try to do so as adults.

Skills are nurtured very early in life by parents, who then turn their children over to preschools and primary schools. The expected path for young people is to continue on to secondary school, when decisions are made about whether to enter the labor force, marry, and go on to higher education. These decisions may need government sup-

port because some of the gains to schooling accrue to society rather than individuals. Governments also try to level the playing field for rich and poor, so that those with the greatest aptitude attain the most schooling.

Some countries are more successful at managing this transition than others. Several East Asian governments have done it so well that it has been called a miracle.[12] Much as one would want to believe in miracles, many other countries are much less likely to see them. Why?

- Despite dramatic recent progress in the numbers completing primary school, a Millennium Development Goal, children are not learning as much as they should (box 2).

- Many completing primary school cannot further their education because of a lack of school places, a lack of resources, or a pregnancy—or all three.

- The global wave of economic and technological change is demanding more from workers than basic skills. For example, in many Latin American countries, supply has not kept up with the rising demand for skills.[13] The problem is not only one

---

B O X 2   *The poor quality of basic education severely limits opportunities for young people*

The dramatic recent progress in the numbers of children completing primary schools, a Millennium Development Goal, does not fully address country needs because the children are not learning as much as they should. Many, even those who reach lower secondary levels, can hardly read or write and are unprepared to cope with the practicalities of daily life. In several African countries, half or fewer of all young women ages 15–24 can read a simple sentence after three years of primary school (chapter 3)—and in Ghana and Zambia after even grade 6 (left panel of figure). Even among those who go on to lower secondary (typically grades 7–9), preparation is low.

The gap is not limited to book learning. Many young people do not know basic facts that could save their lives, such as what causes HIV/AIDS, at a time when many begin sexual activity. Knowledge about condom use is very low regardless of grade attained in both high- and low-HIV-prevalence countries (far right figure). The risks are even higher because the use of condoms is typically lower

than the rates of knowledge would imply. Such ignorance can be devastating. In Kenya, the probability that a 20-year-old will die before

reaching age 40 is projected to be 36 percent in 2010—without AIDS it would have been 8 percent.[14]

There are big gaps in the book knowledge and life knowledge of young people

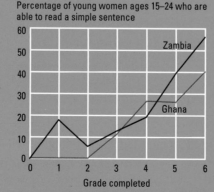

Percentage of young women ages 15–24 who are able to read a simple sentence

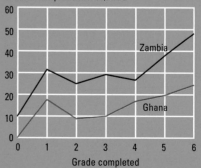

Percentage of young women ages 15–24 who know condom use prevents HIV/AIDS

Source: Authors' calculations from Demographic and Health Surveys.
Note: Zambia has a high prevalence of HIV/AIDS.

Figure 9 Transitions seen through three lenses focus policies and magnify impact

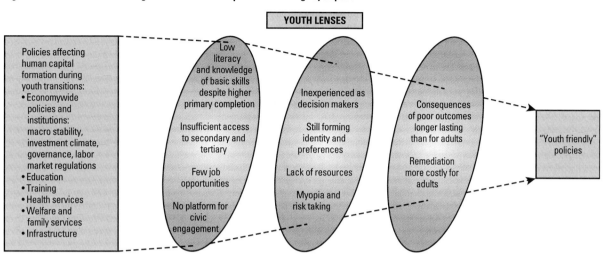

YOUTH LENSES

Policies affecting human capital formation during youth transitions:
• Economywide policies and institutions: macro stability, investment climate, governance, labor market regulations
• Education
• Training
• Health services
• Welfare and family services
• Infrastructure

Low literacy and knowledge of basic skills despite higher primary completion

Insufficient access to secondary and tertiary

Few job opportunities

No platform for civic engagement

Inexperienced as decision makers

Still forming identity and preferences

Lack of resources

Myopia and risk taking

Consequences of poor outcomes longer lasting than for adults

Remediation more costly for adults

"Youth friendly" policies

Opportunities   **Capabilities**   **Second chances**

the capabilities to grasp them are blunted or misdirected. Having better decision-making capabilities (agency) can lead to frustration if the opportunities are far below aspirations. Not having second chances can lead to a free fall in outcomes. Some of the lenses loom larger in some transitions than in others. In the transitions toward sustaining a healthy lifestyle and forming families, for example, outcomes are influenced most by young people's behavior, so the emphasis would be on capabilities.

Viewing economywide and sectoral policies through these lenses make them "youth friendly" by identifying gaps and setting priorities. The need to narrow gaps does not necessarily mean that the benevolent hand of government should do all the heavy lifting—even if well intentioned, many governments lack the resources and capacity to provide all the necessary investments. Instead, public policy needs to improve the climate for young people, with the support of their families, to invest in themselves—by addressing the costs, risks, and perceived returns of investing in people, just as they should do for firms. The next three sections fill the right side of figure 9 with examples of specific policies and programs.

Policies to broaden opportunities

Developing and deploying youth's human capital become special challenges as the numbers surviving childhood diseases and completing primary school grow. Not addressing these challenges passes poverty to succeeding generations, because the poor outcomes of young people today are transmitted to their children. Countries that have broken out of this spiral have improved the basic skills of adolescents and young adults, met demands for even higher-order skills, and smoothed the start of young people's work and civic lives.

Improving basic skills— intervene earlier in the life cycle and focus on quality

The lesson from the massive education expansion in the 1980s and 1990s is clear—expanding places rapidly can come at the cost of quality, reflected in high enrollment rates but low achievement. In Morocco and Namibia, more than 80 percent of school children stay until the last grade of primary education, but fewer than 20 percent have minimum mastery of the material (chapter 3). Young people are already paying the price; many of the large numbers of adolescents completing primary education do not know enough to be literate and numerate members of society. A youth lens thus reinforces the point—well documented in worldwide monitoring reports[18]—to improve the balance between expanding primary enrollments and ensuring a minimum quality standard.

What should countries do? First, measure quality well. Quantity may have been stressed because it is easier to measure enrollment and completion rates than learning outcomes. This is slowly changing with the introduction of standardized tests comparable across schools within and across countries.[19]

Second, consider the system of learning over the entire life cycle rather than as standalone pre-primary, primary, secondary, and tertiary education. For many countries this means improving the foundations before the children reach adolescence through early investments in nutrition, health, and psycho-social development. In countries as diverse as Jamaica, the Philippines, Turkey, and the United States,[20] enriched child care and preschool programs have led to higher achievement test scores, higher graduation rates from high school, and even lower crime rates for participants well into their twenties (figure 10).

Establishing the basic skills for a well-functioning society may require making lower secondary school universal, as many countries are doing. Again, this should not come at the cost of quality. Setting standards, developing accreditation and evaluation systems, training and motivating teachers, and increasing the accountability of school administrators to parents,

students, and local communities are only some of the measures (chapter 3). Because a focus on quality is not costless, what can be deferred until upper secondary and beyond is the selection and specialization that some countries have from early grades. In Chile's secondary education reform, for example, all vocational specialization moved to upper secondary school, better establishing a solid academic base.

Meeting the demand for higher order skills—improve the relevance of upper secondary and tertiary education

Even as countries struggle with basic needs, the global economy demands more technical and behavioral skills, especially those formed during the ages 15–24. Competition has driven up the demand for skill-intensive technological innovation in Asia and Latin America, much of it in export industries, which tend to use disproportionately more young people (chapter 4).

This pressure can be eased if upper secondary schools and universities turn out more students. But simply increasing quantity is not enough because content and how it is delivered matters most. If quality is low or if what is learned is not relevant in the job market, unemployment rates can be high even for some of the most highly educated. Countries like South Africa are trying to respond to employers' demand for quality and relevance by revamping upper secondary curricula to emphasize practical thinking and behavioral skills and offering more of a blend of academic and vocational subjects (chapter 3). Policies that link educational institutions with prospective employers from the private sector through regular consultations and joint university-industry research projects help, as in China.

Such reforms can be costly because of the high unit cost of educating students beyond the basics. Teacher shortages in math and the sciences are especially acute in Sub-Saharan Africa. Efficiency gains may be possible through better incentives for administrators and teachers, such as performance-based pay schemes now being tried in some Latin American countries (chapter 3).

Figure 10   Early childhood interventions (at ages 1–5) can have long-lasting effects on young people (at ages 13–18)

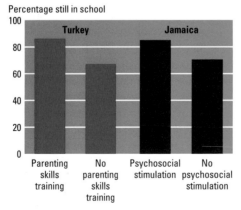

Percentage still in school

Sources: Walker and others (2005) and Kagitcibasi, Sunar, and Bekman (2001).

Note: In Turkey, the intervention was for four years between ages 3 and 9, and involved both parenting skills training and daycare. Only the parenting skills had an effect at the followup at ages 13–15. In Jamaica, children ages 1–2 received two years of professional psychosocial stimulation, and follow-up was at ages 17–18. Both are controlled impact evaluations.

Many educational systems can also expand and improve by diversifying their funding sources. Families already contribute significantly to the cost of tertiary education in some countries—up to 80 percent of the cost in high-performing economies with relatively high enrollment rates such as Chile and the Republic of Korea—when they feel they are getting value for money. Countries such as the Slovak Republic, Turkey, and Uruguay, where private funds contribute 20 percent or less of the total cost of tertiary levels,[21] could mobilize more resources through fees, public-private partnerships, income-generating activities (consultancies, leasing unused property), and donor support.

Programs that enable rich and poor to compete more evenly are only beginning to be tried. What is clear is that "free tuition" for universities is neither financially sustainable nor directing benefits to the poor, because so few poor students seek entry to tertiary institutions. In Uruguay, more than 60 percent of those enjoying free tuition in public tertiary institutions come from the two richest quintiles.[22] Loans or targeted scholarships to students from disadvantaged families could be both efficient and sustainable. For example, some countries subsidize private secondary and tertiary institutions according to the number of low-income students they enroll. The institutions apply for the subsidies and are then screened to meet quality standards (chapter 3).

Accumulating skills on the job— ease barriers to start work and facilitate mobility

Broadening opportunities for young people's employment works best when premised on economywide growth that stimulates demand: a rising tide lifts young people's boats, as well as everyone else's.[23] In many economies, an export orientation and foreign direct investment expanded the demand for young workers. Such policies have been cited, along with sound basic education, as a source of growth to explain the "East Asian miracle."[24] In Indonesia, in heavily export-oriented sectors such as electronics and textiles, youth employment shares are more than twice the national average—truly "youth intensive" sectors (chapter 4). They have had a particularly stimulating effect on previously excluded groups, such as young women in Penang, Malaysia, whose entry into the labor force 20–30 years ago fueled the growth in a fledgling electronics industry and altered social stereotypes about women. So policies that open the economy to free trade tend to be youth friendly. A youth lens would not necessarily change these policies—it would merely strengthen the argument for pursuing them in the first place.

A youth lens may also mean that some general policies need to be changed once the implications for youth are taken into account. Such is the case for labor market regulations that affect new entrants disproportionately. Policies that limit flexibility and mobility across sectors tend to lengthen the transition to work and constrain young people more than others. Employment protection laws in Latin American and OECD countries can increase the unemployment rate for young people (chapter 4). If minimum wages are set too high, they may discourage employment of the unskilled, mostly young workers who are only beginning their working lives. These are not arguments for scrapping all such laws and regulations. Instead, they are a call to develop policies that provide adequate protection without stifling opportunities for already disadvantaged groups.

In poorer countries such as Burkina Faso, The Gambia, Nicaragua, Paraguay, Rwanda, and Sierra Leone, many of the young are more likely to begin work in the informal sector (chapter 4). Although this sector will not solve all issues of youth employment—even selling on the street requires some sales skills and language skills and conditions can be harsh—evidence suggests that it can be a remarkably resilient and productive stepping stone, sometimes to formal employment.

If these jobs are to be the first rungs rather than the last stop up the skill ladder, youth have to be able to move freely to seize the opportunities that arise. Practical training that combines occupational and behavioral skills can make young people more mobile. But the track record of schools and even large public national training institutions in providing such skills has, at best, been mixed. Are there alternatives? Advanced countries' experiences with formal apprenticeships and internships, which provide a "structured work experience," hold lessons for middle-income countries that are rapidly developing a modern wage sector. In other countries, traditional apprenticeships in informal sector firms are more common, and incentives can be used to improve quality and encourage innovation, as in Kenya's Jua Kali program (chapter 4).

Another option for the young is self-employment. Some are entrepreneurs of necessity, others by opportunity. Both types face constraints made more binding by their age, such as access to capital and to business networks. Programs to provide seed capital to build financing and contacts have started in Latin America.

> *"We only have observer status when things are decided in this community."*
>
> Young person,
> Bonthe District, Sierra Leone
> February 2006

Geographic mobility also broadens opportunities, and the young are a disproportionately large share of all migrants, both to urban areas and to other countries. In China, 118 million rural dwellers have sought employment outside their home villages, and because of the rising productivity in rural areas, this has not significantly reduced agricultural production. But the migrants do not have the same access to social services as those with an urban residence permit. Nor do they enjoy the full range of social security and safety net benefits, contributing to social pressures. Policies that smooth the transition to cities and across borders, such as recognizing the rights of migrants, would be efficient and equitable as are now being introduced in China.

Young people represent a large proportion of the world's international migrants. Migration broadens the opportunities to work (chapter 8). It also expands options for education, especially in higher education. Opportunities for secondary education back home also can be broadened thanks to remittances from migrant parents or other relatives. Measures in both sending and recipient countries can ensure that migrants take these opportunities (box 3).

Participating in civic life— enhance youth voice in policy and service delivery

Opportunities to be recognized and heard as citizens, and to be included in community initiatives, are important for the delivery of services that affect young people directly. *World*

BOX 3 *International migration offers opportunities and risks for youth*

The probability of migrating internationally peaks in the late teens and early twenties (see figure), so youth make up a disproportionate share of the world's migrants—and often also a large share of the return migrants. About a third of the migrant flow from all developing countries are ages 12 to 24, and half are ages 12 to 29. The youth bulge in developing countries and the aging populations in most developed countries will further increase the demand for migration over the coming years. Even so, much of the youth demand for legal migration is unmet, with 50 to 90 percent in some countries reporting that they would migrate, usually temporarily, if they had the opportunity. So the young are more likely to resort to illegal migration and to fall victim to trafficking than older age groups.

Youth migration has large direct effects on growth and poverty reduction through remittances and the return of migrants with skills acquired abroad. It can thus be a very important way for youth to use and develop their human capital to help reduce poverty in their own countries.

Easing immigration restrictions for temporary workers would be one way developed countries could help. To maximize the development impacts, developing countries need policies that

- increase the benefits from their existing youth migrants, such as lowering remittance costs, providing access to finance, and for returning migrants, recognizing the skills gained abroad;

- expand the opportunities for other youth to migrate by reducing high passport costs, removing legal restrictions on emigration, and developing active bilateral work arrangements;

- mitigate the risks of migration through information campaigns to reduce trafficking and the spread of infectious diseases, and through broadening the opportunities for work at home;

- facilitate the return of migrants who have gained useful overseas experience by improving the investment climate at home.

Source: Authors.

Mexicans migrate young and return to Mexico young

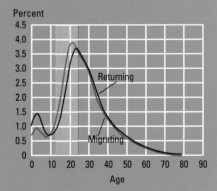

Source: Authors.
Note: Shaded portion represents 12–24 age range.

Development Report 2004[25] referred to this engagement as "client power," arguing that it can make providers more responsive to those who matter—the beneficiaries. Voice also matters because young people's disposition toward citizenship tends to be durable, and participating early in life is a good predictor of ability and willingness to engage in the future. How can governments give that voice more prominence and not be threatened by it?

For most young people, direct consultation and recognition through their participation in policy decisions and implementation may be a more important platform than, say, voting. Such opportunities include not only state-sponsored channels but also social and civil organizations, such as rural associations in West Africa (*kafoolu*), samba schools and sports clubs in Brazil, and 4-H and Scouts everywhere. National service, whether military or civil, is another channel countries have explored for active participation. The successful youth service programs emphasize flexibility, youth input, accountability, and organizational autonomy in their design (chapter 7).

Often the young are more likely to have opportunities to be heard and have a more direct impact in local settings. In Ceará, Brazil, youth had a chance to review the state budget and identify initiatives previously not on the agenda. The effect of broadening such opportunities is not simply to ensure stability—it is often a way to get better outcomes. It is also a good way to develop skills in decision making.

Policies that enhance capabilities: Youth as decision makers

The second youth lens focuses on the need to help young people decide more capably among life's opportunities. When young people enter adolescence, the most important decisions are made for them by their parents and the elders in their families. As they get older, decision making shifts from parents and families to youth themselves. The speed of the shift varies greatly for the different transitions. In some societies, the transition comes early. For many others, it comes only for some decisions—and at an older age. For some, such as young women in traditional societies where decision making simply shifts from parents to husbands, independence never comes.

These differences are well illustrated in the responses to an international survey of 15- to 24-year-olds that queries who has the most influence on decisions about marriage, education, and occupation (figure 11). Very few young Bangladeshi women think they have the most influence on their schooling or marriage choices. In contrast, Albanian, Malaysian, and Romanian youth feel remarkably empowered to decide for themselves. Ethiopians, Iraqis, and Tajiks are mixed. The

"[The] majority of youth in Georgia now realize that the key factor . . . in finding proper jobs lies in themselves."

Young person,
Tbilisi, Georgia
December 2005

Figure 11 Who has the final say? The percentage of young women (ages 15–24) who feel they themselves have had the most influence on key life transitions varies greatly across societies

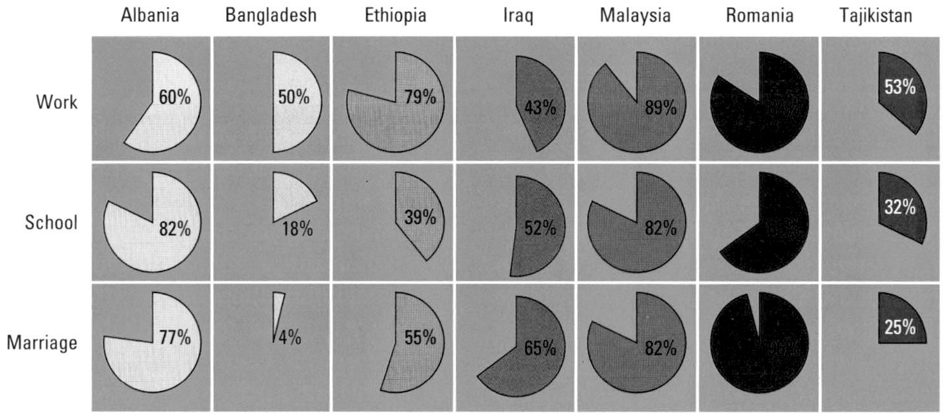

Source: WDR 2007 InterMedia surveys.
Note: The figure shows the percentage of people ages 15–24 who answered "myself" (rather than parents, government, or other) to the question: "Thinking of [each transition: your current or most recent occupation, your years of schooling, and your marriage partner], who has had the most influence?"

results for males mirror these proportions with a few exceptions (chapter 2). Iraqi males feel less in control about work and school than females; Bangladeshi males feel significantly more in control than females about work and marriage, but not about school.

Even if there is no outright independence, young people everywhere make important decisions that can affect their futures, even in what are seemingly tradition-bound communities. Young primary school completers may dutifully enroll in secondary school to please their parents but their own efforts will be important to their success. Young couples may be prohibited by laws from marrying too young but can still have sexual encounters that could lead to unwanted pregnancies. That is, they are exercising their "agency," defined by social scientists as the ability of young people to define their goals and to act on them.[26]

Agency needs to be recognized. This might be as simple as ensuring that young people have legal identity, including the basic documentation often crucial for access to basic services. But recognition alone is not sufficient—agency must be informed, resourced, and responsible. That is, if it is to help young people take advantage of existing opportunities, it must be "capable." What determines this capability? Access to information, command over real resources, and the ability to process and act on the information. Policies can help in all three.

Informing youth

Young people know a lot. Their literacy rates are much higher than before. They are also much more frequent users of one of the most ubiquitous sources of information now available—the Internet (chapter 8). However, there is much more to know and young people's knowledge base to inform key decisions about human capital investment and risk-taking behavior is often deficient. Recall the low rates of knowledge of condom use among young females in Africa, even those who are educated (see box 2). A survey of otherwise well-informed and educated Vietnamese youth ages 14–25 conducted in 2003 indicates that fewer than 60 percent of rural youth had ever heard of syphilis or gonorrhea.[27] In a country

where traffic accidents are the leading cause of death and serious injury for those ages 15–19 and where motorbike use by urban young people exceeds 70 percent, only about a quarter use a helmet—many are simply not convinced of its protective value.

What can be done to better inform youth about the benefits and costs of investing in their human capital? Successful interventions use schools, use the broader media, improve the content of dissemination campaigns, and harness new technology.

Improve the curricula in and convey the value of schools. Inculcating life skills in schools is the surest way to enhance the capabilities of young people. This goes beyond skills needed for further schooling and work. School-based reproductive health education programs can increase knowledge and the adoption of safe sexual behavior.[28] A school-based sex education intervention in Kenya—providing young girls with specific information, such as the prevalence of HIV infections among older men—reduced pregnancies (chapter 5). And there is no evidence that sex education increases sexual activity among youth.

However, it is not enough just to intervene in schools, because so many youth in developing countries drop out. This is often because of poverty, but it may also be that young people are not well informed about the benefits of continuing their education. In the Dominican Republic, simply telling young boys about the "real" earnings premium to education, a fairly cheap intervention, increased secondary completion (box 4).

Examine options outside schools. How best to target those who have dropped out or never sought education? Success in containing the spread of HIV/AIDS in Cambodia and Thailand is associated with structured information campaigns that worked through media and information providers.[29]

While it is difficult to establish that a campaign causes the desired effects because of many other influences, a few rigorous studies have attempted to solve the attribution problem. The Better Life Options program provides a combination of various services to young women (ages 12–20) in periurban slums and rural areas in India. It disseminates information on reproductive health and services, provides vocational training, and promotes women's empowerment through recreational events and dissemination of information material. A multivariate analysis indicates that those in the program were significantly more involved in key life decisions—such as spending in the household, when to marry, and whether to continue education—than those who were not.[30]

Harvest worldwide knowledge through new technologies, such as the Internet, to inform youth. A better climate for private investment in technology is important for young people. They are especially likely to use communal modes of access, such as Internet cafes, so government regulations to allow easy entry of firms into these sectors would help. A reform of the licensing process in Algeria that made it more affordable to obtain authorization to provide Internet service led to an explosion of Internet cafes between 1998 and 2000 (chapter 8). However, because much of the information on the Internet would be in a foreign language, efforts to kick start local content are needed. Many youth also need guidance on how to avoid the risks of using the Internet and to learn how to find reliable information among the mass of content available.

Improve the delivery and management of information to ensure that what should be taught is taught well. Some who purport to be trainers are often poorly trained themselves. Addressing this in developing countries requires training the trainers better and improving their incentives. School-based career guidance services show some promise in Chile, the Philippines, Poland, Romania, the Russian Federation, South Africa, and Turkey. One consistent finding is that success depends on the information available to the counselors (chapter 3).

The consequences of ill-informed conclusions, because of the "noise" in the information flow, can be profound. Many studies show that young people tend to overestimate the amount of sexual activity and high-risk behaviors in the population, putting more pressure on them to conform (chapter 5). In

---

BOX 4 *Knowing what's good for you: Telling young people about the benefits of school can affect outcomes*

Do young boys know the value of schooling? Not always. In the Dominican Republic a survey of boys in 2001 enrolled in the final year of primary school compared the returns they perceived to continuing their education with the actual returns in terms of differences in earnings from age-earnings profiles. It found that they accurately estimated the returns to completing primary school (but not completing secondary school) consistently with estimated earnings profiles. However, they severely underestimated the returns to completing secondary school. The measured actual average earnings gains (from surveys) between secondary and primary completion, at about 1,300 Dominican pesos (about $200), was 10 times the perceived gain of 140 Dominican pesos (about $21) (figure). The differences were most pronounced for the youth in the poorest households.

Some students at randomly selected schools were then given information about the estimated actual earnings profiles. Follow-up surveys in 2005 indicate that those who were given the information were 12 percent more likely to be attending school in the following school year relative to those who did not.

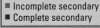
The measured actual earnings gains for completing secondary education in the Dominican Republic are much higher than the perceived gains

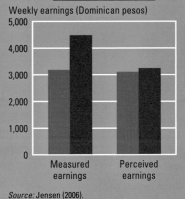

Source: Jensen (2006).

---

many societies, especially as the young seek their identity, peers could have at least as much influence on decisions as families or schools. So, informing a young person can have spillover effects on others. Programs have begun to include them as part-time service providers, such as Jamaica's Health Ministry, which encourages peer-to-peer learning to combat HIV/AIDS.

Helping young people command resources

Because young people are only beginning to be financially independent, they naturally confront more constraints on their consumption and investment decisions. Indeed, one of the reasons that the age of leaving home is getting later even in rich countries is that young adults rely on their families to get on a firmer economic footing. For those from poor families, or for those who for one reason or another (orphanhood, broken families) can no longer rely on family resources, the result could be a rocky start on the road to a sustainable livelihood— and for young females, a weak negotiating position within families, especially regarding marriage and childbearing.

Choosing to invest in skills presents substantial costs to young people. Out-of-pocket costs tend to vary—for the half of all university students in private universities in Argentina, Brazil, Chile, and Colombia, they range from 30 percent to 100 percent of GDP per capita.[31] Even for students in free public universities the opportunity costs are substantial. Because of the big personal payoffs to higher education, such costs would not be a binding constraint if liquidity were not an issue. But it is. A recent study from Mexico showed that households are less likely to send their offspring to university if their income falls temporarily, even if their permanent long-term income remains unchanged.[32]

The obvious way to lift this constraint is to provide credit. Because commercial loans are not available to the poorest students, who do not have the collateral or parental guarantees to back them up, such credit schemes could not function effectively for students without government support. Moreover, the pressures on the young to begin a livelihood are high enough even without having to pay back a debt that is many multiples of initial earnings. And many public institutions have found it difficult to administer such schemes because of low repayment rates, especially given the many episodes of youth unemployment. Australia has pioneered a system that makes repayment contingent on graduates' incomes, as tracked in tax systems. Middle-income countries such as Thailand are only now starting to try such

schemes, which are worth monitoring and evaluating. For countries with poorly developed income tax systems, alternatives such as targeted school vouchers and individual learning accounts, which encourage savings for education, may be better (chapter 3).

The income constraint is binding in poorer countries even for secondary education. Because parents are the main means of support for young people at this age, some subsidies to encourage enrollment target the household, but the transfers are conditional on achieving youth-related outcomes. Mexico's Oportunidades provides such an incentive by giving larger transfers to households if young females (versus males) stay in school. In rural areas, girls' enrollment in all three years of middle school increased much more than that of boys (figure 12).

Some innovative programs have channeled subsidies directly to students, particularly young girls—partly as an inducement for them to perform well in school but also to ensure that they "own" the decision to attend, circumventing age-old biases against girls' schooling. The Bangladesh Female Secondary Stipend Assistance Program (FSSAP) targets girls ages 11–14, transferring a monthly payment to bank accounts in the girls' names, contingent on them staying unmarried and performing well enough to pass in school (chapter 6). This program has yet to be rigorously evaluated, but it has been associated with the enormous increase in girls' enrollment there.[33] Such incentive-based schemes may not work too well if they force the provider to only increase quantity and not quality. Concerns about learning outcomes in the first round of FSSAP are being addressed in subsequent programs.

Such programs do more than help young girls go to school. They also highlight the role of resources in enhancing the capability of young women as decision-making agents within the family. Some early marriages are arranged more for the convenience of families and parents than for the young couple. While many are successful, there still are outrages, illegal in almost all countries, such as the exchange of very young brides, some less than 12 years old, to much older men for a debt cancellation. Poor young women are also more likely to succumb to pressure to

Figure 12   It pays to go to school

Percentage increase in middle school enrollment due to Mexico's Oportunidades 1997–2001

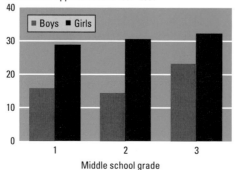

Source: Parker (2003).

accept money or goods in exchange for sex, increasing their risk of sexually transmitted infections. Helping them earn a living or providing credit and savings may empower them to withstand the pressure to put their health and future at risk (chapter 6).

Young people, unable to earn a living by working for others, often work for themselves. Some seize opportunities voluntarily; others do so out of necessity—but the barrier of finance is common to all. It takes money to make money. The young, even if they have the brightest of prospects, have no credit ratings, are inexperienced, and can offer no collateral to borrow money to start a livelihood. More programs now try to help such young entrepreneurs, but they still need to be evaluated rigorously. Early lessons from Latin America's Endeavor programs, providing financing and technical assistance to young people, are promising (chapter 4).

Enhancing the capacity to decide well

Young people, once resourced and informed, still have to filter and assess the information—so much more of it, given the Internet—and consider the consequences of their actions. The process of evaluating information and acting on that evaluation is difficult enough even for the most confident. For many young people, it is more complicated because they are still seeking their identities. The process of developing a person's sense of self has been used by some economists to explain seemingly irrational acts that put human capital at risk, including youth's tendency to engage in risky behavior, such as joining violence-prone gangs, despite the low expected economic payoffs to such activities (chapter 2).

The ability to process information starts to develop early in school. But many education systems fail because they emphasize rote learning of facts. Few emphasize thinking and behavioral skills—motivation, persistence, cooperation, team-building, the ability to manage risk and conflict—that help individuals process information and come to sensible, informed decisions. These programs have been well tested in developed country settings such as the Netherlands and the United States and are now beginning to be tried in developing countries as well (chapter 3).

Sometimes changing attitudes requires changing the environment for learning—to thwart entrenched practices, some not even recognized, that channel behavior. Research from secondary schools in Thailand indicates that girls who study in single-sex environments do better in math and develop more leadership skills than girls in mixed-sex environments, a finding consistent with research in developed countries.[34] Another example includes U.S. residential job-training programs, which allow participants to avoid interactions in their own disadvantaged neighborhoods and thus develop their self-image. The programs are more successful than those that try to save money by not offering the expensive housing component.[35]

Coming to the correct decision can also be influenced by incentives, especially if the young do not take into account the effects on others (or on themselves in the long run)—even if they had the information and knew how to decide for themselves. In Indonesia, an increase in the price of cigarettes is estimated to affect consumption for the young more than it does for adults, a finding consistent with those in richer countries.[36] By contrast, banning cigarette and alcohol advertisements and setting minimum ages for drinking attempt to increase the "price" of such behaviors, but their impact tends to be weak.

Policies to offer second chances

Broadening opportunities available to young people and helping them choose wisely among them are the priorities, especially because remediation is costly. Yet many cannot take advantage of these opportunities, even if offered. What can be done for the 19-year-old whose poor parents took her out of school at the age of 9? Or her twin brother who is still in primary school? What about the unemployed 23-year-old who has just started a family but never learned any on-the-job skills because he could not find work in the formal sector? Or the petty pickpocket incarcerated in an adult jail along with hardened criminals? What are the options for those who have been dealt life's proverbial bad hand?

Some young people have undesirable outcomes because they have had their opportunities restricted—others, because they chose the wrong path. More than half

"[Many] of my acquaintances [whom] I met during some [previous] phase of my life . . . are dead, in jail or crippled. Marcos [a youth activist] introduced me to the [second chance] movement. . . . I've participated in meetings, met the people. . . We've started to be integrated as a community, [to] develop a conscience . . . to get out of the drug trade."

—Bruno, 21,
Ceará, Brazil
May 2006

of all HIV/AIDS infections occur among young people under 25, most instances due to voluntary sexual behavior or intravenous drug use (chapter 5). Half of all murders and violent crimes in Jamaica are committed by young males 18–25, who make up 10 percent of the population.[37] This is not totally unexpected, because behavioral research shows young people to be less risk-averse than older people[38] and criminal activity is a risky business.

Policies that help youth recover from bad outcomes can provide a safety net and benefit society well into the future. Referred to in this Report as second chances, they must be well designed, well targeted, and well coordinated, and give the right incentives to beneficiaries.

Targeting programs finely

Because of the high cost of second-chance programs, it is important to direct them to the neediest youth, such as orphans and those from families too poor to provide a safety net. Interventions that use means testing, geographic targeting, and self-selection are all associated with getting a larger share of the benefits to the lower two quintiles of the population.

Aside from avoiding errors of inclusion (giving subsidies to those who do not need them) it is important to avoid errors of exclusion—leaving out young people who need to be reached. This is especially true regarding health risks, because some risky behaviors may not have an immediate and discernible impact on health. More than 100 million young people are afflicted by sexually transmitted infections (STIs), including HIV, every year. Some infections are easily treated if identified early. Many, however, go unnoticed (especially when initial symptoms are mild) unless diagnosed by trained health workers. In South Africa, many reproductive health services are not easily accessible by young people; when they do go, they feel that facility staff are judgmental and hostile. It might not be surprising, then, that those who contract STIs would rather go to traditional healers than to low-quality and high-cost formal services. In Nigeria, providing school students with STI education and training pharmacists and private doctors to treat STIs in adolescents increased the uptake of STI services among sexually experienced students and reduced the incidence of STIs (chapter 5).

Integrating second chances with mainstream programs

Countries have programs that try to mitigate the effects of undesirable human development outcomes for youth: youth rehabilitation programs, treatment programs for those infected with communicable diseases, and retraining programs for dropouts. Many of them are small and disconnected from each other, risking very costly parallel programs. Worse, they may not allow for reentry into mainstream programs.

Coordination is the key. Graduate equivalency, for example, allows dropouts to take classes that will eventually get them the equivalent of a primary or secondary diploma. Even without the paper certificate, getting the equivalent skills would help. The Underprivileged Children Education Program (UCEP) in Bangladesh helps 10- to 16-year-olds who have dropped out of primary school—the aim is to educate them for three years and direct them into UCEP-run vocational programs. Studies show that UCEP, which served 36,000 students in 2002, has costs per student roughly the equivalent of the regular school system (around $20 per year). At the tertiary level the community college system in the United States, designed originally to provide second chances for adults, is now being used increasingly as a second-chance program by young high school graduates—three-quarters of all remedial students are in community colleges.

Mainstream programs have to be flexible so that early mistakes do not turn into permanent liabilities. Some countries stream students as young as 10 into differing ability schools, while others keep the schools comprehensive. A recent study across 18 countries, comparing the performance of these students on standardized international secondary-level tests, finds that early tracking not only increases education inequality (there is no catching up despite the segregation) but may also lessen performance.[39]

Rehabilitation with accountability

Rehabilitation is very costly, but the payoffs are highest for young people who still have a lifetime of potential productivity ahead of them. For those who commit crimes at a young age, they must be made to face the consequences of their actions without being made to lose hope. Many of these young people—some with relatively minor misdemeanors, some simply homeless—are often incarcerated along with hardened criminals. In the United States, where more than 10,000 juveniles are housed in adult facilities, harsher prison conditions are associated with higher recidivism rates (chapter 7). Consequences should be commensurate with the gravity of the crime, and programs should facilitate the reintegration of these young people into healthy and productive roles in society.

Some interventions (chapter 7) have overcome the limited capacity of court systems, such as the Justice on Wheels program in the Philippines, where judges travel to correctional facilities around the country to speed up the trial process. As an alternative to traditional *retributive* justice, more than 80 countries have *restorative* justice programs to promote rehabilitation. The programs provide opportunities for victims and offenders to meet, and to agree on a plan of restitution. The most famous of these is the Truth and Reconciliation program in South Africa instituted after apartheid.

Young people have been involved in conflicts in every part of the globe: estimates suggest that 300,000 under the age of 18 are now or have recently been involved in armed conflict, and another 500,000 have been recruited into military or paramilitary forces.[40] Experience with disarmament, demobilization, and rehabilitation programs shows that it is possible for young combatants to reconstruct their lives in peacetime. Ex-combatants clearly require skills training to prepare them for post-conflict life, but they also need medical and psychosocial support to overcome the traumas they have suffered. Young female ex-combatants may have a distinct set of needs that may not be addressed by programs designed for male soldiers.

Any remediation program confronts what economists call moral hazard. If someone knows that the consequences of risk-taking behavior are mitigated by a government program or by insurance, that person might engage in more risk-taking than warranted. Some express fear that the availability of antiretroviral therapy could cause young people to take fewer precautions. Indeed, in Kenya, condom use fell after the government announced reported "cures" for AIDS.[41] The solution is not to deny second chances like treatment—that would be unethical as well as wasteful. Instead, it is to build in incentives that encourage the care-taking behavior to persist even as people undergo treatment. Programs that enhance both capability and second chances are more likely to succeed.

This concept is well illustrated in vocational training programs for out-of-school youth. In a variety of country settings the programs tend not to pass cost-benefit tests. However, when training is provided as part of a comprehensive package that gives recipients the incentives and information to find jobs—such as employment services, counseling, and life-skills training—they have better outcomes. Jovenes programs in Latin America, targeted to training disadvantaged youth, ages 16–29, can have significant effects on employability and earnings. The training may also be costly, but the costs compare well to other human capital development programs for young people (chapter 4).

Moving forward

The broad policy directions recommended in this report—divided according to the youth lenses of opportunities, capabilities, and second chances—are summarized in table 1. Some of the actions and programs require a reallocation of resources. These include the recommendations to attend to quality in the development of basic skills for adolescents and young adults, as governments press ahead with meeting quantitative targets for children. In countries that have already met their quantity and quality targets, the priority is to expand access to upper secondary and tertiary education, especially by stimulating the demand for education.

Public spending alone will not do the trick. Policies must stimulate young people, their parents, and their communities to invest in themselves. The Report describes the failures in markets, institutions, and policies that contribute to an unfavorable climate for human capital investments in

"When it comes to 'youth making a difference in communities' I think the value of youth has been underestimated everywhere. Youth are excellent in delivering grass roots levels development projects at minimal budgets and very effectively. Due to the fact that they are involved at the grass roots level, they can easily implement a project without the bureaucracy of organizations . . . they often have a lower cost base too."

—Shasheen, 20,
Australia
June 2006

Table 1 Policy goals, directions, actions, and programs

Broaden opportunities for young people to develop their human capital		Develop capabilities of young people as decision-making agents		Offer second chances to manage consequences of bad outcomes that occur early in life	
Policy goals	*Policy actions and programs*	*Policy goals*	*Policy actions and programs*	*Policy goals*	*Policy actions and programs*
Children enter adolescence with basic skills for further learning and practical living	Improve quality at primary and lower secondary	Young people have appropriate command over resources that affect human capital decisions	Targeted scholarships based on merit and need, conditional on outcomes (Bangladesh Female Secondary Stipend Program)	Allow young people to regain access to services that safeguard and develop human capital	Demand-driven programs that help youth reenter mainstream education systems (graduate equivalency)
	Universalize lower secondary		Micro credit for youth		Treatment for HIV/AIDS for young people
	Redesign inflexible educational systems to be more diverse and to integrate academic with life skills (Chile Education Reform)		Income-contingent loans (e.g., Australia and Thailand)		Retraining programs linked well to labor demand (e.g., Latin America's Jovenes)
	Motivate teachers with incentives	Young have sufficient and accurate information about human capital needs and constraints, and programs to address them	School-based information, education, and communication campaigns (Kenya)	Give hope to those who have committed crimes or who were combatants in armed conflict	Restorative justice and rehabilitation programs that are cost-effective (e.g., Romania, South Africa Truth and Reconciliation)
	Address demand-side constraints among girls through women teachers, improved school environments		Better Life Options Curriculum (India)		
			Job counseling programs (e.g., Philippines Overseas Workers Program)		
Young people enter labor force at the right time and are mobile to be able to accumulate higher-order skills	Align minimum wage with market realities		Curriculum reform to stress noncognitive skills training		
	Break down barriers to mobility (e.g., relax overly rigid employment protection, residence regulations)	Support decision-making by recognizing identity, and giving incentives to shift behavior	Include students in school decision making		
			Cash transfers conditional on outcomes (e.g., Mexico's Oportunidades)		
All young people are given a voice in civic life	Recognize youth as significant stakeholders in public institutions and as legal entities (e.g., policy consultations in Ceará, Brazil)		Cigarette taxes		

young people. The good news is that reforms to correct for these failures may not be as costly to the public purse as direct investment. The bad news is that they may require more difficult political trade-offs. For example, the returns to investing in young people would be substantially enhanced by trade and labor market reforms that deploy human capital more efficiently through more open competition—but this may threaten older workers who would like to maintain their entitlements. Measures that enhance capability and offer second chances may be controversial too. Some societies see decision making in the hands of the young as a threat or consider it too costly to mitigate the effects of bad decisions, even if the young were not responsible for them.

If countries are to mobilize the economic and political resources to stimulate reform, they will have to resolve three issues (chapter 9):

- *Better coordination and integration with national policy.* Youth issues by nature cut across sectors, while most policies that influence them are set within sectors (box 5). So the challenge of coordination looms large. Countries that have experienced success are those that have drawn up a coherent national framework for youth, supported by all ministries. This framework needs to be well integrated into national policy planning and budgeting (like the poverty reduction strategy processes), rather than be seen as standalone programs run by underfunded and overmandated youth ministries, which are more effective as coordinating bodies.

- *Stronger voice.* Young people's lack of voice means they are a weak constituency for reform. Parents do not represent the views and aspirations of young adults like they do for younger children.

Yet youth may lack the opportunities or self-confidence to represent themselves in public forums. Young people need to be encouraged to participate more fully in public life. Governments and other agencies need to learn to communicate with them, make their programs attractive to them, and tap their immense talents as partners in service delivery.

- *More evaluation.* The dearth of rigorously evaluated youth-oriented programs and policies can undermine the credibility of them, even if most are promising. Preparing this Report was a challenge because of this gap—studies like the one in box 5 were fairly rare. Addressing this gap requires capacity building in government and incentives to use evidenced-based criteria in deciding among programs. Because such knowledge is a public good, it also requires international funding. The policies and programs mentioned in table 1 include not only those that have been rigorously evaluated, but those that appear to be promising based on professional judgments. Otherwise it would have been a patchy table indeed.

Some issues raised in this Report may never be resolved. After all, parents have been complaining about their teenagers (and vice versa) for a long time. Such issues are part of human maturation and outside the realm of development economics. But the Report also identifies other "actionable" concerns about the development of youth's human capital—concerns that, if unaddressed, can put all development at risk. Fortunately, examples abound of young people, supported by good policies and institutions, who have not only coped but flourished, thereby contributing to the future of all generations.

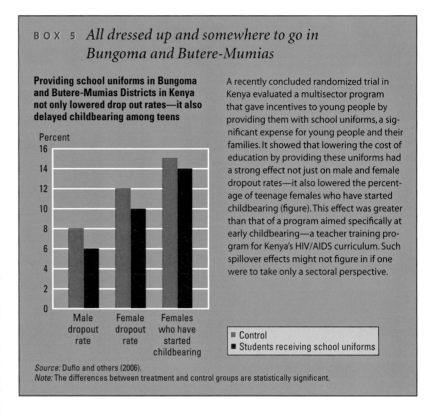

B O X 5 *All dressed up and somewhere to go in Bungoma and Butere-Mumias*

Providing school uniforms in Bungoma and Butere-Mumias Districts in Kenya not only lowered drop out rates—it also delayed childbearing among teens

A recently concluded randomized trial in Kenya evaluated a multisector program that gave incentives to young people by providing them with school uniforms, a significant expense for young people and their families. It showed that lowering the cost of education by providing these uniforms had a strong effect not just on male and female dropout rates—it also lowered the percentage of teenage females who have started childbearing (figure). This effect was greater than that of a program aimed specifically at early childbearing—a teacher training program for Kenya's HIV/AIDS curriculum. Such spillover effects might not figure in if one were to take only a sectoral perspective.

■ Control
■ Students receiving school uniforms

Source: Duflo and others (2006).
Note: The differences between treatment and control groups are statistically significant.

Launched in 1997 by Chilean university students as a summer project to provide minimum living conditions for the poor, a program mobilized 4,000 volunteers to build 2,156 homes in the poorest parts of southern Chile in the first two years. By 2004, Un Techo Para Chile had built more than 24,000 basic housing units and recruited more than 18,000 volunteers each year. The group has also developed initiatives on technical training, education, microcredit, health, judicial services, and community service. The initiative has also spawned Un Techo Para mi País to share its experiences with other countries across Latin America. (http://www.untechoparachile.cl/)

Why now, and how?

PART I

DEVELOPING COUNTRIES' POPULATIONS HAVE more young people than ever; indeed, in many countries, there are more young people now than there likely will ever be, because of falling fertility. This presents challenges but many more rewards—if policies and institutions for the next generation of workers, household heads, citizens, and leaders are well designed and implemented. Hard to do, but, as some countries have shown, not impossible.

Opportunity. The capability to choose. Another chance when choices go wrong. These are the lenses through which policies must be viewed to examine whether they create the right climate for investment in the human capital of the young.

Youth, poverty reduction, and growth

The developing world's 1.3 billion young people ages 12–24 are its next generation of economic and social actors. Making sure that they are well prepared for their futures—as workers, entrepreneurs, parents, citizens, and community leaders—is thus enormously important to the course of poverty reduction and growth. Because human development is cumulative, missed opportunities to invest in and prepare this generation will be extremely costly to reverse, both for young people and for society.

That it is hard for children to recover from early setbacks in human development is well recognized. New circumstances, however, mean that many developing country governments now have to deal with the needs of those a little older—with next-generation issues of human capital development among youth—if they wish to consolidate and build on the gains so far. Rising primary school completion rates have put enormous pressure on higher levels of education, even in the poorest countries. Even as primary education becomes more widespread throughout the developing world, changes in technology mean that young people need more than basic skills to compete successfully in the job market. As a result of the epidemiological transition from communicable to noncommunicable diseases, along with the emergence of new diseases such as HIV/AIDS, young people are exposed to a different range of health risks than before. Finally, changes in the political landscape and the growth of civil society have altered the meaning of citizenship—and with it, what young people need to learn to engage effectively in community and society.

Even as the development needs of the young come into sharper focus, the demographic transition under way in most developing countries is creating an enormous opportunity to invest more in their human capital because of the decline in the ratio of dependents (children and elderly) to workers. This could even lead to a demographic dividend—an acceleration in the rate of growth, as witnessed by some countries in East Asia—if the right policies are in place to employ the growing labor force.

In countries where the demographic transition is yet to get under way (a handful of countries in Sub-Saharan Africa), a case can still be made for paying attention to young people because of the changing health landscape and the need to engage young people effectively as workers and citizens. At the same time service delivery will need to focus on basic education and health services for children and mothers, essential for lowering infant mortality and fertility. In countries where the demographic transition is far advanced (as in some countries in East Asia and some former transition economies), there is a strong case for investing in the young before the rising fiscal burden of a growing elderly population heightens the trade-offs between the young and the old.

How well are countries preparing this next wave of workers, entrepreneurs, parents, and citizens? The answer varies. Despite enormous progress with primary schooling in the poorest countries, many young people cannot read. In other developing countries many of the young, especially from the poorest households, stumble on the way from primary to secondary school. In still others, the main obstacle is continuing from secondary to higher education. Considering other dimensions important to reducing poverty and sustaining growth—such as improving the quality of formal schooling to provide skills relevant to the changing needs of the labor market, or the knowledge and ability to avoid risky health behaviors—it is clear that much remains to be done.

As developing countries focus on their young, at least five dimensions—or transitions—are relevant from a development perspective. Already mentioned are learning, going to work, and avoiding risks to health. As a fourth dimension, young people also need to learn how to become good parents. Finally, as democratization brings greater representation and civil liberties, they need to learn how to engage as citizens. For countries that address the challenges of these five transitions—learning, going to work, staying healthy, forming families, and exercising citizenship—the payoffs can be enormous.

Young people are critical to further progress with poverty reduction and growth

Poverty in the developing world has declined significantly in the last 20 years, with the deepest reductions in East Asia (with and without China) and South Asia (with and without India). As a result, the developing world is likely to meet the Millennium Development Goal of reducing poverty. However, all regions other than East Asia and South Asia will fall short.[1]

What can be done to reduce poverty more widely? Past *World Development Report*s have articulated strategies based on the building blocks of economic growth, human capital, empowerment, and social protection.[2] The blocks are mutually dependent, so they are like the wheels of an "all-wheel drive" vehicle, complementing each other to navigate difficult terrain.

Young people and poverty reduction

Where do young people fit into this? This Report considers young people as, broadly speaking, those in the age group 12–24 years (box 1.1). Youth is a period of intense learning, when people can acquire the

"Early marriage spells doom for children because they end up being like their parents."

Young person, Abuja, Nigeria
December 2005

BOX 1.1 *What is youth?*

Youth is a transitional phase from childhood to adulthood when young people, through a process of intense physiological, psychological, social, and economic change, gradually come to be recognized—and to recognize themselves—as adults. So it is more a stage in life than an age. It can also be a period of great energy, enthusiasm, and creativity giving rise to the expression that you are "as young as you feel," which is especially popular among those who are well past their youth!

For research and policy it is useful to pin down the period of youth more precisely. Perspectives on the most relevant age range vary across disciplines. In the health field youth is associated with the ages of physical maturation that begins with menarche for girls and more gradually for boys, typically between the ages of 10 and 16. In the social sciences youth is defined by the acquisition of various adult statuses, marked by events such as menarche, leaving school, employment, marriage, and voting, with the recognition that becoming an adult is a lengthy, self-reinforcing process, often extending into the twenties. Social psychologists argue that the subjective experience of feeling adult matters at least as much as the objective markers of adulthood, such as age or a particular

status. While much research is based in developed countries, it suggests that young people in their late teens and early twenties often see themselves as not yet adult. Some argue that this prolonged period of semi-autonomy can be viewed as a new life stage in which young people experiment with adult roles but do not fully commit to them.

Laws in most countries designate ages when people can be treated as adults and are thus no longer offered the protections of childhood. One can thus change from being a child to being an adult overnight. But the age at which school attendance is no longer compulsory, and employment is legally permitted typically ranges between 11 and 16 years. Legal responsibility for crime can begin earlier, but individuals are generally not charged as adults until around 16. Political participation through voting is postponed, typically to around 18 or later. Likewise, service in the military, whether compulsory or voluntary, is often restricted until age 18. The purchase of cigarettes, in countries where there are restrictions on sales to minors, is allowed from around 15 to 18. Consumption of alcohol, where it is legally prohibited for minors, is allowed from around 18 to 21, though in some cases it is prohibited until the age of 25.

National policies on youth typically establish an age range for beneficiaries. The lower bound ranges from around 12 years (Jordan) to around 18 years (Bangladesh). In some cases it is not strictly defined, as in Hungary, where the youth secretariat deals with both 0- to 14-year-olds and 15- to 26-year-olds. The upper bound ranges from around 24 (Jamaica) to even 35 or 40 (Kenya, Pakistan).

The UN's World Program of Action for Youth defines "youth" as people ages 15–24, while the World Health Organization (WHO) and UNICEF use the terms "adolescent" for those 10–19, "youth" for those 15–24, and "young people" for those 10–24. The wider band of 10–24 years used by these agencies recognizes that many policies directed at youth often need to influence outcomes before the age of 15.

Recognizing the diversity in perspective, this Report uses different ranges depending on the context. However, the focus, by and large, is on the age range 12–24, when important foundations are laid for learning and skills. The Report uses the terms "youth" and "young people" interchangeably.

Source: Fussell (2006).

"One of my neighbors is an intelligent girl, but she could not register at school because her mom did not have the 250 lempiras [about $13] she needed for the matriculation."

Young person, Honduras
January 2006

"Education is anything but inclusive."

Disabled young person,
Recife, Brazil
January 2006

human capital they need to move themselves and their families out of poverty (definition 1.1). Not confined to the skills needed to become an economically productive adult, learning extends to other aspects of life such as navigating health risks and becoming a responsible spouse or parent or citizen.[3] It can happen in several ways, often through the formal school system, but also through learning from parents, peers, family, community, and work experience. Because the capacity for learning is so great relative to older ages, missed opportunities—to acquire skills in school or on the job, or good health habits, or the desire to engage in community and society—can be extremely difficult to reverse.

The high cost of remedying missed opportunities is easiest to appreciate in formal schooling. For many, youth marks the transition from primary to secondary school. Dropout rates can be very sharp at this stage, especially in countries that have made primary education universal (see figure 1 in the overview). Those who drop out at this stage typically never return—in part because few countries have programs of remedial education to ease the transition back into school, or provide formal equivalency with school degrees. The competing demands of work and, for young women, of family and children are further obstacles to returning to school. Discouragement and stigma can also play a role, and there is a question of whether cognitive development, once arrested, can be resumed, especially if the gaps are long (chapter 3). Similar arguments apply to other missed opportunities, such as learning from continuing employment (chapter 4) or civic engagement (chapter 7).

Building human capacity early is important not just for the future opportunities open to young people but also to mitigate the intergenerational transmission of poverty. More educated youth are more willing to control family size and invest in the health and well-being of their offspring. The impacts are particularly strong for women.[4] In all developing regions the average number of children born is significantly lower for women with at least secondary education. Maternal education strongly influences

child health and birth weight. Throughout the developing world, but especially in the low-income regions of South Asia and Sub-Saharan Africa, the percentage of children immunized is higher when mothers have some secondary education.[5]

Parental schooling is also important for the cognitive development of children. Evidence from Ecuador shows that the more educated the parents, the greater the positive impacts on the cognitive development of children as young as three years—impacts that become more pronounced as children grow older.[6] These findings hold even when controlling for the better health of children of more educated parents.

Given the importance of building human capital in youth, it comes as no surprise that this stage of life is given some prominence in the international commitment to development as reflected in the Millennium Development Goals. Seven of the eight goals relate to outcomes for young people either directly or indirectly (box 1.2).

Many aspects of human capital development among the young are, however, not covered by the Millennium Development Goals. Preparing young people to be active citizens is notably absent. Within education, the quality of education is not sufficiently emphasized, while the health goals do not take into account health risks beyond HIV/AIDS and those arising from motherhood.

Young people and equity

Poverty reduction is more than a reduction in absolute deprivation. Relative deprivation or inequity is also enormously important.[7] A concern for equity leads to an emphasis on early intervention to build human capacity because inequity—or "inequality of opportunity" in the parlance of last year's *World Development Report*—quickly becomes deeply entrenched. In developing countries where basic education has become widespread, many inequalities of opportunity—at least as they relate to schooling—appear in youth as poor young people drop out of school, or receive poorer quality education than the rich (chapter 3). For many young women from poor households, youth marks the entry into early marriage or early childbearing, effectively sealing off further opportunities for

---

BOX 1.2   *"The Millennium Development Goals are not about youth, right?" No, wrong!*

Although the widespread impression is that the Millennium Development Goals are about providing basic services to children, seven of the eight goals have outcomes that relate to young people.

Education outcomes for the young are explicitly targeted both as a part of achieving universal primary education (goal 2), and promoting gender equality and empowering women (goal 3). The high risk of HIV/AIDS faced by young people, especially in Sub-Saharan Africa, is targeted through three indicators relating to how well the young are informed of risks, to infection rates among young pregnant women, and to risks facing orphans—all critical to combating the spread of HIV/AIDS (goal 6). The role of young people as stakeholders in the future of international development is recognized through an emphasis on employment opportunities for them as a part of building a global partnership for international development (goal 8).

Even where young people are not the explicit focus, their involvement can be important to achieving goals. Young women contribute 20–30 percent of total fertility in high-fertility countries and upward of 50 percent in low-fertility regimes (chapter 6). Given the well-recognized links between female schooling, fertility, and child health, the education of young women and their ongoing reproductive health needs are thus critical to meeting goal 4 on child mortality and goal 5 on improving maternal health. All in all, making sure that young people have the opportunity to build and use human capital—whether through better schooling, better health, or more productive employment—will take the world a long way toward meeting goal 1, eradicating extreme poverty and hunger.

Seven out of the eight Millennium Development Goals target youth outcomes

Millennium Development Goal	Direct or indirect youth-specific target
Goal 1. Eradicate extreme poverty and hunger	Indirect
Goal 2. Achieve universal primary education	Target 8. Literacy rate of 15- to 24-year-olds
Goal 3. Promote gender equality and empower women	Target 9. Ratio of girls to boys in primary, secondary, and tertiary education Target 10. Ratio of literate women to men, ages 15–24
Goal 4. Reduce child mortality	Indirect
Goal 5. Improve maternal health	Indirect
Goal 6. Combat HIV/AIDS, malaria, and other diseases	Target 18. HIV prevalence among pregnant women ages 15–24 years Target 19. Percentage of population ages 15–24 years with comprehensive and correct knowledge of HIV/AIDS Target 20. Ratio of school attendance of orphans to school attendance of nonorphans ages 10–14 years
Goal 8. Develop a global partnership for development	Target 45. Unemployment rate of young people ages 15–24, by sex

Source: Authors. For Millennium Development Goals and targets see http://unstats.un.org/unsd/mi/mi_goals.asp.

---

schooling or employment (chapters 5 and 6). Solidarity with other human beings, and attitudes toward those who are ethnically or religiously different, are also formed in youth and can be important to young people's sense of identity and how they relate to others in society (chapter 7). Youth can thus be an important period for promoting equality of opportunity and allowing individuals to attain their full potential.

Young people and growth

Youth is an important stage of life for building the human capital that allows young people to escape poverty and lead better and more fulfilling lives. The human capital formed in youth—whether in skill levels, or health, or civic and societal engagement—is also an important determinant of long-term growth.

The most compelling evidence is on the microeconomic side. Schooling is persistently found to increase productivity, as reflected in earnings. As discussed below, average earnings for those with secondary and particularly tertiary education have risen over time because of the growing demand for higher skilled workers. The evidence extends beyond the wage sector—educated farmers are more likely to adopt new technologies, and almost all studies on agricultural productivity show that better educated farmers get higher returns on their land.[8] Many studies have documented the importance of a large pool of educated workers—particularly if they are educated to the secondary level—for knowledge spillovers and for foreign direct investment.[9] Lower computer penetration and productivity in Latin America and the Caribbean compared with the East Asian economies has been attributed to the lower proportion of the workforce with secondary schooling.[10]

Macroeconomic models also suggest large potential impacts on growth and living standards. The strongest evidence relates to the impact of HIV/AIDS on growth and productivity. HIV/AIDS disproportionately affects young people ages 15–24 in high prevalence countries, where they account for more than half of new infections. In South Africa, where prevalence is over 20 percent, the unchecked spread of the epi-

"When we work, [...] there remains no time or energy for depression, juvenile delinquency, aggression, and the like."

Young person, Nepal
January 2006

BOX 1.3 — *Losing a decade—what HIV/AIDS is doing to human capital accumulation and growth in Kenya*

Young people in Kenya, as in most parts of the world, confront the real choice between continuing their educations and starting to work. They also become sexually active, with all the gratifications and risks that entails, including contracting such sexually transmitted diseases as HIV/AIDS. Somewhat later, as young adults, they choose partners, have children, and take on the responsibilities of family life. To examine the impact of these decisions on human capital and long-term growth, Bell, Bruhns, and Gersbach (2006) set up an overlapping generations model in which the wellspring of growth is human capital accumulation.

In the model, the formation of human capital involves the intergenerational transmission of knowledge and abilities through both child rearing and formal education. The growth process can be derailed by the failure to expand human capital as a result of poor quality schooling or the limited expansion in schooling, or premature adult mortality from HIV/AIDS. In Kenya, the victims of AIDS are overwhelmingly young adults or those in the early prime years, most with children to raise and care for.

A parent's death does more than destroy the victim's human capital. It also weakens the mechanism to form human capital in the next generation and beyond. Why? Because the affected family's lifetime income shrinks, and with it the means to finance children's education, and because children lose the parental knowledge and guidance that complement formal education.

The model suggests that as a result of HIV/AIDS, national income in Kenya will be roughly halved by 2040 (box figure). Per capita income growth, faltering since the 1980s in Kenya, takes half a decade longer to recover to 1990 levels in the AIDS scenario than without AIDS. By 2040, per capita income is 15 percent lower than without AIDS. Note that with higher population in the no-AIDS scenario, per capita income is actually lower until 2010 than in the AIDS scenario.

The reductions in growth are driven in large part by the setback in the spread of secondary education, which both lowers the productivity of school leavers and weakens the transmission of human capital to their children. By 2040, HIV/AIDS delays human capital attainment on average by about a decade.

HIV/AIDS can have a big impact on the growth of national and per capita income in Kenya

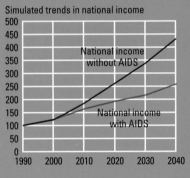

Simulated trends in national income

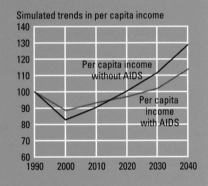

Simulated trends in per capita income

Source: Bell, Bruhns, and Gersbach (2006).

demic is estimated to reduce the growth of GDP in the range 0.8 to 1.5 percentage points a year.[11] In Kenya, where the epidemic is hitting a peak currently, one estimate suggests it will take more than 40 years for per capita income to recover to 1990 levels (box 1.3). In Russia, with its smaller but more rapidly growing epidemic, GDP may decline by 10 percent in 2020 if no attempt is made to limit the spread of the disease.[12]

More conventional approaches to estimating macroeconomic effects, through cross-country regression analysis, provide less clear-cut evidence.[13] In part it is difficult to measure human capital consistently across countries, let alone that which is formed in youth, other than through fairly crude measures such as completed years of schooling. Plus weaknesses of institutions or demand mean than human capital does not consistently add to growth everywhere. However, one attempt to get beyond quantity finds a robust relationship between growth and the quality of human capital embodied in the labor force.[14]

Young people are also an enormous resource for growth in the short run. In many developing countries, they form the largest group of job seekers. Their share in the unemployed is upward of 50 percent in most countries in the Middle East and North Africa, and upward of 40 percent in the Caribbean. Having young people sit idle is costly in forgone output. Estimates indicate that lowering youth unemployment could raise GDP by anywhere from 0.3 to 2.7 percent in a range of Caribbean countries[15] based on forgone earnings alone.

Failing to direct young people into productive pursuits can prove costly in other ways. In many countries crime often peaks in this age group and can hurt the investment climate. In Jamaica, youth 17–29 are responsible for more than half of all prosecuted crime except arson.[16] A 1 percent reduction in youth crime could increase tourist flows, and raise tourism revenues by J$40 million (about $1 million), or 4 percent.[17]

How the challenges confronting young people have changed

Not only is human capital development in youth important to poverty reduction and growth, changing circumstances mean that many developing countries have to focus more on this stage than ever before.

Expansion in access to basic education

In many of the poorest countries, progress with providing basic education to children means that governments are now confronted with the learning needs of those who are somewhat older—youth. Despite outstanding challenges, primary completion rates have increased substantially, particularly in South Asia, Sub-Saharan Africa, and Latin America and the Caribbean. Combined with the larger number of children of graduating age, the pressure on education systems at levels above primary is enormous (figure 1.1). The only region in the world experiencing little pressure on this account is Europe and Central Asia, where falling fertility is reducing the number of primary school graduates.

Building on the gains to primary schooling requires balancing opportunities for postprimary schooling with the expansion of primary schooling. In countries where the gains to primary completion are recent, the main challenge is providing access to secondary education, especially lower secondary. In other countries that have been successful in providing access to secondary (especially lower secondary) education, the balanced expansion of access to upper secondary and tertiary education is more of an issue. But throughout the developing world, as schooling becomes more widespread, the education system also needs to recognize that students are becoming more diverse and may require more options for learning in keeping with their different interests and abilities.

Rising demand for workers with higher education

The global context is changing in other ways. Unlike 20 years ago, when earnings of workers with secondary and tertiary education were low relative to those with primary education in many developing countries, earnings have now risen substantially, particularly for workers with tertiary education but also, in some countries, for those with secondary education.[18] In Latin America and the Caribbean, labor market returns to those who completed primary or secondary education have declined sharply, while the returns to those with tertiary education have increased (figure 1.2a). In Ghana there has been a marked increase in the return to university education over time, and as a result, those returns are significantly higher than returns to primary than they were in the past. In Vietnam, returns to both tertiary and upper secondary (high school) have risen relative to primary (figure 1.2b).

The rising premium on higher education reflects the growing demand for skills driven in large part by the spread of new technologies.[19] Twenty years ago the expansion of trade was expected to increase the demand for unskilled workers in developing countries. However, the spread of new technologies to developing countries has sharply increased the demand for skilled workers, substantially increasing returns even as the supply of skilled workers has increased. Recent research suggests that the increase in the number of skilled workers may have in fact boosted skill-biased technological change and raised the demand for skills.[20]

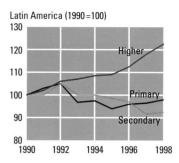

Figure 1.2a Returns to higher education have risen over time

Latin America (1990=100)

Source: Behrman, Birdsall, and Szekely (2003).
Note: Estimates are based on log wage regressions for 30- to 55-year-old urban males that control for various factors affecting earnings, based on 71 sample surveys from 18 countries with an average sample per year of over 7,000 individuals.

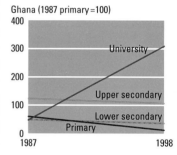
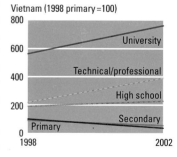

Figure 1.2b Returns to higher education have also risen relative to primary schooling

Ghana (1987 primary=100)

Vietnam (1998 primary=100)

Source: Gian and others (2006); and Schultz (2003).
Note: For Ghana, estimates are based on log wage regressions for 35- to 54-year-old males with controls for post-schooling experience and other factors. For Vietnam, estimates are based on log wage regressions for workers ages 18–65 whose primary employment was in the wage sector.

Figure 1.1 The number of children completing primary school has risen in most regions

Number of primary school graduates in 2003 (1990=100)

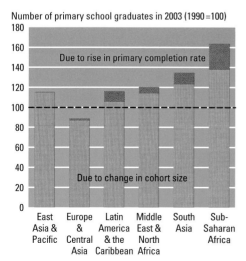

Source: World Bank, UNESCO Institute for Statistics (UIS), and OECD (2006) for primary completion rates; World Bank (2006h).

Figure 1.3 People today participate more in political processes and have greater civil rights and liberties

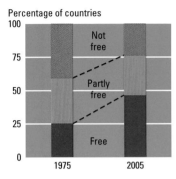

Percentage of countries

Source: Freedom House (2006).
Note: The freedom ratings are a composite of two measures that relate to political rights and civil liberties. Each is ranked on a scale from 1 (least free) to 7 (most free). See http://www .freedomhouse.org for details.

The growing demand for skills has increased the value of further education and made it more important for growth. Indeed, in many countries building a workforce with higher order skills is an important part of improving the climate for investment, acquiring a competitive edge, and generally maintaining the engine of growth. Because much of the return to higher education—especially tertiary education—is private, rising returns are not an argument for public funding, or at least for public funding that goes beyond the need for equity of access. It does draw attention, however, to important changes in how the global market is rewarding skills.

New health risks

The health environment has also changed. As infant and child health has gradually improved, new diseases have emerged. As a result, sexual initiation and sexual experimentation in youth carries far greater risks than before, especially in some Sub-Saharan African countries with very high HIV-prevalence rates. Outside Sub-Saharan Africa, ongoing progress with tackling communicable diseases, both new and old, means that noncommunicable diseases and injuries have risen in prominence for young people. The greater coverage of roads and vehicular traffic is contributing to road fatalities. In Vietnam, road traffic accidents are the most important cause of death among young men.[21] Tobacco is now marketed far more aggressively to young people

in developing countries, and illicit drugs are available more readily.[22]

The changing nature of politics and the growth of civil society

The number of countries in which people cannot participate freely in the political process or where there is limited freedom of expression or belief has declined significantly from 4 in 10 countries in 1975 to 1 in 4 in 2005 (figure 1.3). And the number of electoral democracies has vastly increased. Many of the gains have come since the fall of the Berlin Wall and the end of communism in Eastern Europe and the former Soviet Union. With greater democratization in the developing world there has been a tendency toward decentralizing public decision making to lower levels of government[23] and toward more civic participation through civil society organizations, community interest groups, and other nongovernmental organizations.[24] This has increased the opportunities for people to participate in political activity and exercise their voice through a wide range of forums. Preparing young people for their rights and responsibilities as citizens—building their social capital for this kind of engagement—has thus become more important.

Globalization and new technologies

Young people are growing up in a more global world. Information flows have increased substantially because of the greater reach of global media, movies, music, and other cultural exports, though access varies significantly. Freer trade has expanded the goods and services that people are exposed to. And greater mobility—seen in rapid urbanization and the flows of people across borders—has increased awareness of consumption possibilities. New technologies, such as the Internet and mobile telephony, have a strong following among youth. New data collected for this Report show that young people are among the primary users of the Internet, accounting for 40 percent or more of Internet users in a range of developing countries. Access, however, varies from less than 1 percent of youth in Ethiopia to more than 50 percent in China (figure 1.4).

Figure 1.4 While access to the Internet varies greatly, young people dominate usage

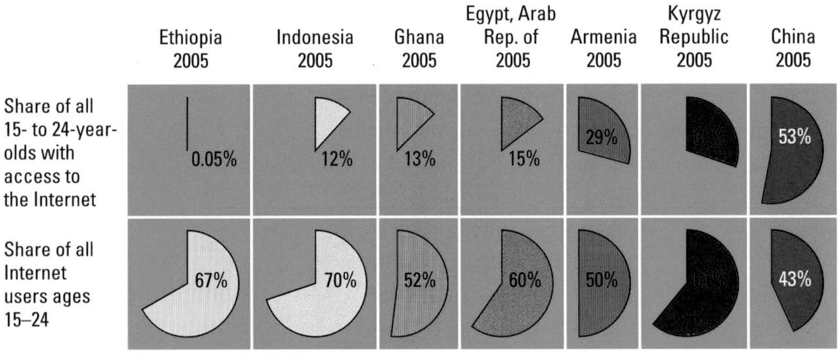

	Ethiopia 2005	Indonesia 2005	Ghana 2005	Egypt, Arab Rep. of 2005	Armenia 2005	Kyrgyz Republic 2005	China 2005
Share of all 15- to 24-year-olds with access to the Internet	0.05%	12%	13%	15%	29%		53%
Share of all Internet users ages 15–24	67%	70%	52%	60%	50%		43%

Source: WDR 2007 InterMedia surveys.
Note: "Access to the Internet" is defined as having used the Internet in the four weeks before the survey.

The impact of new information and communications technologies is likely to vary both across and within countries because of differences in access. At one end of the spectrum, young people in many middle-income countries, especially if urban or middle class, have easy access to information through radio or television or the Internet. At the other end, large numbers of young people, especially in low-income countries, continue to have very limited access not only to new sources of information, but even to traditional sources such as radio and television.

The effects of exposure to more information can be both positive and negative. The Internet is an important source of information for many young people on matters related to sexual and reproductive health, especially where little is provided in school or through the family. Both old and new media, however, can expose the young to unfiltered, beguiling, or confusing images of sex and violence. Both types of media can also promote exaggerated images of Western consumption and lead to frustration if opportunities are not commensurate with the expectations young people have formed.

The impact of greater exposure to media also depends on the local culture and its response to imports. In many parts of the developing world, the resurgence of religious movements has acted as a countervailing influence to the more permissive attitudes sometimes purveyed by the media. These movements have been associated with changes in the behavior and attitudes of young people toward sex and marriage (promoting virginity before marriage) and health (leading to a rejection of the use of alcohol and drugs).[25]

Do numbers matter? How demographic changes affect opportunities for youth

Even as changing circumstances increase the need to focus on human capital development for youth, many developing countries are helped by favorable demographic changes that are creating a unique opportunity to invest in youth.

Largest numbers ever

The current cohort of young people in developing countries is the largest the world has ever seen—around 1.3 billion.[26] On current projections, the number of 12- to 24-year-olds will reach a maximum of 1.5 billion in 2035 and decline only gradually thereafter. Numbers are at a plateau because birth rates are falling. Combined with a slowdown in the increase in the number of women of childbearing age, cohorts are at or near a maximum in many countries and in the developing world as a whole (see spotlight on differing demographics following this chapter).

The plateau hides distinct regional trends (figure 1.5). At one end, the numbers of youth in East Asia (dominated by China) have peaked and are set to decline. The same is true of Europe and Central Asia. At the other end, the youth population in Sub-Saharan Africa, already more than four times its 1950 level, is projected to continue growing rapidly into the foreseeable future.[27] South Asia, Latin America and the Caribbean, and the Middle East and North Africa are between the two extremes. Numbers in Latin America and the Caribbean have reached a peak, or a long plateau; those in South Asia and the Middle East and North Africa are expected to grow slowly until they peak in the next 25 years or so.

Figure 1.5   Trends in the developing world's population of young people vary significantly across regions

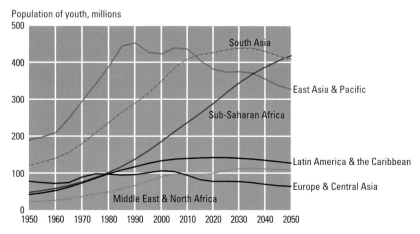

Population of youth, millions

Source: United Nations (2005b), medium variant.

Falling relative shares—
with a few exceptions

Absolute numbers are interesting—but only to a point. It is not clear that this is a critical variable unless inputs to economic and social well-being (factors of production) are in fixed supply. Some of these factors, such as land, may indeed be relatively fixed in supply, though the supply of land has been relatively unimportant in explaining economic growth, wages, or poverty during the last 50 years of rapid population growth.[28] Other inputs, such as physical capital (machinery and infrastructure) can be expanded.

Evidence from developed countries suggests that the size of youth cohorts relative to older workers is more important for long-term outcomes than absolute numbers. The postwar baby boom in Organisation for Economic Co-operation and Development (OECD) countries resulted in a relatively large number of young people entering the labor market in the 1970s (see the spotlight on baby booms following chapter 4). This cohort experienced lower wages and higher unemployment than preceding generations.

Studies that examine whether there were long-term effects—or scarring—from these negative early experiences are varied. Some conclude that the impact of being in a relatively large youth cohort tends to diminish over time, in some cases disappearing. Others find more persistent effects, especially among those with lower education (chapter 4). Caution is needed in deriving conclusions for developing countries, but note that the baby boom generation is broadly comparable in relative size to the large youth cohorts entering the labor market in developing countries today.[29]

The difference is that in most developing countries, the relative size of youth cohorts is shrinking. Figure 1.6 shows countries in different stages of the demographic transition—China is far along, while Sierra Leone is lagging. Other than in Sierra Leone, the highest peak of the youth population relative to the population of older workers occurred in the 1970s or 1980s. The declines in this ratio since then have been considerable, ranging from 25 percent to 50 percent. For a small group of countries (Sierra Leone is one of them), relative sizes are still increasing. Others in this group are Afghanistan, Chad, Democratic Republic of Congo, Equatorial Guinea, Ethiopia, Guinea-Bissau, Liberia, Niger, Republic of Congo, and Somalia. Except for Afghanistan, the countries in this group are in Sub-Saharan Africa.[30]

The fact that the relative size of youth cohorts is declining in most developing countries means that the negative effect of being part of a large cohort, strong though it may be, is declining. However, for the small group of countries where relative sizes are set to grow, the rising relative size of cohorts could well aggravate difficult employment conditions for young people—if the right macroeconomic and labor market policies are lacking.[31]

A window of opportunity
from falling dependency

The declining relative size of youth cohorts signals the decline in the ratio of dependents (children and elderly) to working population that occurs during the demographic transition. (The convention is to define children as those below 15 and the elderly as those above 65.) The trajectory of the relative size of youth cohorts mirrors the dependency ratio, diverging significantly only when the demographic transition is so far advanced that the rising burden of the elderly on the working population pushes up the dependency ratio (figure 1.6).

This decline in dependency (the rise in the ratio of working population to the nonworking population) during the demographic transition can boost economic growth.[32] The strongest evidence comes from East Asia where between 25 and 40 percent of the rapid growth between 1965 and 1990 in Japan, Hong Kong (China), the Republic of Korea, and Singapore has been attributed to the higher growth of the working age population.[33]

The potential for enhanced growth through a demographic dividend arises for two reasons. First, the rise in labor supply per capita, reinforced by the increase in female labor supply that often accompanies fertility decline, increases potential output per capita. Of course, this greater

Figure 1.6   The relative size of youth cohorts is declining in most of the developing world, as is the dependency ratio

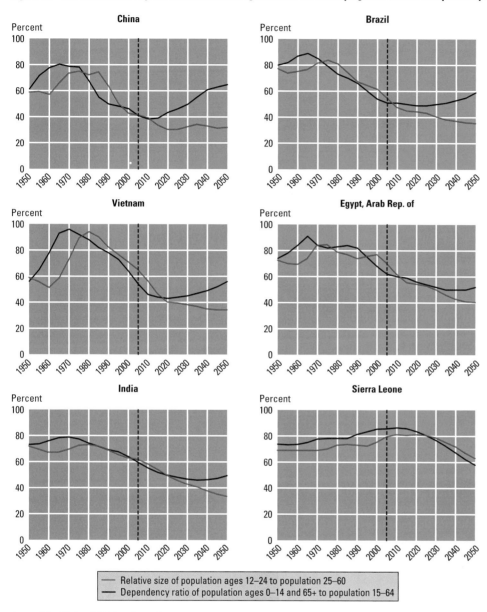

Relative size of population ages 12–24 to population 25–60
Dependency ratio of population ages 0–14 and 65+ to population 15–64

Source: United Nations (2005b), medium variant.
Note: Dotted line represents 2005.

labor supply would need to be productively employed. Second, higher savings and investment per capita associated with the rising share of the working age population (more likely to be in the saving phase of the life cycle than the rest of the population) could also boost growth. Countries in East Asia were particularly successful in absorbing their growing cohorts of new labor market entrants. Savings also grew, though it remains unclear whether this can be attributed to the rising share of the

working age population, because the micro evidence is not consistent with a life-cycle hypothesis of saving.[34] Other factors—such as rising life expectancy—may have contributed to rising savings.[35]

This literature on the pathways for the demographic dividend is not conclusive, but the idea of a demographic dividend from changes in the dependency ratio has practical significance for public expenditures. Funded by taxes on income or consumption, those expenditures are likely to

"We young women are not prepared to become mothers. I would like to continue my studies, but since I have had my daughter my options have changed, because I have many more obligations now. I hope that this will not be a barrier for me to succeed in life."

Eylin, 19, Honduras
January 2006

be affected by the ratio of the tax-paying population to the beneficiary population. Dependents are typically net beneficiaries rather than net taxpayers, depending on governments to finance primary and secondary schooling, postsecondary education (in many cases), training programs, health programs, and pensions. Early in the demographic transition, when the population of elderly is small, the main net beneficiaries are children and youth. With dependents and youth cohorts falling in size relative to the tax-paying population in many developing countries, the economic circumstances for investing public resources in children and youth are likely to improve. In a country with a 25 percent decline in the dependency ratio, every real or baht or lira or rupee collected in taxes from each working age person could pay for a 33 percent increase in spending per dependent, compared with the year of the peak ratio. This increased investment can help build the human capital of children and youth, which can have subsequent positive effects on growth.

Not every developing country has declining dependency ratios. In the countries such as Sierra Leone, mentioned earlier, the dependency ratio is still rising because the demographic transition is not yet under way.[36] There, rising dependency ratios are steadily reducing the resources available per child and young person, possibly leading to a vicious cycle of underinvestment and low growth. Without serious efforts to lower child mortality and fertility, this situation is not going to change. For the other developing countries, circumstances have never been better. Just as a changing world is increasing the need for policy to focus on the young, demographic changes are making it easier to do so. This surely is good news.

The window of opportunity presented by declining dependency ratios will also close, however, earlier in some countries than in others. Many developing countries are set to become more like developed countries, which already face the consequences of rising dependency caused by the rising share of the elderly in the

population. In China, which underwent an early and fairly rapid fertility transition, dependency ratios will start increasing as early as 2010 because of the rapid aging of the population. Other countries expected to see an increase in dependency in the next decade include Armenia, Georgia, and Thailand. The pressure to increase spending on the elderly will likely generate pressures to raise taxes, cut expenditures (including those on children and youth), or both. So there is no time like the present for investing in the young.

How prepared are youth for today's challenges? A glass half empty

How well are countries building the human capital of their young? The overall picture is one of steady progress in averages but uneven improvement across different dimensions of human capital and different groups. Thus, much more remains to be done.

Education levels have been rising worldwide, and today's youth cohorts have on average more years of schooling than their predecessors. On conventional measures of health, such as mortality in childhood or height-for-age, they are also the healthiest generation by far. Outside countries with a very high prevalence of HIV/AIDS and some parts of the former Soviet Union afflicted with premature male mortality, their chances of surviving to old age are higher than ever before.[37] These are achievements to be proud of, but the averages hide enormous differences across and within countries.

At one end of the spectrum are young people in almost every developing country who have had the benefit of good secondary education. They can be expected to go on to university. Some may even pursue an advanced degree in a developed country. In a country such as Niger, many more young people go on to study in France than in tertiary education institutions at home (chapter 8). While well off youth in developing countries may have experimented with alcohol and drugs or engaged in sex while at school, their good prospects, their means to deal with poor outcomes, and

Figure 1.7   Many young people from poor households do not have the most basic skill of literacy

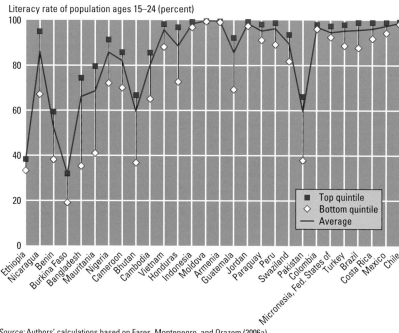

Literacy rate of population ages 15–24 (percent)

Legend:
- ■ Top quintile
- ◇ Bottom quintile
- — Average

Countries (x-axis): Ethiopia, Nicaragua, Benin, Burkina Faso, Bangladesh, Mauritania, Nigeria, Cameroon, Bhutan, Cambodia, Vietnam, Honduras, Indonesia, Moldova, Armenia, Guatemala, Jordan, Paraguay, Peru, Swaziland, Pakistan, Colombia, Micronesia, Fed. States of, Turkey, Brazil, Costa Rica, Mexico, Chile

Source: Authors' calculations based on Fares, Montenegro, and Orazem (2006a).
Note: Countries are ordered from lowest to highest GDP per capita (PPP).

possibly their greater awareness mean that this experimentation is less likely to have adverse consequences. Because they have access to better quality education, many will have developed "softer" life skills, such as working in teams or handling difficult situations with confidence. Finally, being the children of more educated and wealthier parents, many may be developing a sense of their place in community and society.

At the other end of the spectrum are a vast number of young people for whom the opportunities look very different. Many either did not attend school as children or dropped out too early to acquire even the most basic skills, leaving more than 130 million 15- to 24-year-olds illiterate. Most of them are in South Asia and Sub-Saharan Africa, more of them women than men (figure 1.7). For those who progress through school, average grade completed shows a similar pattern, with rich young-sters completing more years of school than poor youngsters (box 1.4).

For poor young people with little or no education, life's opportunities are restricted. Young men with little or no education face enormous disadvantages in the labor market. Many may have worked as children. The International Labor Organization (ILO) estimates there were 84 mil-lion 12- to 14-year-olds working in 2000.[38] As child laborers grow older they face very limited options for employment and earn-ings. For many poor young women, their limited (or nonexistent) education is asso-ciated with early marriage, which is still high in a number of countries (chapter 6). Many studies from Sub-Saharan Africa find that early marriage increases the risk of HIV/AIDS among women because of the higher frequency of sexual contact within marriage. Young women are more likely to bear children at an early age if they are from poor households (box 1.4). This combination of poverty and low education means that they are not well-placed to take care of themselves or their offspring, per-petuating poverty.

Between the two ends of the spectrum are the vast swath of today's young people. Many of them are still in primary school, having started late and frequently repeat-ing grades. Late starts are more common in postconflict environments: in Cambo-dia, 15 percent of 15- to 19-year-olds were enrolled in primary school in 2001. Others will have made it through primary school

BOX 1.4   *A youth perspective on equity and development*

World Development Report 2006 made a case for focusing on inequalities in key dimensions of opportunity—such as education, health, and the capacity to participate in society—because these inequalities tend to perpetuate themselves, both across groups in societies and over time. This can result in inequality traps, which some groups or people are unable to escape. This is detrimental on both intrinsic grounds, because people cannot realize their full potential, and on instrumental grounds, because inequality traps can curtail growth and dynamism.

Many inequalities become entrenched in youth because of the vastly different opportunities confronting youngsters from different economic backgrounds.

We have already discussed how differences in literacy—the most basic of skills—affect the future income-earning potential of youngsters and the economic prospects of their families.

But even among those who go to school, opportunities are vastly different (figure 1).

As might be expected, per capita income and schooling attainment among 15- to 24-year-olds are broadly correlated. In many low-income countries, though, young people from the poorest 20 percent of households cannot aspire to complete the primary cycle (six years). On the other hand, those from the richest 20 percent of households can expect to do so almost everywhere. Among those from poor households, girls are far less likely to complete primary school than boys. These differences, in addition to perpetuating poverty, are an enormous cost to society—with the poor unable to make the most of their talents.

Young people's access to productive jobs, which allow them to build skills and experience, also varies enormously between those from rich and poor households (figure 2). Youngsters from poor households are far less

likely to find paid employment outside the home than those from rich households, in some cases by a substantial margin. The contrast is particularly striking in countries such as Bolivia, Panama, and Paraguay.

For young women, puberty and adolescence often mark the divergence in opportunity with their male counterparts (see spotlight on gender following chapter 2), differences heightened by poverty. Poor young women are not only less likely than their richer sisters to complete primary schooling—they are also far more likely to bear children before the age of 15 (figure 3), which can be detrimental to their health and well-being and that of their children. The life trajectories of 15- to 24-year-old women from poor households can thus be very circumscribed.

Addressing these inequalities is an important part of addressing inequality of opportunity by allowing young people to participate more fully in their societies.

Opportunities for young people at school and work vary enormously between rich and poor

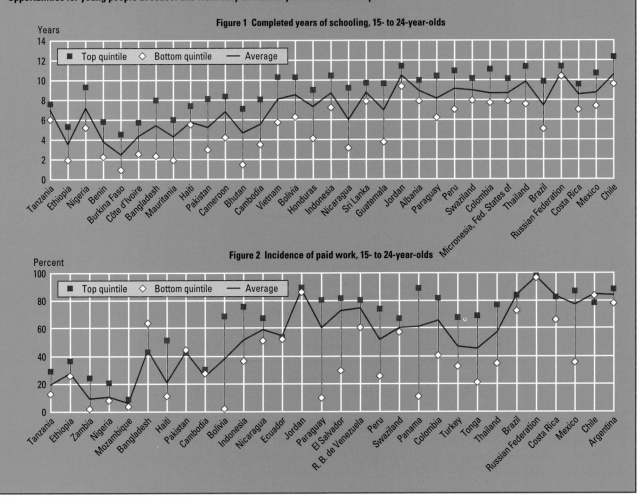

Figure 1 Completed years of schooling, 15- to 24-year-olds

Figure 2 Incidence of paid work, 15- to 24-year-olds

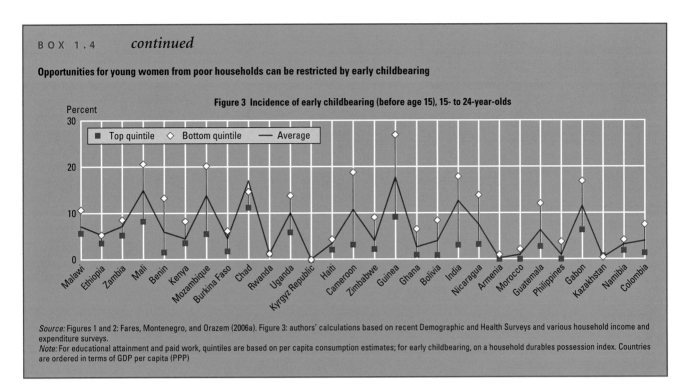

B O X 1 . 4   *continued*

Opportunities for young women from poor households can be restricted by early childbearing

Figure 3 Incidence of early childbearing (before age 15), 15- to 24-year-olds

Source: Figures 1 and 2: Fares, Montenegro, and Orazem (2006a). Figure 3: authors' calculations based on recent Demographic and Health Surveys and various household income and expenditure surveys.
Note: For educational attainment and paid work, quintiles are based on per capita consumption estimates; for early childbearing, on a household durables possession index. Countries are ordered in terms of GDP per capita (PPP)

on time, but they may have faltered in the transition to secondary school—because of poor access to schools, a curriculum that fails to engage and instruct, and high costs (including opportunity costs), especially for the poor. Still others will be progressing through secondary school, for the most part, acquiring fewer skills for work and life than young people in developed countries. Those who are from poor families will learn even less than those from richer backgrounds (chapter 3).

The challenges young people confront go beyond acquiring skills relevant to the labor market and extend to skills to navigate health risks and engage constructively in community and society. Many young people remain far from well-informed about the consequences of excessive consumption of alcohol or drugs or engaging in unprotected sex. Knowledge of how to prevent HIV/AIDS, which is nowhere near universal, is in many cases confined to a very small proportion of young people (chapter 5). Regular consumption of tobacco is very common in many developing countries: upward of a quarter of 15- to 24-year-old men currently smoke regularly

in Armenia (44 percent), Indonesia (58 percent), Mexico (29 percent), and Nepal (55 percent).[39] Many developing countries provide civic instruction at school, but it is only as effective as the teaching methods, which can leave much to be desired (chapter 7). Opportunities to participate in the community—whether in school councils, community organizations, or local governments—vary substantially both across and within countries (chapters 3 and 7).

Finally, many young people cannot find work. Unemployment rates for young people, which are higher than those for adults all over the world, are five to seven times the adult unemployment rates in some developing countries (chapter 4). Unemployment is not the only problem, as many young people are stuck in low productivity jobs or are neither in work or school.

All these problems set back the human capital development of young people.

What should policy makers focus on? The five transitions

Much of what governments need to focus on to make young people fulfill their

"Regarding the young gang members, it is not a matter that they cannot study. The problem is that . . . the teachers are very strict, authoritarian. During lessons, only the teachers talk, they do not discuss [things] with the students. Young people can study, but they are not motivated."

Elvis, 21, Peru
January 2006

potential and contribute to their own well-being and that of society has already been touched on. Young people need to continue learning to build skills and acquire human capital. Skill-building needs to cover not only the skills for work, because young people need to learn to manage a range of health risks. They also need to be adequately prepared to become parents to reduce the intergenerational transmission of poverty that occurs because of the failure to plan and space births, and nurture children appropriately. They need also to learn to become actively engaged as citizens in the communities and societies in which they live.

The five dimensions—learning, going to work, staying healthy, forming families, and exercising citizenship—are referred to in the social science literature as "transitions." The term "transition" is a little misleading because some of the dimensions, such as going to work or forming a family, have more of an element of transition than others. All, however, are critical for poverty reduction and growth because they relate to building, maintaining, using, and reproducing human capital. Recent research also highlights these five transitions, emphasizing that success in

the transition to adulthood requires the development of human capital, the capability to make competent choices, and the development of a sense of well-being.[40]

When exactly these transitions occur varies by age, and one can think of three distinct phases when different transitions might be more evident. In the early phase, roughly ages 12–14, the focus is more likely to be on learning. In the middle phase, ages 15–18 or 15–20, learning continues but work begins to come into greater prominence. Many behaviors that endanger health increase with age and so can be more important at this stage. At the upper end of this range, young people may begin to formally exercise citizenship through voting, and for many young women this may also be a phase of childbearing. In the late phase, ages 18–24, work and childbearing assume greater importance.

How these transitions play out naturally varies by country and individual. In Haiti, a poor and largely rural economy, the early phase of ages 12–14 is dominated by primary school (figure 1.8). By age 14 more than a quarter of 12- to 24-year-olds continue to be enrolled in primary school—which formally ends at 12 years—owing to repetition and delayed or interrupted primary schooling. A smaller proportion of 12- to 24-year-olds are enrolled in secondary school. As young people progress through the teens, enrollment in secondary school declines, falling quite sharply in the late teens. Girls have uniformly lower enrollment than boys. Labor market attachment rises with age but picks up particularly after the ages of 15–16, more for boys than for girls.

Experimentation with tobacco in Haiti also rises with age but is low overall, a common finding in many low-income environments where access to tobacco products is constrained by income. Engaging in sex is more common, with 30 percent of females and 50 percent of males reporting having had sex by the age of 16. Reported differences between the sexes can be large, with women understood to under report and men to over report sexual activity. Marriage is not common for young men before age 24, but it rises quite sharply for women after age 18.

BOX 1.5   *Work and marriage for men in the Middle East and North Africa*

Countries in the Middle East and North Africa (MENA) have increased schooling among both young men and young women. In 1960, women over age 15 had less than one year of schooling on average, but in 2000 more than 4.5 years. Men's average years of schooling rose from around 1.5 years to more than 6. As a result, the MENA region now has schooling levels around the developing country average.

MENA's unemployment rates, however, are among the highest in the world, leaving over one in four young men and women in search of employment. In part, high unemployment reflects growth rates lower than the developing country average. The failure to find employment is also the result of schooling systems that do not impart market-relevant learning and skills. In addition, labor markets protect the rights

of incumbents, making it difficult for new entrants—typically youth.

Difficulties in transitioning to work have devalued education credentials and fostered cynicism among successive cohorts of youth. Another consequence has been a delay in marriage, particularly for young men. The MENA region stands out for having one of the highest declines in the proportion of ever-married men in the 20–24 year age group since the 1970s. Qualitative studies point to a sense of frustration among young men at their inability to start forming families. However, more research is needed to establish the consequences of these trends on family and society.

Source: National Research Council and Institute of Medicine (2005); Mensch, Singh, and Casterline (2006).

Figure 1.8   The transitions for Haitians ages 12–24

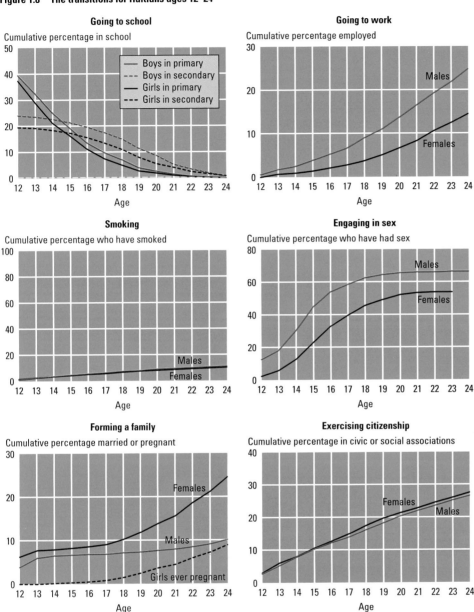

Source: Authors' calculations based on Enquête sur les Conditions de Vie en Haiti (2001).

By 24, nearly a quarter of young women are married and nearly 10 percent have borne children. Participation in civic or social associations outside the home rises almost uniformly from age 12 onward, slowing as young people approach their mid-twenties.

In Chile, an upper-middle-income country, the five transitions are both similar to and different from those in Haiti (figure 1.9). A good proportion of young people are still in primary school until age 14, but the proportion in secondary schools is higher. Very few young people remain in primary school after age 15 and in secondary after age 18. Labor market engagement rises with age but sharply increases after age 18, as opposed to ages 15–16 in Haiti. Engagement in civic associations rises over this age range and looks very similar to that in Haiti.

The big difference from Haiti is in health behavior and family formation. Experimentation with alcohol, tobacco, and drugs is

Figure 1.9   The transitions for Chileans ages 12–24

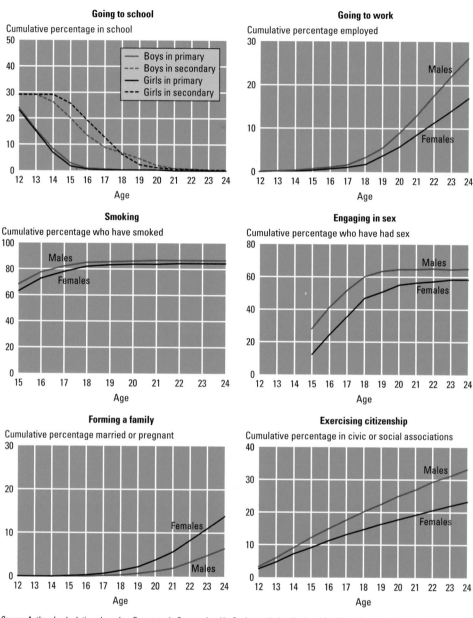

Source: Authors' calculations based on Encuesta de Caracterización Socioeconómica Nacional (2003) and Encuesta Nacional de Juventud (2000).

much higher among Chilean youth, with more than two-thirds of young people having tried one of these substances by age 16. Many young people also report that they engage in sex at a fairly young age—more than 20 percent of females and 40 percent of males report having had sex by age 16. These figures are comparable to those reported by youngsters in Haiti. However, Chile's incidence of marriage among 12- to 24-year-olds is lower than Haiti's.

The five transitions, though discussed separately, interact. Some of the inter-relationships are obvious, such as longer schooling delaying labor force entry, or childbearing reducing labor market attachment (at least temporarily). Some are less obvious, such as the relationship between work and marriage for men (box 1.5). For governments that create a policy environment conducive to all the transitions, the payoffs can be enormous.

Differing demographics

Most young people today are born into smaller families than their parents, but there are many more of them than in their parents' generation. The developing world as a whole and many countries are seeing a peak in the numbers of youth because population momentum—the inertia in population growth related to the large size of the childbearing population—is being gradually overtaken by falling fertility. Now at 1.3 billion, the population of young people is expected to grow slowly into the foreseeable future because the continuing growth in youth populations in Sub-Saharan Africa, Middle East and North Africa, and South Asia will counter the slow declines in East Asia and Europe and Central Asia.

Why youth populations are approaching a peak

Why are youth populations so large? Recall the main elements of the demographic transition. Before the demographic transition, death rates and birth rates are high and in balance, implying low rates of population growth. The demographic transition begins with a decline in death rates. With death rates falling, birth rates typically remain high for some period, accelerating population growth. Eventually birth rates also fall, slowing population growth. The transition ends when birth rates and death rates have both stabilized at a new low level, implying a return to low (or zero) population growth.

High-income countries went through a demographic transition in the 1800s and early 1900s and had a long and slow decline in mortality. The gap between birth rates and death rates was never very large, and population growth rates rarely exceeded 1 percent a year.

The demographic transition in developing countries is quantitatively very different. Death rates declined very fast in the 1950s and 1960s, generating population growth rates in excess of 4 percent a year in some countries. The timing of fertility decline has varied, but it occurred in many developing countries in the 1960s, when world population growth hit a peak of around 2 percent a year. The rapid population growth of the 1960s—the "population explosion"—is the origin of today's large youth cohorts. Today's youth are the children of the population explosion generation.

Consider Brazil (figure 1).[1] The demographic transition was already well under way by 1950, with the death rate having fallen to 15 per 1,000, while the birth rate was almost 45 per 1,000. Population growth was about 2.8 percent a year, higher than ever experienced by high-income countries when they went through the demographic transition. Although the birth rate was falling in the 1950s, death rates were falling faster, causing a peak population growth rate of 3.0 percent in 1960–65. This was also when world population growth rates reached their historic peak.

Birth cohorts grew rapidly in the 1950s in response to the rapid decline in death rates (figure 2), driven largely by declines in infant and child mortality. Cohort size leveled off in the late 1960s and early 1970s,

reflecting the rapid decline in fertility rates that began in the 1960s. Cohort size then grew rapidly again in the late 1970s, reaching a peak in 1982, driven by what demographers call population momentum—the increase in the size of the childbearing population as the birth cohorts of the 1950s reached childbearing age.

The experience for other developing countries is similar to Brazil's, with differences only in the timing of the largest surviving birth cohort. With the large declines in fertility starting around the 1960s, the developing world as a whole is now approaching a plateau in youth numbers. There are now 1.3 billion young people ages 12–24 in the developing world, a number expected to grow to 1.5 billion in 2035 and begin declining thereafter.

Country patterns are distinct

Depending on the timing and speed of fertility decline, countries can expect to see different trajectories of number of youth (figure 3). Four distinct patterns are the result of a complex interaction between fertility, mortality, and population momentum.

Group 1. Countries in this group typically experienced an early transition to low

Figure 1   The demographic transition in Brazil led to a peak in population growth during 1960–65

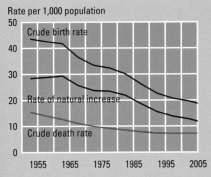

Rate per 1,000 population

Source: United Nations (2005b), medium variant.

Figure 2   The largest surviving birth cohort in Brazil was born in 1982

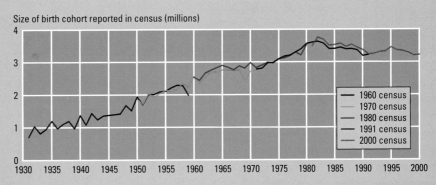

Size of birth cohort reported in census (millions)

— 1960 census
— 1970 census
— 1980 census
— 1991 census
— 2000 census

Source: Lam (2006)

Figure 3   Country trends in youth population vary significantly

Population ages 12–24 (1950=100)

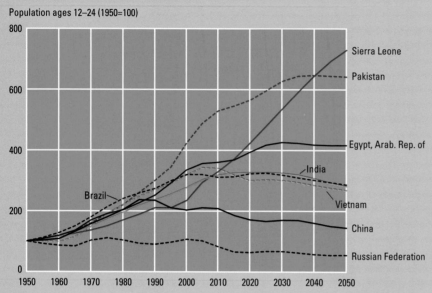

Source: United Nations (2005b), medium variant.

fertility and have seen a peak in their youth numbers (China, Russia). Other countries in this group include Albania, Armenia, Cuba, Georgia, Mauritius, Poland, and Thailand.

Group 2. Countries in this group experienced the fertility transition somewhat later than the first group and are seeing a peak about now (2000–10). In some cases the peak is relatively sharp (Vietnam). In others there is a long plateau, with countries projected to experience 20 to 30 years of relatively constant youth populations after they reach their peak (Brazil).[2] Other countries in this group include Argentina, Chile, Costa Rica, the Islamic Republic of Iran, Indonesia, South Africa, Sri Lanka, and Turkey.

Group 3. Countries in this group will experience a peak between 2010 and 2030, for some relatively sharp (India) and for others long drawn (the Arab Republic of Egypt).[3] Other countries in this group include Bangladesh, Malaysia, Nicaragua, Peru, and the Philippines.

Group 4. Countries in this group will not experience a peak in the foreseeable future (Pakistan, Sierra Leone). For most the fertility transition is halted, proceeding slowly, or yet to get under way. Other countries in this group include Afghanistan, Cambodia, Chad, Republic of Congo, Democratic Republic of Congo, Equatorial Guinea, Eritrea, Ethiopia, Guatemala, Guinea-Bissau, Kenya, the Lao People's Democratic Republic, Liberia, Mozambique, Niger, Nigeria, Pakistan, Rwanda, Senegal, Somalia, Uganda, and the Republic of Yemen.

Within this group there are marked differences in countries. Some with very late fertility declines, such as the Democratic Republic of Congo and Sierra Leone, are projected to have continuing rapid growth of the youth population for the next several decades. Dependency ratios have yet to fall, so resources available per youth are falling, and youth cohorts are growing relative to older workers, intensifying the pressure on the labor market from new entrants. Others such as Pakistan and Senegal are projected to have slower growth. Dependency ratios are falling, steadily improving the economic circumstances for investing in youth. Also falling is the relative size of youth cohorts, easing labor market pressures.

These distinct country patterns underpin the approaching plateau in the absolute number of young people in the developing world. While numbers are declining in several countries, they are countered by increases elsewhere. At the regional level, East Asia and Europe and Central Asia are already experiencing contraction, while Middle East and North Africa, South Asia, and Sub-Saharan Africa are set to grow, the latter the fastest.

Opportunities, capabilities, second chances: A framework for policy

chapter 2

Navigating through the transitions of the next generation of workers, leaders, and entrepreneurs offers great potential (and poses great risks) for growth and poverty reduction in developing countries. The human and social capital of the young will determine national incomes. Their decisions, as the next generation heading households, communities, work forces, and nations, will affect the welfare of everyone else in society. How can policies help?

Governments already do many things that affect the lives of young people—from setting the broad economic context in which they live and work, to providing education, to setting laws about early marriage, voting, and child labor. Are these activities sufficient or even appropriate? How can they be improved? This chapter suggests that

a youth lens on these policies would focus them on three broad directions (figure 2.1):

- Broadening the *opportunities* for young people to develop skills and use them productively.
- Helping them acquire the *capabilities* to make good decisions in pursuing those opportunities.
- Offering them *second chances,* to recover from bad decisions, either by them or by others, such as their governments or families.

Governments provide education and health services for youth and set the broad economic policies and regulations for labor markets where they work. A youth lens on policies, however, reveals important gaps. In many countries the quick and massive

Figure 2.1 Transitions seen through three lenses focus policies and magnify impact

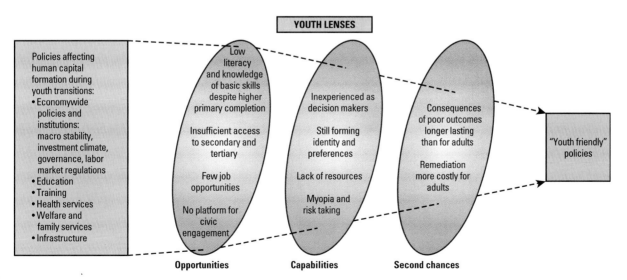

Source: Authors.

expansion of primary education has resulted in unprecedented pressure for places at secondary schools but not always transmitted literacy and basic life skills. Labor market regulations may have very different effects on younger workers than on older workers. Youth in many developing countries lack a platform for civic engagement. Therefore, policy makers need to improve access to services that help the young develop and preserve their human capital. They also need to give them ways of beginning to use that human capital to sustain their livelihoods and participate fully in community life.

At some point (the exact age varies across cultures) young people make their own decisions to seize (and in some cases create) these opportunities. Choosing well from an expanded set of opportunities depends on developing the capability to define one's goals and act on them—one's agency. Youth must make these choices at a time when they are acquiring an identity and are inexperienced as decision makers. Governments can help by providing information and tools to manage the risks that many youth confront for the first time. In some cases, government policies also need to enhance the role of young people as decision-making agents, particularly adolescent girls in societies where they are further behind in skills or where they are unable to choose for themselves.

Because many young people are deprived of opportunities to develop their human capital or participate responsibly in the decisions that affect them, they need second chances. The consequences of not offering those chances will reverberate for decades afterward, not only as youth become the next generation of workers and leaders, but also as they become parents who influence the succeeding generations. These programs for second chances can be costly, but not as costly as remediation for adults. To lower costs, the programs should be well integrated in the overall delivery system for developing human capital. They also need to target those who need them most, resolve moral hazards if they encourage risk-taking, and supplement rather than replace family-based safety nets.

In sum, the three broad policy directions that emanate from a youth lens imply that governments need not only reorient spending and publicly provided services but also improve the climate for young people and their families to invest in themselves. These are the "youth friendly policies" (figure 2.1) that the rest of the Report elaborates. Just as the three lenses have to be aligned for the image to be in focus, so must policies be well-coordinated to have maximum impact. Opportunities can be missed if the capabilities to grasp them are blunted or misdirected. Having better decision-making capabilities (agency) can lead to frustration if the opportunities are too far below aspirations. Not having second chances can lead to a free fall in outcomes, regardless of the opportunities or capabilities.

This framework derives directly from the human capital model familiar to economists (box 2.1). It is also important to add a gender filter to the youth lens. The youth transitions vary for males and females. Societies that try to protect the well-being of young girls often wind up restricting their opportunities and capabilities for schooling and meeting health needs. (See the spotlight on a gender filter on the youth lens following this chapter.)

Broadening opportunities

Economywide and sectoral policies affect the opportunities for human capital investment. Public financing, provision, and regulation of education and health systems have largely determined not only the number and quality of skilled workers available to the economy, but also of skilled parents and active citizens available to families and communities. Economywide policies for aggregate public spending, the labor market, external trade, and the money supply affect growth and investment—and thus influence how many workers of different skills will be demanded. To what extent are countries' human capital policies and institutions adequately providing opportunities for young people to develop their future skills—broadly defined to include not just work, but also social

---

BOX 2.1   *Applying the human capital model to young people*

[P]eoples of the world differ enormously in productivity; ... these differences are in turn largely related to ... the accumulation of knowledge and the maintenance of health. The concept of investment in human capital simply organizes and stresses these basic truths ... I would venture the judgment that human capital is going to be an important part of the thinking about development, income distribution, labor turnover, and many other problems for a long time to come."

—Gary Becker (1964) in *Human Capital*

If the true test of the value of an economic theory is longevity, the human capital model passes with flying colors. Its basics are simple and empirically testable (and generally validated). An individual will invest in his or her human capital—an additional year of schooling, on-the-job training, or acquiring a healthy lifestyle—as long as the marginal gain from that investment exceeds its added cost. The gains extend over a lifetime and are discounted to the present. If some of these gains accrue to others, governments need to stimulate individuals to take them into account in making decisions. Public action may also be needed if poor individuals cannot mobilize the resources to finance the investment now, despite a promise of big gains in the future.

Like all basic models, the elegance comes at the price of simplifying assumptions—assumptions that have led to extensions that this Report uses to analyze the hard realities facing youth in developing countries.

To whom are policy makers accountable?
One set of these assumptions has to do with the ability and willingness of government to correct for the failure of the market so as to optimize the welfare of all. Government policy makers do not always behave as the benevolent

dictators the models would have them be, dutifully correcting for externalities and equalizing opportunities for all. Instead, their behavior may depend on their accountability. Is it to the ultimate beneficiaries? Is it to their supervisors? Or is it to special interest groups, to voters at large, or even to their own families or pockets? Getting that right will determine outcomes, as examined in *World Development Report 2004*.[1] If these policy makers do not feel accountable to young people, or if young people do not have a platform for holding providers accountable, a gap in youth's opportunities for human capital investment may result (box 2.2).

Who makes investment decisions?
A second set of assumptions has to do with who is making the decisions about investing in human capital. The model assumes that a young person makes his or her own decisions. The age range 12–24 is precisely when the locus of decision making shifts from parents or households—and in most cases, both parties have a say in the final outcome. But how much say does each party have? How do they resolve conflicts if they have different views—such as whether the young person should work and contribute to the household income or go to school? Economic models have tended to treat children as passive receivers of parental decisions.[2] In some societies this assumption is a stretch of reality, a point especially obvious to parents with teenagers; in others it may very well describe how youth's opportunities can be limited by social conventions. The model's extensions include bargaining among household members to determine human capital investments.

Are investors in human capital well informed decision makers?
A third set of assumptions concerns the motives and preferences of the young person as a decision maker. The model assumes that the human capital investor is well-informed about the benefits and costs, discounts the future appropriately at the prevailing economic discount rate, accounts for the riskiness of the investment by comparing it rationally with other risky assets, and has well-formed views, not just about their present preferences, but about future desired consumption bundles as well.

For many young people, the reality is that they are inexperienced decision makers who are only selectively informed about the risks, costs, and benefits of most human capital investments. Some tend to be more myopic and impatient than adults, which may lead them to discount the value of long-term investments like human capital. They are still forming their own identities, too, so that their own preferences for consumption are still evolving and may be easily influenced by peers. Extensions of the basic model, discussed more in boxes 2.7 and 2.9, include the explicit modeling of information asymmetries, identity formation, the dynamic effects of cumulative learning, and the synthesis of behavioral science with economic thinking.[3]

The broad policy lenses of opportunities, capabilities, and second chances come directly from the human capital model and its extensions as applied to young people. The rest of this chapter shows how.

Source: Authors.

---

skills? What would this "youth lens" imply for the priorities for public action?

The answers are far from easy because some constraints on young people vary greatly across countries while others are more common. This section focuses on the following policy priorities:

- Improve the quality and relevance of services that enhance basic skills, such as literacy and knowledge about health outcomes, especially for low- and some middle-income countries that have raced to meet quantitative targets for education for all.

- For countries that have long been able to provide access to primary and lower secondary education of acceptable quality, address barriers to expanding opportunities for building higher level skills in upper secondary and tertiary institutions.

- For all countries, help people build skills at work while they are young and most apt to learn from work experiences—and start toward an independent livelihood.

- For all countries, provide opportunities for young people to be heard and to participate in civic life outside the family—to build their skills for exercising citizenship.

Addressing these priorities poses difficult (but not insurmountable) challenges for government. Services beyond the basic mean higher unit costs, both for providers and for beneficiaries, who face greater opportunity costs. The case for public intervention is not as strong for upper secondary and higher education as it is for primary.

Improving the quality and relevance of services that enhance basic skills

A youth lens points to improving the quality of basic services for children as well as for young adults, especially in countries that have recently improved quantitative indicators of primary school enrollment. Despite the higher primary completion rates, many children enter adolescence ill-prepared for work, further schooling, and the practicalities of coping with life in a more connected and complex world. Literacy and numeracy, the backbones of the arguments to justify public subsidies to primary education, are often not in place by grade 6.[4] The most recent UNESCO report to monitor the Education for All (EFA) campaign puts it starkly: "Simply focusing on quantitative goals such as universal primary education will not deliver EFA.... [I]n many parts of the world, an enormous gap prevails between the numbers who are graduating from schools and those among them who have managed to master a minimum set of cognitive skills."[5] Fewer than a third of children in the countries named in figure 2.2 achieved minimum mastery of the relevant topic by grades 4–6, even though the average net enrollment rate was about 65 percent.

Improper health practices mean that many children enter adolescence stunted and malnourished. More than 40 percent of all 10- to 14-year-olds in Cameroon, Guatemala, Nepal, and the Philippines are anemic.[6] Ill health puts them at a disadvantage when they go to school or work. For men and women who work in urban Brazil, a 1 percent increase in height leads to a 2.0 to 2.4 percent increase in wages or earnings.[7]

Because many children enter adolescence on the proverbial wrong foot, the first priority is still their adequate preparation.

Figure 2.2   Attending is not always learning

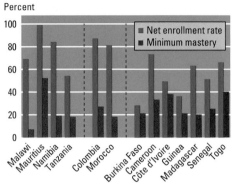

| | Grade 6 reading test, 1995 | Grade 4 reading test, 2001 | Grade 5 French test, 1990 |

Source: UNESCO (2004b).
Note: Net enrollment ratio is the ratio of the number of children of official school age (as defined by the national education system) who are enrolled in school to the population of the corresponding official school age. Minimum mastery is calculated by multiplying the percentage of children in the study who have achieved the minimum standard by the percentage of children who made it to grade 5. The grade 5 reading test is SACMEQ (Southern and Eastern Africa Consortium for Monitoring Education). The grade 4 reading test is PIRLS (Progress in International Literacy Study), which determines the percent of students with reading scores above the 25th percentile of the international benchmark. The grade 5 French test is PASEC (Programme d'Analyse des Systèmes Educatifs de la Confemen).

Basic services have lasting impacts well into young adulthood in both developed and developing countries. Aside from primary schooling and basic health care of those age 6 and older, early childhood development programs, such as enriched child care, increase the probability of graduating from high school and attending college—and reduce the likelihood of being charged with a crime.[8] Studies in the Philippines find that nutritional status at a young age leads to academic success, as measured by greater chances of school enrollment and lower repetition rates, even by the time students are 11 years old.[9] In Turkey, a mother-child education program providing early enrichment for young children and training and support for mothers increased educational attainment, reduced delinquency, and improved the status of mothers in the family.[10]

One could go further and extend the basic agenda to include grades 6–9 (or roughly middle school). These are grades necessary to consolidate the gains, and in some cases remediate the missed opportunities, from earlier grades. Many students in these grades are adolescents 12–15 years old. Many countries are already expanding their definition of basic education to include this age.[11] As countries embark on these extensions, however, the lesson from the attempt to universalize primary is clear—ignore quality at your peril. A balanced approach that improves quality along with quantity may mean higher costs, but there will be savings as well, because higher quality education implies less repetition.[12]

Addressing barriers to expanding opportunities for building higher level skills beyond literacy, numeracy, and basic health knowledge

Countries need to broaden opportunities in postbasic services—in upper-secondary, technical, and higher education, and in training centers and informal settings, including the workplace. On this, there is an emerging consensus, especially for middle-income countries (chapter 1). But how can already strapped governments afford to pay

for these services, which are more expensive per learner, for all who want them? They cannot, under present circumstances. There are two ways out: one is to have more options to finance these services, the other, to make delivery even more efficient.

Financing and targeting. Students and their families are already paying for a big part of these costs, especially at tertiary levels, in countries as diverse as Côte d'Ivoire, Indonesia, the Republic of Korea, and Paraguay (figure 2.3). This would not be especially worrisome if all promising young people could afford to finance such training, because the returns accrue mostly to the individual student. More often than not, however, large numbers of poor (and some not so poor) are unable to finance it. With private spending on higher education exceeding 60 percent of GDP per capita in Benin and Côte d'Ivoire, it is not surprising that tertiary enrollment rates are below 5 percent—and very few of those attending are poor. Guaranteed free universal access to higher education would hardly be a solution—it is neither fiscally feasible nor equitable because poor young people are severely underrepresented among the pool of secondary completers and could probably not afford to forgo work. Best would be providing a financial environment for institutions to offer student loans. Because this takes time and scarce management resources to develop, scholarships—tightly targeted to the poor and merit-based—would be warranted to encourage promising youth from low-income families.

Spending cost-effectively. For governments already struggling financially with providing primary education and basic health care, it is even more important to pay attention to cost effectiveness. Because basic services are failing poor young people, the lessons of *World Development Report 2004*[13] are relevant here, especially those on strengthening the accountability of service providers to clients and citizens (box 2.2). The lessons apply perhaps even more strongly, because many of the services used

Figure 2.3   Private funds finance a big part of tertiary education costs in diverse countries

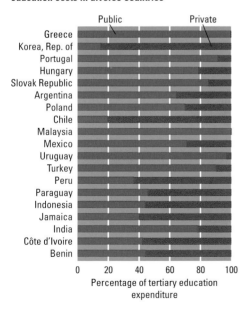

Percentage of tertiary education expenditure

Source: Calculated from UNESCO (2005).
Note: Countries are ordered by (PPP adjusted) GDP per capita from top to bottom.

BOX 2.2   *Making services work for poor young people—*
World Development Report 2004 redux, with a youth lens

World Development Report 2004: Making Services Work for Poor People developed a framework for improving delivery in such services as education and health. The framework unbundles the delivery chain into the relationships between three sets of actors. As *clients*—patients in clinics or students in schools and their parents—they are the ultimate beneficiaries of services. They have a relationship with the frontline *providers,* who are schoolteachers and doctors, for example. In a competitive-market transaction the consumer holds the service provider accountable through the power of the purse—by paying for satisfactory service or taking his or her business elsewhere. However, for services such as health and education there is often no direct financial accountability of the provider to the client, as when service providers are financed by the government. There is then a "long route" of accountability—with clients as citizens influencing *policy makers,* and policy makers influencing providers. When the relationships along this long route break down, service delivery fails.

The recommendations from *World Development Report 2004* center on strengthening the relationships between these three actors:

enhancing the power of clients to hold providers accountable for service delivery; strengthening the voice of citizens to influence, and possibly sanction, policy makers for decisions about service delivery; and ensuring that the compact between policy makers and providers gives the right incentives for the delivery of good services.

Making services work for poor youth is fully consistent with the 2004 Report's framework. Services that work well for the poor will, of course, typically work for poor youth as well. But a youth lens sheds additional light on the framework. As young people age they become actors in their own right. They become an important and independent group of clients. They also become a distinct part of the citizenry, with their own needs, priorities, and goals for policy. Viewing the 2004 Report's framework through a youth lens produces the following implications.

- *Client power*—improves services by empowering youth to actively engage in the provision of services, either by giving them the means to choose among providers or to participate in the management of decentralized delivery (see chapters 3 and 5).

- *Citizen voice*—improves services by increasing the ability of young people to articulate their needs and wants, and ensuring that policy makers listen (see box 2.3 for an example and chapter 7).
- *Provider compact*—improves services by ensuring that providers have the right training, motivation, and incentives to deliver high quality. Examples include contracting with private providers to deliver youth-oriented services, with payment conditional on successful implementation, and by training providers to create more youth-friendly services (chapters 3, 5, and 6).

An overarching recommendation from the 2004 Report rings even more true in the context of youth-oriented services—and echoes through this year's Report. Although a variety of interventions and programs have been tried, little reliable evaluation of their impacts has been undertaken. So to guide youth-oriented policy development, it is urgent to build the knowledge base of what works under what conditions.

Source: Authors.

---

by young people (rather than those used by children) tend to be more expensive per person. The one dimension not emphasized in that agenda, which does not differentiate among generations, is the voice of young people in improving service availability, discussed in box 2.2 and in the next section.

Enhancing opportunities to begin a sustainable livelihood

Human capital, once developed, needs to be used productively to sustain a livelihood. This has long been recognized to be a main path to poverty reduction, because labor is what the poor have in abundance. How the young start off in their working lives has an enormous effect on their later prospects. Because young people are on a very steep part of their learning curves, they can acquire skills quickly when working, an attribute that diminishes with age.[14] For most of them, this means working in the private sector, which in most countries is the largest employer. Policies should ensure that

young people do not start full-time employment too early and that they have free entry and mobility when they are ready.

Start at the right time.   Poverty can force children to work at home or enter the labor market prematurely, encouraging adolescents to drop out of school early. Because dropouts often never return, the short-term income gain to the parents and family comes at the cost of forgone education for the child. Their chances of being able to read, for example, may fall because literacy rates increase significantly as individuals go from no schooling to 1–3 years of schooling and then again to 4–6 years.[15]

Cash incentives to remain in school may enable youth to stay long enough to acquire a threshold level of basic skills that are difficult to accumulate outside the school setting. Literacy and numeracy would also provide a strong base for more advanced skills, which help in insulating one during downturns. The East Asian financial crisis of 1997–98 hit the least-skilled and other marginal workers—women, young workers, the less educated, recent school dropouts, and first-time job seekers—in Korea the hardest. Young workers ages 15–29 accounted for the lion's share of job destruction, especially young female workers.[16] Job recovery also took longer for the less-educated young worker. Similarly in Argentina, workers with less education took longer to be reabsorbed into the labor force after its recent financial crisis.[17]

Free entry into the labor market. The young continue to gain skills after they enter the labor market, but because they are inexperienced, their unemployment rates tend to be higher than those of adults. For industrial countries, the unemployment rate of young people ages 15–24 is two to three times that of adults, and for some developing countries up to five to seven times (chapter 4). These differences may not matter so much if they are due to the natural search for jobs. However, they are an enormous problem if young people, unemployed for the first few years of their working lives, become basically unemployable thereafter, at least in the formal sector.

What policies could ease entry of young people into the labor market? Broadening opportunities for young people's employment is best premised on economywide growth that stimulates demand: a rising tide lifts the boats of young people and everyone else. Some of these policies unintentionally have a disproportionately large effect on young people. In many economies, such as those in East Asia, exports and foreign direct investment expanded the demand for young workers and were a principal source for growth explaining the East Asian Miracle.[18] They have had a particularly stimulating effect on increasing the labor force participation of previously excluded groups, such as young women (box 2.3).

At the same time, some broadly based policies, especially those regulating the labor market, can hurt new entrants disproportionately. For example, minimum wages are sometimes set too high, and some studies in the United States and Latin America have

---

BOX 2.3   *A tale of two exports: How electronics in Malaysia and garments in Bangladesh promoted work for young women in traditional societies*

Malaysia in the 1970s and 1980s and Bangladesh in the 1980s and 1990s experienced rapid increases in the labor force participation of young women, especially in some export industries.[19] In Malaysia the electronics assembly sector attracted a steady stream of young women from rural areas to the state of Penang. Similarly, the garment sector in Bangladesh drew many young women from rural areas to such cities as Chittagong and Dhaka.

Women constituted 90 percent of the garment workforce in Bangladesh and the semiconductor assembly workforce in Malaysia. These sectors provided many young women with their first opportunities to enter the labor force: 93 percent of female workers in Bangladesh's garment sector and two-thirds of women in Malaysia's electronics sector had no previous work experience.

The previous generation of Malaysian women had neither the educational attainment nor the employment opportunities of their daughters—nor the modern lifestyle associated with wage employment. Case studies from Bangladesh reveal that young women preferred working in the garment industry to agriculture or domestic service. Work in the garment sector meant higher wages and social status. Though factory work was strenuous, those who did it had higher self esteem and autonomy. In a survey of Bangladeshi garment workers, 90 percent of young female respondents had a high opinion of themselves, compared with 57 percent of female workers in nonexport industries.

The salaries of these young women enhanced their status within their families as well as benefited their families. Their wages could contribute up to 43 percent of household incomes in Bangladesh. A 1995 study indicated that 80 percent of families of female garment workers would fall below the poverty line without their daughters' salaries. While these contributions did not always improve their bargaining power in the household, they seem to have had more inputs into some key decisions, such as the timing of marriage. In Malaysia work before marriage has become the norm. Young women working in Bangladesh's garment sector, having also delayed marriage, expect greater influence in the choice of their marriage partner, as had already occurred in Malaysia.

Some long-term economic and social effects are unclear. Once married, young women tended to leave wage employment, and most young women expect to work only three or four years. Aside from the short tenure, many of the jobs were tedious, low-skilled, had limited upward mobility, and were managed in traditional patriarchal ways. Young women experienced greater autonomy as they migrated to urban settings, but were sometimes stigmatized for having a more Western, individualistic lifestyle. Nevertheless, what is clear is that these young women in Bangladesh and Malaysia have broken some new ground and in the process contributed economically to their families and societies.

Sources: Ackerman (1996); Amin and others (1998); Chaudhuri and Paul-Majumder (1995); Kibria (1995); Ong (1987); Paul-Majumder and Begum (2000); and Rahman (1995).

found that they can reduce the employment of youth.[20] Employment protection laws provide stability to those already employed, but could inhibit employers from taking a risk in hiring promising but inexperienced workers. A study of 15 Latin American and Caribbean and 28 Organisation for Economic Co-operation and Development (OECD) countries found the impact of such regulations on young people's employment rates to be more than twice that on prime-age male workers'.[21] Overly generous social protection schemes have the same effect.

Social attitudes, including discrimination by employers and the reluctance of families to let young people work outside the home, can also suppress opportunities, especially for females. Young women already contribute much to the economy through unpaid work at home, work notoriously missing from GDP estimates.[22] The entry of such a trained and motivated pool into the formal labor force can produce higher growth because they are a large share of the population relative to those not working, even without a dramatic fertility transition. Discriminatory practices can change, too, as countries develop, though some social norms are remarkably resilient (see examples in the spotlight on gender following this chapter).

Mobility.   Once employed, young people tend to be highly mobile, more so than older workers. Changing jobs is one way of getting better jobs and in the process accumulating human capital. Policies and institutions that hinder mobility thus especially affect the young.

Except for the lucky (or the well-connected), many young people start work in the informal sector. Some thrive there, especially those who manage to set up successful businesses. This is a fairly small proportion of the labor force (chapter 4) and a fairly limited and risky route. For many young people who find it difficult to get credit, self-employment is a survival strategy, discussed later in this chapter. Moreover, because success in business can be elusive, many would-

be entrepreneurs end up working for someone else at one time or another.

For the bulk of the young workforce, the surest way to a better job that provides adequate training and skill-building opportunities is to move eventually into the formal sector. Here, again, policies that provide an incentive for the private sector to hire young people will be important. In Côte d'Ivoire, Rwanda, and Senegal in the late 1990s and early 2000s, because of the small size of the formal sector and overly high expectations, the unemployment rate for those with postsecondary education was seven to eight times that for those with just primary education.[23] Pursuing investment climate improvements for firms can create more and better jobs, as discussed in *World Development Report 2005*.[24]

The lack of domestic opportunities has pushed young people to look outside their local environment, including outside the country. Most of the world's migrants are young. Because they are some of the best and the brightest, many observers are concerned about the brain drain (chapter 8). Policies to get the most from international migration include improving the infrastructure for migrants to send remittances, enabling migrants to stay connected with their home countries, and encouraging the successful return of young migrants. They also include better access to information on jobs, as in the Philippines.

Opening opportunities to be heard outside the family

The skills and the desire to interact with the broader community and engage in civic life are also formed early (chapter 7). Moreover, having a voice expands opportunities for better service. ("Voice" is shorthand to indicate not just expression but recognition and inclusion—a chance to contribute to society and be acknowledged.) *World Development Report 2004* argued that the voice of the beneficiary, the poor person, can be routed directly through contact with the service provider or indirectly through influence on policy makers, who then direct providers to deliver better services (see box 2.2).[25]

This is true for all in society, but for young people—only beginning to make their voices heard outside the home, less patient with incremental change, and searching for their identity—the opportunities for expressing voice through voting or consultation are perhaps even more relevant. Opportunities to speak out are particularly important because their parents may not fully represent their interests, as discussed more fully below. The absence of such opportunities can make alternative forms of expression, such as violent behavior, more attractive.

Indirect routes of accountability—from citizens to policy makers to service providers—may become more important as people vote or otherwise make their views known after age 18, officially, but in practice, much later. For most young people, such indirect routes are not available. Direct consultation and recognition through participation in implementing development projects or in setting budgets are also key (box 2.4). The young are more likely to have opportunities to be heard and have an impact in local (rather than national) settings.

The effect of broadening such opportunities is not simply to ensure stability—it is often a way to get better outcomes if the young can use their creative energies productively. It is a marvelous way to develop skills in decision making, the topic of the next section.

Developing the capabilities of young people as decision-making agents

With an expanded array of opportunities, how should one choose among them? And who should choose? The extent to which young people participate in decisions that affect how they acquire skills, begin to work, and express a voice varies across countries, societies, and cultures. This section explores how young people can contribute enormously to their own

---

BOX 2.4   *Young people's voice in budget setting improved outcomes in Ceará, Brazil*

CEDECA (Centro de Defesa da Criança e do Adolescente)-Ceará started "Children and Young People in Action—Participating in Budget Work," in Fortaleza, a city with more than 2 million people, in 2002. (CEDECA-Ceará educates citizens on the importance of Brazil's budget process.)

After identifying 50 young people from different areas of Fortaleza, CEDECA-Ceará trained them on budget content and process. The training covered public administration, political organizations, budget legislation, revenues, expenditures, the budget cycle, budget execution, ways for civil society to engage with the budget process, and the roles of executive, legislative, and judicial authorities.

The 50 young people researched and documented the needs of young people in various parts of Fortaleza by making visits and taking photographs. Having learned to analyze municipal budgets and interpret the results, they engaged with the Fortaleza city government's formal budget process. In 2003 they submitted 33 amendments to the budget proposal for 2004, related to programs for education, drugs, and sexual abuse.

According to respondents, for the first time in the city of Fortaleza, the debate on the budget was marked by the participation of young people who contributed to the discussions in a competent manner. To add value to their proposed amendments, they gathered in front of the Town Hall on the day of the budget vote. There was a mixture of surprise and incredulity among the councilors. They could not believe that a group of young people could understand the budget, present proposals, make their voices heard, and above all protect the right to participation in the drafting of policies aimed at them.

Of the 33 suggested amendments to the 2004 budget, three passed. The project has since scaled up. The young people in the project are now training others. CEDECA-Ceará says that their efforts resulted in an additional allocation of $400,000 to children and young people in 2004 and $760,000 in 2005.

The government of Sweden is supporting an evaluation of the effects of the project on social and private outcomes, and its results are expected to be ready in the near future.

Source: Swedish International Development Agency (SIDA) (2005).

---

well-being, and that of the nation, if policy makers recognize young people as decision-making agents who define their own goals and act on them.[26]

Recognizing agency is not enough—it must be resourced, informed, and responsible. That is, it must be "capable." What determines this capability? The section highlights the importance of addressing the most important issues youth confront as they participate more in decision making:

- Having access to sound information—necessary because young people have had less opportunity to learn from life than adults.
- Commanding real resources—necessary because young people may not be able to afford to invest in themselves, even if they have promising prospects.

"Many parents fear for their children and would 'ask' them to follow their way of doing things, without allowing youth to try new things, for fear of the danger."

Young person, Thailand
December 2005

Figure 2.4   Who has the final say? Young people's influence on their own key transitions varies greatly across societies and for males and females

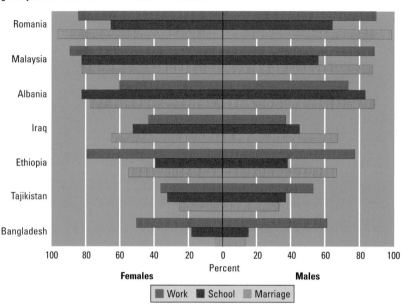

Source: WDR 2007 InterMedia surveys.
Note: The figure shows the percentage of people ages 15–24 who answered "myself" (rather than parents, government, or other) to the question: "Thinking of [each transition: your current or most recent occupation; your years of schooling; and your marriage partner], who has had the most influence?"

> - Deciding judiciously—necessary in the light of their evolving preferences in their search for identity.

Young people make more— and more important— decisions as they age

Parents, or adult guardians, make most decisions affecting the schooling, health, social life, and general well-being of children. As children age they gradually begin to exert more control over many decisions affecting their lives. Those who are 24 make different decisions from those who are 12—in a process that some have called a progression from adolescence to emerging adulthood.[27] The pace of this shift (and the decisions) varies widely across countries and cultures and may have nothing to do with level of development. A 2005–06 survey in a set of diverse countries asked whether young people ages 15–24 felt that they themselves had the most influence regarding decisions across the important transitions of education, marriage, and work (figure 2.4). Despite the variations, at least half the youth surveyed felt in most cases that they had the most influence. Notable exceptions are Bangladeshis and Tajiks regarding marriage and school.[28]

Understanding more about the nature and consequences of choosing among life's opportunities is critical to effective government policy. Where parents, older relatives, or community leaders do most of the deciding, their incentives, resources, and constraints matter most (see box 2.5). However, even when young people do not have outright decision-making responsibilities until they are young adults above 18 or even older, they can still exercise considerable agency early on.

This independence is perhaps most obvious for schooling and health behaviors, which are most difficult for adults to monitor and control. Young primary school completers may dutifully enroll in secondary education in accord with their parents' wishes, but they will not necessarily go to class or study hard enough. The state may

---

BOX 2.5   Seen but not heard: Who decides when to drop out of school? Or when to marry? Or do anything else?

Who participates in the decision to drop out? A survey in Pakistan found big differences. More than three-quarters of male youths (ages 20–24) report a role in the decision to leave school, but fewer than a quarter of the responsible adults felt that young males should be involved. Similarly, nearly 50 percent of female youths report a role in this decision, while only 11 percent of adult respondents felt that young females should play a role.

A third of respondents (ages 15–24) reported a role in the decision to drop out of school but that they were not able to express an opinion during household discussions on this issue. While the contrasting percentages may represent only the difference between a desired norm and actual practice, they call into question both the actual agency exercised by adolescents and youth and the reliability and veracity of adult responses.

Generational differences in views go beyond education—and beyond Pakistan.

For example, psychologists have conducted experiments to show that "pro-social" behavior develops with age. According to Kohlberg (1973) it is around the age of 12 that individuals start to go beyond behaving according to rules and regulations and more as a matter of fulfilling obligations to others. Most of the experimental work supporting these hypotheses has been done in developed countries.

The findings point to the need to understand better the role of young people in the decision making of households. Models of household behavior should treat children not as "dormant agents," but, like spousal pairs, as negotiating partners in a bargaining game (see box 2.7). Some recent historical analysis uses expenditure data from the U.S. in 1917–19 to show that youths were also able to amass bargaining power in the household as a result of their work.

Sources: Moehling (2005) and Sathar and others (2002).

impose minimum ages at which young people may marry, and parents may try to impose rules about whom young people will see, but sexual activity may (and does) take place surreptitiously. Adolescents can express their agency even in seeking work opportunities. A study of 21 villages in 1998 in the Indian state of Karnataka, all just over 100 kilometers from the technology hub of Bangalore, indicates that 12 percent of all boys ages 10–14 were current or returned migrants. Of these, almost a third were considered strongly "autonomous migrants"—they left without any parental pressure or even involvement in decision making or in facilitating work or living arrangements.[29]

So, applying a youth lens means that policy, in addition to addressing parents, needs to account directly for the behavior of young people, even when they are very young or living in what are seemingly traditional settings. How? By enhancing their access to information, their command over resources, and their skills to decide.

Supporting the search for information

Young people know a lot. And because they are on average better educated than previous generations, their rates of literacy are much higher, especially in low-income countries, where the literacy rate of those 15–24 is 75 percent, compared with 59 percent for those 35–44.[30] Indeed, the effect of this literacy is greater if one of these young people happens to live in a household where all others are illiterate—because this would enable a transfer of information to those who cannot read, especially important in remote areas where using fertilizer and other technologies or following a regimen for the treatment of tuberculosis entails understanding directions. Researchers argue that such proxy literacy, the exposure of households to people who are literate, would add another third to India's literacy rate.[31] Young people are also much more frequent users of the most ubiquitous source of information now available worldwide—the Internet (chapters 1 and 8). Household surveys

from Albania, Bulgaria, and China indicate that simply having a youth in a household increases the likelihood of adopting new technologies.[32]

What more is there to know? Plenty. Young people's general knowledge may not extend to human capital investment and risk-taking behavior. A 2003 survey of otherwise well-informed and educated Vietnamese youths ages 14–25 indicates that fewer than 60 percent of rural youths had ever heard of syphilis or gonorrhea. Only about a third had heard of the menstrual cycle. In a country where traffic accidents are the leading cause of death and serious injury for those ages 15–19 and where motorbike use by urban young people exceeds 70 percent, only about a quarter use a helmet—many were simply not convinced of its protective value.[33]

The availability of some information is doubtless rooted in social norms for topics appropriate for discussion. A recent survey in Russia quotes a 20-year-old woman from the North Caucasus as saying: "I am interested in diseases and infections transferred sexually. The problem is that I cannot ask my parents, because my breeding does not allow me to discuss such issues with [them]." Instead, the most common source of health information cited by young people is television.[34] Peers, some equally ill informed, are often an alternative to families or schools as a source of information.

The consequence is ill-informed conclusions because the noise in the information flow can be profound. Many studies show that young people tend to overestimate sexual activity and other high-risk behaviors in the population, putting more pressure on them to conform.[35]

What can be done? Three main avenues can be followed to address the problem. One is to improve the curriculum already being taught in existing institutions. School-based reproductive health education programs can be effective in increasing knowledge and the adoption of safe sexual behavior (chapters 5 and 6). Moreover, evaluations have found

"I would support young people [having] freedom in decision making mechanisms. And also, in Turkey, I would work for eliminating 'family dominance' in young people's choices and decisions."

Sezin, 22, Eskisehir, Turkey
December 2005

no evidence that sex education increases sexual activity among youth.[36] Such programs are clearly not enough, however. There are concerns, too, that sex education programs reach only a select group—those still in school.

A second avenue is to develop options outside the traditional institutions of skill formation, including social marketing of reproductive health services targeted to youth, peer counseling programs, mass media programs, and workplace and community outreach services targeted to youth. These programs can promote good reproductive health if targeted to the right audience and linked to services already in place. (Otherwise they may simply lead to unmet demand.) Although not subjected to rigorous evaluation, they have been tried in Cambodia, Thailand, and Uganda—countries that have contained the spread of HIV/AIDS.

These programs need to address the source of the information gap. In the absence of information, people will act based on their own perceptions. Teenage girls in Kenya, when asked about the age patterns of HIV, massively underestimated the prevalence of the disease among males in their late twenties, making them more complacent about "sugar daddies." A randomized intervention provided HIV profiles by gender and led to a closer matching among like-age groups.[37]

An information gap also occurs when youngsters observe trends from a very select sample. In the Dominican Republic in 2001 a survey of boys enrolled in the final year of primary school accurately estimated the returns to completing primary school consistently with estimated earnings profiles but severely underestimated the returns to having a high school degree. This was because they based their estimates on observing the wages only of youth who remained in the neighborhood after completing secondary schools (the high earners moved out). Students at randomly selected schools were then given information of the estimated actual earnings profiles. Follow-up surveys in 2005 indicate that those given the information were 12 percent more likely to be attending school in the follow-

ing school year relative to those who were not given the information.[38]

A third way is that purveyors of information must themselves be well trained and motivated with the right incentives. Recent research on absenteeism among service providers in health and education, discussed in *World Development Report 2004,* shows that this is easier said than done. In Latin America, teaching quality responds to the level and structure of compensation. However, a review of seven country initiatives indicates that for an incentive scheme to work, it must be very selective, of sufficient size, and very closely linked to monitorable performance.[39]

Using peers is also a promising mechanism for transmitting knowledge, but peers are no panacea, for they too must be informed—and they must be a positive influence. For example, U.S. residential job-training programs, which allow participants to avoid interactions in their dysfunctional neighborhoods and develop their own self-image, are more successful than programs that do not have the expensive housing component.[40]

Helping the young command resources

Of the observable markers of transition—such as completing school, leaving home, beginning one's work life, marrying and becoming a parent—financial independence seems to be the best predictor of self-perceived adulthood, in rich and poor countries alike.[41] In this Report's Bangladesh consultations, the recurring phrase was "*nijer paye darano*"—that is, "standing on one's feet." It refers to economic independence—not having to depend on parents or other family members for livelihoods.[42] As young people begin to be financially independent, they naturally confront more severe restraints on their own consumption and investment decisions.

For the nonpoor who can still rely on resources from families, this is not as much of an issue. Indeed, one of the reasons that the age of leaving home is getting later even in richer countries is that young adults rely on their families to get a firmer economic footing. In France and Germany, the share of young men ages 20–24 living in the parental home increased from around 56 percent in 1986 to 62 percent in 1994; in Italy the increase was steeper, from 50 percent to 66 percent, even among men 25–29.[43] For those from poor families, however, or for those who for one reason or another (such as orphanhood or family breakup) can no longer rely on family resources, the result could lead to underinvestment in human capital, to a bad start on the road to a sustainable livelihood, and, for females, to a weak negotiating position in marriage.

Resources for investing in human capital. Young people who have to make choices about investing in skill formation are confronted with substantial costs (see figure 2.3). Out-of-pocket costs tend to vary—for the half of university students in private universities in Argentina, Brazil, Chile, and Colombia, they range from 30 percent of GDP per capita to 100 percent.[44] Even for those at free public universities, the opportunity costs are substantial. Because of the high payoffs to tertiary education in those countries, such costs would not be an issue unless liquidity were a binding constraint—and it is. A recent study for Mexico found that households with the same permanent income are less likely to send their offspring to university if they had a bad year economically.[45] In many countries, parents lack the wherewithal to pay for such schooling directly or simply expect that young people will contribute significantly as they get older. But will young people do so, since they face more binding resource constraints?

The obvious way to ease this constraint is to provide credit to the student—she who benefits pays, even if it's later on. In advanced countries where students bear a significant burden of the cost, education is financed by students who take out loans. Such credit schemes could not work without government support, because commercial loans are not available to the poorest students, who lack the collateral or parental guarantees to back them up. Moreover, the pressures to begin earning a livelihood are high enough even without the enormous responsibility of having to pay back a debt

that is many multiples of initial earnings. Some promising schemes to mitigate these issues are being offered, such as loans that make repayments contingent on income actually earned (see box 3.6 in chapter 3).

Resources for starting a livelihood. Aside from being a barrier to education, inexperience and lack of collateral can also hinder youths who have the motivation and skill to start new businesses. Evidence indicates that liquidity is more of a constraint on young entrepreneurs than on more established ones. Their lack of a credit history and their inexperience puts them at a disadvantage to adults. This is a tricky area because it would not be prudent to direct government funds to subsidize risky commercial ventures. Some recent experiments to expand microcredit to young people may point to a promising avenue (box 2.6).

Strengthening negotiating positions in families and among peers. Emerging research shows that command over resources is an important way to enhance the agency of young women in marriages, especially ones arranged more for the convenience of families and parents than the young couple.

> **BOX 2.6**   *Is microcredit an answer to relieving the young's resource constraints?*
>
> Microcredit has enhanced opportunities for poor people in countries like Bangladesh. It supplies credit in areas too poor or remote to be served by traditional banks. Through group lending, microcredit provides poor people, especially women, with a viable alternative to the collateral required for traditional loans. Group membership serves as a monitoring device to ensure that each member makes her loan payment, thus absorbing part of the risk. Research shows that it has improved the income-earning opportunities of women. Because young people also lack collateral, can microcredit open doors for them? Would such a system work for a group that is, on average, more mobile and perhaps less risk-averse?
>
> The final answers are not known, but analysis of data from Bangladesh may be indicative of microcredit's promise. There, young people (ages 12–24) have taken advantage of microcredit loans. Ten percent of youth have gotten a loan, compared with 33 percent of all adults. Of all loans to youth, the majority come from microcredit institutions (73 percent). Of all who were eligible to receive loans in 1999, 17 percent received their first loan before the age of 25. There is no indication that young people's loans ran into disproportionately more problems than those to adults. They tended to pay similar interest rates and to use them for similar activities.
>
> Initiatives have been undertaken recently to broaden the use of microcredit schemes as a way to channel resources and empower young people. It is important to evaluate these experiences and to share their lessons.
>
> *Source:* Data calculated from Khandker (2005).

Indeed, in some societies, young people, especially girls, are never empowered to make decisions themselves. That power simply shifts from the parent to other older people, such as the husband or mother-in-law.[46] Poor youths are also more likely to succumb to pressures to accept money or goods in exchange for sex, putting them at increased risk of HIV and other sexually transmitted infections. Many young people take up smoking because of peer pressure.

Programs that help young people earn a living or that provide credit may also empower them to withstand social or peer pressure to engage in risky behavior. An evaluation of the justly celebrated micro-credit programs in Bangladesh showed that they had an effect on education, health, and labor market outcomes of both men and women—and that credit to women had the greatest impact on variables associated with women's power and independence.[47]

Helping young people to decide well

Information, once received, has to be filtered and assessed before it can be acted on. This is difficult even for the most confident of people, and it can be paralyzing for those unaccustomed to the analytic processes of decision making. To some extent this could be addressed in schools. Educational systems that emphasize memorization and rote learning may teach facts but fail to inculcate the analytical skills to come to well-informed decisions.

Such life skills can be taught in schools with changes to the curricula. Sometimes this requires changing the environment for learning to counteract well-entrenched

---

BOX 2.7   *Are youths rational (at least according to economists)?*

There have been three ways of modeling what separates youths from adults, based on some recent literature reviews. They are based on traditional economic analysis, developmental psychology, and the intersection of the two, behavioral economics.

Traditional economic analysis. In this framework, dictated by expected utility maximization, as long as benefits exceed costs in present value, an activity will be pursued, and the same goes for risky activity. Even addictive activities, like smoking, are considered rationally by forward-looking agents who choose their own optimal consumption, fully cognizant of long-run negative consequences. Disparities between youths and adults thus do not rely on variant psychologies or levels of rationality, but can result from income differences or sensitivity to price. Indeed, preliminary evidence suggests that, in the decision to pursue risky activities, youths are quite sensitive to economic factors, spawning incentives to curb teen smoking. Gruber (2001) cites a U.S. government study that concludes that increasing the price of cigarettes is the most reliable method for reducing teen smoking.

Developmental psychology. Unlike traditional economic analysis, developmental psychology treats the decision making of youths and adults as separate processes. In some studies, the factors youths take into account when making decisions or formulating opinions are a subset of those used by adults, while in other cases, youths and adults consider different factors altogether, or with significantly different

weights. Halpern-Felsher and Cauffman (2001) found adults to be more competent decision makers than youths when asked about the short- and long-run costs and benefits of different interventions such as cosmetic surgery or whether to participate in an experimental medical study. Competence was measured by consideration of all options, risks, and long-term consequences. The differences were particularly striking between adults and younger adolescents (those in the 6th and 8th grades).

There is evidence that youth and adults use different considerations in decisions. When asked about the perceived consequences of such risky activities as smoking, drinking, and drug use, youths considered consequences involving social reactions more than adults. Steinberg and Cauffman (1996) show an inverted-U relationship between age and susceptibility of peer influences. Susceptibility increases between childhood and early adolescence, peaking around age 14, and declines during the high school years.

Behavioral economics. According to behavioral economics, incongruous behavior and decision making by youths and adults may be the upshot of different perspectives regarding the future. First, younger people are more likely to heavily discount the future over the present. Activities with high short-run benefits or high long-run costs (or both), and underinvestment in activities with both high short-run costs and high long-run benefits would be the result.

Second, future utility can also be affected by projection bias—the tendency of people to

overappreciate their current preferences and project them onto their future preferences without duly taking into account the effects of changes in their situations in the interim. For example, while increased education can bring a young man better job prospects as an adult, he may underestimate the importance of a good job to him in his adulthood because his current preferences do not put great weight on job opportunities.

Third, risk-taking is affected by past engagement in risky behavior. Suppose that one has engaged in a risky activity in the past, the outcome of which—good or bad—is still uncertain, and is now choosing whether to repeat the same activity. If the activity brings short-run gratification, the higher the probability of a bad outcome, the more likely one will engage in it again, because the marginal risk is decreased. The implications are frightening. The higher the risk of contracting AIDS from unprotected sex, the more likely someone who has had unsafe sex in the past will do so again. The worse the long-term effects of drugs, the higher the probability that someone who has so much as experimented with them will become a regular user.

So economists would generally say that youths are probably quite rational, given their preferences, the resources they command, and the perceived costs of their actions. Whether youths would say the same of economists is another matter.

Source: Basu, Ku, and Zarghamee (2006).

practices that channel behavior, some of which may not even be recognized. Research from secondary schools in Thailand indicates that girls who study in single-sex environments do better in math and develop more leadership skills than girls in mixed-sex environments, a finding consistent with research in developed countries.[48]

For many young people, however, it is more than a matter of learning decision-making skills. Because many youths are still seeking their identity, their decisions are more complicated. The process of developing a person's sense of self has been used by some economists to explain seemingly irrational acts, including young people's tendency to engage in risky behavior, such as joining violence-prone gangs, despite the low expected economic payoffs to such activities.[49] The search for identity, and the influence of peer groups on a young person, go some way toward explaining how much risk a person is willing to take and how much to discount the future relative to the present. Experimental results show, for example, that young people tend to take greater risks in driving automobiles when there are peers present than do older adults in a similar situation (box 2.7).

Coming to the correct decision for someone who discounts future costs too heavily, or who adopts risk-taking behavior to belong to a group, requires making that person aware of future consequences and forcing him or her to confront them. Incentives can sometimes influence such decisions, especially if the young would not take the effects on others (or on themselves in the long run) into account, even if they had the information and knew how to decide for themselves. In the United States, higher cigarette prices significantly reduce smoking by young people.[50] In Indonesia, a 1 percent increase in the price of cigarettes reduces consumption by about a third of a percentage point.[51] By contrast, banning cigarette and alcohol advertisements and setting minimum ages for drinking are attempts to increase the price of such behaviors, but evidence suggests that their impact tends to be weak (chapter 5).

Innovative schemes that have channeled subsidies directly to young girls—partly

as an inducement for them to perform well in school but also to ensure that they "own" the decision to attend, circumventing age-old biases against girls' schooling. The Bangladesh Female Secondary School Stipend program, targeted to girls ages 11–14, transfers money to a bank account for girls directly, contingent on their performing well and staying unmarried. While rigorous impact evaluation has yet to be done, indications are that this was a major factor in the large increase in girls' secondary school enrollment in the country (see chapters 3 and 6).

Offering second chances

Broadening the opportunities available to young people for services and the start of a sustainable livelihood, and helping them choose wisely among them, are the priorities. Many young people cannot take advantage of these opportunities, however, because they were ill prepared during younger ages. The worldwide median primary school completion rate is now approaching 85 percent, but many countries and regions still lag behind (Sub-Saharan Africa is at 55 percent) either because children have dropped out or never went to school in the first place (box 2.8).[52] In countries ravaged by civil war, the proportion could amount to an entire school-age generation (see the spotlight on Sierra Leone following chapter 7).

Bad nutrition at an early age can also diminish life chances for many young people. Height may reflect previous health investments and is accepted as a proxy for earning ability later in life.[53] Many people are disabled and cannot take advantage of opportunities—estimates vary widely, but they range around 75 million to 150 million of those ages 10–24.[54]

Inevitably, some young people will choose or be led down the wrong path. Early childbearing is still a problem in many developing countries. More than half of all infections of HIV/AIDS occur among young people under 25. In the United States, those ages 15–19, 7 percent of the population, account for more than a fifth of the arrests for violent offenses and roughly a third of

---

BOX 2.8   *Even those still in school need second chances*

A sound primary education (six years) is relevant for youth not only as a foundation; for many young adults, it is also the place where they are still learning. Some have repeated many years. Others started school very late. Still others are trying to get back into the educational system after many years away—in postconflict countries, perhaps a generation of school-age kids.

The age-enrollment profiles for different educational levels show that, although some poorer countries such as Vietnam have managed to get their young people through primary levels more or less on time, others such as Malawi have not (see

the figure). Malawi has an enrollment rate of almost 75 percent for all its 15-year-olds, compared with 70 percent for Vietnam, but almost all the Vietnamese kids are in secondary level, compared with only about 5 percent for Malawi. The situation persists for older children. Malawi has a higher enrollment rate for 19-year-olds than Vietnam, but half of them are still in primary school. What programs would be needed to make sure that they are educated to the same levels as those who are much younger? Vietnam has no such issue with age-mixing: all 19-year-olds in school are already at secondary levels.

Large numbers of older youth are still in primary school in some countries

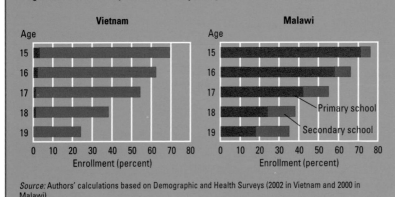

Source: Authors' calculations based on Demographic and Health Surveys (2002 in Vietnam and 2000 in Malawi).

"The system in my country … does not track down those [who] 'drop out' in time to ensure that they do not end up becoming a liability to the world. That is what is happening here; thousands of young people walking aimlessly in the streets [with no] jobs, no social services, and therefore nothing."

Chernor, 21, Sierra Leone
September 2005

those for all property crimes.[55] Figures are difficult to get in developing countries, but there is evidence for some Caribbean countries, such as Jamaica, where nearly half the murders and more than half the crimes are committed by young people, mostly males, between the ages of 17 and 25.[56]

Why second chances? Mitigating the effects of past policies and behaviors

These undesirable outcomes are partly a legacy of past policies and practices that failed to deliver the basic services so important to the foundations for better youth outcomes. Apart from not spending enough for these services, the failure to spend properly has had enormous implications that were documented well in *World Development Report 2004* (see box 2.2).[57] Undesirable outcomes are also a legacy of family and community

strictures. Early marriage, deep-rooted in some societies, can close off opportunities prematurely.

Bad outcomes are also, however, partly the result of the misjudgments of young people inexperienced in decision making and less averse to risk. Even though adults and youths are not that different in their ability to carry out decisions about risky situations, experimental results show that youths differ in how they value the consequences of choices. This could be due to myopia, or to a preference for immediate gratification. It could also be linked to the search for identity—a subject of endless fascination to academics (see box 2.6). The differences in valuing the consequences of choices could have tremendous effects, especially when the costs of actions are borne now—such as going to school or using contraception—but the payoffs occur farther in the future.[58]

Recent research also shows that these attitudes may also have physiological roots. Brain imaging indicates that the part of the brain governing the ability to assess risk matures last, around the early twenties (box 2.9).

How such biological development affects behavior is not clear, but it offers yet another possible explanation for the observed willingness of the young to take more risks than adults. In some countries the insurance market takes account of this difference. The car insurance industry is well aware of the penchant for the young to indulge in risk taking. In Ireland a 19-year-old pays almost three times more than a 29-year-old for car insurance.[59] Companies have long offered incentives to reward responsible past behavior, such as a good track record. Some have even reportedly offered to reward future behavior, such as good grades, presumed to be associated with prudence. However, such insurance markets are thin in developing countries and fail to protect the vast majority. For example, the one insurance market that young people could use is motor insurance, given that the leading cause of death among males outside Africa is injury, most caused by vehicular accidents. The spread of this industry is confined to only a few

BOX 2.9 *Brain development among youth: Neuroscience meets social science*

A decade ago, the prevailing notion was that brain growth ended at about the age of 2 years. Since then, we have learned that brain growth continues well into adolescence (between ages 10 and 19) and into young adulthood (see the figure below). During this period the brain undergoes a series of changes, and parts of the brain associated with social skills, problem solving, and identifying emotions mature only by the early twenties. However, this process of brain development cannot entirely explain adolescent decision making and behavior. Nor does it override the effect of the environment—parents, schools, communities—in which young people live.

Brain development: arborization and pruning

The brain is made up of nerve cells—about 10 billion of them—connected by branches or dendrites. These branches move information from one cell to another, but these connections are not soldered together; rather, there are spaces between the branch of one cell and the body of another. These spaces are called *synapses,* and information moves from cell to cell across these spaces by releasing tiny packets of chemicals. When there are abnormalities in the chemicals in the synapses, a variety of clinical conditions result, such as depression and attention-deficit and hyperactivity disorders.

Different parts of the brain handle different activities—that much is well-known. What is new is the finding that during adolescence certain areas of the brain grow in size and other regions become more efficient. For example, the area of the brain responsible for language more than doubles in size between ages 8 and 14. Consequently, language acquisition is optimal at those ages. So, too, connections grow and strengthen between the brain stem and the spinal cord, increasing the connections between the emotions and what the body feels. Throughout childhood and adolescence, more and more nerve cells grow sheaths around them called white matter or myelin. This is like building a superhighway, allowing information to be interpreted and recalled much faster than was ever possible as a young child.

These structural changes are only some of the brain's alterations during adolescence. Another major change is called "pruning." Throughout early childhood, the number of connections between cells increase, and because the process is much like the growth of branches on a tree, it is called arborization. It allows a child's brain to be very excitable—which is why children seem to be perpetual motion machines. In adolescence, many of those branches die—through pruning. The brain is less excitable but also more efficient in carrying information.

The pruning follows a consistent pattern throughout adolescence and young adulthood

starting at the back of the brain and ending at the prefrontal cortex. The prefrontal cortex regulates impulses, risk taking, planning, decision making, empathy, and insight. Research also shows that the cerebellum, recently discovered to be important for mathematics, music, decision making, social skills, and understanding humor, continues to grow through adolescence and well into emerging adulthood. The last structure of the brain to stop growing, it develops until the mid-twenties.

Implications for social policies

What does this new brain research mean for understanding adolescent decision making and behavior? Although much more research is needed before definitive policies can be recommended based on the new brain research, it suggests some interesting policy considerations:

- The loss of neuronal excitation in adolescence is associated with a rise in depression, especially among adolescent females, suggesting a biological basis for the epidemiological finding that gender differences in depression start around the time of puberty. These biological changes combine with external sources of stress to increase the risk of suicide for youth in many countries of the world.

- As the brain matures during adolescence, alternations in the synaptic chemicals may influence learning (drugs for attention-deficit disorders improve information transfer at the level of the neuronal synapse). For example, antidepressive drugs may allow for certain excitatory neurotransmitters to stay in the space between two brain cells longer than

otherwise.

- Learning and teaching strategies should be timed to increase neurodevelopmental capacities. Because neurodevelopmental maturation occurs at different chronological ages for different people, their inability to grasp a concept at one age does not mean that they are unable to learn the material. This speaks to the risk of educational "tracking" based on comprehension or performance examinations at a young age.

- Without a fully mature prefrontal cortex, adolescents may be more impulsive than adults and perhaps more susceptible to peer influences. This impulsiveness—especially in reactive decision making, as when faced with a situation or threatened to make an immediate decision—suggests the value of second-chance programs.

It is, however, too early in the research to draw definitive conclusions about brain development and behavior. Also, physical development interacts with the social environments to determine behaviors and outcomes. So parental behaviors and expectations, effective schools, communities that are youth oriented and supportive, all make a difference in determining young people's behavior and how well they learn complex decision-making skills.

Source: Blum (2006).

Timeline of brain development

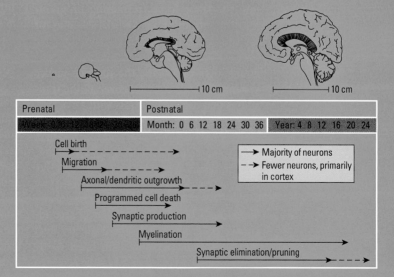

Source: Andersen (2003).

developing countries and its penetration is shallow in middle- and low-income economies, where average premiums per capita are only a tenth of those in high-income economies.[60]

What's to be done?

Given the legacy of past policies and behaviors, and the many market failures, what's to be done? Remediation tends to be relatively costly for many of the transitions, which is why early attention to basic needs for younger children, as well as broadening opportunities for young people and helping them decide wisely, are essential. It is difficult to get precise estimates because remedial programs are so different from the original ones. A rough order of magnitude comparing adult basic literacy programs with primary education programs in Bangladesh and Senegal yields a range of differences that make the former one to three times as costly, even without taking into account their opportunity costs.[61] So, the first lesson: try to get it right the first time.

Beyond prevention, countries rightly have many programs that try to mitigate the effects of undesirable but sadly inevitable youth outcomes. These include reinvesting in human capital (adult literacy programs), treating those infected with communicable diseases, providing drug rehabilitation, integrating the long-term unemployed into the labor force (retraining programs for dropouts and public works schemes for the young), and reintegrating young people into the social fabric (demobilization programs after civil wars, the juvenile justice system). These programs cover all the transitions that the Report deals with.

Three other lessons seem to matter most: target programs closely, coordinate them with mainstream "first-chance" programs, and mitigate without encouraging risky behavior (or encouraging moral hazard).

Targeting.   Because of the cost of second-chance programs, it is important to direct them to the neediest, as with other costly schemes. Many young people have access to family resources that can act as a safety net.

In richer countries, the incidence of returning to the parental home, at least temporarily, has increased after a failed marriage or relationship, job loss, or devastating illness. Households able to cope with this are less at risk and therefore need less subsidy than young people who have frayed family connections, especially in developing countries. There is evidence, for example, that young people return home in smaller numbers if they are from families that have experienced the death of a parent or divorce.[62] Orphans are thus more vulnerable and a priority for social programs.

Another reason for targeting is that some programs that mean to benefit mostly youths but do not identify them as the main beneficiary may fail to reach the neediest, who may not seek the service if they are less aware of where it is. This is why campaigns to address reproductive health, such as postnatal care services for very young mothers (chapter 5), are so aggressive at social marketing.

Coordinating with the mainstream.   Second-chance programs tend to be disconnected, run as separate initiatives by NGOs or agencies (chapter 9). The lesson from the few analyses of these programs is that integration and coordination make them more effective. To avoid the danger of developing very costly parallel programs, it is important to ensure reentry. One example is graduate equivalency programs, which allow dropouts from secondary systems to take classes that will eventually get them the equivalent of a secondary diploma (chapter 3). Another is the U.S. community college system. Designed originally to provide second chances for adults, it is now being used increasingly by young high school graduates as a second-chance program—three-quarters of all remedial students are in community colleges.[63]

By the same token, it is important for mainstream programs to be flexible so that early mistakes do not turn into permanent liabilities. Some countries track students as young as age 10 into differing ability schools—while others keep schools

"I used to steal cellular phones, but that is dangerous. They can put you to prison and even kill you. I did that because I wanted money and under the influence of my gang. I quit that life and now I can walk the streets again . . ."

Freddy, 16, Honduras
January 2006

comprehensive. A recent study of countries' achievements over time shows that early tracking not only increases education inequality (there is no catching up despite segregation) but may also lower performance.[64]

Remediation with accountability. No one doubts that all people, including youths, should face the consequences of their risky behaviors—for their own good and for society's. In the case of criminal behavior, moral justice and deterrence demand it. After one has strayed, though, what is best for society? Rehabilitation is very costly, but the payoffs are highest for young people who still have a lifetime of potential productivity ahead of them. For those who commit crimes at a young age, what is most critical is that they face the consequences of their action without being made to lose hope. In the Philippines, 3,700 children are reported to be in adult jails, "in conditions detrimental to their health and well-being."[65] Many of them—some with relatively minor misdemeanors, some homeless—are incarcerated with hardened criminals. The consequences should be commensurate with the gravity of the crime, and programs should allow young people to rehabilitate themselves where that is possible and appropriate—"restorative" rather than "retributive" justice, in the parlance of chapter 7. More demobilization programs are being designed to rehabilitate young combatants (see the spotlight on Sierra Leone following chapter 7).

Any remediation program confronts what economists call a moral hazard. If someone knows that the consequences of his or her risk-taking behavior are mitigated by a government program or insurance, that person may engage in more risk-taking behavior than warranted. There has been some fear that the availability of antiretroviral therapy for HIV may cause young people to take fewer precautions. In Kenya, condom use fell after the government announced reported "cures" for AIDS (chapter 5). The solution to such problems is not to deny second chances,

such as treatment. That would be unethical as well as wasteful. Instead, it is to build incentives that encourage the care-taking behavior to persist even in treatment.

———

The three pathways implied by the youth lenses in the framework discussed here—opportunities, capabilities, and second chances—need to be applied to each of the transitions introduced in chapter 1. Sustained greater spending on the basics, especially quality, is a top priority in the poorest countries. In others, more attention to upper secondary and tertiary education is key. However, it is not all about spending. Equally important is to ensure that young people, with the support of their families, are stimulated to invest in themselves. As with any investment, improving the climate for investing in human capital can raise the returns and lower the risks. The returns in the form of a good job and an active civic life can be enhanced by policies that level the opportunities for young and old alike. Prudence in taking health risks can be encouraged by the right incentives.

The youth lenses must be aligned to get the most impact. An illustration of the magnitude of this joint effect can be seen by considering the returns to a hypothetical secondary education project using data from the Dominican Republic, Indonesia, and Mexico.[66] Take a project that enhances opportunities by building enough schools to achieve a gain in upper secondary enrollment to 57 percent from 52 percent of the relevant age cohort. Earnings and cost data for Mexico indicate that such a project would have a benefit-to-cost ratio of 1.03 in present value terms—an acceptable return on investment that broadens opportunities.

Recent research shows that secondary students severely underestimate the real returns to completing secondary school.[67] A project that not only provided another secondary school seat but also enhanced the capability of young people simply by providing information to correct their misperceptions of the returns to education, would raise the enrollment rate to 62 percent. The benefit-to-cost ratio for this project would be 1.68—a much better investment.

Finally, a project that makes the investment less risky for youth would increase enrollment even more. The risk could be in the form of an economic shock that would make secondary education unaffordable, forcing them to drop out—a waste of resources. If a student or her family had the insurance of a scholarship scheme in the event of an income shock (a second chance), enrollments would rise to 69 percent. Such a program, combined with the first two, would have a benefit-to-cost ratio of 2.15—better, yet again.

The framework introduced here must be applied in a way that takes into account different economic, demographic, and social environments. Some countries deal well with the next generation of development challenges—others, less so. Countries could also be characterized by the speed at which young people start to make decisions for themselves: in traditional societies the young make fewer decisions about major life transitions, and in others they exercise independence faster than their predecessors. How countries can apply the principles in these different settings across each of the transitions is the subject of part 2.

A gender filter on the youth lens

Gender differences emerge sharply with the onset of puberty, affecting the life trajectories of girls and boys in profoundly different ways. Governments have a range of policy levers to counter the inequalities in opportunities, capabilities, and second chances of young women and men. Some policies are not targeted—they equalize opportunities indirectly by addressing constraints. But disadvantaged from the start, many young women also need directly targeted programs to help them catch up.

Life trajectories diverge early—and permanently—for adolescent girls and boys

Initiation rites in puberty, which vary from circumcision ceremonies in some African societies to debutante balls in the Americas, signal the break with the homogeneity of childhood and the emergence of gender-based expectations for girls and boys. With these rites of passage, the lives of young men and women begin to follow social trajectories defined by gender. Gender-defined roles and responsibilities tend to curtail girls' opportunities and decision-making capabilities but broaden those of boys. In some societies girls are married very young. In others, families severely restrict girls' freedom to protect their virginity before marriage.[1] In still others, adolescent girls often become pregnant and have children outside marriage.[2] These gendered trajectories for young women and men are revealed in gender differences in youth outcomes.

The interplay of differences in sex (biology) and gender (society) also shapes the different disease burdens for adolescent boys and girls. In addition to health risks associated with early and frequent childbearing, young women ages 15–29 suffer disproportionately from HIV/AIDS, unipolar depressive disorders, panic disorders, and fires. Rape and domestic violence account for 5–16 percent of healthy years of life lost by women of reproductive age.[3] In contrast, young men suffer more from disabilities related to violence, alcohol use, and accidents,[4] patterns similar to those in high-income countries, suggesting common risk-taking behaviors and underscoring the global nature of the problems of violence and drugs in adolescent males.

In education, the trend has been toward gender convergence, marking one area where girls' transition to adulthood has undergone significant change. Across countries, school attendance and labor force participation rates have risen faster for young women than young men, in both the 15–19 and 20–24 age groups.[5] However, the schooling experience can still be gender-sensitive. For example, in Kenya where adolescents attend mixed schools and are fairly free to associate with the opposite sex, teachers view girls negatively, often saying that they are too lazy or less capable than boys are to learn.[6]

Time-use studies indicate other differences in the lives of adolescent girls and boys. The amount of time devoted to work, paid or unpaid, rises with age for boys and girls, but girls tend to work more hours than boys, spending long hours fetching water and firewood, cleaning and cooking, and minding younger siblings.[7] Time-use studies in Kenya, India, Nicaragua, Pakistan, and South Africa show that, on average, girls ages 15–29 work about one hour more a day than boys.[8]

For young women in many regions, the transition from school to work does not take place or is interrupted because of marriage and childbearing or because it is socially unacceptable for them to work for pay. Compared to young women, men are more likely to work for pay—especially if they are not enrolled in school—and to work less on domestic chores and unpaid economic activities.[9] The pressures on boys to earn income may explain the rise in school dropout rates for boys.[10] Girls who are not in school are more likely to participate in unpaid domestic work and household surveys may not capture such work. This is evident, for example, in the percentage of "idle" girls in many developing countries: by age 14 the proportion of girls who are absent from both school and paid employment in six developing countries ranged from 6 percent in Nepal to 44 percent in the Republic of Yemen.[11]

Programs that equalize opportunities can reduce gender disparities

Broadening opportunities so that young men and women have better access to services will reduce gender disparities. Governments have a range of policy levers—pricing policies, legal and regulatory reform, better designed service delivery, selected investments in infrastructure—that could have equalizing effects even without gender-based targeting. How? Through alleviating the constraints that disadvantage girls. Some could reduce the relative costs associated with investing in girls' productive skills. Others could increase the information to counter labor market biases against girls, or increase infrastructure investments that ease the burden of household work for girls.

Consider the gender-specific impact of an ostensibly gender-neutral program, such as building more schools in rural areas. More schools should benefit both boys and girls, but studies show different effects for boys and girls. In countries as diverse as Pakistan and Ghana, reducing the distance to a secondary school elicits greater responsiveness in schooling for girls than for boys, partly because girls' enrollment is lower to begin with and because distance is a bigger constraint for girls, for whom personal security is a concern for parents.[12]

Trade policies also can have disproportionately larger effects on young women's employment opportunities. Take Bangladesh, where young women joined the export-driven textile sector in large numbers, increasing their wages dramatically. The increase in women's employment and earnings enhanced their bargaining power within their households.[13] Gender-informed health safety in the workplace and other regulations to ensure good employment conditions for female workers should increase the gains for young women even more—and

Percentage increase in middle school enrollment due to Oportunidades in rural areas in Mexico by sex and grade, 1997–2001

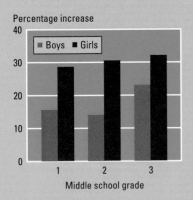

Percentage increase

Source: Parker (2003).

counter the consequences of their inexperience in the workforce.

In addition to general policies and programs, gender-targeted programs must be implemented especially because gender-defined transitions to adulthood often severely limit girls' voice or exposure to information. When low-income families are forced to ration spending on education, health care, and nutrition, girls and young women tend to bear much of the costs. As household incomes rise, spending on these items also rises, with girls and young women often benefiting proportionately. For example, giving larger cash transfers to families to send and keep girls in schools, as with Oportunidades in Mexico, has increased enrollment for girls (see the figure).

A pilot education project in the province of Balochistan, Pakistan, subsidized the establishment of private neighborhood schools. Parents were given the financial resources and technical assistance to contract a school operator to open a neighborhood private school, with the financial resources being tied to the number of girls enrolled in the new school. Opening a new neighborhood school increased girls' enrollments by 33 percentage points, a far larger effect than on boys' enrollments. This project was for primary education. Because distance to school is an even greater worry for secondary school girls in Pakistan, the relative gains for girls of greater school availability at secondary level is likely to be even higher.[14]

Facilitating young women's school-to-work transition requires targeted training programs and labor intermediation services. To attract young women, Chile Joven, an employment training and traineeship program for low-income, high-risk youth, included awareness campaigns for the business sector to recruit women, offered child care services, provided gender training for trainers, and expanded the traineeships in firms for young women. Sixty-five percent of participants found a job on finishing the program, and 70 percent of them found a job in their area of study, proportions much higher than for the control group, and the returns to labor market performance were better for women than for men.[15] Similarly, the youth job training program ProJoven in Peru—created in 1997 to help economically disadvantaged youths ages 16–24 to enter the formal labor market—increased real incomes and reduced the gender wage gap. Fifty-four percent of the participants were young women. Before the program, young men were earning 45 percent more than women—after, only 2.7 percent more.[16]

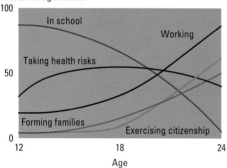

The young founders of Grupo Cultural Afro Reggae, after losing many friends to the violence and drug trade in the *favelas* of Rio de Janeiro, decided that a teenage death should no longer be accepted or expected. They created a program of music, dance, and cultural workshops to steer children and youth away from the drug trade and violence of the favelas—and to break down stereotypes and communicate with broader society. (http://www.afroreggae.org.br/)

Transitions

PART II

EVERY GENERATION GOES THROUGH TRANSITIONS. For infants, it is the process of weaning. For those about to enter the "golden years," it is the process of retiring. For what this Report has been calling the next generation of workers, households heads, and leaders, the following five transitions can be anticipated:

- Learning as adolescents and young adults
- Beginning to work
- Taking risks that impact health
- Forming families
- Exercising active citizenship

When and how these transitions occur vary enormously across countries. But the patterns can be represented in a highly stylized (but empirically based) way in the figure. At the age of 12, most children are in school. They start to leave school shortly thereafter and almost all are out by age 24. Children begin to work at an early age in developing countries but most do not work full time until they are at least teenagers. Young people also begin to engage in risk-taking behaviors, such as having sex, smoking, trying drugs, which have possible health implications. Young people start puberty early but form families later. Finally, young people gradually begin to make themselves heard outside the family and to exercise citizenship.

The chapters in this part of the Report discuss how countries can address the challenges posed by these overlapping transitions, by passing country policies through the three lenses of opportunity, capability, and second chances.

Percent of age cohort

Learning for work and life

chapter 3

Young people need to acquire the right knowledge and skills to become productive workers, good parents, and responsible citizens. Learning takes place in many environments—home, school, the workplace—but most investments in learning take place in schools. Those investments need to happen during childhood and adolescence, and the investments in adolescence are needed to make earlier investments pay off.

Despite great progress in primary schooling in developing countries, the preparation of youth for work and life is very low, just as demand for skills and knowledge is rising. Past education policies focused on increasing the number of people who go through the education system, rather than learning that takes place in schools. This chapter asserts that, to improve the skills of young people for work and life, education opportunities must be made more relevant to the needs of *all* young people as learners and future workers, parents, and citizens, and young people need to be provided with the tools to develop their capabilities so they can make the most of opportunities.

This involves improving educational preparation for adolescence by providing quality basic education (including lower secondary) for all. It also involves meeting the growing demand for postbasic skills, by providing diverse and flexible learning options in upper secondary and higher education; by implementing a relevant curriculum that teaches practical subjects, thinking skills, and behavioral skills; and by connecting school and work. To be successful, these reforms must be abetted by teachers who are well-prepared and motivated as well as schools that are accountable for student learning.

Education opportunities are not enough when young people cannot benefit from them. Young people make important decisions about their own education, but face constraints in doing so. Enabling them to make better education choices requires developing their behavioral skills and involving them as stakeholders in their own education, as well as providing better information about learning options and the job market and providing the financial incentives to make better choices.

Learning opportunities need to be provided for all, including young people who failed to acquire basic skills the first time around. Society cannot afford to neglect them—without second chances, these young people and their families would be condemned to poverty. Governments should therefore develop a system of remedial education, equivalency programs, literacy programs, and skills training that takes into account the diversity of these young people.

Educational preparation of youth for work and life is low

The demand for workers with postprimary education, particularly tertiary education, is increasing as a result of skill-based technological change and the growing importance of knowledge (chapter 1). Rising primary completion rates are substantially increasing the number of potential secondary-school goers. At the same time, many children in South Asia and Sub-Saharan Africa drop out before completing primary school (or never start).

The transition to secondary school remains a barrier around the world, even in countries with high primary completion rates. Why? Because of demand factors—low levels of preparedness, the perceived irrelevance of secondary schooling, and the high direct and indirect costs—and because of low physical access to secondary schools.

Figure 3.1   The transition to secondary school is a stumbling block for many young people

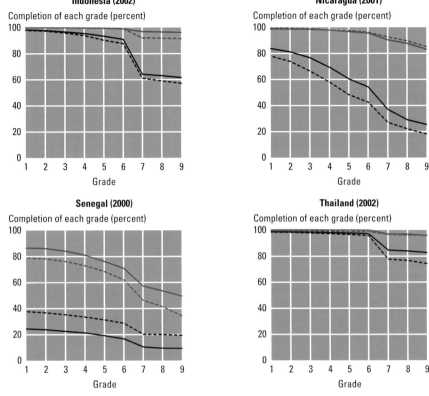

Source: http://econ.worldbank.org/projects/edattain. Kaplan-Meier estimates based on nationally representative samples of 10- to 19-year-olds.
Note: The richest 20 percent and poorest 40 percent are derived from an index of assets and housing characteristics. Secondary school typically starts in grade 7.

The transition to secondary school is especially a problem for the poor (figure 3.1). In middle-income countries such as Indonesia and Thailand, the poorest 40 percent experience a sharp drop in the proportion completing the transition from primary to secondary; in poorer countries such as Nicaragua and Senegal, the drop in completion rates begins earlier, before plunging even faster during the transition. In many countries, particularly in South Asia and Sub-Saharan Africa, gender differences tend to get accentuated in the transition to secondary school and remain large.

The educational preparation of youth for work and life is very low in developing countries, particularly among the poor. The average performance of adolescents in the poorest countries on Programme for International Student Assessment (PISA)

tests—which evaluate 15-year-olds' abilities to apply basic skills—is approximately 20 percent lower than the Organisation for Economic Co-operation and Development (OECD) average of 500 (figure 3.2), and worse for the poorest quintile of the students in these countries. In some countries, such as Mexico, performance is substantially lower than in others at similar incomes.

These numbers are all the more worrisome because the students in these assessments are a select group. Those who have already dropped out of school—likely the poorest and lowest performing—are not included. In Brazil, only slightly more than 60 percent of 15-year-olds are in school in grades 7 and above. These low levels of learning achievement in secondary schools reflect in part the failure of primary and secondary schools to provide the basic skills

Figure 3.2   Learning achievement in poor countries can be very low

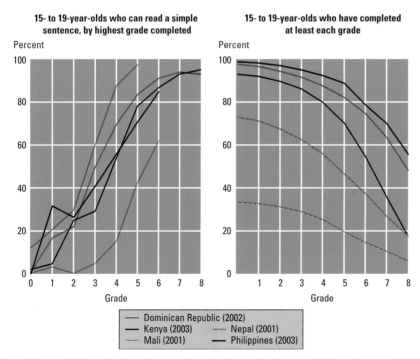

Mathematics

Score

600

500

400

300

200

■ Richest quintile of students
— Average score
◇ Poorest quintile of students

Indonesia, Thailand, Tunisia, Russian Federation, Brazil, Turkey, Uruguay, Slovak Republic, Poland, Mexico, Hungary, Czech Republic, Rep. of Korea, United States

Proportion of 15-year-olds in school
(grade 7 and above)

Percent

100

80

60

40

20

0

Indonesia, Thailand, Tunisia, Russian Federation, Brazil, Turkey, Uruguay, Slovak Republic, Poland, Mexico, Hungary, Czech Republic, Rep. of Korea, United States

Source: Authors' analysis of PISA data.
Note: Countries ordered by gross national income (GNI) per capita in 2003, from lowest to highest.

needed for work and life. They also reflect inequalities in access to good schools. Most of the difference in test scores between the poor and the rich is explained by their attending different schools.

Figure 3.3   The ability to read a simple sentence increases with schooling, but few acquire even that most basic skill

15- to 19-year-olds who can read a simple sentence, by highest grade completed

Percent

100

80

60

40

20

0

0 1 2 3 4 5 6 7 8

Grade

15- to 19-year-olds who have completed at least each grade

Percent

100

80

60

40

20

0

1 2 3 4 5 6 7 8

Grade

— Dominican Republic (2002)
— Kenya (2003)   — Nepal (2001)
— Mali (2001)   — Philippines (2003)

Source: http://econ.worldbank.org/projects/edattain and additional authors' analysis of Demographic and Health Surveys data.

The many children who stop in primary school or drop out before completing it acquire only minimal skills along the way. In Mali, only about 20 percent of 15- to 19-year-olds had completed the primary cycle of six years of schooling—of those, only 60 percent could read a simple sentence (figure 3.3). In Nepal 15- to 19-year-olds who had completed the five years of the primary cycle could typically read a sentence—but among the close to 30 percent who make it no further than grade 3, fewer than 60 percent could read a sentence.

Rising demand for postprimary education and poor preparation for work and life pose three policy challenges:

• Expanding postprimary learning opportunities to meet increasing demand, while increasing the readiness for, and quality of, postprimary education. Although the measured expansion of secondary education opportunities (that maintain a minimum level of quality) is most relevant for countries with increasing demand for secondary education (Brazil, Mexico), improving learning achievement is most relevant for countries with high secondary education coverage (Hungary, South Africa).

• Enhancing young people's ability to make the most of these opportunities by alleviating the decision-making, information, and financial constraints they face. This challenge is most relevant in countries where the opportunities exist (secondary schools) but many young people do not take advantage of them (Morocco, Thailand).

- Providing second-chance learning opportunities for out-of-school youth who lack the basic skills for work and life, which is most relevant for countries with significant numbers of young people who never went to school or dropped out before completing primary school (Pakistan, Senegal).

A solid foundation: Improving the readiness for postprimary education

Learning is a life-cycle process, in which the timing and continuity of investments matter.[1] Investments in learning need to happen during childhood and adolescence; failures to invest at this stage are very costly to remedy later. Learning is most intense in childhood and adolescence, when physical and intellectual capabilities are growing rapidly. From a neurological perspective, childhood and adolescence are critical periods for the normal development of most skills—there is no good substitute for investments during these years (see definition 3.1 of skills and knowledge). For example, language skills are much more easily acquired by children than adults. Different abilities are formed at different stages of the life cycle—although language skills are hard to develop after adolescence, behavioral skills (such as motivation, persistence, self-confidence, and self-discipline) can still be developed through a person's early twenties (box 3.1).[2]

Because learning is cumulative, investments in learning during childhood and adolescence have larger returns than later investments because they increase the productivity of those later investments. For example, early childhood interventions can increase subsequent learning achievement. Also, the impact of job training programs on earnings is typically larger for those who have more schooling.[3] Investments during adolescence are also needed to make child-

hood investments pay off. For example, the effect of preschool interventions on learning achievement may not persist without appropriate further schooling investments. In the U.S. Head Start preschool program, the initial improvements in test scores often vanish among children who attend poor quality schools.[4]

Investments during early childhood reap significant dividends, and can reduce the intergenerational transmission of inequality. Many young children in developing countries suffer profound deficits in nutrition, health, and cognitive and socio-emotional development very early in their lives, with lifelong consequences for educational achievement, employment, and earnings.[5] A study in Ecuador demonstrates that large differences in language acquisition among children from different socioeconomic backgrounds become larger as they mature, partly because of differences in child health and parenting skills.[6] Programs that combine health, parenting skills, and preschool education are likely to be most successful, and rigorous evaluations of programs in Argentina, Jamaica, and the Philippines demonstrate their effectiveness in developing countries.[7] Such programs must be combined with efforts to improve later education for those investments to have the greatest effect.

Early entry, adequate progress, and learning basic literacy and numeracy in primary school are keys to success in postprimary education. In many countries, however, youths are still attending primary school, particularly in Africa and Latin America. The proportions of primary students beyond the primary school age are 34 percent in Brazil, 28 percent in Kenya, and 27 percent in the Lao People's Democratic Republic.[8] Overage enrollment is mainly due to repetition in Brazil, late school entry in Kenya, and a combination of the two in Lao PDR. In rural Bangladesh, late school entry and grade repetition in primary school reduce the chances of going to secondary school and completing it. Making school entry at age 6 compulsory and secondary school more available increase the chances of starting secondary school.[9]

DEFINITION 3.1
Skills and knowledge

The types of skills discussed in this Report include *thinking skills* (critical and creative thinking), *behavioral skills* (perseverance, self-discipline, teamwork, the ability to negotiate conflict and manage risks), *specific knowledge* (including numeracy and literacy), and *vocational skills* (a mix of specific knowledge and skills to perform jobs that rely on clearly defined tasks).

Basic skills denote the set of minimal abilities needed for further learning, work, and life, including numeracy and literacy and basic levels of behavioral skills such as perseverance, self-discipline, and self-confidence. *Postbasic skills* include thinking skills, higher order behavioral skills (decision-making skills, teamwork, the ability to negotiate conflict and manage risks), specific knowledge applied to real-life situations, and vocational skills.

BOX 3.1   *The ignored side of skills development: Building behavioral skills for school, work, and life*

Some high IQ people can fail in life because they lack self-discipline, while low IQ individuals can do well thanks to motivation and persistence.

Several studies in countries as diverse as India and the United States show that job stability and dependability are the traits most valued by employers. Yet academic and policy discussions focus almost exclusively on mastery of specific knowledge. Although it is some-times believed that behavioral skills cannot be measured, psychologists have developed tests to measure these skills—and they are used by companies to screen workers.[10]

Behavioral skills, developed from a very early age through late youth, have long-lasting effects on schooling, work, and social outcomes. They incorporate many traits, including motivation, persistence, self-discipline, self-confidence, and the ability to weigh options and come to a deci-sion (decision-making skills). They also include social skills, such as teamwork and the ability to negotiate conflict and to resist peer pressure.

Significant differences in behavioral skills appear across income levels at early ages and persist over time. The long-term impacts of early childhood interventions come mainly from the social skills and motivation they impart to children and the better home environment they produce. In the United States, behavioral skills measured at ages 14–24 reduce the probability of dropping out of high school and increase the probability of attending college, which in turn

leads to higher wages. They affect employment and the choice of occupation. They also lead to significant declines in smoking, marijuana use, participation in illegal activities, and teenage pregnancy and marriage.

School-based programs
School-based mentoring programs provide evidence of the malleability and importance of behavior in adolescence. A randomized impact evaluation of the Big Brother–Big Sister mentor-ing program in the United States shows that it reduced the likelihood to have initiated drug or alcohol use, to hit someone, to miss school, or to lie to parents. It also led to higher grades and greater competency in school and work. The Quantum Opportunity Program, which offered disadvantaged minority students long-term mentoring and financial incentives for activities aimed at improving social and labor market skills, led to higher high school graduation rates and lower arrest rates. Such programs have not yet been tried in developing countries.

Several classroom-based programs to teach behavioral skills directly have also produced persistent effects in controlled studies in the United States and the Netherlands. Their sucess-ful role in reducing risky health behavior has been most frequently evaluated, but they also improve academic and other behavioral out-comes. Such programs often have curricula and teaching methods that can be adapted to other

country contexts. The Lion's Quest program in the United States is being tried in Japan, and nonformal teaching methods are being used by many programs in many developing countries, although none been well evaluated yet (see box 3.2).

Programs outside school
The Make a Connection program strengthens the connections of young people to their com-munities, to their families and peers, and to themselves by developing such behavioral skills as self-confidence, motivation, teamwork, and conflict management, as well as critical and creative thinking skills; together they are often referred as "life skills." It operates in 25 countries, including Brazil, China, the Russian Federation, and South Africa, adapted to local needs. In the Philippines, it targets indigenous out-of-school youth. The program lasts for about 13 months and includes training in identity, cultural appre-ciation, and leadership, after which participants identify livelihood projects and are eligible for loans to finance them. Self-reported retrospec-tive information reveals significant effects on employment, school reentry, and community service.

Sources: Bowles and Gintis (1976); Carneiro and Heckman (2003); Cunha and others (2005); Hahn (1999); Hahn, Lanspery, and Leavitt (2005); Heck-man, Stixrud, and Urzua (2006); Schweinhart, Barnes, and Weikart (1993); Sternberg (1985); and Zins and others (2004).

Improving the quality of primary educa-tion requires a renewed emphasis on basic literacy and numeracy combined with some of the policies mentioned later in the chap-ter, such as student-centered teaching meth-ods, teachers who are well-prepared and motivated, and schools that are accountable for student learning. Supplementary reme-dial education can also play an important role (see second chances section).

Enhancing postprimary education opportunities

The postprimary education system should serve the diverse needs of young people as learners and future workers, parents, and citizens. This section shows what is needed to do this:

- Provide quality basic education (primary plus lower secondary) for all, as well as

a diverse and flexible menu of learning options, so that young people can fulfill their potential.

- Make school curricula more relevant by teaching practical subjects, think-ing skills, and behavioral skills as well as blending the academic and voca-tional curricula in upper secondary. In addition, strengthening the connection between school and work facilitates the school-to-work transition.

- Hire motivated and well-prepared teach-ers and make schools accountable for student learning to ensure success of education reform.

- Implement cost-sharing strategies, public-private partnerships, and efficiency-enhancing mechanisms to finance the expansion and improvement of postpri-mary education.

Expanding options and improving the organization of postprimary education

Providing basic education for all. Countries can provide all youth with basic skills for work and life by deferring selection and specialization until after lower secondary and by making lower secondary school part of the basic and compulsory education cycle. International test scores show that early tracking significantly increases inequality in learning achievement—and reduces learning.[11] The secondary education reform in Chile moved all vocational specialization to the upper secondary school. This allows time for building a solid academic base for later occupational specialization. Deferring selection and specialization can be combined with compulsory schooling laws, which have been shown to have a positive effect on educational attainment and other social outcomes.[12]

In Tanzania and Tunisia, using entrance exams to strictly ration the number of students progressing to secondary led to overcrowding in primary school and lower student performance overall.[13] Early tracking or selection may also create or perpetuate social exclusion, as in some Caribbean countries that sort students into better and worse schools according to test scores, each with a different uniform.[14] Where there are fiscal constraints on expanding lower secondary, more places can be created by a combination of sharing costs (with a compensating demand-side mechanism for the poor) and working with the private sector (see finance section below). For example, Tanzania discouraged private schools, but Kenya allowed them and even provided some subsidies—and during the 1960s and 1970s secondary school enrollment in Kenya expanded much faster than in Tanzania.

Building schools can meet increases in demand for secondary education, but these investments will not necessarily increase school participation or reduce inequality in many developing countries. A study using data from 21 developing countries shows that most rural residents live within fairly easy reach of a formal primary school but not a secondary school.[15] It finds there is typically a small negative relationship between school participation and distance to secondary school, and little evidence that increasing school availability reduces inequality in enrollment by household wealth or gender.

Diversifying education options while ensuring quality. Upper secondary and higher education have to accommodate diverse student needs, interests, and capabilities—diversity that increases as they expand and become mass systems. The vocational education sector in developing countries is small (22 percent of student enrollment) relative to that in OECD countries. Upper secondary is still heavily directed to more academic university degrees, with programs oriented to the labor market playing a marginal role. However, graduation rates are higher in systems geared to work (Malaysia) than in those geared to university (Argentina and Chile).[16]

Higher education is also heavily concentrated on more academic university degrees, though this is slowly changing with the appearance of new institutions, including technical institutes offering short-term degrees, community colleges, polytechnics, distance education centers, and open universities. Shorter and more occupationally oriented programs have half or more of the students in China, Jamaica, Malaysia, and Zimbabwe.[17]

The expansion and diversification of postprimary education systems can be greatly facilitated by reaching out to the private sector through public-private partnerships. Governments should encourage private participation while ensuring quality standards. The share of the private sector is larger in higher education (33 percent) than in upper secondary (25 percent).[18] In upper secondary, the share has remained stable or declined in most countries, but it has increased in tertiary, especially in Brazil and Peru. Despite some positive trends, there is still more room for private sector involvement in postprimary education.

Public-private partnerships allow systems to expand in a fiscally constrained environment, particularly in the more expensive tertiary sector, and improve learning outcomes and efficiency overall by increasing choices and injecting competition. For that competition to work, public institutions need sufficient autonomy and resources to manage for results (see finance section below) and private institutions need to be accountable for meeting well-defined quality standards.

Several studies conclude that governments should provide information and quality assurance while promoting diversity.[19] Few developing countries have accreditation and evaluation systems for higher education, resulting in a proliferation of low-quality private providers (as in Cambodia). Chile and the Republic of Korea set quality standards lower at the entry point (licensing) to give new institutions the chance to grow, and later make the standards more stringent (accreditation) for both public and private institutions to allow fair competition.

"School prepares spectators instead of creators."

Young person,
Buenos Aires, Argentina
December 2005

A flexible education system. Diversified postbasic education systems need enough flexibility to allow students to experiment and develop their full potential. Open systems can facilitate student mobility by recognizing relevant prior experience, degree equivalencies, and credits earned elsewhere. Recent reforms in secondary education have upgraded previously terminal vocational tracks, allowing vocational education graduates entry to tertiary education after taking school-leaving examinations. For example, vocational graduates in South Africa and Tunisia can now qualify for any higher education institution.

For tertiary education, many institutions throughout the world have adopted credit-based courses, including single institutions (the University of Niger), networks of institutions (such as the Indian Institutes of Technology), and entire national university systems (as in Thailand).[20] In Colombia, people already in the labor market can get university-equivalent certification through any accredited training institution. Many young people need to combine school and work, and they can be accommodated—through, for example, part-time education. Today, part-time tertiary education accounts for only 5 percent of enrollment in university in developing countries, and 13 percent in non-university programs.[21]

For the noncompulsory and more expensive upper secondary sector, using competitive entrance examinations will help ease fiscal pressures, but financing mechanisms similar to those for lower secondary (described above) will also create more spaces. Those who do not pass the examination will need to be offered alternative learning options (vocational) and the possibility of going on to higher education. Well-designed higher education admission tests are likely to be beneficial, because educating the most capable students can foster innovation, driving the economy. Georgia recently reformed its tertiary entrance exam, which limited access and improved the quality of students, but a remaining challenge is to provide learning alternatives to those who failed to make the cut.[22]

Improving the relevance and quality of postprimary education

The low learning achievement in developing countries shows that schools are failing to prepare young people for work and life. A high-quality education system must improve the relevance of school curricula by teaching students the practical knowledge, thinking, and behavioral skills demanded by the labor market; using teaching methods that lead to high learning achievement; and blending the academic and vocational curricula. It must, in addition, strengthen the connection between school and the local economy to facilitate the school-to-work transition and boost economic development. The success of these reforms relies on motivated and well-prepared teachers, who ensure a safe school environment, as well as schools that are accountable for student learning.

Improving the relevance of school curricula. In many developing countries, the secondary curriculum is not relevant to the social and economic needs of students. Nor is it taught in a way that maximizes learning attainment or keeps students engaged in school.[23] Sometimes, it is relevant only to the needs of a few privileged students. In addition, few countries routinely assess their curricula for relevance and effectiveness. Comparative analysis of national secondary curricula between 1985 and 2000 shows very little change.[24] The tertiary education curricula also have many of the same problems.[25] In some countries, however, both secondary and tertiary institutions have begun to teach more practical subjects and become more responsive to the labor market.

Although curricula and teaching methods have remained largely unchanged, labor markets are demanding workers who have strong thinking and interpersonal skills. Job tasks requiring problem-solving and communication skills have grown steadily since the 1970s in the United States while manual and routine cognitive tasks have declined. Surveys of employers and workers in several developing countries, such as India and Malaysia, also indicate an increasing demand for communication skills, which is unmet by current education systems.[26] Entrepreneurship also requires thinking skills to solve problems and such behavioral skills as self confidence and leadership.[27] So, in today's complex and changing environment, the challenge is to build skills that allow young people to think critically and creatively, to process information, to make decisions, to manage conflict, and to work in teams.

Teaching such life skills can be integrated into every aspect of the curriculum through discovery-oriented teaching methods that include interactive learning, applying knowledge to real-life problems, integrating teamwork and peer tutoring into the learning process, and inviting student input into the structure and subject matter of lessons. It can be difficult for teachers to use such methods while ensuring students learn the core material, and some developing countries have found it particularly difficult to implement this type of reform,[28] so teaching life skills as a separate subject may be better (box 3.2). For example, Japan and South Africa have recently included life skills as a subject in their secondary school curricula.

The teaching of such skills should be accompanied by efforts to reform the traditional methods used to teach other subjects. Structured, student-centered teaching methods, which even inexperienced teachers can use successfully, are effective and well evaluated, in both developed and developing countries.[29] The structured teaching model consists of presenting the material in a progression from simple to complex, pausing to check for student understanding, and eliciting active participation from all students. To improve teaching methods or develop a life-skills curriculum, teachers should have adequate materials and training, with routine assessments of student progress and of the teaching methods and life-skills curriculum.[30] Information and communication technologies can also facilitate teaching and learning (chapter 8).

To provide the practical skills demanded in the labor market, new subject areas need to be added to the secondary curriculum without overloading it,[31] including science, technology, economics, and foreign languages—accompanied by renewed emphasis on basic mathematics and reading. Computer literacy is becoming a baseline requirement for many jobs, and the demand for high-skilled information communications technology workers has increased.[32] The command of international languages, particularly English, is becoming an asset for adopting technology and for communicating

---

BOX 3.2   *Life skills programs and nonformal teaching methods in schools*

Young people need problem-solving skills, not only to succeed in the labor market but also to process information for a healthy life, to participate as citizens, and to care for their families. In fact, many of what are called "life skills" programs combine teaching of behavioral and thinking skills with practical information about health, citizenship, or financial literacy. Many governments have worked with nongovernmental organizations (NGOs) to provide nonformal life skills programs both to students in school and to youth out of school.

The programs sometimes use peer educators. For example, Student Partnerships Worldwide (SPW), working in several countries in Africa and South Asia, trains young people (those just finished with secondary school) to teach life skills and health education in schools using nonformal education methods. Some very preliminary evidence suggests that such programs may affect health knowledge (chapter 5), peer educators' future outcomes, and academic outcomes. Such programs merit careful evaluation, and the U.S. National Institutes of Health is doing a clinical trial of an SPW program in Zimbabwe, which will provide clear evidence on health outcomes, to be finished in 2007. Some governments (India and Zambia) have also begun to cooperate with NGOs to train regular teachers in nonformal education. Life-skills programs that emphasize civic and peace education are operating in several countries, including the Arab Republic of Egypt, Georgia, and Liberia; they seem promising, although they have not been formally evaluated (chapter 7).

Source: UZ-UCSF (http://www.uz-ucsf.co.zw/research/researchprojects/current/rds.html)..

with other countries, although basic literacy is best acquired in local languages.[33] Teaching financial literacy narrows the knowledge gap between the rich and the poor and enables young people to make wiser financial choices.[34]

The general and vocational curricula should be more integrated. The skills demanded by young people and labor markets go beyond and cut across the traditional division between general and vocational curricula. Postponing vocational education until upper secondary and connecting it to higher education are two ways to integrate vocational and general education. Also needed is greater blending of content, bringing more vocational content into the general curriculum (Botswana, Ghana, and Kenya) and more vocationally relevant academic subjects (science, mathematics, language) into the vocational curriculum. The curriculum reform in Chile moved vocational education to high school and increased the academic content of vocational education to a third of the total teaching time. Specialized courses were added to the general curriculum for students in the academic strand to choose from, while vocational specialties were streamlined, their content and practices redesigned to give students flexible skills.[35]

Strengthening the connection between school and work. Strengthening the connection is the best way to make school more relevant to work and to facilitate the school-to-work transition. Career academies in the United States combine academic and technical curricula around a career theme and establish partnerships with local employers to provide work-based learning opportunities. The academies reduce dropout rates and improve school engagement among students least likely to do well in a regular school environment. They also improve the labor market prospects of young people, but sometimes they benefit young men more than young women.[36] The successful German "dual system" combining part-time schooling with work has been tried in several countries in Asia, Africa, and Latin America. Success has been limited, however, because of the inability to create jobs for apprentices

and sustainable employment thereafter.[37] In Japan, full-time schooling is followed by full-time employment in enterprises closely connected with the school. (For more on apprenticeships, see chapter 4.)

Effective feedback from the labor market and regular consultations with employers and alumni are indispensable for adjusting curricula to meet changing needs, as in Chile, where vocational training institutes are governed by representatives of employers, workers, and the government (see chapter 4). Formal university-industry partnerships are rare in developing countries, though there are interesting experiences. Universities and research institutes have contributed much to the growth of the Chinese economy. In Beijing, such institutions collaborate with local industry through joint projects and technology transfers and establish firms (spin-offs) to commercialize their inventions. Some of those firms (Lenovo, Tongfang) are among the largest Chinese high-technology firms.[38]

Increasing the preparedness and motivation of teachers. Without teachers who are motivated and well-prepared, reforms to improve the quality and relevance of curricula are unlikely to be successful. Teachers are often not well-prepared, however—either in their knowledge of the material or in their use of effective teaching methods, particularly when it comes to the learning needs of youth.[39] Teacher absenteeism is significant (24 percent in India), and teacher shortages block the expansion of secondary education, especially in Africa.[40] Teachers also sometimes perpetuate or exacerbate violence and harassment in schools, which affects education outcomes (box 3.3). Despite the imperatives, few countries have effective training, incentive, and accountability systems.

To ensure that teachers are well-prepared, education and training are important. Secondary school teachers need to know a large amount of material and be able to interact successfully with independent-minded students. There is little evidence of the impact of teacher training on student learning,[41] but research suggests some lessons. Ideally,

"Education should be more interactive. . . . during the lessons, only the teachers talk, they do not discuss with the students, the young people can study, but they are not motivated."

Young person, Lima, Peru
January 2006

BOX 3.3   *Violence and harassment in schools*

The teacher beat me once ... so I waited for school to end and when the teacher left the school building I beat him up worse. I haven't gone back to school since.
Basti boy, Bangladesh[46]

Violence and harassment in schools is common in many countries. Despite its negative impact on the school outcomes of all students, data are not routinely collected. The pervasiveness of sexual abuse, particularly of girls, by teachers and other students has been documented in some countries in Sub-Saharan Africa—6 percent of 10- to 24-year-olds in Kenya report having been sexually abused by a teacher. Corporal punishment of students, particularly boys, by teachers is common in many countries—25 percent of 10- to 24-year-olds in Kenya report being physically abused by a teacher, and a study in Egypt demonstrated that teacher abuse

increases dropouts. In some countries, students are discriminated against and physically abused on the basis of caste (Dalit children in Uttar Pradesh, India), social status, or disabilities. Students in Latin American countries, who were consulted for this report, said that fear of violence in schools leads to dropping out.

South Africa, where violence in schools is widespread, has recently implemented some corrective policies including dismissing teachers who commit serious offenses, such as having sex with students, and prohibiting corporal punishment. There is still no system, however, for students to file complaints. Implementing such regulations may not be enough to change pervasive cultural attitudes. For example, nearly a third of young men in Johannesburg schools say that forcing sex on someone you know is not sexual

violence and that women who were raped "asked for it." About half of teachers surveyed in Kenya say that having sex with a student should not result in dismissal or other serious action.

Integrating training, incentives, and other accountability mechanisms is likely to be most effective. For example, a pilot in Ghana and Malawi is trying to address sexual violence in schools by improving codes of conduct for teachers; addressing the attitudes of students, community members, and teachers; and developing referral and support systems for students who lodge complaints.

Sources: Dréze and Gazdar (1997); Human Rights Watch (2001b); Interagency Gender Working Group (2005); Lloyd, Mensch, and Clark (2000); Lloyd (2003); World Bank (2005s); and World Bank (2003a).

solid preservice should be combined with regular in-service training that is designed to improve teaching practice as well as foster the sharing of experience among teachers and allow teachers to provide feedback on the effectiveness of curriculum reform. If there are fiscal constraints, research suggests that in-service training is especially effective and is sometimes less costly.[42] Training should also take into account specific needs assessments—and be designed to help foster positive interactions with students, which increases the likelihood that students will exert effort and stay in school (discussed below).

Incentives, if well designed and well implemented, can motivate teachers and make them accountable for performance. Chile more than doubled average teacher salaries in the 1990s, and the quality of students entering teaching programs increased, suggesting that the level of teacher salaries matters.[43] Performance-based incentives are, in principle, superior to across-the-board increases in teacher salaries—on both fiscal and efficiency grounds. But there has been little experience with them—few teachers are accountable for what they do in the classroom.

In practice, the impact of incentive programs in countries as diverse as Chile, India, and Mexico has been reduced by implementation constraints (resistance from teachers, indifference of headmasters and

parents) and design flaws (small incentives, little link to actual performance).[44] Also, while in some cases program-induced improvements in student outcomes come from better quality teaching, in other cases these improvements are the result of teachers misreporting scores, teaching to the test, or excluding low-achieving students. There is some evidence in support of performance awards based on student progress rather than levels of student performance, and awards based on school-level average progress—which promote team work—rather than progress at the class level.[45] To ensure teaching quality, incentives need to be combined with quality training, good working conditions, some teacher autonomy, opportunities for professional development, and school autonomy in hiring teachers.

Increasing system accountability for performance. The *World Development Report 2004* shows that additional public spending on education will not improve learning unless motivated providers can take the required actions (see box 2.2).[47] So frontline providers—school principals and teachers—should be given enough autonomy and resources to manage for results and be made accountable for those results. Two building blocks of accountability are providing information on performance to students, their families, and other stake-

"The teacher pretends to teach, the student pretends to learn, and the state pretends that it fulfills its role."

Young person, Recife, Brazil
January 2006

BOX 3.4   *Georgia: Fighting corruption in higher education*

For years, university entrance examinations were an opportunity for bribery. Corrupt officials favored candidates who either had personal connections or had bribed the members of the examination committee. Well-off students who paid the right professors could get advance tips on examination topics. This meant students were not selected on the basis of merit.

In 2005 a new law on higher education made the unified national examinations mandatory for all potential students seeking to enroll in a higher education institution in Georgia. A high level of security surrounded the testing process in July 2005. Candidates were identified by a barcode on each exam paper to ensure confidentiality in grading. Examination booklets were printed in a secure facility overseas. Each testing center was equipped with surveillance cameras and TV monitors that let students' relatives observe the examination process.

"Young people are no longer afraid, when they take university exams, that other people will pay money and get in instead of them," says Maka, a third-year law student in Tbilisi. Faculty have also reported significant improvements in the competence and commitment of students, allowing students to finish their education sooner.

The new exam is part of the broad slate of reforms to increase the quality of education, including a new national curriculum, building up teacher training capacity, and introducing per capita financing to schools.

Source: National Assessment and Examination Center (2005).

holders; and engaging their participation in school management. Youth participation in school management, covered later in this chapter, has been very limited.

Although many developing countries now collect national data on student achievement, the information is rarely made public and used to hold teachers and schools accountable for performance (through social accountability, accreditation, funding allocation, or performance-based pay). A large civil society initiative in India, the Annual Survey of Education Report (ASER), collects regular data on literacy and numeracy skills of school children in rural India. The program also has a strategy for dissemination and community mobilization, which includes the preparation of annual regional reports and brief summaries at the district level. The 2005 survey includes key findings for policy:[48] 31 percent of 11- to 14-year-olds need remedial language instruction (they cannot read a story text with some long sentences), 47 percent need remedial numeracy instruction (they cannot do division), 23 percent of teachers were absent (on average, per school), and 8 percent of schools had no teacher present at all.

Improving governance in education requires more than just strengthening accountability for performance. For example, curtailing corruption requires a comprehensive strategy that improves accountability systems but also addresses a number of other constraints, including the institutions that underpin the delivery of services. The reform measures introduced in Georgia to fight corruption in higher education illustrate the effectiveness of combining a unified examination system, control mechanisms, and improved transparency (box 3.4).

Financing the expansion and improvement of postprimary education

In selecting the right set of education reforms, countries must consider the state of their education systems (how well they prepare youth for work and life), the needs of their young people, and their overall development priorities. This choice is constrained by a country's available resources and its ability to use innovative ways to finance large-scale reforms. Some countries will choose reforms that require relatively few resources and still have a fairly large impact. Others will take on comprehensive reforms that require a large amount of additional resources.

Financing the types of reforms recommended in this chapter is possible, even for poor countries, but choosing the right type of reform is critical. Investments in quality and relevance can lead to substantial improvements in enrollment and learning. One-time investments can have long-term impacts. For example, a recent project targeting poor lower secondary schools in Guyana included curriculum reform, student assessment, and training and materials for teachers and principals, which only required a one-time 6 percent increase in school expenditures. It was associated with large increases in test scores and in the number of students completing lower secondary school.[49] The success led the government to adopt the changes in all lower secondary schools and to reform the upper secondary curriculum.

While some fast-growing developing countries can rely on economic growth to finance improvements in the education system, most other countries will need additional resources from a combination

---

BOX 3.5   *Chile's higher education: Diversifying the sources of funding*

Chile financed a big expansion in higher education in recent years by charging students tuition, encouraging diversified funding sources, and allocating of public subsidies innovatively. Thanks to sizable private contributions, it increased tertiary enrollment to about 42 percent of the 18–24 age group while being among the Latin American countries that allocate the least public funding to tertiary education relative to GDP.

Significant student contributions have provided the fiscal space to reorient state subsidies to core public sector responsibilities. A priority has been to increase access to income-contingent student loans for students unable to finance their studies. Financial support is determined by the student's socioeconomic profile, while tuition fees are set according to

the research and teaching efficiency of the institution they attend. The system thus gives institutions an incentive to improve their efficiency while enhancing access for less-privileged groups.

Public support incentives are designed to encourage universities to be responsive to both students needs and national priorities. About 7 percent of public support is allocated based on the ability of institutions to attract the students who receive the highest scores in the university admission exam. Universities receive funds by proposing projects to a competitive investment fund for improving the quality of technical, undergraduate, and graduate tertiary education. This approach has generated reforms closely linked to national priorities: improving the quality of teacher education, reforming the

undergraduate degree structure, and increasing the production of PhDs.

A remaining flaw in the financing system is the lack of accountability for results. The system allocates recurrent funds per student to traditional universities based on historical levels—but in 2006 pilot performance agreements are being negotiated between each institution and the ministry of education. The objectives are to link campus missions to national and regional priorities, university autonomy to public accountability, and institutional performance to government funding. The agreements, to run for three years, will contain funding commitments, agreed targets, and indicators to monitor progress.

Sources: Bernasconi and Rojas (2004) and Thorn, Holm-Nielsen, and Jeppesen (2004).

---

of cost-sharing, public-private partnerships, and efficiency enhancements—and some will need help from donors. Chile's higher education system shows how blending funding sources can expand and improve tertiary education (box 3.5). Korea's responsive education policy, strong demand for quality, and partnership with the private sector allowed the secondary education sector to expand without compromising quality (box 3.6). Burkina Faso successfully financed improvements in access to, and the relevance of,

---

BOX 3.6   *Korea's secondary education: Expansion without sacrificing quality*

Korea's secondary schools do well on many fronts. Access is easy and equitable: gross enrollment at the secondary level is at 90 percent, for both boys and girls. Korean students score at the top in such international evaluations as PISA and Trends in International Mathematics and Science Study (TIMSS). Schools are adequately funded—more than 2.4 percent of Korea's GDP is spent on secondary education, a third of that privately.

Where did such achievements come from? First, building a strong education sector was part of Korea's economic development strategies as early as the 1950s. Dynamic and motivated institutions promptly implemented policies to expand education. Second, from the earliest days the focus was on access and quality for all, motivated by the desire to bring educated workers into the workforce. Third, parents contributed to the expansion's costs because of the high value they placed on quality education.

In Korea, compulsory basic education includes primary and lower secondary. Primary education is free, but parents must pay tuition for secondary schools. One in five lower secondary students and more than half of high-school students attend private schools. Forty percent of high school students are enrolled in technical and vocational schools.

Korea focused on one education cycle at a time, starting with basic education. In the 1950s

and 1960s, when public funds mainly targeted primary education, secondary schools financed almost half their expenses through parent teacher associations. However, the rapid expansion of primary education put enormous pressure on secondary schools, and student competition for good secondary schools increased. In preparation for entrance exams—"examination hell"—students often repeated grades, and families paid up to a quarter of their income for private tutoring.

In the face of criticism, the government implemented a national equalization program in 1968, eliminating entrance examinations and instituting a lottery for schools in high demand. Secondary school enrollment soared, and private providers stepped up to provide the needed capacity. The equalization program guaranteed any deficit in operating cost (but not in capital cost) of all private schools. By 1971, most private schools were receiving direct financial assistance, subsidies, and tax exemptions. In return, they gave up control over key decisions (curriculum, tuition rates, and teacher salaries).

The equalization program for lower secondary, while improving enrollment, removed the competition among the elite schools, and quality at the top declined. Examination hell resurfaced at the end of the lower secondary cycle,

and with declining quality; students preparing for entrance exams relied on private tutoring even more. In response, the government adopted an equalization program for upper secondary in 1974, opening high school entry. The program also aimed to narrow the quality gap between urban and rural high schools and increase enrollment in vocational schools to meet demand from the fast-growing manufacturing sector. Without any curriculum change, however, vocational education remained largely a terminal track, and enrollment did not change much.

Although the combination of private funding and public control worked well in the earlier years of expansion, concerns about quality grew. In response, the government carried out a series of reforms in secondary education starting in 1999 and increased public funding to the sector by 7 percent annually until 2003. It relaxed controls over school management, instituted school councils to facilitate parental involvement, and legalized teachers unions. The curriculum reform introduced foreign languages and information technology at earlier ages and emphasized student-centered learning. There are also efforts to improve vocational curricula and link vocational high schools with technical colleges.

Sources: Gill and Chon-Sun (2000) and Kim (2002).

postprimary education by reducing subsidies and charging fees for tertiary education.

Improving efficiency. Efficiency gains can be achieved by using formula funding to education institutions, particularly when they have greater autonomy. More developing countries are moving from traditional line-item budgeting to direct formula funding, which channels funds to schools for operating expenditures according to some known rule, such as enrollment.[50] With block grants, as opposed to earmarked grants, schools have discretion over the use of funds (as with autonomous schools in Nicaragua). School autonomy over personnel management and process decisions (hiring teachers, choosing textbooks, allocating budgets within schools) is related to superior student performance.[51]

Formula funding, particularly block grants, can bring several efficiency benefits—increasing transparency and accountability, reducing corruption, making funding more predictable (which allows better planning), and increasing flexibility (for block grants).[52] It can also be combined with other efficiency-enhancing mechanisms, such as competitive funding and performance-based funding—but it requires good management capacity.

Cost sharing. Appropriate cost sharing and demand-side financing can generate the needed resources equitably. Governments should finance more of the compulsory phase of secondary education, because of higher social benefits and lower unit costs relative to later education. Individuals, their families, and communities should finance more of postcompulsory education, particularly tertiary education. Contributions from those able and willing to pay can promote engagement and accountability.[53] To ensure equitable access, fees and other cost-sharing mechanisms need to be accompanied by well-designed and balanced demand-side financing packages (covered later in this chapter). Such packages include needs-based grants at the lower secondary level, as well as grants that are needs- and merit-based, loans, and savings schemes at the upper secondary and tertiary levels.

Public-private partnerships. Public-private partnerships can expand and improve postprimary education. In addition to alleviating fiscal constraints, they improve learning outcomes and efficiency by increasing choice and competition. Analysis of PISA data shows that private competition is associated with higher test scores, and systems combining private operation with public funding do best.[54] Partnerships vary depending on the services procured and, though still uncommon in developing countries, a few lessons are emerging.[55]

Contracting with schools to enroll publicly funded students (used extensively) has rapidly expanded access to education while avoiding large public capital costs. Voucher-type programs have been implemented in a few developing countries, including Chile, Colombia, Côte d'Ivoire, and the Czech Republic. Their positive impact for beneficiaries has been established (Colombia)[56] but the overall effects are still inconclusive. Vouchers are also found to improve performance in public school through increased competition (the Czech Republic).[57]

Contracting a private actor to operate a public school can a have positive impact on enrollment. Colombia's Colegios en Concesión turns over the management of some public schools to private institutions through a competitive bidding process. Concession schools are paid less per student than regular public schools, must accept all students, and must meet outcome targets for test scores and dropout rates. They are carefully monitored and evaluated—dropout rates have been lower in concession schools, and the competition has also reduced dropout rates in nearby public schools.[58] Contracting for support services (meal provision, facility maintenance) is used extensively, usually with good results. Contracting for professional services (such as curriculum design) is also easy to specify and monitor. Contracting for management services is difficult to implement, not least because of the challenge of identifying measurable and verifiable performance criteria. A few countries are experimenting with contracts for private financing and construction of schools.

Better education choices by young people

As young people mature, they take more control of their education, but some constraints prevent them from benefiting from their learning opportunities. They lack the motivation to learn because they have poor behavioral skills and not much of a say in their own education. They lack information on postprimary education opportunities and the labor market—and have limited access to resources. They face competing options to schooling—work and family—as well as alternative learning options. Helping young people make better education choices requires better decision-making skills, incentives to exert effort, and their involvement as stakeholders in their education. Financial incentives that permit better choices (such as conditional cash transfers or vouchers) and better information about learning options and work possibilities (such as school-based career advisory services) lead to better education decisions.

Motivating and involving students

As young people reach adolescence, they start deciding how much effort to spend on studying and whether to go to school (see figure 2.4). Their decisions indicate their preferences for education—preferences influenced by peers, parents, teachers, and schools that shape their environment. Their ability to successfully act on those preferences is determined by their behavioral skills and psychological well-being. Many young people gradually develop control over their education decisions, while others—young women, orphans, those with disabilities, and those from stigmatized groups—face additional barriers to effective decision making.

Well-designed policies can affect both the preferences for education and the incentives to learn. For example, outcomes can be improved by affecting how peers influence each other, by increasing young people's connectedness to schools, by directly rewarding effort, by developing their decision-making capacity, by responding to their input in the school-level policy-making process, and by reducing social exclusion. For younger adolescents more dependent on guardians, policies should also take into account the preferences and parenting skills of guardians.

Parents affect student behavior, beyond simply influencing the decision to attend school, by affecting a young person's preference for education through the home environment, and by helping to develop their children's behavioral skills. In India, part of the relationship between maternal literacy and child schooling reflects the effects of maternal schooling on the study hours of children.[59] In Rwanda, a guardian's preference for education explains part of the correlation between the education of guardians and children. The strongest evidence comes from the positive impacts on education of programs that emphasize parenting quality to build behavioral skills of children, either directly or through mentors.[60]

Improving the incentives to learn. Social mechanisms (such as peer influence and the social accountability of teachers) and direct economic incentives can influence the effort to learn. Some evidence suggests that the efforts of students, teachers, and parents are jointly determined[61]; thus, to be successful, interventions will often need to take into account the role of peers, teachers, and parents and their preferences and incentives. It is the independent influence of peers on students, however, that has been the most rigorously evaluated, and research shows that even randomly selected peer groups (such as classmates or roommates) affect the behavior of students and education outcomes.[62]

Influencing peer interactions by sorting students into different groups can have an important impact on both academic and social outcomes.[63] In fact, many countries sort students into schools based on their ability, and in countries where there has been ethnic conflict, students are sometimes sorted into classes based on ethnicity. There is some evidence indicating that diversity of student achievement or social groups within a school or classroom might negatively affect student achievement in secondary school. A study in China demonstrates that the diversity of academic achievement has a negative effect on the test scores of poorly performing secondary students.[64] Other evidence suggests, however, that policies to sort students in classes by ability are usually ineffective, because ability varies by specific task and students progress at different rates.[65] Some types of social interactions between young people from different groups can also have positive effects on outcomes such as trust and tolerance.[66]

It is likely that what matters is not the level of diversity, but the classroom context— whether it is competitive or cooperative. Controlled experiments indicate that classroom activities that require cooperation among students from different ethnic groups can improve tolerance (cross-group friendships) and empathy across groups. Such cooperative policies in socially and academically diverse classrooms also improve test scores, as well as behavioral skills such as self-confidence.[67]

A merit scholarship program for girls in Kenya shows how economic incentives that take social mechanisms into account can influence effort.[68] The test scores of the girls who had a good chance of getting a scholarship improved, which can be explained by the economic incentive of the scholarship. The test scores of boys and lower-ability girls also improved as did student and teacher attendance, perhaps as the result of peer influence or the complementarity of student and teacher effort in the classroom. Teacher attendance may have increased as a result of providing the correct economic incentives for parents to hold teachers socially accountable. The program also can be more cost-effective than some typical education programs (figure 3.4).

Increasing students' engagement with schools is one way to raise student effort in school and reduce the likelihood of dropping out. If students identify with their schools, the importance of other social identities can be reduced allowing schools to shape student preferences for the effort to study.[69] This effect may be best quantified by research on school climate and school connectedness, often determined by asking students if they feel like they belong in school, feel connected to it, or like it. The answer to this question matters, and asking it can capture several important aspects

of education that are difficult to measure (such as how teachers interact with students). Data from more than 40 countries show a strong association between school climate and test scores,[70] and evidence from the United States and the Caribbean shows that school connectedness predicts school dropout and health outcomes.[71]

Can such factors be affected by policy? Yes. Reforms specifically designed to increase students' connectedness with schools and teachers, such as the Seattle Social Development Project in the United States, improved academic achievement and other student behaviors.[72] (Poor schools in many countries have high connectedness through simple efforts to engage students.) Often such reforms are comprehensive and rely on a combination of policies similar to those recommended throughout this chapter:

- Training teachers to enhance students' identification with school through student encouragement, student input into lessons, group learning, and group academic competitions.
- Increasing youth participation in school policy.
- Teaching behavioral skills, which can increase student confidence and motivation.
- Teaching through drama, sports, and arts.

Decision-making capability—building behavioral skills and reducing social barriers. Even if students value education and prefer to study, they may not have the capability to act on their preferences, perhaps because they lack behavioral skills or psychological capacity. Yet motivation, persistence, self-discipline, cooperation, and effective decision making are rarely taught in schools. This is a major gap, because the impact of behavioral skills on education outcomes and the ability of schools to teach those skills have been empirically demonstrated (see box 3.1).

A student's ability to make decisions can also be affected by his or her mental health. Research from developed countries indicates the negative effect of mental health disorders on school attainment.[73] While in general mental health has been less stud-

"Studying is only for the people of higher caste, not for ones of lower caste like me."

Young person, Nepal
January 2006

Figure 3.4   Influencing effort directly can be a cost-effective way to improve learning in Kenya

Cost per pupil of 0.1 standard deviation gain in test scores ($)

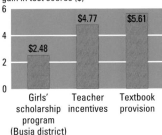

Source: Kremer, Miguel, and Thornton (2004).
Note: The scholarship program had no effect in neighboring Teso district, where it was associated with a natural calamity.

ied in developing countries, posttraumatic stress disorder is known to affect as much as a third of the youth population in post-conflict countries, and a study from Algeria, Cambodia, Ethiopia, and Gaza demonstrated its effect on schooling.[74] Thus, safeguarding mental health can be an important investment in school outcomes.[75]

Negative social perceptions can affect students' decision-making capabilities. Social and cultural norms in many countries exclude some groups from education, primarily girls and young women,[76] although ethnicity, caste, and disability are also dimensions of exclusion. Extensive ethnographic research has long found pervasive attempts by teachers and administrators to discourage students from continuing in school if they belong to traditionally excluded social groups (including the poor).[77] This can affect education decisions by lowering young people's self-perception or by leading them to believe (sometimes accurately) that schools and labor markets will not reward their effort. Evidence from Kenya demonstrates that teacher attitudes about adolescent girls' ability to learn predicts their dropout decisions.[78] In Uttar Pradesh, India, an experiment indicates that students from the lowest castes perform worse when a student's caste is announced before taking a cognitive skills test—indicating that low-caste students believe that teachers who care about caste will not reward them for high performance.[79]

Programs may aim to increase the benefits to young women or their families of overcoming social barriers (through financial incentives such as targeted merit scholarships and conditional cash transfers) or they may aim to reduce the effect of social barriers on decisions by trying to raise self-perception (through, for example, setting up bank accounts for girls, as in Bangladesh). Programs may also be designed to reduce the social barriers themselves (information campaigns, training of teachers). In some environments, especially where physical violence is a concern, programs should be careful to target not only the excluded, but groups who perpetuate social exclusion.

Young people as stakeholders in school policy. The *World Development Report 2004* recognized "client power" in improving the delivery of basic public services such as primary education, with parents and communities viewed as the clients of the education system. Young people are the beneficiaries of the education system and, starting in adolescence, they often begin to make important decisions about their education, and so become actors in their own right (chapter 2). Also, secondary and tertiary institutions usually serve a much broader area than primary schools, making traditional community management less effective as an accountability tool.

Students can exercise their client power through many institutional mechanisms. They can set up students councils, be elected to school boards, or be consulted more broadly on the design of rules, policies, and curricula at the school or classroom level. Students can also provide feedback about teachers. In most countries, however, student participation is limited or nonexistent. Nor are there many evaluations of student participation. The studies typically focus on the personal outcomes of participants rather than on the impact of student-influenced policies on the quality of school life or academic outcomes.[80] Student participation can also have an impact on behavioral skills (as students become decision makers) and other forms of civic engagement.

Student participation improves school environment and relations. Many education providers are reluctant to allow student participation, but one careful analysis of 75 studies (mostly in England) found that even in secondary schools where school management and parents were initially reluctant to institute reforms, no school reversed the reforms, and both teachers and students reported better interactions and improved student behavioral skills as a result of more student participation.[81] A major challenge is that some education providers are willing only to allow token or symbolic participation, which prevents students from having a substantial impact on policy.

Some developing countries have significant student participation, at least in tertiary institutions. South Africa's Student

Leadership Council defended student rights during apartheid and provided training for future political leaders (including Nelson Mandela).[82] Recent reforms of universities in Russia and secondary schools in the former Yugoslav Republic of Macedonia have increased the role of students in school management, giving them as much as 30 percent of the voting rights on some university councils. In a survey of the alumni of one university in Russia, most listed such participation as the single most useful aspect of their education.[83]

Providing information on opportunities for learning and work

Postprimary education decisions are based on private information on the supply and quality of education opportunities available to young individuals, and an understanding of how they translate into education and labor market outcomes. Imperfect information about education makes schools and teachers less accountable and young individuals less able to make good choices and influence school quality, while the uncertainty young people face about the future returns to education leads to inefficiencies and underinvestments.

Good information on learning opportunities leads to better choices. It allows individuals to monitor the performance of schools and teachers and to influence school quality. Information on learning options can also have a real impact on choices, particularly for the poor. Yet there are very few information programs around the world. The U.K. Aimhigher program targets disadvantaged 13- to 19-year-olds, raising their awareness of higher education opportunities well in advance. It posts information on higher education on a web portal, and it provides mentoring and visits to institutions of higher learning. An initial evaluation shows positive effects on promotion rates and test performance—and mixed results on intentions to go on for higher education.[84] School-based career guidance services—which provide information on education and job market opportunities as well as counseling—are being introduced in a few developing countries (discussed later in the chapter in box 3.7).

Young people partly base schooling decisions on expected economic returns, particularly when it comes to the decision to attend university. Results from a study of Indonesia show that students choose to enter upper secondary school on the basis of expected returns.[85] However, uncertainty about future labor market returns prevents some young people from making the education decision that is best for them, generating inefficiency. If people are risk averse, this uncertainty also leads to underinvestment in education. The study from Indonesia also finds substantial uncertainty about future returns to upper secondary and higher education. Those from poor families face more uncertainty than those from richer households. Overall, 11 percent of young people would change their education choices under full certainty—13 percent of the poor and 10 percent of the nonpoor. Because of this uncertainty, the poor tend to underinvest in education more than the rich.

Providing young people with information on labor market opportunities and payoffs to different levels and types of schooling can allow them to make more educated guesses about their future returns, which makes their decisions more efficient. An experiment in the Dominican Republic increased the likelihood of continuing in school by 12 percent, by providing information to students enrolled in the last year of primary education about the returns to secondary education.[86] That the poor are not more responsive to information about future returns indicates that direct and indirect pecuniary costs and nonpecuniary costs such as low behavioral skills (low aspirations, for example) do much to limit access to postcompulsory education in Indonesia.[87] Thus, the policies needed for poor people to go to upper secondary would include some combination of grants, income-contingent loans, mentoring, and information.[88]

Providing financial incentives to alleviate constraints to better choices

Resources matter for schooling decisions when young individuals and their families face imperfect credit markets that prevent them from borrowing against future income. Young people may also be financially constrained when their parents have sufficient resources or access to credit but are unwilling to finance investments in education. Also, young people in postprimary education face competing options to schooling—work and family—as well as alternative learning options.

Credit constraints in schooling.

In most developing countries there is a strong relationship between poverty and school progress, particularly in the transitions to lower and upper secondary school (figure 3.5). Is that link between income and schooling explained by credit constraints? Not necessarily, or at least not entirely. Other factors correlated with income also explain the differences in school progress between the poor and the rich, including inequality in access to physical facilities.

The school attainment differences between the poor and the rich are also explained by the difference in skill readiness for secondary and higher education. The rich tend to attend schools of higher quality than the poor and have a better environment for skills formation. The quality of schooling affects the motivation for continuing in school and the academic readiness for subsequent education. A large part of the association between income and college attendance in the United States is due to long-term factors that affect readiness for college by increasing cognitive and behavioral skills, not to short-term financial constraints at the time of the college decision.[89] The policy implication is to shift the focus from tuition subsidies to getting individuals ready for college through learning investments before college.

However, more young people in developing countries are likely to face credit constraints in gaining access to secondary and higher education than in developed countries. Credit markets are less developed and direct financial support for schooling is often much more limited, justifying the need for policies to address them. Many studies

look at the relationship between income and schooling,[90] but few look explicitly at how credit constraints affect the demand for education. Such constraints determine college attendance in Mexico, though the effect is small, and in rural Pakistan they explain secondary school completion and postsecondary school attendance more than secondary school entry.[91]

Competing options and schooling. In low- and lower-middle-income countries, many of those of secondary school age work (figure 3.6). With age, school participation diminishes while work participation increases. In poor countries such as Cambodia, the trade-off between school and work becomes more of a problem at the age of secondary school entry—43 percent of boys are already working by ages 10–12. Conditions have been improving there, however, as young people stay longer in school and start work later. Most working children can combine work responsibilities with schooling, though with age, working students become a smaller group relative to full-time workers—by ages 13–15, 62 percent of Bolivian working males are already out of school.[92] Young people from the poorest quintile are less likely to attend school exclusively, and more likely to work, than those from the richest. In some countries, girls are less likely to be working outside the home,

Figure 3.5 More rich children than poor children completing primary school make it to higher levels

Percentage of primary school graduates who reach each level

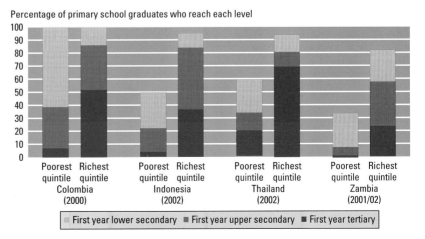

Source: http://econ.worldbank.org/projects/edattain.

Figure 3.6 Adolescents in many low-income and lower-middle-income countries combine school and work

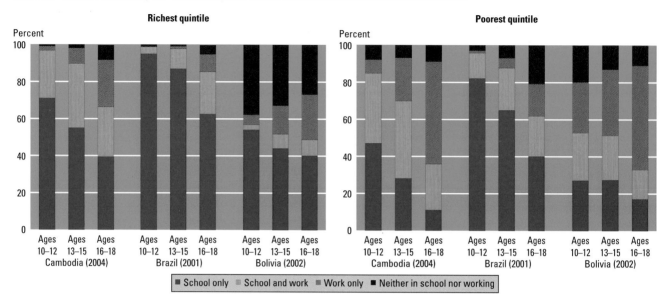

Source: Authors' calculations based on Fares, Montenegro, and Orazem (2006a).

"They [young people] don't go to school because they have a family to take care of, they cannot continue to rely on the good will of their own parents."

Young person, Peru
January 2006

but they are more likely to be engaged in domestic work (for the countries in figure 3.6 the distribution of school and work is similar for boys and girls).[93]

Working can impair schooling and learning, particularly at younger ages. A study conducted in Vietnam finds that if children ages 8–13 work while in school, it reduces school enrollment and educational attainment five years later.[94] In rural Bangladesh, working while attending primary school has a sizable negative effect on the transition to secondary school—and starting to work while attending secondary school has even larger negative effects on secondary school completion.[95] A study of 11 countries in Latin America and the Caribbean finds sizable negative effects on both mathematics and language test scores among primary school students.[96] (For more on child labor, see chapter 4.)

Girls who marry early or bear children at an early age are also more likely to have less schooling.[97] The secondary school dropouts attributed to pregnancy range between 10 and 20 percent in most countries in Africa.[98] The relationship also works the other way: in Guatemala, school attainment increases the age at which young women first marry or become a parent.[99]

Conditional cash transfers. Addressing credit constraints requires identifying the target population, and then designing the appropriate package of demand-side financing mechanisms for postprimary education that also account for the opportunity costs from competing choices. Credit constraints on the demand for education at the lower secondary level can be addressed through needs-based grants (scholarships, conditional cash transfers, vouchers), given the externalities associated with basic education. Even when lower secondary education is free of school fees, students and their families must incur other direct and indirect private costs, making a case for grants targeted to the poor. At the upper secondary and tertiary levels, credit constraints can be alleviated with a combination of well-targeted grants, loans, and savings schemes.

In designing such a package, it is also important to think of the education system as a whole—to avoid imbalances and bottlenecks. For example, the success of Oportunidades in Mexico and Bolsa Família in Brazil increases the pressure on the postcompulsory system. It is thus necessary to anticipate the rising number of individuals completing basic education and willing to study further.

Conditional cash transfers can increase the demand for schooling both directly (through increased income) and by reducing the incidence of work (by compensating for the forgone income from work). Introduced in the late 1990s, particularly in Latin America, they provide cash to poor young people conditional on school attendance, and are quickly becoming popular in other parts of the world.[100] Mexico's Oportunidades, the best documented, has increased secondary school attendance rates by 8 percent, the transition to secondary school by nearly 20 percent, and grade attainment by 10 percent, with significantly larger effects for girls than for boys.[101] The impact on enrollment is mainly due to the condition for attendance.[102] Oportunidades is not inexpensive, but the net benefit is substantial.[103] Efficiency can be increased by targeting and calibrating the size of the grants.[104]

Part of the positive impact of conditional cash transfers on school enrollment comes from a reduction in work. But the transfers alone do not appear to be enough to reduce work significantly, which is important for policy makers concerned about child labor and how child labor affects academic performance. A substantial number of children continue to combine both work and school under Oportunidades. The program increases the number of children in school and reduces the number of children who are working, but does not necessarily reduce the hours worked of children who also attend school. Also, Oportunidades increases the likelihood that young people will stay in school when a household experiences a shock, but does not prevent parents from resorting to child work in response to a shock.[105] Evidence from rural Brazil suggests that after-school programs may be a good complement to the conditionality on school attendance.[106]

Conditional cash transfers and other policies that reduce the price of schooling (fee waivers) have been used to weaken the attraction of activities that compete with girls' schooling. Under the secondary school stipend for girls in Bangladesh (see box 6.5), girls received a stipend conditional on secondary school attendance and delaying marriage until age 18. The stipend has been associated with postponing marriage and increasing schooling.[107]

School vouchers. A promising tool to address credit constraints and school quality, school vouchers are publicly provided for students to enroll in the school of their choice. Beyond the potential effect of vouchers on their beneficiaries, vouchers can increase competition among schools and thus increase the quality of the system. They also allow enrollment to increase without additional public capital costs. However, they can have a detrimental effect on the (lower quality) schools that (higher performing) voucher recipients leave, at least in the short run.

A few developing countries have used vouchers, including Chile, Colombia, and the Czech Republic. Colombia's voucher program offered vouchers to poor individuals to attend private schools and had a positive impact on learning, which persisted over the long run.[108] More evidence is needed, though, on the overall impact of vouchers, including the impact on nonbeneficiaries. Vouchers for secondary or even tertiary education should be targeted to the poor (with possible refinement for merit at the upper levels). Choice should be open to any accredited school (public or private), supported by publicly provided information on these schools.

Loans. Well-designed loan programs, combined with grants targeted to need and merit, can allow postcompulsory education to expand equitably. Grants, when affordable, are likely to be more appropriate for upper secondary education than for higher education—the ratio of social to private benefits is likely to be higher in upper secondary, and grants in upper secondary are likely to be more progressive. To improve cost-effectiveness, they should be specifically targeted to the poor who are most likely to benefit from the grant on the basis of merit.[109] The higher cost of tertiary education makes student loans particularly useful, but well-designed loans are hard to implement in low-income countries.

Income-contingent loans are superior to conventional loans (box 3.7). They generate the needed resources in the face of limited fiscal capacity. By deferring payments until individuals start working and reach a certain income, they have lower default rates, promote more equitable access and loan repayment, and increase efficiency by addressing uncertainty about future earnings and facilitating consumption smoothing. However, they are hard to implement and may be a realistic option only for some middle-income countries.

Individual learning accounts. The easy implementation and attractive features—induced savings, consumption smoothing, and a low public burden—of individual learning accounts make up a promising financing option for middle-income countries. Individual learning accounts, which are becoming more popular in OECD countries, encourage savings for education while providing vouchers to individuals inter-

ested in pursuing further education. The amount an individual is entitled to depends on the amount saved and the kind of training desired. In Brazil, a graduation incentive for primary and secondary education, Poupança Escola, was introduced as part of the first version of Bolsa Escola in the Federal District.[110] Oportunidades in Mexico introduced Jovenes con Oportunidades, through which conditional cash transfer beneficiaries accumulate points from the last year of lower secondary until the end of secondary school. Credit points are converted into a savings account and deposited into individual accounts in the National Savings Bank, which beneficiaries can tap for further study or to start a business if they complete upper secondary before turning 22.

Young people lack adequate information, financial resources, academic readiness, and decision-making skills. Addressing these complementary constraints requires policies that integrate information, mentoring, academic support, and financial incentives (box 3.8).

BOX 3.7   *Income-contingent loans*

A well-designed loan system has three characteristics—income-contingent repayments, an efficient interest rate, and adequate size.

Income-contingent repayments. A conventional loan involves repayments of a fixed amount per month, with the risk that low-income borrowers may default, while income-contingent repayments are a percentage of the borrower's earnings—often collected alongside income tax or social security contributions, and thus have built-in insurance against an inability to repay because the loan repayment falls if a borrower's income falls. They thus assist borrowers by protecting them from uncertain returns to human capital investments and promote equity because this uncertainty is more of a deterrent for the poor. They assist lenders by using the government's power to collect taxes as a substitute for physical collateral. After Australia introduced income-contingent loans in 1989, participation in higher education increased, particularly among women.

Efficient interest rate. The interest rate should be broadly equal to the government's cost of borrowing. Some countries, such as Australia and the United Kingdom, offer loans at a zero real interest rate, but because of the resulting fiscal pressures loans are too small, access is limited, and university income is reduced. Interest rate

subsides are also deeply regressive because graduates, rather than students, make repayments. Targeted interest subsidies may still be an option, however, for people with low earnings or who are out of the labor force. In some loan programs, unpaid debt is eventually forgiven.

Adequate size. Loans should be large enough to make education and training feasible, but small enough so that most individuals can repay, with a cap both in annual amount and duration. Income-contingent loans have a long repayment period and small monthly payments so they are friendlier to other borrowing (say, to start a business), because lenders typically look at monthly income net of loan repayments. The purpose of a loan is to allow young people to redistribute resources to themselves over their lifetimes, so loans should in principle be available to all qualified applicants. Without a government guarantee, private sector lenders would charge a high risk premium, so if governments face serious cash-flow constraints it may be necessary to restrict loans to the poor.

Beware the implementation requirements. Policy makers invariably underestimate the institutional requirements. A particular error is to focus on lending *policy,* with inadequate attention, time, or resources for loan *administration.* A country should not embark on a loan scheme without

- a reliable system of identifying individuals, which is the responsibility of national government;
- the capacity to keep records (amount borrowed), a responsibility of the loans administration;
- the capacity to collect repayments, ideally through the tax or the social security system; and
- the capacity to track income, ideally through income taxes or social security contributions.

Given the requirements, it is not surprising that successful income-contingent loans in advanced economies—including Australia, New Zealand, the Netherlands, Sweden, and the United Kingdom—are not echoed in poorer countries. Chile and South Africa have such schemes on a small scale, with repayments collected by universities, a method that has proven unsatisfactory. Both schemes have had some success, but would be fiscally costly on a larger scale. Thailand is planning to introduce an income-contingent loan scheme in 2006, the success of which will depend greatly on the effectiveness of income tax collection. Designing a cost-effective repayment mechanism in poorer countries should be at the top of the policy-maker agenda.

Sources: Barr (2004) and Chapman (forthcoming).

Offering second chances

Poverty, economic shocks, and bad schools force many young people to leave school without having acquired the basic skills they need for work and life. Large numbers also begin school late or never start. Allowing these youths to remain illiterate or semi-literate and unskilled throughout their lives is costly for them, their families, and their communities. Second-chance programs have effects on behavior beyond schooling and work that should be considered in evaluating their full effects. For example, reduced crime accounts for a substantial part of the benefit of the Job Corps program in the United States.[111]

Many countries operate a variety of programs to get out-of-school youths back into school or in informal training courses—and illiterate young adults into literacy programs. Few countries, however, have a system of second chances that meets the diverse needs of young people. The high cost of operating such a system may be one reason. Another may be the need for innovative solutions and effective partnerships. Few countries have pilot tested and evaluated such programs.

The needs of out-of-school youths are diverse because they leave school at different points in the schooling cycle, with different levels of skill attainment. Some have never attended school and are functionally illiterate. Others have dropped out before completing basic education. Still others have completed basic education but did not acquire basic skills. Even among youths who have the same skills (or lack thereof), the second chances likely to be appealing and effective depend on the age of the young person.[112] Second chances also need to be tailored to the local environment, which might be rural or urban in either a low- or middle-income country.

This diversity adds to the challenge of providing a system of well-targeted second chances. Addressing diversity, while scaling up enrollments, is greatly facilitated by reaching out to the private sector and NGOs. Government in these programs may be most effective as a standard setter, regulator, and funder (along with international donors), and less as a provider.

A policy and organizational framework for second chances—clearly linked to the

---

Integrated approaches address the many constraints on young people

Developed countries have integrated programs targeted to disadvantaged youth in secondary school to help them go to college, and have found them to be effective. Similar to the U.K.'s Aimhigher, the U.S.'s Upper Bound Program focuses more on preparing for college but does not provide financial assistance. Its impacts on high school and college performance are generally limited but large for those with low educational expectations and at academically high risk.

In Mexico, a new World Bank-funded program recognizes that the limited access of disadvantaged youth to college needs to be addressed by a combination of targeted financial assistance (a mixture of loans and grants), academic support for poor and talented students in secondary schools to prepare them for college, and the diffusion of information about higher education opportunities and labor market outcomes through a Web-based labor-market observatory.

School-based career guidance services can help students make better educational and career choices by providing them with information and skills. A review of the limited evidence on these programs in developed countries found positive effects for career decision making and maturity. Some middle-income and transitional economies are also introducing these services, namely Chile, the Philippines, Poland, Romania, Russia, South Africa, and Turkey. Most common is to provide guidance counselors, who have a broad mandate but focus on student learning and behavioral problems. The official ratio of counselors to students is, however, very low (1:500 in the Philippines, 1:800 in Romania), and counselors generally do not deal with education and career choices.

Sources: Johnson (1996); Myers and Schirm (1999); and Watts and Fretwell (2004).

---

formal school system and informed by the demands from the labor market and society—is often missing. In its place are numerous programs that focus on disadvantaged youths but are not linked to each other or to the school system.

Young people still in school: Remedial education

For those still in school, one policy response has been to offer poorly performing students supplementary instruction. Programs identify at-risk students at the primary level and provide better grounding for them when they reach the secondary—but identifying who needs such instruction is a key step. In some developed countries, such as Australia, Canada, and the United States, the results of standardized tests trigger a supplementary tutoring program. This may be challenging to implement in many developing countries because standardized testing is nonexistent or much less frequent, so rather than using standardized tests, the successful Balsakhi program in India allowed teachers to informally identify students that were falling behind.

In many countries, however, the growing numbers of students who take after-school tutoring may be driven largely by teach-

"If we could go to school in the evenings, or for a few hours in the middle of the day, we could pull rickshaws during part of the day, and go to school for the rest. We cannot be in school the whole day, we need to earn money."

Basti boy, Kalayanpur, Bangladesh
January 2006

ers who seek other sources of income, with families bearing the costs. Teachers have a perverse incentive to create demand for their time in after-school tutoring by resisting improvements in their regular classroom hours. For this reason, Hong Kong (China) and Turkey prohibit teachers from providing supplementary tutoring for their own students.[113] Such a policy should accompany any effort to provide remedial education.

Well-designed remedial programs have proven to be successful in improving school outcomes for students of different ages and in very diverse environments, and often help the most disadvantaged students.

- In 1999, Israel implemented a remedial education program to boost the percentage of students in the secondary academic track who earn matriculation certificates. The program targeted 10th through 12th graders who needed additional instruction to pass the matriculation exams, usually determined by failing marks and teacher assessments. The program increased the probability of participating students earning a matriculation certificate by 22 percent.[114]

- In India a large remedial education program for younger children also had positive results.[115] Young women from the community teach basic literacy and numeracy skills to primary school pupils who have not mastered the expected competencies. It could be that class size matters more for children falling behind their peers: not capable of following the standard curriculum, they need individual, nonthreatening attention from a teacher.

Young people who are out of school

Equivalency programs. To appeal to out-of-school youth, second-chance programs must take into account why young people dropped out or never attended school, the challenges they will face to stay in a program, and how they can be integrated into the formal education sector or find employment. All these vary by age, skill, and the local environment. Equivalency, literacy, and job training programs may serve different youth populations, but their common aim of providing competencies for work and life requires a more integrated approach: literacy and equivalency programs that include life skills and vocational training, and vocational training programs that include life skills.

Equivalency systems use more practical curricula, more flexible schedules, and less formal instruction methods than regular schools. They depend on a strong partnership between the formal education sector, private providers of programs, and prospective employers (box 3.9). Without this partnership, the graduates of equivalency systems will be left holding diplomas that allow neither reintegration into the regular school system nor employment in jobs requiring a certain level of competency.

The mode of delivery must take into account why young people dropped out. For example, to bring programs closer to homes in rural areas of Mexico, the Telesecundaria program offers lessons by video, while in the urban slums of Bangladesh, programs rent rooms rather than build schools to solve a supply shortage. Knowing that even small costs can be a barrier to enrollment for the poorest, successful programs provide textbooks, notebooks, and pencils. To accommodate the pressure for adolescents

---

BOX 3.9 *Reaching out-of-school youth in Bangladesh*

Two NGOs in Bangladesh—the Bangladesh Rural Advancement Committee (BRAC) and the Underprivileged Children's Education Program (UCEP)—have provided education to many young people. In a comparative study by UNICEF, students from both programs performed much better on general tests than did students in the Department of Non-formal Education's own Hard-to-Reach schools program, although more rigorous impact evaluations are needed.

The two programs rely on many of the same principles, but their mechanics differ. Both target the poorest and thus provide schools and all materials in the areas where the poorest people live. If a school is to be opened in an area, or students are targeted to begin the program, parents are involved before school starts, and continuing parental involvement is expected. The feedback of parents, teachers, and students is regularly solicited, and the curricula have undergone continuing revisions. A simplified version of the standard government

curriculum—focusing on Bangla, math, and social science—allows students to progress at a fast pace, maintaining their interest and permitting them to catch up to other young people.

BRAC and UCEP tailor their delivery to target young people of different ages and skill levels. BRAC's Non-formal Primary Education Program targets younger people (ages 8–10) and reintegrates them into the formal education system. Their curriculum was adjusted to include English so that students make a smooth transition to the formal education system. UCEP targets older students (ages 10–16), and thus emphasizes speed (providing two grades of education in each year), completeness (providing five or eight years of general schooling), and feeds students into UCEP-run vocational programs, which then integrate students directly into the private sector.

Source: Eusuf and Associates and Center on Social Research and Human Development (2002).

to work, the Tutorial Learning System in Colombia allows students in rural areas and their facilitators to determine the preferred schedule and pace. This greater flexibility should not, however, come at the expense of educational quality.

Aspects of the school environment—social support, curriculum, learning methods—must be properly adapted because they affect both why young people dropped out of the formal school system, and whether they will stay in an equivalency program. For younger adolescents the support of parents can reduce attrition and boost student performance, so involving parents in the early stages of a program is likely to pay off. In addition, programs that emphasize social support and emotional connections—by keeping the same group of students and teacher together over a multiyear program (Colombia's Tutorial Learning System)—tend to have lower dropout rates than programs whose flexibility comes at the expense of such support and continuity (Nonformal Education Project in the Philippines).[116]

Successful equivalency programs that hope to reintegrate people in the formal education system often use teaching methods that are similar to those recommended above for formal schools—student-centered learning, regular assessment, and remedial sessions to involve students in their learning progress (box 3.9). Programs for older youth, however, often use very different approaches. The Mexican National Institute for Adult Education (INEA) has developed an innovative education model for out-of-school individuals 15 or older to learn how to complete the equivalent of primary, lower secondary, or upper secondary education. It provides a curriculum based on acquiring skills for work and life through a flexible system of modules—individuals can choose among the modules and the length of the program is attuned to their needs, covering subjects such as health and civic education and vocational skills.

Literacy programs. The poorest countries in the developing world, and large pockets of disadvantaged groups in better-off countries, have out-of-school youths who are illiterate. Despite the magnitude (137 million youth), the illiteracy problem has been largely neglected by governments and donors, but there are signs of renewed interest—literacy is now part of the Millennium Development Goals and the Education for All goals.

The past neglect is partly due to poor results of literacy programs, but there is room for adapting programs to the needs of participants. Many countries carried out literacy campaigns in the 1960s through 1980s through government-led, top-down brief courses that offered no follow-up. The uptake of eligible participants was limited, and about 50 percent of them dropped out. Of those who stayed on, about half passed literacy tests, and about a quarter eventually regressed to illiteracy. So only a quarter of participants acquired stable literacy skills. Dropout rates fell and completion rates improved for these programs in the 1990s, but the literacy outcomes were still modest.[117]

A key aspect of the improvement was the shift to more contextual and demand-driven models. Attracting enrollees and keeping them interested is a big challenge. Many countries operate adult literacy programs that teach not only reading, writing, and arithmetic but also job and life skills relevant to the local context. Several programs in Africa involve the local community, churches, and businesses. They apply active learning and other participatory methods for instruction in local languages, and they include postprogram follow-up, such as reading activities, to solidify literacy skills. Examples include the Senegal Pilot Female Literacy Project and the Ghana Functional Literacy Project, which require at least 300 hours of instruction over 18–21 months. The cost of the Ghana program is $24 per enrolled learner per cycle and $43 per successful literate graduate per cycle. (None of these programs has been subject to a rigorous impact evaluation.)

Job training. Vocational training programs for out-of-school youth can be more cost-effective by improving targeting, and ensuring that programs are complemented with other services and tailored to the needs of local labor markets. Evidence from developed and developing countries shows low rates of return to most training programs, and few programs pass cost-benefit tests.[118] Vocational training is most effective for those at the high end of the wage distribution but often has less effect for those at the bottom, illustrating the complementarity of skills.[119] Programs also tend to be more effective when they include on-the-job training and employer sponsorship. Vocational programs for youth are most likely to improve the employment and earnings prospects of participants when training is provided as part of a comprehensive package that includes employment services, counseling, and life skills.[120] Examples include the Jovenes and Entra 21 programs in Latin America (see chapter 4 for more on training programs).

Table 3.1 Summary of youth education policies

	Proven successful	Promising but unproven	Unlikely to be successful
Opportunities			
Universal lower secondary to provide basic skills	Compulsory schooling laws (R. B. de Venezuela)	Moving vocational tracks to upper secondary (Chile)	Early tracking and selection (Tanzania and Tunisia)
Diversification with flexibility of postbasic education	Allowing private sector entry and private-public partnerships (Colombia) Providing quality assurance and information (Chile and Rep. of Korea) Fostering competition (autonomy, performance-based funding) (Chile)	No terminal vocational tracks (South Africa and Tunisia) Transferable credit-based courses (Thailand) Part-time schooling (Argentina and Russian Federation)	Unregulated private sector (Cambodia)
Improving quality and relevance of education for work and life	Teaching quality Continuous, needs-based teacher training with follow-up Well-designed and negotiated performance-based pay (Chile)	Making the curriculum more relevant Practical, thinking, and behavioral skills (South Africa) Blending of vocational and general curricula (Chile) Better connection to work and local economy (China's university-local economy linkages, U.S. Career Academies and Germany dual system) School Accountability Disseminating information on school performance (Chile)	Teacher incentives based on narrow test scores (Chile, Kenya, and Mexico)
Capabilities			
Motivating students	Developing behavioral skills (U.S. Big Brother/Big Sister and Philippines Make a Connection) Improving school connectedness with students (United States) Improving incentives to exert effort (merit scholarships for girls in Kenya)	Including students in school policy decision making (Georgia and Russian Federation) Young person–based conditional cash transfers (Bangladesh stipends for girls)	
Providing better information	Information on education opportunities (U.K. Aimhigher)	School-based career guidance services (Poland and Turkey)	
Financial incentives to alleviate constraints to better choices	Conditional cash transfers (Mexico Oportunidades) Vouchers (or beneficiaries) in Colombia	Income-contingent loans (Australia and Thailand) Individual learning accounts (Mexico)	
Second chances			
Remedial education	Testing to determine eligibility (Israel) Combining with other services (information, financial incentives, mentoring) (U.S. Upward Bound Program)		Supplementary teaching parallel to regular classes provided by the same teachers (Cambodia)
Equivalency programs		Group classes with flexible schedules (Colombia) Simplified and practical curriculum, life skills (Mexico) Mechanisms to smooth transition to formal education or work (Bangladesh)	Individual, self-paced programs (Philippines)
Literacy programs		Beneficiary participation in design (Bangladesh) Combination with skills training (Senegal and Ghana) Built-in follow-up mechanisms (Bangladesh) Partnerships with private sector and NGOs (Bangladesh and Brazil)	
Vocational training	Combining with life skills (Jovenes and Entra 21 in Latin America)		

Governments can help improve the skills of young people for work and life by implementing policies that meet their needs. The balance and sequencing of education policies across the three dimensions—postprimary education opportunities, tools to enhance education decision making, and second-chance education options—as well as prioritization among them (basic skills rather than postbasic skills) depends on the state of a country's education system (how it performs in preparing youth for work and life), its level of development, its overall development priorities, and the priorities of its young people. For example, young people consulted in Bangladesh demanded more part-time schooling, while those from Georgia set the teaching of decision-making skills as a priority.[121] This Report proposes the following key areas of policy action (table 3.1):

- Improve educational preparation for adolescence by building a strong foundation and providing quality basic education (including lower secondary) for all. Relevant to most developing countries, this should be a priority for low-income countries where large numbers of young people do not attain the basic skills needed for further study, work, and life.

- To meet the growing demand for postbasic skills, provide diverse and flexible postbasic learning options; a relevant curriculum that teaches practical subjects, thinking skills, and behavioral skills; and connection between school and work—all abetted by teachers who are well-prepared and motivated. This should be a priority for middle-income countries where most young people are equipped with adequate levels of basic skills and there is an increasing demand for postbasic skills (from primary school or from the labor market).

- To enable young people to make better education choices, develop their behavioral skills, involve them as stakeholders in their own education, and provide them with financial incentives and good information. This applies to all countries, but financial incentives should be a priority for countries where many young people do not go to secondary school even though the facilities exist.

- To meet the learning needs of young people who failed to acquire basic skills the first time around, develop a system of remedial education, equivalency programs, literacy programs, and skills training that takes into account their diverse needs and economic conditions. This is a priority for countries with large numbers of young people who are out of school and lack basic skills, particularly countries that have "lost generations" of young people.

Vietnam has been experiencing a period of unprecedented economic growth and poverty reduction. The youth cohort today is larger, more educated, healthier, and more enthusiastic than ever before. However, growth has not fixed all problems. Indeed, it may have brought some new ones for Vietnamese youth: exposure to new health risks, difficult conditions among rural migrants, frustration from the inability to find jobs that match their higher levels of education, and the inadequacy of the skills produced by the education system relative to the changing needs of the labor market.[1]

Starting in 1986, Vietnam gradually shifted from a centrally planned system to a socialist market economy. It doubled its GDP in the 1990s and more than halved the poverty rate from 58 percent in 1993 to 20 percent in 2004. Fueling these changes was a disciplined, hard-working, and fast-learning young population. More than half of its 83 million people are under 25 years old, and 27 percent are between 12 and 24.

Youth in Vietnam today are more educated, healthier, and more optimistic than ever before. The lower secondary school completion rate increased from 25 percent in 1992 to 62 percent in 2002 (see the figure). Although disparities remain, the improvements have been widely shared, with females, rural youth, ethnic minorities, and the poor benefiting proportionally more. The first Survey Assessment of Vietnamese Youth—conducted in 2003 and consisting of a household-based sample of 7,584 youth ages 14–25—shows that most Vietnamese youth are hopeful about the future, believing that they have more opportunities and a brighter future than their parents.[2]

Vietnamese youth have become substantially more educated

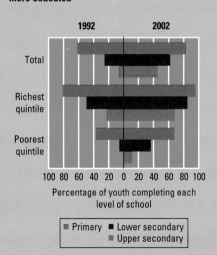

Percentage of youth completing each level of school

■ Primary ■ Lower secondary
■ Upper secondary

Source: Staff estimates based on nationally representative household surveys in 1992 and 2002.

Emerging health risks

Greater wealth and changing lifestyles have increased the exposure of youth to new technologies, mass media, and global culture—45 percent of urban youth have used the Internet. This is creating tension between traditional and modern values. It has also led to new health risks, such as drug use, HIV/AIDS, unwanted pregnancies and abortions, and traffic accidents. Well over half of all reported cases of HIV infections are injecting drug users. Youth make up a growing share of HIV/AIDS infections—from 10 percent in 1994 to about 40 percent today.

Information gaps—fewer than 60 percent of rural youth had ever heard of syphilis or gonorrhea, and 45 percent of youth reported not knowing how to use a condom—and negative attitudes toward condom use—only about 15 percent of youth have ever used a contraceptive method—make young people vulnerable to sex-related health risks.

Young women are especially vulnerable to sex-related health risks because of their limited decision-making power and the lack of comprehensive sex education. The cultural stigmatization of risky health and social behaviors as "social evils," particularly as they relate to HIV/AIDS, has been a major impediment in delivering prevention and care to vulnerable groups and in developing effective behavior change communication. Vietnam lacks youth-specific health policies to address the impact of HIV/AIDS and substance abuse.

A few programs have begun to fill this gap through life skills education and youth reproductive health services. UNICEF, in partnership with the Ministry of Education and Training, the Vietnam Women's Union, and the Vietnam Youth Association, provides healthy living and life skills for youth, focusing on ethnic minorities and young women. The program includes life skills education for 120 lower secondary schools, and its success has led the Ministry of Education to work toward mainstreaming the activities into the lower secondary curriculum. It also includes community-based Healthy Living Clubs to reach out-of-school adolescents and equip them with the knowledge and practical skills to respond to and cope with substance abuse, unprotected teenage sexual relationships, and the risk of HIV/AIDS.

In the last 10 years, road deaths have increased fourfold—from 3,000 a year to almost 13,000. Road accidents on a motorcycle are now the leading cause of death for youth ages 15–24. Motorbike racing and limited helmet use (only 25 percent of young drivers wear helmets) are the main behavioral factors behind these figures. The costs are also borne by the society as a whole: road injuries consume 75 percent of medical care budgets in urban hospitals.

The Asia Injury Prevention Foundation is working with the Ministry of Education and Training to introduce a Traffic Safety Education curriculum in primary schools. More is needed, however, on road safety enforcement.

Managing rural-urban migration

The surge in business activity has led to a huge increase in the demand for labor, with major shifts from agriculture to nonagricultural activities and migration from rural to urban areas. Between 1994 and 1999, more than 4 million people seeking better employment and economic opportunities moved across provincial borders, with more than 53 percent moving into urban centers, particularly Hanoi and Ho Chi Minh City. Over half these internal migrants were younger than 25 years old, with the highest rate for those ages 20–24. Migration has been happening at a very fast pace: the 2004 population census of Ho Chi Minh City uncovered 420,000 more people living in the city than authorities had predicted. Migrants there make up about 30 percent of the population, and outnumber permanent residents in 7 of 24 districts.

This massive migration wave, by itself, puts pressure on services and jobs and creates tension with the local population. Under the registration system, migrants need to get permanent registration status in their new places before they can use such services as public schools, health insurance, housing, and microcredit. Access to permanent residence status, however, is very limited, putting migrants at high risk.

In Ho Chi Minh City, about 40 percent of children (ages 11–14) of short-term and seasonal migrants are out of school, compared with 15 percent of children of nonpermanent migrants, who have resided for over six months and can demonstrate permanent employment. Older youth are at even greater risk: 80 percent of short-term and seasonal migrants and 53 percent of nonpermanent migrants 15 to 18 years old have dropped out of school, compared with 34 percent of permanent residents.

Migrants tend to work in small firms and the informal sector where they enjoy little protection in terms of collective bargaining, fair wages, and other benefits. Migrants also lack access to public microcredit to start a new business.

A revision or elimination of the household registration system has been debated in the National Assembly. A proposal to tie the budget for public services to actual (and frequently updated) population counts is also being considered. Beyond improved access to general services, however, few social protection programs are targeted to vulnerable migrants.

Action Aid recently began offering holistic assistance to the migrant community, including evening classes delivering basic education for children out of school, HIV information, commercial sex worker outreach and services, and a microcredit scheme to support livelihood development. Marie Stopes International provides health services for youth migrants through mobile clinics and site-based clinics in industrial zones.

Managing expectations and improving the relevance of education

About 1.4 million young Vietnamese enter the labor market each year. They are becoming better educated—the relative supply of workers with primary education to those with upper secondary education or higher is growing rapidly—and have high expectations about their futures. The large number of better prepared and more enthusiastic youth entering the labor market creates enormous opportunities, but also substantial risks if they are not productively employed.

The increase in the return to upper secondary and tertiary education relative to primary education between 1992 and 2002 indicates an increase in the relative demand for workers with upper secondary education or higher. Returns between 2002 and 2004 have dropped, however, suggesting that the supply of educated workers is beginning to outpace demand. As a result, many young people are taking on jobs well below their education level or are underemployed. They risk becoming frustrated.

The key policy challenge is the inadequacy of the skills produced by the education system to meet the changing needs of the labor market. About 50 percent of firms in the textiles and chemical sectors consider skilled labor to be inadequate for their needs. About 60 percent of young workers with vocational and college education need further training right after they become employed. Software companies also report that local IT training institutions fail to produce qualified graduates, and that they have to spend at least one year retraining 80–90 percent of recruits.

Although Vietnam has greatly increased the number of people that go through the school system, the curriculum and teaching methods have not kept pace. The curriculum in upper secondary and tertiary education (and even vocational education) remains too theoretical, providing little variety. Youth consulted in Ho Chi Minh City and Hanoi complained about the irrelevance of the curriculum and teaching being too passive and not interactive.

Although some training takes place in firms, it does not cover the training needs of many who struggle to be productively employed. This is particularly the case of youth who were left behind in the country's bonanza, who find themselves without the basic skills for work and life. There are, however, some examples of second-chance programs run by nongovernmental organizations (NGOs) that target these individuals.

The Blue Dragon Children's Foundation is an Australian organization that supports children and youth ages 7–20 from disadvantaged backgrounds (including street children). A contract is set up with each child, specifying objectives, the program to achieve them, and the obligations. The program provides integrated services, including scholarships, food and lodging, health assistance, English and computer skills, recreational activities, and counseling. The program also facilitates access to other successful NGO programs (e.g., KOTO) that provide vocational training for disadvantaged youth with at least lower secondary schooling. KOTO combines hospitality training with life skills training and hands-on experience. Trainees are provided with housing, food, medical insurance, and a training allowance.

Youth policy development

Young people are increasingly seen as an instrumental force for driving the country's future, but cultural perspectives that view this group as immature and needing guidance and control, persist. This has implications for youth policies, which are often problem oriented. Some positive changes in youth policy are under way. The National Youth Development Strategy by 2010 and the first Law on Youth have recently been adopted, and a Master Plan for Youth Health is currently being developed. And some youth have been consulted on these and other government plans.

Going to work

chapter 4

Once young people are in the labor market, they begin to reap the benefits of earlier investment in education and health, and continue to develop the skills needed for a productive livelihood. A successful transition to work for today's many young people can accelerate poverty reduction through better allocation of their labor, and boost economic growth. Some youth, however, encounter roadblocks: some go to work too early, others cannot enter the work force, still others get stuck in low productivity work.

Because most learning occurs at the beginning of the work life, initial experiences can have long-lasting effects. Difficulties in entering the labor market can persist and be very costly to mitigate. Poverty and slow economic growth can exacerbate poor youth outcomes such as child labor, school dropout rates, and joblessness. The lack of access to insurance and information and the unintended consequences of some labor market policies magnify the impact of household poverty and slow economic growth.

Correcting for these failures requires the right mix of policies to ensure that enough opportunities are available for young people, that their skills match employment opportunities, and that second-chance options protect those who fall behind. Some policies, such as improving the investment climate or enhancing the functioning of the labor market, are not youth specific, but have a disproportionate impact on youth. Other interventions are youth specific and should be designed to fit the country context. In most middle-income countries, the priority is to reform labor market institutions and to build more bridges between school and work to better accommodate new entrants. In most low-income countries building on basic skills and providing a springboard to

reintegrate the most vulnerable will allow youth to gain productive employment.

The chapter starts by documenting the challenges youth are facing in their transition to work along with their consequences in the short and long terms. The next section shows why general policies will not solve all the constraints youth face so that a youth-specific approach is needed in the labor market. The last three sections discuss the policy options that could support the opportunity, capability, and second-chance pillars of the Report's policy framework in the transition to work.

Youth challenges in the labor market

By age 24, almost all youth in developing countries have left school and entered a new stage in life—some to begin wage work, some to engage in home enterprise, some to form households and raise families, and some to do combinations of these activities. Over the past 30 years, the age of leaving school has risen in every region in the world except Africa.[1] The increased educational attainment associated with this should have improved the transition to work and led to greater success once employed. Indeed it has, but too many youth still face significant challenges in their path to work. The main obstacles are starting too early, failing to enter the labor market, and having difficulties moving across jobs and up the skill chain. The effect of these obstacles on skill accumulation, future performance in the labor market, and economic development are long lasting.

Starting too early

Some young people never attend school, and many others begin working at very young ages. An average of 14 percent of

Figure 4.1   Child labor is highest in Africa

Percentage of children economically active

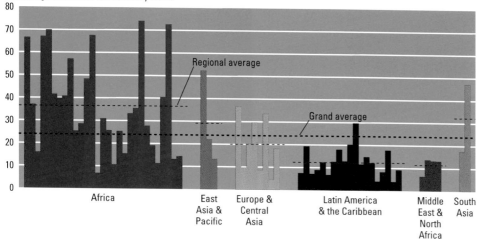

Source: Fares and Raju (2006).
Note: Regional (dotted horizontal lines) and grand (solid horizontal line) means are calculated by weighting country child economic activity rates by country child population (7–14 years).

the population ages 10–30 in 82 developing countries have never attended school. Child labor is prevalent among this group, but it is also common among those who entered school. The International Labour Organization (ILO) estimates that despite an 11 percent drop in the incidence of child labor between 2000 and 2004, 218 million are still trapped in child labor.[2] In 65 countries, about 21 percent of children under age 15 are economically active (figure 4.1). The estimate likely understates child work because it is difficult to measure work outside the market and because child labor is characterized by short spells missed by surveys.[3] The highest reported rates are in Sub-Saharan Africa, averaging 35 percent. In seven of 29 African countries, more that half the children between ages 7 and 14 are working (figure 4.1).

A consensus against the very visible and worst form of child labor is reflected in the large number of countries ratifying ILO convention 182 on the Worst Form of Child Labor. However, the majority of children are not working under such harsh visible conditions. The reality is quite complicated. Many working children combine school with work. In 29 countries in Sub-Saharan Africa, an estimated 52 percent of children working were also attending school, while in 19 countries in Latin America as many as 78

percent of working children were estimated to be attending school.

About 70 percent of child laborers are in agriculture, predominantly in unpaid family work. Fewer than 10 percent are in manufacturing.[4] For many poor families, child labor represents a significant share of household income. For example, in Brazilian households in which children work, child labor represents 17 percent of urban household income and 22 percent of rural household income. The unfortunate trade-off is that children who sacrifice schooling when young are likely to be poor as adults.[5]

Recently completed research has improved our understanding of the determinants and consequences of child labor.[6] Many adolescents work while in school, but the effect of doing so is unclear (chapter 3). For young adults, working may enable them to finance upper secondary and tertiary education that would otherwise be unaffordable. The problem is with younger people—work appears to be more damaging to school attainment because prematurely dropping out of school reduces the amount that youth learn while in school. A negative association between work and the test scores of 8th graders is found in a majority of countries. [7] Poorer schooling outcomes also lead to poorer earnings later in life. In Brazil, boys who entered the work force before age 12 earned 20 percent less per hour and were 8 percent more likely to be in the lowest income quintile than boys who started working after age 12.[8]

Leaving school too early is costly for later productivity. The forgone earnings and the lack of skill accumulation can make it much more difficult to escape poverty as an adult. In 61 countries, the estimated average return per year of schooling was 7.3 percent for men and 9.8 percent for women.[9] The returns are highly correlated within countries, so markets that reward schooling for men also reward women, and markets that reward urban residents also reward those in rural areas. These returns suggest that across a wide array of countries at all stages of development, education offers substantial wage returns—not only to urban male youth, but to women and rural youth as well.

Children of parents who worked as children are more likely to work at young ages, holding other household attributes constant, suggesting that child labor recurs across generations and may be a means by which poverty is passed on from parent to child.[10] Child labor can also have temporary or permanent adverse health consequences that can hinder future earning capacity.[11]

Failing to enter the labor market

Many young males and females face significant difficulties entering the labor market. This employment difficulty can be measured differently depending on the country context and youth characteristics (box 4.1). According to most measures, youth are more

---

BOX 4.1 *Measuring youth activity in the transition to work*

Conclusions about youth labor market outcomes differ depending on how youth time allocations are measured. For example, youth who are not employed in the formal market may be spending time productively in school or in informal production activities or they may also be actively seeking work (see figure below).

The standard labor market indicators in developed countries are the unemployment rate, the employment rate, and the labor force participation rate. Youth are considered employed if they work at least one hour for a wage in the weeks prior to the survey but also if they work in unpaid labor for an enterprise owned by their households. To be considered unemployed, an individual must be not employed but actively seeking work. The labor force participation rate is the share of the population either employed or unemployed, and the unemployment rate is the share of the labor force that is unemployed. The employment rate is the share of the population that is employed. Two other measures are used in developing-country settings: the proportion of the population neither in the labor force nor in school, and the proportion of the population neither working nor in school (the jobless rate).

No one measure provides a complete picture of the labor market for youth, so multiple measures are needed to analyze youth labor markets in developing economies. For a sample of 91 developing countries, these indicators are not perfectly correlated. There is an inverse correlation between the unemployment rate and the employment rate, and a weaker inverse correlation between the unemployment rate and the labor force participation rate. According to the level of country development and the gender and education of youth, the relevant indicator could vary. The following list indicates the caveats of each indicator and suggests alternatives:

- The unemployment rate is a measure of difficulty of finding work. In middle-income countries the ratio of youth to adult unemployment rate is telling, but short-term and long-term unemployment need to be distinguished. In low-income countries, the youth unemployment rate is very low, and relevant only for the more educated and better off portion of the population.
- The employment rate for youth does not account for school enrollment and the type of work. Using the population out of school as a reference group allows for better comparability with adults, while looking at the sector of work, hours of work, and measures of earning shed light on the quality of employment and underemployment.
- "Out of school and out of work" is a measure of unused human capital but not for girls involved in household activities. The relative ratio for males in this group indicates the extent of discouraged youth who withdrew from the work force.
- Youth employment is considered informal if the job is unpaid or if the job includes no benefits such as participation in the country's social security system. High rates of informality are a signal that youth are finding less permanent, low-quality jobs.
- Combining school and work is potentially harmful for the very young, and could be an indicator of the risk of early school exit.

Source: Fares, Montenegro, and Orazem (2006a).

An illustration of youth time use

	In the labor force	Not in the labor force
Employed Formal market		**Not in the labor force and not in school**
Informal market	**Enrolled in school** Working	Not working
Unemployed		

likely to be unemployed than adults. Significant variation in unemployment exists between urban and rural sectors, between developed and developing countries, as well as between poor and rich households. Young females are more likely than young males to stay out of the labor force. Early difficulties in finding employment can have long-lasting effects on employment later in life.

Young people have a hard time finding employment. Survey data from 60 developing countries suggest that, after leaving school, youth spend an average of 1.4 years in temporary or intermittent work and spells of joblessness before permanently entering stable employment.[12] This estimated duration varies widely between countries and estimation methodologies, but could reach above four years in some instances. In many countries in Eastern Europe, Latin America, and the former Soviet Union, youth entering the labor market experienced long spells of unemployment.[13] Initial failure in finding a job can lead to persistent joblessness for young people, especially in weak economies.

In every region the difficulty youth face in entering the labor market is evident in higher unemployment rates for young men and women than for older workers. Youth make up 25 percent of the working-age population worldwide, but 47 percent of the unemployed. The estimated global unemployment rate for youth increased steadily from 11.7 percent in 1993 to 14.4 percent in 2003. It varies widely across regions, from a low of 7.0 percent in East Asia to 13.4 percent in industrial economies to a high of 25.0 percent in the Middle East and North Africa.[14] Across all markets the youth unemployment rate is two to three times higher than the adult unemployment rate, regardless of the level of aggregate unemployment (figure 4.2). The high unemployment rate among youth in some countries has made unemployment in these countries a youth problem. In the Arab Republic of Egypt, Indonesia, Qatar, and the Syrian Arab Republic, youth make up more than 60 percent of the unemployed.[15] In most developing countries, the youth unemployment rate is higher in urban than in rural areas, and is estimated to be higher for young women than for young men.[16]

Figure 4.2   Unemployment is higher for youths than for adults

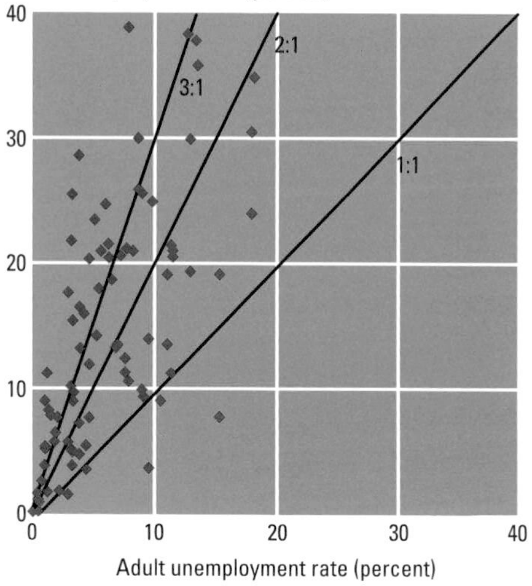

Youth unemployment rate (percent)

Adult unemployment rate (percent)

Source: Fares, Montenegro, and Orazem (2006a).
Note: The 1:1 line represents the cases in which the estimated unemployment among youth and adults is identical. The 2:1 (and 3:1) lines represent cases in which estimated youth unemployment is twice (three times) as high as adult unemployment. Each data point in the graph represents one country.

In most countries, the less skilled youth are more likely to face difficulties in finding work compared with more skilled youth. However, in some developing countries the unemployment rate is very high even among educated youth, a great concern to many countries in the Middle East and North Africa. In Tunisia, where the unemployment rate for 20- to 24-year-olds is more than three times higher than the rate for those over 40, it is more than 40 percent for youth with higher education compared to about 25 percent for those with primary education.[17] The disadvantage faced by the most educated persists over several years after entry into the labor force. The cross-sectional pattern implies that it takes an estimated 10 years for the unemployment rate for Tunisians with postsecondary education to drop below that of the less educated.

Unemployment is only one symptom of problems in the labor market. Within poor countries, youth unemployment is concentrated among those who are educated and from high-income families. Other dimensions in the labor market must be examined to assess the ease or the difficulty for young people to integrate themselves in the labor market. Some youth are neither working nor in school (box 4.2); other poor young people cannot afford to stay unemployed, most have to work. So the incidence of unemployment may be low, although youth are still mired in poverty. In the poorest countries, youth unemployment rates are very low and employment rates are very high (figure 4.3). As country income increases the incidence of unemployment among youth also increases—a likely reflection of available alternative income sources and safety nets that make it possible to be unemployed. Youth employment rates also fall as per capita income increases because youth devote more time to schooling.

The effects of these difficulties are lasting. An initial period of unstable employment upon leaving school is common and not of great concern if young people eventually move into more stable jobs, but this is not

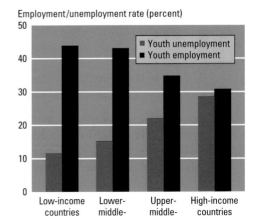

Figure 4.3   Where young people cannot afford to be unemployed, youth unemployment is low and employment is high

Employment/unemployment rate (percent)

Source: Fares, Montenegro, and Orazem (2006a).

always the case. The duration of unemployment for some is very high. For example, in 2000, more than an estimated 60 percent of unemployed youth remained unemployed for more than six months in the Czech Republic, Hungary, and the Slovak Republic.[18] In both Brazil and Chile, youth cohorts that entered the labor market during recessions faced an atypically high likelihood of unemployment during the recession and persistently high unemployment for several more years even after recovery began.[19] In Bosnia and Herzegovina, youth's difficult entry into the labor market led to low future earnings (box 4.3).

Long spells of unemployment can discourage youth from remaining in the labor force, leading to a high incidence of youth out of school and work (see box 4.2). The delays in finding work are important at this age because young people need the early experience to build on their basic education and to continue to acquire skills relevant to the labor market. Being either unemployed or out of the workforce for a long time can limit the accumulation of human capital young people need to get better integrated into the workplace and find productive employment.

During repeated spells of unemployment, young men and women in Canada and the United States increase their uptake of training, stay longer in school, delay marriage,

---

BOX 4.2   *Some youths are neither in the labor force nor studying*

In many countries, the proportion of youth who are neither in the labor force nor in school is too large to dismiss as a problem of measurement or as a temporary phenomenon. A cross-country comparison of young men and women reveals important differences in these proportions across gender and relative to adults (see the figure):

- *Differences in levels.* Female observations almost always lie to the right of male observations, implying a higher incidence for females relative to males.
- *Differences in ratios.* Most observations for men lie above the 45 degree line, where the estimated incidences for youth and adults are identical, implying that young men are systematically more likely to fall in this group than adult men. The pattern is not replicated for females.

Some of the high estimates may be attributable to measurement problems, particularly for young women working in their households. In Tanzania, the main reason young women said they were not looking for work was their household responsibilities. For young men, it was the lack of market work.

The data reveal important differences between males and females in this group—males are predominately discouraged workers, while females are engaged in

The incidence of young females neither in the labor force nor studying is higher than for young males, which is higher than for adult males

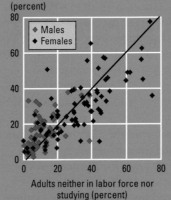

Youth neither in labor force nor studying (percent)

Adults neither in labor force nor studying (percent)

Source: Fares, Montenegro, and Orazem (2006a).
Note: The 45 degree line represents the cases in which the estimated incidence of neither working nor studying among young and adults are identical. Each data point in the graph represents one country.

nonmarket activities. Youth who are neither attaining marketable skills in school nor using those skills in productive work are a wasted resource in the economy, so mechanisms need to be found to tap that resource.

BOX 4.3   *Early unemployment persists in Bosnia and Herzegovina*

In Bosnia and Herzegovina, despite the end of the civil conflict in the late 1990s, youth have had significant difficulties entering the labor market and experienced excessive instability in their early years of the transition to work. In 2004, the unemployment rate was 62 percent for those between 15 and 19 years old, and 37 percent for those between 20 and 24 years old, compared to 22 percent for adults in the same year. These outcomes persist in the first few years of youth experience in the labor market. Among those 15–24 who were unemployed in 2001, 77 percent were jobless one year later, and 58 percent were still jobless three years later. Even among youth employed in 2001, a third of them were jobless in 2002, and a quarter of them were still jobless in 2004.[20]

Controlling for young workers' characteristics (for example, gender, education, marital status), those who suffered a spell of unemployment or inactivity at any point over the 2001–02 period were also found to have faced a greater likelihood of unemployment or joblessness (both inactivity and unemployment) in 2004. Among young workers, the experience of joblessness is associated with about 11 percent greater probability of unemployment and 30 percent greater probability of joblessness. The effect on earnings is also significant. For all workers in Bosnia and Herzegovina, a spell of joblessness is associated with lower wages.

Poor transition probabilities in Bosnia and Herzegovina, 2001–04 *(percent)*

	Employment status in 2002			Employment status in 2004		
	Inactive	**Unemployed**	**Employed**	**Inactive**	**Unemployed**	**Employed**
Employment Status in 2001						
All						
Inactive	73	12	14	63	15	21
Unemployed	32	34	34	30	27	43
All employed	13	07	81	13	08	79
Ages 15–24						
Inactive	71	17	12	53	21	26
Unemployed	36	41	23	26	32	42
All employed	22	12	66	11	15	74

Source: Fares and Tiongson (2006).
Note: "Inactive" is defined as being out of school and out of the labor force.

---

and continue to live with their parents.[21] Not all these options are available in developing countries. When productive options are not available for jobless youth, there is a greater likelihood that they will enter activities damaging to themselves and society. Youth difficulties in the labor market increased crime rates in France, and increased the probability of incarceration in the United States.[22] Similarly, in Sri Lanka, where the proportion of long-term unemployed young people exceeds that of adults, high youth unemployment was cited as the main cause for large-scale unrest of Sinhalese youth from the rural south. The second insurgency from 1987–91 brought the country to the verge of collapse and left 40,000–60,000 dead or missing, most of them youth.[23]

Getting stuck in jobs that do not build human capital

Youth and adult employment are positively correlated—as adult employment rises, youth employment also increases. But youth are less likely to be employed compared to older men and women. Even after adjusting for school enrollment, the difference between youths' and adults' employment rates persists. Among youth, the employment rate for young men is always higher than the employment rate for young women, partly reflecting a stronger attachment to the labor force among males—but also reflecting the additional difficulties many young women face in going to work and the greater proportion of them engaged in home production, not included in measured employment.

When working, youth often are found in low-paying jobs or unpaid family work. For 74 developing countries with data, only 25 percent of working youth in low-income countries are in paid work, with the proportion rising with country income, to 57 percent for the middle-income group and 74 percent for the high-income group. Even those who are paid are less likely to have access to social security compared with

"I am positive for my future. I'm sure I will find a job sooner or later and the first job doesn't mean a job that I will do my whole life. The most important thing for me is to improve myself."

Xiangju, university student,
China
December 2005

older workers. In these 74 countries, it is not uncommon to find the incidence of unpaid work to be two to four times higher for youths than adults (chapter 1).

Starting in a low-paying job, or being mismatched early on with the wrong type of employment, would not have severe consequences if youth can move to more productive opportunities. Indeed, during the early transition to work, youth are expected to be experimenting with different types of employment, and evidence indicates that such early turnover will enhance subsequent job matches, reflected in higher productivity and higher earnings for youth.[24] However, not all youth are mobile. In Burkina Faso, more than 90 percent of teenagers between 15 and 19 with no education started working as family helpers in 1993, falling only to about 80 percent five years later.[25] Higher education does increase mobility. More than 80 percent of teenagers between 15 and 19 with some secondary education started working as family helpers in 1993, and this share fell to about 40 percent five years later. While initial differences were not as large, those with higher education moved out to find better productive work much more quickly.

Does starting in informal or unpaid work rather than formal-sector work lead to different employment and wage outcomes? Where informality is widespread, the informal sector is an important stepping stone in the transition from school to work for those who have the choice. In Latin America the vast majority of apprenticeship occurs in the informal sector, and new entrants might choose the informal sector to acquire the skills needed for the labor market.[26] In Albania, Argentina, Georgia, Hungary, Poland, Russia, Ukraine, and República Bolivariana de Venezuela, youth gain substantially when they move from the informal to the formal sector.[27] The wage gains from the move are significantly greater for youths than for older workers. Youths also benefit from faster wage growth once in the formal sector, both in comparison with older workers and in comparison with their counterparts in the informal sector. Some, however, become stuck in informal low-paying jobs that offer no opportunity to further develop their human capital.

Figure 4.4   Returns to experience are highest for the young

Percent return to one year of additional experience

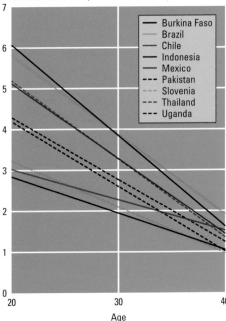

Source: Fares, Montenegro, and Orazem (2006b).

On entering the labor market, youth may have the opportunity to obtain formal and on-the-job training, with a large impact on their eventual earnings. Young workers have the fastest wage increases during this period of learning on the job, and the rate slows as workers age (figure 4.4). Returns to an additional one year of experience at age 20 increase earnings by up to 6 percent. However, holding everything else constant, an additional year of experience at age 40 increases earnings by less than 3 percent. The more skills acquired in the early work career, the more the worker can earn later on. In more than four-fifths of the countries analyzed, earnings peaked after age 40, with an average peak in earnings at age 47. At the peak, earnings were on average 2.5 times the starting wage, indicating considerable skill development after leaving school, most of it in the first few years on the job. Youth who lose the chance to acquire these skills after leaving school because of early labor market difficulties may face a career of lower skills and poorer pay. Indeed, in Hungary, initial career success drives later labor market outcomes.[28]

The effect on poverty and social outcomes should not be understated. In many countries, some households with working youth are still poor, even after factoring in youth earnings. Because the most abundant asset of the poor is labor, if poor households are unable to escape poverty even when their youth work, it is unlikely that they will do so through other means. This puts the policy issues for poverty alleviation in stark focus. The overwhelming evidence is that better schooling helps youth make an easier transition from school to work and enjoy greater success. More stable employment and earnings also ease the next transition into marriage and household formation. However, the poorest households cannot meet their current consumption needs without the income earned through their children's labor, so their children's schooling and potential escape from poverty is sacrificed for current subsistence.

What makes youth vulnerable in the labor market?

Youth labor market outcomes are affected by general trends in poverty and economic growth. Because of the severe income constraints in low-income countries, households may have no choice but to send children to work, while in slow-growing economies, youth have significant difficulties in finding work.

The incidence of child labor is high in the Sub-Saharan Africa and South Asia regions, characterized mostly by low-income countries (see figure 4.1). This relationship, however, is not linear and indicates that at very low levels of income, the effect of changes in per capita income on the incidence of child labor is the highest. Significant variation also occurs in the incidence of child labor even at similar levels of income, which indicates that factors other than poverty could increase or reduce the incidence of child labor. Some families and children have low perceived returns to education, while others face borrowing (and other) constraints to finance their children's schooling. Microanalysis for Burkina Faso and Guatemala shows that the incidence of child labor increases when poor families are faced with income shocks.[29] Conditional cash transfer programs such as

PETI (Program to Eradicate Child Labor) in Brazil were shown to be successful already in reducing child labor incidence by providing support to income-constrained families conditional on their children attending school and after-school programs.

Young people suffer disproportionately from weakening labor markets. Cross-country analyses from developed and developing countries show that increased labor demand always improves employment and increases labor force participation among youth.[30] In Brazil in the 1980s and 1990s, employment rates for adults during economic downturns and expansions varied only slightly from the trend, but movements were much greater for young males and females.[31] The differences in employment fluctuations are even more apparent in Chile. The employment rate for young males is consistently below that of adults, partly because a large share of those between 15 and 24 years old are enrolled in school and also because of the greater difficulties youth face in their transition to work. However, the difference is not constant and varies widely over time. During the economic slowdowns of 1974, 1982, and 1998, the employment rate for young males, adjusted for school attendance, declined at least twice as much as that for adult males (figure 4.5).

What is contributing to the vulnerability of youth in the labor market? Four factors:

- In some countries, large cohorts of new entrants and higher female participation rates will continue to add pressure on the youth labor market.

Figure 4.5   In Chile employment is more responsive to demand fluctuations for young males than for adults

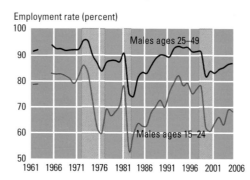

Employment rate (percent)

Source: Fares and Montenegro (2006).
Note: Shaded portions represent periods of economic slowdown. Employment series are adjusted for school enrollment.

- Poor access to information and credit leads to premature exit from school, perpetuating skill mismatches.
- Policy failures have unintended consequences on youth employment and widen the gaps between youth and adults in the labor market.
- Social institutions hinder the full participation of many youth, particularly girls, in skill acquisition and work.

Large youth cohorts

Several developing countries around the world are experiencing larger youth cohorts (see spotlight on differing demographics following chapter 1). In some, particularly in Sub-Saharan Africa, the share of youth in the population will continue to rise for the next few decades, adding pressure on the youth labor market. Indeed, earlier baby booms in developed countries increased youth unemployment (see spotlight on baby booms following chapter 4).

In 32 developing and transition countries, a 10 percent increase in the youth share of the population increased youth unemployment by an estimated 6 percent between 1980 and 2000.[32] In Ethiopia, local labor markets with the largest share of youth in the population had the lowest youth employment rates, with the effect more pronounced among uneducated youth.[33] Thus, countries with rising youth cohorts will face increasing challenges in absorbing youth in jobs.

Even where the youth share of the population is decreasing, the underlying increase in female participation rates will limit the impact of slower population growth as larger shares of young females in these cohorts look for employment in the labor market.[34] Rising educational attainment has had a particularly important effect on the labor supply choices for women. As women acquire more education, they increasingly move out of traditional household or agricultural production activities and enter wage work. Rising female education levels and the associated rise in female participation in wage work have another effect—they are strongly inversely correlated with country fertility rates.[35]

Lack of access to information and credit

Leaving school to start work before acquiring the relevant skills limits the ability of youth to take advantage of future work opportunities (chapter 3). Poor households with limited access to credit, facing income or health shocks, might have no option but to withdraw their children from school and send them to work. Low expected returns to education might also cause early school dropout and entry to work. Because of information failures, households may undervalue the potential returns from schooling, particularly when jobs requiring education are in urban areas and the household is rural. These information failures are greatest in households with poorly educated parents.

Another reason for low expected returns is that policies restrict youth from moving easily from one job to another, from one area to another, or from one industry to another. The Heritage Foundation Economic Freedom Index measures how a country's economic institutions allow people to work, produce, consume, and invest in the ways they feel are most productive.[36] Returns to schooling average 9.9 percent in the group of developing countries where workers are freer to seek economic advantage, but 6.4 percent in the less mobile group (figure 4.6). This is consistent with theoretical work that ties returns to human capital to economic mobility across alternative sectors and occupations.

Lack of access to information reduces the effectiveness of job search and prolongs joblessness among youth. Not knowing the available opportunities in the labor market and how to prepare for them reduce the likelihood of youth developing the right skills and finding the appropriate job for their skills. The information asymmetry makes employers less confident in hiring new entrants because they are not certain about their productivity. It also increases turnover as youth and employers learn more about the quality of their employment relationship.

Restrictive labor market institutions

Labor market institutions—such as unemployment insurance, employment protec-

Figure 4.6   Returns to education are higher for workers who are more mobile

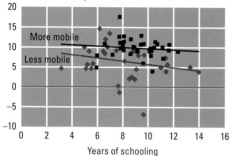

Return to education (percent)

Source: Fares, Montenegro, and Orazem (2006b).
Note: "More mobile" countries have an average return to education of 9.9 percent; "less mobile" countries have an average return to education of 6.4 percent. Countries are classified as "more mobile" and "less mobile" according to the Heritage Foundation Economic Freedom Index. Each data point in the graph represents one country.

tion laws, and the minimum wage—came into being in response to the suffering of the unemployed and the exploitation of workers. Despite good intentions, those institutions are less than optimal in many countries. Their design might have been poor to start with, circumstances and the economic environment might have changed, and political considerations might have given institutions a life and shape of their own. Reforming these institutions has long been on the agenda in many countries.[37] Some of these institutions have a disproportionate effect on youth.

Employment protection laws are effective in protecting jobs and preventing job loss, but also raise hiring costs, putting young people at a disadvantage.[38] *World Development Report 2005* and *Doing Business 2006* show that employment regulations can be more stringent in developing countries than in industrial countries. High firing costs reduce layoffs as well as job creation in firms and limit the entry of new firms, disproportionately burdening youth in the labor market.[39] Furthermore, reduced turnover increases the duration of unemployment. This effect, combined with the lasting impact of long, early unemployment spells, impairs youth outcomes and future prospects. In Chile, where job security provisions depend on job tenure, employment was biased against young workers. Stricter employment protection laws meant lower wages and employ-

ment rates for young workers.[40] The adverse impact of such regulations on young workers' employment rates was more than twice that on prime-age male workers in 15 Latin American and Caribbean countries and 28 Organisation for Economic Co-operation and Development (OECD) countries in the 1980s and 1990s.[41]

Because youth are more likely to be at the bottom of the wage distribution, changes in the minimum wage will naturally have a larger impact (positive or negative) on them. In Brazil, an increase in the minimum wage led to greater job loss for female, young, and low-skilled workers whose wages were clustered around the minimum. In Chile, minimum wages reduced the overall employment probabilities of youth, particularly the unskilled.[42] Even when the informal sector is large, as in Latin America, minimum wages in the formal sector spill over into wages in the informal sector.[43] As a consequence, youth in the informal sector are also affected by changes in the minimum wage.

When public sector wages and benefits are more generous than private sector compensation, a strong incentive arises for young (usually educated) school leavers to queue for government jobs and stay unemployed for some time after graduation. Substantial wage premiums in the public sector—coupled with job security, tenure, prestige, and other nonwage benefits—influence the decision to voluntarily hold out until a public sector job opportunity opens. In Morocco, the starting hourly wage in the public sector is 42.5 percent higher than in the private sector.[44] This leads to a strong preference for public employment among highly educated young Moroccans. In Tunisia, the public sector wage premium is 18 percent, again leading the young to queue for jobs in the public sector rather than accept less attractive private sector jobs.[45] In Ethiopia, a large share of the unemployed youth aspired to work in the public sector because of the perceived high benefits.[46]

These results are not unique to Ethiopia, Morocco, and Tunisia. Earnings regressions for 39 developing countries reveal a public wage premium in 25 countries, on average about 26 percent, controlling for individual characteristics. For other countries such as

"Young people are deprived of secure jobs; their unemployment rate is well above the national average."

Jérémie, law student, France

Cambodia and Vietnam, the public wage premium is negative.[47] In Latin America the public wage premium is much higher for women than men. In several countries in Latin America and in Indonesia, the public wage premium also varies with skill levels.[48]

Inhibiting social institutions, especially for young females

In all regions over the past three decades, labor force participation rates have risen for young women, coincident with rising female educational attainment and falling fertility rates. In some regions, however, rising female education levels have not translated into dramatic increases in labor force participation rates for young women. Social institutions and norms could be a reason. A simple cross-country regression for 128 countries shows that religion alone can explain about one-third of the variation in female participation rates.[49]

Social norms can also affect whether young women succeed in the labor market. In Egypt, women, whose average education level has increased enormously, stay close to home and refrain from driving—limiting their job mobility. While young males increased their commuting distance to work between 1988 and 1998, young women did not, limiting their access to paid employment outside government. The least educated women are the most disadvantaged, confined either to domestic work or to non-wage work in home-based enterprises and subsistence agriculture.[50]

Broadening labor market opportunities

In all countries, a good investment climate lets the private sector expand, helps trade flourish, and allows the country to attract foreign direct investment, all needed for job creation. Youth can contribute to the growth of these sectors, but steps are needed to mitigate the effect of market and policy failures that disproportionately affect youth. The steps will differ depending on a country's level of development. In middle-income countries and countries where labor market institutions are more binding and likely to be enforced, reforming labor mar-ket institutions is a priority. In low-income countries, with large informal sectors and dominance of the rural economy, reforming institutions will have limited impact. Thus, expanding alternatives in the rural sector, promoting sectoral and regional mobility, and reducing child labor are most urgent.

Improving the investment climate

Economic growth and job creation benefit most participants in the labor market, youth included. When labor demand is strong, youth employment and labor force participation for both males and females increases while the unemployment rate for youth goes down.[51] Because the private sector should lead in job creation, a good investment climate is needed to allow firms to form and expand. *World Development Report 2005* argued that governments should create a better investment climate by tackling unjustified costs, risks, and barriers to competition. They can do this by ensuring political stability and security, improving the regulatory and tax climate for investment, providing needed infrastructure, and improving information on vacancies for job seekers.

Expanding world trade has shifted production around the world. Because the young are the most able to respond to the growing demand for labor, these shifts favor young workers. In Indonesia, industries with youth employment shares more than twice the national average are concentrated in electronics and textile manufacturing, heavily engaged in exporting. The young workers in these youth-intensive exporting sectors are disproportionately well-educated— 47 percent have completed secondary schooling, compared with 11 percent of other employed youth. Similarly, in Vietnam 20 percent of the young workers in those sectors have completed secondary school, compared with 8 percent in other sectors, and in Brazil 41 percent, compared with 15 percent.

Youth-intensive exporting sectors seem to target young female workers, who make up 74 percent of employed youth in those sectors in Indonesia and Vietnam, compared with 46–50 percent in other sectors. Young workers in exporting firms are better paid than their counterparts elsewhere.

Figure 4.7   Productivity and earnings increased faster for youth relative to older workers in Slovenia during the transition, (1992–2001)

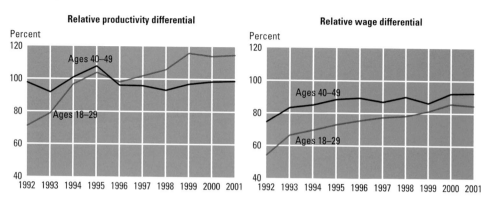

Source: Vodopivec (2005).
Note: The figures show relative productivity and earnings of different age groups compared to a reference group of people ages 50 and above, whose productivity and earnings were normalized to 100 percent.

In Indonesia, young workers in the export sector were paid 30 percent more than young workers in other sectors and 20 percent more than young workers in other manufacturing. Young workers may also be attracted to exporting firms and those with at least some foreign ownership, because of the greater likelihood of training.[52]

The young may be particularly attractive to firms in the new and growing sectors of the economy because they are more adaptable than older workers to new production methods. During the Estonian transition, the relative share of employment and the returns to experience rose faster for the young.[53] In Slovenia, wages and labor productivity rose faster for the youngest workers (figure 4.7). In the early 1990s, younger workers were the least productive age group in the labor market. The productivity of those between 18 and 29 years old was about 70 percent of the productivity of those 50 years and older. Around 1996, young workers' productivity caught up with that of 40- to 49-year-olds, and by 2001 youth had become the most productive. At the same time, earnings rose at a pace faster for the young than for older workers, closing significantly the gap in earnings with older workers.

Industrial growth led by foreign direct investment was initiated partly due to the availability of cheaper young labor. However, the dynamic growth process increased the demand for a highly skilled and highly edu-

cated labor force able to adapt to new technology with appropriate knowledge, skills, and behavior. In several Latin American countries, this has boosted high-skilled wages.[54] The experiences of Thailand and Malaysia suggest that government has a role to play in reducing the negative production externalities caused by accelerating wage increases, in turn caused by shortages in quality labor.[55] Evidence suggests that opportunities in export-oriented sectors can provide incentives for youth to acquire more skills. Among 48 developing countries, increases in apparel and shoe exports as a share of GDP were found to be positively associated with subsequent upturns in both male and female secondary school enrollment. For the average country, a doubling of apparel and footwear exports as a share of GDP raises female secondary school attendance by 20–25 percent.[56]

Reforming institutions

World Development Report 2006 discusses why governments intervene in the labor market and how poorly designed or inappropriate policies can make conditions worse for equity and efficiency. As shown earlier, these policies disproportionately affect youth. In high-income countries, the result is a reduction in the employment rate for young people and an increase in the incidence and duration of unemployment (see spotlight on baby booms following chapter 4). In low- and middle-income countries, the result is a

---

BOX 4.4   *Reforming part of the labor market has been no substitute for comprehensive reform in Spain and France*

Spain and France have suffered from high unemployment among youth over the last two decades. Both governments have experimented with partial labor market reforms as a means to reduce the youth unemployment problem.

In Spain, the initial reform in the early 1990s was intended to increase employment flows among youth by making it less costly for firms to hire young workers. Lowering the firing costs for entry level jobs without changing the costs for regular jobs may have increased firms' willingness to hire new workers but also made them reluctant to retain these workers. The result of this policy was a systematic rise in the use of temporary contracts for young workers, without an increase in permanent and stable employment. Over 30 percent of employment became temporary, while unemployment remained as high as 24 percent. Spain had to move to broader reforms in 1997. Policies such as reductions of payroll tax and dismissal costs proved to be effective in reducing overall unemployment, particularly for the young. Youth unemployment decreased from about 40 percent in 1995 to 20 percent in 2000.

In France, youth unemployment rates have remained above 20 percent since the 1990s. In 2006, the government proposed a contract for first employment (Contrat Première Embauche, CPE) that would have allowed employers to fire workers under 26 within a two-year trial period without giving a reason. It was hoped that employers would be more likely to recruit young people if they knew they could be fired readily and that this would reduce youth unemployment. Students, with the support of workers' unions and opposition parties, demonstrated against the new law and forced a showdown with the government, leading to the withdrawal of the proposed law.

Some decried the lack of consultation. Analysts also argued that the CPE reinforced the market segmentation already in place since the introduction of the fixed duration contract, the Contrat à Durée Déterminée, CDD, a partial reform in 1979. The proportion of those employed under the CDD rose from 3 percent in 1983 to 17 percent in 2000. This substantially increased turnover without a reduction in unemployment duration.

The lesson: Because partial reform, as in Spain in the early 1990s, tends to reinforce market segmentation, it is a poor substitute for broad reform, and its public support and effectiveness are limited. Another alternative, suggested by analysts in France, could be a more gradual approach that deemphasizes the segmented labor market for different age groups—perhaps a progressive contract in which protection gradually increases as a worker's tenure rises.

Sources: Blanchard (2006); Blanchard and Landier (2001); Cahuc and Carcillo (2006); Kugler (2004); and Kugler, Jimeno, and Henanz (2003).

---

segmented labor market—one comprising a small number of workers who benefit from greater employment and income security and another comprising a large number of young workers alternating between short spells of employment and joblessness, with little access to security and opportunities to develop their human capital.[57]

Broad, not piecemeal, labor market reform. To protect those currently employed, some governments have experimented with modest labor market reforms, but because partial reforms tend to reinforce market segmentation, the results were not favorable (box 4.4). For policy makers, a move from partial reform toward more general and comprehensive reform will benefit employment creation with a disproportionate effect on youth. The level of protection has to be balanced with the flexibility needed to encourage job creation. In 1990, Colombia introduced a labor market reform that substantially reduced the costs of dismissing workers. The reform increased turnover for formal sector workers relative to nonformal but also reduced the length of unemployment spells, particularly for youth and for more educated workers.[58]

At any general level of protection, firms will need additional incentives to employ and train young inexperienced workers. Analysts advise against jumps in protection from one type of employment to another—jumps likely to segment the market (box 4.4). A more progressive contract is preferred, where protection increases gradually with tenure with no large discrete changes in protection.[59] Such contracts provide incentives for firms to invest in young workers as their productivity increases with longer tenure.

A similar approach applies to the minimum wage, intended to protect workers' wages from falling to very low levels. In many developing countries, however, the minimum wage is high. In Chile, Colombia, Costa Rica, Nicaragua, Panama, Peru, and República Bolivariana de Venezuela, it exceeded 50 percent of the median wage for workers ages 26–40 between 1980 and 2000.[60] Yet many workers receive much less than the minimum wage because of weak enforcement. Young workers' wages tend to be concentrated at the lower end of the wage distribution anyway. For example, in Russia the share of young workers with labor market earnings below 30 percent of the median wage is estimated at 38 percent for 2002, in Indonesia at 35 percent for 2003, and in Ghana at 52 percent for 1998.[61]

Several countries have differentiated the minimum wage by age to mitigate the effects on youth employment. Setting a lower minimum wage for youth reduces the disemployment effects by keeping it profitable for firms to hire and train young inexperienced workers.[62] Below-minimum apprenticeship wages significantly increased the job opportunities for young graduates in Chile.[63] Lower wages should be intended to subsidize on-the-job training so youth can develop the skills needed to increase their productivity and future earnings.

In many countries where the public sector offers higher wages and more generous benefits and employment security, educated youth remain out of work while waiting for openings in the public sector. Closing the gap in pay and benefits between the public and the private sector, or at least reducing the incentive to wait for a public sector opening, will reduce youth unemployment among the most educated. Closing the gap in information, promoting opportunities in the private sector, and aligning higher education more with labor market demands will shorten the long queues of young men and women waiting for public sector jobs. Governments also have to signal a willingness to move from job guarantees (explicit or implicit) to a more competitive process for entry into the public sector, perhaps by making the application process merit based. In Turkey, the requirement of passing a set of examinations to apply for a government post shortened the queue for public sector jobs and shifted graduates to the pursuit of other careers.

Direct employment creation. Wage subsidies to private firms have sometimes encouraged employers to hire new entrants.[64] In a world where wages cannot adjust to compensate for the risks firms might perceive from hiring inexperienced young workers, subsidies will have an effect on hiring and dismissal policies of employers. Several evaluations of wage subsidy schemes in European countries are available. Almost all studies find a large beneficial impact on employment.[65] While encouraging, these findings do not usually take into account potential displacement effects or deadweight loss that may be associated with wage subsidy schemes.

Better design of wage subsidies and better targeting are needed to ensure that young hires do not gain employment at the expense of other employees, and that the subsidy goes to those employers who would not have hired young workers in the absence of this additional financial incentive. Evidence from the Czech Republic, Hungary, and Poland demonstrates that youth-specific wage subsidies can be of particular benefit if they are well targeted to the most disadvantaged, with females with lower educational attainment benefiting the most. In OECD countries, wage subsidies work best for unemployed youth, especially those from more disadvantaged backgrounds.[66]

Differences in the target group, eligibility criteria, assignment to participation, type of jobs, and duration and amount of subsidies will play a role in the effectiveness of these programs. These programs exhibit large variations. In Belgium, the "employment plan" offers two-year subsidies for employers through a reduction in social insurance contribution, of up to 25 percent of the gross wage in the first year and around 17 percent of the gross wage in the second year of the subsidy. In Sweden, a program targeting the long-term unemployed offers employment subsidies for six months. In the Slovak Republic, two-year subsidies were offered both in the public and private sector. Because wage subsidies are costly and less effective in economies with large informal sectors, their applicability is limited mostly to middle-income countries. Even in middle-income countries, however, the financial constraints mean that programs have to be well-targeted and be of limited duration.[67]

Expanding rural opportunities

In many developing countries, many youth still live in rural areas. For rural youth, employment opportunities are not only in agriculture but also off farm. Including rural towns, the rural nonfarm sector accounts for about 40 percent of full-time rural employment in Asia and Latin America and 20 percent in Sub-Saharan Africa.[68] The history of economic development has shown that development of the nonfarm sector is tied to improved productivity on the farm. As technological innovations raise

"[Working in government] is stable, with higher social status and more space for future development as a government official."

Jingxiao, university student,
China
December 2005

BOX 4.5   *Off-farm opportunities for youth in Palanpur, India*

The nonfarm economy has expanded greatly in the North Indian village of Palanpur in the past decades. In the mid-1980s, more than a third of village income came from nonagricultural activities, and more than 70 villagers were employed regularly or semi-regularly in the nonfarm sector (of a working-age male population of about 250). Visits to the village in the 1990s and in 2005 indicate that the expansion of nonfarm occupations has not abated.

Many young male villagers from Palanpur hold semi-regular jobs in industrial workshops and bakeries in the nearby towns of Chandausi and Moradabad. Employment contracts are often piecework, offering fairly high incomes in return for

hard work and, in some cases, exposure to health hazards.

Although employment outside Palanpur is highly valued by villagers, particularly the young eager to venture beyond the village, access remains limited. Why? Because of social status (proxied by caste and education levels), wealth (bribes need to be paid), and outside contacts (a "recommendation" is often required).

Palanpur is located in socially conservative rural Uttar Pradesh, and outside employment opportunities are generally confined to males. Elsewhere, nonfarm jobs are also accessible to women.

Source: Lanjouw and Stern (2006).

---

productivity on the farm, labor is freed up to move to the nonfarm sector.[69]

The range of opportunities in rural areas is far wider than might be apparent at first glance. The rural nonfarm economy generates 30–50 percent of rural incomes throughout the developing world, shares that continue to grow.[70] In some instances, the high share is a result of crop failures or other adverse shocks to the farm sector. In most cases, however, rising productivity growth in the agriculture sector raises farm income and hence the demand for goods produced outside agriculture. Rising agriculture labor productivity also frees up labor to work off farm.

The rural nonfarm economy, extremely heterogeneous, provides an important source of youth employment throughout the developing world. In Latin America, about half the youth population ages 15–24 in rural areas, and more than 65 percent of those ages 25–34, work in nonagricultural activities. In 15 countries in this region, the higher share of youth employment in several nonagricultural sectors compared to employment in agriculture bears out the importance of the rural nonfarm economy.[71] In rural India, the likelihood of moving into nonfarm casual occupations peaks at age 22, and in Brazil at around 33.[72]

Because young people are the most mobile, they are the most likely to switch sectors to take advantage of new opportunities,

including those in other countries (see chapter 8). So policies to develop the nonfarm sector will have a particularly pronounced effect on youth, even if not targeted at them.[73] For example, the promotion of small and medium rural enterprises that use imported technologies could have a differential impact on youth, given their advantage in using new technologies, as with Taiwan, China's promotion of rural manufacturing. As subcontractors, rural firms can acquire inputs, technical know-how, and links to external markets, increasing their attractiveness to young workers.[74] As education levels for rural youth improve, they can enter a broader range of nonagricultural occupations. In rural India and in Brazil, better educated youth have a higher likelihood of moving into highly productive nonfarm work.[75] Some of these new off-farm opportunities involve physically demanding and hazardous work (box 4.5). As transportation and economic integration reach the small towns scattered throughout rural areas, rural youth gain better access to urban opportunities without the need to migrate.

Facilitating mobility

For 29 developing countries with data, youth are 40 percent more likely than older people to move from rural to urban areas or to move across urban areas. Those who move have better employment outcomes, with mobility correlated negatively with youth unemployment and positively with employment and labor force participation.[76]

The Chinese rural-urban migration typifies the pattern.[77] Rural migrants tend to be younger than 35. Two-thirds are male. Half are single. Female migrants are younger and less likely to be married. Rural migrants are more educated than rural residents who did not migrate: 66 percent had a lower secondary school education, compared with 40 percent of rural residents who did not migrate. Rural migrants are less educated than urban residents, and so tend to fill the least skilled jobs available in cities. Even so, the incentives to migrate are clearly economic. Per capita urban incomes are more than three times those in rural areas, and the gap is rising. Even though rural migrants are paid half of what similarly skilled urban residents are paid, their pay is still well above that of workers in rural areas. Many rural migrants send money back to their relatives in rural areas, representing 13 percent of Chinese rural income in 2003.

Rural migrants nevertheless face real disadvantages relative to urban workers. In China, migrant workers have little legal recourse to compel payment, few receive health insurance or pensions, and few have good access to social services. China makes this explicit by the restriction on establishing legal residency in urban areas. These restrictions imply that total employment in the city is artificially smaller than its most efficient size. Allowing employment to grow to its peak efficient level could raise production by as much as 35 percent.[78] Rural migrants without residency permits have to pay significantly more for education, health, and other public services.[79] The government clearly recognized these issues, and is making policy changes to gradually delink the residency permit system from its welfare program, and to strengthen enforcement of labor regulations.[80]

Restrictions on rural-urban migration, not unique to China, show up in various guises in many countries. Such restrictions tend to depress wages in rural areas relative to urban areas, whereas allowing population flows out of rural areas tends to raise wages for those remaining in rural villages, and benefits the country as a whole by improving efficient allocation of labor.[81] Many youth also pursue opportunities to work overseas, whether they are from rural or urban areas. Issues of international migration, including country policies, are taken up in chapter 8.

Choosing to work and developing the skills to do so

Young people around the world ask, when should I start to work? What kind of job do I want? How do I look for it? How do I get ready for work? Preparing youth for employment starts with general education that provides the foundation for later acquisition of vocational skills. These vocational skills are acquired in the formal education system and beyond—in apprenticeship, work experience, and nonformal training.

Those who want to work on their own need information, mentoring, and credit.

Skill development beyond schools

In middle-income countries with growing industrial sectors, the bridges between school and work, meant to address youth's lack of work experience and severe skill mismatches, take the form of formal apprenticeships or bringing work experience into the school context. In low-income countries with limited formal schooling, traditional apprenticeships are more widespread and more likely to provide the initial experience and skills youth need. In all countries, training systems must not only prepare youths for entry to work, but provide pathways for continual learning over a lifetime in response to changing technologies and global economic requirements. Increasing the incentives for firms to train and to reform training systems is essential.

Formal apprenticeship schemes. Germany's "dual system" combines part-time schooling with work and apprenticeship. Employer involvement ensures that the skills offered fit the needs of employers, reducing the likelihood of skill mismatches. The program has wide coverage: more than half of all youth undertake an apprenticeship. As in Germany, alternative school-based paths to qualifications in France, the United Kingdom, and the United States are associated with rather selective improvements in early labor market experience.[82] Overall, the strongest evidence favoring formal apprenticeships is the positive impact on employment for young men, and on earnings for young women.

Do apprenticeships apply to developing countries? Probably not, in their current format, because of the small share of employment in the modern wage sector, the slow growth of wage employment and jobs for new apprentices, and the weakness of institutions.[83] Some developing countries have tried the dual system, but with no clear pattern of success. The Mubarak-Kohl initiative in Egypt, launched to introduce the dual system in 1995, illustrates the challenges to starting such initiatives. Early reports from the ILO indicated resistance in the public education system and the absence of private sector umbrella organizations to manage joint training courses.[84]

"Lack of experience is the main barrier that young people face while seeking employment, because most employers prefer a few years of work experience."

— Rahat, 24, Bangladesh

To succeed, these programs need to move beyond the traditional craft and technical trades and provide more general content as a foundation for occupational specialization. This could reduce mismatches in growing sectors, promote adaptability, and reduce gender bias. The United Kingdom's Modern Apprenticeship program offers apprenticeships in nontraditional trades in business administration, retailing, catering, personal care, and information technology; women constitute nearly half the apprentices. Australia's New Apprenticeships combine practical work and structured training, leading to nationally recognized qualification in more than 500 occupations. It is not clear how well these types of programs will perform in low-income countries.[85]

Traditional apprenticeships in low-income countries. Formal apprenticeships in the modern wage sector may be less relevant in many developing countries, where self-employment and the growth of microenterprises in the informal sector have accounted for an expanded share of employment over the past three decades. In Ghana, 80–90 percent of all basic skills training comes from traditional apprenticeships, compared with 5–10 percent from public training institutions and 10–15 percent from nongovernment sources.[86] Across West Africa, it is common to find more apprentices than wage employees in informal sector firms.[87] The strengths of traditional apprenticeships, while not carefully evaluated, are their practical orientation, self-regulation, and self-financing. They cater to individuals who lack the educational requirements for formal training (rural and urban poor), and they are generally cost-effective. However, they favor young men, screen out applicants from very poor households, perpetuate traditional technologies, and lack standards and quality assurance.[88]

Steps to strengthen traditional apprenticeship include improving literacy and the basic education of apprentices, opening access to new technologies, improving the pedagogical and technical skills of master craftsmen, and certifying skills attained. In Kenya's Jua Kali, the informal sector, vouchers enhanced the access of master craftsmen to new technologies and upgraded their skills, improv-

ing the quality and relevance of the training they could offer apprentices.[89] The vouchers helped create a market for training that encouraged new sources of supply and competition. Providing literacy and basic education for apprentices and certifying their skills on completion also improve outcomes.

Training by employers. Bringing work experience into the schooling context can improve the youth transition to work (chapter 3); at the same time employers provide and finance training on and off the job long after youth exit school. As a source of skills for youths, employers are often overlooked in favor of public training programs. Surveys conducted by the World Bank in 37 countries covering 18,217 manufacturing firms show that enterprises are active trainers.[90] Nearly 60 percent of firms in East Asia and the Pacific provide training with the share falling to just under 20 percent in the Middle East and North Africa.

Leaving training to enterprises does not, however, ensure access for all to training. Enterprises often are less likely to invest in skills widely used by other enterprises for fear of losing trained workers and their investment. Thus, not all firms will train, nor will all workers in enterprises be trained. In Colombia, Indonesia, Malaysia, Mexico, and Taiwan, China, large manufacturing firms are more likely to train than smaller ones.[91] Kenya, Zambia, and Zimbabwe show a similar pattern, with manufacturing firms employing 151 or more workers being twice as likely to invest in external training for their workers as those employing 51 to 150, and more than 10 times as likely as those with firms of 10 or fewer workers. Firms with a higher likelihood of training are those that export, have foreign investment, and adopt new technologies—and they are more likely to train workers with more education.[92] Other firms will need financial incentives to train young inexperienced workers. Policies can also condition the participation in other programs (like wage subsidies for new entrants) on the provision of training for young workers.

Technical and vocational education and training. Because not all firms can pro-

"To avoid jobs like house servants and cleaners, youth programs can include training in other jobs like catering, carpentry, and building."

Jack, 16, Zambia

vide training and because not all young workers benefit from employer training, public interventions are needed. Training offered by employers is relevant and effective, but that provided by the public sector is subject to question. Rigid, low-quality training systems disconnected from labor markets have led many countries to reform their programs. Nonformal training systems outside formal education are changing the way providers are governed, managed, and financed (chapter 3). China, Chile, the Islamic Republic of Iran, the Republic of Korea, Malaysia, Mozambique, and Singapore, recognizing the fiscal limits of public provision, have opened the doors to public-private partnerships to diversify financing for training, promote sustainability, and improve access and relevance. In Latin America, but also other regions, the roles of government as financier and provider of training (Servicio Nacional de Aprendizaje or SENA, for example) are being reassessed for national training agencies.[93] Specialized training agencies, responsible for training policies and strategies, are assuming a larger role in policy development and management of training expenditures instead of provision. These are also opening more competition between public and private providers to improve quality and relevance of the training offered.

In Mauritius, the Industrial Vocational Training Board has split the financing and provision of training and adopted a competitive model for procuring training services. Argentina and Chile have similar national bodies. In Chile, the Servicio Nacional de Capacitación y Empleo (SENCE), a specialized agency of the Ministry of Labor, maintains no capacity for the provision of training and instead procures training services from other public and private providers for target groups. Competition promotes efficiency in delivery and more closely links training to market demands, shifting the financing model for training from supply-driven to demand-driven.[94]

Overall, training systems are moving away from a narrow focus on inputs for training, with more instructors, workshops, and equipment—to a focus on outcomes, with attention to skills standards set by employers and competency-based delivery by a mixture of public and private provision, measuring performance in terms of job placement and increased worker productivity. Curricula developed in a modular fashion promote flexible entry and exit for training consistent with a lifelong learning model. Sound monitoring and evaluation programs are important in guiding reforms, policy development, and market operations.

Starting work on their own: Self-employment and youth entrepreneurs

Many young people in the labor market work in businesses they have started on their own.[95] Some are entrepreneurs by necessity, others by opportunity.[96] In Latin America, 13 percent of those 16–24 are in entrepreneurial activities, the great majority (12 percent) self-employed; only 1 percent are employers. The self-employed are generally less educated and poorer than employers. Women make up about one-third of the self-employed entrepreneurs and about one-quarter of the employers.

Of the unemployed in Peru in 1998, 18 percent became self-employed by 2001, compared with only 6 percent in Nicaragua (table 4.1). The higher self-employment in Peru explains part of the lower persistence of joblessness in Peru. About half the young

Table 4.1 Employment transitions for youth (ages 16–30)

Status in 1998	Status in 2001			
	Unemployed or inactive (%)	Employee (%)	Self-employed (%)	Employer (%)
Peru				
Unemployed or inactive	33	24	18	2
Employee	7	28	13	1
Self-employed	13	25	52	1
Employer	9	9	55	27
Nicaragua				
Unemployed or inactive	60	18	7	0
Employee	25	59	23	17
Self-employed	11	23	45	9
Employer	3	17	40	31

Source: Llisteri and others (2006).
Note: Not included in the table are students and those in unpaid family work.

"I do not want to be a babshahi [Bengali word for businessman, implying small businessman]. I want to be a bijnizman [after the English word, implying large scale business]."

Male young person, Bangladesh

people self-employed in 1998 were still self-employed three years later. Nine percent of the self-employed in Nicaragua had become employers within three years, but only 1 percent in Peru. And only a third of employers in 1998 continued to be employers in 2001, the majority becoming self-employed or paid employed. All in all, these patterns suggest that self-employment is a faster route to paid employment, but if it persists over the medium term, it is not likely to create additional jobs.

In Latin American countries, about half of entrepreneurs felt motivated to strike out on their own just after secondary and tertiary school and during their first labor experience, using the knowledge, skills, and contacts they had acquired.[97] They come mainly from middle- or upper-middle-class families, about half of them from families with at least one entrepreneurial parent. More than half are graduates starting their business within two years of leaving university. This small group is responsible for a disproportionate part of the jobs created by new companies. In Argentina, for instance, five years after their creation, about 6 percent of the new firms are responsible for 60 percent of the jobs in survivor firms from that cohort.[98]

These entrepreneurs face several constraints to creating and growing a venture: access to financing, to formal networks, and to clients, suppliers, and skilled workers. The Global Entrepreneurship Monitor indicates only a very small share of these entrepreneurships are able to succeed. Young Latin American entrepreneurs face higher transaction costs than those in East Asia. Most of them use their networks (mainly production networks of clients and suppliers and social networks of family and friends) to overcome obstacles and make their ventures grow. General policies that enhance the environment for doing business are not youth-specific but are needed to facilitate entrepreneurship in general.

However, because youth lack the networks, experience, and collateral of adults, they face additional constraints. Several new programs to promote entrepreneurship have been initiated in Latin America, but they are fairly new and have not been formally evaluated. They are targeted to

entrepreneurs with high-growth potential, frequently founded by young middle-class people. Universities, business schools, private foundations, incubators, angel investor networks, and, more recently, some governments provide direct support to the entrepreneur—networking, incubation, mentoring, and financing. For example, Endeavor (a program in Argentina, Brazil, Chile, Mexico, and Uruguay) helps young ventures in a second round of growth mainly through networking (with private investors) and mentoring.

The public sector in some countries has started to support entrepreneurs close to or just after start-up. The Umsobomvu Youth Fund is a development fund in South Africa created by the government to support access to information, skills development, and financial support for people under age 35. Softex in Brazil, a public-private partnership, targets university students in software, providing training courses, technical assistance, and networking support. In Chile, a seed capital program led by CORFO (Corporación de Fomento de la Producción) provides finance and technical assistance to entrepreneurs, operating a public-private partnership with universities and incubators to identify and evaluate the most promising ventures and prepare them for seed capital. This program was replicated by the Buenos Aires Emprende 1 and scaled up by Emprende 2 by large public universities and trade chambers fostering software entrepreneurs.

Providing a springboard to reintegrate the most vulnerable

Vulnerable young people—those who started work too early, never attended school, failed to acquire literacy, or never made it to the workforce—need a second chance. Some disadvantaged youth—such as those with disabilities, ethnic minorities, and orphans—never had even a first chance. Providing them with the relevant skills to enter or reenter the workforce reduces inequities in the labor market and increases their productivity and ability to break out of poverty traps. Because second chances are costly, they have to be well-targeted, designed to increase youth skills, and geared to labor market needs. Because young people in need of second chances are usually vulnerable along several dimensions, programs have to be comprehensive.

Second-chance programs are costly but needed

Policies and programs for second chances are typically costly and rarely successful. Meager and Evans (1998) observe that "it is rapidly becoming conventional wisdom in the policy evaluation literature that labor market training and re-training schemes for the unemployed have not lived up to expectations." A recent review of 19 programs, five of them in transition and developing countries, shows that training programs rarely improve the employment and earnings of young participants.[99] The results underline the importance of having universal access to first-chance policies and programs. In some cases, however, the costs of not intervening are overwhelming, and if well designed, second chances could be cost effective.

An estimated 8.4 million children are engaged in what international conventions call the "unconditional worst" forms of child labor, which include child trafficking, prostitution, and other forms of extremely hazardous work. About 10–12 percent of the population in developing countries is estimated to be disabled, and some evidence suggests they are disproportionately poor.[100] Young people with disabilities, as well as youth from ethnic minority groups, invariably face more difficulties finding employment, despite the evidence that they can be productive given the right support (box 4.6). From an equity perspective, public intervention is needed to support the most vulnerable and to offer them a second chance to reintegrate into the workplace. For the very young, some second-chance opportunities could reintegrate them into the education system (chapter 3). For the large pool of low-skilled unemployed youth, a second chance could help them move into productive work.

What might make for successful programs?

Not enough evaluations of youth employment interventions are available to provide

---

BOX 4.6   *Employing youth with disabilities*

In addition to the usual challenges youth face finding employment, disabled youth face a lack of access to jobs and employment centers because of stigma and other barriers. In particular, disabled people have often been denied an education: About one-third of all children not in primary school have a disability. In Brazil, while 55 percent of 18- to 19-year-olds are employed, only 29 percent of physically disabled youths and 24 percent of mentally disabled youths have jobs. This lack of education and employment sets them up for a lifetime of poverty. In Serbia and Montenegro, 70 percent of disabled people are poor and only 13 percent have access to employment. In Sri Lanka, over 80 percent of the disabled are unemployed.

Evidence from OECD countries shows that disabled youth can be quite productive given the right attitudes and supports, doubly important because disabled youth have greater difficulty recovering from an unsuccessful school-to-work transition. Some OECD countries have instituted national policies on school-to-work transition for disabled youth.

Experience from low- and middle-income countries also demonstrates that disabled youth can be integrated into the labor market. In Egypt, Ethiopia, and Uganda, organizations are empowering disabled youths and their parents to plan for and pursue employment. In Pakistan many disabled youth are employed at Independent Living Centers.

The Salva Vita Foundation in Hungary has run a program since 1996 to integrate the disabled into the general workforce:

- The Supported Employment Service assists in job placement, offers training, and helps solve problems at work.

- The Employees' Club provides individual and group follow-up for clients who have found employment through the Supported Employment Service.

- The Work Experience Program integrates employment into the school curriculum.

Sources: Bercovich (2004); World Bank (2004c); Stapleton and Burkhauser (2003); Tudawe (2001); and www.salvavita.hu.

---

guidance in selecting the right model.[101] Experience suggests, however, that interventions need to require that youth are either working or actively searching for work, provide the skills relevant to integrate or reintegrate them into work, and be delivered efficiently in response to local demand.

Beneficiaries have to work or look for work. Unlike other interventions, such as cash transfers or unemployment insurance, interventions targeting youth need to include either work or active search as conditions to benefit from the programs. Programs in the public sector that focus on the provision of public works to produce needed public goods and services provide good opportunities for young workers, particularly the low skilled and rural, to acquire initial work experience. Few evaluations have tested whether these programs improve the chances of participants to enter the labor market and enhance employment in the private sector. One positive example is Argentina's Trabajar program, which had a significant impact on participants' current income.[102] There

"Discrimination forms the biggest challenge given the social exclusion of disabled persons from society. Most of the disabled youth haven't accomplished their education due to lack of support, hence they have a skill deficit [relative to] the job market."

Frederick, 23, Kenya

is also some evidence of lagged gains from past participation. Among continuing participants in this program, about half felt that it improved their chances of getting a job, two-thirds that it gave them a marketable skill, and about one-third that it expanded their contacts.[103]

The African AGETIP (Agence d'Exécution des Travaux d'Intérêt Publique) programs combine efforts to build public infrastructure such as roads, buildings, and sanitation systems, with efforts to provide jobs and training for unemployed youth. Construction firms that get the contracts also agree to use relatively labor-intensive practices to use local inexperienced youth who receive training funded by AGETIP. The youth are hired on a temporary basis, but the training and work experience are important inroads to later, more permanent employment. Because the public works projects are local, they can be targeted geographically to assist relatively poor, uneducated, or unemployed areas of the population.

The evaluation of the first seven years of the AGETIP program in Senegal found that the number of engineering firms more than tripled, the number of construction firms increased fivefold, and 35,000 person-years of employment were generated. Unfortunately, governance can be an issue.[104] Public works projects require transparency and oversight to ensure that the projects are targeted to the poor, that only worthy projects are funded, that the money is used wisely, and that inexperienced youth are trained.

Public works provide good targeting for other youth interventions that could increase the likelihood of youth finding better employment opportunities beyond the program. Argentina's Proempleo experiment in 1998–2002 tested mechanisms to help participants in the public works program (Trabajar) find employment in the private sector. It assessed whether wage subsidies and specialized training could assist participants in the transition from workfare to regular work. The wage subsidy increased the probability of becoming employed in the private sector by 9 percentage points for young participants under 30.[105] The wage subsidy and training programs raised private sector employment by 13 percentage points. Interestingly, effects for older cohorts were insignificant, so the successes were confined to youth.

Public employment services should also require youth to be active in job searching. In Korea, the Philippines, and Thailand, however, young people make little use of state labor offices.[106] In those countries, employment offices have been transformed into one-stop centers giving job seekers access to job search assistance and placement in vocational training. In Korea, however, only 5.8 percent of the unemployed found jobs through the public employment services, and even that may overestimate the impact because there were no proper controls to measure the placement rate for people not using the service.

An interesting recent example of private involvement from Brazil is the First Job program started in Curitiba municipality, financed by the local government. It aims to link youth with firms in the municipality (no evaluation is available yet). Another promising public employment program is JobsNet, a quickly growing job-matching agency in Sri Lanka.[107]

Programs should provide the relevant skills. Comprehensive programs that provide training as part of a package that includes basic education, employment services, and social services are more likely to have better success. Entra 21, a global effort intended to prepare 19,000 disadvantaged youth for jobs requiring information and communication technology in 18 countries in Latin America, placed at least 40 percent of the targeted youth in employment. The programs offer a complete range of services, including not just technical and life-skills training but also job placement services, internships, and advice in developing self-employment initiatives. A meta-analysis of six Entra 21 projects revealed a higher than expected job placement rate among 2,890 youths.[108] Employment rates rose from 15 percent at the start to 54 percent 6–12 months later. Most jobs were in the formal sector, permanent, and paid the minimum wage or higher. Although most youth opted for salaried employment, in several coun-

Joven programs increased employment and earnings for some disadvantaged youths

The Joven programs offer comprehensive training to unemployed and economically disadvantaged youths 16 to 29 years of age, aiming to improve their human and social capital and employability. The demand-driven model has been customized throughout Argentina, Chile, Colombia, the Dominican Republic, Panama, Paraguay, Peru, and República Bolivariana de Venezuela. Technical training and internship experiences with employers are combined with basic life skills and other support services to ensure social integration and job readiness (see table). Private and public institutions—contracted through public bidding mechanisms—provide the training and organize the internships.

The programs target the poor, and more than 60 percent of participants come from low-income families. The highest education level completed by beneficiaries was secondary, with significant participation by school dropouts (50 percent in Chile Joven). Other targeting criteria, such as employment, gender, and age, also applied. Most beneficiaries had precarious employment conditions before the program. In Argentina 83 percent of participants, and in Chile 57 percent were unemployed. Women were fairly equally represented in Chile, while Argentina had the lowest female participation (about 40 percent). Targeting focused on 16- to 24-year-olds, about 70 percent of all participants.[109]

Employment

The programs increased the probability of beneficiaries finding employment upon graduation, especially for women. In Argentina, the program increased the probability of employment for young adult women (21 years and older) by about 10 percentage points over a control group. In Chile the program increased the probability of employment 21 percentage points, with strongly significant results for youths 21 and younger.

Earnings

In Argentina the program increased monthly wages by about 10 percent over a control group, with results more favorable for young males and adult females. In Chile one study showed a negative impact on wages of -8.8 percent, led by a reduction of wages in the formal sector. Subsequent analyses found a positive impact on earnings approaching 26 percent, strongly significant for youths 21 and younger. In absolute terms the wage impact was higher for men, but in a comparison of pre- and postprogram earnings, women had a slightly higher increase relative to men.

Costs and benefits

With the given underlying cost per trainee and the impact on employment and earnings, the net present value (NPV) of the program can be calculated (given a discount rate, usually assumed to be 5 percent). While costly, these programs in Argentina and Chile have positive NPVs, with a higher NPV in Chile compared to Argentina. It is important to note that this calculation does not take into account the externalities from the program such as better health outcomes and reductions in risky behavior among participants. In this sense, the estimates are likely to provide only a lower bound of the NPV. It is also important to note that with the exception of forgone earnings, the party incurring the direct costs (public funds) is different from the party benefiting from the program—the participants.

Sources: Aedo and Nuñez (2001); Aedo and Pizarro Valdivia (2004); de Moura Castro (1999); Elias and others (2004); Inter-American Development Bank (2005); and Santiago Consultores Asociados (1999).

Costs and impact of programs varies across countries

	Argentina	Chile
	Proyecto Joven	Chile Joven
Coverage (people)	116,000	165,000
Cost per trainee ($)	2,000	730–930
Private benefits		
Impact on employment (percentage point increase)	10	21
Impact on earnings (percentage point increase)	10	26

tries as many as a quarter set up their own micro businesses.

Employers surveyed by Entra 21 value the combination of life skills and technical skills developed by the program, rating youths' life skills as satisfactory to highly satisfactory in meeting their companies' needs. More than 70 percent of employers said the graduates' potential as workers was equal to or greater than that of other employees in similar positions, and more than 90 percent in four projects rated graduates' overall performance as better than or equal to that of workers in similar positions.

In Argentina, Chile, Peru, and Uruguay the Joven programs have been widely recognized as successful in reaching disadvantaged youth (box 4.7). Their targeting of low-income youths has improved labor placement and earnings for their beneficiaries across Latin America. Critical to their success is the nature of the training—from technical to life skills and from lectures to internships—and the sound support services and course certifications that foster youth's continuing participation.

Skill development should respond to local demand and promote competition among providers. Among the important factors behind the success of the Joven programs are that the demand-oriented approach fosters private participation—and that

Table 4.2 Summary of youth employment policy directions and examples of programs

	Proven successful	Promising but unproven	Unlikely to be successful
Opportunities			
Creating jobs	Trade openness: youth-intensive exporting sectors (Indonesia and Vietnam) Market-oriented reform (Slovenia and Estonia) General labor market reform (Colombia) When minimum wages are too binding, lowering youth minimum wage (Chile)	Wage subsidies and private sector incentives, targeted to unskilled and unemployed (Hungary, Poland, and the Czech Republic)	Schemes guaranteeing public sector jobs for the educated (Morocco, Egypt, Sri Lanka, and Ethiopia) Wage-setting institutions that compress wages (overly high minimum wages, Chile and Brazil) Overly restrictive employment protection laws (Chile, Latin American and Caribbean countries, and OECD countries) Partial labor market reform (reducing employment protection for youth only, or temporary contracts) increases youth turnover, but segments the market (France and Spain)
Reducing child labor	Conditional cash transfers for children vulnerable to child labor (PETI in Brazil, PROGRESA in Mexico, and Human Development Bond Project (BDH) in Ecuador)		
Facilitating mobility	Support for rural nonfarm employment (Taiwan, China's promotion of rural manufacturing)		Restrictions on rural migrants
Capabilities			
Skills development	Apprenticeship programs: successful in Germany, unproven in developing countries Traditional apprenticeship with access to new technologies for master craftsmen (Kenya's Jua Kali program) Enterprise-based training (Ghana, Kenya, and Zimbabwe)	New apprenticeship programs (the United Kingdom and Australia offering apprenticeships in new service sectors) Traditional apprenticeships in the informal sector (mixed evidence from Sub-Saharan Africa) Jobs Net, Sri Lanka matching agency Training vouchers (Malaysia) Reforming training institutes to introduce competition among private and public providers (Mauritius Industrial Vocational Training Board, Chile Servicio National de Capacitación y Empleo)	Slovenia's capitalization program (for entrepreneurs)
Self-employment		Self-employment assistance (Hungary and Poland) Promotion of entrepreneurship (Endeavor program in Argentina, Brazil, Chile, Mexico, and Uruguay) Softex (Brazil) public-private partnership for entrepreneurs Chile CORFO and Buenos Aires Emprende 1 and 2 Empowering youth with disabilities (Pakistan's Independent Living Centers)	
Second chances	Bundled programs (comprehensive) providing training, placement, mentoring, and the like (U.S. Job Corps, Joven programs in Argentina, Chile, Peru, and Uruguay) Public works programs (in low-income countries targeted to the low-skilled and unemployed youth) Proempleo program in Argentina combines public works and wage subsidies	Entra 21 programs including training, soft skills, internship (18 countries in Latin America and the Caribbean) Reintegrating youth with disabilities into the labor market (Hungary Salva Vita Foundation on supported employment and work experience program) AGETIP (Senegal) public works targeting youth Colectivo integral de Desarrollo in Peru Public employment services (Korea, the Philippines, and Thailand)	

competition is promoted among training providers. Transferring the Joven model to other developing countries requires strong institutions to manage a decentralized program and to coordinate the goals and operations of training institutions and participating companies. It also requires continual evaluation of the quality of the courses and internships and the performance of training institutions.

In sum, roadblocks on the way to work have implications for youth themselves and on development and poverty reduction efforts. Policy makers need to consider strategies to delay youth from going to work too early, to smooth the entry to the workforce, and to allow movement toward better quality work (table 4.2). In all countries, a better investment climate, a well-functioning labor market, and an expanding nonfarm rural sector broaden employment opportunities for everybody, and youth could benefit more than adults. Other interventions are youth-specific, designed to fit individual country contexts:

- In middle-income countries, reforming labor market institutions to better accommodate new entrants and providing financial incentives for firms to hire young workers will broaden youth opportunities. Building more bridges between school and work and increasing access to information will enhance the ability of youth to take advantage of these opportunities.

- In low-income countries, building on basic skills through better-designed formal and informal apprenticeship will improve relevance to the needs of a changing labor market and facilitate youth transition to work. A mix of public work programs, wage subsidies, internships, and training provides a springboard to reintegrate the most vulnerable back into productive employment.

Do baby booms lead to employment busts? Not in OECD countries

The post–World War II OECD baby boom offers lessons on how to absorb large youth cohorts into the labor market. What groups are most affected? What policies help youth most? Do bad policy choices cause more damage to youth employment prospects than large youth populations?

Youth unemployment in OECD countries is due to weak demand and bad policy and not the baby boom

One year after the end of World War II and for about 20 years thereafter, the G-7 countries experienced a surge in the birth rate relative to periods before and since. As a result, an unusually large share of youth entered the labor force from the mid-1960s until the early 1980s, with the peak occurring between 1967 and 1973 (figure 1). Since then, the youth share of the labor market has fallen steadily.

One might expect that youth in the baby boom cohorts would have had much more difficulty finding work than would the relatively small youth cohorts entering the labor market in the 1990s. The opposite is true, however: average youth unemployment rates across the G-7 countries are 7 percentage points higher than during the peak of the baby boom. In contrast, adult

Figure 1   Youth unemployment rates for the G-7 countries are higher now than during the baby boom

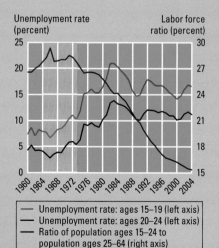

Unemployment rate (percent) — left axis / Labor force ratio (percent) — right axis

— Unemployment rate: ages 15–19 (left axis)
— Unemployment rate: ages 20–24 (left axis)
— Ratio of population ages 15–24 to population ages 25–64 (right axis)

Source: Authors' compilations based on data provided by OECD Database on Labour Force Statistics.
Note: Shaded portion of the figure indicates peak baby boom entry years.

unemployment rates in the G-7 countries have risen less than 2 percentage points.

Youth unemployment rates did rise modestly as the baby boom cohort entered the labor market. However, the unemployment rates are affected much more by the overall strength of the labor market.[1] Youth unemployment is extremely sensitive to the business cycle: youth benefit greatly when labor demand is increasing, but suffer disproportionately when the economy is in recession or growing slowly. One lesson from the Organisation for Economic Co-operation and Development (OECD) countries is that even a modest deterioration in the strength of labor demand, measured by the rising unemployment rate for older workers in OECD countries, has increased the difficulty in the transition from school to work.

The less educated and minority youth have the greatest problems with unemployment

Are youth receiving too much education so that they become overqualified for the jobs that are available? No. Evidence suggests that the least educated face the greatest mismatch between skills and job vacancies. In almost every industrial economy, average unemployment rates fall as years of schooling increase.

Nor does job training tend to reduce the disadvantage faced by the less educated. The gap in access to jobs continues as the cohorts age because the most educated get the most job training. College graduates in OECD countries are seven times more likely to receive training than are high school dropouts. Similarly dramatic gaps in access to training exist between the highest and lowest literacy groups.

Unemployment rates are uniformly higher for minority youth in OECD countries. Such groups are atypically disadvantaged by recessions and by policies that tend to limit new job creation. They are also atypically disadvantaged in completing edu-

cation, compounding disadvantages related to discrimination in the labor market. In France, where government statistics do not recognize ethnicity, youth unemployment rates in predominantly ethnic urban enclaves are around 40 percent, nearly twice the already high French average.

High youth unemployment can cause youth and the country permanent harm

Does early unemployment cause permanent scarring of youth, resulting in employment difficulties later in life? Answers vary. In the United States, most studies find that spells of unemployment after leaving school do not result in persistent unemployment later in life. This corresponds to fairly high transition rates from unemployment into employment: 46 percent of unemployed youth are employed one month later.

Corresponding transition rates in France, Germany, and the United Kingdom are much lower, ranging from 4 to 14 percent, and more evidence indicates that early unemployment results in persistent unemployment. One-third of the unemployed in France have been unemployed more than a year, compared with 8.5 percent in the United States. The persistent adverse effects of early unemployment on later employment stability can last seven years in France, compared with two in the United States.[2] The degree of persistence appears to respond to business cycles, with less permanent damage from early unemployment in economies experiencing job growth. In addition, the scarring effect of early unemployment tends to be greatest for the least educated and for disadvantaged youth.[3]

Weak youth labor markets tend to delay other transitions. In Europe, the average age at which youth leave the home has increased, especially in southern European countries. In Italy, 80 percent of males ages 18–30 still live with their parents, compared with 25 percent in the United States. Across OECD countries, the average age of marriage has increased while the average number of children per household has fallen.

Weakening youth labor markets have at least a partial role in explaining these changes in life transitions. Youth tend to delay leaving their parents' homes during recessions. Differences in the relative strength of country youth labor markets can explain observed differences across countries in the average age of home leaving.[4] In Germany and Spain, the likelihood of leaving home increases significantly with youth employment status and labor earnings.[5]

When youth face constraints in access to legal employment, they may engage in illegal activities. Studies in the United States and the United Kingdom show that weakening wages for low-skilled youth are correlated with increases in criminal activity.[6] Less consistent evidence links long-term youth unemployment with crime, although discontent with high rates of youth unemployment in minority communities has been cited as a contributing factor to unrest. One recent study in France shows that cities with higher youth unemployment have higher rates of burglaries, thefts, and drug offenses.[7]

Efforts to protect job security do not help and may hinder youth

The youth unemployment problem appears to be exacerbated by policies aimed at preserving jobs. Many countries have enacted Employment Protection Legislation (EPL) that makes it more difficult or costly for firms to lay off workers. These policies are designed to insure workers against income loss from fluctuations in labor demand. However, such legislation also makes it more costly for firms to hire workers, thus stricter EPL tends to depress the rate of new job creation.[8]

These adverse consequences of EPL are borne mostly by groups that are disproportionately first-time job seekers, so youth tend to be atypically disadvantaged.[9] Because EPL appears to retard new job creation, it can also heighten the persistent effects of early unemployment on employment prospects later in life.

Stricter employment protection legislation does not appear to create unemployment problems for older workers and may even insulate them from competition with

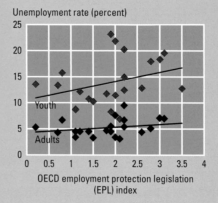

Figure 2 Employment protection hurt OECD youth, but not adults, in 2003

Unemployment rate (percent)

OECD employment protection legislation (EPL) index

Source: Authors' compilations based on information presented in OECD (2004).
Note: In the figure, youth are those ages 15–24; adults are those ages 25–54. Correlation with EPL index is 0.32 for youth and 0.27 for adults. Each data point in the graph represents one country.

younger workers (figure 2). In eras of both large and small youth cohorts, stricter EPL is correlated with higher youth unemployment rates.

Similar findings hold for legislation that diminishes wage flexibility, such as high minimum wages or extending union-negotiated wages to nonunion workers. Such policies reduce wage inequality across workers, but risk making it too expensive to hire those lacking schooling or prior labor market experience.

Many of the countries with the strongest youth labor market outcomes over the past 15 years (Ireland, the Netherlands, New Zealand, the United Kingdom, the United States) have tended to be those with rising wage inequality. The implication is that wage flexibility has helped these economies to adjust to shocks and to create new job opportunities for youth, but at a cost of increased income disparities in the population.[10]

Countries with stronger EPL have experienced growth in temporary and fixed-term jobs that are frequently exempt from firing restrictions. This allows new job growth, but it creates dual labor markets with protected jobs held predominantly by "insiders" (older male workers) and temporary jobs held by "outsiders" (women, minorities, and youth). Insiders have an incentive to maintain and expand employ-

ment protection, which protects their jobs at the expense of youth and other outsiders. Perhaps that is why all but a few countries have found it so difficult to relax the employment protection, even when their youth unemployment rates are so high.

Efforts to fix the youth labor market have mixed success

OECD countries have used various policies to try to fix youth unemployment. One option that appears unsuccessful is to try to "make room" for youth employment by encouraging older workers to retire. The limited evidence suggests that older and younger workers may be complements and not substitutes in production. Countries with higher retirement ages for men and women have higher employment rates for male and female youth.[11] Similarly, efforts in France to limit hours of work to force firms to hire additional workers appear not to have resulted in appreciable job growth.

The average OECD country spends around 2 percent of GDP on active labor market policies, with training being the largest component of those expenditures. Public expenditures are only about one-tenth of the total, however, and private training is weighted heavily toward the most educated. Private training is unlikely to offer a significant second-chance option for those who failed to attain a sufficient level of prior education. Publicly subsidized training tends to have the greatest success with more-educated recipients.

The experience of youth training programs in Europe suggests that they have improved the transition to employment but that the impact on earnings is more mixed.[12]

Of other active labor market policies, job search assistance and wage subsidies appear to be the most promising for raising employment rates of disadvantaged youth, but public employment programs have not worked. Evidence also suggests that youth are more successful in transitioning to employment in countries where unemployment benefits are conditioned on active job search and willingness to accept jobs when offered.[13]

Growing up healthy

If death rates are the benchmark, the young are a healthy group, and today's young are healthier than at any time in history. This presents an unprecedented opportunity for further investment and growth. Young people in developing countries have a mortality rate of less than 3 percent, down significantly over the past 20 years, and a fraction of that for infants and adults.[1]

Average mortality is a misleading measure, however, because it does not reflect the behavior that puts health at risk later in life. A more appropriate benchmark would reflect such behaviors as tobacco use, drug use, excessive alcohol consumption, sexual behavior that increases the likelihood of sexually transmitted diseases, and inadequate diet and physical activity. These behaviors affect youth while they are still young: for example, unprotected sex can lead to HIV infection or an unplanned pregnancy. However, most of the adverse consequences show up only when they grow older, in such noncommunicable diseases as lung cancer, diabetes, and heart disease.

Good health is not equally available to all young people. Although mortality among young people is low on average, and young people are fairly healthy, their likelihood of premature death is much higher in poor countries. The average 15-year-old boy has a 90 percent chance of surviving to the age of 60 in Western Europe or North America, but only a 50 percent chance in Sub-Saharan Africa, primarily due to the spread of communicable diseases such as AIDS. In countries hardest hit by AIDS, the probability is only 20 percent.[2]

Young people today have access to a much broader range of choices than previously available, in a vastly different environment, which makes it harder to choose appropriately and to avoid behavior that puts their health at risk. Awareness of the consequences of decisions for health, and of ways to avoid ill health, is very low among young people, especially girls, and only a small percentage of those aware actually adopt safe behavior. Young people are thus likely to make uninformed decisions about behaviors that put their health at risk.

Risky behavior during youth can deplete productive human capital many years into the future. Long after tobacco smoking peaked in the United States, tobacco was the single largest cause of all lung cancer deaths, and about half of those who died were still in middle age. In some developing countries today, close to half of all young men are smokers. Similarly, HIV develops into AIDS with a lag of up to 10 years, taking its toll on people in their prime working ages. In many developing countries, new HIV infections affect young people disproportionately. The costs of treating AIDS and such chronic diseases as cancers, diabetes, and heart disease are high, and the treatments often ineffective.

The best way to avoid the future loss of productive human capital and steep increases in future health care expenditure is to modify health behavior during youth, when habits are still being learned. Policies to promote better health for young people rest on three legs. First, give them the knowledge to help them make informed choices about their behavior—and the skills to negotiate safe behavior with peers and partners. Second, create an environment for the young to practice healthful behavior, making risky behavior costly, and limiting the opportunities for it. Third, for young people harmed by poor health decisions or environments, provide health services, treatment, and rehabilitation. Broadening access to these services—whether dealing with unwanted pregnancies, obesity, or drug addiction—will minimize the long-term consequences and lead to better health.

The health concerns facing young people differ greatly around the world. As the Global Burden of Diseases project shows, leading causes of death and disability for young people include injuries in Latin America and HIV/AIDS in Africa.[3] This chapter focuses on the factors that are common to all youth health issues. Rather than focusing on specific health outcomes, the chapter presents a framework to develop policies that encourage healthier behavior among youth.

Promoting the health of young people stimulates growth and reduces poverty and health care expenditures

Although the death rate for young people ages 12–24 is less than 3 percent, and young people are generally healthy, their continuing health and survival into adulthood are at risk, largely because of their behavior as youth. It has been estimated that nearly two-thirds of premature deaths and one-third of the total disease burden of adults can be associated with conditions or behavior begun in youth.[4] Policies that encourage healthful behavior among youth, by improving their productivity and health as adults, will have ripple effects on the economy.

Impact on poverty reduction and growth

Risky health behavior during youth can deplete the economy of productive human capital for many years into the future. The prevalence of smoking among U.S. males peaked before 1945, but since then, with smoking rates more or less unchanged, the deaths attributed to lung cancer increased nearly fourfold, and among smokers twentyfold (figure 5.1). Some developing countries, in which half of young men are smokers, face the burden of enormous health costs in 20 or 30 years.

Heavy alcohol consumption and drug use reduce productivity and increase absenteeism and other health-related costs to firms and individuals.[5] Drug abuse is concentrated among 18- to 25-year-olds—

Figure 5.1   In the United States, mortality from lung cancer among men increased dramatically for nearly 40 years after smoking peaked

Deaths per 100,000 males

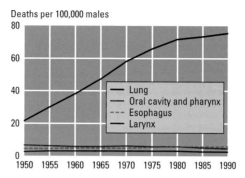

Source: Centers for Disease Control and Prevention (1993).
Note: Deaths per 100,000 population are standardized to the 1970 age distribution of the U.S. population.

just when they are entering the workforce. It can make a job search more difficult, and being unemployed can make drug abuse more attractive. Unemployment and illicit drug-taking are strongly correlated, in both developed and developing countries. In Colombia, the prevalence of cocaine use was 4.1 percent for the unemployed, 0.4 percent for the employed.[6] In Russia, severe alcohol consumption is associated with a higher probability of job loss.[7] Countries with higher rates of alcohol consumption among youth also report higher rates of motor vehicle deaths and suicides among youth. More than half of deaths due to homicide or traffic accidents in South Africa and Brazil had blood alcohol levels in excess of legal limits.[8] Traffic accidents are among the leading causes of death and disability in developing countries. Accidents are estimated to cost low- and middle-income countries $65 billion per year, or between 1 and 1.5 percent of gross national product.[9]

Safe health behavior, by contrast, can encourage greater investment in productive human and physical capital. Longer life expectancy may lead to higher investments in secondary school, just as higher mortality due to HIV/AIDS may reduce the gains from investments in children accumulated during the past generation. HIV and AIDS reduce savings and investments in productive physical capital among the poor, thus reducing the likelihood that poor youths escape poverty.[10] African parents have responded to the higher mortality risk from HIV/AIDS by having more children and providing each of them with less education.[11]

Impact on health care expenditures

Addictions, exercise patterns, and eating habits are hard to change, harder as people mature and become set in their ways. A longitudinal study from Indonesia finds that the proportion of men who smoked in 2000 was almost identical to the proportion who had ever smoked since 1993, suggesting that very few smokers quit.[12] Modifying health behavior during youth, when habits are still being learned, is a much more effective means of preventing unsustainable increases in health care expenditures. Treatment, especially for such noncommunicable diseases as cancers, diabetes, and heart disease, is expensive and often ineffective. In adulthood, when adverse health consequences become visible, both the behavior and the consequences are irreversible.

Consider the consequences. Smoking increases the risk of general health problems, the susceptibility to severe respiratory illnesses, and the risk of dying from lung cancer.[13] Excessive alcohol consumption leads to greater alcohol dependence, more alcohol-related injuries, and other psychological and physical problems later in life. Substance abuse can lead to addictions; to circulatory, respiratory, and digestive diseases; to accidental overdose; and to the greater risk of acquiring HIV and AIDS. Poor nutrition and a lack of exercise can lead to obesity, which causes hypertension, cardiovascular diseases, type-2 diabetes, and many other chronic diseases in youth and adulthood.[14] Early sex, unprotected sex, and having multiple partners can lead to HIV/AIDS and other sexually transmitted diseases. Almost all HIV infections in 2001 in Africa and parts of Latin America, and about a quarter in Eastern Europe, can be attributed to unsafe sex.[15]

Now consider the costs. Providing health care to a drug addict costs about 80 percent more than providing it to an average person in the same age group,[16] and by one estimate, tobacco use results in a global net loss of $200 billion a year.[17] Individual country studies estimate the net cost of tobacco use at between 0.03 percent and 0.40 percent of GDP—costs expected to rise as young smokers age and begin to suffer the consequences.[18]

Caring for AIDS patients is squeezing the resources and care available to HIV-negative patients. In South Africa, patients are turned away from hospitals because of limited beds,[19] and Kenya has seen higher mortality among HIV-negative patients.[20] From 1988 to 1992, the average number of people admitted per day to a Nairobi hospital who were *not* infected with HIV fell by 18 percent while the number of HIV-infected more than doubled.[21] Although there is no evidence that health workers risk infection more than the general population, the fear of infection, plus the greater demand for health care and the overwhelming tide of dying patients, has accelerated their burnout.[22]

Public intervention is needed to promote youth health

Governments around the world try to reduce risky behavior—through tobacco control; regulation of alcohol consumption; and public messages about diet, nutrition, and safe sex. Such public intervention is justified because of market failures that dominate health behavior and cause individuals to make privately and socially inferior health decisions, and these market failures are magnified for young people. Private markets do not facilitate optimal decision making by individuals for a number of reasons. One problem is that individuals have incomplete information about the consequences of their behavior over time. They do not know whether or when they might face the adverse consequences of their behavior. Unprotected sex and excess tobacco and alcohol consumption are risky, but the risks are difficult for young people to quantify (see boxes 2.7 and 2.9). They might find risky behavior attractive or convenient in the short run, or believe that experimenting with such behavior is safe, or be coerced into engaging in it.

Even if the consequences of poor environments or decisions are purely private, public action can still be justified—on the grounds of merit or concern for equality. Good health is often accepted as a *merit good:* something socially accepted as beneficial for people, regardless of their feelings in the matter. Equity also matters, because the poor are likely to be less healthy than the nonpoor. This is most obviously manifest in differences in life expectancy. In Brazil, the life expectancy for young men between the ages of 10 and 19 from the poorest quintile is 38.0 years, and for young women 35.8 years. For young men from the wealthiest quintile, it rises to 49.7 and for young women to 53.1. Poverty cuts 12 years from the expected life of a young man, and more than 17 years from the life of a young woman.[23]

The rest of the section describes only some of the risky health behaviors—unprotected sex, tobacco use, drug use, excessive alcohol consumption, physical inactivity, and unhealthy diet—that arise from the market failures described above. While governments intervene in these areas in many ways, these measures must be better designed to address the unique market failures young people face when making choices about their behavior.

Health behavior, imperfect information, and inequality

Individuals may not have good information about the risks they face today, even if they understand the risks over time. Some information, such as HIV status, is easily withheld from partners, and during the early and more virulent stages of many infections, infected persons may be unaware of their true status. These external risks are also present where individuals suffer from the behavior of others over which they have no control. The most obvious case is second-hand tobacco smoke, but other ostensibly private behaviors can have consequences for others, especially if the costs of later treatment are passed on to the wider community.

Imperfect information and risky sex. More than half the young in many countries are sexually active, and data from surveys conducted between the late 1990s and 2004 show that the proportion who initiated sexual activity before the age of 15 is increasing.[24] A significant proportion of youth in developing countries—especially girls—are sexually active within marriage or informal unions, but many unmarried youth are also sexually active. Evidence indicates that the

age at menarche (first menstruation) has declined for girls, and the average age at marriage is increasing.[25] A study based on 27 Sub-Saharan African countries shows that this rise in age at marriage is linked to the increase in the percentage of young people who engage in premarital sex.[26]

Imperfect knowledge about consequences can lead people to engage in unprotected sex. Fewer than half of sexually active young people use condoms, even though unprotected sex is the greatest risk factor for HIV transmission in most areas of the world (figure 5.2). Even in countries where HIV prevalence is high, a large proportion of young people engage in unprotected sex. These young people are at greater risk of HIV infection. In Mozambique, a country with moderately high HIV prevalence, sexual activity among youth is common, but condom use is low. The share of sexually active boys using condoms ranges from 20 percent in Mali to about 50 percent in Zambia. Condom use is higher among unmarried sexually active girls than among married girls. In Uganda, slightly more than 50 percent of all unmarried girls used condoms the last time they had sex, compared with only 3 percent of married girls.

Condom use may be lower among young married women than unmarried women because they are planning to bear children. But in Burkina Faso, Kenya, and

Figure 5.2 **Sexually active youth are unlikely to use condoms, even where HIV prevalence is high**

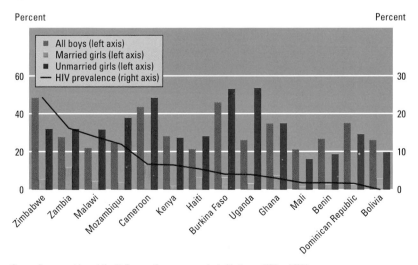

Source: Demographic and Health Surveys for surveys conducted between 1997 and 2004.
Note: Left axis of figure refers to 15- to 24-year-olds who reported using a condom at most recent sexual intercourse.

Zambia fewer than a third of married girls who did not use condoms were planning a pregnancy within two years—the rest were trying to avoid pregnancy.[27] Unprotected sex increases the risk that married young girls will become infected, and recent data from Sub-Saharan Africa show that HIV incidence is growing fastest among young married women. This is primarily because younger women are married to older men, who have a higher chance of being infected (through risky sex with partners outside marriage).[28] One study in rural Uganda found that the HIV infection rate among married women under 20 was nearly three times that of unmarried women under 20 (17 percent compared with 6 percent).[29]

Unequal power and risky sex. Risky sexual behavior is more likely to occur among poor youth, who are in a weaker position to negotiate safe sex, and are more likely to experience coerced sex and sex for exchange.[30] Forced sex exposes young women to the risks of HIV and other sexually transmitted diseases, risks heightened by injuries from physical violence.[31] More than 20 percent of women attending antenatal clinics in Soweto, South Africa, reported having had sex with a "non-primary" male partner in exchange for goods or money.[32] Data from DHS surveys around the world indicate that 13 percent of unmarried women between the ages of 15 and 19 received money or gifts in exchange for sex in the four weeks preceding the survey.[33]

The "sugar daddy" phenomenon is widely observed in Africa and other settings. A survey of 45 studies in Sub-Saharan Africa reports that sex with older unmarried partners is widely accepted among adolescent girls in many countries.[34] There is some evidence that the HIV epidemic has increased the incidence of sex between older men and younger women, as men seek to avoid infection.[35] Women who report transactional sex, controlling for age and number of partners, were 50 percent more likely to be HIV-positive.

Health behavior, habit formation, and irreversibility

Young people lack information partly because they lack experience. Youth is a time of experimentation; this experimentation is partly intended to acquire information about behavior, choices, and consequences, as well as to form a sense of identity and belonging. People, young and old, choose behaviors because of the pleasure and benefits they yield. The pleasure from some of these behaviors is fleeting, while the costs can persist. Experimentation can lead to habits and addictions, which can be destructive and extremely difficult to break.

Preferences may be time-inconsistent, and behaviors can have irreversible consequences. In the future, today's youth will most likely wish they had made different decisions when they were young, especially if they begin to suffer the consequences. For many of these adverse consequences, it is not possible in later life to undo the damage caused by earlier behavior. Treatment, especially for such noncommunicable diseases as cancer, diabetes, and heart disease, is expensive and often ineffective.

Alcohol, tobacco, and drugs. Alcohol is the most widely consumed drug in the world: about half those 15 and older have consumed alcohol in the past year.[36] Patterns are difficult to interpret, because moderate drinking—even by youth—is accepted in many countries. The proportion of young people who report drinking generally exceeds 60 percent, of whom 10 to 30 percent engage in binge drinking (figure 5.3).[37] In the United Kingdom, young people between 16 and 24 are the heaviest drinkers in the population, and the least likely to abstain from drinking.[38] Limited data from developing countries suggest that young people are beginning to drink alcohol at earlier ages. Boys are more likely than girls to drink alcohol, and to drink heavily, though consumption among girls in some countries (especially in Latin America) has begun to approach or even surpass that of young men.

Early initiation of alcohol use is correlated with a greater likelihood of both alcohol dependence and alcohol-related injury. A study of hospitals in three cities in South Africa found that 61 percent of patients admitted to trauma units in these cities were alcohol-positive, including 74 per-

Figure 5.3   Alcohol consumption is common among 15- to 19-year-olds in some countries

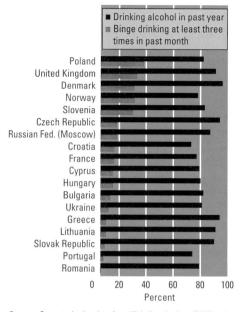

Sources: Computed using data from Hibbell and others (2000) and Bloomfield and others (2003).
Note: "Binge drinking" is defined as consuming five or more drinks in a row.

Figure 5.4   Many young people, especially young men, consume tobacco

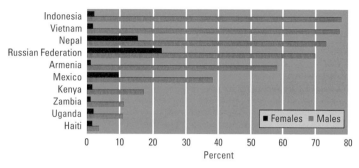

Sources: Indonesia Adolescent and Youth Survey (2002–03) of 15- to 24-year-olds; Mexico current smoking prevalence is based on survey of urban 14- to 22-year-olds; Vietnam Ministry of Health and General Statistics Office, UNICEF, and WHO (2005) surveys of 14- to 25-year-olds; Russia Longitudinal Monitoring Survey (Round 6) (15- to 24-year-olds). Remaining data was obtained from MEASURE Demographic and Health Surveys conducted between 2000 and 2004 (15- to 24-year-olds).
Note: Figure refers to youth who report currently smoking cigarettes or pipes or using other tobacco products.

cent of violence cases, 54 percent of traffic collisions, and 30 percent of trauma from other accidents.[39] Young people who abuse alcohol and drugs are more likely to commit crimes, and substance abuse is a major risk factor in violence.[40] Examination of 960 people arrested in nine police stations in three cities in South Africa found that 22 percent were under the influence of alcohol when the alleged crime took place.[41]

Per capita consumption of tobacco is declining in developed countries, but rising in many developing countries, for both men and women. Between 1970 and 1990, tobacco consumption is estimated to have increased by about 3.4 percent a year in low- and middle-income countries,[42] and people are beginning to smoke at younger ages.[43] Reported use of cigarettes, pipes, and chewing tobacco varies widely (figure 5.4). Most smokers in Indonesia consume clove cigarettes, which contain twice the tar, nicotine, and carbon monoxide of American cigarettes, and smoking among 15- to 19-year-olds rose from 32 percent in 1993 to 43 percent in 2000.[44] Fewer girls than boys report tobacco use, though it may be increasing among girls in developing countries.[45]

Few young people experiment with illegal drugs, and an even smaller number go on to develop long-term chronic problems. Even so, measures to prevent experimental use are worthwhile to avoid addiction and the acute and possibly fatal reactions with even limited experimental use. Young people in developed and developing countries experiment with cannabis, amphetamines, cocaine, heroin, and inhaling solvents, glue, and gasoline. Inhaling volatile chemicals, relatively neglected by policy makers, is extremely dangerous, and acute intoxication can be fatal. Young people are more likely to abuse solvents because they are easily available in homes and shops, and street children are especially vulnerable (box 5.1).

BOX 5.1   *Street children abusing drugs*

The World Health Organization's Substance Abuse Department identifies inhalation of volatile substances as a particular problem of street children. It recommends that prevention and interventions are urgently needed to deal with the almost universal use of organic inhalants among street children in developing countries.

Cairo has a large and rapidly growing population of street children (150,000 in 2001). Nearly two-thirds of those surveyed regularly abuse drugs or solvents. Of those who consumed illicit substances, 97 percent reported sniffing glue. Other substances include cannabis, hashish, solvents, and prescription medication. They take drugs because of peer pressure, to relieve the pressures of the street, to help them sleep, and to help them endure pain, violence, and

hunger. There are no direct comparisons among non-street youth; but a recent study of Egyptian university students found that 7 percent had ever tried cannabis, and 18 percent had ever used solvents.

A study of street children (ages 15–16) in Karachi, Lahore, Peshawar, and Quetta in Pakistan found that of those who had used drugs, 90 percent inhaled glue, gasoline, or paint thinner, all easily available from the local market. Nearly two-thirds of them reported having used these substances for more than two years. Roughly three-quarters had never been to school. They beg, clean cars, and scavenge through garbage, spending half what they earn on drugs.

Sources: Refaat (2004); United Nations Office on Drugs and Crime (2004); UNODCCP (2002); and WHO (1999).

The prevalence of illegal drug use is highest in developed countries but increasing in developing countries. In many regions, especially Central Asia, prevalence now approaches developed country levels.[46] (Estimates of drug abuse by young people are available only from a few small studies, mainly for school students.) There are an estimated 13 million injecting drug users worldwide, 78 percent of them in developing and transition countries, the majority young.[47] Potentially deadly in itself, injecting drug use increases the risk of acquiring HIV through the sharing of infected needles and the exchange of body fluids.

Diet and exercise. More sedentary lifestyles, along with high intakes of salt and saturated fats and low intakes of vegetables and fruits, can lead to obesity, high blood pressure, high blood cholesterol, and such noncommunicable diseases as heart disease and diabetes. The consequences of poor diets can be passed from generation to generation: babies born to malnourished mothers are at significantly higher risk of being overweight or obese in adulthood.[48]

The health consequences of poor diets and physical inactivity have generally been considered diseases of the affluent. However, these noncommunicable diseases, far from being affluent-country lifestyle diseases, appear with greater frequency in populations undergoing rapid socioeconomic improvement with better access to food and shifts in diets.[49] Data from China, the Arab Republic of Egypt, India, Mexico, the Philippines, and South Africa reveal a marked shift over the last 20 years toward diets high in saturated fat, sugar, and refined foods, while the share of cereals, legumes, pulses, and nuts remained stable or declined.[50]

Being overweight is rapidly becoming more prevalent in low- and middle-income countries, where incidence is increasing especially rapidly among poor households.[51] A recent survey from rural Mexico of low-income households found that 60 percent of adult women and more than 50 percent of adult men were overweight.[52] In many countries young people are more likely to be overweight than underweight, with girls especially at risk (figure 5.5). This partly reflects signifi-

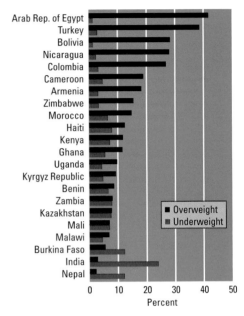

Figure 5.5   Many young women in developing countries are overweight

Source: Demographic and Health Surveys conducted between 2000 and 2003.
Note: Anthropometric measurements were taken for all married and unmarried women interviewed. BMI-for-age cutoffs from a reference population were used to classify 15- to 24-year-old women as overweight (above the 85th percentile cutoff) and underweight (below the 5th percentile cutoff).

cant sex-based differences in patterns of diet and exercise. In urban Mexico, only a third of young girls report exercising, compared with more than half of all boys.[53]

The health consequences of poor diets and lack of exercise are becoming more prevalent in many developing countries. In large cities in China, the prevalence of hypertension among those 18 years and older increased from less than 12 percent in 1991 to 19 percent in 2002, and the prevalence of type-2 diabetes increased from 4.6 percent to 6.1 percent. In Egypt and Mexico, the prevalence of diabetes has been estimated at 10 percent.[54]

Nutritional habits and outcomes are stable over time, so there are great benefits to intervening during youth when habits are being formed. Longitudinal data in Guatemala show that being overweight or obese as a youth significantly raises the chance of becoming obese in adulthood (figure 5.6).

In many ways the risks facing young people today are greater, and consequences poten-

Figure 5.6 Being overweight as a youth increases the chances of being overweight as an adult

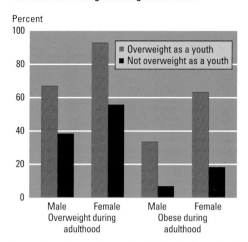

Source: Personal communication with Alexis Murphy, International Food Policy Research Institute, 2005 (using INCAP Longitudinal Study, Guatemala, 1987–2004, IFPRI).
Note: Overweight is body mass index (BMI) greater than 25 and obese is BMI greater than 30, such that individuals who are obese are also considered overweight.

Figure 5.7 The proportion of 15- to 24-year-olds infected with HIV is high, especially among girls

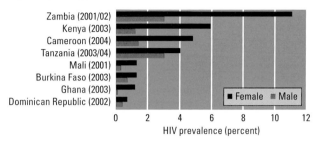

Sources: Demographic and Health Surveys and Tanzania HIV/AIDS Indicator Survey.

tially more deadly, than for previous generations. This is most obvious in the spread of HIV and AIDS, increasingly prevalent among young people (figure 5.7), and dramatically increasing the risks of unprotected sex. Today's young people also have access to more calorie-dense foods, which, combined with more sedentary lifestyles, are making young people obese and leading to hypertension, heart disease, and diabetes. Adding to this is the aggressive marketing of tobacco products and the increase in smoking around the world. So the broader opportunities open to young people make it harder to choose appropriately and to avoid risky behavior.

Strengthening young people's capability to practice healthy behavior

A central element of health promotion is providing health education to change youth behavior and encourage adoption of healthy behaviors. However, behavior change is one of the most difficult goals to achieve in health promotion. In recent years, experience with health education, particularly in the context of HIV prevention, shows changing knowledge alone may not change behavior.[55] But evidence from Uganda and Eastern Zimbabwe suggests that behavior change is possible. Young people there

are delaying sex, and this has resulted in a drop in HIV incidence.[56] A few evaluated programs suggest that providing culturally appropriate teaching about health risks and increasing the capability of young people to practice healthy behavior (including negotiating safe sex with partners) are more likely to change behavior.

Providing young people with schooling can be an effective way to change their behavior. Evidence shows that there is a strong relationship between education and health. Healthy decisions are promoted by education and economic growth, which raises the prospect of higher lifetime earnings and a better life in the future. A stronger sense of an attainable and prosperous future can encourage individuals to make good health and survival more likely. Education, often called a "social vaccine," is considered by many to protect young people from engaging in risky behaviors (box 5.2).[57] Policies that improve young people's access to education can also be effective behavior-change policies. Chapters 3 and 4 discuss ways in which young people's access to education and labor market opportunities can be improved. In this chapter, we focus on investments in improving health behavior, of which formal health education is only one—albeit important—determining factor.[58]

Information is necessary to change behavior

Many countries have health education programs, especially for school-going youth. However, evidence of the efficacy of school-based health education programs is mixed, with variations in effectiveness depending

"We are aware that we drink alcohol and that we consume drugs and we have sexual relations with different girls. We want to change but we do not have a great deal of will to do that."

Young male gang member,
Comas, Peru
January 2006

BOX 5.2   *The role of education in behavior change*

Studies from developing and developed countries show that more education is associated with healthier lifestyle choices, be it smoking, drinking, sex, or use of seatbelts when driving. In Indonesia, poor and uneducated youth are more likely to smoke cigarettes, and higher education is associated with reduced smoking. In urban Mexico, youth who expected to complete secondary school were less likely to smoke, engage in risky sex, or drink alcohol. In rural Kenya, where many students do not expect to complete their education because of high costs, free uniforms (and sex education) significantly reduced risky sex, evidenced by a drop in pregnancies among schoolgirls. In the United States, those who attend and are more engaged in school are less likely to engage in risky behavior. Better prospects for current and lifetime employment, earnings, and wages also reduce the chance that they engage in risky behavior. In South African communities where youth wages and employment are high, young people are also more likely to use condoms. HIV prevalence in Uganda, thought to be higher among the educated in the early stages of the epidemic in Sub-Saharan Africa, is negatively related to education.

Why does education lead to the adoption of healthy behaviors? The observed relationship between schooling and less risky behavior is partly explained by the fact that education raises the private returns to remaining healthy. Education gives young people a sense of the future and the ability to imagine themselves in the future in a way that has some value today. It also improves their earning prospects and other life opportunities. This gives educated young people a stronger incentive to engage in safe behavior. Finally, education also gives people the ability to better process health information. All of these reasons might explain why educated people are more likely to adopt healthy behaviors. But these observed associations could also be partly explained by a "selection effect"—those youth who value their future also attend school.

Sources: Blum and Nelson-Mmari (2004); De Walque (2004); Dupas (2006); Gertler and others (2006); Gruber (2001); Kaufman and Stavrou (2004); Kenkel (2000); Strauss and Thomas (1995); Witoelar, Rukumnuaykit, and Strauss (2005); and World Bank (1999b).

---

partly on the outcome evaluated. Health education can include information about clean water and sanitation, nutrition, substance abuse, infectious diseases, violence, and sexual and reproductive health. A school-based program of the Partnership for Child Development in Tanzania's Lushoto district provided education for helminth (worm) infection and personal hygiene. At the outset of the project, no schools provided drinking water or water for hand washing after using the latrine. By the end of the first year, all schools in the intervention area were doing both. Knowledge and practices improved in the intervention schools but not in the comparison schools. A follow-up survey 15 months later found that many of the healthy behaviors were maintained in the intervention schools.[59]

School-based health education programs. Most evaluations of school-based programs have focused on sex education, which can increase knowledge and encourage adop-

tion of safe sexual behavior.[60] School programs can reach a large number of young people in countries where enrollment rates are high; and enrollments—especially in primary school—have grown significantly, increasing the potential audience for school-based health information campaigns. The structured school environment is conducive to teaching young people about their bodies and about safe health behavior. The programs offer a chance to reach large numbers of young people and their teachers, as well as an opportunity to institutionalize sex education and broaden its impact when ministries of education make it official policy. No evidence indicates that sex education increases sexual activity among youth.[61]

A randomized evaluation in Namibia showed that health education given to children promoted safe sex behavior (box 5.3). A summary of 21 school-based sex education programs in developing countries found that nearly all had a positive influence on reproductive health knowledge and attitudes.[62] However, not all of those studies assessed behavior. Of the few that did, one found an increase in condom use in the short term among sexually active youth ages 11–14 in Jamaica, but the effect disappeared in the long term. Programs in Chile, Mexico, and Uganda also included younger teenagers and found less sexual activity and greater use of contraceptives among those sexually active.

Using mass media and social marketing to reach all youth. School-based programs exclude those youth not in school. And these programs are mostly provided in secondary school, after many young people have left school (chapter 3) and after many young people have already begun having sex. Broadly based information, education, and communication programs aim to change the health of young people through social marketing and community-wide public information campaigns. In addition to curriculum-based health education and sex education programs in schools, such efforts include youth development programs through youth centers, and the use of mass media, to influence the knowledge, attitudes, and behavior of young people.

Mass media can inform youth and the community about health issues and, in principle, shape attitudes, beliefs, and behaviors. Mass media campaigns raise knowledge significantly, but their impact on behavior is limited. Social Marketing for Adolescent Sexual Health (SMASH) in Botswana, Cameroon, Guinea, and South Africa changed knowledge but not behavior.[63] The Arte y Parte program (Paraguay) and the Promotion of Youth Responsibility project (Zimbabwe) reached similar conclusions.

Broadcast media, with their wide reach, can increase awareness, though there is little evidence that they change behavior. The television drama *Sexto Sentido* in Nicaragua attracts 70 percent of the entire TV-viewing audience, and 80 percent of 13- to 17-year-olds.[64] Even more impressive, the wildly popular dramas *Soul City* and *Soul Buddyz* in South Africa are watched by 13 million people each week, and the entire campaign (radio, television, and print) reaches an estimated 16 million people each week. Evaluations of *Soul City* consistently show that viewers and readers are more aware of health risks and healthy choices. However, the studies have not controlled for preexisting differences between viewers and non-viewers. Nor have they examined changes in behavior or such objectively measured outcomes as pregnancy and incidence of sexually transmitted infection (STI).[65]

Youth development programs and peer education programs vary widely in design and goals. Youth development programs focus on life options and skills, educational aspirations, vocational opportunities, and psychosocial development needs. They may or may not address reproductive health, but the many program components can act together to promote a healthy lifestyle. One group of young people consulted during the preparation of this Report suggested both cultural and content-specific ways in which information on HIV/AIDS and reproductive health could be made more effective and attractive to youth. These included making the content short and specific, keeping the message "real, close to daily life," integrating

---

BOX 5.3   *Reducing HIV risk in Namibia*

The Namibia Ministry of Youth and Sport developed My Future is My Choice, a curriculum-based program derived from the Focus on Kids curriculum for African-American youth ages 9–15 in public housing in the United States. It included basic information about reproductive biology, HIV/AIDS, substance abuse, and violence, as well as communication and decision-making skills, over 14 sessions. The intervention was randomly assigned to young people in grades 9 to 11 (15- to 18-years-old) in 10 secondary schools.

Participants displayed improved knowledge of HIV/AIDS, reproduction, and the use of condoms relative to the control group. A few indicators of attitudes toward sexual intercourse also improved for participants. They were more likely than controls to have used a condom in the immediate follow-up period and more likely to report that they intended to use condoms in the next six months.

After 12 months, participants who entered the program as virgins were more likely to have remained virgins than those in the control group (especially among girls), though the percentage who reported remaining virgins fell dramatically among both groups. Condom knowledge and competence remained strong after 12 months: participants were more likely to report that they knew where to find condoms and how to use them, and were more likely to report that they could successfully negotiate condom use with their unwilling partners.

The results were based on self-reported behavior, which the authors acknowledge is subject to bias. They note that it would be useful if future studies could also examine the effect on biological outcomes (such as pregnancy and HIV and sexually transmitted infections rates).

Sources: Fitzgerald and others (1999) and Stanton and others (1999).

---

the messages into television programs and advertisements, and asking pop stars to perform specific HIV/AIDS songs.[66]

Peer programs recruit and train a core group of youth to serve as role models and to provide information, referrals to services, and contraceptives to their peers. They typically include several elements important to health promotion and development: strong identification with the social and cultural environment of the target group, promotion of social norms and values supportive of positive attitudes and health behavior, and involvement of young people in programs designed for them. They take advantage of the fact that many young people prefer to interact with others similar to themselves and commonly identify peers as one of their primary sources for reproductive health information.

There are few well-controlled evaluations of peer education programs. One in Peru improved knowledge and attitudes, reduced the proportion of sexually active males, and increased contraceptive use. The West African Youth Initiative in Ghana and Nigeria reduced risky sexual behaviors in the intervention area, and the Entre Nous Jeunes Program in Cameroon increased condom use.[67]

"We don't know how to get knowledge about sex. It has always been a topic that can't be talked about in public."

Male university freshman, 18, China
December 2005

Information is not always enough—preferences matter too

Interventions to change behavior—such as the Abstain, Be faithful, use Condoms (ABC) campaign—have been the mainstays of HIV prevention since the 1990s. These programs rely on informing people about behaviors that can protect them from becoming infected. Uganda's success in halting the rise of HIV infections has been attributed to a combination of these interventions.[68] In many other countries, knowledge of these approaches is low despite the promotion of ABC messages (figure 5.8).

Even among those who know the ABC messages of the HIV/AIDS campaigns, few put their knowledge into practice. Among youth who report that condoms protect against HIV, few actually use them (figure 5.9). Low rates of condom use are found even among those who know how to obtain them.

Young people with more education are more aware than those with less education that condoms can prevent HIV transmission, and they are more likely to use condoms. Among all young people, however, the wide gap between knowledge and behavior is not eliminated by education. In fact, knowledge of condoms is more responsive to education than is condom use (figure 5.10), so that the gap between knowledge and behavior increases with education.

People engage in risky behavior because it yields benefits. Unprotected sex, smoking, and drinking alcohol can be perceived as providing short-term goods for the person engaging in these activities. There is also a significant time lag between the activity (which provides a benefit) and the manifestation of harmful consequences, and the risk that the individual faces is uncertain. The symptoms of AIDS, for example, are apparent only some years after exposure to the virus, and the risk of being infected with each act of sexual intercourse is on the order of 0.1 percent, with the probability varying enormously across individuals.[69] Low values on the future relative to the present, and perceptions of invulnerability can affect the willingness of young people to translate better knowledge about safe health practices into safer behavior. This is clearly evident in sex, but it applies to any other risky behavior.

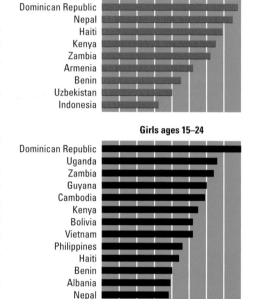

Figure 5.8   Knowledge of the ABCs (Abstain—Be faithful—use Condoms) to avoid HIV prevention is low among young people

Boys ages 15–24

Dominican Republic
Nepal
Haiti
Kenya
Zambia
Armenia
Benin
Uzbekistan
Indonesia

Girls ages 15–24

Dominican Republic
Uganda
Zambia
Guyana
Cambodia
Kenya
Bolivia
Vietnam
Philippines
Haiti
Benin
Albania
Nepal
Armenia
Morocco
Uzbekistan
Indonesia
Turkmenistan
Tajikistan

0 10 20 30 40 50 60 70 80
Knowledge of HIV prevention methods (percent)

Sources: HIV/AIDS Indicator Database (MEASURE DHS) and surveys conducted 2000–04.
Note: Knowledge of HIV-prevention methods is the composite of two components (prompted). The figure represents the percentage of respondents who, in response to a prompted question, say that people can protect themselves from contracting HIV by using condoms or having sex only with one faithful, uninfected partner.

The influence of peers, as well as cultural and historical norms, may influence individual behavior, and peers may encourage risk-taking or discourage risk aversion. For example, it may be unseemly for young women to argue about sex with a partner, or to insist on condoms, or even to discuss sex at all. And even occasional behavior can quickly become habitual.[70] That is why it is essential to intervene when people are young and in the process of forming habits and identities.

Changing preferences to narrow the knowledge-behavior gap

Even when young people receive information on healthy behavior, they may make choices that put their health at risk. Interventions to change behavior have traditionally focused on the design and content of information campaigns, on the assumption that with the right information young people will make better choices. But as this chapter has shown, it is also necessary to address the formation of preferences and decision-making capabilities.

The design and content of health information campaigns. Many issues relating to health education, particularly sex education, still need to be resolved. Programs vary widely in what is taught, at what age, in what setting, by whom, and in what manner. Often, funding is low, and teachers are not trained to deliver the information effectively. In many cases programs are offered only in high school after many youth are already sexually active. Despite the fact that no evidence suggests that sex education increases sexual activity among youth, not all countries include sex education as a part of their school health program.[71] Most countries provide information to secondary students, fewer to primary students (table 5.1). Many provide information on nutrition, but in only a very few does this include information on obesity.

Providing accurate and specific information is more effective than providing vague or general information. School-based HIV/STI programs were more likely to have an impact on behavior than general reproductive health programs.[72] A school-based sex education intervention in Kenya that provided young girls with information about the higher prevalence of HIV infection among older men reduced the incidence of intergenerational sex and significantly reduced pregnancies among girls—in a setting where age-mixing is quite common.[73] Messages must provide a range of options: programs providing only one message—say, on abstinence—will not reduce STIs. The information must be reinforced by repeated exposure, too. Those that include multiple sessions, over a number of years, are more effective than those that merely provide information once or a few times.[74]

Health information campaigns must take into account the ability of the target audience to absorb the messages. Many

Figure 5.9   Knowing that condoms prevent HIV does not always lead to condom use

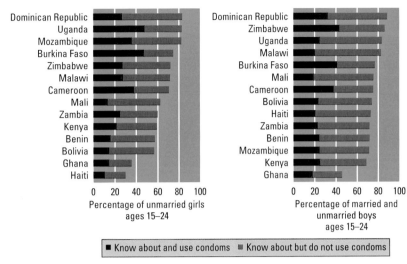

Know about and use condoms ▪ Know about but do not use condoms

Source: Demographic and Health Surveys conducted between 1997 and 2003.
Note: The total length of each bar represents the percentage of sexually active young people who know that condoms can prevent HIV transmission.

Figure 5.10   Knowing that condoms prevent HIV increases with education, but so does the gap between knowledge and behavior

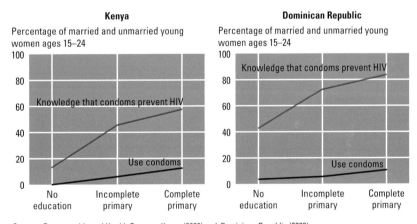

Sources: Demographic and Health Surveys: Kenya (2003) and Dominican Republic (2002).
Note: "Know that condoms prevent HIV" includes those who know condoms can prevent HIV transmission. "Use condoms" is based on the sample of those surveyed who know condoms can prevent HIV transmission.

young people in schools do not learn basic literacy and numeracy skills, raising questions about the effectiveness of the health education curriculum (chapter 3). An HIV information campaign in Uganda benefited better-educated participants more than it did those with less education.[75] If all young people are to be reached, the content of the program and the way it is delivered must be tailored to reach them.

Changing attitudes and preferences directly. In recent years, evidence that information is

Table 5.1 Proportion of countries that include specific health topics in the school curriculum *(percent)*

Region	HIV/AIDS in primary school	HIV/AIDS in secondary school	Substance abuse (including alcohol)	Tobacco	Nutrition	Specifically obesity	Number of countries
Sub-Saharan Africa	93	86	46	54	79	7	28
South Asia (except India)	0	100	75	75	75	25	4
Indian states	13	100	13	13	100	13	8
East Asia and Pacific	83	100	100	83	100	50	6
Latin America and the Caribbean	0	100	85	62	85	46	13
Middle East and North Africa	33	67	0	0	67	33	3

Source: Partnership for Child Development (2006).
Note: **Sub-Saharan Africa** includes Benin, Burkina Faso, Cameroon, Côte d'Ivoire, Chad, the Democratic Republic of Congo, Eritrea, Ethiopia, Gabon, The Gambia, Ghana, Guinea, Kenya, Liberia, Madagascar, Malawi, Mali, Mauritania, Mozambique, Niger, Nigeria, Rwanda, Senegal, Sierra Leone, Tanzania, Togo, Uganda, and Zambia. **South Asia** includes Bangladesh, Bhutan, Nepal, and Sri Lanka. **Indian states** include Andhra Pradesh, Gujarat, Karnataka, Maharashtra, Manipur, Nagaland, Tamil Nadu, and Uttar Pradesh. **East Asia and Pacific** includes Cambodia, Indonesia, the Lao People's Democratic Republic, the Philippines, Thailand, and Vietnam. **Latin America and Caribbean** includes Argentina, The Bahamas, Barbados, Belize, Brazil, Chile, Guyana, Jamaica, Mexico, Panama, St. Vincent and the Grenadines, Trinidad and Tobago, and Uruguay. **Middle East and North Africa** includes Egypt, Islamic Republic of Iran, and Israel.

"Many in Vietnam think that sex education is giving youth the 'key' to certain behaviors/activities, but it is better to give [them] the key rather than let [them] get lost in difficult situations."

Young notetaker at the youth consultation in Ho Chi Minh City, Vietnam April 2006

necessary but not sufficient to change health behavior has led to interventions designed to change preferences, either by fiat or by persuasion. The experience to date suggests that dictating behavior change, that is, forcing people to make certain choices, is not likely to be successful. Virginity pledges and abstinence-until-marriage programs have garnered much popular attention, complicating evaluation and interpretation. A survey of published research from developed countries in 2001 found no evidence that they had any lasting impact on sexual activity or risks.[76] Other research has found that virginity pledges may delay first sex, but have no impact on STI incidence or pregnancy, because those who pledged were much less likely to use contraception than nonpledging youth once they engaged in sex.[77]

Mental health services can change the incentives for youth to make healthy decisions, because depression and low self-esteem can lead to excessive risk-taking. Similarly, many studies, primarily from developed countries, suggest that regular physical activity and sports can lower the risk of many chronic diseases of adulthood, reduce stress and depression, and improve self-esteem.[78] Sports programs also disseminate information, empower the young, and keep idle youths occupied and away from crime.[79] The Mathare Youth Sports Association in Kenya, in addition to organizing sports, engages thousands of young slum residents in community-development activities and provides them with information on HIV and other issues (chapter 7).[80]

As box 5.2 shows, education has at least two beneficial consequences for health behavior, in addition to simply providing a conduit for information. First, it can enhance the ability of individuals to absorb the information, and second, it can change expectations and attitudes about the future. For example, people with more education are more likely to value the future more highly and discount the future more slowly (see box 2.7); and those with higher discount rates—or a higher relative value of the present—are more likely to be obese.[81]

Enhancing a young person's sense of the future is one of the prime objectives of health interventions that focus on "life skills." These include the ability to think critically, to be assertive, and to understand the influence of community, family, and gender in decision making. One life-skills program among youth in Kenya found that male participants were more likely to report condom use, and female participants were more likely to report fewer sexual partners, than among the control group.[82] Many life-skills programs involve young people as peer educators to provide information (box 5.4). Preliminary anecdotal results from the ongoing Regai Dzive Shiri project in Zimbabwe include the observation that "girls walk with their heads high" and that boys complain that "they are more difficult to seduce these days"![83]

The need for well-designed evaluations. Behavior that is private, hard to verify, and that is the subject of strong cultural norms is difficult to change. For these reasons, the impact of health education programs designed to affect this behavior has proven extremely difficult to evaluate. For example, sex education may affect both knowledge and some self-reported behavior,[84] but there is little evidence that these programs have a beneficial impact on objectively measured outcomes. Most studies tend to evaluate changes in knowledge, rather than changes in behavior.

Alford, Cheetham, and Hauser (2005) reviewed nearly 200 studies of youth-oriented health interventions, of which 10 met their criteria for success in both intervention and evaluation. Of those 10, only two showed any positive impact on objectively measured health status. A series of reviews conducted by Kirby, Lepore, and Ryan (2005) and Kirby, Laris, and Rolleri (2005) found strong evidence of program impact on knowledge, values, and self-reported behavior. Of the 83 studies reviewed in Kirby, Laris, and Rolleri (2005), two-thirds found a significant positive impact on self-reported sexual behaviors or outcomes. However, only 9 of those 83 include biomarkers, and of those 9, only 3 report a positive impact on health outcomes.

Studies that do look at behavior tend to rely on self-reported behavior, which can be subject to reporting bias. A three-year evaluation of a school-based, family-life education program in Jamaica found that young people in the schools that received the intervention were more likely than those in a comparison group to report their sexual activity inconsistently.[85] For the effects of health education programs to be reliably estimated, objective outcomes, such as pregnancies or prevalence of STIs, must be used. Those outcomes will be evident only with a lag, and studies must be prepared to assess behavior over a suitable length of time.

Enhancing opportunities to make healthy choices

Having better access to health services can encourage young people to practice safe behavior. Conversely, restricting opportunities to make poor choices may also be beneficial. The set of available opportunities can be altered by changing their availability directly, or by changing prices. For tobacco use and alcohol consumption, taxes, advertising bans, and sales restrictions can reduce demand.

Improving access to health services

Informing youth about practicing safe sex can increase condom use, if they have access to pharmacies or clinics that distribute condoms.[86] Social marketing of condoms can improve young people's uptake of condoms through pharmacies and retail outlets. The Horizon Jeunes program in Cameroon combines health education efforts with condom distribution by peer educators. As part of a countrywide social marketing campaign, the program increased condom use by young women (box 5.4).[87] Condoms can also be distributed to young people where they get together, such as at youth centers. The goal of this approach is to reach young people in a comfortable environment where they also have access to recreational activities. However, experience from interventions in Latin America and Africa have shown that such centers are not effective at changing the behavior of sexually active youth.[88]

The coordination of multiple condom promotion strategies is needed to reach all youth—married and unmarried, in and out of school. Often, however, reproductive health programs are separate from programs to prevent STIs. Funding as well as interventions are often separate for condoms intended for contraceptive use (distributed by family planning services) and those to prevent STIs and HIV transmission (distributed through STI services, HIV testing and counseling services, and condom social marketing campaigns).

BOX 5.4   *Social marketing can change behavior— Horizon Jeunes in Cameroon*

Horizon Jeunes, a reproductive health program targeted to urban youth ages 12 to 22 both in and out of school, was framed within the national social marketing campaign. It sent out two main messages to youth through various channels: to delay the initiation of sex, and if they chose to have sex to use condoms to prevent HIV and STIs. Youth-friendly, the program had peer educators distribute the Prudence Plus condoms promoted in the national campaign. It also encouraged providers to serve unmarried young women, often denied services by reproductive health providers.

Horizon Jeunes added to young people's knowledge of reproductive health and changed behavior. The proportion of females who ever used condoms rose from 58 percent to 76 percent in the treatment group, compared with a decline from 53 percent to 50 percent in the control group.

Source: Alford, Cheetham, and Hauser (2005).

This separation is a problem because young married women are less likely to use condoms, which are widely regarded as less effective at preventing unwanted pregnancies than other contraceptives. This leaves young married couples vulnerable to STIs. However, young people who perceive the risk of acquiring STIs to be low may not use condoms and therefore leave themselves vulnerable to unwanted pregnancies. Promoting condoms as "dual protection" rather than only as "safe sex" may increase the uptake of condoms and protect both married and unmarried young people from STIs and unintended pregnancies.[89]

Changing prices and incentives

Young people's choices respond to changes in prices and incomes, as well as to the existence of health services. In rural Kenya, a randomized controlled experiment providing free uniforms (along with sex education) significantly reduced risky sex, as evinced by a drop in pregnancy incidence among schoolgirls.[90] General poverty alleviation programs targeted at youth or families with youth can increase the opportunities available to young people, and conditional cash transfers can provide additional incentives for healthy choices. The Oportunidades program in Mexico provided incentives for young people to remain in school, where they received health information and periodic health services (see chapter 3). In addition to the beneficial effects on schooling, the program led to reduced smoking and alcohol consumption for all youth, and an increase in the age of sexual debut among girls.[91]

Most governments levy taxes on tobacco and alcohol, which increases prices. In general, young people are more price-sensitive than adults.[92] If the price of cigarettes rises, they are less likely to take up smoking, and those who have begun smoking are more likely to quit. In Indonesia, where the prevalence of smoking among men is high, 15- to 24-year-old males were more responsive to cigarette prices than older males.[93] Alcohol consumption also declines with increases in price. Among high school students in the United States, a 10 percent increase in the price of alcohol will reduce alcohol consumption by 4–5 percent, and binge drinking by 20 percent. There is similar evidence on the consumption of illicit drugs: a 10 percent increase in the price of marijuana will reduce marijuana use by 5 percent; and price increases in marijuana, cocaine, and heroin reduce both arrests and hospital admissions associated with drug consumption. Changes in prices can explain most of the observed changes in binge drinking and marijuana use by high school seniors between 1975 and 2003.[94]

Cigarette smoking tends to be more sensitive to price in low-income countries than in high-income countries. For example, it is estimated that a price rise of 10 percent for a pack of cigarettes reduces demand for cigarettes by 6–10 percent in China, and only 4 percent in the United States.[95] One reason for the difference could be that low-income countries have a larger share of young people than high-income countries, and young people are more price-sensitive than adults. Poorer people are also more price-sensitive than wealthier.[96]

In addition to raising prices through taxation, comprehensive bans on advertising and product promotions, age restrictions on sales, and prominent health warning labels can reduce the consumption of tobacco and alcohol. Comprehensive bans on cigarette advertising and promotion reduced smoking in some high-income countries, although partial bans had little or no effect.[97] Studies based on cross-country analysis find no link between advertising and sales restrictions and reduced smoking.[98] However, a study of 100 countries comparing consumption trends over time found that consumption fell much more steeply in countries that had nearly complete bans on advertising, compared with countries with no such bans. Health warning labels on cigarette packs, though effective in reducing tobacco consumption among adults, may not discourage youth from smoking, because they are more likely to buy single cigarettes than packs.[99]

Young people are exposed to a wide variety of tobacco control policies, including advertising restrictions, health warnings, and prohibitions on the sale of tobacco to minors. There is little consistency in policies: some countries ban advertising without restricting sales to minors; others ban sales to minors but do not restrict advertising. The independent effect of each policy is difficult to identify. Interventions to reduce the consumption of these potentially harmful substances are more effective if implemented jointly: for example, tobacco control is more effective if it includes both advertising bans and higher taxes.[100]

Policies to reduce consumption of harmful substances can have unintended consequences. In 1985, Russia restricted alcohol sales and raised the legal age for alcohol consumption. This dramatically improved life expectancy among men, but it also increased the use of harmful alcohol substitutes (box 5.5).

What if prevention fails? Helping young people deal with the adverse consequences of poor health behavior or misfortune

Despite good information and the freedom to make independent decisions, we are all susceptible to poor health outcomes. Occasionally we make poor choices: in spite of the overwhelming evidence of the harmful effects of tobacco, more than a billion people smoke worldwide.[101] Occasionally we fall victim to the external effects of the private decisions of others, or to the failure of government to provide services, or we are coerced into making risky choices. A vital function of youth health services is to help young people overcome the adverse consequences of risky health behavior. They may be addicted to tobacco or drugs, or infected with sexually transmitted diseases, or have an unintended pregnancy. They need support to recover to a healthy life: abortion services, sexual health services, maternal and child health services, drug rehabilitation services. They also need cessation and rehabilitation programs to help them stop the behavior that is causing the harm.

Programs to help youth overcome addiction

A supportive environment is needed to encourage tobacco consumers in their attempts to quit. Treating tobacco depen-

---

BOX 5.5   *Russia limited the sale of alcohol, and deaths and illnesses fell*

In 1985, President Gorbachev implemented anti-alcohol legislation to limit alcohol sales and raise the legal purchasing age to 21. Alcohol consumption fell, but only by 26 percent, despite a 63 percent decrease in sales. The consumption of unregistered alcohol, including moonshine, nearly doubled, and increases were also seen in substance abuse and related poisoning, especially among youth.

Overall, life expectancy among males improved. Even so, the law was repealed after three years. With the liberalization of alcohol sales and relaxation of administrative controls, alcohol psychosis increased. Surveys show a substantial increase in alcohol consumption between 1992 and 1994, consistent with a sharp price reduction.

Source: World Bank (2005d).

---

dence should be part of a comprehensive tobacco-control policy. Many people are able to quit smoking successfully on their own and with some guidance (box 5.6).[102] However, some young smokers might have developed a strong dependence on nicotine and could benefit from nicotine replacement interventions to address the physiological aspects, such as tobacco dependence and tobacco withdrawal.[103]

Strong evidence from controlled trials indicate the benefits of treatment for drug abuse, including significantly fewer drug-related health and social problems. Those improvements translate into substantial reductions in social problems and societal costs, including reduced crime, violence, and incarceration.[104] Many countries—primarily in Asia and the former Soviet Union—are introducing methadone maintenance therapy and needle and syringe exchange

---

BOX 5.6   *Technology can help change young people's behavior: Using text messages in New Zealand to reduce smoking*

In New Zealand, as in many countries around the world, mobile phone ownership is high and text messaging very popular. An intervention in New Zealand used text messaging to help youth quit smoking. Information on individual participants was used to create personalized text messages providing advice, support, and distraction. Participants could also communicate with others with similar characteristics ("quit buddies").

Participants randomly assigned to a treatment group received five personalized messages per day, those in a control group received general information only once in two weeks. All participants were between 19 and 30, half of them female.

After six weeks, 28 percent in the treatment group had quit smoking, more than twice the percentage in the control group. Given the widespread use of mobile telephone technology, this type of intervention might be easily replicated in different regions.

Sources: Rodgers and others (2005) and Internet Safety Group (2005).

programs. There is similarly strong evidence that these programs reduce the risk of HIV infection.[105] Two international studies found that average seroprevalence decreased in cities with exchange programs, and increased in cities without them.[106]

Improving access to health services for treatment of sexually transmitted infections

More than 100 million STIs other than HIV occur every year around the world among people under 25 (figure 5.11).[107] Most are easily treated, without severe or lasting consequences, if diagnosed and treated early. Treating STIs prevents HIV/AIDS transmission, because STIs facilitate the sexual transmission of HIV, particularly syphilis, chancroid, and genital herpes, which produce genital ulcers.[108] Many infections, however, go unnoticed, especially among women and girls, who may show no symptoms or signs so mild that they are unrecognizable. In Nigeria, providing school students with STI health education and training providers (pharmacists and private doctors) to treat

STI in adolescents increased the uptake of STI services among sexually experienced students and significantly reduced the incidence of STIs.[109]

Unmarried adolescents are often denied services in countries where premarital sex is frowned upon. In Ghana, services were denied to young or unmarried clients, and to married women who could not demonstrate the consent of their spouses.[110] Even where young people are legally protected, reproductive health services may be out of reach. In South Africa, many reproductive health services are not easily accessible by youth, and young people feel that facility staff are judgmental and hostile.[111] In Nigeria, adolescents who contracted an STI would go to a traditional healer rather than use formal reproductive health services because of the high cost and low quality.[112]

For these reasons, making clinics youth-friendly—training doctors and nurses to deal with young clients, having clinic hours that are convenient for youth, and offering space where young people can consult with providers in privacy—may encourage young people to use health services for treatment. Evaluations of youth-friendly health services have so far not shown any evidence that they increase the use of health services by young people.[113] The interventions that do seem to increase their use of treatment services are health information that teaches them to recognize symptoms of STIs and referrals to trained providers, as in the Nigeria program.

Antiretroviral therapy (ART) can turn AIDS from a certain death sentence to a manageable (though severely unpleasant) chronic condition. Treatment remains prohibitively expensive, and current international efforts to provide ART are already overwhelming the capacity of many hard-hit developing countries, even though only a small percentage of those clinically eligible for treatment actually receive it. Public provision of ART may be feasible and affordable in cases where the epidemic is limited.[114] There have been no well-controlled studies of the impact of treatment on prevention, but some simulation models show that treatment can enhance the effectiveness of

Figure 5.11   Reported STI incidence varies among youths in Sub-Saharan Africa

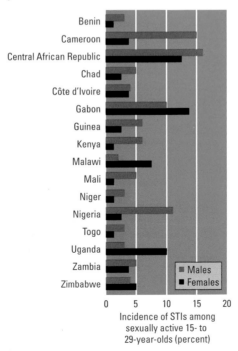

Incidence of STIs among sexually active 15- to 29-year-olds (percent)

Source: Bankole and others (2004).

prevention.[115] Other simulations caution that an exclusive focus on treatment will increase incidence, partly due to the neglect of other, more conventional interventions, and partly due to the incentive effects of treatment.[116]

Simulations in South Africa show that full coverage of ART could avert up to 1.7 million deaths and 860,000 orphans by 2010.[117] Some empirical evidence suggests that ART will reduce the costs associated with hospital care and treatment of opportunistic infections due to AIDS. One study from Brazil estimated that ART averted 358,000 hospital admissions between 1996 and 2002, saving US$2.2 billion.[118] HIV-positive injecting drug users, predominantly young, also benefit from ART treatment,[119] but little attention goes to treatment and care for injecting drug users living with HIV/AIDS.[120] Among those who do receive treatment, allocations do not favor youth.[121]

Providing access to emergency contraception and safe abortion services

One potential outcome of unprotected sex is unplanned pregnancy. For unmarried young women, such pregnancies can bring immense social costs, especially in countries where family networks do not support out-of-wedlock births. It is not surprising, then, that each year millions of young women undergo unsafe and illegal abortions. Women opting to terminate pregnancies using unsafe methods are predominantly young and unmarried, particularly in Sub-Saharan Africa and Latin America and the Caribbean. In Sub-Saharan Africa, about 60 percent of women who have unsafe abortions are 15–24 years old. In Latin America and the Caribbean, young women make up about 43 percent of those who undergo unsafe abortions.[122] In Kenya, Nigeria, and Tanzania, adolescent girls make up more than half of the women admitted to the hospital for complications following illicit abortions, adding to the costs of already under-resourced health systems.[123] Access to safe abortion services is thus critical for young women to avoid further damage to their health.

Not all unprotected sex has to result in an unwanted pregnancy (where young women are forced to consider abortion as an option). Access to emergency contraception can effectively prevent unwanted pregnancy in such cases, but it is typically not provided as part of reproductive health services in developing countries.[124] Even when young people know about emergency contraception, few are well informed about its use.[125]

Safe abortion services and emergency contraception are, however, highly controversial in many countries. Where abortions are illegal or restricted, the percentage of unsafe abortions and maternal deaths arising from them tends to be very high. This is evident in Romania, where maternal death dropped dramatically when abortion was legalized.[126] Where legalizing abortion is not feasible, the access for young people to modern contraceptive methods must be strengthened.

Ensuring that girls have access to safe abortion services and postabortion care will greatly reduce the associated health risks of unplanned pregnancy. One possible approach is to link contraceptive services (including emergency contraception), abortion, and postabortion care, making them part of maternal health service delivery.[127] Access to postabortion care can be strengthened through outreach by trained midwives. Where the public sector cannot provide abortion or postabortion care, private clinics are viable alternatives, if they are regulated to ensure safe procedures.

Feedback effects of treatment programs

Do programs to cope with or mitigate the consequences of bad choices affect the decision to engage in risky behavior in the first place? Can treatment programs have positive feedback for prevention? Or might there be negative feedback, or moral hazards? If so, can we design "incentive-compatible" interventions to minimize poor choices and still protect those with poor outcomes?

There is some legitimate concern that providing second chances will encourage moral hazard—that is, if the costs of some risky actions are not borne by individuals, they will behave more carelessly, or in a way that increases risks to themselves or others. For instance, health insurance may cause people to take greater risks with their health, or consume more health services than they would in the absence of insurance.[128]

No evidence suggests that the availability of emergency contraception will increase the incidence of unprotected sex. Of the women attending a family planning clinic in Pune, India, those who received pills and information were not significantly more likely to have unprotected sex—and not one of these woman used emergency contraception more than once over the course of the year.[129] In the United Kingdom, only 4 percent of those using emergency contraception reported using it more than twice in a year, so they presumably were not using it as a substitute for regular contraception.[130]

It has been suggested that ART will discourage risk aversion and increase risky sexual behavior.[131] Studies of men who have sex with men in Europe and the United States have shown that potent ART may induce both HIV-positive and HIV-negative men to engage in riskier behavior than they would in the absence of such therapies.[132] A long-term study of condom use in Kenya—during a period when two reported "cures" for AIDS were announced and widely touted by government leaders—found that after each announcement, sex workers reported a substantial drop in condom use. Eventually the ineffectiveness of these drugs against AIDS became apparent, and condom use increased.[133]

———

The interventions affecting the health of young people can be loosely distinguished as those that affect the *opportunities* and *capabilities* for healthy choices and those that offer *second-chance* services for those who require assistance to cope or recover. Table 5.2 summarizes the evidence of interventions known to work in promoting youth health and those that are promising, but for which claims of effectiveness have yet to be verified.

Evidence indicates that young people do respond to policies that alter the set of available opportunities. This is most clearly seen in the impact on young people of changes in prices and incomes, such as the imposition of cigarette taxes and the distribution of conditional cash transfers. This chapter has argued, however, that the most significant determinant of healthy behavior in youth—and of health in adulthood—is the capability of young people to make the right decisions.

Some health promotion interventions have changed behavior, such as sanitation and hand-washing—as has information provided to parents to improve the health of young children, such as breastfeeding. Behavioral interventions have emphasized health education, on the assumption that individuals lack information and that more information will allow them to make healthier choices. A key policy recommendation in countries where information is missing, or misinformation rife, is to establish standards and provide information about behavior and consequences. As table 5.2 shows, school health education varies greatly around the world. In some regions, information on HIV is provided only in secondary schools, after many young people have become sexually active.

As this chapter has shown, information is essential to healthy decision making; but it may not be sufficient, especially for decisions about such private issues as food and sex. Behavior in these areas is extremely difficult to influence. More evidence will improve understanding and the design of policies. In these difficult areas, experience provides three clear directions about health information campaigns. First, target younger people rather than older youths: information about safe sex has a stronger and more lasting impact if delivered prior to the initiation of sexual activity. Second, repeated exposure to health messages is more effective than one single exposure. Third, provide specific information that addresses the real problems facing young people. This is best seen in the program in Kenya that provided specific information

Table 5.2 Summary of policies to improve young people's health and health behavior

	Proven successful	Promising but unproven	Unlikely to be successful
Opportunities			
Opportunities to make healthy choices			
Providing services to change behavior		Treatment for depression and mental health Sports programs and programs promoting physical fitness	Youth centers (more likely to attract boys, older youth)
Using taxes, advertising bans, and sales restrictions	Price controls and taxes (for tobacco and alcohol) Total advertising bans, restrictions on sales to minors (tobacco and alcohol)		Partial advertising bans on tobacco and alcohol
Capabilities			
Strengthening ability to practice healthy behavior			
School-based health education	Curriculum-based sex education combining basic reproductive health information with communication and decision-making skills (Namibia's My Future is My Choice) Curriculum-based programs providing culturally relevant information about risky sex and specific information about health risks (rural Kenya, randomized evaluation)	Health education on tobacco, alcohol, and drug abuse Health education promoting healthy diet, physical activity Abstinence-only programs (to delay initiation of sexual activity)	Abstinence-only programs (to delay transmission of STIs, HIV, and pregnancy)
Mass media and social marketing	Mass media campaigns combined with peer education and trained providers in Cameroon (Horizon Jeunes)	Social Marketing for Adolescent Sexual Health (SMASH) program in four African countries—program effective in increasing condom use only in Cameroon (no evidence of behavior change in Botswana, Guinea, and South Africa) Radio, television plus telephone hotline and peer education— Sexto Sentido (Nicaragua), LoveLife (South Africa)	Program promoting only abstinence (to delay transmission of STIs, HIV, and pregnancy)
Second chances			
Minimizing consequences of risky behavior			
HIV/AIDS and sexual and reproductive health services	STI treatment and counseling—increased use of private physicians to treat STIs in two cities in Nigeria (Benin City and Ekpoma) Providing emergency contraception and abortion services ART (to minimize consequences of HIV infection) Providing postabortion care	ART (to prevent HIV transmission) "Youth-friendly" sexual health and family planning health services	
Treatment of addictions and cessation programs	"Harm reduction"—needle exchange, methadone substitution		

to young women on the higher HIV prevalence in older partners.[134]

Second-chance health services—especially legalized abortion, harm reduction for injecting drug users, and STI treatment—are essential to minimize the adverse consequences of poor decisions and poor environments. The benefits of these second-chance services accrue both to the young people served and to the broader society, in terms of reduced expenditure on curative care, lower infectious disease prevalence, and spillover effects on welfare, security, and economic growth.

Persistent inequality is one of the most important concerns in an economy that is otherwise growing and making progress in reducing poverty. Inequality in human development outcomes among Brazil's youth endangers future progress. In particular, a shortage of labor market and educational opportunities for vulnerable groups reinforces the intergenerational transmission of poverty and leads to continuing inequality. Brazil is developing a cross-sectoral approach to break this cycle.

Brazil, an industrial power with the largest population in Latin America and the Caribbean, has made big strides in reducing the poverty that continues to afflict millions of its people. Brazil's literacy and tertiary enrollment rates are on par with other Latin American countries such as Colombia and Mexico, but averages mask the disparities that affect millions of poor young people.[1]

- Youth (15–24 years old) from the poorest decile (10 percent) of families have a formal sector employment rate of 4 percent, one-eighth the national average for the age group—and barely a tenth of the national average employment rate of adults. In contrast, those from the richest decile have a formal sector employment rate of 50 percent, one-third higher than the national average for the age group.[2]

- Youth from the poorest decile of families have a 14 percent illiteracy rate, three times the national average (by age 12, half the youth from the poorest families have left school). The corresponding rate for those from the wealthiest decile is 0.3 percent.

- By age 14, young women from poor neighborhoods have begun their transition to motherhood—compared with age 17 among girls from the wealthiest households.[3]

Because inequalities of opportunity are easily transmitted across generations, investing in its young people is key to Brazil's long-run poverty reduction strategy. A recent analysis of the main household survey indicates that more than a fifth of the total earnings inequality in Brazil can be explained by four variables: parental schooling, father's occupation, race, and region of birth,[4] with the human capital of the parents most important.

Brazil is trying to address these inequalities by targeting disadvantaged youth directly and by coordinating the actions of diverse providers.

Targeting disadvantaged youth

Brazil has a rich portfolio of public and private programs to expand opportunities, enhance capabilities, and provide second chances to its youth. It is guaranteeing universal access to antiretroviral medication, part of an HIV/AIDS strategy that is considered to be an international model. In education, it is providing more funds to local municipalities to address high repetition rates and the poor quality of secondary school services. It has also begun to look for responses that cut across transitions and sectors, with the Bolsa Familia, ProJovem, Abrindo Espaços, and health education programs for males and females.

Bolsa Família

For so many overage students, the opportunity cost of staying in school is high. The perceived benefit of staying in school beyond a few grades of primary is low and the forgone earnings can be significant.[5] To alleviate the opportunity and direct costs to attending school, Brazil was one of the first countries to experiment with conditional cash transfers for school attendance. Bolsa Escola (School Scholarship), emerged first at the state level, and paid families a monthly stipend if all of their children ages 7–14 attended school.[6] School attendance increased more for beneficiaries than for a control group. In 2001, the program was expanded to the national level and in 2004 the federal government launched the Bolsa Família (Family Grants) program merging the Bolsa Escola with other conditional cash transfer programs.[7] While an impact evaluation of the Bolsa Família program is just starting, a 2005 study concludes that among the lower-income deciles, the stipend can make a difference of 11.5 percent in school enrollment. To expand the program to youth, the government has been discussing the possibility of adapting Bolsa Família's education incentives by (a) providing bonuses for secondary school graduation, (b) increasing the

value of the transfer for older youth to stay in school (recognizing the higher opportunity cost), or (c) extending attendance conditions to youth ages 16–18, which would capture secondary school enrollment (or a combination of the three).

ProJovem

The Brazilian government recognizes that young people who have left school may wish to further their education. In fact, approximately 20 percent of working youth return to school.[8] The Educação de Jovens e Adultos program is an adult education class that focuses on literacy for adults and youth who have left school. In addition, a new program—ProJovem—is being piloted. Going beyond literacy for youth (ages 18–24) who have left school, it instead offers a full curriculum that covers mathematics, languages, job preparedness, and citizenship, among other topics; a two-week volunteer project; and career and general support services to youth while they are participating in, and shortly after leaving, the program.

Abrindo Espaços

Social exclusion is hypothesized to be a driving factor behind youth violence. The Open School Program in Pernambuco, started in 2000 as a partnership between local government and UNESCO, keeps schools in the poorest and most violent neighborhoods open during weekends, offering children and youth an array of cultural and athletic activities to keep them off the streets and to allow them to express themselves in a peaceful manner. A UNESCO study shows that participating schools have experienced a 60 percent reduction in violence.[9] The program, now known as Abrindo Espaços (opening spaces), has since been expanded to Rio de Janeiro, Bahia, São Paulo, and Rio Grande do Sul, and is showing positive results.[10] Also, schools that entered the program earlier had greater success, suggesting increased impact over time.[11]

Health education

Given early sexual initiation among youth combined with risky sexual behavior (as defined by the lack of use of contraceptives), programs addressing youth are of particular importance in preventing teenage pregnancies and the spread of sexually transmitted diseases. In 2003 the Ministries of Health and Education launched a controversial pilot program of condom distribution to schools in five municipalities. In 2004 the program was extended to 205 municipalities responsible for almost half of all HIV/AIDS cases in Brazil. The program has the additional benefit of preventing teenage pregnancies, now accounting for 25 percent of all births in Brazil. The program was expected to reach 900 public schools attended by about a half million students. While this particular initiative has not been evaluated, similar programs for the general population have been part of Brazil's successful strategy of curbing the fast spread of HIV/AIDS.

Gender: Bring the boys in

Unsafe and early sexual behavior is often attributed to gender-related roles: boys attempting to prove their masculinity and girls without the bargaining power to negotiate the situation. Rather than leaving the responsibility to girls, as in so many programs, Program H in Brazil has instead worked to give greater agency to boys by altering the way they think about gender roles and behaviors, with the hope of changing their sexual choices and expectations.[12]

The program was evaluated in three of Rio's favelas, two of which had the program and the third of which did not. The evaluation found that six months after the program ended, there was greater condom use among program participants, less incidence of new sexually transmitted infections, and a significant improvement on the Gender Equitable Men scale,[13] relative to the control site. While there were some shortcomings in the evaluation methodology, Program H's experience shows that its approach is promising for healthy sexual behavior.[14]

Coordinating policies to target poor youth in a highly decentralized state

Recently, Brazil has taken steps to enhance coordination among the various players in youth policy:

- The recent creation of the Secretaria da Juventude (Youth Secretariat) allows for a central guiding body strategically positioned within the Secretaria Geral to facilitate collaboration across ministries and develop a national strategy. By focusing on developing national priorities and guidelines to enable actions at the local level through technical and financial support, it aims to leverage public and private budgets for maximum impact. Other ministries are also doing this with their own youth strategies.

- The youth themselves are mobilizing at both the community and national levels. The recently organized Vozes Jovens have developed a proposal for a national youth policy. This group of leaders from youth nongovernmental organizations (NGOs) both strengthens the NGO movement and gives youth voice on the national stage.

- State and local governments have developed youth strategies and are channeling federal and their own resources to local civil society organizations and private sector firms to implement programs. Better coordination between the state and local levels in terms of defining target groups, priorities, and the division of labor at each level of government would allow for greater efficiency in the delivery of services. For example, the federal government of Brazil is using tax and expenditure incentives to municipalities and states to increase secondary school enrollment via a financing mechanism known as the FUNDEB (Fundo de Desenvolvimento e Manutenção do Ensino Básico e Valorização do Magisterio).

- NGOs are already very active in implementing programs and giving feedback to government at all levels. Helping to align local priorities, further encouraging the work of the NGOs through incentives and support from government (financial and technical), and improving program design through the development of monitoring and evaluation systems will further enhance civil society's role.

Forming families

chapter 6

As young people form families, their ability to plan safe childbearing and raise healthy children depends on their education, nutritional status, and health knowledge—and on their use of health services. Many young men and women are not well prepared. They lack knowledge of good health practices, and available maternal and child health services may not fully meet the needs of first-time parents. Malnutrition, especially micronutrient deficiencies, are common among young women, who in many parts of the world become mothers when they are still teenagers, elevating the health risks for both mother and baby.

Young parents' decisions about the timing and number of children affect population growth and so directly affect economic development. If young people choose to have smaller families, the decline in births can bring about a rise in the share of the working age population, a potential bonus for countries with the right supporting policies.

Nutrition and reproductive health services are among the most important human capital investments that prepare young people to become the next generation of parents, helping them plan births and ensure the health of mother and child. Failing to provide a young mother with adequate nutrition before and during pregnancy increases the risk of low birth weight infants. Low birth weight infants are less likely to survive the first year of life. Low birth weight also causes irreversible damage to a child's ability to learn in school and be productive in the labor force. It increases susceptibility to chronic health conditions in adulthood, such as coronary heart disease.

Policies to broaden the opportunities for young men and women to be better prepared for parenthood include improving access to reproductive and child health services and to nutrition services. Programs aimed at delaying marriage can also give young girls the opportunity to avoid entering motherhood too early. Because a young woman's nutritional status before pregnancy can significantly affect the baby's health, nutritional services should reach young women before and during pregnancy.

Strengthening decision-making capabilities, particularly in reproductive health and the nutrition and care of infants, will help young men and women prepare for parenthood. Health education can stimulate demand for child health and nutrition services, particularly if it also targets young men. Teaching life skills to young people can encourage them to delay marriage and to use health services. Early child development programs that promote parenting and child care skills can also develop the decision-making skills of young parents.

Second-chance programs can help teenage mothers overcome obstacles posed by low education and poor employment opportunities. Because most teenage mothers are from poor households, such programs must address the disadvantages of poor socioeconomic status.

Preparing for family formation is good for growth and poverty reduction

Young people's transition to parenthood can have a lasting impact on the economy and demographic trends in a country because in most countries, first births—the entry into parenthood—take place during youth. Nearly 60 percent of girls in developing countries become mothers before age 25. Boys make this transition a bit later, becoming fathers between 25 and 29.[1] This difference largely reflects gender differences in the age of marriage.[2] For many reasons, including societal pressures, newlyweds make a swift transition to parenthood (box 6.1). With the marriage age increasing for women and men in most countries, the interval between marrying and having the first child is becoming shorter: most become parents within a year and a half of marriage.[3]

Impact on growth and poverty reduction

Preparing youth for the transition to family formation so that they can plan childbearing, have a safe pregnancy, and raise healthy children has an impact on productivity and savings, which affect economic growth and poverty reduction. Parents' labor supply and productivity increase because they can plan childbearing more effectively. Young children deter mothers' participation in work, particularly paid work, as in urban Morocco.[4] So having fewer unintended births can facilitate young women's participation in the labor force. Helping couples attain their desired family size—both through reduced child mortality and through planned births—also increases parental investment in their children's education, nutrition, and health. Because the survival of children can encourage couples to save, these higher savings can have an additional impact on growth.

Avoiding pregnancies at a very young age, having fewer unintended pregnancies, and spacing births prevent the depletion of mothers' health and reduce the risk of maternal and child mortality and ill health. Female genital mutilation, practiced in parts of Sub-Saharan Africa, can also exacerbate the health risks to young mothers.[5] Young women in many countries face the risk of becoming mothers at a very young age, largely because of early marriage (box 6.1). More than 10 percent of 15- to 19-year-old females are mothers in Sub-Saharan Africa, South Asia, and Latin America (figure 6.1). In Bangladesh and Mozambique, more than 30 percent of 15- to 19-year-old females are mothers or pregnant. Pregnant adolescents face higher risks of maternal mortality, delivery complications, obstructed labor, and premature delivery, mainly because their own physical growth

---

> **BOX 6.1**   *The sequencing of marriage and childbearing*
>
> Marriage may be a precondition for childbearing in many parts of the world, but the trend varies across countries. In many developed countries, such as the United States and France, and in some parts of Latin America and Africa, out-of-wedlock childbearing is common. For example, in the United States, births to unmarried women account for nearly 30 percent of all births, which is the result of both an increased proportion of unmarried women and their higher fertility.
>
> In many other parts of the world, such as Africa, South Asia, and Muslim societies, marriage is the only recognized state in which childbearing is permitted. The timing and cultural norms associated with marriage can significantly affect the quality of married life. The biggest concern is physical abuse by partners. In South Asia, violence by husbands, sometimes linked to dowry payments, is one of the major causes of death among young women.
>
> Early marriage, and hence early childbearing, is prevalent in many regions of the world. The proportion of girls marrying before age 18 ranges from less than 20 percent in Central Asia to more than 60 percent in Bangladesh, Guinea, and Mali. A very early transition to marriage, before age 15, is also notable in some parts of the world. For
>
> example, in Mali, nearly 36 percent of young women were married by age 15.
>
> Although the causal effect of the age at marriage on various outcomes remains to be resolved (especially in developing countries), its association with negative outcomes for women is well documented. Early marriage is associated with early childbearing and higher fertility. Women who marry early are also more likely to have less say in decision making in a marriage. Increased risk of domestic violence is also associated with early marriage.
>
> Strikingly, studies report early marriage as a risk factor in acquiring HIV/AIDS for girls. In Kenya and Zambia in 1997–98, HIV infection rates were 48–65 percent higher among married girls than sexually active unmarried girls of similar ages. A similar pattern is found in other Sub-Saharan African countries. Studies find that high HIV/AIDS prevalence among young married girls is associated with greater frequency of unprotected sex with an older partner who is more likely to be infected by HIV than younger men.
>
> *Sources:* Bruce and Clark (2004); Buvinic (1998); Clark (2004); Eltigani (2000); Jensen and Thornton (2003); Lesthaeghe and Moors (2000); Singh and Samara (1996); Upchurch, Lillard, and Panis (2002); and Willis and Haaga (1996).

---

is incomplete. The risks are heightened for girls who become pregnant very soon after menarche. Pregnancy-related illnesses associated with early, frequent, or closely spaced pregnancies drain women's productivity, jeopardize their income-earning capacity, and contribute to their poverty.[6]

Pregnancy-related illnesses are a significant cause of death among young women ages 15–29. In South Asia, Sub-Saharan Africa, and the Middle East and North Africa, regions with high fertility, between 15 and 20 percent of all female deaths arise from pregnancy-related causes. Reducing those deaths has strong intergenerational benefits. Children benefit from lower maternal mortality because those who lose a parent are much more vulnerable, partly because of the loss of resources and partly because of the lack of parental care. In Indonesia, children whose mothers die are less likely to start school and are less healthy than other children.[7] In Ethiopia, children

Figure 6.1 Teenage motherhood is common in some regions

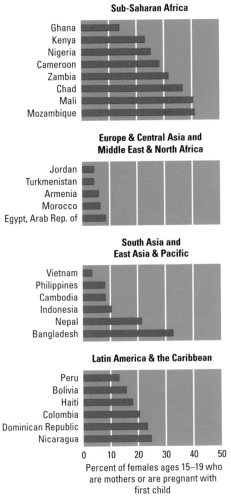

Sub-Saharan Africa

Ghana
Kenya
Nigeria
Cameroon
Zambia
Chad
Mali
Mozambique

Europe & Central Asia and
Middle East & North Africa

Jordan
Turkmenistan
Armenia
Morocco
Egypt, Arab Rep. of

South Asia and
East Asia & Pacific

Vietnam
Philippines
Cambodia
Indonesia
Nepal
Bangladesh

Latin America & the Caribbean

Peru
Bolivia
Haiti
Colombia
Dominican Republic
Nicaragua

0   10   20   30   40   50
Percent of females ages 15–19 who
are mothers or are pregnant with
first child

Sources: ORC Macro (2006) and MEASURE DHS STAT Compiler (surveys conducted between 2000 and 2005).

Figure 6.2 The share of youth fertility is high in countries with low fertility

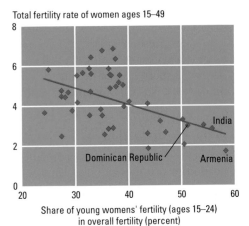

Total fertility rate of women ages 15–49

India
Dominican Republic
Armenia

Share of young womens' fertility (ages 15–24)
in overall fertility (percent)

Sources: ORC Macro (2005) and MEASURE DHS STAT Compiler (surveys conducted between 2000 and 2004).

whose mothers succumbed to AIDS show less psychological well-being and lower participation in schooling.[8]

Impact on growth through demographic trends

The fertility decline witnessed around the world in the past 20 years has led to a concentration of births among women ages 15–24. As fertility begins to decline, childbearing patterns change in three ways: women may delay their first birth, space their births, or stop having children at an earlier age than previous cohorts. Even though women's marriage age has increased, the average gap between marriage and the first birth has fallen,[9] suggesting very little net delay in

the start of childbearing. In some countries evidence indicates that women are stopping childbearing earlier than did previous cohorts of women. In India in the late 1990s, there was a roughly one year drop in the age when women stopped childbearing, from 30.2 years (among women ages 45–49) to 28.7 years (among women ages 40–44).[10]

The compression of childbearing during youth is visible in the large share of births to young women in countries where fertility is low (figure 6.2). In many countries, births among 15- to 24-year-olds account for 30–50 percent of all births. In the Dominican Republic and India, where fertility rates are lower than three births per woman, births among 15- to 24-year-old women constitute close to 50 percent of all births. In Armenia, with fewer than two births per woman, the youth share is 60 percent.

Because of their larger share in fertility, young people's decisions about parenthood will shape future demographic trends: as more couples are better able to plan their births, both fertility and mortality will decline, and the share of working-age population will rise. With the right set of supporting conditions, an economy can reap the benefits for growth of having more workers with fewer dependents (chapter 1). In some African countries, such as Chad, however, young women can expect to have six children or more during their lifetime.[11] In these countries, preparing young couples for family formation will spur the decline in fertility and in dependency ratios, offering a window of opportunity to benefit from a larger working-age population.

Preparation for family formation is poor

Many factors determine when young men and women become parents, the number of children they have, and how they raise their children. In some settings young people make these decisions, while in others, parents or extended family make the decisions for them (chapter 2). To some extent, these are purely private decisions that do not merit public intervention. However, there is a role for public investment in areas that will ensure safe passage through a first pregnancy and beyond, because young people may underinvest in family planning or maternal health services relative to the level that might be socially optimal.

Most governments finance maternal health services because of the positive externalities of the improved health of the (as yet unborn) child. Governments also provide these services because of the low demand on the part of prospective parents who have little education, little information, and are poor. A further justification for government investment in supporting the transition to parenthood is to ensure equity. Publicly financed or provided services broaden access to those who would otherwise not be able to avail themselves of the services, particularly women and adolescent girls.[12]

Among the many factors influencing family formation is the position of young women in their parents' households. A position of disadvantage can push them into pregnancy at a very young age, and it can also lead to lower investments in education, with significant consequences for the transition to parenthood (box 6.2). Young men's labor market outcomes are associated with the timing of transition to marriage and parenthood. Evidence from the Arab Republic of Egypt, the Philippines, Thailand, and Vietnam suggests that poverty and a lack of financial security are reasons for men to delay marriage. In rural Ethiopia, the unavailability of land is associated with delayed marriage for men.[13] Research

from the United States suggests that labor market outcomes for men are linked to parenthood: fathers' earnings increase when they have children.[14]

While the nature of unions may vary, marriage or forming a union is a key transition in life. For many young people and their families, timing of marriage is affected by economic pressures and expected gender roles (box 6.3). Once married, newlyweds make joint decisions about contraceptive use and the timing of births. Discord between spouses in the demand for children can also affect the couples' use of contraceptives or maternal health care.

In addition to these factors, nutrition and reproductive health are important for a successful transition to family formation. Good nutrition and reproductive health have big payoffs for the young when they make the transition to parenthood. Young women who are underweight or who suffer from micronutrient deficiencies before pregnancy are more likely to have low birth weight infants.[15] Preventing low birth weight infants brings very high returns for the child: lower infant mortality, better cognitive ability, and reduced

---

BOX 6.2 *Education shapes family formation*

Young women and men today are more educated than previous generations were when they become parents. Better educated parents plan safer childbearing and invest more in their children's education and health. Compared with the past, young people today are also more likely to marry later and have more say in whom and when they marry. Some attribute the decline in arranged marriages and the shift of marriage decision making from parents to young people to the increased education of women.

There is also a strong link between female education and reduced childbearing in almost all countries. In some countries, even a few years of attending primary school reduces the number of children ever born, and secondary education has a stronger impact. Mothers' education is also associated with reductions in desired family size and increases in contraceptive use.

In some countries, the push toward universal primary education in the 1990s and the incentives to girls to continue beyond primary have stimulated girls' enrollment in secondary school, evident in the educa-

tional attainment of teenage mothers in some countries. In Bangladesh during the 1990s, the percentage of teenage mothers who had ever enrolled in secondary school rose from 16 percent to 26 percent. To the extent that mothers' education is associated with better health outcomes, children of teen mothers may suffer fewer disadvantages today.

Expanding schooling and employment opportunities can delay entry into motherhood. A study from Guatemala spanning 35 years suggests that women delayed childbearing because of increased schooling. Using rich panel data, the study shows that education has a significant causal effect on age at parenting for women but not for men. Every additional grade of school attainment delayed the mean age of first parenthood for females by 0.52–0.87 years. It also reduced the probability of becoming teenage mothers (before age 18) by 14 to 23 percent.

Sources: Behrman and others (2006); Mensch, Singh, and Casterline (2005); and National Research Council and Institute of Medicine (2005).

BOX 6.3   *Voices of Bangladeshi youth: Searching for the ideal spouse*

There is considerable agreement on what constitutes an "ideal" partner—of either sex. For both parties, education and good character is considered desirable. However, boys seek girls with good looks and girls seek boys with family wealth or a job. In Sylhet, an "ideal" husband is somebody who is established and honest and an "ideal" wife is somebody who is shongshari (good at household tasks), has good character, and is good looking. The Hindu male group in Chittagong is cynical about what brides look for in a boy: "all the girls want in a husband is money—none of the other characteristics matter. If a boy has money, he will get a bride." The Kalyanpur *basti* (slum) boys had

a lot more discussion on what constitutes a good woman, and they seemed quite concerned about the "morality" of women today—particularly of their "easy" female colleagues in the garment factories. The Kalyanpur basti girls, however, were quite cynical in their comments about a good husband: "a bad husband is someone who beats you in public, in front of everyone; a good husband is someone who beats you quietly, at home, so no one realizes."

Source: Ali and others (2006); Consultation meetings carried out with 23 youth groups (ages 10–27) in Chittagong, Dhaka, Rajshahi, and Sylhet, Bangladesh, January 2006.

---

chance of acquiring noncommunicable disease in adulthood. It also improves labor productivity in adulthood, with the economic benefits close to $510 per infant prevented from falling into low birth weight.[16] Fathers' nutrition can indirectly affect child health through the effect on household income. Well-nourished fathers are more productive in the labor market and have higher earnings.[17]

First-time parents experience health risks—for the mother and the baby. For example, firstborn children have a greater likelihood of dying within the first four weeks of life, perhaps due to a lack of health knowledge and to inappropriate care. HIV/AIDS poses an additional concern for young people starting a family. Because young women are more likely to marry older men, they face a greater risk of acquiring HIV.[18] That is why the incidence of HIV is higher among young women than young men in populations where the disease is prevalent, as in some Sub-Saharan African countries (chapter 5). This pattern will also emerge in low HIV-prevalence countries, such as India, where infections are spread mostly through sexual contact. Not having access to relevant information, counseling, and testing during pregnancy increases the risk of mother-to-child transmission of the virus.

As the rest of the section shows, undernutrition is not as widespread among the

young as it once was, but micronutrient deficiencies remain common. While the use of family planning, maternal, and child health services has increased in many countries, in others it remains low. Even where the use of services has increased, women may not receive all services, particularly hurting first-time mothers. Moreover, young women and men are poorly informed about sex and child health. Governments intervene in nutrition, family planning, and maternal and child health in almost all countries. The gaps described here suggest that these interventions have to be more effective in reaching young men and women.

Youth suffer from nutritional deficiencies

A young woman's height can indicate whether she risks having a difficult delivery, because small stature is often related to small pelvic size. The risk of having a baby with a low birth weight is also higher for mothers who are short. Low maternal weight and micronutrient deficiency before and during pregnancy can cause low birth weight infants.[19]

In most developing countries, young girls appear on average to be well nourished, with heights greater than levels that signal obstetric risks (140–150 centimeters). Other than South Asian countries and a few countries in Latin America, the proportion of 15- to 24-year-olds shorter than 145 centimeters is 3 percent or less. Bangladesh, India, and Nepal have the highest prevalence of young girls who are stunted, ranging from close to 16 percent of 20- to 24-year-olds in Bangladesh and Nepal to 13 percent in India (figure 6.3). Among Latin American countries for which data are available, Peru has the highest prevalence, with close to 14 percent of 15- to 24-year-olds shorter than 145 centimeters. The prevalence of underweight young women ages 15–24 is less than 3 percent in Colombia, Egypt, Nicaragua, and Turkey, but is high in South Asia. In most countries, the percentage of young people who are overweight is greater than the proportion underweight (chapter 5).

In contrast to their generally good nutritional status, young people suffer from micronutrient deficiencies. Anemia, the

Figure 6.3   Young women of short stature risk developing obstetric complications

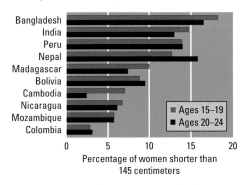

Percentage of women shorter than 145 centimeters

■ Ages 15–19
■ Ages 20–24

Sources: ORC Macro (2006) and MEASURE DHS STAT Compiler (surveys conducted between 1998 and 2005).

Figure 6.4   Anemia is highly prevalent among young women

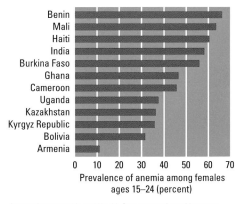

Prevalence of anemia among females ages 15–24 (percent)

Source: Demographic and Health Surveys conducted between 1998 and 2004.
Note: Anemia is defined as hemoglobin (Hb) content in blood of less than 12 grams/deciliter (includes mild, moderate, and severe anemia). Adjustments in these cutoff points were made for women living at altitudes above 1,000 meters and for women who smoke, since both groups require more hemoglobin (Centers for Disease Control and Prevention (1998). Figure represents married and unmarried young women ages 15–24.

outcome of multiple micronutrient deficiencies, is prevalent among young people in most developing countries (box 6.4). During adolescence, the nutritional requirements for iron increase because of rapid growth and so does the risk of iron deficiency. Among boys the risk subsides after their growth spurt. Among girls and women, however, menstruation increases the risk of iron deficiency throughout the childbearing years.[20] Anemia is highly prevalent among young women ages 15–24, including those who are pregnant (figure 6.4).[21] In Benin, Mali, Haiti, and India, more than 50 percent of girls are anemic. In Egypt, close to 30 percent of boys ages 11–19 suffer from anemia.[22] In the United States and Europe, the prevalence of anemia among women and children is 7 to 12 percent.

Young people are not well informed—and are less likely to use key services

Sexual and reproductive health knowledge is low among young people. Among sexually active youth in Nigerian schools, awareness of the risk of pregnancy from the first sexual encounter is very low.[23] Nor are young people able to identify the time of month when the risk of pregnancy is highest. Even married girls, who are most likely to be regularly engaging in sex, were no more knowledgeable than unmarried girls.[24] Of young people ages 15–24 in Indonesia,[25] 21 percent of girls and 28 percent of boys did not know any of the signs of puberty's physical changes for the opposite sex. Of those who

knew the signs, most reported that friends were the source of the information.

In Bangladesh few teenage mothers could identify life-threatening conditions during pregnancy. Only about 5 percent knew about conditions such as severe headaches, high blood pressure, and pre-eclampsia, that might threaten the life of the mother during pregnancy or delivery. Nearly 50 percent of teenage mothers reported not seeking any assistance for maternal complications.[26]

Young couples are less likely to use contraceptives than older couples, evident in the percentage of women by age who report using any method of contraception (figure 6.5). In Peru, 64 percent of 30- to 34-year-old women use contraceptives, nearly seven

Figure 6.5 Young women are less likely to use contraceptives than older women

Percentage of sexually active young women, married and unmarried, who use contraceptives

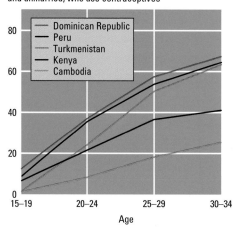

Sources: ORC Macro (2006) and MEASURE DHS STAT Compiler (surveys conducted between 2000 and 2005).

Figure 6.6 Young mothers do not get full care during antenatal visits

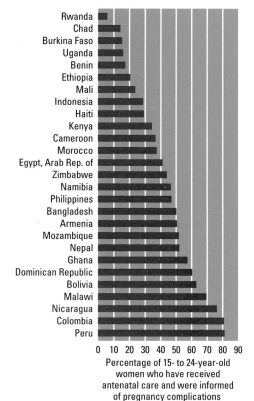

Percentage of 15- to 24-year-old women who have received antenatal care and were informed of pregnancy complications

Source: Demographic and Health Surveys conducted between 1998 and 2003.
Note: Data shown are restricted to women who used antenatal care for their latest infants during the three years prior to the survey.

"I don't think information about bearing and fostering children I have obtained is enough, and we can't obtain this information from school and family."

University student, China
December 2005

times the proportion for 15- to 19-year-olds, perhaps because young couples want to have children soon after marriage. Or it could be that family planning services emphasize methods that help women stop births (for example, sterilization) rather than space births, so older women ready to stop may be more likely to use these services than younger women just starting their families. Another constraint for unmarried women is the difficulty of obtaining contraceptives. In some countries, laws regulate young women's access to contraceptives. Restrictions may include minimum age requirements and requirements that young women be married and have spousal approval.[27]

In Bangladesh, India, Mali, and Pakistan, the use of maternal health services, particularly antenatal care, is low among young women. Price, including travel and waiting time, determines health care use by all women.[28] For young women and first-time parents, a lack of knowledge about the need for preventive care during pregnancy could be an additional factor. Girls' lower bargaining power also reduces their ability to negotiate with their husbands and in-laws about the need for care during pregnancy. In rural Pakistan, the mobility of adolescent girls is highly constrained, making it difficult for them to seek services.[29]

In many countries in Latin America and Sub-Saharan Africa, commensurate with the general high use of antenatal care, the percentage of young women receiving such care is also high, ranging from 80 percent to 100 percent.[30] However, even where the use of antenatal care is high, young mothers who receive antenatal care do not receive full care. First pregnancies are at a higher risk of neonatal mortality, and informing women of potential complications is an important component of care for young mothers. In most countries for which data are available, young mothers who used antenatal care were more likely to get checkups, such as measurements of blood pressure, but unlikely to be told about pregnancy complications (figure 6.6). In many countries where anemia is prevalent, iron supplements are offered as part of antenatal care. But in Cambodia, where anemia affects more than half of all young women, fewer than a quarter of mothers received iron supplements during antenatal care.[31]

Parenting skills help parents interpret infant and young child behaviors, as does knowledge about their health, nutrition, and developmental needs. Young mothers and fathers tend to be less aware of signs of childhood illnesses and of ways to treat them. Knowledge of oral rehydration therapy (ORT), a simple and effective response to a child's dehydration during episodes of diarrhea, remains low in many countries, particularly among young men and teenage mothers. In Peru, only about half of all teenage mothers were aware of ORT salts, compared with 80 percent of 25- to 29-year-old mothers. Even in Indonesia, where awareness is close to 100 percent among older mothers, only 85 percent of teenage mothers knew about ORT salts. In Kenya, only 40 percent of young men ages 15–24 had heard of ORT, compared with 60 percent of older men.[32]

Providing opportunities for youth to prepare for parenthood

Opportunities for young men and women to become better prepared for family life can be broadened by improving their access to family planning, maternal, child health, and nutrition services. Financial incentives can also increase the opportunities for people, particularly the poor, to use health services. Most of the programs have not been specifically targeted to young people, but they offer promising approaches to preparing young people for parenthood. Efforts to prevent early marriage can broaden young girls' opportunities to avoid early motherhood and help them avoid all the associated adverse health consequences.

Improving access to health services

Young men and women are less likely to use family planning, maternal, and child health services—access being a key issue. One way to improve access is to provide "youth-friendly" services where providers are trained in catering to young people's needs. Making antenatal and postnatal services friendlier for young mothers has been tried in several countries, but no rigorous evaluations are available.[33] An example of a promising program is a hospital-based breastfeeding program for adolescent mothers in Mexico that was associated with increased antenatal visits by program recipients.[34]

Because mobility can be a constraint, outreach services (rather than fixed-site delivery) can also make a difference. In such settings, providing mass-media health information campaigns that reach all in the community can stimulate the demand for services. There are no health outreach programs that target youth, but the success of programs targeting all couples in their childbearing years suggests that outreach can be effective.[35] The doorstep delivery program in rural Bangladesh (Matlab district) significantly increased the uptake of antenatal and postnatal care services.[36] The Lady Health Worker Program in Pakistan has been effective for women of all reproductive age groups.[37]

Increasing men's uptake of reproductive health and family planning services improves their health and the likelihood that couples are protected from sexually transmitted infections (STIs) and unintended pregnancies (see the spotlight on Brazil). Men who need care for sexually transmitted diseases may not seek it from maternal and child health and family planning clinics, largely viewed as women's services. They may be more attracted to separate facilities that can provide them with STI and family planning services.

Engaging the private sector in public-private partnership can improve the availability of reproductive health services for women, with limited involvement and resources from the government. If governments find it controversial to deliver such services to young people, contracting them out can reach young women, as in Colombia.[38] The social marketing of condoms prevents STIs and HIV, but the few evaluations available do not provide evidence on preventing unintended pregnancies.[39] Promoting condoms as "dual protection" rather than only as "safe sex" may increase

"If young people have free access to family planning methods, we could understand the consequences of our actions and could be more conscious about our behavior, and could be more careful."

Young person, Cuzco, Peru
January 2006

the uptake of condoms and protect both married and unmarried young people from sexually transmitted infections and unintended pregnancies.[40]

As discussed in chapter 5, integrating STI and HIV services with reproductive health services can encourage greater use of both. This is particularly important in Sub-Saharan Africa, where HIV prevalence is already high—and in India, where prevalence, though low, is increasing among young married women. Integration can ensure that young women receive counseling about HIV and mother-to-child transmission of the virus when they go for antenatal checkups. Few women, however, receive such counseling or even opportunities for testing. The feasibility and effectiveness of integration, given the resource constraints facing most developing countries, are debatable—and no evaluations are available.[41]

Improving access to nutrition services

The World Health Organization recommends that if an adolescent is still growing, adequate weight gain and nutrient intakes must be ensured to prevent poor pregnancy outcomes. Because iron deficiency is often accompanied by other micronutrient deficiencies (vitamin A, folate), food-based approaches are likely to improve young people's diets. Fortifying foods and providing supplements are fairly inexpensive—and successful—ways of reducing micronutrient deficiencies. Where anemia is highly prevalent, food fortification may not be sufficient, and iron supplements may be necessary.[42] School-based iron supplementation programs can be effective in reaching adolescents in countries where enrollment rates are high. It has been estimated that the benefit-cost ratio of iron supplementation for secondary school students ranges between 26 and 45—that is, one dollar invested in iron supplementation will yield 26 to 45 dollars in return.[43]

Information on anemia in the population is often lacking, and surveys that measure anemia prevalence can help in developing health intervention programs to prevent it. Many countries provide iron and folic acid as supplements to pregnant women to prevent anemia during pregnancy. Because pre-pregnancy nutritional status has a significant effect on the newborn's health, nutritional measures should also target girls before they become mothers. Although providing supplements over a long period has proven difficult, because they have to be taken daily and they sometimes have side effects, school-based iron-supplementation programs have been found to be effective.[44] Results from a recent survey by the Partnership for Child Development of school health policies in selected countries shows that although a number of countries offer iron supplementation to school children, many countries such as Benin and Cameroon, where close to 50 percent or more of young girls are anemic (figure 6.4), do not offer such services in schools.[45]

Nutrition services must be an important dimension of antenatal and postnatal care services for teen mothers. Pregnant teenagers are at high obstetric risk, particularly if short or underweight before pregnancy. Close monitoring of teenage mothers' nutritional status has been recommended, because adequate weight gain may even be more critical for them than for older mothers.[46] Nutrition and weight monitoring are not always easily implemented, and health providers must be able to give women context-specific dietary advice. In addition to iron supplementation, vitamin A, zinc, and calcium supplementation can also be particularly beneficial for teen mothers, because they are at a higher risk of pregnancy-induced hypertension and pre-eclampsia. Teen mothers might also need postpartum nutritional care, such as diet counseling and support for breastfeeding.

Offering financial incentives

Conditional cash transfers have been effective in increasing the use of preventive health care by poor households. Although these programs have not been targeted to young parents, they offer a promising approach to increasing the uptake of preventive health services by first-time parents. Mexico and Nicaragua have provided cash transfers conditional on household members' participation in health and nutrition workshops and on visits to the health center. Mexico's Oportunidades increased nutrition monitoring, immunization rates, and antenatal care visits. Growth-monitoring visits increased by an estimated 30 to 60 percent, and children under 5 had fewer illnesses than children outside the program.[47] Nicaragua's Red de Protección Social also promotes children's participation in nutrition monitoring and the timely immunization of children.[48]

Preventing early marriage

A delay in early marriage, one way to prevent teen pregnancies, is likely to yield benefits for child health as well. For example, in Guatemala delaying marriage for girls improves the chances of their children surviving past age 5.[49] Many countries have laws specifying the minimum age for girls and boys to marry, with or without parental consent. In 50 of 81 countries examined, the minimum age for marriage is at least 18 for both males and females,[50] and in 32 countries it is lower for girls than for boys. Over time the legal minimum age at marriage for girls has risen, but it is difficult to enforce where vital registration systems are weak. A minimum age is also more likely to be effective when young girls, particularly those from poorer households, have opportunities to attend school and improve their livelihoods.

Norms about marriage age are culturally sensitive issues, and where there are strong taboos against premarital sex, daughters' early marriage might appear to be a desirable option for parents. Efforts to prevent early marriage must therefore involve parents and the community as well as young people themselves. One such program is the Apni Beti, Apna Dhan ("our daughter, our wealth") scheme in the Indian state of Haryana, launched in October 1994 to raise awareness about the importance of the girl-child and to reverse gender discrimination. It honors mothers of girls with a small monetary award (Rs. 500, or $16) to cover post-delivery needs of the mother for the birth of a daughter, paid within 15 days of birth. It also endows each girl with a longer-term monetary investment of Rs. 2,500 ($80) in government securities within three months of her birth, which she can claim when she turns 18, if still unmarried. In 1995, the Haryana government expanded the scheme by offering a higher maturity amount (from Rs. 25,000 [$800] to Rs. 30,000 [$960]) for girls who agree to defer cashing in their securities. The program has not been evaluated for short-term outcomes or long-term objectives.[51]

Strengthening young people's decision-making capabilities to prepare for parenthood

Young people need good information to make better choices about the timing of births, the health services to use, and the right child care and feeding practices. Programs to strengthen their decision-making capabilities in reproductive health, nutrition, and the care of young children include health education, parenting and early child development services, and life skills education—for young men as well as young women.

Providing health information to young men and women

Informing young people can be effective in preparing them for the transition to parenthood. Many governments offer such information as part of their school health program as well as under broader nutrition programs.

Sex education to prevent early childbearing. Sex education programs delivered to unmarried youth—whether school based or through mass media—can increase knowledge among young women and men. Knowledge, however, may not be sufficient to change behavior (chapter 5). As described in chapter 5, most evaluations of sex education programs have relied on self-reported behavior, which may not reveal the true program impact. However, evidence from impact evaluations suggests that sex education can be effective in changing behavior. In Kenya, an impact evaluation of an intervention that provided female primary students with sex education that included specific information about the risk of getting HIV from sex with older men reduced teenage childbearing.[52] In Chile, the school-based sex education intervention Adolescence: Time of Choices increased the use of contraceptives and reduced the incidence of teen pregnancy.[53]

Reproductive health education programs for couples. Reproductive health programs provide health education to married couples, but few evaluations are available.[54]

- A program in Bangladesh provides newlyweds with reproductive health information and services before they have children. All newly married couples are registered by a family planning fieldworker during a home visit, establishing a relationship with the couple and providing the opportunity to deliver family planning information. The fieldworker also provides referrals to health clinics for maternal and child health care.

- The Population Council's First-Time Parents Project in two cities in India provides reproductive and sexual health knowledge targeted not only to married young girls but also to their husbands, mothers, mothers-in-law, health care providers, and the community.

- A community-based approach to married girls' reproductive health in the Indian state of Maharashtra tests the effectiveness of delivering information through community-based organizations along with improving the quality and content of public services by training health providers. It also targets girls' husbands and mothers-in-law.

Information targeted to men. Providing information to men about safe motherhood and child health services can increase the couples' uptake of maternal and child health services (box 6.5). The Suami Siaga ("alert husband") campaign in Indonesia shows that mass media campaigns can increase husbands' involvement in safe motherhood. Suami Siaga and Desa Siaga ("alert village") were part of public awareness campaigns implemented with the five-year safe motherhood program. Between 1998 and 2002, Suami Siaga targeted husbands ages 15 to 45

from low or middle socioeconomic status, and promoted their involvement in the pregnancy, preparation for the delivery, and any potential emergency through various mass media campaigns and training programs. Desa Siaga focused on getting the whole community involved in safe motherhood, arranging transport to hospitals, providing funds, donating blood, and being alert to emergencies during childbirth. Although not rigorously evaluated for impact, monitoring reports show that husbands and wives exposed to the Siaga programs were more likely to have more knowledge of signs of emergency than their unexposed counterparts and more likely to have delivered at health facilities or with midwives.[55]

Nutrition education. School-based health education programs can encourage healthy eating and physical activity. Such programs must include messages promoting the consumption of a variety of fruits and vegetables—and moderation in saturated fats.[56] Young people must also be encouraged to consume foods rich in iron. Educating mothers about rest during pregnancy and appropriate child feeding practices have been part of successful nutrition programs in India (Tamil Nadu), Indonesia, and Thailand.

Like all health education programs, bringing about change in diet habits through nutrition education is difficult (chapter 5). An evaluation of the Bangladesh Integrated Nutrition Program (BINP) raised knowledge about appropriate nutrition-related behaviors, but most mothers did not practice them.[57] Poverty and time constraints were a major reason. Nor did the program adequately involve husbands and mothers-in-law, perhaps preventing many young mothers from practicing new behavior. Some behavioral change efforts, such as hand washing to prevent diarrhea, were found to be effective.[58] This program also had innovative components, such as targeting adolescent girls through the creation of Adolescent Girls Forums. In one subdistrict covered by the BINP, newlyweds were targeted to test whether it is more cost-effective to address first pregnancies and work with couples until their child's 24th month, rather than aiming to cover all young children and

"In order to help our students to gain better knowledge, we organize events at SOS village [space for free discussion on reproductive health issues]."

Do, 22, male university student in Hanoi and chairperson of the Reproductive Health Club of his university March 2006 pregnant women in a community. Results from an evaluation of this newlyweds initiative is not yet available.[59]

Provide parenting skills and early childhood development services

Parenting skills can improve child development. One such skill is knowledge of when an infant is ready for complementary feeding. In addition to this skill, parents must also follow practices such as active or interactive feeding, selecting foods suited to the child's emerging motor capacities and taste preferences, and talking and playing with the child during the meal. Early childhood development programs in Ecuador and Jamaica show that responsive and interactive parenting to support psychological development in children can offset many of the adverse consequences of childhood malnutrition on cognitive development.[60] In Jamaica, nutritional supplementation for undernourished children and psychosocial stimulation improved mental development.

Formal child care services can also support mothers who want to work. Extensive research from the United States suggests that the price of child care affects mothers' labor force participation.[61] In urban Guatemala, the higher price of formal child care facilities reduces hours worked by mothers. Children attending the *Hogares Comunitarios* child care facilities in urban Guatemala had better dietary and micronutrient intakes than their counterparts who did not.[62] In Vietnam, where average fertility and family size are low, 41 percent of urban mothers use formal sources of child care (schools and institutional care) while 46 percent of rural mothers rely on extended family members.[63] In Kenya, the high costs of early childhood development programs discourage households from using formal child care facilities and reduces mothers' participation in work. The school enrollment of older children, mainly girls, is also affected.[64]

Teaching young women life skills

Most life skills programs for girls, married or unmarried, also provide health information, family life education, and livelihood training. Gaining such skills empowers

---

BOX 6.5   *Grameen Bank's "Sixteen Decisions"— convincing men to have fewer children*

A study estimating the impact of male and female participation in microcredit programs in rural Bangladesh found that men's participation in the program reduced fertility. Among the four microcredit programs in the study, participation in Grameen Bank had the largest effect—surprising because men spend more time working and less time childrearing. So the effect for men could not be the result of greater livelihood opportunities from microcredit.

Authors attribute the finding to men's exposure to social development activities that are part of the microcredit programs, activities that may have altered men's attitudes. Grameen Bank teaches its participants the value of small families (among other social issues, such as girls' education). Having a small family is one of the "sixteen decisions" that members must promise to obey. The effect of men's exposure to such messages highlights the importance of targeting men in information and education campaigns for family planning and reproductive health.

Source: Pitt and others (1999).

---

women. For example, participation in microcredit programs has increased the use of formal health care by women. In urban Malaysia, women's unearned income (a proxy for their bargaining power) increased the demand for maternal care.[65]

Evaluations based on randomized control experiments of youth-focused interventions in this area are rare, but impact assessments of a few programs provide some guidance for effective interventions. One is the Better Life Options program in India,[66] initiated by the Centre for Development and Population Activities in 1987. Targeting out-of-school young women ages 12–20, it offers various services in periurban slums and rural areas—offering knowledge of reproductive health and services, providing vocational training, and promoting women's empowerment through recreational events. Results from treatment and control group comparisons indicate that the program improved the welfare of young women—delaying marriage, increasing knowledge of reproductive health, strengthening decision-making skills, and increasing the use of health care services (figure 6.7).

A quasi-experimental study in Nepal reveals that an integrated reproductive health program targeted to youth ages 14–21 had a large significant impact on behavior, such as the use of reproductive health care services, teenage pregnancy, and marrying young. A distinctive feature of the intervention was that it also involved

Figure 6.7 In India, acquiring life skills can stimulate young women's demand for health services

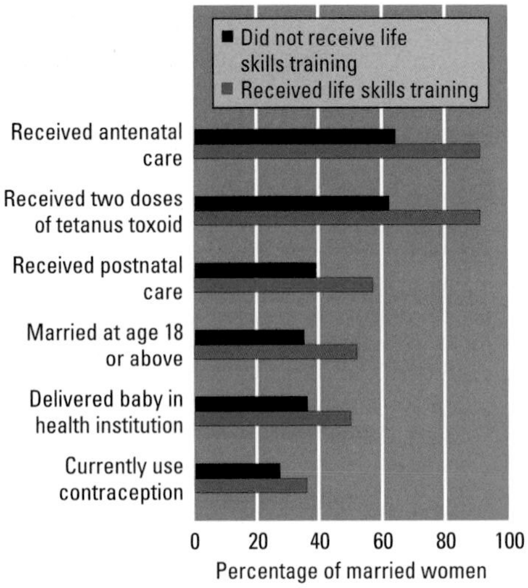

Source: Center for Development and Population Activities (CEDPA) (2001).

adults, teachers, and health care providers in assessing the needs of youth and designing delivery mechanisms. This may have contributed to the success of the program.[67]

Like the Better Life Options program, the life skills program of the Indian Institute for Health Management in Pachod in rural Maharashtra operates in rural areas and urban slums and targets out-of-school females ages 12–18. Offering a one-year course one hour each weekday evening, led by women trained in health and nutrition, literacy, and life skills, it had a significant impact on delaying marriage for the young women.[68]

Giving young women resources to delay marriage

Interventions that encourage girls' schooling—scholarships, vouchers, free books, and uniforms—can also discourage early marriage and hence early pregnancy. The well-known secondary school stipend program in Bangladesh (box 6.6) is promising because girls' average age at marriage is so low there. But it is not clear, because of the lack of a comprehensive evaluation, whether it delayed marriage for girls—a study of two villages found that it did.[69] Better employment opportunities for young women, such as the increased job opportunities in garment factories in Bangladesh, can also delay marriage.[70]

Supporting those who become mothers at an early age

Girls who become mothers at a very young age need to overcome consequences such as interrupted schooling. Young mothers may discontinue school because of lack of family or community support and the physical demands of pregnancy and childbirth. Others may drop out of school when they marry, then later face difficulties in finding paid work and earning a living. Because most teenage mothers are from poor households, second-chance programs must address their disadvantages.

Flexible school policies

Flexible school and social policies can mitigate the adverse effects of teen pregnancy. In the United States, where teen pregnancy is among the highest in the developed world,[71] it is often regarded as a public health problem because teen mothers and their children are also more likely to have higher poverty rates and greater dependence on the welfare system.

Some U.S. studies find a significant causal impact of teenage childbearing on schooling and earnings, while others find that a good part of the consequences can be attributed to prior social and economic disadvantages and not to teenage childbearing. The results, rather than being contradictory, might reflect different periods of time.[72] In the 1960s and 1970s, when social conditions made it difficult for girls to cope with pregnancy, teen mothers faced irreversible consequences. Over time, better access to second-chance programs ensuring school continuation for teen mothers may have reduced the causal impact of teen pregnancy on a range of outcomes. High school equivalency programs and welfare programs help teen mothers make up for their low income and catch up with their schooling. School systems also adapted to the education of pregnant and parenting teenagers, and this might have kept them in school.

Evidence from South Africa suggests that such supportive schooling policies helped teen mothers catch up and complete their education.[73] More countries in Sub-Saharan Africa and Latin America allow for more liberal reentry policies, and some even allow pregnant girls to remain in school during pregnancy (Burkina Faso, Cameroon, Chile, Peru). This is an improvement from the 1990s, when most countries in Sub-Saharan Africa required expulsion of pregnant girls. The implementation of these policies has not been documented, and their effects have not been evaluated.[74]

Integrated programs to meet the diverse needs of a teen mother

Since 1977, the Women's Center of Jamaica Foundation has supported unmarried teen mothers in an integrated program that meets many needs of very young mothers.[75] Offering teen mothers a chance to complete their education, it encourages young girls to avoid repeating pregnancy during their teenage years. It also offers them vocational training and day care.

The program provides formal schooling for pregnant girls ages 12–16—and personal and group counseling about the challenges of teen pregnancy and motherhood. It makes referrals to local hospitals and clinics for health services, including family planning. It also offers practical services to support young mothers during and after their pregnancies, such as day care for infants, classes in parenting and child nutrition, and information about women's and children's legal rights. It also provides job skills training and vocational training and placement for women ages 18–24. No rigorous evaluations are available, but the program appears to have improved the lives of teen mothers in Jamaica. Program benefits were transmitted across generations: all children of program participants were enrolled in school, and none of the teenage daughters of participants had pregnancies. Most girls in the program had only one child.[76]

Many policies and programs for nutrition and reproductive health can prepare young people to form families (table 6.1). Countries with widespread anemia must give priority to nutritional interventions. This chapter has shown that anemia is highly prevalent among young women in a number

---

BOX 6.6 *Cash transfers conditional on delaying marriage to promote school attendance for girls in Bangladesh*

In 1977 a local NGO in Bangladesh began a small project to provide secondary school stipends to girls who had completed primary school, on the condition that their parents agreed to delay their marriage. In 1994, with support from the International Development Association, the program evolved into the Female Secondary School Assistance Project (FSSAP), covering all 460 rural subdistricts in the country.

The conditions for continuing participation were that girls would agree to

- attend school for at least 75 percent of the school year,
- obtain at least 45 percent marks on average in final examinations, and
- remain unmarried until completing the secondary school certificate exam.

Each recipient was allowed to withdraw cash from the bank independently. An extensive information campaign was conducted to raise public awareness of the importance of female education. The project also took steps to enhance the school infrastructure, recruit female teachers, and provide occupational training to girls leaving school.

According to an operational evaluation, the project increased girls' enrollments. There were serious concerns, however, about the impact on educational performance. In 1999, only a quarter of the girls who received stipends in grade 10 passed the secondary school certificate exam, less than the nationwide secondary school completion rate for girls. This could be because some schools may have inflated enrollment and attendance data to meet performance targets. The evaluation also found no evidence that the program led to a rise in girls' age at marriage.

The first phase of the FSSAP neither collected baseline data nor established an external control group, which made it impossible to carry out an impact evaluation. To remedy this, a rigorous evaluation component was added in the second phase of the FSSAP (initiated in March 2002).

Sources: Bhatnagar and others (2003); Khandker, Pitt, and Fuwa (2003); and World Bank (2003c).

of countries and that iron supplementation programs may not always reach them. Few countries where anemia is a problem have a national program of iron supplementation. Use of antenatal care, during which iron supplements are typically offered to anemic mothers, is far from universal in some regions, particularly South Asia. Even where most mothers use antenatal care (and where anemia is common), only a small percentage report receiving iron supplements. There is also scope to improve young girls' access to iron supplementation through school-based health programs.

This chapter has also identified countries that need to pay more attention to intervention in increasing knowledge on reproductive health. On average, a high percentage of young people use reproductive health services such as antenatal care in medical clinics. However, of those who used the service, the percentage with critical knowledge about topics such as pregnancy complications and

Table 6.1   Programs and interventions that prepare youth for transition to family formation

	Proven successful	Promising but unproven	Unlikely to be successful
Opportunities			
Improving access to services	Conditional cash transfers for use preventive health services (Mexico and Nicaragua) *(first-time parents were not the focus of program)*	Reorienting reproductive health, family planning services, and safe motherhood services to youth needs	
	Micronutrient supplementation and food fortification for children and for young women before and during pregnancy	• Training providers to deal with youth • Family planning outreach (doorstep delivery) to youth	
	Family planning and maternal and child health programs *(not targeted to young mothers)*	Engaging the private sector • Contracting out family planning services in some countries (Profamilia in Colombia) • Public-private partnerships • Social marketing of contraceptives	
		Integrating STI and HIV services with family planning and maternal and child health (integrating condom distribution)	
		Increasing men's uptake of reproductive health and contraceptive services	
Preventing early marriage		Legislation setting a minimum age at marriage; banning child marriage	
		Delaying girls' marriage by offering financial incentives to parents (for example, Our Daughter, Our Wealth program in Haryana, India)	
Capabilities			
Providing health and nutrition education	School-based sex education to prevent teen pregnancy (Chile, Adolescence: Time of Choices)	Reproductive health education and education about safe motherhood and child health to	Programs offering information that is a) general in content; b) not culturally relevant
	Nutrition education to mothers to improve child nutritional status through feeding practices (hand washing in rural Bangladesh) *(not necessarily targeted to young mothers)*	• Young pregnant girls (Mexico, hospital-based programs) • Newlyweds (Bangladesh Integrated Nutrition Program, Bangladesh Newlyweds Program; India, First-time Parents Project, Community Based Approach to Married Girls' Reproductive Health Project) • Men (Suami Siaga in Indonesia)	
		Nutrition education to improve young people's dietary intakes, especially those programs directed to teenage mothers	
Teaching parenting skills	Early child services and responsive parenting skills (Jamaica and Ecuador) *(not targeted to young or first-time parents)*		
Empowering young women		Conditional cash transfers to young women (Bangladesh Female Secondary School Stipend Program)	
		Life skills plus livelihood training—(Better Life Options Program in India)	
Second chances			
Supporting teen mothers with flexible school policies		School policies allowing pregnant girls to continue in school or to return after delivery	
		School equivalency programs	
Integrating programs		Combining child care and the opportunity to learn livelihood skills (Women's Center of Jamaica Foundation)	

infant care is low in many African countries and some countries in Latin America and South Asia (see figure 6.6). These countries must invest further in quality and delivery mechanisms for reproductive health care services.

Most programs that have been shown to enhance reproductive health effectively do not explicitly focus on youth (table 6.1). This chapter has highlighted some of the interventions that can help to prepare youth for the transition to parenthood. Promising pro-grams have three features in common (table 6.1). First, they target youth and have youth-friendly components. Second, they focus on more than the transition to parenthood because this transition is interlinked with other transitions such as school and work, both associated with socioeconomic back-ground. Third, because transition to forming families involves multiple decision makers in various cultural settings, they involve not just the young couple, but also parents, teachers, caregivers, and the community.

Exercising citizenship

c h a p t e r 7

Consider what young people can accomplish: Days after the October 2005 earthquake in Pakistan, news began circulating that coordination problems among relief agencies were keeping aid from reaching those who needed it most. A group of 24 students from Lahore University of Management Sciences volunteered to be the first surveyors of devastated villages. Sleeping in tents, traveling by foot and in borrowed cars, these young men and women—between the ages of 18 and 22—surveyed 3,500 households, assessing needs and delivering supplies. Since then they have conducted a second, more in-depth survey of 200 households—covering some 32,000 individuals to date. Their data helped donors and relief agencies target their efforts and save lives.[1]

It is during their youth that people start to participate in social and political life on their own, and decide which skills to acquire, where to work, and with whom to develop intimate relationships. They can vote for the first time. Many choose, or are required, to serve in the military. Some join clubs or sports teams. They might decide, along with others in their religious institution, to provide care for extremely sick AIDS patients in their community. They might deliberate over whether to assume the debt a neighbor owes to the village moneylender. Some have staged protests because fees at their schools were too high, others because community leaders ostracized a supposedly immodest young woman. All these roles—both social and, in the broad sense of the word, political—are aspects of citizenship.

Citizenship is an ideal in social movements and political life, but the meaning of the term is elusive because almost any relationship between individuals and communities can be cast as an aspect of citizenship. The simplest definition is that to

be a citizen is to be a member of a political community and to enjoy the privileges and protections, as well as the incumbent obligations, associated with community membership.[2] Citizenship has both *passive* and *active* dimensions. Individuals, simply by being community members, receive rights and privileges—the right to a free education, the right to a legal identity, and, in liberal democracies, the right to vote, to a fair trial, and to associate with others. They also take on obligations to pay taxes, and to serve in the military where required. Active citizenship emphasizes how individuals should hold public officials accountable for their actions, demand justice for themselves and others, tolerate people who are ethnically or religiously different, and feel solidarity with their fellow citizens and human beings.

Public action to nurture good citizens is important because markets cannot do it alone—nor can mere social participation (too many social institutions are exclusionary or worse). It is also important because collective action, public accountability, caring for kin and community, and environmental stewardship are so much more difficult without an active citizenry. Even if Kant was right when he wrote that the problem of good government can be solved even "for a race of devils," the solution would be expensive and unpleasant (box 7.1).

This chapter examines the transition that young people undergo as they become citizens and the policies that might support them, first reviewing data on youth citizenship at the global level. Although young people might be growing less interested in politics and more disaffected from mainstream institutions in high-income and many middle-income countries, that does not appear so in several low-income countries, where interest in politics, and confidence

---

BOX 7.1   *What is citizenship?*

Historically, the status of citizens was contrasted to the state of slaves and others supposedly without the capacity to use reason to shape the common destiny of communities. The ideal of citizenship has also, at various times, and in various places, emphasized equal participation in and obedience to the community, advocated participation in social life, and described a zone of private life that the state ought not violate. Citizenship also has been used to refer to a shared way of life and the willingness to defend it against outsiders. Citizenship is now often used to suggest human dignity, and many social and political movements, such as movements for health and education rights, are cast as efforts to enhance citizenship. The rights associated with citizenship, particularly in developing countries, have in recent decades expanded to encompass the requisites of freedom—social and economic

goods, such as employment and access to basic services—and not only political and civil immunities and privileges.[3]

That is the ideal of citizenship. The reality, of course, has always been, and continues to become, more complex. For example, de facto legal rules throughout much of Africa ascribe rights—regarding not only religion and family matters but also land ownership and economic opportunities—to the chiefs of ethnic and linguistic groups, not to individuals. This practice reflects the colonial distinction between individualist rights for urban residents and group-based privileges for "peasants."[4]

The two main elements of contemporary citizenship—shared identity and rights—are becoming unbundled as legal resident aliens receive rights of access to basic public services in many countries (and even the right to vote in national elections in Chile, Malawi, New

Zealand, Uruguay), as the numbers of undocumented aliens, asylum seekers, and refugees increase, and as countries carve out export processing zones and other areas with different legal rights and obligations.[5]

The ideal of universal, equal citizenship does not specify the state's relationship to ethnic minorities. Should subnational electoral and administrative boundaries correspond to ethno-linguistic divisions? And what languages should be taught in schools?[6] Some states have stripped ethnic minorities of national citizenship to shed the costs of providing services to groups that do not support the dominant regime, making hundreds of thousands stateless in the last decade.[7] In many countries, women continue to face legally sanctioned and cultural barriers to own and inherit property, participate in politics, or receive an education.

---

in the civil service and private business are increasing.

The chapter next explains why youth citizenship is crucial for development outcomes. The youth experience of citizenship is formative and has lasting effects on the extent and kind of political participation throughout life. Citizenship affects development outcomes through three channels: by enhancing the human and social capital of individuals, by promoting government accountability for basic service delivery, and by enhancing the overall climate for investment and private decision making.

The chapter then moves to the three policy areas developed throughout this Report: opportunities, capabilities, and second chances. The opportunities available for youth to develop active citizenship depend on the principles and customs that structure the political and social spaces throughout a nation. Countries have promoted youth citizenship in several ways, including lowering the voting age and establishing youth councils and consultative bodies, military service, and national and community service. Such opportunities for political and social participation, if flexible and well-designed, can support active citizenship.

The section on capabilities develops the notion that the adoption of political and social roles is a process of identity forma-

tion for youth and that a young person's identity emerges through recognition from those who count. Possessing a legal identity and having work are both important. The clearest and most equitable policy for promoting the capability of young people is to make sure that all young people possess legal identities as full citizens. Two specific policies can promote youth capabilities in citizenship: civic education and programs of youth development and youth action. The absence of agency can lead youth to choose negative social roles, including gang membership and participation in personal and political violence.

Because many young people are attracted to, and experiment with, social defiance—and because many governments and societies fail to protect youth—legally recognized second chances are crucial. The chapter analyzes policies to give second chances to young people who have committed crimes and to child soldiers; young offenders can benefit from restorative justice programs, and former child combatants from assistance in reintegrating with their home communities.

Youth participation: Rising, declining, or both?

Concerns about the civic dispositions of young people are not new. In the eighth century BCE Hesiod observed: "I see no hope for the future of our people if they are dependent on the frivolous youth of today, for certainly all youth are reckless beyond words." Condorcet argued in 1782 that, as a rule, every generation appears less virtuous than its predecessors. As always, the virtue of young people is a preoccupation in many, probably most, places in the world.

How well-founded are concerns about contemporary youth? Are young people less involved citizens than their parents? Citizenship is a composite of complex and culturally differentiated identities, attitudes, and behaviors. For youth in high-income countries, some measurable declines—in political participation, interest in politics, and membership in civic organizations—have been widely documented. Youth sections of political parties in Belgium have lost more than 60 percent of their numbers since the 1980s. Membership in youth organizations in Sweden fell from 220,000 in 1972 to less than 50,000 in 1993. Almost all the decline in Canadian voter turnout can be attributed to the lower rate of voting among young people today, compared to their counterparts 30 or 40 years ago.[8]

A three-generation, longitudinal analysis that separates life-cycle and generational effects finds a sharp decline in social trust among American youth.[9] In recent decades newspaper reading, watching politics on TV, knowledge of current events, voting, and the belief that voting is a civic duty have all fallen among youth in almost all established democracies.[10] These changes reflect a decline in both opportunities for participation and civic interest on the part of youth, although alternative forms of civic participation may be emerging. Indicators of environmental activism and participation in protests, for instance, are up among young people in established democracies.[11]

Is declining interest visible in developing countries? Apparently not, at least not in low-income countries. Analyses of data from the World Values Survey suggest that, for low-income countries, youth interest in politics might actually be rising. It has been rising in China, India, and Nigeria, but falling elsewhere (figure 7.1). Related questions in the survey—How important is politics in

"Although youths want to participate in politics and raise their concerns and priorities, they are unable to do so because political leaders have their own agendas and self-interests, which detaches youths from active involvement in politics and social life."

Chandan, 20, Nepal
January 2006

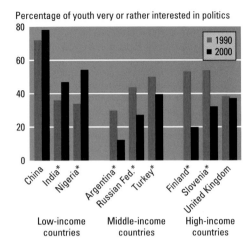

Figure 7.1   Interest in politics is on the rise among youth ages 18–24 in low-income countries

Percentage of youth very or rather interested in politics

Source: Authors' calculations from World Values Survey 1990–2000 (Inglehart and others (2004)).
*Difference significant at < 5 percent.

your life? How often do you discuss politics with friends?—exhibit the same trends. Another way to look at this is to compare political interest among young people with that of older age groups. The proportion of young people in most middle- and high-income countries who think that politics is important is about half that for older age groups, or even less. But in China, India, Nigeria, Vietnam, and Zimbabwe, young people are at least as interested in politics as older people (table 7.1). In Indonesia and the Islamic Republic of Iran, interest in politics is highest among the young, and steadily declines with age.

These differences in participation coincide with an equally distinct pattern in youth attitudes. In the low-income countries sampled, there is evidence of growing confidence in many national institutions, confidence that appears to be falling in many middle- and high-income countries. Whereas youth in middle- and high-income countries have less confidence in the civil service than a decade ago, the reverse is true in low-income countries (figure 7.2). Confidence in the press among youth is down or unchanged over the last decade in middle- and high-income countries, but rising in low-income countries. Strikingly, in low- and lower-middle-income countries—such as China, India, Russia, and Vietnam—

young people are most likely to believe that business should be privately owned, in contrast to the pattern in high-income countries—France, Japan, and the United States (table 7.2). Indonesian youth in 2000 were less likely to believe that business should be privately owned, but this might reflect their heightened political awareness during the financial crisis.

Girls are less likely than boys to participate in political activities. Gender disparities in political interest (How often do you discuss politics with friends?) are generally larger in low-income countries (table 7.3). This is related to the large gap in educational and participatory opportunities for girls and young women in low-income societies (including informal opportunities, such as spaces to play). That leaves girls less interested in public life, which in a vicious circle leaves the interests of girls and young women underrepresented in public institutions. Recent data from Sierra Leone show that girls are much less likely than boys to attend community meetings, and when they do attend, they are much less likely to speak (see spotlight on Sierra Leone following chapter 7). Among urban slum dwellers in Rio de Janeiro, boys score significantly higher than girls on every dimension of citizenship, including political participation, membership in community or civic organizations (excluding churches), seeking out government agencies, and having official legal documents.[12]

The declining interest and confidence in mainstream political institutions among youth in middle- and high-income countries may be due to other coincident transformations that are less pronounced in low-income countries. The technologies that have lowered information and coordination costs might also have increased the relative power of firms, civil society organizations, and other nonstate actors, and in the process reduced the power, prestige, and legitimacy of the state—and the incentive to participate in traditional politics. Young people might have less interest and trust in political life as aging populations push political debates toward the concerns of older citizens, and as income inequality increases.[13] Substitute forms of participation

Table 7.1 Do young people care less about politics than older groups? Not everywhere

	Age group			
	18–29	30–44	45–64	65+
Low-income countries				
India	46.3	45.3	43.5	40.5
Indonesia	53.3	41.7	28.4	18.9
Nigeria	54.9	50.3	47.5	53.9
Uganda	45.7	54.4	58.5	—
Vietnam	76.9	79.4	82.0	80.7
Zimbabwe	31.6	30.3	33.7	25.3
Middle-income countries				
Albania	26.1	44.3	47.6	44.0
Argentina	13.0	19.4	19.9	25.8
Bosnia and Herzegovina	29.3	39.7	44.6	51.7
China	74.7	65.3	74.8	83.3
Iran, Islamic Rep. of	61.9	57.4	45.5	32.1
Korea, Republic of	38.5	47.2	60.3	71.4
Poland	30.6	37.4	53.2	41.5
Russian Federation	28.8	37.8	47.8	39.8
Venezuela, R. B. de	22.2	25.3	27.6	24.2
High-income countries				
Canada	34.9	46.2	56.7	55.5
Finland	22.1	21.5	35.1	32.8
France	27.2	34.7	40.5	42.6
Iceland	36.8	53.3	53.4	62.9
Japan	43.7	48.9	75.7	84.1
United States	58.5	59.3	71.6	83.5

Source: Authors' calculations from World Values Survey 2000 (Inglehart and others (2004)).
Note: — = Not available. Table represents percentage of respondents in each age group reporting very or rather interested in politics.

Figure 7.2 Young people's confidence in the civil service is increasing in low-income countries

Percentage of youth reporting great or a lot of confidence in civil service

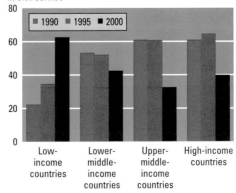

Source: Authors' calculations from World Values Survey 1990–2000 (Inglehart and others (2004)).
Note: The sample of countries is restricted to those with data from all three waves of the survey.

Table 7.2 Should private ownership of business be increased?

	Age group			
	18–29	30–44	45–64	65+
Low-income countries				
India	19.3	18.2	19.4	16.5
Indonesia	4.9	8.0	13.3	18.0
Uganda	39.4	40.1	41.5	—
Vietnam	15.0	14.3	11.6	10.0
Zimbabwe	33.8	34.9	43.2	30.0
Middle-income countries				
Albania	21.0	22.4	18.7	19.8
Argentina	13.4	15.2	20.9	19.9
Bosnia and Herzegovina	19.8	15.3	15.2	13.6
China	10.5	8.1	4.8	—
Iran, Islamic Rep. of	8.6	10.3	8.0	3.7
Korea, Republic of	7.0	9.4	14.3	11.1
Poland	12.1	9.1	9.6	4.6
Russian Federation	14.9	8.4	6.0	5.6
Venezuela, R. B. de	17.0	21.0	25.0	23.0
High-income countries				
Canada	14.3	18.8	17.1	25.1
Finland	5.7	8.2	11.9	13.2
France	14.7	17.4	21.9	25.2
Iceland	13.5	18.4	19.9	21.4
Japan	4.9	6.5	8.3	17.5
United States	24.8	24.3	26.4	34.2

Source: Authors' calculations from World Values Survey 2000 (Inglehart and others (2004)).
Note: — = Not available. Table represents percentage in each age group reporting that private ownership of business should be increased.

that are more opportunistic and less stable might have increased but are not yet being measured—such as "monitoring citizenship," in which individuals evaluate governments from afar through electronic media; targeted protests; or "checkbook activism," in which individuals spend money on consumer goods and nongovernmental organizations (NGOs) that match their values.[14]

Whether trends in youth participation and attitudes in low-income countries will, as incomes rise, begin to reverse themselves and resemble the declines visible in richer countries remains to be seen, as do the effects of these declines on youth engagement in politics and social relationships in middle- and high-income countries. Note that these trends of youth political engagement hardly encapsulate political citizenship, let alone the social dimensions of citizenship.

A more meaningful set of indicators of youth citizenship, which countries could assemble with new household and official data, would include the share of youth without identity papers, the share of youth in presentence detention, measures of local political or civic knowledge, and the percentage of youth who answer yes to the question, "Have you ever worked together with someone or some group to solve a problem in the community where you live?"

What youth citizenship means for adult citizenship and development

Patterns of behavior endure: political participation in adulthood is largely determined by participation in youth.[15] Young people learn political beliefs and behavior from those around them, and over time these orientations become habits, even if young people leave their socializing group behind. Consider voting habits, which are stable over time.[16] The first voting experience is challenging: young people might not know how to register to vote, where polling places are located, and perhaps have not developed an understanding of where candidates and parties stand on issues. Moreover, their peers, from whom they learn, are typically nonvoters. Some young citizens overcome these obstacles and become habitual voters, but others do not. Whereas parental education and income, as well as peer effects, help young citizens overcome these voting "start-up" costs, these socioeconomic and demographic effects diminish over time as voting (or nonvoting) tendencies become habitual.[17]

Conversely, political exclusion during youth has lifelong consequences. Although voting rates among women in the United States gradually approached those among men over the 20th century, the group of women who came of age before female enfranchisement in 1920 exhibited lower voting rates than their male counterparts over their entire lives.[18]

The lasting impact of early political behavior is visible in other areas, though it is generally stronger for symbolic attachments (party affiliation) and the extent of participation than for other political variables, such as location on the left-right political scale or attitudes toward specific policies. A study comparing young individuals who participated in intense and dangerous political activism with individuals who were going to participate, but for some reason did not, found that those who participated were more involved in politics and displayed more concern for civil rights issues over the course of their lives. Another study tracking lifelong participation among successive cohorts of high school students found significant continuities in civic engagement and social trust over the life span.[19]

Participation in civic life promotes shared growth

Active citizenship can broaden the access of previously excluded groups to opportunities for growth and higher living standards, most obviously in the empowerment of women. Participants in the Women's Empowerment Program in Nepal were more likely than nonparticipants to initiate community development activities and campaigns against domestic violence, alcohol, and gambling. They had more influence on household expenditures, and they better understood the importance of keeping their daughters in school. Legal and political empowerment includes informing people of their rights and providing the disadvantaged with opportunities to effect and exercise these rights. The Panchayat Raj program in India has empowered women and previously marginalized groups (*dalits*) and led to some increase in participatory democracy.[20]

Active citizenship also facilitates collective action, which can yield more effective and better targeted public services.[21] Community involvement is particularly effective in managing such local public goods as water supply, sanitation, forests, roads, schools, and health clinics.[22] In some areas, the participation of older youths in decision making enhances service quality. Student-university co-management councils in Russia aim to reduce corruption in higher education (chapter 9). The municipality of Fortaleza, Brazil, improved budget processes and outcomes by including young people in the deliberations (box 2.4).

Table 7.3 Women (ages 18–29) are less likely to discuss politics with friends

	Overall	Men	Women
Low-income			
India	60.3	76.0	40.4*
Indonesia	82.4	88.0	77.0**
Nigeria	74.7	82.9	66.0*
Uganda	73.0	73.6	72.4
Vietnam	75.8	82.1	69.9*
Zimbabwe	44.0	58.6	30.9*
Middle-income			
Albania	70.5	81.9	60.9*
Argentina	46.3	49.2	43.3
Bosnia and Herzegovina	60.8	69.2	53.0*
China	82.4	87.7	78.3
Iran, Islamic Rep. of	76.7	79.7	73.5*
Korea, Republic of	70.4	69.9	70.8
Poland	72.0	72.6	71.4
Russian Federation	70.3	74.0	66.4
Venezuela, R. B. de	53.6	57.1	49.6
High-income			
Canada	57.9	64.4	51.0*
Finland	62.7	64.2	60.8
France	52.0	62.9	42.5*
Iceland	66.3	60.9	72.5
Japan	45.0	58.5	34.6*
United States	65.1	67.1	61.9
Overall	64.4	69.7	59.2*

Source: Authors' calculations from World Values Survey 2000 (Inglehart and others (2004)).
Note: Table represents percentage of respondents in each age group reporting that they sometimes discuss politics with friends.
* Difference between men and women significant at < 5 percent.
** Difference between men and women significant at < 10 percent.

Citizen participation is greater in democracies than nondemocracies, almost by definition, and some evidence indicates that democracies, on balance, have better development outcomes than authoritarian governments. However, untangling the effects of democracy and economic growth runs into problems of identifying causal pathways, imperfect measures of democracy and participation, selection bias related to differences in regime durability, and the absence of reliable data. Some observers conclude that democracy has a modest or near-zero net effect on growth, with a possibly positive effect during initial democratization and a possibly negative effect later on

Alluring, Fascinating
Beautiful, Charming
Mere descriptions all
That we have never seen
All around us there is but one image
Tell me, is this to be my fate?
No sir! No sir! Accountability and
nothing but Accountability

. . .

How long will it take?
For this dream to be realized

The answer to all these questions...
Accountability, only Accountability
Accountability, Accountability
Accountability, only Accountability

Junoon, *Ehtesaab*[27]

as interest groups mobilize.[23] More secure property rights, associated with constitutional limits on the state and vigilance on the part of rival institutions, seem to promote growth.[24]

Democratic participation also enhances development outcomes indirectly—reducing corruption, improving governance, increasing the demand for human capital investment, and preparing for and preventing disasters. Democracies—insofar as they improve governance—reduce corruption, which in turn stimulates technological change and spurs productivity. In countries with the best civil liberties, public investments have an economic rate of return between 8 and 22 percentage points higher than the rate in countries with the worst civil liberties. Voting rights and participation explain which countries expand access to education, itself crucial for economic growth. Famously, democratic countries avoid calamitous outcomes, such as famines.[25]

Crime and the fear of crime and violence are widely acknowledged to depress private investment among both households and firms. Between 1984 and 1996, civil war cost Sri Lanka most of its tourists, and the estimated equivalent of $1.6 to $2.8 billion, or between 13 and 23 percent of GDP. The total cost of the war—in lost human capital, law and order, and investments—weighs most heavily on the poor and the young. School enrollment is lower among households in Colombian municipalities where homicide rates are above the national median. Crime and violence can have international spillover effects: tourism in Turkey has been significantly reduced by violence in Greece.[26]

Significant group-based social exclusion is also a source of violence and conflict. Some observers express concerns that the size of youth cohorts in many developing countries predisposes countries toward war, but the evidence on this is mixed (box 7.2). Most kinds of political violence—whether interstate conflict or war, civil war, riots, or terror—have roots in grievances and perceived injustices. As Trotsky observed, however, "The mere existence of privations is not enough to cause an insurrection; if it were, the masses would always be in revolt."

Political violence requires a motive, but also a group identity and the subsequent socialization of individuals into a fighting mode—and then an opportunity to engage in violence. Democracy may at first increase the opportunities to stage conflict as the repressive powers of the state are dismantled, and only subsequently reduce the motive to fight, after democratic institutions channel and satisfy group-based grievances. The result would be an inverted U-shaped relationship between democracy and the risk of civil war, a proposition supported by recent findings.[28]

BOX 7.2 *Do large youth cohorts cause violence? Maybe, if economic growth rates are low*

Samuel P. Huntington and Robert D. Kaplan have both argued that demographic dynamics portend conflict and violence across the developing world.[29] Their argument is that members of large cohorts, relative to those in their parents' cohort, experience reduced opportunities in life: more childhood poverty, less parental attention and supervision, and greater influence of peers relative to adults.[30] Their lower economic status, in turn, leads to lower fertility rates, higher female labor force participation rates, later marriage, and higher rates of divorce and out-of-wedlock birth when compared to the preceding cohort.[31]

Researchers across diverse disciplines have looked for the effects of cohort size on crime, drug use, wars, political alienation, and civic knowledge.[32] While cohort effects have been found for political views and behavior as well as for civic knowledge in some contexts, they are mitigated by national sociopolitical factors in others. The correlation between youth cohort size and crime and violence is stronger in rapidly growing cities, exacerbated by HIV/AIDS and competition for cropland and fresh water.[33]

Urdal (2004) finds no evidence for Huntington's claim that societies with larger youth cohorts are particularly war-prone, nor do large youth cohorts appear to lead to anarchy. Urdal does find that cohort size can increase the propensity for conflict among countries with poor economic performance. It seems that a large youth cohort can aggravate the tensions caused by poor growth but does not by itself lead to conflict. Similarly, others argue that "multiple demographic stress factors tend to exacerbate each other's effects, expose more of a population and more geographic areas to tensions, and test developing country governments with complex challenges."[34] Thus, the risk of civil conflict for countries in the early or middle phases of their demographic transition may be heightened by an interaction of demographic factors with each other and with nondemographic factors.

Very little of this research focuses on the effects of cohort sizes for developing countries.[35] In recent decades, the importance of cohort size has diminished due to changing sociopolitical and demographic dynamics, such as shifts in gender roles and values.

Youth can be political actors while still in their youth

Investing in youth citizenship affects patterns of participation, development priorities, and thus development outcomes, as young people age. But youth are important not merely because they are future adults: they can define and achieve positive change today. The political, moral, and even stylistic choices of youth help society see what is culturally important and achieve what is politically possible. Writing between the World Wars, Mannheim noted that the emergence of youth permits a society to achieve "fresh contact" with its cultural and social possibilities, and this fresh contact "facilitates re-evaluations of our inventory and teaches us both to forget that which is no longer useful and to covet that which has yet to be won."[36]

It is no accident that a new generation of young leaders has been involved in the transition to democracy and economic openness in Latin American countries, the political reforms in Eastern and Central Europe, and the adoption of new information technologies everywhere. Less embedded in older patronage and exchange networks than adults, they are positioned to exploit new political, social, and economic conditions.[37] It also makes sense that young people everywhere tend to be more receptive to emerging values and worldviews, such as environmentalism (figure 7.3). Young people have been crucial participants in China's anti-imperialist and democratic movement that began in Beijing on May 4, 1919; the 1942 Quit India movement; the prodemocracy movement in South Africa following the Soweto uprising in 1976; and the Otpor youth movement in the former Yugoslavia between 1998 and 2000 (box 7.3).

Opportunities for political participation and active citizenship

As young people encounter their society's main social institutions, they learn the privileges and protections their communities provide, the tasks their communities require, and what they can do to improve those institutions. Social institutions both teach young people how others regard them and estab-

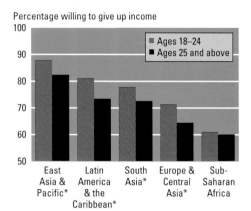

Figure 7.3 Young people are more willing than older people to give up income to prevent environmental pollution

Percentage willing to give up income

Source: Authors' calculations based on World Values Survey 1990–2000 (Inglehart and others (2004)).
* Difference significant at < 5 percent.

lish (or deny) opportunities for young people to participate in public life. This section addresses the participatory aspect of institutions—the next, how institutions shape the social identities of young people. Every institution does both, but for ease of exposition this section focuses on the opportunities to participate in elections, youth councils, the military, and national or civic service.

The quality of participatory opportunities depends on a society's constitutional framework—the formal rules and informal practices that suffuse its political and social spaces. Institutions based on liberal democratic principles teach young people the beliefs, skills, and habits of active citizenship—through the ways nondiscrimination and personal liberty are incorporated in schools, legal systems, health clinics, and village leadership councils. Rules for unionization gave rise to labor rights activism in Europe. Social rules associated with plantation economies promoted forced labor arrangements and limited political activism in Guatemala, Guyana, and elsewhere in Latin America. More recently, in Brazil, mobilization to oust the military government led to a new constitution in 1988 with a specific right to health care, which in turn promoted citizen mobilization to provide antiretroviral drugs to all AIDS patients.[38]

Young people have more opportunities to participate in public life than ever before,

BOX 7.3   *The Otpor youth movement in the former Yugoslavia*

When older generations in positions of power are beholden to vested interests and are morally compromised, young people can have the independence and moral courage to stand up to these institutions—whether parents or government officials or corporations. Young people's lack of experience can be a political asset. Free from prevailing norms and protocol, they can challenge failed policies and procedures.

The Otpor ("Resistance") youth movement in the former Yugoslavia, which played a key role in removing Slobodan Milosevic from power, relied on these traits. Otpor began in four universities, where young people used simple protest tactics and principles of nonviolence to express their dissatisfaction with the Milosevic regime and their disillusionment with political parties and the political process.[39] Participants had a hands-on approach to building sup-port for the movement, starting within their families, schools, and communities, under the radar of Serb authorities. They communicated their slogans and symbols through graffiti, badges, T-shirts, and other media. Belgrade was covered with Otpor slogans and its protest symbol, the black fist.

Gathering strength through their grass-roots work and partnerships with student groups and trade unions, Otpor's demonstrations against military tribunals and a public communications campaign spread the movement into the provinces and to older age groups. This mounting pressure brought early elections. When Milosevic tried to annul the election results in September 2000, Otpor conducted national protests that led to the installation of a new legitimately elected president.[40]

Source: La Cava and others (2006).

in the sense that there is "more democracy in more places" than at any time in human history. About 60 percent of the world's countries are democracies (121 of 193), up from about a quarter in 1974 (41 of 150).[41] In addition, the recent trend toward political decentralization has expanded opportunities to participate in subnational politics. Brazil, India, Indonesia, Italy, Mexico, Nigeria, Uganda, and the United Kingdom are among the many countries that have recently taken significant decentralization initiatives.[42] New technologies have also lowered the cost of acquiring information on social and political life.

However, the evidence that youth participation and interest in politics has declined as democratic institutions have become more widespread suggests that competitive elections are not enough to genuinely expand the opportunities for active citizenship. In many countries, the democratic transitions are incomplete, with persistent authoritarian enclaves, such as secret police; continuing clientelism; concentrations of power that limit participation, political competition, and accountability; and the emergence of lawless zones where the state is weak.

These themes emerge clearly in a 30-year study of *favelados*—urban slum dwellers—in Rio de Janeiro, Brazil. As each succeed-ing generation became better educated and more politically astute, and more committed to democratic ideals, it also became more aware of its exclusion from citizenship. It grew more cynical and less willing to participate in what it perceived to be a closed and corrupt system run by and for the elite. For many, particularly for youth, the main contact with the state is now the police, widely considered more disrespectful and needlessly violent than drug dealers. As drug factions emerged and began to negotiate votes on the community's behalf, the few tangible benefits the communities received from old-style clientelist politicians disappeared (box 7.4).

Promoting active citizenship among youth requires more than allowing more young people to vote and hold office. The constitutional framework involves the broad opportunity structure of the society, not just elections. Steps to enhance that opportunity structure include establishing institutions of accountability in government, widening access to justice, and enhancing civil society advocacy and participation.

Participating in elections

The opportunity to vote is perhaps the most hallowed form of political participation in electoral democracies. Recognizing this, and aiming to enhance the involvement of young people in public life, most democracies now set the voting age at 18 (107 of 121 countries with available data), and as low as 15 (in the Islamic Republic of Iran). Because of varying rules for the accessibility and voluntariness of voting, and the timing of national elections, it is difficult to compare voting rates across countries. It is widely recognized, however, that young people are less likely to vote than adults, and that youth voting rates have been declining in many middle- and high-income countries.[43] The percentage of urban youth in Chile registered to vote steadily declined between 1997 and 2003 (figure 7.4). This may be related to global patterns, as well as to potential fines and imprisonment in Chile for failing to vote once registered.

There are two alternative explanations for the difference in voting rates between young people and adults. First, young people may vote less frequently because they have less experience with politics and are less socially and politically integrated than adults. Alternatively, young people may be decreasingly interested in and more excluded from political life. The decline in overall turnout observed in many countries between 1965 and 1999 may be due to life-cycle effects, paradoxically exacerbated by the decision to lower the voting age to 18. It may be that well-prepared voting cohorts are being replaced by younger, less well-prepared ones, who first vote just when they leave home.[44] Overall, young people are voting at lower rates than they did in previous generations.[45]

While developing countries such as Bolivia and India have lowered their voting ages, no studies have been found that track the subsequent effect on youth or adult turnout. Because there is evidence that voting is a habit, reforms that lower the voting age should be combined with efforts to incorporate young people into public life, and perhaps to ritualize their first voting experience. For example, a proposal to lower the voting age to 16, combined with more intensive "citizenship education" in schools, is being discussed in the United Kingdom.[46] Turnout is also related to illiteracy and economic indicators, but evidence also suggests that relative educational levels, not the absolute amount of education, determine voting behavior for individuals.[47]

Randomized trials of "get-out-the-vote" campaigns in the United States show that phone canvassing increased young voter turnout by 5.0 percentage points, and face-to-face canvassing by 8.5 percentage points. The cost per vote ranged from $12 to $20.[48] In developing countries, capacity constraints often translate into out-of-date voter rolls and cumbersome registration processes. However, these constraints may be overcome in ways that are not prohibitively expensive: a voter roll of 75 million people in 83 electoral districts in Bangladesh was digitized and reproduced on CD-ROMs to allow voters to check their names before the elections—a first in the country's history.[49] Some countries have legally codified youth involvement in governance, such as the Philippines through the Youth in Nation-Building Act—an important first step in encouraging youth to vote.

BOX 7.4   *The citizenship of Big George— from youth to adulthood*

Jorge Paivo Pinto (not his real name), known as "Big George," came to Rio de Janeiro from a small city in the Northeast when he was 16 years old. He is the fifth of 19 children, nine of whom died from malnutrition. His parents were illiterate rural workers, and he never went to school. He traveled all over the country during his military service, an experience that developed his political awareness.

While still young, he was among the early invaders of a squatter settlement in the industrial North Zone of Rio, and he led the fight against eviction. By 1968 he was a highly respected leader within the community, and he spearheaded the struggles to obtain electricity, water, sewerage, paved pathways, and concrete steps on the muddy hillsides.

Rio's citizens had earlier lost the right to vote for mayor, governor, and president, but they could still elect their own city councilmen (*vereadores*). George remained president of the Residents' Association and negotiated with the city council on behalf of the community. Democracy was restored in 1984–85, and citizen action, nonprofit organizations, and political parties blossomed. This was also when the drug traffic started to appear within the favelas. It was felt that the police protected the rich neighborhoods, but looked the other way in the poor favelas, the locations of choice for the drug trade.

The drug trade attracted both money and weapons to the favelas, and drug dealers began to exert more influence, taking over the Residents' Association, community organizations, and even the local school. George was forced to move to a more remote area of the favela, but he continued to upgrade community life, fighting for a health clinic, daycare, and better school quality—and to be a respected leader in his own right, angering the dealers even more. The lights on his street were shot out each night. Bullet holes punctured the water tank on his roof and riddled his house with pockmarks. Youth gangs doing drugs congregated in front of his entranceway. Finally, in 2004, after several death threats and much pleading by his family, he moved out.

The majority of the people interviewed in Rio's slums do not feel like citizens. They do not even feel like *gente* (people). Experience has taught them to be cynical. The police are not held accountable for extrajudicial action, including murder—and the justice system and the political system are "complicitous in maintaining the privilege of the privileged," as George's son explained.

Source: Perlman and Anthony (2006).

Figure 7.4   Fewer youth are registering to vote in urban Chile

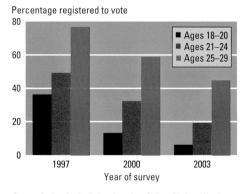

Source: Authors' calculations based on Chilean National Youth Surveys 1997–2003.

Youth councils promote citizenship

Many countries do not permit young people to hold national political office. For instance, the Philippines requires individuals to be 40 years of age to serve as president, 35 as a senator, and 25 as a member of the house of representatives. (Some offices of local governments in the Philippines are open to individuals as young as 18). Even if young people could hold national office, either through a lowering of age cutoffs or official set-asides for youth, it is not obvious that national priorities would move in a direction favorable to youth interests. Youth representatives could be too few in number, possess heterogeneous priorities, or cease to identify with other youth once they obtain positions of influence (chapter 9), with no change in the outcome.

Many countries promote advisory youth assemblies, councils, or parliaments. Some, such as those in Slovenia and Zimbabwe, bring together local youth representatives at the national level. Regional structures include the European Youth Forum, the Latin American Youth Forum, and the African Youth Parliament. Assemblies also operate in many locales, including the Youth Council of Catalunya and the Youth Parliament of Ryazan, Russia. In the municipality of Barra Mansa, in Rio de Janeiro, Brazil, children ages 9–15 help set expenditure priorities. In the Philippines, the councils are open to youths ages 15–21.

These initiatives can promote civic engagement—research shows that participation in student government (and other extracurricular activities and volunteering) is strongly correlated with other civic behaviors, such as volunteering and voting in adulthood.[50] But there are few data on youth participants in representative bodies—or on those whom they represent. Preconditions for successful youth involvement in decision making include commitment from the top leadership to youth involvement, prior support by the organization for young people in decision-making roles, strong advocacy by adult leaders for youth participation in decision making, and pressure by young people to increase their involvement in governance.[51] Without a strong sense of purpose or a clear set of objectives, a sense of disempowerment and tokenism can set in.[52] The objective of some of these councils is to advise governments on how to improve services provided for youth, but there is little evidence on whether any youth parliaments have enhanced the quality of youth services or the governance of service delivery.

Perhaps the most important drawback is that these initiatives are necessarily small, typically targeting those already motivated to participate. In Nepal, boys were more likely to participate than girls, and higher caste youths more likely than others.[53] Moldova's youth parliament (implemented with the support of an NGO) involved 450 children in four years, and because of concerns about who was included and the small scale of involvement, "was eventually phased out in favor of concentrating on the development of effective models of local youth participation capable of reaching greater numbers of young people."[54] Moldova then moved to youth councils as forums for youth representation and empowerment—the councils were operating in 25 percent of all localities in Moldova in 2005.

Military service has disparate impacts

Wars and armies have been crucibles of national identity, particularly in multiethnic societies. The former Yugoslav People's Army was one of that country's only national institutions, and conscription was one of the few common national experiences. When the armed forces attach themselves to the nation and not to a particular regime or social group, they can be liberal, modernizing institutions. For young people, military service can provide opportunities to learn skills and integrate into national society, particularly for disadvantaged ethnic and racial minorities who have few other opportunities for advancement. In the United States, active duty service has large positive returns for African-Americans, while it depresses earnings for whites and women. Among almost all countries sampled in a recent international survey, the majority of young people (ages 15–24) remain favorably disposed to military service, even more than to mandatory national service (table 7.4). And in most of these countries, young women tend to favor both national and military service at higher rates than young men.[55]

Although some have argued that required military service can promote citizenship, conscription is unevenly applied in both developed and developing countries, favoring the wealthier classes. The result is that it is more likely to harm rather than promote

Table 7.4   Youth opinions on military and national service in 2005 *(percentage agreeing or strongly agreeing)*

The government should require all young people to perform one or two years of national service

	Albania	Bangladesh	Ethiopia[a]	Iraq	Malaysia	Romania	Tajikistan
Ages 25+	77	84	54	38	76	75	90
Ages 15–24	**51**	**84**	**44**	**46**	**69**	**59**	**84**
Male	43	86	44	44	67	55	79
Female	60	82	43	48	72	64	89
Working	53	88	43	46	70	60	83
Not working	50	82	44	46	69	58	92
High socioeconomic status	57	79	—	21	93	54	86
Low socioeconomic status	48	86	—	39	70	60	82

Military service is a good experience for young people

	Albania	Bangladesh	Ethiopia[a]	Iraq	Malaysia	Romania	Tajikistan
Ages 25+	89	86	54	43	88	81	90
Ages 15–24	**70**	**90**	**46**	**54**	**84**	**69**	**85**
Male	60	91	43	48	85	61	79
Female	81	90	49	60	83	78	91
Working	71	94	42	56	85	63	91
Not working	70	89	49	52	84	70	84
High socioeconomic status	81	89	—	60	93	61	89
Low socioeconomic status	65	92	—	80	87	72	78

Source: WDR 2007 InterMedia surveys.
— = Not available.
a. Not a representative sample—Addis Ababa and Tigray regions are not included in the survey.

a democratic conception of citizenship premised on equal rights and obligations.[56] The military draft is equivalent to an income tax on conscriptees, with an associated decline in annual earnings of as much as 15 percent and a reduction in the incentive for families to invest in their children's education. The tax is also regressive because many developing countries establish exemptions to conscription, such as medical eligibility and deferments for continuing education, and because wealthier families are better positioned to take advantage of these exemptions, either directly or through connections and bribes. In Russia, poor, low-educated, and rural households were much more likely to have their sons enlisted, and the lifetime losses they incurred were large—about 15 percent of annual income. The costs are not limited to conscripts themselves. Research conducted for this report suggests that military service significantly increased the likelihood of subsequent criminal activity.[57]

The effects are compounded if one considers the risk of military service for health and well-being: even in the absence of combat participation, military service can result in rape, physical assault, and psychological trauma.[58] Data from the United States show that military service also has significantly adverse consequences for later (post-service) health. Cohorts with higher participation in military service subsequently suffered higher premature mortality, primarily due to ischemic heart disease and lung cancer.[59]

Community and national service: Involve young people in design, and give them choices

Some countries, such as Brazil, France, Germany, and Israel, offer young people service programs as alternatives to voluntary or required military duty. In other countries, among them Ghana, Indonesia, Nigeria, South Africa, and a number in Latin America, governments have required skilled young people, such as newly educated physicians or university graduates, to perform national service. In some cases, NGOs sponsor voluntary service programs (Servicio País in Chile), and in others the government contributes financing (Green Corps in Australia). The Mathare Youth Sports Association in Nairobi, Kenya, and the Cambodian Volunteers for Community Development were both established by young people. Service programs also vary in the length of service, compensation for participants, the extent to which different social groups mix, the activities youth engage in, the structure of supervision, and extent of youth input. Their objectives are to provide youth with opportunities for civic participation, instill civic virtues, build livelihood skills, and contribute to community well-being.

Voluntary service programs promote civic engagement. A rigorous longitudinal study of the AmeriCorps National Civilian Community Corps program in the United States compared civic and political outcomes for program participants with those for young people who applied to the program but did not participate. It found that the program increased civic engagement (though not the likelihood of voting). Systematic evaluations of community service programs are difficult to conduct because the very characteristics of successful programs—organizational autonomy and youth initiative—are confounded by selection effects that make impact hard to measure. Nevertheless, many service programs from around the world, such as VivaRio in Brazil, have produced passionate advocates and highly supportive former participants.[60]

One risk for service programs is that mandates applied to young people can become mandates for institutions, such as schools, to produce services (in this case opportunities for civic engagement), with many of the general problems associated with the delivery of public services. This underscores the importance of flexibility, youth input, and organizational autonomy in the design of service programs (box 7.5). In addition, elements common to successful youth service programs appear to include recognition afforded to youth for socially valued (as opposed to token) work, a manageable size so that par-

ticipants know each other and staff, and the presence of accountability standards.[61]

Acquiring an identity and a sense of belonging

Youth is the period of acquiring an identity. Erik Erikson put the challenge of identity this way: "from among all the possible and imaginable relations, [a young person] must make a series of ever-narrowing selections of personal, occupational, sexual, and ideological commitments."[62] Children typically make any number of imaginary choices, but for young people the choices are real and in some respects irreversible. Success in the transition to active citizenship entails, in Erikson's words, feeling "at home" in one's society, knowing "where one is going," possessing the "inner assuredness of anticipated recognition from those who count." For youth, who are *those who count*? Families are important, of course, as are peers. As young people grow older, however, those who count are increasingly drawn from institutions of society—teachers, police, employers.

A young person, viewed favorably, is more likely to feel invited to participate in public and economic life—social recognition promotes active citizenship. A longitudinal study of youth in Estonia found that a measure of a young person's self-esteem predicted the likelihood of starting a business years later. Similarly, having a goal of attending secondary school, controlling for family background, was related to secondary school completion. Conversely, social invisibility, discrimination, mistreatment at the hands of powerful institutions, and stark inequalities of opportunity can lead young people to suffer not only in material terms but in their sense of who they are and what they can do. Commenting on the need for spending money, a young Malagasy man said, "If I go out without shoes, it's as if I'm not a man." A sense of belonging is important to the performance of any organization, whether family, firm, or nation: "from the classroom to the boardroom, . . . a sense of identity and attachment to an organization is critical to well-functioning enterprises."[63]

At the extreme, young people can assume that the labels society applies to them are in fact true because, for most people, it is better to have a negatively valued identity than no identity. In addition, when states fail to establish, or actively repress, inclusive identities for youth, or fail to provide for the needs of citizens, resentment and oppositional identifications emerge. For example, the marginalized young descendants of North African immigrants to France speak a countercultural antilanguage, *verlan*, which arose in the politicized *banlieues* (suburbs) of the 1970s, because it deliberately obscures meaning, and carries elements of defiance, indifference, and heroism. On the computer of a young man arrested in Italy for alleged political extremism was a song that repeated the words "I am a terrorist, I am a terrorist," over and over, suggesting an aspect of glory even in that label.[64]

Social organizations provide spaces for young people to develop a sense of belonging. They include social and civil organizations, such as religious groups, rural associations in West Africa (*kafoolu*), samba schools and sports teams in Brazil, clubs such as 4-H and Scouts, and environmental protection movements. To promote a sense of belonging and active citizenship, public policy for social organizations should be permissive, with few requirements for formation and reporting.

This section examines four institutions that young people encounter, through which they learn how others regard them, and with or against which they begin to identify themselves: the state and the documents of formal citizenship, schools, employers, and official and NGO youth groups. Young people sometimes turn, when these and other formal institutions fail to recognize them, to informal groups whose identities include opposition to society's formal institutions. So the section also examines the motives and consequences of gang membership and political extremism.

A legal identity

Actions, or omissions, on the part of the state affect whether, and how, a young person comes to feel recognized in society. These include a legal identity—a passport, an identification card, and other basic documentation often crucial for access to basic

---

BOX 7.5   *Promoting voluntary and independent opportunities*

More research is needed on the kinds of opportunities that best stimulate youth citizenship and on government initiatives promoting them. The research so far suggests that conscription, while an instrument of nation-building in some contexts, is often applied inequitably, with negative consequences for poverty alleviation and solidarity. Service programs to promote civic engagement are more effective when young people have choices about the activities they want to participate in and are involved in their design.

Too often, political leaders have used the energy and vitality of young people as instruments of state power. The Hitlerjugend (Hitler Youth) in Germany was a notorious instance of state-sponsored opportunities for youth civic engagement that destroyed, rather than created, the kinds of state-society relationships that facilitate accountability and transparency. Less well known, but perhaps for that reason more striking, were youth-led groups, such as the Edelweiss Pirates and the White Rose, who despite the threat of execution, resisted the National Socialists.[65] The exploitation of the energy and strength of young people for state power is evident in the youth wings of political parties—associated with attacks on rival groups in Côte d'Ivoire, Indonesia, Russia, Rwanda, Zimbabwe, and elsewhere.[66] Precisely because state-sponsored youth participation has been (and can be) exploitative, participatory programs must promote youth involvement in their design and objectives, and emphasize organizational autonomy for the coordinating institutions.

---

services. According to UNICEF, more than half of all births in developing countries are unregistered.[67] A study in Brazil using data from 2001 found that of children not enrolled in school, 8 percent did not enroll for lack of documentation, about the same percentage who did not do so because they lacked money for school-related expenses.[68]

At older ages, the lack of documentation impedes young people's entry into the formal labor market (chapter 4). The high cost of obtaining passports in many countries bears especially heavily on poor and credit-constrained young people (chapter 8). Internal migration in China, Vietnam, and elsewhere results in "floating populations," composed significantly of young people who lack residence cards and other identity cards legally required to obtain housing, education, and health care—and without which they remain excluded from society (see spotlight on Vietnamese youth—managing prosperity, following chapter 3).[69] Taking steps to make basic legal identity more available to young people could increase their sense of belonging to society by opening crucial services and social institutions to them.

The mixed impact of schools on citizenship

Aspects of civics in school policies—whether to pledge allegiance to the flag or

"When a youth gets citizenship, he or she needs to realize that he or she has now transited from a nobody to a somebody."

Young person, Nepal
January 2006

sing the national anthem—are political flash-points in Japan and elsewhere. The reason: schooling is inherently political in the sense that, over the long term, it establishes a particular understanding of citizenship and the nation. Both directly through school policies and social science classes—and indirectly through the practices and choices of educators, communities, and peers—schools endorse certain virtues for students (chapter 3). Lee Kuan Yew of Singapore, in a discussion of multiculturalism, education, and nation-building, argued that a good citizen defends his country, protects his wife and children, respects elders, is a good neighbor, and is "clean, neat, punctual, and well mannered." Advocates of democratic education emphasize nondiscrimination, respect for the rights of others, holding public officials accountable for actions, the ability to deliberate and state publicly the reasons for choices, respect for the rights of others, and shared solidarity.[70]

Although schools promote national identity over the long run, it is not clear whether civic education promotes citizenship in the short run. Most recent studies on the impact of civic education rely on self-reported student behaviors and have difficulty establishing causal relationships. Data from the International Association for the Evaluation of Educational Achievement Civic Education Study, based on nationally representative samples of 14-year-olds in 28 countries, showed that increased civic knowledge was correlated with self-reported engagement and citizenship-oriented attitudes.[71] In the United States, students who took at least three courses in social studies were more likely to register to vote, to vote, and to perform volunteer work.[72]

Evaluations have repeatedly found, however, that civic education classes have a weak effect on school-age children.[73] Out-of-school civic education in Zambia changed knowledge rather than behavior, and the impact was mediated by educational attainment. Civics lessons in South Africa were effective only if the methods were participatory, if civics classes met more than once a week, and if students found their teachers charismatic.[74]

In the South African program, obstacles to participation included resistance by school officials and teachers to allow an NGO to conduct the civics sessions, despite the stated goal of weekly sessions; and crime and political struggles within the provincial and local governments. Those obstacles suggest a general problem that might explain why civics courses, although able to promote civic knowledge, have almost no impact on "the development of democratic attitudes and behaviors." [75] Students learn as much, and probably more, about citizenship from the broader school culture than from civics classes, and the broader school culture usually replicates the patterns of exclusion and hierarchy in society.

In service-learning programs, students work outside the school to meet real community needs. Teachers incorporate those outside activities into the curriculum, and students examine what they have experienced and receive recognition for their contributions. Service learning can promote social awareness, increase social connectedness, and reduce smoking, alcohol abuse, and unwanted pregnancies. The programs appear promising, but almost all available studies have been in high-income countries, and outcomes seem to vary with the quality of the program offered.[76]

Religious schools, which typically enjoy a degree of curricular autonomy from the state, often address values and social ideals more directly than state schools. The Jesuit Fé y Alegria schools in República Bolivariana de Venezuela and elsewhere in Latin America attempt to integrate community building, skills training, and leadership development into many of their programs. In many of the Mujahid group of *madrassas* in the Indian state of Kerala, girls outnumber boys, and the schools stress women's rights and empowerment for girls.[77] There is a danger, however, that some religious schools indoctrinate students, vilify outsiders, or undermine equality of opportunity for boys and girls. In Jordan, the government is promoting a new religious curriculum and textbooks that would highlight human rights and democratic ideas within Islam and eliminate negative references to adherents of other religions.

Recognition through work

Employment can instill a sense of competence, autonomy outside the home, and social standing. It facilitates the development of social capital and the means to start one's family, which itself promotes social belonging and confers a protective effect on youth (chapter 6). In rural Botswana, working is the crucial element of *go itirela*, or "making oneself socially" a part of the community. There is evidence that higher rates of youth unemployment lead to more burglaries, thefts, and drug offenses. Unemployed young people are more likely to feel alienated, express less confidence in existing political systems, talk less about politics, and more frequently support revolutionary ideas than their employed peers.[78]

Work is particularly important for young women, for whom it is sometimes the only culturally acceptable experience in the public sphere. Expanding women's access to credit and targeting agricultural extension and technology to women can enhance their sense of belonging and value (chapter 4). Working adolescents, especially young women who are engaged in intense or solitary occupations, such as domestic or household labor, may feel isolated if they are unable to socialize with their peers.[79]

Youth development and youth action programs

Youth development programs combine sports, mentoring, theater, life skills, leadership training, peace building, and livelihood skills, usually in a defined geographic area. Typically, their goals are to build self-confidence, trust, and problem-solving skills. However, there are few persuasive evaluations of these programs, and most do not link program characteristics to the assets and developmental processes believed important for youth development.

Short-term or intermittent contact, such as that characterizing "part-time, uniformed clubs," may not provide the sustained environment to develop relationships of trust, perhaps because of the lack of opportunities for one-to-one contact.[80] A U.S. program that focused on poor adolescents in high-risk neighborhoods—and included education, community service, skills development, and financial incentives over four years—increased positive attitudes and community service, though it was prohibitively expensive for developing countries.[81]

Youth development programs have been implemented in municipalities in Colombia and more widely in FYR Macedonia, but evaluations are not yet available. Obstacles to the successful application of youth development programs in developing countries include skepticism of parents, a tendency to focus on young men in urban areas, and a social reluctance in many places to mix with individuals of other classes and ethnic groups.

Youth action programs encourage social activism and community involvement more explicitly than youth development programs (spotlight on youth action following chapter 9). Young people have been key participants in political movements as diverse as street demonstrations in support of the adoption of the Convention of the Rights of the Child in Brazil and school-based clubs that advocate evaluations of teacher performance in Romania. But programs encouraging activism are fairly new and remain unproven. Many rely on education, and while there is evidence that peer education benefits the educators, there is less evidence that it benefits the target group.[82] The programs tend to focus on a small core of youth, such as those with proven leadership skills, and might not reach those most in need.

Youth, gangs, and crime

Identity, status, and belonging are important reasons for young people, usually young men, to join gangs. Membership can provide prestige or status among friends, opportunities for association, excitement, and money, and a sense of belonging and identity for marginalized young people. In some areas young people are actively recruited into gangs.[83] Fieldwork from urban Nicaragua illustrates the commonly observed phenomenon that poor and marginalized young people band together to create opportunities and identities denied them by prevailing social structures.[84]

Some young people join gangs to rebel against authority. Others want to be accepted by a group of peers. Still others are attracted to the group's rituals and roles. Gang members may feel better after joining—with more self-esteem, fewer symptoms of depression or anxiety, and an improved sense of physical health, as well.

They may also feel competent, optimistic, in control, and accepted by their peers.[85]

The few long-term studies of gang membership have identified "risk factors" for belonging to a gang and committing a crime. These include community characteristics (weak social integration and the prevalence of violence and availability of illegal drugs), family characteristics (poverty, poor parental supervision, or parental absence), and individual characteristics (depression, poor commitment to school, illicit drug use, and peers who are gang members).[86] Young women, in particular, might turn to gangs for protection, even where gangs are not widespread. A recent survey reveals that 88 percent of young sex workers in Nicaragua reported being friends with a gang member, and in Panama 92 percent. Among those who were not sex workers, only 37 percent in Nicaragua reported having gang members as friends, and 47 percent in Panama.[87]

The state, or its local police and politicians, can fuel gang activity. In the 1980s, politicians in Rio de Janeiro armed supporters and gangs in their garrison communities, and local police were caught negotiating an arms deal with drug traffickers in 2004. In other countries gang leaders pay extortion money or bribes to police. In Jamaica, Nigeria, the Philippines, and elsewhere, local governments, the military, and senior politicians have directly armed and collaborated with ganglike militias.[88]

Where the state or local authority and other formal institutions appear to have broken down, and where the incidence of crime is high, young people may band together for protection, or to provide services. In some cases, these groups—which can include "youth patrols" and other service-oriented associations—can evolve into criminal gangs. The Bakassi Boys began in 1998 in the Nigerian city of Aba as an officially sanctioned response to petty crime in the market. A group of young people was organized by local traders, with the support of local politicians, to patrol the market and chase out criminals. This group quickly turned vigilante and took the initiative to summarily execute those they suspected of crime. By 2002 the Bakassi Boys had themselves begun to commit organized crimes, including kidnapping and extortion.[89]

Serious offenses by gang members are infrequent—on average, fewer than 10 percent of boys are charged with violent crimes, and an even smaller number of boys (6–7 percent) is responsible for the majority of serious violent crimes. Most offenses involve boys who commit minor crimes against property, and most boys grow out of it.[90] But gang membership is dangerous—the likelihood of being killed is many times higher for gang members than for the general population.[91]

Young gang members commit a disproportionate share of offenses, both violent and nonviolent, and the influence of gang membership on violence is greater than the influence of violent nongang peers. Youths commit more serious and violent acts while they are gang members than they do after they leave the gang. In some countries, the number and share of crimes committed by young people have increased significantly in recent years. In Eastern and Central Europe, youth crime more than doubled in the first six years after transition. Similarly, juvenile offenses increased after apartheid restrictions were lifted in Namibia.[92]

Evidence of the efficacy of interventions—diversion programs—to prevent young people from joining gangs, to encourage them to leave, or to prevent gang violence is limited. The few programs properly evaluated show ambiguous effects. Criminalization and suppression are the most common official responses to gangs, but they are the least effective. Successful interventions must address the underlying marginalization, discrimination, lack of opportunities, and hopelessness that afflict young people.[93]

For those who have not yet joined a gang or even committed a crime, but are at substantial risk of doing so, several diversion programs have been designed and evaluated in the United States. Some have even shown measurable benefits. However, the resources and time they require—in costs and in trained individuals to provide services to at-risk youth and their families—make them less than appropriate for most developing-country contexts.

Peace education programs promote tolerance and conflict resolution skills among youth living in areas of potential conflict, whether among rival gangs or rival ethnic or religious groups. One such program in Ecuador provided students with extracurricular training in creative arts as well as workshops on the risks of teenage pregnancy and drug and alcohol use. Interviews with beneficiaries of this multipronged approach revealed that students who participated in the project developed an awareness of the sociopolitical landscape around them and had much greater confidence in expressing their opinions and a higher sense of self-esteem than before.[94]

Juvenile crime is positively associated with local unemployment and poverty, and decreases with family income and education.[95] Youth crime also responds to jobs and changes in wages. Falling wages in the United States in the 1970s and 1980s were partly responsible for the increase in youth crime.[96] Programs to combat crime are less effective if they do not take into account the alternative opportunities for schooling and work.

The widespread availability of guns increases death rates from violence. Reducing the spread of small arms would have a significant impact on violence. Most of the trade in guns among youths is already illegal, but possible interventions include licensing, regulation, and a ban on carrying guns. Youth homicide rates are highest in Latin America. In 1995, there were nearly 13,000 homicides among young people ages 10 to 29 in Colombia, or 84 per 100,000. The municipal governments of Cali and Bogotá, Colombia, banned the carrying of guns on certain days known to have higher homicide rates (weekends and holidays), and there were fewer homicides when the ban was in effect. In Bogotá that effort was part of a comprehensive set of interventions to reduce youth violence that included administrative reform and municipal accountability; public awareness and antiviolence mobilization; reduction in alcohol consumption; public order and the restoration of urban spaces; local community-based security councils; additional funds for policing, domestic violence, and child abuse prevention; and alternative conflict resolution.[97]

Young people and political violence

There appears to be no single reason for individuals to join organizations promoting political violence. Most who engage in political violence are young men, and many—though not all—are students. Many members of the Taliban (*taliban* means "students") were recruited from madrassas in Pakistan and Afghanistan, although the vast majority of madrassas do not foment conflict or hatred, and only a small minority of madrassa students become involved in political violence. Studies conflict on the propensity of young people to be involved in terrorism. Some argue that the majority are under 25, others that young people are not more likely to be involved. Yet even in widespread violent political movements, young people play a small role. Of course, the vast majority of young people are not involved. And as with crime, their involvement in radical movements, even with terrorism, is often temporary.[98]

A study of 250 West German terrorists found that as many as a quarter had lost at least one parent by age 14, suggesting that the disposition toward political violence might be related to a kind of psychological loss. Other studies argue, however, that neither psychopathology nor socioeconomic deprivation drive people toward political violence. In some cases, participants in political violence were more educated and wealthier than their counterparts in the general population, and in others they were more likely to come from working-class backgrounds.[99] Terrorist organizations might be selecting more educated individuals for difficult operations or leadership.

This suggests that interventions to prevent political violence need to go beyond providing educational and economic opportunities. Social and political inclusion, in addition to improved economic opportunities, can drain crucial support for violent groups. Organizations promoting political violence resemble gangs and cults in the socialization process: social contacts and the social environment promote a sense of belonging to the organization. This has been observed among immigrants in England, global terrorists, and the Weather Underground in the United States. In addition, the calling to political violence might, like gang membership, be a way to overcome a fragmented inner identity with something believed to be more transcendent and higher. Young people "want to believe, with every sinew of their existence."[100]

Young people need legally recognized second chances

Young people develop their identities by joining an organization, trying a job, or falling in with a crowd. They discover how well those roles fit with their self-conception and their aspirations, trying on new roles that fit better, and then adjusting their aspirations again. Sometimes the most dangerous roles and identities seem most real, a precarious moment for youth. Erikson puts it this way: if societal authorities "diagnose and treat as a criminal, as a constitutional misfit, as a derelict doomed by his upbringing, or indeed as a deranged patient a young person who, for reasons of personal or social marginality, is close to choosing a negative identity, that young person may well put his energy into becoming exactly what the careless and fearful community expects him to be—and make a total job of it."[101]

Two of the most dangerous roles for youth are criminals and soldiers. And two practices of legally recognized second chances for their social belonging and political inclusion are criminal due process and the reintegration of child soldiers. It is important not to criminalize young people's experimentation. It is also important to avoid, whenever possible, their incarceration—not only because it promotes stigma and a negative identity but because of the effects on the health and well-being of young inmates and detainees. Where criminal justice systems are underdeveloped, many youth wait in overcrowded and dangerous prison for months, even years, before seeing a lawyer or a judge. Many child soldiers joined insurgent groups because they were abducted or because their choices and abilities were severely circumscribed by poverty and social dislocation. While they engage in (and suffer) extraordinary violence

"Youth rebel because we have a different perspective, different tastes, and because we've grown up within different cultures."

Young person, Honduras
January 2006

as combatants, measures to reconcile them to their home communities, and to assist in their reintegration, are critical for them and, in some cases, for regional stability.

Restorative justice for young people

Experimenting with social defiance is almost universal. Between 70 percent and 80 percent of children have committed at least one—usually petty—offense, most often unreported and undiscovered. Young people are often vulnerable to arrest and detention for "status crimes," offenses that stem from the status of the offender rather than the offense committed. Most common among these are statutes against vagrancy or loitering. A 1997 report by Human Rights Watch found that 1,800 young people were imprisoned in Kenya for "destitution and vagrancy," and a further 500 for being "beyond parental control." Egyptian police often arrest children they deem "vulnerable to delinquency" or "vulnerable to danger," categories delineated in Egypt's Child Law.[102]

Criminal behavior does begin in youth.[103] Data from South Africa show that 60 percent of repeat offenders committed their first crimes by age 19, and 82 percent by age 25.[104] But the evidence is clear that the way to prevent continued criminal behavior is not to punish young criminals excessively: do not impose harsh penalties, do not incarcerate youths with adults, provide access to justice, and promote restorative justice rather than incarceration.

Avoid harsh penalties. Many countries impose harsh penalties for the young. Between 1996 and 2001, 11 individuals are known to have been executed for crimes committed when they were under age 18, eight in the United States. (In 2005 the U.S. Supreme Court abolished the death penalty for offenders younger than age 18.) The Democratic Republic of Congo, the Islamic Republic of Iran, and Nigeria each carried out one such execution; each has since expressly renounced the practice, which violates the Convention on the Rights of the Child and the International Covenant on Civil and Political Rights.[105] Other harsh penalties often inflicted on young people include severe corporal punishment and excessive, long-term imprisonment, particularly for victimless crimes. The rate at which young people are imprisoned varies enormously across countries (figure 7.5). Some countries have fewer youth in prison than expected given the size of the youth population, average income, and schooling. This may be because youth crime rates are low, or because they have established alternative methods to deal with young criminals.

Young people respond to increases in the severity of punishment and the likelihood of punishment by reducing criminal behavior. But juvenile punishment does not deter later criminal behavior, and even in the short run individuals with either the most minor or the most serious criminal histories are not significantly deterred. Premature or excessive punishment, including incarceration and social stigma, can lead young people to continue to participate in criminal activity or violence. Harsher prison conditions are associated with higher recidivism rates. Reintegration, treatment, and restoration help young people find ways to belong, to feel both personally and socially valued. Obviously, policies allowing second chances need to be balanced with the legitimate purpose of deterring violence.[106]

Do not incarcerate youths with adults. Many countries have laws or regulations forbidding the incarceration of young people with adults, but the laws are routinely ignored—either deliberately or because of insufficient capacity in juvenile or adult prisons. Estimates suggest that more than 10,000 U.S. juveniles are housed in adult criminal justice settings each year. Juvenile offenders sentenced to adult prison are more likely than both their peers within juvenile facilities and adults serving time alongside them to re-offend on release from prison. Peer effects for various categories of theft, burglary, and felony drug and weapons crimes suggest limiting the exposure of less experienced criminals—the young—to those with more "criminal capital."[107]

Prisons are also extremely high-risk environments for the transmission of HIV and other communicable diseases. They are overcrowded, provide poor nutrition and limited health care, promote unprotected sex and unsafe tattooing, and continue illicit drug use

Figure 7.5 Countries incarcerate young people at very different rates

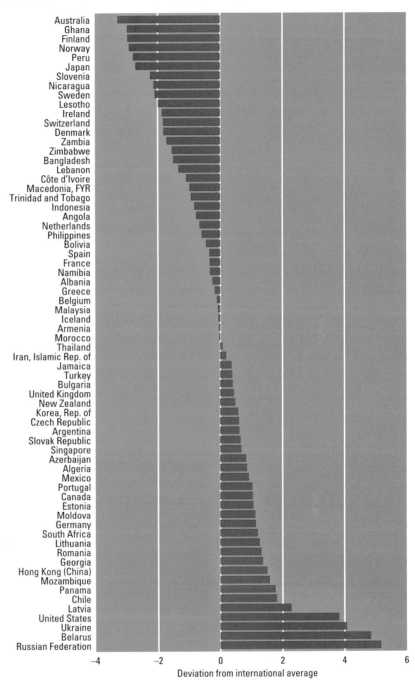

Deviation from international average

Source: Authors' calculations based on data from International Center for Prison Studies (2003).
Note: This figure shows international differences in incarceration rates among youth, in standard deviations from the international mean, controlling for youth population size, GDP per capita, and gross secondary enrollment.

and unsafe injecting practices. Syringe-sharing rates are higher in prisons than among injecting drug users outside prison.[108] Juvenile inmates in adult facilities were five times more likely to be sexually assaulted, twice as likely to be beaten by staff, and eight times more likely to commit suicide than juveniles held in juvenile facilities.[109]

Provide access to justice. Many young people in developing countries languish in prisons for months, sometimes years, before encountering a lawyer, a judge, or anyone who might establish their innocence. Most countries do not have even basic data on access to justice for youth, such as the number of young people in pretrial detention. Initiatives that attempt to overcome limited court capacity and bring legal support to incarcerated youth—such as the Justice on Wheels Program in the Philippines, where judges travel to correctional facilities and process detainees—appear promising. Also important are efforts, such as those recommended in a South African Criminal Justice System White Paper, to separate those awaiting trial from sentenced criminals, to separate organizational responsibility for detainees from responsibility for inmates, and to monitor the length of stay of detainees.[110]

Promote restorative justice rather than incarceration. Other interventions make young offenders aware of the future they face if they continue their criminal behavior. The most famous are the "Scared Straight" programs, which expose young people to inmates in adult prisons. However, they appear to do more harm than good. A review of nine randomized controlled trials finds that, relative to doing nothing, these programs are likely to increase delinquency.[111] Similarly, alternative residential camps that impose military discipline on residents ("boot camps") do not reduce recidivism.[112]

Restorative (in contrast to retributive) justice provides opportunities for victims and offenders to meet face-to-face, talk about the crime, express concerns, and work out a plan for restitution (box 7.6). Almost unknown 30 years ago, it is widespread today, both for adults and young people, with thousands of programs in individual jurisdictions in more than 80 countries.[113] These programs, and their requirements for offenders, differ across jurisdictions—for example, they are not universally a substitute for incarceration. Best known among them is the South African "Truth and Reconciliation Commission" following the transition to democracy in the 1990s.[114] Other examples include victim-offender mediation programs in Bucharest and Craiovia, Romania, and a public-private alliance supporting alternative justice programs managed by the AlvarAlice Foundation in Cali, Colombia.

Recent reviews of the impact of restorative justice programs on participant welfare and the likelihood of recidivism show

"Ocassionally they call us rebels because we dress poorly or ridiculously."

Young person, Honduras
January 2006

BOX 7.6 *Last chance in Texas*

Candace's parents were drug dealers. By the time she was nine, her father was dead and she had been raped and injected with heroin. Forced to steal to keep her younger siblings from starvation, Candace ended up with a friend of her mother's who exposed her to crack cocaine and tried to lure her into prostitution. At 13, she ran away with her 23-year-old boyfriend; together, they robbed 120 convenience stores in six months. Candace was arrested and sentenced to the Giddings State School in Texas—home to the Capital Offenders program for rehabilitative youth justice.

The school seeks to make youth offenders confront defining events in their lives and the crimes they have committed. It teaches students to take responsibility for their lives. This can be difficult for students whose traumatic early experiences have shaped their senses of right and wrong (see box 2.9 on brain development).

Guided by therapists, youth immerse themselves in detailed accounts of their lives and crimes. Students repeatedly reenact their crimes, playing both themselves and their victims. Participants are thus taught to empathize both with their victims and their inner selves. Students spend their time in Giddings learning things that were not taught in their homes—communication, introspection, and the ability to accept criticism without reacting angrily.

Youth who go through the Capital Offenders program demonstrate lower recidivism rates than those incarcerated elsewhere. Only 10 percent of students released from Giddings had been rearrested in the 36 months after their release, compared to 74 percent of all youth parolees in a recent study in California.

While these findings are impressive, the program is costly. However, the average young person incarcerated for a 40-year sentence in the Texas Department of Criminal Justice costs the state $626,000, not including the cost of crimes committed by those who reoffend. The average cost of rehabilitation at Giddings for that same person would come to about $160,000—a quarter of the cost of incarceration.

Candace spent 70 months in Giddings. After she had struggled to complete the Capital Offenders program the first time, she asked to repeat it. The parole committee at Giddings asked her, "How are you a different person than when you arrived?" She replied "I came here so locked in my feelings, there was no way I could understand them. Everything Giddings has to offer, I took advantage of. I earned myself some distance from myself."

Source: Candace's life story and Giddings program details excerpted from Hubner (2005).

BOX 7.7 *Private sector interventions to deter youth crime*

On February 15, 2003, three members of a youth gang known as La Placita entered the grounds of C.A. Ron de Santa Teresa (CARST), a rum distillery in the town of El Consejo, Aragua State, República Bolivariana de Venezuela, and assaulted a security guard. One of the youths was found by the company's security manager. The chief executive officer of CARST, 34-year-old Alberto Vollmer, describes the event:

Our head of security, Jimin, caught one of the guys after three days, and took him to the police. But the police here, it's not like the States. They look on the computer: "Wanted for this, this, and this. Ah." The worst prison you can imagine is the best alternative. Otherwise, they take you out in the jeep—which means you're dead. Jimin calls me up and says, "Listen, the police are taking this guy out to execute him. Green light or red light?" I said,

"No, no, red light. Bring him over here." They didn't want to give him over. But Jimin finally bought the guy for 50,000 bolivares. That's something like 23 bucks. Amazing, no? Twenty-three dollars, the difference between life and death.[116]

Alberto met with the young man, and proposed that the youths pay for the damage they had caused by working for the company without pay for three months. He accepted the offer, and on the following Monday showed up at the company's doors together with 22 other members of the gang.

The company responded by starting the Alcatraz Project. Many of the young people were poorly educated, many had drug problems, and many had committed serious crimes, including

murder. They agreed to work for the company during the mornings; in the afternoons they were given basic education, instruction in values and legal issues, drug counseling, and sports activities.

At the end of the first three months, the project recruited a second cohort from a rival gang, and then a third gang came asking to join the project. More than 100 young people have gone through the program. State Police report a 35 percent drop in crime in the district; but as of April 2004, only one of the project's graduates had found outside employment. The rest were working temporary jobs at Hacienda Santa Teresa.

Sources: Brandt (2005); de Cordoba (2004); and Gonzalez and Marquez (2005).

---

fairly consistent results, both from randomized controlled trials and other methods. Victims and offenders who participated in restorative processes were more satisfied than those who went through the courts. In general, offenders in restorative justice programs were more likely to complete restitution agreements, and less likely to reoffend, than those in control groups. Of the studies that matched participants to nonparticipants, only one found that participants had a slightly higher risk of reoffending than nonparticipants. The evaluation and adoption of restorative justice programs are complicated by the fact that they are almost always voluntary. Those who refuse to participate may not have benefited from the program even if they had participated. Some may refuse out of fear that these extrajudicial programs do not guarantee legal due process: the accused must admit guilt to avoid trial, and may not be informed of their legal rights.[115] Restorative justice programs need not be administered by the state. They can be initiated by private firms or individuals, as a complement or alternative to official justice systems (box 7.7).

Rehabilitation for young combatants

An estimated 300,000 children under age 18, who represent 10 percent of global combatants, either are fighting in wars or have been recently demobilized. (If the age group were expanded to include youths to age 24, the figures would be substantially larger.)

Between 30,000 and 50,000 child soldiers are engaged in the conflicts in the Democratic Republic of Congo, 30 percent of all combatants there. About 100,000 children have fought in Sudan's two-decade civil war. Some 100,000 Iranian children fought and died in the war with Iraq. Myanmar has more than 75,000 child soldiers serving both in the state army and with its armed rivals. Some 70–80 percent of combatants in Colombian guerilla and paramilitary units were under the age of 25. The UN estimates that more than 50 states have actively recruited another 500,000 children into military and paramilitary forces.[117]

A large percentage of child combatants—as many as one-third—are abducted or otherwise pressed into fighting. Other young people join because of family poverty and social marginality: armies and militias offer youth employment, food, shelter, and social membership—and in many cases the promise of booty, including sex, drugs, and material goods. A third of the fighters in the civil war in Sierra Leone had lost at least one parent, and 60 percent had been displaced from their homes before the war started; most were uneducated and poor. Political marginalization and the lack of economic opportunities encouraged the formation of factions among rural youth. Some young people are motivated by revenge: 15 percent of young recruits in Colombia had a sibling who was killed before their recruitment.[118]

The range of pain and loss for surviving ex-combatants includes almost every dimension of social and economic well-being: injury, exposure to disease, psychological trauma, sexual abuse, social isolation, poverty, lost education. Strikingly, there is some evidence that these effects might be worse for youths than for children, possibly because children are more resilient, or perhaps because they suffer fewer stigmas, than youths (box 7.8).

Programs to give these soldiers a second chance in life usually comprise disarmament, demobilization, and rehabilitation (DDR). To prevent re-recruitment, revenge, and abuse, it is important during the demobilization process to house underage combatants separately from older youth and adults. Rehabilitation should also include medical and psychosocial support. A survey of child soldiers in Africa found that 50 percent regularly had severe nightmares, and 25 percent suffered some form of mutism. At camps in Uganda, 70 to 80 percent of female child soldiers and 60 percent of males tested positive for one or more sexually transmitted diseases. Drug addiction and battle injuries such as amputation are common, as are the sexual abuse and rape of girl soldiers, often recruited to serve the militia leaders.[119]

Linking programs to development planning is particularly important in countries such as Liberia, where as many as 10 percent of the male working-age population will go through such programs. Ex-combatants and potential new recruits need help in obtaining skills, jobs, and self-employment opportunities consistent with foreseeable labor market trends and the needs of their

---

BOX 7.8   *War-affected youth in Uganda*

Youth suffer more than any other age group from war violence, yet not all war-affected youth receive equal attention and resources. In northern Uganda, for instance, services for children are more common than those for young adults. However, according to a recent survey of 750 youth combatants and noncombatants in northern Uganda, young adults are at least as badly affected by war as children (and in some cases more so).

The rebel Lord's Resistance Army (LRA) has terrorized northern Uganda for two decades. More than 1.5 million people have been displaced; tens of thousands have been attacked, maimed, or killed; and almost one-third of the population has lost a family member to war violence. At least 66,000 youth are thought to have been forcibly recruited into the LRA. The rebels have focused on abducting males between the ages of 13 and 18, but people of all ages and both sexes have been taken. The duration of abductions ranges from one day to 10 years. Two-thirds of them are severely beaten, a fifth are forced to kill, and nearly 10 percent are forced to murder a family member or friend to bind them to the group.

The consequences of abduction and forced soldiering on youth are severe. Those who had been abducted are more than three times as likely to have a serious physical injury or illness that impedes their ability to work. Abductees are twice as likely to report difficulties in family relations. In a society where kin are crucial to success, such discord can be ruinous. Abductees have nearly a year less education—a substantial amount when median educational attainment is

Figure 1   Among ex-combatants in Uganda, adult literacy rates are lower than those of adolescents

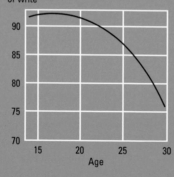

Percentage of respondents who can read or write

only seven years—and they are twice as likely to be illiterate. Those who were abducted earn significantly lower wages. Abduction, however, has few long-term psychological consequences on the majority of youth, and is only weakly associated with symptoms of emotional distress.

Although most programs and policies are focused on children, young adults who were abducted seem to have fared at least as poorly as those under age 18. And by some measures, young adults are doing even worse than children. Young adults are less likely to be literate (figure 1); they also earn lower wages (figure 2), most likely because they were pulled out of school at a critical stage and have had fewer

Figure 2   Postconflict earnings in Uganda decrease more for young adult combatants than for child combatants

Earnings gap between combatants and noncombatants ($)

opportunities to return to rebuild their human capital.

There are few resources available to young adults affected by the conflict. Those abducted after the age of 17 were less likely to have passed through a reintegration center (the principal intervention available in the area) before going back to the community. And fewer young adults than children report receiving assistance from NGOs. Some NGO staff complain that donor funds are more forthcoming for child soldiers than young adults.

Source: Annan, Blattman, and Horton (2006), available at www.sway-uganda.org.

local communities. Also needed are complaint mechanisms—to begin to reverse the political exclusion that was itself a source of the conflict and to address injustices that occurred in the conflict. Some of these rights-based approaches could emphasize the needs of youth "floating populations," such as those who worked in the diamond mines in Sierra Leone, by granting computer-generated identity cards.[120]

If large benefits are targeted toward ex-combatants and little to the larger rural populations, young people will have an incentive to become new combatants. Similarly, focusing exclusively on collecting the weapons of ex-combatants without also taking steps to limit arms trading ignores the fact that most postconflict environments are awash in weaponry. DDR programs thus need to think not only about ex-combatants but about the broader young population and the large reservoir of potential new recruits.[121] Female ex-combatants have a distinct set of medical, psychosocial, education, and employment needs, yet DDR programs tend to tailor services for young men.

The few evaluations of rehabilitation and reintegration programs show mixed success. The Emergency Demobilization and Reintegration Project in Bosnia and Herzegovina focused on training and counseling for employment, and included a quasi-experimental evaluation component. It increased wage employment and earnings, even among youth, and the largest impact on employment was among participants with very little education.[122] In Liberia and Sierra Leone, the vast majority of DDR participants reported successful reintegration into economic, social, and political life, but nonparticipants in the DDR process fared as well as participants. Young ex-combatants, like young noncombatants, still face considerable problems, primarily due to their lack of education and skills and the absence of job opportunities.[123]

Perhaps Kofi Annan put it best:

"No one is born a good citizen; no nation is born a democracy. Rather, both are processes that continue to evolve over a lifetime. Young people must be included from birth. A society that cuts off from its youth severs its lifeline."[124]

The task of nation-building is never complete; it must be renewed for every generation. Countries can promote youth citizenship not only by establishing broad liberal democratic principles, but by making every institution with which youth come into contact a venue for inclusion, solidarity, and participation. The participation of young people is important because it builds the capabilities of future decision makers, and because their involvement can improve the quality of services that governments provide.

Which institutions are most important for youth citizenship, and how can they be improved? For many of the policies discussed in this Report, there are few evaluated interventions for youth citizenship. This makes direct comparisons, cost-benefit estimates, and priority setting difficult. Youth programs suffer from the weaknesses of "youth" as an interest group—widespread stigmatization, constrained voice, and short-term identification on the part of its members (chapter 9). Even so, some general lessons emerge from the evidence presented in this chapter (table 7.5). Lowering the voting age, particularly if combined with social and educational support, might help young people develop a pattern of participation at the polls that will persist over their lifetimes. Voluntary service opportunities might be combined with life-skills training, vocational training, and public works programs (chapters 3, 4, and 5) to develop not only civic attitudes, but actual economic opportunities for young people, which can give them the sense that their lives have a purpose and direction. Military service, while widely praised as developing the skills of disadvantaged youth, carries long-term economic and health risks for the young people that participate and is not obviously superior to nonmilitary economic opportunities. Military conscription tends to be inequitably enforced.

Many young people lack any legal identity whatsoever, without which they cannot use basic services, and which contributes to the sense of exclusion and personal inefficacy that they experience. Ensuring that every young person possesses the documenta-

Table 7.5   Summary of citizenship policy directions and examples of programs

	Proven successful	Promising but unproven	Unlikely to be successful
Opportunities			
Fostering active youth participation		Lowering the voting age to 15 or 16 with social support (United Kingdom); local youth councils (Moldova)	
Not all opportunities are equal		Military conscription (U.S. minorities)	Military conscription (Russian Federation)
Giving youth choices		Voluntary service opportunities run by civil society (Kenya, Cambodia, and Chile)	
Capabilities			
Building safe spaces and trust	Ban on firearms (Colombia)	Youth development programs (Colombia and FYR Macedonia), but there are problems of scale	In-school traditional civics education (South Africa and Zambia)
Encouraging activism		Youth action programs including issue advocacy (Romania and Brazil), but there are problems of scale	
Recognizing youth as individuals and leaders		Legal recognition and documentation (Brazil) Service learning (United States)	
Second chances			
Providing alternatives to incarceration	Restorative justice (South Africa)	Access to justice for youth (Philippines)	Harsh penalties, such as capital punishment (Democratic Republic of Congo, Islamic Republic of Iran, Nigeria, and the United States) and prolonged imprisonment for victimless crimes
Providing resources needed for reintegration into society		Disarmament, demobilization, and rehabilitation programs (Sierra Leone and Uganda)	Excessive imprisonment (Russian Federation, Belarus, Ukraine, and the United States)

tion to secure the rights and privileges of national citizenship ought to be a priority for governments. An additional priority is to create secure and safe spaces for young people. The most successful anti-violence and crime prevention efforts have included a comprehensive list of interventions, including the enforcement of a ban on firearms in particularly volatile locales and events. Traditional civics classes tend to have little effect on civic attitudes, probably because those classes are swamped by the wider school culture. School safety and inclusion (chapter 3) can enhance citizen-ship learning and socialization, as might service-learning programs.

Criminal justice reform should be a top-level priority for governments. Too many young people are incarcerated for indefinite periods, without access to legal assistance, on the basis of obscure or vague charges. For young people, restorative justice programs should be used in place of incarceration wherever possible. In societies emerging from wars or conflicts, programs that demobilize, disarm, and reintegrate ex-combatants, and that provide opportunities to all youth, are crucial for security and development.

Rebuilding lives and institutions in Sierra Leone

After a brutal civil war, young people in Sierra Leone are trying simultaneously to build their lives and their country. Institutions and infrastructure are now being rebuilt, but opportunities are still limited. The country's 1.5 million young people need a second chance to build their skills; they need opportunities to engage in productive employment; and they need the opportunity to help rebuild social institutions for better governance. Youth make up more than a quarter of the population; they are desperate to learn, to work, to start families, and to contribute to their country's growth and development.

Sierra Leone has emerged from a decade-long conflict that displaced nearly half of the population, destroyed much of the economy and its productive capacity, and halted any progress in the development of human capital. The social costs have been incalculable. Sierra Leone is today relatively stable, but overcoming the legacy of the war and of prewar mismanagement remains an enormous challenge. The country's renewal must address widespread corruption, inefficient public services, and low investment in critical economic and social areas.

Nowhere is this more evident than in the indicators of human capital. The country ranks 176 of 177 in the human development index, and 70 percent of the population lives in poverty. Life expectancy at birth declined to 34 years in 2002, from 42 years in 1990.[1] Maternal mortality rates are among the highest in the world; teenage pregnancy rates are high, as are rates of sexually transmitted infection among youth. HIV prevalence is low (1.5 percent), although many of the factors that facilitate explosive increases in HIV can be found in Sierra Leone, including widespread sexual abuse, high unemployment, chronic poverty, and commercial sex work and informal exchanges of sex for goods and services.[2] Roughly 40 percent of 12- to 24-year-olds and 63 percent of 25- to 35-year-olds have never attended school. Only 20 percent of 25- to 35-year-olds have finished primary school.[3] All people, young and old, consistently rank education among their highest priorities, as do ex-combatants in rehabilitation programs.[4]

Sierra Leone defines youth as the period between ages 15 and 35; according to this definition, 34 percent of the population are youth. Using this Report's definition of youth, 26 percent are between 12 and 24, and 16 percent are between 25 and 35. Only 39 percent of these older youth are male, reflecting the impact of violence and migration on male youth during the conflict.[5]

With substantial assistance from the international community, the government is trying to establish three pathways for its 1.5 million young people: improve basic human capital services, enhance opportunities for productive employment, and encourage civic participation to rebuild social capital.

Human development—basic health and education for youth

Private and public investment in human development is increasing, and the government, together with local communities, has rebuilt many of the schools and clinics that were destroyed during the war. To respond to the high demand for second-chance education, programs such as Complementary Rapid Education for Primary Schools (CREPS) provides condensed education to youth forced to leave school during the conflict, benefiting about 110,000 pupils in 2004.

The government introduced free primary education for all in 2001, but many schools are supported by contributions from parents and their communities.[6] These contributions supplement official resources—paying for supplies and repairs to buildings, and even supporting additional teachers—but they can also deter students of poorer families from attending school. The vast majority of teachers report that they are rarely paid on time; this may contribute to a teacher absence rate of 22 percent and to the practice of holding private tutoring sessions outside of school.

Progress on education is being made in spite of these many obstacles: primary enrollment has doubled since 2001; gross primary enrollment is more than 150 percent. About half of sixth-graders are older than 13, reflecting the return to schooling of many who were denied education when younger, as well as grade repetition. While access to primary school has increased significantly in the last couple of years,

many rural locations do not have qualified teachers, resulting in overcrowding and frustration. The government's target is to provide universal primary education by 2015. Access to secondary education has also doubled since 2001, but the number of places has not kept pace with demand.[7] Besides rebuilding schools, as elsewhere in the developing world, the quality of education must be improved so that graduates are equipped with the skills the market seeks.

Shared growth—youth employment and opportunities

Sixteen percent of the population lives in Freetown; the vast majority live in small agricultural communities. Many rural youth are migrating to urban areas, especially those who feel they have limited opportunities in rural areas. Underemployment is common among both urban and rural youth, and formal-sector employment is extremely rare: 3 percent of youth are employed in the public sector, and 2 percent in the nonagricultural private sector.

While some young people would like more training, especially in areas such as business development, many others are concerned about access to land and credit. Some young people who have received skills training lack the tools required to practice their trades and have no resources to purchase them. In a survey of ex-combatants who had received some training and were working, only 28 percent had used their new skills to secure a job.[8] Young people in focus groups also express the belief that "connections" are needed for formal sector employment. And while land is abundant, elders in many rural areas maintain strict control over land allocation, deterring youth from farming.[9]

The lack of opportunities for young people in Sierra Leone has already had devastating consequences. Are there lessons from elsewhere? In many postwar economies, such as Somalia, Angola, and

Mozambique, much of the population is likely to be engaged in "gray" or informal economic activities as the primary means for survival.[10] These activities are essential for young people who have few alternatives for sustainable livelihoods or entry into the labor market. Participation in the informal sector is also a response to the lack of credit, information, or institutions that are required for a formal sector to function. As one review of the rehabilitation experiences of youth in Croatia concluded, it would be unfortunate if the continued lack of opportunities left youth "with little else but dreams."[11]

These examples show that it is important to focus on today's youth through short-term interventions, such as public works programs. But ultimately investments and policy changes are required for broadly based economic growth in the medium and longer term. Key among these investments is rehabilitating the country's physical infrastructure and social institutions.

Rebuilding trust—youth voice and governance

Traditional society is strictly hierarchical. Village elders maintain control over land, the allocation of labor, and marriage. Young people feel excluded from decision making in many communities. They are significantly less likely to believe that they can change unjust policies or laws; they attend fewer community meetings, and are less likely to speak during meetings. This is especially true among young women (see the figure). Community youth leaders, who are appointed rather than chosen by youth themselves, may not represent the interests of young people: half are over 35, and a tenth are over 50.[12]

Participation and voice are lower among youth and women in Sierra Leone

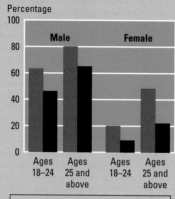

Source: Miguel, Glennerster, and Whiteside (2006) and Whiteside and others (2006).

Opportunities for the expression of voice are growing: many paramount chiefs were chosen in competitive elections following the end of the war, and the country held local elections in 2004—the first in a generation. Participation among young people was very high in these elections, and many local councilors represent a new generation of politicians.

Elders and policy makers often use the term "youth" with disdain and trepidation, to describe those—especially male—youth who are unable to provide for a family and are a potential threat to peace and stability. There is widespread concern that without better opportunities, the resentment may result in renewed violence. A recent social assessment for Sierra Leone found that the conflict was fought primarily by marginalized young people, especially from rural areas, who lacked education and access to livelihood opportunities.[13] The rebel forces took advantage of the "void of opportunities," as one young person described it, to recruit soldiers for the war. Another youth, when asked why he joined the rebels, responded, "I had never been offered anything, they provided me new shoes and clothes."[14]

The indescribable violence of the civil war created suspicion and fear, particularly of ex-combatants, making it difficult for some to return home. Reintegrating ex-combatants and other displaced people has been an enormous challenge, yet millions have returned home, and almost all ex-combatants have been reintegrated into society. Many communities have developed strong informal networks and local institutions, partly as a reaction to the breakdown of national structures; and there is some evidence that these social networks and institutions are strongest in those parts of the country that were hardest hit by the war.[15]

Experience in other postconflict countries suggests that the active participation of young people is a significant determinant of their satisfaction with reintegration. Increased participation may also enhance access to basic services, psychosocial well-being, and social capital.[16] In turn, young people are key to postwar economic and political reforms, improving the effectiveness of rehabilitation efforts, and the transition from crisis to development. The experiences of countries as diverse as Mozambique, Sri Lanka, and Vietnam show that addressing the needs of youth and managing the transition from crisis to development requires flexibility, local knowledge, and the inclusive participation of all stakeholders.[17]

In FYR Macedonia, university students were tired of paying bribes and having their professors accept them. They launched a public campaign to raise awareness of the levels of corruption, attract other students to their anticorruption campaign, and lobby for reform that would foster a more transparent university environment. The media embraced their campaign, and reform is under way to change the higher education law. (http://www.studentitezasebe.org.mk/)

Across transitions and next steps

PART III

INCREASINGLY, YOUTH'S TRANSITIONS ALSO CROSS national borders. This is occurring physically, through the large representation of young people among migrants, and virtually, through the young's disproportionately high and ever increasing use of new technologies. Both present worrisome risks and enormous opportunities.

What next? Implementing policies that affect young people face three challenges. One is that the youth "lens" is a cross-sectoral one, but most policies that affect youth are set sectorally. Another is that young people are a weak constituency for reform because, underrepresented in both civic forums and by their families, they lack voice. Finally, there is a paucity of proven success stories.

Moving and communicating across borders

Young people today live in a world integrated by faster movements across borders—movements of goods, capital, information, technology, ideas, and people. This chapter focuses on the two international movements in which youth play the most major roles: international migration and the spread of information and ideas through information and communication technologies (ICTs). Youth involvement in these two global movements can enhance growth and alleviate poverty. It can also broaden their opportunities, enhance their capabilities, and give them second chances when things go wrong in their many transitions.

Young people's opportunities widen when they can migrate to work abroad or use today's technologies to acquire new skills and get better jobs at home. More developing-country students are studying overseas and at home through online education programs. New interactive technologies are providing unprecedented amounts of information to youth, allowing them to become more informed decision makers and to communicate more with youth in other countries.

One problem is that young people in many developing countries have few legal options to migrate, leading to illegal migration and trafficking. A second is that the rapid expansion in mobile phone and ICT use has yet to reach many young workers. The challenge for policy is to extend the benefits of migration and ICTs to more developing country youth—and to enhance their development impact while mitigating the new risks.

Receiving countries can do more for poverty reduction and development by providing more opportunities for less-skilled young migrants—through seasonal and temporary worker programs and by letting the youth who do migrate use and build their human capital. Sending countries can also do more to increase the development impact of youth migration. The benefits from existing young migrants can be increased—by lowering the costs of sending remittances and facilitating return migration. They can also expand the opportunities for other youth to migrate by avoiding hefty passport costs and restrictive legal conditions on emigration—and setting up more agreements for labor migration. And they can mitigate trafficking and illegality by providing more information on the risks of moving and living abroad and by implementing policies that foster more domestic opportunities for work.

A youth lens on ICTs suggests that governments need to pay more attention to particular types of regulations, in addition to their broad regulatory and competition policies. Communal access to new ICTs is more important for younger individuals than older, so regulations that allow easy entry for prepaid phone card operators, Internet cafés, and village phones can have large payoffs for youth. Policy makers should do more to use ICTs to communicate and interact with youth on government policy and to promote local language content. Policy makers also need to experiment with helping the first generation of youth using these new technologies to do so in a responsible and safe way, mitigating the risks of child pornography, cyber bullying, and other such dangers.

Youth and international migration

In 2005, an estimated 190 million of the world's people lived outside their country of birth, 49.6 percent of them women, 50.4 percent men.[1] Of the world's migrants, 82 percent come from developing countries, with Bangladesh, China, India, Mexico, Russia, and Ukraine sending the largest numbers.[2] Small island countries have the largest proportions of migrants (box 8.1).

New analysis for this Report shows the propensity to migrate increasing over the teenage years, peaking in the early twenties in many destination countries, such as Spain and the United States (figure 8.1). Migrants to developing countries, such as South Africa, are more heavily concentrated among youth. Countries with very skill-intensive immigration criteria, such as Canada, receive fewer youth migrants. Twelve- to fourteen-year-olds are less likely to migrate to developed countries than younger children, who are more likely to be accompanying their parents.

Young people make up a higher proportion of the flow of international migrants than the stock (table 8.1). Thus, the average youth immigrant is much more likely to have recently arrived in the host country than older migrants. The proportion of youth migrants varies across destination countries, ranging from a low of 17–20 percent of the flow into Canada and Russia to a high of 50 percent of Nicaraguans migrating to Costa Rica and women migrating to Côte d'Ivoire. Less age-specific information is available on refugees, but youth are also a large share of asylum seekers in some countries.[3] Overall, about a third of the migrants from developing countries are youths, perhaps 20–25 percent of the stock. Broadening the definition of youth to also include 25- to 29-year-olds gives them half the migrant flow and a third of the stock. Based on these patterns, 32–39 million youth migrants are from developing countries.

Youths are more likely to migrate because of individual, family, and community factors

Why are people most likely to migrate when young? The classic economic explanation is that migration is an investment, requiring individuals to incur costs to generate the return from higher incomes.[4] Young people are likely to face lower costs in moving and have higher lifetime returns. Expected returns can be higher because they have more of their human capital in education than in job-specific skills than do older workers—and longer working lives. The forgone earnings from migrating are also likely to be lower for youth, especially in countries with high levels of youth unemployment and strict seniority rules that reduce wages more for the young.

While the motive for migrating for work may be greater for the young, policy conditions and personal circumstances determine the ability to act on it. When the only legal options for migration are through high-skilled immigration categories—requiring tertiary education or substantial job experience—migrants are less likely to be youth. Only 17 percent of the flow of Chinese immigrants to the United States are ages

"[I]mmigration by youth should be viewed as resourceful and not as opportunistic."

Young person, Kenya
November 2005

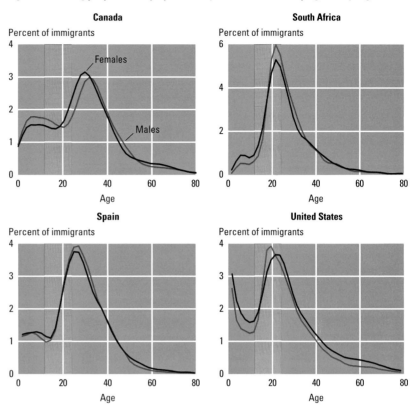

Figure 8.1   Young people add disproportionately to the flow of developing country migrants

Source: McKenzie (2006a).
Note: Shaded portions indicate the 12–24 age range. Height of each curve represents percent of the flow of total migrants into the country who are of a given age.

BOX 8.1   *Small islands, large migrations*

Youths growing up in small island states have among the highest likelihood of migrating of youth in any country. The average island country with a population under 1.5 million has 17 percent of its citizens overseas, though several have more than 30 percent abroad (table 1). Migration is even more dramatic from some of the smallest islands. Niue has a resident population of 1,761, with 5,328 Niue-born living in New Zealand. Comparison of the 1997 and 2001 Niue censuses suggests that 28 percent of all 15- to 24-year-olds left the country in these four years.

Many of these small islands have high rates of youth unemployment that, together with the need to obtain tertiary education abroad, drive migration. Many of the wage jobs are in the public sector, which often places a premium on seniority, limiting entry positions for young people.

Other aspects of living in a small country can also spur youth migration. A 2005 survey of Tongans asked about the importance of different reasons for choosing to apply (or not) to a special immigration quota that New Zealand reserves for 18- to 45-year-old Tongans each year (table 2). Youth who applied to migrate gave better public services in New Zealand as the most important reason for migrating, along with joining family networks and earning higher wages. However, 82 percent of youth also reported that the chance for a better social life in New Zealand was an important or somewhat important reason for applying.

Whereas paying for education is an important motive, fewer youth are interested in migrating to overcome credit constraints associated with buying a house or starting a business. Of youth who did not apply to migrate, 100 percent say that a lack of information was the main reason, while concerns about the cost of airfares and English language abilities are also important. Broadening the opportunity for youth to migrate therefore requires better quality English language education in schools—and perhaps loan programs. And providing them with more information on migration opportunities can enhance their ability to choose.

Many of these small island states benefit heavily from the remittances sent by international migrants: 31 percent of GDP in Tonga, 12 percent in Samoa, and 11 percent in Kiribati. But there are fears that many of these young migrants will never return, and that countries will lose many of their most dynamic workers. Recent developments in information and communication technologies may increase options at home through distance education and access to job opportunities across borders.

Sources: McKenzie (2006b) and World Bank (2005i).

Table 1   Migrants living abroad

	Population (thousands)	Percent migrants		Population (thousands)	Percent migrants
Africa			**Pacific Islands**		
Cape Verde	470	18.7	Fiji	835	13.5
Comoros	600	3.2	Kiribati	96	2.4
Mauritius	1,222	6.9	Marshall Islands	53	13.0
São Tomé and Principe	157	8.5	Micronesia, Federated States of	125	12.2
Seychelles	84	8.7	Palau	20	20.2
Caribbean			Samoa	178	35.1
Antigua and Barbuda	79	28.9	Solomon Islands	457	0.5
Dominica	71	32.0	Tonga	102	31.1
Grenada	106	23.8	Vanuatu	210	1.0
St. Kitts and Nevis	47	38.5	*South Asia*		
St. Lucia	161	17.5	Maldives	293	0.8
St. Vincent and Grenadines	109	31.1			
Trinidad and Tobago	1,313	18.8			

Source: McKenzie (2006b).

Table 2   Reasons for Tongan youth to apply, or not apply, to migrate to New Zealand

	Percent saying reason is very important	Percent saying reason is somewhat important
Main reasons given for applying to migrate		
Better public services such as health care in New Zealand	71	25
To be with family members already in New Zealand	68	21
To earn higher wages in New Zealand	43	50
Better social life	43	39
To earn money for school fees in Tonga	11	64
To earn money to build a better house in Tonga	7	25
To earn money to start a business in Tonga	7	7
Main reasons given for not applying to migrate		
Did not know the requirements	100	0
Do not want to move away from family members	22	17
Cannot afford the cost of an airfare to New Zealand	22	11
Do not feel my English is good enough	17	39

Source: Pacific-Island New Zealand Migration Survey, Tonga.
Note: Applicant results for 18- to 24-year-olds, nonapplicant results for 18- to 30-year-olds due to small sample size.

Table 8.1   Youth make up a large share of developing country migrants

Destination	From[a]	Source	Age range	Proportion of migrants who are youth				Proportion of youth migrants who are female	
				Migrant flow		Migrant stock			
				Males	Females	Males	Females	Flow	Stock
Argentina	Developing	c	12 to 24	31.7	41.9	8.4	9.6	65.3	57.3
Brazil	All	c	10 to 24	20.7	29.8	5.8	6.7	56.8	50.3
Canada	Developing	c	12 to 24	19.7	20.0	15.9	14.3	51.1	49.2
Chile	All	c	10 to 24	32.9	31.6	31.5	29.9	51.4	50.9
Costa Rica	Nicaragua	c	10 to 24	50.1	49.4	34.6	34.5	53.6	50.0
Côte d'Ivoire	All	c	12 to 24	34.2	50.2	17.2	27.1	48.3	46.4
Oman	All	c	10 to 24	—	—	9.5	19.7	—	42.4
Russian Federation	All	l	14 to 24	18.7	16.7	—	—	33.5	—
South Africa	Developing	c	12 to 24	46.0	44.8	20.4	23.3	38.8	41.4
Spain	Developing	c	12 to 24	26.7	26.9	46.7	45.5	47.9	48.1
United Kingdom	Developing	c	12 to 24	30.9	34.5	14.7	14.4	55.1	50.2
United States	Developing	c	12 to 24	36.7	31.1	19.5	16.6	41.6	45.4

Source: McKenzie (2006a).
Note: — = Not available, c = census or survey-based measure, l = legal flow of permanent residents.
a. "Developing" indicates developing country migrants only. "All" indicates all immigrants to this country.

12–24, compared with more than 40 percent from Mexico, Honduras, Guatemala, and El Salvador, for whom family migration and illegal channels are more important.[5]

Family factors. The decision to migrate is often a decision of the family, not just an individual, particularly in developing countries, where imperfect credit and insurance markets create a rationale for migrating to diversify risk and finance costly household investment activities. Households can send one of their members and count on remittances to help them cope with financial crises and natural disasters. They will select the member not just based on who has the greatest individual gains from migrating— but also consider the household functions the member performs and the likelihood of remitting money. In many societies parents exhibit greater control over daughters than sons, so young women may be especially likely to be sent for family reasons.

Community factors. Once some young people have migrated, community factors make it more likely that other youth will migrate too. One reason is the migrant social network, which lowers the costs and increases the benefits of migrating. Because youth are more likely to migrate, a young potential migrant is more likely to have a recent migrant in his or her peer network than an older individual, and so may be more likely to benefit from the migrant network. Over time, a culture of migration can develop in a community, with migration becoming a rite of passage for youth, and with those not migrating considered lazy and unenterprising.[6]

Why is youth migration a development issue?

This Report argues that investing in youth is crucial for a country's long-run development. Migration offers a way for young people to earn a higher return on these investments, and to gain more skills through education and work experience abroad. However, while migration usually results in large increases in income for the individual,[7] governments may be concerned that many of the externalities associated with having a more educated and skilled population will be lost if youth migrate. The degree of concern depends on whether young migrants ever return, the age at which they return, and the skills they bring with them.

Many migrants do return. Studies of legal migrants to the United States, West Germany, and Switzerland in the 1960s and 1970s found that between half and four-fifths of migrants returned to their country of origin. A more recent study of Mexican migrants to the United States estimated that half the migrants returned within two years and almost 70 percent within 10 years.[8] Moreover, new research for this Report shows that migrants tend to return at relatively young ages (figure 8.2), giving them long periods of productive life in their home countries to use the skills and wealth acquired abroad. For example, the average youth migrant from Mexico returns at age 24 after spending three years abroad, while the average youth migrant from Albania returns at age 25 after seven months abroad. Although return migrants may migrate again, the likelihood of further migration falls after age 25—leading many return migrants to work for most of their lives in their home countries.

This temporary migration of youth can have large impacts on poverty reduction and development. The World Bank's *Global Economic Prospects 2006* estimated that a 3 percent increase in the global stock of migrants by 2025 would boost global income by $356 billion and developing country incomes by 1.8 percent a year.[9] This is more than the gains from removing all remaining barri-

ers to free trade. Because many of these new migrants would be young people, much of this aggregate impact will be the result of youth migration. The return of young migrants with education, skills, and income acquired abroad is likely to have a larger impact on development than the return of older individuals, because young migrants will still have most of their working lives ahead of them in their home countries.

Even migrants who do not return can continue to have sizable impacts on the development of their home countries. Remittances sent back to developing countries amounted to $167 billion in 2005,[10] with a large share coming from young migrants. One recent review concluded that remittances are especially likely to be higher when migrants are young but married, with family behind at home.[11] Over longer periods young migrants who stay in their destination countries can continue to support development at home through involvement in diaspora networks that facilitate trade and technology transfers.

Even so, some migrants will not return. If they are highly skilled, this gives rise to fears of brain drain in the sending countries. This is most evident in the health sector, where the migration of nurses and doctors has had large impacts in some countries. For example, in 2002 at least 11,000 Sub-Saharan physicians were licensed and practicing in Canada, the United Kingdom, and the United States.[12] As a result, the public health sectors in several countries have large vacancy rates, hampering efforts to scale up health interventions. The fear of brain drain is much lower for youth migration, because the majority of youth migrants are not highly skilled. Governments may still be concerned, however, if the state has financed expensive tertiary education, only to see students leave after graduation. Where higher education is mostly financed privately, as in the Philippines, this is not as much of a concern.

How does international migration affect youth transitions?

Youth migration also matters for development because it provides new opportunities—and new risks—for the youth

Figure 8.2   Migrants from developing countries tend to return home at a relatively young age

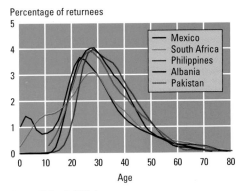

Percentage of returnees

Legend:
- Mexico
- South Africa
- Philippines
- Albania
- Pakistan

Source: McKenzie (2006a).
Note: Height of each curve represents percent of the flow of total migrants into the country who are of a given age.

transitions. Young people may migrate to work, to attend school in another country, to get married or follow a spouse, or to become a citizen of another country. The prospect and process of migration may, in turn, affect decisions about schooling in the potential migrant's home country. It may also affect the health knowledge, fertility decisions, and health behavior of the migrant. It may affect the transition to work of young people who do not migrate. It may also affect the degree of civic engagement.

The exact interactions between migration and youth transitions vary according to the age and gender of the migrant and to the circumstances in the sending and receiving countries (figure 8.3). The likelihood of working and being married increases with age, while younger migrants are more likely to be attending school and accompanied by parents. Female migrants are less likely to be working and more likely to be married than males of the same age.

Migrant youths tend to work in a small number of occupations and not use all their skills. Migration broadens the opportunity to work but only in certain occupations. The most frequent jobs for young men are physically intensive, as construction laborers and agricultural workers. Young migrant women are most likely to work as domestics, cashiers, sales clerks, and waitresses and cooks. While many of these jobs are stereotypically immigrant jobs in some countries, youth are more likely to be working in many of these jobs than older migrants. For example, young female migrants to the United States are 2.7 times more likely to be a waitress as recent female migrants ages 35 to 50 and 3.4 times more likely to be a cashier.

The few occupations that young migrants tend to cluster in have low barriers to entry and require little previous experience and education. Many of these jobs, considered of low status in developed countries, offer little career advancement. Such jobs were traditionally filled by teenagers in developed countries, whose declining labor-force participation creates additional demand for immigrant youth to fill them. The native-born youth who do work in receiving countries are much less inclined to engage in

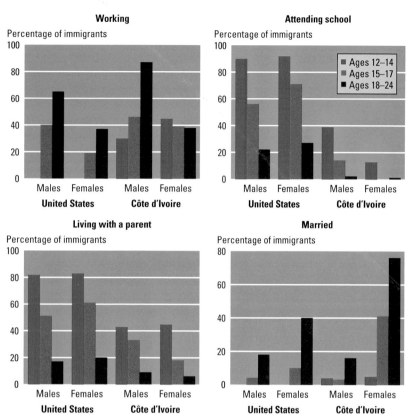

Figure 8.3 Patterns of migration and youth transitions vary according to age, gender, and circumstance

Source: McKenzie (2006a).
Note: Work and marriage rates were not asked of 12- to 14-year-olds in the United States, and are presumed to be close to zero.

some of these occupations than are migrant youth. In Spain, 35 percent of recent female youth migrants do domestic work, compared to less than 5 percent of native female youth workers. In Argentina, 25 percent of male migrant youth work in construction and building, compared to less than 7 percent of native male youth.[13]

Many developing country youth migrants have less education than the average in the country they are moving to, but even youth who migrate with high levels of education may have difficulty obtaining jobs in the fields in which they are trained. The probability of a migrant with a bachelor's degree finding a skilled job varies considerably by country of origin, reflecting in part the quality and language of education in the home country.[14] Thus, educated Indians have much higher probabilities of being employed in skilled jobs in the United States than educated Mexicans.

A further barrier is widespread occupational licensing, which makes it illegal for anyone without a license to perform the job. Such restrictions are estimated to cover 18 percent of American workers and many occupations in the European Union. They cover not only professional occupations such as medicine and law, which youth are less likely to be trained in, but also less skilled occupations such as hairdressing and cosmetology.[15] The difficulties young skilled migrants face in transferring qualifications across countries can push even highly skilled migrant youth to work in many of the same occupations as their less skilled counterparts.

Migration by some young people can improve the labor market prospects of other youth in sending countries, a safety valve in times of high unemployment. Albania, Algeria, El Salvador, Jamaica, Mexico, the Philippines, and Turkey all have more than 10 percent of their labor force abroad, and evidence indicates that these large outflows increase the wages and employment prospects of those left behind. One study found that a 10 percent reduction through emigration in the number of male Mexican workers in a skill group increased the average wage of remaining workers in that skill group by 4 percent.[16] However, because individuals with more education were more likely to migrate, emigration increased the wages of remaining workers more for individuals with higher levels of education, increasing wage inequality among remaining workers.

Migrating for education—and educating to migrate. The chance to obtain an education in another country is one of the main motives for youth migration. Parents who migrate with their children often consider schooling to be one of the most important reasons for their decision. A recent survey of Tongan migrants to New Zealand found that 87 percent of parents reported the desire to have their children educated in New Zealand as a very important motive for migrating, even more than the 76 percent viewing the opportunity to earn higher wages as very important.[17] Parental migration can also broaden the opportunities for

educating the children remaining at home. Studies in El Salvador and the Philippines have found remittances to lower the probability of children dropping out of school.[18]

Although older migrant youth are more likely to be working than in school, tertiary study abroad is a large and growing industry. It often serves as one of the only legal ways for youth from developing countries to enter developed countries—and provides opportunities to turn migration for education into that for work. The number of non-OECD students studying in OECD countries shot up by 59 percent between 2000 and 2002.[19] Although only a small number of developing countries send a large number of students abroad, opportunities to migrate to obtain a tertiary education are very important for individuals in countries with limited domestic tertiary education systems. An extreme example is Niger, which has more tertiary students in France than in its seven domestic tertiary institutions. The number of students abroad from Albania, Cameroon, Jamaica, Kenya, and Malaysia exceeds 20 percent of the number of tertiary students at home.[20]

The prospect of migration may also affect the incentives to become educated at home. Recent literature suggests the possibility of a "brain gain," in which migration improves the incentives to acquire education for the pool of workers considering migrating. Because some of these individuals will not migrate, the average human capital level in a country may, in theory, be higher than in a situation where no one migrates. In some contexts, education decisions do seem to be very closely geared to the requirements of the global labor market. An example is the Philippines, with high rates of private education in fields that shift in response to international demand.[21] The prospect of migration is also driving part of the demand for learning global languages in many countries.

Conversely, when legal channels for migration are limited and domestic education is poorly rewarded in overseas labor markets, potential migrants may choose less education. There is evidence for this among Mexican migrants. A survey of students in the state of Zacatecas revealed that students with migrants in their families expressed less desire for continuing their education to university.[22] This appears to outweigh any remittance effect on the education of 16- to 18-year-olds, so the net effect of having a migrant parent is to lower the education of their children.[23]

Young migrants are especially vulnerable to HIV/AIDS, but migration to developed countries also offers possibilities for greater health knowledge. Migration has been identified as a key factor in the spread and prevalence of HIV/AIDS in Southern and Western Africa. Migrants also have higher incidence rates than the general population in other parts of the world. It is estimated that returned migrant workers accounted for 41 percent of all diagnosed HIV/AIDS cases in Bangladesh, 32 percent in the Philippines, and 25 percent in Sri Lanka in 2004.[24] Major reasons for the greater vulnerability of migrants are their tendency to engage in risky sexual behavior and their lower access to information and prevention services.

Migration for many young migrants involves prolonged periods of separation from their spouses and the watchful eyes of family. For example, more than 90 percent of African migrant mine workers in South Africa live in single-sex hostels, with easy access to commercial sex workers.[25] Loneliness, separation, and the anonymity of being a foreigner can increase the chance of risky sexual activities. Trafficking victims in the sex industry are also at high risk of HIV/AIDS. But because of cultural and language barriers and a lack of financial resources, they have little access to information and prevention services. Undocumented migrants are especially vulnerable because they may avoid contact with any official government services for fear of deportation.

Although the circumstances accompanying migration often have the potential to increase health risks, migration to countries with good infrastructure can lead migrants to acquire more health knowledge. Research shows a strong effect of Mexican migration to the United States on the acquisition of knowledge about different contraceptive practices. Women in households with a migrant member knew more about methods of contraception than women in non-migrant households, with the effect stronger if the household had a female migrant. This greater health knowledge, coupled with the higher household income from migration, improved birth outcomes. Children born to mothers in migrant households had higher birth weights and were less likely to die in their first year of life.[26]

Migration and civic engagement—uncertain identities, but potential exists for engagement and positive change. Migration can disrupt the process of becoming an active citizen in one's home country. Young people who plan to migrate permanently or for long periods face conflicting desires to assimilate and to maintain their culture and national identities, while youth migrating for shorter periods may find themselves isolated from opportunities to take part in society in either country. Even so, there are avenues for migrant youth to take part in community organizations and civil society. Governments are also providing more options for formal participation in home country politics through absentee voting and dual citizenship.

Many formal immigrant groups, such as Latino hometown associations in the United States, tend to be led by older and more established migrants, with youth less likely to be involved unless their parents are around. But such societies can offer social opportunities and a sense of community for recent arrivals. They may be particularly important for young women working as domestic workers or in other occupations that offer little contact with the outside world. Like youth at home, immigrant youth are often more inclined to participate in less structured community activities. A study of Haitian youth in Miami found that the most common activities were helping non-English speakers or senior citizens in their neighborhoods, and helping peers through counseling or tutoring.[27] However, many admitted ignorance of both the opportunities for civic participation and how to take advantage of them.

While public opinion and news coverage often focus more on the minority of

"Here in New Zealand there's heaps of places where you can smoke and drink, whereas if you were in Samoa and you drink and smoke and one person knows you, then the whole village will know that you smoke, because everyone knows each other really well."

Ann, 20, Samoan migrant
August 2005

"Illegal immigrants can get injured or even die when trying to cross the American border. If they make it, they might improve their lot a bit, but over time and due to the little communication with them, they don't feel close to their families anymore. I don't know if that's worth it in the end."

Guadalupe, 18, Honduras
January 2006

Figure 8.4   Youth are more likely than older people to migrate illegally

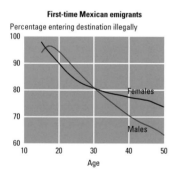

First-time Mexican emigrants

Percentage entering destination illegally

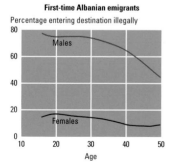

First-time Albanian emigrants

Percentage entering destination illegally

Note: Calculated from the Mexican Encuesta Nacional de la Dinámica Demográfica 1997 and the Albanian Living Standards Measurement Survey 2005.

immigrant youth who join gangs, a review of empirical evidence from the United States found immigrants to be generally less involved in crime than similarly situated groups of natives.[28] This was attributed to the greater likelihood of immigrants to be employed than poor native workers living in similar areas. Immigrants may also face high costs of being caught, such as being deported, making them less likely to commit crimes. However, some sending countries have faced a rise in gang activity because of the deportation of young migrants. An example is the emergence in El Salvador of the Mara Salvatrucha gang, founded by Salvadoran immigrants in the United States, many of whom were deported back to El Salvador after committing crimes in the United States.

Enhancing the opportunity for youth migrants to participate formally as citizens in their home countries is the increase in absentee voting rights and dual citizenship in many countries. In 1998, at least 43 countries allowed their citizens to vote from abroad, although many migrants face logistical and informational obstacles in exercising this right.[29] A number of developing countries have decided to allow their emigrants to vote since then, including Mexico, Mozambique, and the Philippines. The votes of migrants can push for institutional change in their home countries. Analysis of the votes cast by Czech and Polish migrants in their recent national elections found evidence that migrants' voting behavior was influenced by the institutional environment in their host country, with those living in western democracies more likely to favor center-right parties.[30] This could be even more so for youth, who may be less invested in the institutions of their home countries.

Youth migration can also be riskier

The strong motives for youth to migrate result in a demand to migrate that exceeds the supply of legal opportunities. Therefore, youth may consciously choose to migrate illegally, seen in the higher probabilities of younger migrants being undocumented in data from both Mexico and Albania (figure 8.4). Young women are

less likely to migrate illegally than men in Albania. Even in Mexico, when women do migrate illegally, they do it in a safer way than men, traveling with others and using a paid guide.[31] Less systematic recent evidence comes from newspaper stories of young African men trying to cross into Europe through the cities of Melilla and Ceuta in October 2005. Such illegal migration brings the risk of arrest, robbery, and death. In 2005 at least 460 people died crossing the border from Mexico to the United States, 75 percent of them male, 35 percent ages 12 to 24.[32]

Young people also constitute the majority of victims of human trafficking.[33] Measurement is difficult because of the clandestine nature of trafficking, but it is estimated that between 600,000 and 800,000 people are trafficked across borders each year.[34] The majority of victims are female, although an increasing number of males are also affected. Data on victims assisted by the International Organization for Migration indicate that 81 percent between 2001 and 2005 were female, and 71 percent ages 14 to 25. A study in South Eastern Europe found that the vast majority of girls are recruited by personal contacts or newspaper advertisements, offering them work. Younger victims may be volunteered by parents in exchange for a monthly allowance, without the parents necessarily understanding the conditions in which their child will be working. Many victims ending up in the sex industry are recruited under false promises of employment in other industries.[35]

With the demand for youth migration growing, how can policies enhance the development impact?

A large number of youth in many developing countries express a strong desire to migrate, especially for short durations: 91 percent of Albanians, 88 percent of Romanians, 80 percent of Ethiopians, 78 percent of Bangladeshis, 76 percent of Iraqis, 60 percent of Tajiks, and 57 percent of Malaysians say they would migrate if they had the legal opportunity, but fewer than 23 percent would move permanently (figure 8.5). The pressure is reflected in long wait lists for some of the legal opportunities available. In October 2005, brothers and sisters of migrants from China, India, Mexico, and the Philippines all had waits in excess of 10 years to be able to enter the United States through the family reunification category.[36] Given limited legal options, some of this pressure spills into illegal immigration.

The youth bulge in many developing countries (see spotlight on differing demographics following chapter 1) and aging in most developed countries is likely to increase the demand for international migration over the coming years. Without further migration the labor forces in Europe, Russia, and high-income East Asia and the Pacific is projected to fall by 43 million between 2005 and 2025, while it is projected to rise by 19 million in China, 77 million in Latin America and the Caribbean, 82 million in the Middle East, North Africa, and Turkey, 93 million in low- and middle-income East Asian and Pacific countries, 211 million in Sub-Saharan Africa, and 292 million in South and Central Asia.[37]

This will increase demand for international youth migration for three main reasons. First, because youth have the highest propensity to migrate, the rising number of youth in developing countries will increase the number of potential migrants. Second, a larger youth cohort can increase unemployment and lower wages in developing countries, while the smaller youth cohort in developed countries can push up wages (chapter 4). So the economic gains from migration will rise, increasing the likelihood of migrating for each youth. Third, as more youth migrate, the size of the migrant network will increase, further increasing the motive for other youth to migrate.

History provides support for the predictions that a larger youth cohort results in more outmigration. Migration patterns from Western Europe to the New World between 1820 and 1913 show a large and positive effect of youth cohort size on emigration, with almost half the additional births ultimately emigrating. Similar size effects have been calculated for intra-Africa migration in the late 20th century. The effect

Figure 8.5 Leave a light on for them—most young people wish to migrate temporarily

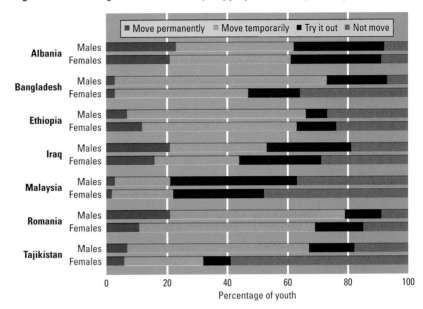

Source: WDR 2007 InterMedia surveys. In the survey, youth ages 15–24 were asked "If it were possible for you legally to move to another country to work, would you?"

of cohort size is lower when policies restrict migration, but a study of migration into the United States over 1971–98 reveals that the share of the sending-country population in the 15–29 year age group is a significant predictor of migration, raising emigration rates from Latin America by 11 percent over those from Western Europe.[38] Based on these historical estimates and demographic projections, it is predicted that the annual flow of emigrants out of Sub-Saharan Africa will rise by between 1.5 million and 2.1 million by 2025.[39]

Receiving countries can increase the benefits by providing more opportunities for youth to migrate, perhaps through temporary worker programs—and by letting migrants develop and use their human capital. Many developed countries have targeted their immigration systems at highly skilled workers, providing developing country youth with few options for legal migration. With aging societies and rising incomes fueling demand for the services that young, less-skilled migrants typically perform, developed countries stand to gain from more youth migration. However, receiving countries typically worry that an influx of migrants reduces employment or lowers wages for native workers.

A very large literature tries to measure the effect of immigration on the wages of natives. A recent meta-analysis of 344 estimates concluded the average effect on the wages of natives is significant but small, with a 1 percent increase in immigrants lowering wages of native workers by 0.11 percent.[40] While other studies have found larger effects, the most recent research from the United States and the United Kingdom also finds little evidence that immigration has had adverse effects on native workers in these countries.[41] Cross-country evidence in Europe has found more negative effects in countries with more rigid labor markets, which restrict hiring and firing, with the effect greater for young men. As a result, youth immigration into Denmark, Switzerland, and the United Kingdom, which have fairly flexible markets, has less effect on native workers than immigration into France, Germany, Italy, and Spain, which have higher business entry costs and more labor market restrictions.[42]

The early experience following the accession of eight Eastern European countries to the European Union (EU) shows broadly positive impacts of increased migration for the receiving countries. Twelve of the EU15 member countries elected to maintain restrictions on migration from these new member states during a transitional period, while Ireland, Sweden, and the United Kingdom allowed immediate free movement of workers. The majority of workers moving under this scheme were young: 83 percent of new registered workers from the accession countries in the United Kingdom were 18–34, and 44 percent were 18–24.[43] Initial assessments have concluded that the main impact of these flows was to increase output and employment, relieving labor market shortages and having little impact on native workers.[44]

A second concern of receiving countries is the potential difficulties associated with assimilation of migrants from different cultural backgrounds. This is an area of active policy debate in many developed countries, and is largely beyond the scope of the developing country focus of this Report, except to note that youth migrants generally are able to assimilate more easily, and that acquisition of the host country language is widely found to be of fundamental importance in allowing permanent migrants to integrate. This provides a further reason for bringing global languages into the curriculum in developing countries with high outmigration (chapter 3). Temporary and seasonal work programs offer one avenue for receiving countries to reap many of the benefits of more youth migration while lessening the perceived costs of assimilating migrants. Many youth in developing countries express a desire to migrate for a short period (see figure 8.5), allowing them to save money to buy a house, open a business, or achieve other goals in their home countries.

Several temporary worker programs are youth-specific. The Seasonal Agricultural Workers Scheme in the United Kingdom allows full-time students ages 18 and over who live outside the European Economic Area to work for six months in seasonal agricultural work. Participants can apply to take part again after three months out of the country. The Working Holidaymaker Scheme in the United Kingdom allows 17- to 30-year-olds from Commonwealth countries to work for up to 12 months of a two-year stay.[45] Australia, Canada, and New Zealand also employ working holiday schemes open to 18- to 30-year-olds, but these cover only a few middle-income countries. Such schemes provide some opportunities for youth migration, but requiring participants to be full-time students or have enough funds to support themselves for their first few months of "holiday" limits poor, less-skilled youth from participating.

The main concern of developed countries is whether temporary workers will return home at the end of the work period. Experience is mixed, and further policy experimentation is needed. One of the key factors appears to be whether workers can return with a reasonable expectation of being able to work again in a subsequent year. Canada's seasonal agricultural workers' program is a possible model, with employers free to request the same workers again the next year.[46] Of the 15,123 workers who entered in 2004, only 1.5 percent went absent before the end of the contract, and almost all are estimated to have returned home. In contrast, the previous version of the United Kingdom's seasonal agricultural worker program did not allow the opportunity to return, and had estimated overstays of 5–10 percent.

Developing countries can maximize the development impact of youth migration through policies that increase the benefits from existing migrants... There is considerable scope for policy interventions in sending countries to increase the development benefits from their existing stocks of youth migrants. One area of recent policy focus is the high cost of sending remittances, which reduces the amount received by relatives back home and acts as a disincentive to remit. Because young migrants are more likely to be migrating without the papers to establish bank accounts and have less experience with the financial system, high remittance costs may be even more of a barrier. Only 31 percent of 18- to 24-year-old recent migrants in the United States have bank accounts, compared with 65 percent of 25- to 50-year-old recent migrants.[47]

Policies to lower the remittance costs include providing information to migrants on the costs of using different methods (as with Mexico's consulates in the United States), delivering financial education to migrants before leaving (as in the Philippines), and developing the financial infrastructure for receiving remittances through competition policy and the lack of onerous regulations.[48] Such policies offer the potential for considerable gains in remittances: a study of Tongan migrants in New Zealand estimated that reducing the cost of sending money to that prevailing in the more competitive world markets would increase their remittances by 28 percent.[49]

Sending countries can also benefit through policies that facilitate the successful return of young migrants. One part of this is sound macroeconomic policy, which can generate expectations of improving conditions. Not surprisingly, youth are more likely to migrate when facing poor domestic labor markets (box 8.2). Many temporary migrants decide to return to enjoy the higher purchasing power at home. Evidence also suggests that the return decisions of some migrants are driven by the desire to achieve a certain target level of savings abroad, which can be used to start businesses on returning home.[50] Young people find it particularly hard to access

financial institutions and obtain credit for business start-ups, so programs that enhance access to credit can be beneficial.

Several countries have tried to attract back their most highly skilled migrants, with mixed success.[51] Such programs are rarely directed at young migrants, who are less likely to be highly skilled. One broader issue that does affect youth is the difficulty migrants often find in having the qualifications they gained abroad recognized back home. This also affects youth indirectly through their tertiary education systems. For example, Romanian academics often find it hard to get masters and doctoral degrees earned in Germany and the United States recognized, and so are reluctant to return.[52]

"I am a girl. I can't go working in other cities. My brothers could never tolerate it."

Female, 20, Morocco[53]

BOX 8.2 *Poor job prospects fuel migration in Morocco*

In the nine communities visited in Morocco for the *Moving out of Poverty* study, youth express great frustration at the difficulty of obtaining good jobs locally. "Graduates are a thousand times more numerous than the existing posts," exclaims a young man from Foum Zaouia, while in the opinion of one young woman from Bir Anzarane, the few good jobs to be had are "via corruption, via mediation, via favoritism, and via closeness." Training or job placement services seem to be far out of reach for most youth, even those with college degrees. As for setting up their own businesses, young men and women express interest but also discouragement due to weak markets, high taxes, complex procedures, the inability to access credit, and the lack of their own funds.

Faced with these conditions, youth widely identify migration overseas as the best, if not the only, means to get ahead. Young men say their goal is "to save regularly to be able to buy a work contract abroad at 60,000 DH [Moroccan dirhams] (more than $6,550) or to migrate illegally, which costs between 20,000 and 30,000 DH per person." Over 70 percent of Moroccan 18- to 24-year-old migrants in Spain are men, and over half of the women who migrate are married to another migrant.[54] Young women face more restrictions, saying parents are reluctant to let them work outside the home, let alone in a big city or another country. "The girl is always supervised," explains a young women from Igourramene-Tizi.

Migration is viewed extremely favorably by adults in these study communities,

who identify migration as one of the main factors helping the best-off households, and a way out of poverty. "The only period of moving up in our life was between 2000 and 2005, and the reason for this was my son's emigration to Spain," says one woman in Foum Zaouia, who now plans to send her other son abroad. If youth feel pushed by their families to migrate, they do not speak of it in those terms, although a joke from Tamessa-Tissyan-Azendo may be revealing on this subject: "A mother sends her son to work in a faraway city. When he comes back after three years, the mother, instead of welcoming and hugging him, says to him: 'Oh! Why do you come back so early, did you forget something?'"

Youth reveal more mixed emotions about migration than adults. Several express uneasiness about having to leave their villages, and the resulting separation of families. Those with insufficient funds to migrate internationally may migrate internally and speak of difficult working conditions in the cities of Morocco. "We suffer and the conditions of work are very hard. Most of us work only in construction yards ...whatever the job we do, the income is minimal." Even so, others welcome the potential new surroundings, and the escape from family tensions over being out of work and clashes between modern and traditional ways. "What all of us really wish is to go to Europe. Here we can't even communicate with our parents. Also, there is nothing for us to do," says a young man from the village of Bir Anzarane.

Source: Narayan and Petesch (2006).

... through policies that expand the opportunities for other youth to migrate... Despite the benefits from migration, country policies can inhibit the opportunities for young people to emigrate.[55] One barrier is the cost and time of obtaining a passport, the most fundamental document of legal identity for migrants (chapter 7). Data on passport costs in 127 countries show that one in every 10 charges more than 10 percent of average annual per capita income for a passport. Reducing passport costs by 1 percent of per capita income is associated with a 0.75 percent increase in emigrants per capita. Because young people are likely to have less accumulated savings, high passport costs may be more of a barrier than for older migrants.

Several countries inhibit emigration through legal barriers on the right of women to emigrate, which in some cases apply only to young women (table 8.2). These countries have 5–6 percent fewer migrants per capita than countries with similar levels of income, population, and governance that do not employ such restrictions. Faced with these restrictions, young women who wish to migrate must do so through alternative channels, increasing the risk of trafficking.

In addition to removing restrictive policies, countries can take more active measures to broaden the range of migration opportunities available to youth. The best established example is the Philippines, which in 2005 sent 1 million of its citizens overseas as contract workers. On average, youth ages 18–24 constituted 31 percent of all female migrants, and 15 percent of all male migrants.[56] The Philippine government licenses recruitment agencies and markets its workers worldwide, signing 56 bilateral treaties with receiving countries. A network of attachés and welfare officers operates worldwide, acting as resources and advocates for the overseas workers. In addition to broadening opportunities for migration, the government provides pre-employment orientations. Potential migrants are told about cultural differences in the country they are considering—and given information on illegal recruitment, methods for sending money, and phone numbers to use in case of grievances.

. . . and through policies that mitigate the risks associated with international migration. The risks of trafficking and illegal migration can be mitigated, first, by broadening opportunities for other forms of work, both domestically and abroad. Promoting the entry of disadvantaged youth into the labor force in developing countries can lessen the desire to leave (chapter 4), but large income differentials, missing credit markets, and a desire to experience life in other countries will still provide strong incentives to leave. Providing legal forms of temporary migration thus acts as an alternative to illegality, the only form of migration available to many youth. Second, information campaigns and legal steps can promote the agency of youth, helping them become less vulnerable to the false promises of traffickers and giving them legal recourse when being sold by family members. Third, victims of trafficking can be given a second chance for life back home—by working with developing country governments to ensure that victims are not treated as criminals and can receive help in returning.

Sending countries should lessen the risks of HIV/AIDS affecting their migrants, especially given the potential spread of the disease to the nonmigrant population. The two main policies are to promote information and prevention activities in the sending areas and to work with receiving countries to create an environment for migrants less conducive to the spread of HIV/AIDS. For example, predeparture orientation semi-

Table 8.2 Countries that restrict the right of women to emigrate

Married women require their husband's permission but no restriction on unmarried women	Restrictions on both married and unmarried women
Congo, Dem. Rep. of	Afghanistan
Gabon	Iran, Islamic Rep. of
Uganda (when travelling with children)	Jordan
	Kuwait (unmarried women under 21)
Unmarried women require their father's permission but no restriction on married women	Libya
	Qatar (women under 30)
Egypt, Arab Rep. of (women under 21)	Saudi Arabia
	Sudan
	Swaziland
	United Arab Emirates
	Yemen, Republic of

Source: McKenzie (2005).

nars in Bangladesh, Indonesia, the Philippines, and Vietnam all inform migrants about HIV/AIDS, while prevention activities in Thailand are held in some of the main sending villages, allowing spouses and other family members to obtain information as well.

The higher risk associated with the separation of migrants and their partners can be reduced by working with receiving countries to enable the spouse or partner to accompany the migrant. While single-sex hostel environments for migrants are the norm in mining and construction in some receiving countries, studies have shown the potential of family housing to dramatically reduce the incidence of HIV.[57] Cameroon provides an example, with villages built to support immigrants working and living with their families at an oil pipeline construction site.

Youth and the global flow of information and ideas

The first few years of the new millennium saw extremely rapid increases in Internet, mobile phone, and computer use in developing countries. Between 2000 and 2003, the developing world gained more than one-quarter of a billion Internet users and almost half a billion mobile phones. These new technologies are growing much faster than older information and communication technologies (ICTs) such as television, radio, mainline telephones, and newspapers (definition 8.1 and table 8.3). Mobile phones have overtaken mainline phones in coverage in many parts of the world, and there are more Internet users per 1,000 people than there are daily newspapers purchased in every region except South Asia. Even so, Internet use remains low in poorer developing countries, and radios and televisions are much more prevalent.

Rapid growth in ICT use among young people

Although young and old alike watch television and listen to the radio, young people are the main users of the new ICTs, especially the Internet and more advanced features of mobile phones such as text

messaging, also known as short messaging service (SMS). In a typical age pattern, youth were the first adopters of the Internet in the Kyrgyz Republic and account for most of the growth in users between 2001 and 2005 (figure 8.6). Data from surveys in 2005 show that youth accounted for 43 percent of all Internet users ages 15 and older in China, 50 percent in Armenia, 53 percent in Bolivia, 60 percent in Egypt, 61 percent in the Kyrgyz Republic, and 70 percent in Indonesia. These proportions, similar to those for 2002 and 2003, suggest that approximately 130–160 million of the 269 million new Internet users between 2000 and 2003 were ages 15 to 24.

Although youth are more likely than older age groups to use the new ICTs, the use among youth varies dramatically. Across countries surveyed in 2005, the share of 15- to 24-year-olds who have ever used the Internet varies from less than 1 percent in Ethiopia to 12 percent in Indonesia, 13 percent in Ghana, 15 percent in Egypt, 29 percent in Armenia, and 53 percent in China. The digital divide also occurs within

> **DEFINITION 8.1**
> *ICTs*
>
> Information and communication technologies (ICTs) consist of hardware, software, networks, and media for the collection, storage, processing, transmission, and presentation of information (voice, data, text, images), as well as related services. Communication technologies consist of a range of communication media and devices, including print, telephone, fax, radio, television, video, audio, computer, and the Internet.
>
> *Source:* Neto and others (2005).

Table 8.3 Catching up fast: The rise of new technologies

	EAP	ECA	LAC	MENA	SA	SSA	Low income	Middle income	High income
Usage rate per 1,000 people									
"Old" ICT									
Daily newspapers	60	—	61	—	59	12	44	55	—
Radios	287	447	410	273	112	198	137	344	425
Telephone mainlines	161	228	170	133	39	11	32	177	393
Television sets	314	408	290	205	81	63	78	319	362
"New" ICT									
Internet users	68	161	106	46	10	20	16	117	279
Mobile phones	195	301	246	85	23	51	23	224	785
Personal computers	26	73	67	31	7	12	7	42	284
Annual per capita growth since 2000 (%)									
Internet users	41	59	38	39	20	32	63	46	13
Mobile phones	51	48	27	52	87	42	83	43	17
Personal computers	28	18	17	9	27	11	24	20	12
Telephone mainlines	21	1	5	15	12	3	14	12	0
Television sets	10	—	—	5	5	10	4	5	0

Source: World Bank (2006h).
Note: Data are generally for 2002–03, except for newspapers (2000) and radio (1997). High-income countries are non-OECD high income. — = Not available. EAP = East Asia and Pacific; ECA = Europe and Central Asia; LAC = Latin America and the Caribbean; MENA = the Middle East and North Africa; SA = South Asia; SSA = Sub-Saharan Africa.

"The digital divide must be defined as a wider concept than the access to the Internet. Even if you have it, if you do not know how to navigate it you will find nothing in it."

Young person, Argentina
January 2006

countries (table 8.4). Computer and mobile phone ownership and Internet and SMS usage are highest among youth in urban areas and with more education and higher household incomes. In Indonesia, 59 percent of university students had used the Internet and 95 percent SMS, compared with 5 percent or less among youth with only primary education.

The use of these new ICTs is a more communal experience in developing countries than in developed. Many youth do not have computers in their own homes, and instead access the Internet at school or at

Internet cafés (figure 8.7). Access at school varies considerably across countries. Some richer, developing countries have connected many schools, with Chile having 75 percent of schools online. In contrast, data from six Sub-Saharan African countries reveal that fewer than 1 percent of schools are covered.[58] Mobile phone use can also be communal, especially in rural areas. Widespread access to phone resellers in many countries has reduced the barrier to access for young people.

In some countries, young women access the Internet less through these public access points than do young men (figure 8.7). In Ghana, 16.5 percent of male youth use Internet cafés, more than twice the 6.6 percent for female youth. Women may not feel comfortable or may be restricted from attending these public points alone or after certain hours. Even at school, girls may find it harder to gain access. In Sub-Saharan Africa, enrollment rates of boys greatly exceed those of girls, so girls compete with a large number of boys for scarce computer resources.[59] In contrast, young women do not appear to have less access to mobile phones than young men, and may actually use them more in some countries.

Young people are more likely to adopt these new technologies for economic, physiological, and social reasons. As with migration, longer working lives mean that young people have more time to gather the benefits from investing in new technology. The cost of investing in the skills required to learn how to use the new ICTs is also likely to be less for youth, who are better educated than older generations and may receive training through school. Moreover, youth find it easier to acquire complex information-processing tasks. The tendency of youth to use these technologies is amplified by the desire to use these technologies for entertainment, and reinforced through peer learning and network effects: the value of a mobile phone or Internet connection increases when more of one's peers are using it.

As a result of this rapid expansion in ICTs, young people around the world are more able to access information and connect to ideas and people outside their countries. In 2005 it was estimated that there

Figure 8.6   In the Kyrgyz Republic, young people use the Internet more than older people and account for much of its growth

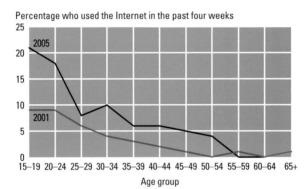

Percentage who used the Internet in the past four weeks

Source: InterMedia national audience surveys.

Table 8.4   The digital divide among Indonesian youth

	Internet use (percent)	Youth with computer in home (percent)	Youth with mobile phone (percent)	SMS use (percent)
All 15- to 24-year-olds	12	5	26	24
Among 15- to 24-year-olds				
Males	16	5	22	22
Females	8	5	31	27
Urban youth	16	7	28	27
Rural youth	6	2	21	18
Primary education or less	3	1	9	5
Secondary education	7	4	19	19
Senior education	20	8	37	35
College or university education	59	28	96	95
Monthly household income				
Above Rp 1,250,000	29	19	57	55
Rp 600,000 to 1,250,000	10	3	33	22
Less than Rp 600,000	5	0	7	7

Source: InterMedia national audience surveys.
Note: Rp = Indonesian rupiah; 1,250,000 Rp is about $128; 600,000 Rp is about $61.

were close to 1 billion Internet users world-wide.[60] A social experiment involving users in 166 countries measured the number of steps required to connect to designated targets and found that the popular notion of "six degrees of separation" between any two people in the Internet world is not too far wrong: the median number of steps required to connect users in different countries was seven.[61] Surveys for this Report show youth to be more likely than 25- to 50-year-olds to communicate with people in other countries (figure 8.8). A remarkable 44 percent of Romanian youth and 74 percent of Albanian youth reported having communicated with someone abroad in the last month. Telephone is the most common means of communication, but SMS and e-mail are also very popular.

Global connectivity and the youth transitions

Although the main reason for many youth to use computers, the Internet, and mobile phones is entertainment—playing games, downloading music, and talking with friends (table 8.5)—the new ICT technologies are having wide-ranging effects on youth transitions. New opportunities for work and study are opening up, and the interactive and decentralized nature of these new technologies is providing youth with many more opportunities to obtain information outside the traditional channels, enhancing their agency. While the majority of youth in many developing countries still do not use the Internet or mobile phones, the experience of those who do shows the possibilities and potential benefits of increased access. Because the spread of these technologies is very new in many developing countries, much of the impact has yet to be carefully evaluated. Thus, in many cases this Report can describe only how the new ICTs are being used to enhance youth transitions, without providing systematic evidence on the magnitude of the effects. Even so, the rapid and continuing growth of ICTs in developing countries suggests that their importance for youth will increase.

Broadening opportunities and providing second chances for work. Business process out-

Figure 8.7 Public Internet access points are important for young people

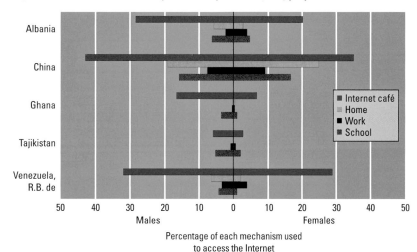

Source: InterMedia national audience surveys.

Figure 8.8 Youth are more likely than older people to communicate with people abroad, especially using new technologies

Percentage of people using each method of communication

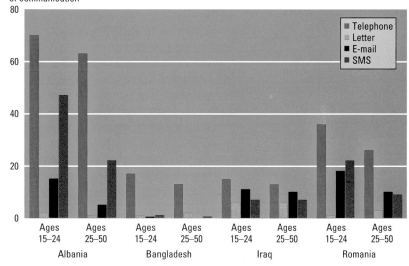

Source: WDR 2007 InterMedia surveys.
Note: The figure reflects communication with people abroad in the past month.

sourcing employed approximately 695,000 people in India in 2004–05.[62] One estimate suggests that 11 percent of all service jobs worldwide, amounting to 160 million jobs, could be carried out remotely.[63] However, actual offshore employment is predicted to only reach 4.1 million by 2008, suggesting considerable scope for future growth. Such employment acts as an alternative to

Table 8.5   What do youth do online?

Percentage of Chinese Internet users ages 16–25 reporting that they sometimes, often, or always use the Internet to:	
Play games	72
Download music	70
Do general browsing	69
Read news	61
Search entertainment information	61
E-mail	53
Online chat	50
Online study	35
Work	31
Check product information	30
Search for medical information	20
Blog	15
Online professional training	11

Source: The Chinese Academy of Social Sciences Internet Survey taken in five cities, January 2005.[64]

"Go to your nearest ICT building, is it accessible to wheelchair users? Will the blind visitors be able to use at least one of the computers? There may be yes for those from the developed countries but in developing countries especially in Africa it is a BIG NO."

Ambrose, Uganda
October 2005

migration, allowing workers to sell their labor overseas without having to leave their country.

The average age of a call center employee in India is 23, with employees more likely to be male and urban and to have upper secondary or tertiary qualifications. While wages are much lower than in developed countries, they are high by developing country standards, creating a new generation of young professionals who are often the first in their families to have a debit card, benefits, and to live alone or with roommates. Other jobs created for youth by ICTs include employment as programmers, Internet café workers, local language Web site developers, and village phone operators.[65]

In addition to directly creating jobs, ICTs provide information about non-ICT job openings to youth. Online job databases, such as one run by the Philippines Department of Labor and Employment, offer information to those with Internet access. In poorer developing countries, mobile phones are particularly important for job information. In South Africa and Tanzania, many respondents identified mobile phones as essential for contacting employers and getting contacted about job openings, particularly in remote areas and areas of high crime.[66] The newer uses of mobile technology are also proving useful for job information. OKN Mobile in Kenya provides a job information service called Kazi560, which sends SMS (text message) job advertisements to job-seekers, who pay a small fee per listing received. The service, with more than 30,000 subscribers, is targeted at poorer workers for whom the cost of job information has been prohibitive—the SMS information is marketed at one-tenth the cost of a newspaper or bus fare into town.[67]

New ICTs also offer the potential for a second chance at work for youth with disabilities, but this promise has yet to be achieved for many disabled youth. Speech synthesizers and text magnifier programs can allow visually impaired youth to use ICTs for work, while e-mail and SMS offer greater flexibility in work-related communication needs for the hearing impaired. Many ICT jobs do not require mobility, and coupled with possibilities for telecom-

muting, this opens options for youth with disabilities.[68] However, young people with disabilities often have among the least access, due to higher likelihoods of low income and education, and to physical barriers such as Internet cafés that are not wheelchair accessible or equipped with the necessary technologies. One example of a self-sustainable business model providing opportunities for disabled youth is Digital Divide Data (DDD), a data outsourcing center in Cambodia that employs only youth who are orphans, land mine victims, physically disabled, or trafficked, with each of the more than 100 employees receiving vocational training and scholarships to continue their education.[69]

ICTs diversify the range of learning opportunities, but lack of education can be a barrier to their use. Distance education has incorporated television and radio for more than 60 years, and these traditional ICTs are still the most cost-effective ICT educational interventions for secondary schooling in many developing countries, helping to meet the challenge of extending schooling beyond primary (chapter 3). For example, Mexico's Telesecundaria program gives those finishing primary school in rural areas a way to continue their schooling without having to travel long distances.[70] More than 1.2 million students in 16,500 locations receive televised lessons, followed by in-class work guided by a teacher. One teacher is used to cover all subjects, rather than the subject matter specialists used in general secondary schools—cutting per student costs in half. But concerns remain about quality, with Telesecundaria students scoring poorly on the international Programme for International Student Assessment tests. The challenge is thus to raise quality while maintaining the low cost.

For tertiary education, the Internet's capacity for two-way interaction offers the greatest promise for improving access and affordability and for providing flexibility to combine work with further study. Several developing countries already cater to substantial numbers of online students, while developing country students also take online classes from developed country universities without having to migrate. For example, close to 1 million students are studying online in China, while the U.S.-based University of Phoenix had students from about 90 countries in 2003.[71] Such programs can expand access and save on costs. Mexico's Tec Milenio uses professors from its parent university to deliver online courses to modestly equipped satellite campuses for one-third the original cost, opening access to young working adults. In other countries, however, poor infrastructure, low incomes, and government regulation limit the access of youth to online education. One approach in these circumstances is to create learning centers that combine online classes with local moderators and technology (box 8.3).

Considerable debate surrounds the cost-effectiveness and justification for public provision of specialized classes in computer skills in poor developing countries. Some initiatives, such as the World Links program in Uganda, lessen digital divides in access and have spillover benefits, with 80 percent of secondary school students in the program indicating that they had taught friends or family members some computer skills.[72] Until costs fall, however, computer provision is unlikely to be financially possible in many poorer developing country educational systems, with the cost of a computer lab amounting to between 2 and 21 times the total discretionary budget per primary student, according to one calculation.[73] Even when computers are provided, a lack of infrastructure and trained personnel can inhibit use: in the Dominican Republic computers sat in their boxes for more than four years at some schools because of inadequate or absent electrical capacity.[74] Using computers already in school for computer-assisted learning can help—a program run by the nongovernmental organization Pratham in India resulted in sizable improvements in mathematics skills.[75]

Although specialized education in ICTs may not be required, a lack of education hampers the use of the new ICTs. A study of mobile phone use in several African countries found that rural uptake of SMS messaging was low because of illiteracy and indigenous language, even though text messages were cheaper than making a call.[76] The

information gains from Internet searches are naturally less for youth who are unable to read, process, and choose among different sources of information, or even spell the words they are looking for. The difficulties are compounded for many developing country youth by the lack of access to content in their native languages. In 2002, 72 percent of the world's Internet pages were in English; 7 percent in German; 6 percent in Japanese; 3 percent in Spanish; 3 percent in French; 2 percent in Italian, Dutch, and Chinese; and 1 percent or less in any other language.[77] Education in global languages, especially English, is thus key to expanding access to global content, together with development of local language Web sites.

Facilitating more informed reproductive health decisions.   The private and anonymous nature of the Internet offers youth the

"I use ICTs to educate children and adolescents about environmental protection and sustainable development as well as to give a possibility to educators and civil society organizations to share visions, information, experiences, etc. regarding this subject."

Cecilia, Argentina
October 2005

BOX 8.3   *Moving in fits and starts with technology—the African Virtual University*

Tertiary education in many Sub-Saharan African countries is hampered by limited resources, empty libraries, and excess demand for classes. The African Virtual University (AVU) uses new technologies to help remedy this problem, increasing access to quality tertiary education in the region by tapping into global knowledge and educational institutions. But its experience illustrates the travails of working with evolving technologies and the challenges currently facing online education in developing countries.

The AVU grew out of a World Bank pilot project initiated in 1997. Its rocky start raised concerns about its viability. Because the ICT infrastructure in Africa was in its infancy, the initial delivery approach used digital video broadcasting over satellite networks, which was very expensive and offered only limited interactivity with teachers. Rapid advances in Internet protocol standards during 1998–2001 made online learning feasible—and African Virtual University's 100 percent satellite-based approach outdated and inefficient.

AVU reassessed its technology options in 2001 to reduce costs and improve the connectivity and efficiency of networks. The delivery approach now consists of a mixed mode methodology, incorporating online and satellite video broadcast courses, pre-packaged learning materials on CD-ROMs and DVDs, chat sessions with the lecturer, and face-to-face in-class sessions with teaching assistants. Supplementary use of the Internet lowered costs significantly, but satellite technology is still needed because of poor telecommunication infrastructure in the region.

The AVU has provided courses to over 24,000 participants. Degree, diploma, certificate, and short-course programs are offered in a range of subjects, including computer science, public health, languages, journalism, accounting, and business administration. Current joint university programs include business studies offered through Curtin University in Australia, and computer science offered through RMIT University in Australia and Laval University in Canada. AVU also provides a digital library, offering access to international journals and e-books, substituting for empty libraries.

The AVU, a work in progress, will need to continue to evolve with technology. African universities still are likely to pay 100 times more for Internet service than institutions in North America. The remaining challenge is finance. The AVU pilot relied too heavily on donor financing and private sector subsidies. The learning centers are now financed through course fees and educational grants from local universities and governments.

Sources: www.avu.org; Halewood and Kenny (2006); International Telecommunication Union (ITU) (2005); and Prakesh (2003).

possibility to discretely access information about reproductive health and sexuality that they may be otherwise too embarrassed to ask or unable to talk about for cultural reasons. One-quarter of young Internet users in Kathmandu, Dakar, and São Paulo reported using the Internet to find information about sex education and health topics (box 8.4).[78] This is particularly important for young women in traditional societies, who tend to have few other opportunities for obtaining this information. All young women who had access to the Internet through the World Links program in Mauritania reported obtaining information on sexuality, puberty, and HIV/AIDS prevention.[79] Although developing country evidence is not available, a randomized experiment among young women at family planning clinics in the United States offers evidence that computer-based aids to contraceptive decisions can improve health knowledge, increase take-up rates, and reduce adolescent pregnancies.[80]

Helping migrants stay connected as citizens. New ICTs are lowering the barriers between migrants and their home communities, enabling them to connect with one another while abroad. High prices for international calls are becoming less of a problem as prepaid phone cards and voice over Internet protocol (VoIP) calls lower the costs of connecting home. Calls to migrant family members are also one of the most common uses for village mobile phones. Online discussion boards and migrant Web sites provide a way for migrants to connect with and meet others from their community and to foster expatriate civic associations. The Haiti Global Village Web site receives 500,000 hits a month, with 80 percent from outside of the country, acting as a central forum for those in the diaspora to discuss community affairs and ways to help their country.[81]

What policies enhance the development impact of youth use of ICTs?

Youth use of ICTs matters indirectly for development outcomes through the impacts on youth transitions—and directly through the large youth contribution to overall ICT use. A few transition and newly industrial countries, such as the Czech Republic, the Slovak Republic, Hong Kong (China), the Republic of Korea, and Singapore, have seen economic growth directly driven by the production of ICTs. But for most developing countries, ICT use rather than ICT production is likely to have a much bigger impact on growth. Substantial evidence from developed countries now shows a strong effect for information technology use on productivity and growth, but this occurred only with a substantial lag after the introduction of these technologies.[82]

The more recent introduction and relatively low use rates in many developing countries suggest that the contribution of ICTs to growth is currently lower than in developed countries,[83] but that the rapid current expansion should contribute to future growth. Positive effects are already beginning to be seen. Recent cross-country work has found that access to the Internet spurs the export performance of developing country firms.[84] At an even more micro level, several studies have documented improvements in prices received by farmers and fishermen, thanks to better access to mobile telephony— fishermen in India, for

---

BOX 8.4	*Staying alive: HIV prevention using ICTs*

More widespread use of television and radio makes these older ICTs the main components in widespread information campaigns to prevent the spread of HIV/AIDS. The 2002 global HIV-prevention campaign Staying Alive was broadcast on television stations that reached nearly 800 million homes, as well as radio stations in 56 countries. Survey results from three cities suggest that people exposed to the campaign were more likely to talk to others about HIV/AIDS and more likely to understand the importance of using condoms, discussing HIV/AIDS with sexual partners, and getting tested for HIV.

The campaign was particularly effective where adapted to local conditions. Although there was a considerable body of material from the United States, the Senegalese participants decided to localize their content based on the fact that, according to one participant, "[t]he countryside and the clothes were too exotic, the references too westernized [and] the images and the

dialogues far too explicit." The Senegalese organizers also focused on radio stations rather than cable television—the primary vehicle for the global campaign. Radio is the most popular and widely available electronic medium in Senegal—96 percent of youth surveyed in Dakar have access to radio compared with 39 percent to cable programming. The proportion of surveyed youth who knew about the campaign in Dakar was 82 percent, but less than one-quarter in São Paulo and Kathmandu, where the campaign was limited to cable.

The Staying Alive campaign continues to produce content for television and radio, but it has also embraced the new ICTs, providing an online Web site (http://www.staying-alive.org/) in 10 languages with information provided in languages and formats designed to appeal to young people, links to a variety of help lines, online discussion boards, and downloads for mobile phones.

Source: Halewood and Kenny (2006).

example, use mobile phones to get information about prices at different ports before deciding where to land their catch.[85]

The most important government policies to foster ICT use are the core elements of any infrastructure policy: sound economic conditions, regulatory policy promoting competition, and complementary infrastructure. Yet uncertain market demand and network externalities may lead the private sector to underprovide access, providing a rationale for further government intervention to serve rural areas. The case is clearest for cellular telephony, due to mounting evidence linking greater access to telephones to several development outcomes.

The Internet is a newer technology, and less evidence is available, making it still too early to recommend direct government provision of Internet infrastructure. However, because the costs of delaying the introduction of ICTs are also difficult to measure, and the development of ICT skills is seen by many to be necessary for workers to take part in the global economy, governments may want to speed the diffusion of this technology. Governments have a mixed record in this area, and those that do choose to directly provide access to underserved areas can learn from countries like Chile, where the Enlaces program combined infrastructure provision with teacher training and decentralized support, leading to widespread use in schools. In the Dominican Republic, however, the provision of computers was not accompanied by complementary infrastructure and personnel, resulting in unused computers in some locations and lack of use for educational purposes in others.[86]

Regardless of their position on direct provision of Internet access, governments can increase the benefits of ICTs for youth. A youth perspective on ICTs reveals that government regulation affecting communal modes of access determine youth access. Regulation can have dramatic effects on the incentives for private entrepreneurs (often youths) to set up Internet cafés. A reform of the licensing process in Algeria made it extremely affordable ($13) to obtain authorization to provide Internet service. The num-

ber of Internet cafés grew from 100 in 1998 to 4,000 in 2000, dramatically expanding youth access and generating many Internet-related jobs.[87] Similarly, regulations allowing easy entry for prepaid phone card operators and long distance phone calls over the Internet can have large payoffs for youth.

Regardless of whether the government is involved in Internet provision, governments can help stimulate demand for new services by providing public service content online. Governments can reach youth through the media they use. They can also kick-start local language content, preventing a vicious cycle in which those who do not speak global languages do not use the Internet because of a dearth of content, while the lack of users acts as a disincentive to local-language Web site creation. The government of Tamil Nadu offers one such example, providing seed support to online initiatives and working with the private sector to decide on a standardized Tamil keyboard and Tamil character encoding scheme. As a result, use of Tamil on the Internet was reported to be far greater than any other Indian language.[88]

The current generation of youth is the first experiencing the Internet in many countries, with all the pros and cons. Parents unfamiliar with the new technology and not present when it is being used thus have little ability to protect young people from some of the dangers. This raises issues of how to teach young people to be safe and responsible users of this new technology, protecting them from some of the risks of unfettered access, such as child pornography, hate groups, stalkers, pedophiles, and cyber bullies. In early December 2005, three of the top five search terms on the Internet, and 68 of the top 200, were sexual.[89] This presents a problem for youth who wish to use the Internet to seek reproductive health information: web-filtering programs can block useful content, while unfiltered searches for teen sex are likely to result in pornographic content. Moreover, parents and society may consider some content appropriate for an 18-year-old but not for a 12-year-old.

Given the vast amount of information available, many youth may be unprepared to sort through and judge what is reliable and what is not. There is thus a need to help

"The use of ICT[s] [has] contributed to the success of community-driven development initiatives by making it possible for project coordinators to source funds . . . through the Internet. ICT[s] ha[ve] also been used in exchange programs, whereby youth exchange ideas on projects that have [been implemented] and projects that are currently being carried out."

Thomas, Zimbabwe
October 2005

youth become safer and more effective users of the Internet. The natural place for this is in schools, but in many countries access to the Internet is available only out of school. So experimentation is needed with alternative mechanisms for teaching youth how to use these new ICTs safely, perhaps through government partnerships with telecenters. Little is known about what works in this area.

Young people are extremely active participants in the global flows of migration and information. What then should be the priorities for governments to take full advantage of this involvement? Table 8.6 provides some first steps. Developing country governments can try to increase the opportunities for their existing migrants by allowing them to retain citizenship links with their home countries, making it easier and cheaper for them to send money home, and removing barriers to their return. But the main priority is for sending countries to work together with receiving countries to work out bilateral arrangements that expand opportunities for

youth to migrate—in a way that is beneficial for both countries and for the migrants themselves. Temporary worker programs offer one promising avenue. Governments also need to experiment more with programs to prevent trafficking, and carry out careful evaluations of these policies.

The main ICT priority for governments is to ensure a good investment climate that allows private companies to serve the growing demand for ICT services, by enacting regulations that provide for easy entry and competition. For youth it is particularly important to also provide good regulatory conditions for modes of communal access, such as village phones and Internet cafes. Governments also need to experiment with ways to provide youth with the skills needed to best take advantage of new technologies, through teaching global languages, providing support for local language content development, and developing ways to teach youth responsible and safe use. Rigorous evaluations of such policies are needed to find out what works and to share lessons across countries.

Table 8.6   Policies for youth in a global world

	Proven successful	Promising but unproven	Unlikely to be successful
Opportunities			
Expanding opportunities for developing country youth to migrate	Bilateral agreements (the Philippines)	Temporary worker programs (Canada's seasonal agricultural workers program)	Skill-based points systems (Australia and Canada)[90]
Increase opportunities for existing migrants	Regulations that allow open entry and competition (multiple countries)	Absentee voting and dual citizenship (Mexico, Mozambique, and others)	Tax incentives to encourage migrant return (Malaysia)
Enhancing access to information and communications	Easy licensing of communal access provision (Internet cafés in Algeria)	Government support for local language content (Tamil Nadu government, India)	Equipping schools with computers without incorporating them into the curriculum (Dominican Republic)
Creating new opportunities to work and study in developing countries	Teaching global languages (India)	Online tertiary education (China and Tec Milenio in Mexico) SMS and online job listings (OKN Mobile, Philippines and Sri Lanka online job listings)	
Capabilities			
Improving knowledge and context surrounding HIV/AIDS	Family housing for young male migrants (Cameroon oil pipeline project)	Pre-orientation seminars for migrants (the Philippines, Thailand) Computer-based contraceptive decision making (U.S. family planning clinics)	Strong censorship of sexual content on the Internet
Creating responsible Internet users		Working with telecenters on education programs	
Second chances			
Preventing trafficking and help victims		Information campaigns and rehabilitation of victims (GTZ program against trafficking in women, BMZ, Germany)	Restrictions on young women's right to exit (Sudan and the Republic of Yemen)
Providing work opportunities for disabled youth		Use of ICT to provide jobs for disabled youth (DDD in Cambodia)	

What donors can do

Donors can help governments undertake policies to broaden opportunities, enhance capabilities, and provide second chances to young people. Key actions for donors: applying the youth lenses of opportunities, capability, and second chances to their own policies, and funding the evaluation of the promising but unproven policies identified in this report.

Determining the extent to which donors are involved in supporting youth outcomes in developing countries is a Herculean task— one that almost defeated the writers of this report! As with national governments, very few donors track program and project activity systematically by age range. The suggestions here are based on information and feedback from a limited number of donors—a comprehensive review is left for others.

Donors through the youth lenses

How do donor policies and programs fare when seen through the "youth lenses" that this Report has used to evaluate country policies? There appear to be large gaps, with considerable scope for greater donor involvement to expand opportunities, enhance agency, and extend second chances.

Broadening opportunities to develop human capital

Much international investment in human capital is focused on improving opportunities for children in education and health in developing countries. This is consistent with the focus on preventive approaches and investment at early ages—a theme emphasized by this report. However, the focus on children and basic services means that youth issues are sometimes neglected. Although those over age 12 form around 30 percent of those in the age range 0–18 in developing countries as a whole, there is little consistent focus on this group.

Given the global size of this youth cohort and the changing nature of the risks and opportunities they confront (chapter 1), complementary programs are needed that build on the earlier investments and address the needs of older children and youth. What more can be done?

An important task is a comprehensive assessment of how present country assistance strategies serve young people. The youth-content of World Bank loans, for example, has grown over the past few years with the focus of youth-oriented lending

evolving from mainly formal education in the late 1990s to areas such as promotion of healthy behavior, livelihoods and employment, nonformal education, and family and community support—which now account for around 40 percent of lending for youth initiatives. Such an assessment can be used to address key questions at the country level. Are there gaps? Are there overlaps? Are interventions sufficiently prioritized?

Answering these questions would require considering synergies across the interventions arising from the multisector nature of youth outcomes—a difficult task for most agencies. For example, many interventions encouraging young people to adopt healthier lifestyles need to occur outside the health sector (chapter 5). Vocational education needs to provide a broader set of skills than those required for immediate employment in an identified sector or industry (chapters 3 and 4).

Much of this work needs to take place in the groups within donor agencies and other organizations that determine country pro-

grams. But it would also be useful to have an overarching strategy to ensure prioritization and to harvest lessons across countries. Donor agencies do this relatively well for well-established sectors such as education and health, but are only beginning to do so for youth (see the box).

Developing the capability of young people as decision-making agents

One of the key issues discussed in this Report is whether young people are recognized as agents who have voice and who make decisions that shape their human capital. There are two activities donors can undertake to promote voice and enhance the decision-making capabilities of young people. One is to do more as global advocates for youth, particularly the most disadvantaged. The other is to involve young people more directly in policy and program development.

As global advocates, donors can further promote the adoption of international conventions, such as the United Nations

---

Organizing bilateral and multilateral youth programs

In 1997, the German federal ministry for economic cooperation and development (BMZ) became one of the first international donors to make children and youth a major thematic area for development assistance. Over the past decade, BMZ has supported a wide range of projects intended to benefit young people. One of its implementation agencies, German Technical Cooperation (GTZ), uses several mechanisms to promote the integration of youth development into its overall strategy, test new youth-oriented projects, and enable coordination across sectors:

- The organizational structure includes health, education, and youth as sectors under the same division. Regional meetings of managers in these three areas are frequently held.

- Heavy investment in knowledge management allows better access to the experiences

of different projects and greater sharing of knowledge across sectors affecting youth.

- New approaches have been tested, including attempts to integrate different fields (education and conflict transformation, information and communication technologies to support vocational training, and peer-to-peer education to prevent HIV/AIDS).

Some multilaterals have also begun to take action. The Inter-American Development Bank was the first development finance agency to establish a youth strategy, and it has become a major funder of youth employment ventures. In 2003, the World Bank appointed a Children and Youth adviser to develop a more youth-focused approach and facilitate coordination across the Bank.

Source: Author's discussions with officials at BMZ and the Inter-American Development Bank.

conventions on trafficking and child labor, which have increased international attention on these issues.[1] By coming together under the Youth Employment Network, donors have played an important role in raising awareness and building commitment to addressing youth unemployment.

However, advocacy needs to be complemented with specific policies and programs to be more effective. For instance, donors (BMZ, Sida), NGOs (Oxfam, Coalition against Trafficking in Women), and international organizations (ILO, International Organization for Migration, and UNICEF) have all supported programs to reduce human trafficking and assist the victims. However, there is very little knowledge sharing, and few of these programs have been evaluated for their effectiveness, making it hard to know what works well. Donors can invest more in pooling knowledge and supporting more rigorous evaluations of their programs.

There has also been action on child labor. The Understanding Children's Work joint research program of the ILO, UNICEF, and the World Bank, initiated under the Oslo Agenda for Action, has advanced the global agenda on children's work. In addition to improving understanding of children's work, it has resulted in greater coordination of the efforts of different government departments and agencies involved in addressing child labor in countries such as the Republic of Yemen. Similar joint efforts could be developed to address the gap in data on youth in general, and the shortage of rigorously evaluated interventions (discussed in chapter 9).

Donors could also draw upon young people more directly in policy and program development. This could be through financial and technical support to young people or their organizations to give them greater means for getting involved in international, national, and local development processes. Inviting youth delegates to the General Assembly of the United Nations is one such initiative. Another is the training provided by the German government to young professionals and future leaders. Youth voice

could also be supported through holding regular consultations with youth as a part of preparing youth-focused reports or projects. In the "Youth as Partners" work of the World Bank, a representative group of youth from different sectors of Brazilian society is regularly convened to provide feedback on the country program. Young people were also directly involved in the preparation of the youth development projects in the Dominican Republic and FYR Macedonia.

Supporting second-chance programs

Many young people need second chances, illustrated most starkly by countries that have "lost generations" due to conflict or political and economic calamities (see spotlight on Sierra Leone following chapter 7). Youth literacy is often low in poor countries, but it is much lower in poor countries recovering from years of conflict, as illustrated by Afghanistan and Sierra Leone in the figure below. While donors have responded strongly by rebuilding schooling infrastructure, often much more is needed to take into account the very different needs

Youth literacy is low in many countries, especially those emerging from conflict

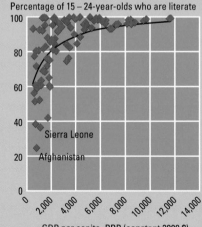

Percentage of 15 – 24-year-olds who are literate

GDP per capita, PPP (constant 2000 $)

Source: Authors' calculations based on Fares, Montenegro, and Orazem (2006a) and World Bank (2006h).
Note: Data shown are for 92 country-year observations from 64 countries. The line shown is the fitted line from a two-tailed tobit regression of literacy on log GDP per capita.

of older learners.[2] Other second-chance programs that could benefit youth include retraining programs well linked to the labor market and cost-effective restorative justice and rehabilitation programs.

Moving forward: Funding evaluation of promising but unproven programs, and sharing lessons across countries

Many programs highlighted in this Report are promising rather than proven, and most need to be adapted to the particular circumstances of individual countries and their youth. Donors can promote adaptation and innovation in program areas that may be too new or too risky for governments; they can also support evaluation. *World Development Report 2004: Making Services Work for Poor People*, highlighted the fact that many donors, including the World Bank, often have resources for evaluation that go unused. A good use of resources would be to evaluate the promising programs identified in this report, such as the following:

- Life-skills education (chapters 3, 4, 5, and 6)

- Provision of information on the returns to education to increase retention in schools (chapter 3)

- Programs that enhance youth citizenship such as school student councils, national service and other service learning programs, student parliaments, and youth leadership development programs (chapters 3 and 7)

- Programs that build skills among poor youth through public works or wage subsidies to firms to hire young new workers (chapter 4)

- Restorative justice programs for young offenders and mobile court systems that deal with young offenders (chapter 7)

- Use of the Internet and SMS to provide job listings, as in Kenya, the Philippines, and Sri Lanka (chapter 4 and chapter 8)

Youth policy: Doing it and getting it right

chapter 9

In a world that demands more than basic skills, expanding the opportunities for young people to learn means going beyond primary schooling. Because building human capital takes more than schooling, it also means including young people more in their communities and societies so that they have opportunities to use their talents at work and to participate as active citizens. Informing and facilitating their decision making—so that they choose well—adds to their success as workers and entrepreneurs, as parents, and as citizens. And for those who have to recover from poor decisions or poor circumstances providing second chances—to make up for missed opportunities—can keep young people from being irrevocably left behind.

For many low-income countries, the priority is to provide quality basic education (including lower secondary education) for young adolescents and, where HIV/AIDS prevalence is high, such as in parts of Sub-Saharan Africa, to safeguard health by preventing transmission among young people who are beginning to be sexually active. Both will help in the transition to work. For many young people in these countries, basic skills for life and work will have to be acquired through second-chance programs. Making full use of young people's skills and providing them further opportunities to build skills on the job will require maintaining an overall macroeconomic environment conducive to growth.

For middle-income and high-growth countries that have already provided mass basic and then secondary education, like those in East Asia and Eastern Europe and the former Soviet Union, the challenge is to develop a tertiary education system and to address new health threats to youth, such as tobacco use, obesity, and road acci-

dents. Second-chance programs will still be needed, but not on the scale of low-income countries. In addition to a macroeconomic climate conducive to growth, countries may need to reform labor market institutions to better accommodate new entrants.

Knowing what to do is not enough—policies directed at young people often fail. Why? For three main reasons: First, influencing youth transitions requires working across many sectors, yet few countries take a coherent approach to establish clear lines of accountability for youth outcomes. Many countries have a vision for young people—typically articulated in a "national youth policy" that fails to set priorities or coordinate action. These policies need to be revisited and revamped. Even where policy is well articulated, it may stand alone from national development policy. Poverty Reduction Strategy Papers in low-income countries are a case in point. Until recently, there was little integration of young people's issues as part of a wider societal effort to combat poverty. This is changing, but not fast enough. Greater capacity is also needed—for analysis, for integration with national policy planning and budgeting processes, for coordinated implementation, and for monitoring and evaluation.

Second, young people often lack voice in the design and implementation of policies that affect them.[1] Governments at all levels also need to be more open to listening to young people, particularly older youth beginning to engage more formally as citizens. As important clients of many public services, young people can improve quality by participating in implementation and providing feedback. Promising experiences of this kind of voice are having an impact on service delivery, as in the anticorruption efforts of tertiary level students in Eastern Europe.

Third, there are few success stories—few policies and programs that have proven effective. Too many policies directed at young people, including many discussed in this Report, are promising but unproven, and this is a serious impediment to wider replication. More needs to be done to find out which policies and programs improve youth outcomes and why. This is not easy, because of spillovers from one youth transition to others, and because some policies may be more effective in combination than on their own. Knowing what works, what does not, and in what circumstances would be of tremendous value in improving policy for all countries.

Youth policy priorities vary by country context

Previous chapters focused on policies to influence investment decisions across five youth transitions: learning, working, staying healthy, forming families, and exercising citizenship. This entire range of policies that influence youth outcomes constitutes what shall be referred to as "youth policy" in this chapter.

We will not repeat these policies here but ask instead: how are the policy recommendations discussed in chapters 3–8 and summarized in the overview of this Report to be customized to each country context? It would seem that at least four dimensions should be considered. First, as discussed in chapter 1, the starting levels of young people's skills and capabilities (their human capital) is the basis on which countries can build. This can be determined from answers to questions such as: what are primary and secondary completion rates? How healthy are young people entering adolescence? What are the main threats to their health in the short and long terms? Are young people building skills through productive employment in the labor market? Are they prepared for parenthood? And are there opportunities for them to participate in community and society?

Second, country income determines the extent to which young people and their families can afford to pay for these investments themselves. It is also a proxy for administra-tive capacity to implement policies and pro-grams. Managing income-contingent loan programs to encourage the take-up of higher education requires high levels of adminis-trative capacity (especially in tax adminis-tration), making such programs difficult to implement in a low-income country. Other financial incentives—such as conditional cash transfers—are found to be effective in a wide range of contexts where many young people do not go to secondary school even though the facilities are there.

The third dimension is the stage of the demographic transition. Is the country proceeding through the demographic tran-sition, and is there a window of opportu-nity from declining dependency? Or is the demographic transition yet to start? If the latter, the resources available for investment in the human capital of children and youth are steadily falling (Chad, Niger). In these countries, an emphasis on basic child and maternal health services is essential to lower fertility and improve the lives of children and youth. At the other end of the spectrum are countries where the window of oppor-tunity from falling dependency will soon close (Armenia, China). These countries should act now before rapid aging results in sharper trade-offs between the needs of the young and those of the elderly.[2]

Fourth is the degree to which young people influence decisions concerning themselves, discussed in chapter 2. In soci-eties where decision making is communal, the family or community may have as much say, or more, in decisions affecting young people (as in Bangladesh). In societies that are more individualistic, the views of young people may be more important to the final decision (as in Malaysia or Romania). While autonomy in decision making bears some relationship to income, some young people in poor countries report as much autonomy in decision making (Ethiopia) as their peers in richer countries (Iraq).[3]

While they may overlap, these dimen-sions are distinct. In general, starting levels of human capital and income are impor-tant in setting priorities for *what* countries should focus on. The stage of the demo-graphic transition indicates the *urgency* for country action. The autonomy of young people in decision making influences *whom* to target and the *type* of intervention.

A very low-income country

Take Sierra Leone (see spotlight following chapter 7). Typical of many countries in Sub-Saharan Africa with very low levels of income and human capital, it is also shifting from postconflict reconstruction to long-term development. However, it has yet to undergo the demographic transition. So, in addition to maintaining sound fundamentals for growth, improving access to and the quality of primary education and primary health care must be a priority. This will give young people the basics for life and work as well as create the conditions for the transition to lower fertility.

Getting children into school is not enough, as many of today's youth in Sierra Leone did not go to school and are now illiterate. Offering them a second chance at school (as undertaken in Ghana's functional literacy program) will improve their chances of doing more remunerative work. Building skills through employment in public works programs in conjunction with or as a complement to basic literacy should also be considered (as with Senegal's Agetip). For many young men directly involved in conflict, rehabilitation that leads to work is essential.

The basic skills for good health and parenting can be imparted through a combination of life-skills training in school (as in Namibia's "My future, my choice" program), through second chance programs, and through social marketing and media campaigns attractive to young people outside schools (as in Horizon Jeunes in Cameroon). Even as young people take greater responsibility themselves, information and outreach—on health risks, on birth spacing, and on other reproductive health issues—should be targeted not just at young people but more broadly at families and communities.

In a society rebuilding itself, institutions should be genuinely open to the participation of young people. Ensuring their legal identity and their representation in local community organizations and imposing milder penalties on young offenders can do much to promote a sense of solidarity.

A fast-growing economy

Vietnam is a low-income country that has gone beyond the basics (see spotlight on Vietnamese youth following chapter 3). Enjoying its demographic dividend, secondary completion rates are high, and a rapidly growing economy readily employs young people. Dependency rates will continue to decline for the next two decades, giving scope to address the challenge of improving the quality of higher education and the risks to young people from the rapid pace of economic and social change.

Vietnam now needs to expand access to a more diverse and flexible upper secondary and tertiary education system, reorienting curricula so that young people learn relevant practical skills (information technology, languages) and life skills (problem-solving, working in teams) while creating stronger connections between school and work (as with the university-industry link in China). Tertiary education could be expanded by reaching out to the private sector (as in Chile). But to ensure its quality—something that many developing countries often get wrong—Vietnam will need good accreditation and evaluation systems (Chile and the Republic of Korea provide good examples). Creating opportunities may not be enough, especially for deserving students from poor or rural backgrounds. So loans or scholarships should be targeted to the needy or those who face the greatest conflict with work (as in Mexico's individual learning accounts).

Health risks in Vietnam are growing due to alcohol and drug abuse, sexually transmitted diseases, and other risky behavior. So, young people could benefit from more information and stronger incentives to make the right decisions. Providing life skills necessary for better health in lower secondary schools could help (South Africa recently reformed its secondary curriculum to include these skills). Given the substantial increase in road accidents among young men, traffic safety is a life skill worth emphasizing.

Outreach and dissemination of information on sexual and reproductive health for youth, the primary decision makers in these matters, need to be undertaken with a respect for confidentiality. Even with the best information, however, many young Vietnamese

"We are not respected in the community; they call us rude and unruly ex-combatants."

Young, commercial bike rider and ex-combatant, Bombali District, Sierra Leone February 2006

"The shortest adult is taller than the tallest youth."

Young person, Tonkolili District, Sierra Leone February 2006

"Teachers. . . . teach theoretically, so this disadvantages youth in learning well and being able to find work."

Young person, Hanoi, Vietnam
March 2006

will stumble, making second-chance programs important. They are also important for vulnerable youth such as street children and commercial sex workers.

Vietnam is increasingly providing more opportunities for youth to participate in public life, but it could do more to legally recognize young migrants to urban areas, whose access to public services is often compromised.

As different as Sierra Leone and Vietnam may be, they present only a small part of the diversity among developing countries in the five transitions of young people, diversity that makes it difficult to draw more general conclusions about where priorities should lie. That is why each country needs to choose policies based on its circumstances.

Youth policy often fails young people

Knowing what to do is in many ways the easy part of devising policy. Making sure it gets done, and done well, is more difficult. Youth policy has had at best mixed success in ensuring smooth transitions for the young, for at least three reasons:

- Poor coordination among policies and sectors that affect youth and limited accountability for youth outcomes
- Weak voice of young people in monitoring and providing feedback on the quality of policy and service delivery
- The paucity of proven successes

Poor coordination and limited accountability

Youth outcomes, extending across the five transitions, are influenced by more than just the health sector or the education sector. Because the transitions overlap—outcomes in one sector are influenced by policies in another—many sectors need to work together when devising policies to influence outcomes. Addressing the difficulties in going to work requires looking beyond the labor market to macroeconomic policy and the investment climate and to the quality of education and training (as discussed in chapter 4). Inculcating citizenship involves learning in school (chapter 7). Raising enrollments requires reconciling the conflicting choices of work and marriage against

education. The success of conditional cash transfers—such as Oportunidades in Mexico, not the standard education sector policy instrument—lies precisely in the fact that they address competing demands on young people's time (see chapters 3 and 6). And with individual transitions as diverse as they are, young people can be hard to reach. Health information and education campaigns have to work across a broad range of sectors to reach young people because they can be in school or out of school, or in work or out of work (see chapters 4 and 5).

Even where there are no spillover effects from one transition to another, there may still be a need for coordination across sectors. Making lower secondary education universal (chapter 3) will in many countries require improvements in transport and other infrastructure to increase physical access to schools. In Vietnam, addressing the high death rate from traffic accidents may require better road safety rules and stronger enforcement (see spotlight on Vietnamese youth following chapter 3). For many young women, taking advantage of opportunities to learn or work may also require relief from some element of domestic drudgery through investments in efficient sources of energy and water (see spotlight on gender following chapter 2).

In most countries, sector ministries are responsible for the bulk of policies that affect youth, while ministries or departments of youth are responsible for youth outcomes (box 9.1). This does not make for clear lines of accountability, because departments of youth typically have little influence over their sector counterparts. In some countries, youth ministries have triggered opposition from sector ministries to the detriment of youth policies. In others, leaders of youth departments are political appointees with no particular interest in developing or monitoring a medium- or long-term vision for youth. With a range of sectors responsible and the lines of accountability weak, no sector is fully accountable—and youth outcomes suffer as a result.

Weak voice in policy formulation and service delivery

Although the interests of young people may be reflected by other, older groups in decision making at the local and national levels,[4] it is striking how seldom young people are consulted on policies that affect them. According to one estimate, about two-thirds of countries with national youth councils, bodies intended to reflect the views of different stakeholders, do not listen to youth nongovernmental organizations (NGOs).[5] Very few young people or youth NGOS are consulted as a part of the poverty reduction strategy process in low-income countries (discussed further below).

Service delivery is another area in which youth are not visible. Even though young people are important clients of public services, they often are not consulted. Yet as direct clients, they can be crucial to improving the quality of service delivery (see box 2.2).[6] Many health services suffer from a very youth-unfriendly image, paying little attention to young people's concerns and needs (see chapter 5). Few school systems recognize young people as stakeholders who can improve the quality of education (see chapter 3). Yet young people have every incentive to hold public services accountable, something they get better at as they mature.

Paucity of proven successes

Few solid evaluations of youth programs in developing countries unambiguously identify the causality from policy to program to effect.[7] This gives youth policy the aura of being soft, lacking in rigor. Much more is known about what affects outcomes in childhood, thanks to a large and growing body of solid evaluations of the impact of early childhood development programs, school nutrition programs, school management reforms, remedial primary education, and so on.[8] As the tables at the end of the chapters 3–8 detail, many programs that are important for expanding opportunities and building capabilities fall into the "promising but unproven" camp. They include most life-skills programs (which many countries are investing more in) and most programs for promoting youth citizenship, including student councils, youth parliaments, and service learning (including national service). The lack of evidence is not confined to expanding opportunities.

BOX 9.1 *What do ministries of youth do?*

Youth issues typically do not command an entire ministry of their own. In most countries, youth issues are dealt with by departments of youth housed within other ministries—typically education (Jamaica and Sweden) or in omnibus ministries responsible for youth as well as sports, culture, social affairs, or local government (India and Singapore).

Their functions vary but broadly consist of developing a framework for youth issues and formulating policy, fostering coordination, collaboration, advocacy, research, technical assistance, and monitoring. The departments sometimes support special programs, outside the traditional line ministries, directed to youth at the national or local level. They may also maintain contact and channels of communication with young people and their organizations.

The role of departments of youth is partly a function of how far countries have progressed in developing and implementing policies for the young. In many Organisation for Economic Co-operation and Development countries where policy development has been well established over several decades, the role of youth departments is mainly policy development, coordination, and monitoring.

In many developing countries only beginning to develop coherent policies toward young people, there is more emphasis on advocacy and advice. In others, departments have moved to policy development (Chile, El Salvador, and Nicaragua) and coordination (Chile).

Source: Mattero (2006).

Except for the Jovenes programs from Latin America (which train out-of-school youth), almost no second-chance programs are rigorously evaluated. Even where evaluations exist, they may be on narrow outcomes. The Jovenes evaluations look largely at impacts on employment and wages, and not the better health or lower crime that may go hand in hand with employment.

Getting it right— by developing a coherent framework and integrating it with national policy

What can be done to ensure that policy is not destined for failure? To increase the chances of success, policy makers must as a start articulate a coherent view of desired outcomes for young people, integrating that view with national planning and implementation mechanisms. This will improve accountability for outcomes. The capacity to implement this strategy at all levels is also required.

A coherent national framework for youth

Accountability is easier to assign if there is a well-articulated set of national objectives for youth, developed with key ministries and stakeholders. This is especially important where countries are decentralizing public service delivery, a growing trend (see

"Many organizations have visited us, but after we explained our situation to them we do not see them again [there is no follow-up]."

Young person, Kissy, Sierra Leone
February 2006

"Youth participation is token and . . . it is frustrating when [the authorities] send you . . . to a meeting and they are not bothered by the sets of recommendations and follow up. . . ."

Rotimi, 22, Nigeria
June 2006

chapter 1). Many initiatives that focus on youth—from smaller schemes responding to the needs of special groups to programs that tackle national issues—often intersect at the local level, where most services that influence youth are provided. Appropriate enough in federal systems, they can be plagued by fragmented effort and poor coordination, especially when services are provided by more than one level of government (such as education in Brazil) or where effects overlap across jurisdictions (as in

HIV/AIDS campaigns). A clear national framework can guide coordination.

However, the policy vision at the country level—often articulated through national youth policy—is usually very narrow in scope. In 2001, 82 percent of all countries had a national youth policy, 89 percent had a designated national youth coordination mechanism, and 60 percent were implementing a national youth program of action. But in 70 percent, national youth policy was focused on the narrow range of concerns of the department of youth, with few links to other youth-serving ministries, such as education, health, or labor.[9] Even where broad, it may not be very strategic, reading more like a laundry list of desirable policies than a strategic program of action.

Revisiting these policy statements can sharpen the focus on youth in conjunction with building a broad constituency for youth outcomes. Having the key economic and finance ministries on board obtains wider ownership of policy among public agencies, as evident from the progress with policy development in areas such as gender, which—like youth—cuts across sector lines (box 9.2). And the development of youth policy would greatly benefit from consultations with young people.[10]

In a national framework, many policies affecting youth outcomes are best addressed within individual sectors. For example, expanding the range of options open to young people in upper secondary school and increasing flexibility among them, recommended in chapter 3, can be tackled largely within the education sector. Making preventive health services more youth friendly, recommended in chapter 5, can also be handled within the health sector. What is required for many policies is that ministries or agencies help rather than hinder the efforts of others. In Chile, the Department of Youth conducts a survey of youth conditions every three years, providing valuable feedback to line ministries on the efficacy of their programs. Departments of youth have limited expertise implementing health or education policies. Some, though, have considerable expertise convening groups of young people and their organizations. This could be put at the disposal of traditional

---

BOX 9.2 *Does addressing gender issues hold lessons for youth policy? The view from East Asia*

Since the Fourth World Conference on Women in Beijing in 1995, governments in East Asia have set up legal and institutional frameworks to promote gender equality. Most have defined and approved gender plans of action, establishing mechanisms and bodies to ensure that gender concerns are adequately addressed at all stages of policy planning and implementation. Departments dedicated to women's empowerment have been elevated to ministries, as in Cambodia and Indonesia, and high-level intersector coordinating bodies have been formed, as in the Lao People's Democratic Republic, the Philippines, and Vietnam.

What needs to be improved?
Weaknesses in implementation and in monitoring and evaluation are common throughout the region, because many relevant public institutions are still weak, lacking resources and capacity, and struggling to define their roles with the more established sectors.

What has been learned?
Four lessons:
Design a comprehensive gender strategy involving all key ministries. A comprehensive gender strategy is needed so that gender concerns are addressed up front in a country's overall development program. All line ministries and specialized agencies should be involved, so that gender equality falls to the Ministry of Women's Affairs. The involvement of the Ministries of Economy and Finance ensures that gender concerns are effectively addressed in the formulation and execution of the national budget. For instance, the interministerial working groups set up in Cambodia involve line ministries in the design of the gender strategy and in specific gender actions. And the 2002 National Strategy for the Advancement of Women in Vietnam sets out the

responsibilities of different government departments.
Build the capacity to mainstream. The agency responsible for making sure that gender concerns are part of sector policy needs strong capacity, as do the sector ministries and other agencies—through suitable mainstreaming mechanisms, adequate budget allocations, and technical training. In some countries (Cambodia), the appointment of gender focal points responsible for incorporating gender issues into sector agendas has been only partly effective, and alternative or complementary mechanisms (interministerial working groups) are being pursued. In most countries, technical training on gender issues has been easily incorporated into general training programs.
Strengthen the women's movement in civil society. Although the position of women in national parliaments has hardly changed over the decade, there has been significant progress with policies that affect women. Much of this is the result of women's stronger voice in civil society to exert pressure for change. In Indonesia, Korea, Mongolia, the Philippines, and Thailand, women's movements have brought about changes in policies and helped implement laws on labor, family, domestic violence, and trafficking.
Monitor and evaluate. Few countries have put adequate systems for impact evaluation in place on time. Suitable indicators and data collection and analysis mechanisms need to be developed from the beginning, involving national statistical institutions and research institutes. In Cambodia and Lao PDR, national statistical systems are being adapted to incorporate disaggregation by sex into national statistics.

Sources: Asian Development Bank and World Bank (2005); Brown, Al-Hamad, and De Paz Nieves (2005); Javate de Dios (2002); World Bank (2005g); and World Bank (2005h).

line ministries that may wish to consult or obtain feedback from young people on the quality of services provided to them.

Coordination is needed, however, in developing an overarching strategy for addressing youth outcomes; assigning clear roles and responsibilities for implementation; getting ministries and agencies, civil society organizations, and the private sector to work with each other; monitoring progress with implementation; and policy development. Coordination in this sense is no different from what is required for other cross-sector objectives of national policy, such as improving gender outcomes. Because youth transitions affect one another, the evaluation of policies and programs also needs to be coordinated.

Integration with national policy planning and implementation mechanisms

Policies are more likely to be successful if youth issues are well integrated into national policy planning and implementation mechanisms, because most of them are implemented by traditional line ministries. Ensuring that they understand their roles and responsibilities builds and maintains a constituency for youth issues.

Integrating youth policies with national development frameworks is in its infancy in most developing countries. In low-income countries, youth issues often sit outside the poverty reduction strategy (PRS) process, failing to tap the various constituencies that support PRS outcomes. Although more recent PRS papers do a better job than older ones of integrating youth outcomes, coverage is still far from universal (box 9.3).

Many middle-income countries suffer from the same poor integration with national development frameworks, perhaps attributable to the strong regional and historical flavor of national youth policy. According to one view, the European Union and the British Commonwealth have traditionally promoted cross-sector, integrated approaches, while the Arab Council of Ministers of Youth and Sports and the Conference of Ministers of Youth and Sports of the French-speaking Communities have

---

BOX 9.3   *Neither seen, nor heard—youth in the poverty reduction strategy process*

For a group that makes up a large share of the population in most low-income countries, young people are underrepresented in the poverty reduction strategy process.

Youth in consultations
In a study of 31 poverty reduction strategy papers (PRSPs) completed by September 2003, around half of the papers (14 PRSPs) were found to be drawn up without consulting youth groups at all as part of their overall consultation process.

Youth in poverty diagnostics
Only one in five papers (6 PRSPs) identified young people as a group vulnerable to poverty. A little over a third (12 PRSPs) identified youth vulnerability to poverty in a minor way, while another one-fifth (6 PRSPs) identified youth as one of several groups vulnerable to poverty (see table 1). In part an issue of how people in this age range get classified, many PRSPs also take a relatively static view of poverty. A more dynamic view would look at factors that predispose individuals to poverty over the long run, such as the failure to acquire an education.

Youth in poverty action plans
Few PRSPs take an integrated view of the needs of young people in their action plans. Just three-quarters of the papers (24 PRSPs) mention young people in their action plans, only a half address youth issues as a key goal. A quarter of action plans do not mention youth at all (see table 2). This is not to say that policies that affect youth outcomes, such as education, do not figure prominently. They do, but not as part of a coherent cross-sector approach to addressing the needs of the young. Even where there is reference to young people in the PRSP action plans, there is little follow through in specific targets or budgetary allocations for implementation.

Progress since 2003 is mixed. Provisional analysis of 55 PRSPs completed by April 2006 suggests that more PRSPs now identify young people as a group vulnerable to poverty. However, a coherent cross-sector approach to youth issues is still lacking.

Table 1   Are youth identified as a group vulnerable to poverty?

	Major focus	Minor focus	One of many	No mention	Total
Number	6	12	6	7	31
Percent	19	39	19	23	100

Table 2   Are youth in PRSP action plans?

	Major focus in key goal	Minor focus in key goal	No mention	Total
Number	17	7	7	31
Percent	55	23	23	100

Source: Curtain (2006) and United Nations (2003).

given more sustained attention to youth and sports than to policy integration.[11] Making progress on integration with national policy is thus relevant in a wide range of contexts.

Integration with budgeting frameworks is equally weak. Only a handful of developing countries systematically track how much is spent on young people, let alone relate it to youth outcomes.[12] This kind of integrated view is essential to making progress with youth policy.

Building capacity

Implementing a coherent and integrated national framework requires strong capacities—for analysis, policy development, implementation, coordination, monitoring, and evaluation. However, those capacities have traditionally been weak in developing countries. In countries with a long history of youth policy, the department of youth plays the role of "champion" and "policeman" of youth policy effectively, as in Sweden (box 9.4); but in many developing countries, departments of youth are under-resourced both in financial resources and in personnel—and thus lack the clout to be effective.

Building this capacity is clearly critical and will take resources, but given what is spent on youth through traditional line ministries, the additional resources are likely to be a small proportion of what is already expended. The ability to hire staff with the right skills is absolutely vital. In addition to analytical skills, staff need to communicate effectively with young people and their organizations and work across traditional sector boundaries. The ability to work with those outside government—including the corporate sector and not-for-profit agencies, both engaged in improving outcomes for young people—is equally important. The work of youth departments is likely to be enhanced by having strong inputs from organizations that represent the interests of young people. So building capacity in youth-serving NGOs is also important.

With youth policy still new in many developing countries, there are few good examples of where capacity has been built effectively. However, in some countries in Latin America, youth agencies are moving in the right direction, focusing less on implementing programs and more on

---

BOX 9.4   *How do developed countries handle youth issues? Consider Sweden*

Sweden has a coherent national framework for youth, well integrated with national policy planning and implementation mechanisms, and with a strong capacity for implementation.

Policy framework
Swedish youth policy stretches back more than 50 years. At the beginning, the main ambition was to create good scope for after-school activities. Policy has since moved on. The foundations of an integrated national youth policy were laid in the mid-1980s, with continuous evolution since.

The latest policy revision—set out in a new youth policy law, Power to Decide, enacted in 2004—provides a new structure for national youth policy with the aim of giving all young people equal opportunities to develop, to be empowered, to gain influence over their everyday lives, and thus to be able to realize their dreams. The target is young people between the ages of 13 and 25. Five main fields have been created to facilitate analysis and coordination—learning and personal development, health and vulnerability, influence and representation,

self-support, and culture and leisure—the five transitions as it were, Swedish style.

Integration with national planning and implementation mechanisms
Swedish youth policy is highly "mainstreamed," well integrated with national policy planning and budgeting processes. Ten or so ministries take responsibility for realizing the established youth policy goals. As in most other countries, government activities are divided into various sectors, each with its own goals and its own budget. All sectors that affect young people are expected to help achieve national youth policy objectives.

Goals are established within each of the sectors for each of the five transitions identified in the new law. This integrates youth policy into the relevant sectors and facilitates realizing and monitoring the overall objectives within the framework of the normal day-to-day activities in the area. Each sector contributing to the national youth policy has its own indicators to measure how it is doing from a youth perspective.

Capacity
The implementation of national youth policy is aided by strong institutions. The Division of Youth Policy at the Ministry of Education, Research and Culture coordinates youth policy within the government. The Minister for Pre-School Education, Youth Affairs, and Adult Learning leads a system in which 20 or more governmental authorities monitor the living conditions of young people.

Most of the responsibility for living conditions of young people in Sweden rests with municipalities. A special agency, the Swedish National Board for Youth Affairs, supports the development of municipal youth policy and monitoring of the objectives of national youth policy. It supplies up-to-date knowledge of young people's living conditions both locally and nationally. It also provides support for the development of knowledge-based intersector youth policy at the municipal level with a high degree of youth influence.

Source: Forum 21, European Journal on Youth Policy, available on line at www.coe.int/youth/forum21.

policy development, coordination, and monitoring (box 9.5). Governments clearly need to experiment and innovate, especially where they may be starting to build capacity from scratch. The lessons from attempts to address other cross-sector issues, such as gender equality, suggest that much can be achieved over a decade (see box 9.2).

The payoff from having a coherent national framework for youth integrated into national policy with capacity for implementation is well illustrated by the model described in chapter 1, projecting the impact of HIV/AIDS in Kenya. As discussed in chapter 1, the model predicts that the HIV/AIDS epidemic will take a heavy toll on growth in Kenya because of its impact on human capital accumulation and in particular on secondary school completion rates. To combat the impact of the epidemic on school enrollment, the government can either act directly on enrollment by providing a subsidy to encourage school attendance or act indirectly to improve young people's health. The model suggests that at plausible discount rates, the net present value of the benefits from the education subsidy lies between 1.7 and 3.5 times that of the costs. Under a combined program—in which the educational subsidy is halved and the other half is spent on measures to combat the epidemic and treat its victims—the net present value of the benefits would be 8.9 to 13.3 times greater than the costs (box 9.6). This striking improvement is due not only to saving lives under the combined intervention but also to the fact that the resulting reduction in expected mortality provides an additional potent incentive to invest in education.

Getting it right— by listening to young people

As the most important clients of policies and services directed at them, the ability of young people to exercise voice, or client power, can be invaluable to ensuring quality. Governments should thus be open to consultation and feedback from young people on the design and implementation of policies that

affect them. Many national youth policies are drawn up without adequate consultation with young people. Even the institutions meant to reflect the voice of young people, such as national youth councils, often fail to do so.[13] Many low-income countries do not consult with youth groups as a part of the PRSP process (see box 9.3). This should be remedied, particularly for older youth, who may be exercising more indirect voice through the ballot box. Efforts to give young people voice need to go beyond the tokenism that often characterizes such attempts. Not only does there need to be a process for listening to young people—there also needs to be a process for careful consideration of the suggestions and feedback that emerge.

An often-voiced criticism of more participatory approaches is the danger that youth elites or other unrepresentative groups will capture the process. With adequate planning, however, a wide representation of young people can be ensured, bringing benefits both to policy making and to young people (box 9.7). Denying young people an adequate

"As youth we are passionate and eager to make a difference. We are like warriors; all we want is just to be heard and given the chance to make a difference."

21-year-old Liberian-American
June 2006

BOX 9.5 *Where departments of youth are headed: Evidence from Latin America*

Over the past two decades, most Latin American countries have aimed to strengthen youth departments (called secretariats, vice ministries, or presidential programs). The record is mixed. A general lesson from the more promising reforms is that youth departments should focus on guiding—rather than implementing— national youth plans.

In countries such as El Salvador and Nicaragua, youth departments have achieved substantial success in contributing to the formulation of national plans, defining priorities, and helping to align sector policies.

In many countries where sector ministries already identify their own priorities for youth policy, the most appropriate contribution of youth departments is to help coordinate such policies.

In countries that have set forth ambitious long-term visions for youth development, such plans need to be translated into short- and medium-term action if there is to be a realistic attempt at implementation.

In Chile, a two-year youth action plan (Chile se Compromete con los Jovenes)

complements the longer-term vision and proposes interventions that are immediate, measurable, and capable of being evaluated. Each intervention has an assigned budget and relies on implementation by designated sector ministries and agencies. Because most programs are implemented by line ministries, the youth agency , INJUV (Instituto Nacional de la Juventud), focuses on coordination among sectors and critical follow-up. INJUV's national survey on youth, conducted every three years, provides sector ministries with critical knowledge upon which to base programs targeting youth. Through its evaluations and research on youth programs, INJUV also contributes to the formulation of policies affecting youth. The next step will require further collaboration with sector ministries to address issues identified in the evaluations related to youth. For many youth agencies, including INJUV, reaching out to youth will also require collaboration with NGOs and youth organizations.

Source: Instituto Mexicano de la Juventud (IMJ), Organización Iberoamericana de la Juventud (OIJ) (2006) and authors.

BOX 9.6   *Successful policy coordination and implementation:*
How health and education policies can work together to combat the AIDS shock

Box 1.3 in chapter 1 discussed one model of how HIV/AIDS could affect human capital accumulation and growth, calibrated using data from Kenya. Here, this model is taken a step further and asks what would be the impact on human capital accumulation and growth of policies to increase enrollments and reduce infection rates among the young.

Education subsidies are modeled assuming that 50 percent of the cost of secondary education is borne by the state and funded by donors. An alternative to this is to reduce the subsidy to education by half and allocate the same stream of outlays to combating the epidemic. Measures that promote education directly, such as school attendance subsidies, increase income by increasing human capital. Measures to combat the epidemic, primarily through reducing infection rates among 15- to 24-year-olds, not only reduce the toll of suffering and death but also promote investments in education by increasing the families' lifetime resources and the expected returns to education investments.

Figures 1 and 2 plot the impact of these interventions on postprimary enrollment and on per capita income. Both measures raise postprimary enrollments, but with different time profiles. The education subsidy, which costs 0.9 percent of GDP in 2000, rising to 1.8 percent of GDP in 2020, has the greatest impact on raising enrollments up to 2020. If some of these funds were allocated instead to health promotion, all the effects of reduced mortality—and the expectation of reduced mortality—on investment in secondary education come into play. In comparison with the direct working of education subsidies, these effects are small at first, but they accumulate over time, so much so that, in the model as calibrated, enrollments are higher under this program from 2020 onward. The combined program would, in fact, cost slightly less—0.8 percent of GDP in 2000, rising to almost 1.8 percent in 2020. Yet it yields higher secondary enrollments by 2030 than an education subsidy alone. This points to an important, long-run synergy between education and health policy.

Both interventions hasten the recovery of per capita income to 1990 levels—that is, they reduce the impact of the AIDS shock. Recovery is fastest under the education subsidy. Even though the combined intervention leads to higher postprimary enrollment and greater human capital in the long run, the lags in the system are such that in 2040, the outer year of the projections, per capita output is higher for the education subsidy.

In view of the very different time paths of the streams of costs and benefits for the two interventions, an evaluation of their social profitability requires that they be discounted at an appropriate (real) rate. Assuming a discount rate of 4 percent, both programs yield significantly higher benefits than costs (see table below). However, the intervention that involves the promotion of health has a benefit-cost ratio roughly three to four times that of the intervention involving educational subsidies alone.

Figure 1. Impact of interventions on per capita income

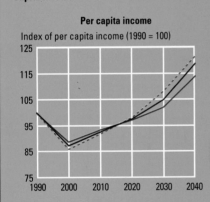

Figure 2. Impact of interventions on postprimary enrollment

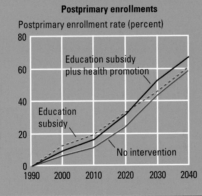

The social profitability of education and health programs

Index	Aggregate GDP benefits/ costs	Per capita GDP benefits/ costs
School attendance subsidy	3.5	2.9
Combined program—school attendance and health promotion	13.3	11.7

Source: Bell, Bruhns, and Gersbach (2006).
Note: All benefits and costs discounted at the rate of 4 percent a year.

---

hearing can lead to less constructive expressions of voice.

The voice of young people can also improve service delivery by monitoring and giving feedback on the quality of services. For example, students and student organizations in Eastern Europe have notched important early wins in the fight against corruption in tertiary education through the exercise of voice. In 2003, a regional network of student NGOs from Albania, Bulgaria, Croatia, FYR Macedonia, Moldova, and Serbia and Montenegro was formed to improve governance in higher education. It focused on changing regulations govern-

ing tertiary education, introducing student rights and mechanisms for student protection, and reducing corruption. The results so far—more effective students' ombudsmen are being instituted in several universities; the monopoly of old-time student unions (often dominated by ruling elites) has ended; and dialogue has been initiated with parliaments, education ministries, and university administrators and faculties to reduce corruption in higher education. While it is too early to say if this process will lead to sustained improvements in issues that particularly affect students, this is a start.[14]

Vozes Jovens: Opening national youth policy to youth voice and participation in Brazil

It should come as no surprise that Brazil's strong civil society has given birth to an energetic youth movement. As part of the government's effort to open up to civil society, it took on the challenge of incorporating the voice of youth into policy development. As a complement to this process, the World Bank initiated a dialog with youth, Vozes Jovens (Youth Voices), to assist in the development of the World Bank's country assistance strategy in Brazil.

Over time the Vozes Jovens grew into a broad dialog on youth issues, independent of the World Bank, involving representatives of the Brazilian government and congress, political parties, other civil society organizations, and the private sector. It provided valuable input for establishing the National Youth Secretariat, which coordinates youth policies at all levels of government.

Vozes Jovens allows youth to express their needs, consolidates efforts of many youth organizations, and most important, institutionalizes youth voice through participation on the National Youth Council, the governing body of the National Youth Secretariat, made up of government and civil society representatives. State governments are now applying the Vozes Jovens methodology, with the states of Ceará and Pernambuco recently hosting Vozes Jovens events to enhance local policies. Today, more than 300 youth organizations participate in local, subnational, and national policy processes.

This process has brought benefits to both the government and young people. According to Minister Luiz Dulci, of the General Secretariat of the Presidency, "Vozes Jovens has been fundamental in contributing to the dialogue the President has launched to ... empower Brazilian youth, and has resulted in the creation of sound policies for the country's youth, such as the second chance program PRO JOVEM, the National Youth Council and the National Youth Secretariat, within two years of President Lula taking office."[15]

The young civil society leader and National Youth Council member Josbertini Clementino notes, "We were able to form our own youth network, Rede Nacional de Juventude-RENAJU, which is represented in the National Youth Council. Vozes Jovens provided young leaders with the opportunity to sit on the National Youth Council, where they can help build the youth policies Brazil needs."[16]

Challenges, however, remain. A truly national youth policy in Brazil requires harmonizing a diverse array of social and political interests (see spotlight on Brazil following chapter 5). Young people also introduce new ways of doing business—different language, different organizing methods, and different ways of presenting cases and results—that need to be incorporated into policy development and programming. There is also a need for greater policy integration at various levels of government, better priority setting across policies, and even more recognition of the diversity of needs among Brazil's youth.

Source: Authors.

Young people can also do a great deal to create opportunities to exercise voice. The spotlight that follows this chapter, by young people and for young people, provides examples of how to go about this.

Getting it right—through monitoring and evaluation

Youth policy, as mentioned previously, is bedeviled by the shortage of solid evaluations establishing the impact of policies and programs on youth outcomes. There is also little consensus on what the most relevant outcomes might be. So establishing priority outcomes and developing a body of evidence on what works, what does not, and in what circumstances are critical to advancing policy.

Monitoring

Because many interrelated outcomes are relevant to poverty reduction and growth, this chapter lists a range of indicators that emerge from the discussions in chapters 3–8 (box 9.8).[17] (The tables at the end of this Report present data on many of these indicators for a large number of countries, disaggregated by sex). The indicators allow benchmarking and country comparisons to monitor progress in different dimensions.

They can be used to arrive at an assessment of the main issues confronting the young, in some cases, serving as an "early warning" on problems (risky health behavior, lack of legal identity). Where there are large disparities within countries, it would be important to go deeper than these countrywide measures to subnational or local estimates.

Owing to the importance of learning in school, several measures are recommended to monitor schooling, including school participation, school completion, and schooling quality. At a minimum, the preparedness of children for postprimary learning could be assessed on the basis of literacy rates at the end of the primary (or early secondary) cycle. More sophisticated measures of learning could also be used, such as those derived from the Programme for International Student Assessment (PISA) and the Trends in International Mathematics and Science Study (TIMSS), which monitor learning at the end of the primary cycle and at the end of compulsory schooling (lower secondary). This would require a substantial expansion in coverage of these tests in developing countries.

Because the productive use of young people's labor is important for both individuals and society, detrimentally early tran-

BOX 9.8   *A youth scorecard? The many indicators of youth development*

In selecting indicators, the focus is on those relevant from a poverty reduction and growth perspective. Some may not be readily available from existing data sources, and are marked with an asterisk; most could be collected with little effort by adding questions to existing survey and census instruments.[18]

Learning	1.	School enrollment by gender
	2.	Primary, lower secondary, and upper secondary completion rates among youth, by gender
	3.	Learning achievement—end-primary and end-secondary—by gender *
Going to work	4.	Incidence of child labor, by gender
	5.	Labor force participation rates, by gender
	6.	Unemployment rates, by gender, for rural and urban youth
	7.	Percentage not at work and not in school, by gender
Staying healthy	8.	Percentage currently using tobacco, by gender
	9.	Percentage currently using drugs including inhalants, by gender *
	10.	Body mass index, by gender *
	11.	Percentage of sexually active youth engaging in unprotected sex, by gender and by marital status
	12.	Percentage of youth with knowledge of how to prevent HIV/AIDS, by gender
	13.	Percentage of 15-year-olds who will die before reaching their 60th birthday, by gender
Forming families	14.	Age specific fertility rates
	15.	Percentage of young women giving birth before 18
	16.	Percentage of young women using antenatal care
Citizenship	17.	Percentage of youth who have worked together with someone else or some group to solve a problem in the community where they live, by gender *
	18.	Percentage of youth who correctly answer a question concerning political knowledge appropriate to the country, by gender *
	19.	Percentage of youth without identity papers, by gender *
	20.	Number of youth in presentence detention, per 100,000 population, by gender*
Moving across	21.	Percentage of youth studying abroad, by gender*
borders and	22.	Percentage of youth working abroad, by gender*
communicating	23.	Percentage of youth migrants returning within 10 years of migrating, by gender*
	24.	Percentage of youth who have used the Internet in the past month, by gender*

Source: Authors' recommendations based on discussions in chapters 3–8 of this book.
* The indicator is not currently collected on a regular basis.

sitions to the labor force could be monitored through the incidence of child labor. Postponed transitions, also costly from a human capital development perspective, could be monitored through measures of unemployment and discouragement (being not at work and not in school). It is not enough to know whether the young are employed. The quality of employment also matters, especially in low-income countries where unemployment may be something of a luxury, but it is notoriously difficult to pin down.

Young people incur multiple threats to their health, so monitoring tobacco use, drug and inhalant use, unsafe sexual activity, body mass, and the probability of dying before the age of 60 can provide estimates of the extent of these risks. Of these measures, statistics on drug and inhalant use and body mass index are not collected systematically in large numbers of developing countries. Because the efficacy of health service delivery for this age group is important for influencing risk-taking behavior, indicators are proposed for both knowledge (of safe sexual practices and methods of preventing HIV/AIDS) and use (antenatal care) among the young. The focus in family formation would be on the incidence of early motherhood (before the age of 18).

Encouraging young people to participate in the broader political and democratic processes of society builds a responsible citizenry, so participation in the local community and broader political awareness are proposed as measures of active and passive citizenship. It would also be important to document government failures to provide legal identity to youngsters—and harsh punishments for young people (presentence detention).

Under migration and communication, the proportion of young people abroad for work and for study is of interest, as is the proportion who return after a reasonably short time. Access to the Internet would also need to be monitored.

All these indicators are either collected routinely or could be collected routinely at little marginal cost. Better monitoring of outcomes for young people is thus within easy reach, and could contribute enormously to the analytical basis for improving policy.

Evaluation

Evaluation is not within easy reach because it is more intensive in both skills and resources. However, concerted efforts could improve the knowledge available for policy making.

Spillovers from one youth transition to others make impact evaluation difficult. For example, the impact of investing in an additional year of schooling for girls beyond primary school would need to take account not only of potential additional earnings (which may be small in societies where female labor force participation is low),

but also the mother's health (through likely lower fertility) and her children's health and mortality.[19] For another example, the impact of reducing crime among youth may have returns that go beyond direct improvements to the safety of local citizens and may include indirect benefits through increases in international tourism and foreign investment. Fully accounting for these spillover effects is important for understanding the full benefits of investing in young people.

These spillover effects also make it more difficult to evaluate youth investments using traditional cost-effectiveness analysis. Such analysis—of, say, cost per disability life year saved or cost per beneficiary placed in employment—is widely used to evaluate investments in health, training, and other activities. It requires a single effectiveness measure for comparing alternative investments, impractical where outcomes are multiple and varied.[20] The alternative would be to use cost-benefit analysis, comparing cost with the monetized sum of

---

BOX 9.9 *Credible proof of a program's success can ensure continuity:*
The case of Oportunidades

Oportunidades (formerly Progresa), one of Mexico's best known "brands," gives cash benefits to poor households conditional on their maintaining the use of education and health services, particularly for children and youth. Introduced in 1997 as a part of an effort to break the intergenerational transmission of poverty, it now covers some 25 million of the poorest people throughout the country, with a budget of about 0.36 percent of GDP in 2005. The evaluation program was designed at the same time as its implementation, permitting rigorous evaluation of a complex program with many components.

What has it achieved?
Oportunidades has boosted enrollments and narrowed the gender gap in secondary school. The bulk of the positive impact on school enrollment lies in higher continuation rates rather than in returns of children who had left school. Grade repetition is lower, as are dropout rates, especially in the critical transition from primary to secondary school. Adolescents engage in less risky health behavior. Qualitative analysis suggests that the program is raising the aspirations of young people, especially those of girls to become teachers and nurses and to put off marrying until they can acquire the necessary skills.

Why has it been successful?
Multisector programs are notoriously difficult to implement because of the complexity of coordinating operations across ministries, with different mandates and sometime conflicting objectives. How have programs such as Oportunidades managed successful implementation?

Central backing. From the beginning, Oportunidades had very strong central backing, including the full confidence of the executive arm of the government, from the president to the finance ministry official who was one of its cofounders. This allowed it to break through bureaucratic logjams and to secure adequate funding despite the usual vicissitudes of annual budget appropriations. Fiscal space permitted the program to grow over time.

Piloting and outreach. Many operational issues that needed to be addressed—such as efficient targeting, the need for better monitoring and evaluation, and interagency coordination—were identified in an early pilot. Great effort before the launch of the program built consensus and support for the program. This effort continues, particularly through educating beneficiaries about their rights.

Apolitical allocations. The program goes to great lengths to avoid any impression of partisan-

ship or close ties with the administration in power. It is run by a new agency that coordinates with the ministries responsible for various government services. The national parliament establishes the program's budget and annually publishes its operating rules and the number of families enrolled. Enrollment is closed for several months before national elections, and payments are not made before voting days in any jurisdiction. A transparent and nonpolitical system for allocating benefits is one of the program's hallmarks.[21]

Rigorous monitoring and evaluation. From its inception the program has emphasized monitoring and rigorous evaluation, collecting baseline data and longitudinal household and service-provider data with treatment and control groups. Initial evaluation was contracted to an outside agency (International Food Policy Research Institute), and continues to this day involving academics from three continents. Credible empirical proof of the program's achievements has been essential to the program's longevity. The program survived a change in presidents, and was even expanded by the new government.

Sources: Bate (2004); Behrman, Sengupta, and Todd (2001); Levy and Rodriguez (2004); Murray (2004); and Schultz (2000).

benefits, but this requires knowledge of the effectiveness of the interventions across the range of potential outcomes, which is rarely available. For example, no evaluations of the Jovenes training programs in Latin America look into the impact on health, civic participation, or crime.

Another aspect of youth policies is that they may be more effective when administered jointly, because outcomes may have common determinants that need to be targeted together. For example, health information and job skills training may be more effective in ensuring that young people obtain and retain a job when offered jointly than when either is offered on its own—because obtaining a job is a function both of being healthy and being qualified. Similarly, discouraging girls (and their parents) from early marriage may be more effective when girls are in school. In the model discussed in box 9.6, targeting both education and health outcomes of young people is more effective in encouraging human capital development than education interventions alone.

Both these features—spillover effects and complementarities across transitions—suggest that when it comes to youth there may be a case for coordinated evaluations of outcomes. Traditional evaluations focus on programs and judge the impact of the program on a specified outcome. Perhaps more relevant for young people would be, what is the most cost-effective way of reaching a given outcome? This may require coordinated evaluations across a range of relevant interventions.

Meeting the challenge is essential to advancing policy development. True, evaluating is expensive, but because the knowledge generated is a public good, there is a strong case for greater donor effort to assist in evaluation. Donor assistance has already advanced the evaluation of policies and programs, but much more remains to be done (see spotlight on donors following chapter 8).

On top of adding to the pool of policy-relevant knowledge, one neglected outcome of rigorous evaluation is the possible benefit of insulating good programs from politics. Oportunidades, the conditional cash transfer program in Mexico, provides a good example. Found to be effective in boosting secondary school enrollment, the evaluation of its outcomes was built in at the outset. This helped ensure the program's longevity (box 9.9). Changes in political leadership during program implementation did not derail the program because its established effectiveness in addressing the long-run causes of poverty was hard for the new government to question.

It's up to you(th)—taking action for development

This Report's simple message to governments and policy makers is that investing in young people is essential for development—and for those investments to be most effective, young people must be included as stakeholders in decisions that affect them. But what can young people do? This spotlight addresses young people directly about how to develop their own capabilities so they can seize the opportunities provided to them, but especially, so they can create opportunities for themselves, for other young people, and for everyone. The spotlight benefited greatly from consultations with youth from many countries who have successfully taken action for development. It was written by young people, for young people.

Young people make a difference

People will decide their lives
People will identify their problems
People will lead to self-help
People will share the fruits

This is the motto of Chamila, Kamili, Wacheeri, and Milmini—four young women from villages in Sri Lanka who are helping young people and all people in their villages overcome poverty. Kamili (age 22) says, "Our problems are village problems, and the village's problems are ours." They have seen resources wasted and misguided projects implemented by those trying to help their villages, but instead of becoming disillusioned with development work they became engaged in it. They sum up their work as "Strengthen the village by increasing your individual capacity."

Powerful older villagers haven't always appreciated their involvement: when Chamila (age 19) was elected to the village council, it would not allow her to take office because of her youth. But the community, remembering her past hard work and cooperation while volunteering on village projects, forced the whole council to resign instead. Chamila was then reinstated with a new council.

These four women are just a few of the hundreds of poor young people (ages 16–25) who are volunteering and working together for community development in Sri Lanka.

Source: Interview with Samantha M. Constant and Sarath K. Guttikunda. Social Accountability Workshop. Gemi Diriya Project, Sri Lanka. March 2006.

This Report recommends that governments should invest in and recognize young people. For it to become reality, young people must seize the initiative and invest—by developing your own capacity, and taking action to make youth investments successful. And as young people in Sri Lanka recognize, (see the box above), all meaningful investments in development can positively affect young people. What can be done and how to do it?

Take action: What can be done

No matter who you are, you can take action as young people to make life better for yourself, and at the same time, for others around you. Some of the poorest boys and girls (ages 12–15) in Malawi and Nepal, for example, have formed sanitation clubs—sometimes in spite of ridicule from their peers—to build latrines and maintain water pumps for their schools, improving their daily experience and the health of their communities.

The many things young people have accomplished fill books and reports,[1] and there are few limitations on the ways young people can contribute to development.

Action can be as simple as developing one's own capabilities—learning about and taking advantage of a training program, a health service, career options—or finding out about and discussing with friends an issue that matters to them (the environment, HIV/AIDS). What you decide to do and how you do it will depend on your skills, your personality, the issues that inspire you, the resources you have available to you, and the circumstances in which you live.

Working with the system

Few societies readily include young people in policy decisions (chapters 7 and 9), but many young people overcome that challenge to volunteer or work for existing NGOs, or cooperate with governments to improve policies. Through youth service organizations in countries such as Kenya, Pakistan, and the Philippines, youth have developed and carried out active solutions to community and national problems. In Mexico 2,000 young people volunteer to improve literacy and civic participation through one of many large programs that involve young people. Young people have a key role in exercising their "client power" to

hold governments accountable—as young people have done in Brazil (see box 2.4), FYR Macedonia, and Russia (chapter 3). And "government" can be anything from a local teacher to a global institution.

Going beyond the system

Many young people decide to start something new, be it an activist campaign for social justice or a motorbike transport business (chapter 7). These youth-led projects usually work best when young people work together, and train the next "next generation" to continue their efforts. Students at one college in the United States started the first student-run think tank in 2004, and already, students at 50 other colleges have joined the network, and lawmakers have begun to use their research.

Young people face many challenges, but every challenge to taking action is an opportunity to take action. Most young people see a lack of jobs as just a challenge to employment. Several large groups of young ex-combatants in Sierra Leone took it as an opportunity and joined together across opposing sides of the conflict to start a motorbike transportation business. By starting a new trade (motorbike transportation did not exist before the war), they avoided the challenges faced by youth breaking into established trades and instead were very successful. Plus, they found a job that they particularly enjoy as young people. As one bike rider (age 18) says, "The war was exciting, but bad. To be a bike rider is exciting and good." Still they had to work to gain the trust of clients, and learn to cooperate with the traditional system: rather than reacting violently to perceived unfair treatment by police, they hired a lawyer.[2]

Tools for action: How to get it done

Young people often face complex challenges, such as lack of information and experience, skeptical and resistant authorities, bureaucracies that favor qualifications over hard work and skills, lack of resources, and lack of recognition for their work. Despite these obstacles, young people can still take action to develop their capability—through persistence, a willingness to experiment, and four basic tools.

Learn

Find out as much you can about how to build skills for your work and your life, about both sides of development issues you are passionate about, about different ways of taking action.

One youth UN delegate from the Netherlands, spent "half a year" lobbying his government to participate in the Millennium Summit, and relied on his expertise on the issues to convince them to allow him to go:

> After a certain time they knew me, they knew that I wasn't just smiling and representing the youth, but also, I could really help them with experts on different youth issues. What I know a lot about because of my work at the Red Cross is HIV/AIDS. But if they wanted to talk with child soldiers, I could help them. . .[3]

How can this be done?

- "Use the power of ICTs to get information," writes a young volunteer in Nigeria (chapter 8). To start, learn from Web sites such as the Development Gateway, the UN, and the World Bank, and the many sites for specific issues and national organizations.*

- Take advantage of programs that provide information to young people, such as Umsobomvu Youth Fund in South Africa, or those that provide information about services for young people (education, jobs), such as the ASER project in India (chapter 3).*

- Learn how to apply for small grants for projects, work with people, and write proposals for the many resources provided by youth organizations, for example, "Global Youth Coalition on HIV/AIDS (GYCA) conducts online courses in proposal writing, advocacy, etc." advises one youth leader.*

Evaluate

Be critical. Question your interests, the circumstances around you, and the poli-cies and actions of those who are supposed to serve you and your community. Reconsider what you already know and what you hear. As you take action, do research to evaluate whether your efforts are making a difference for those you want to help.

- "Asking for advice is the most important tool that we have as youth. . . . My advice to other youth leaders is not to ignore the small people . . . sometimes they know more than those at the top," says a Liberian youth leader.

- Check out TakingITGlobal's youth action guide, search for others, or create your own.*

- Talk with an open mind to people who you think your action will help, and find out what they need—and then adapt your plan to make it work

- Find out about youth involvement in monitoring and evaluation of programs that are designed to serve youth.

Cooperate

If you are going to make change effective, you must work with others: form alliances, collaborate, work collectively. Just as important, learn work to with people who have the power to help.

A young woman from Kenya became the first UN youth delegate from Kenya in 2005 by taking initiative to voice important issues and cooperate with Kenyan officials:

> From the beginning of the year, from my organizational level, I lobbied and advocated for the youth to be included in all the processes on the MDGs. . . . We never missed their meetings, we worked so hard to have our thoughts and ideas put in. When it was time for the ministry to appoint the delegation, they appointed the most active and persistent.[4]

Join a local or national youth organization, or a global network of young people (such as TakingITGlobal, Youth Employment Summit campaign [YES], the Global Youth Action Network) who are taking action. This is an opportunity to find other young people that you can learn from and work with and a way to make your voice heard.*

Voice

You can hold civil servants, social workers, and policy makers accountable. Another important way to use your voice is to inform and learn from other young people.

One young activist from Italy found an alternative way to express her voice in the face of challenges:

> I was tired of taking part in pro-youth consultation processes ending up in nothing, and was tired to keep talking but not having anyone listen. . . . I then decided that I [would] try to change it, and worked toward the aim of setting a youth platform, Youth Action for Change, to make my voice heard—and every other young person for that matter—heard.... The project proved very successful . . .[5]

A youth leader in Singapore says:

> About voice: know how it works. It's difficult to effect any real change if you don't know the political infrastructure....Talk to youth-friendly people in civil service or NGOs which effectively engage with government.

These four tools are just the beginning. Use these and others to motivate your plans and develop capabilities for action.

Who can help

Many groups exist to help young people take action. If you would like their help, make your voice heard. As in the story from Sri Lanka, young people can often have a big impact at the local level. Global youth organizations (mentioned above) are a network for many small, local organizations. At both the local and global levels the UN has worked to include young people. The World Bank has begun to involve youth organizations by providing courses, and by consulting with youth about its programs. At the local level, the World Bank has civil society and youth liaisons in its country offices. At the global level, see the work of the Youth, Development and Peace Network.

In the end, it is up to you—your involvement is crucial to increasing the role of young people and youth issues in efforts to alleviate poverty.

---

*See the following Web sites: Development Gateway: www.developmentgateway.org/youth, GYCA: www.youthaidscoalition.org, Taking IT Global: www.takingitglobal.org, Umsobomvu Youth Fund: www.uyf.org.za, UN: www.un.org/youth, World Bank: www.worldbank.org/childrenandyouth, www.youthink.org, Youth Employment Summit Campaign: www.yesweb.org.

Bibliographical note

This Report draws on a wide range of World Bank documents and on numerous outside sources. Background papers and useful comments were prepared by Arvil Van Adams, Pablo Angelelli, Sarah E. Anthony, Kaushik Basu, Clive Bell, Eric Bettinger, Ramona Bruhns, Pedro Carneiro, Esther Duflo, Pascaline Dupas, Tanja El-Cherkeh, Elizabeth Fussell, Sebastian Galiani, Elena Galliano, Hans Gersbach, Elizabeth Gomart, Juan Pablo Gutierrez, Naomi Halewood, Hugo Kantis, Charles Kenny, Michael Kremer, Hyejin Ku, Gloria La Cava, David Lam, Juan José Llisterri, Minna Mattero, Sarah Michael, Edward Miguel, Alexis Murphy, Zeynep Ozbil, Janice E. Perlman, Agnes Quisumbing, Dhushyanth Raju, Usha Ramakrishna, Martin Rossi, Juan E. Saavedra, Ernesto Schargrodsky, Samuel Simei, Elena Stirbu, Mio Takada, Luis Tejerina, Erwin Tiongson, Andrea Tolciu, Gerold Thilo Vollmer, Kathryn Young, and Homa Zarghamee.

Background papers for the Report are available either on the World Wide Web www.worldbank.org/wdr2007 or through the World Development Report office. The views expressed in these papers are not necessarily those of the World Bank or of this Report.

In addition to commenting on the Report, the following also contributed substantially to preparing boxes and spotlights. Contributions for the spotlights and boxes were provided by Ragui Assaad, Nicholas Barr, Mayra Buvinic, Le Thi Minh Chau, Ernesto Cuadra, Wendy Cunningham, Carmen De Paz Nieves, Ana Cristina Torres Garcia, Andrea Guedes, Juan Carlos Guzman, Richard R. Hopper, Sandra Huang, Peter F. Lanjouw, Kathy Lindert, Cynthia Lloyd, Daniel Mont, Juan Manuel Moreno, Andrew Morrison, Deepa Narayan, Harry Patrinos, Pia Peeters, Patti Petesch, Jenny Petrow, Susana Puerto, Martin Rama, Jamil Salmi, Noala Skinner, Kristian Thorn, Carolyn Turk, Dorte Verner, Zeze Weiss and Yesim Yilmaz.

Many people inside and outside the World Bank gave comments to the team. Valuable comments and contributions were provided by Charlie Abelmann, Daron Acemoglu, Ahmad Ahsan, Harold Alderman, Santiago Levy Algazi, Caridad Araujo, Ana Arjona, Jeffrey Jensen Arnett, Tamar Manuelyan Atinc, Arup Banerji, Sergio Bautista, Kathleen Beegle, Jane Bertrand, Myra L. Betron, Mohini Bhatia, Nancy Birdsall, Andreas Blom, John D. Blomquist, Anthony Bloom, David Bloom, Daniel Kwabena Boakye, Christian Bodewig, Jan Bojö, Gillian Brown, Peter Buckland, Don Bundy, Danielle Carbonneau, Nadereh Chamlou, Nazmul Chaudhury, Samantha M. Constant, Luis Constantino, Richard Curtain, Anis Dani, Amit Dar, Jishnu Das, Maitreyi Das, Monica Das Gupta, Joanna de Berry, Jaikishan Desai, Shantayanan Devarajan, Karen Dillard, Sophia Drewnowski, Antonio Estache, Shahrokh Fardoust, Tazeen Fasih, Manuela Ferro, Armin Fidler, Ariel Fiszbein, Constance A. Flanagan, Shubashis Gangopadhyay, Marito H. Garcia, Ines Garcia-Thoumi, Alan Gelb, Tina George, Maninder Gill, Elena Glinskaya, Rachel Glennerster, Peter Gluckman, Daniela Gressani, Karen Gross, Jon Gruber, Sarath K. Guttikunda, Andrew Hahn, Minna Hahn, Keith Hansen, Inaam Haq, Karla Hoff, Leif Holmberg, Camilla Holmemo, Robert Holzmann, Macartan Humphreys, Ingo Imhoff, Farrukh Iqbal, Shweta Jain, Evangeline Javier, Malathi S. Jayawickrama, Rajendra Dhoj Joshi, Ursila Jung, Jan Kasprzycki-Rosikon, Omer M. Karasapan, Mats Karlsson, Iqbal Kaur, Kei Kawabata, Homi Kharas, Douglas Kirby, Robert Krech, Angela Langenkamp, Frannie Léautier, Danny M. Leipziger, Peter Levine, Santiago Levy, Jeffrey D. Lewis, Samuel Lieberman, David Lindauer, Rick Little, Benjamin Loevinsohn, Elizabeth Laura Lule, Ante Lundberg, Shelly Lundberg, Akiko Maeda, Sam Maimbo, Gift Manase, Viviana Mangiaterra, Ali M. Mansoor, Katherine Marshall, John May, Linda McGinnis, John McIntire, Rekha Menon, Pradeep Mitra, Nancy Murray, Mustapha Kamel Nabli, Ambar Narayan, Claudia Nassif, Sophie Naudeau, Kenneth J. Newcombe, Akihiko Nishio, Tara O'Connell, Eric Olson, Patrick Osewe, Egbe Osifo, Mead Over, Pierella Paci, John Page, Guillermo Perry, Djordjija Petkoski, Susana Pezzullo, Lant Pritchett, Christine Zhen-Wei Qiang, G N V Ramana, William Reese, Ana Revenga, Linda Richter, Pia Rockhold, Ernesto Rodriguez, Halsey Rogers, Khama Rogo, James Rosen, David Rosenblatt, David Ross, James Sackey, Junko Saito, Hussain Samad, Stefano Scarpetta, Norbert Schady, Julian Schweitzer, Shekhar Shah, William Shaw, Carlos Silva-Jauregui, Bachir Souhlal, David Steel, Miguel Szekely, Kaleb Tamiru, Stephanie Tam, Thaisa Tiglao, P. Zafiris Tzannatos, Bernice Van Bronkhorst, Dominique van der Mensbrugghe, Willem Van Eeghen, Tara Vishwanath, Milan Vodopivec, Hermann von Gersdorff, Adam Wagstaff, Mike Walker,

Michel J. Welmond, L. Alan Winters, Katherine Whiteside, Jorge Wong-Valle, David Woollcombe, Ruslan Yemtsov, Deji Young, Tanju Yurukoglu, and Hassan Zaman.

Nazanine Atabaki, Phil Hay, and Christopher Neal assisted the team with consultations and media dissemination. Other valuable production assistance was provided by Madhur Arora, a former WDR program assistant, Gytis Kanchas, Polly Means, Nacer Mohamed Megherbi, Anthony Nathan, Shunalini Sarkar, and Roula I. Yazigi.

Despite efforts to compile a comprehensive list, some who contributed may have been inadvertently omitted. The team apologizes for any oversights and reiterates its gratitude to all who contributed to this Report.

Background papers

Adams, Arvil V. "The Role of Skills Development in the Transition to Work: A Global Review."

Basu, Kaushik, Hyejin Ku, and Homa Zarghamee. "Determinants of Youth Behaviour and Outcomes: A Review of Theory, Evidence and Policy Implications."

Behrman, Jere R., Alexis Murphy, Agnes Quisumbing, Usha Ramakrishna, and Kathyrn Young. "What is the Real Impact of Education on Age of First Parenthood and Family Formation?"

Bell, Clive, Ramona Bruhns, and Hans Gersbach. "Economic Growth, Education and Aids in Kenya Model: A Long-run Analysis."

Carneiro, Pedro, and Cristobal Ridao-Cano. "Heterogeneity and Uncertainty in Returns to High School: The Case of Indonesia."

Carneiro, Pedro, and Cristobal Ridao-Cano. "The Role of Short Term Liquidity Constraints in Explaining Educational Investments in Indonesia."

Duflo, Esther, Pascaline Dupas, Michael Kremer, and Samuel Simei. "Education and HIV/AIDS Prevention: Evidence from a Randomized Evaluation in Western Kenya."

El-Cherkeh, Tanja, Elena Stirbu, and Andrea Tolciu. "Youth Migration to Europe: Potential Impact on the Labour Market of the Countries of Origin."

Fares, Jean, and Claudio E. Montenegro. "Youth Unemployment's Dynamics: Evidence from Brazil (1978–2002) and Chile (1957–2005)."

Fares, Jean, Claudio E. Montenegro, and Peter F. Orazem. "How Are Youth Faring in the Labor Market? Evidence from Around the World."

Fares, Jean, Claudio E. Montenegro, and Peter F. Orazem. "Variation in the Returns to Schooling Across and Within Developing Economies."

Fares, Jean, and Dhushyanth Raju. "Child Labor across the Developing World: Patterns, Correlations and Determinants."

Fares, Jean, and Erwin Tiongson. "Entering the Labor Market and Early Mobility of Youth: Evidence from Panel Estimates in Bosnia and Herzegovina."

Galiani, Sebastián, Martín Rossi, and Ernesto Schargrodsky. "Conscription and Crime."

Gomart, Elizabeth. "Supporting Youth Citizenship: Review of Evidence."

Gorpe, Mehmet Ziya, Jean Fares, and Claudio E. Montenegro. "Public Wage Premium Around the World."

Gutierrez, Juan Pablo. "*Oportunidades* for the Next Generation: Effects of a Conditional Cash Transfer on the Wellbeing of Mexican Youths."

Halewood, Naomi, and Charles Kenny. "Young People and Communications Technologies."

La Cava, Gloria, Zeynep Ozbil, Sarah Michael, Elena Galliano, Minna Mattero, and Mio Takada. "Youth and the Transition to Citizenship: The Role of the State in Promoting Positive Youth Religious and Ethnic Identities and Young People's Role in Peace-Building and Social Change."

Lam, David. "The Demography of Youth in Developing Countries and its Economic Implications."

Llisterri, J., H. Kantis, P. Angelelli, and L. Tejerina. "Youth Entrepreneurship in Latin America."

Mangiaterra, Viviana, and Gerold Vollmer. "Youth Consultations for the WDR 2007: Synthesis Report of Country and Grassroots Consultations."

Mattero, Minna. "Youth Policies and the Institutional Framework."

McKenzie, David J. "A Profile of the World's Young Developing Country Migrants."

Perlman, Janice E., and Sarah E. Anthony. "Citizenship and Youth in the Favelas of Rio de Janeiro."

Background notes

Arjona, Ana. "Understanding Recruitment in Civil Wars."

Blum, Robert. "The Adolescent Brain."

Filmer, Deon, Emmanuel Jimenez, and Annette Richter. "Simulating the Returns to Youth Opportunity Agency and Second Chances."

Graham, Carol and Matthew Hoover. "An Exploration of Civic Activity in Latin America."

Hasan, Amer. "Youth Dispositions Towards Citizenship: Do Constitutional Frameworks Matter?"

Ridao-Cano, Cristobal. "Vietnamese Youth: Managing Prosperity."

Endnotes

Overview

1. This range encompasses those who are recognized officially by the UN as "youth," those ages 15–24, as well as those many classify as adolescents. The wider range is necessary to enable us to discuss transitions from puberty to full-time work.

2. World Bank (1990) and World Bank (2001d).

3. World Bank (2005j).

4. National Research Council and Institute of Medicine (2005) p. 73.

5. Acemoglu (2003).

6. World Bank (2005r).

7. Cohen and Bloom (2005).

8. World Bank (2004e). In a celebrated longitudinal study of Rio de Janeiro's slums (*favelas*), anthropologist Janice Perlman recounts that the youth there had more education than their parents but without perceptibly better jobs. In the late 1960s, parents would warn their children that if they did not stay in school they would end up as garbage collectors. In July 2003, the city opened competition for 400 garbage collector jobs and 12,000 people applied. A high school diploma was the prerequisite (Perlman (2005)).

9. Bloom and Canning (2005).

10. By 2050, 4 of every 10 people will come from today's cohort of those ages 12–24, their children, or their grandchildren. See Lam (2006).

11. Bell, Devarajan, and Gersbach (2006) p. 80.

12. See World Bank (1993a). Precise estimates vary, but about a third of the growth rate of the East Asian tigers over 1960 to 1985 was attributed in this study to sound investments in primary education alone.

13. De Ferranti and others (2003).

14. Bell and others (2004) p. 44.

15. Behrman and others (2005a).

16. Abeyratne (2004).

17. See box 2.1 for a fuller discussion.

18. UNESCO (2004b).

19. Examples are the Trends in International Mathematics and Science Study and Progress in International Reading Literacy Study tests.

20. Garces, Thomas, and Currie (2000); Glewwe, Jacoby, and King (2001); Kagitcibasi, Sunar, and Bekman (2001).

21. UNESCO (2005).

22. World Bank (2005o).

23. Policies to sustain growth are studied at great length in other work and are not discussed here. For a recent review, see World Bank (2005e).

24. Bloom and Canning (2005).

25. World Bank (2003f).

26. Kabeer (1999) and Sen (1985).

27. Vietnam Ministry of Health and General Statistics Office, UNICEF, and WHO (2005).

28. Boyer and Shafer (1997); Cáceres and others (1994); and Eggleston and others (2000).

29. World Bank (2004a).

30. Centre for Development and Population Activities (CEDPA) (2001).

31. De Ferranti and others (2003) p. 97.

32. Jacoby and Skoufias (2002).

33. Arends-Kuenning and Amin (2000).

34. Jimenez and Lockheed (1989).

35. Akerlof and Kranton (2000).

36. Gruber and Zinman (2001) and World Bank (2005j).

37. Hahn and Leavitt (2003).

38. While most of this research has been done in developed countries such as Germany, the experimental result is robust across a number of settings. See Dohmen and others (2005).

39. Hanushek and Wößmann (2005).

40. Singer (2005) and Stohl (2001).

41. Jha and others (2001).

Chapter 1

1. World Bank (2006b).

2. World Bank (1990); World Bank (2001d); and World Bank (2005r).

3. National Research Council and Institute of Medicine (2005).

4. It has proven difficult to convincingly establish causality from education to lower fertility. However, the role of maternal schooling in improving child health has been extensively documented. Grossman (2005a); Knowles and Behrman (2005); Schultz (2002); and World Bank (2001c) are some recent installments to this literature.

5. World Bank (2001c).

6. Paxson and Schady (forthcoming).

7. World Bank (2005r).

8. Jimenez (1995).

9. World Bank (2004e) and World Bank (2005f).

10. De Ferranti and others (2003).

11. Estimates are from a wide range of modeling approaches including computable general equilibrium simulations and various growth models. See Bell, Devarajan, and Gersbach (2006), table 1.

12. World Bank (2002b).

13. Barro (1999) analyzing panel data from 100 countries during 1960–95 finds growth to be positively related to the starting level of

secondary schooling. Pritchett (2001), however, finds no impact of education growth on growth of GDP per capita or growth of total factor productivity using data on 90 countries over the period 1960–85. Neither Barro nor Pritchett take account of schooling quality.

14. Hanushek and Kimko (2000).

15. World Bank (2001b).

16. See Panton quoted in World Bank (2001b).

17. World Bank (2001b).

18. For Latin America and the Caribbean see Behrman, Birdsall, and Szekely (2003) and Sánchez-Páramo and Schady (2003); for the Middle-East, Abu-Ghaida and Connolly (2003); for Sub-Saharan Africa, Schultz (2003); for East Asia, Abu-Ghaida and Connolly (2003); for China, Heckman and Li (2004); and for India, National Research Council and Institute of Medicine (2005).

19. Berman and Machin (2000).

20. Acemoglu (2003).

21. Vietnam Ministry of Health and General Statistics Office, UNICEF, and WHO (2005).

22. National Research Council and Institute of Medicine (2005).

23. World Bank (2000).

24. National Research Council and Institute of Medicine (2005).

25. National Research Council and Institute of Medicine (2005).

26. Projections are based on the United Nations (2005), and assume that fertility follows the medium variant.

27. These projections incorporate the impact of HIV/AIDS. Projections generally suggest that AIDS will hasten the fertility decline and thus hasten the peak in the youth populations. For example, in Botswana the youth population is projected to peak around 2005 but under the alternative "No AIDS" projection it would have continued increasing for several more decades.

28. Johnson (2000) and Lam (2006).

29. Lam (2006).

30. Because the analysis is based on projections from the United Nations' World Population Prospects, it does not cover countries that are missing from this data base. Examples include countries with a population less than 100,000 in 2005 and Timor Leste.

31. Another way of thinking of the pressure of new entrants is in terms of the growth rate of youth cohorts. This, too, peaked in most developing countries in the 1960s and 1970s, at the height of the population explosion, and has been declining since. So although it is still high in many developing countries—at 2–3 percent a year—it is on a downward trend and thus points to an easing of pressure. In the few countries where the fertility transition is not under way, growth rates are not declining.

32. There is a long literature going back to the classic work of Coale and Hoover (1958) and Leff (1969) on how countries with high population growth rates suffered from low savings rates because of the high ratio of children and youth to the working-age population.

33. Bloom and Sachs (1998); Bloom and Williamson (1998); Bloom, Canning, and Malaney (2000); and Mason (2001). The literature largely focuses on Japan, Hong Kong (China), Singapore, and Korea. Bloom and Williamson also include China and Taiwan (China).

34. Deaton and Paxson (1997).

35. Bloom and Canning (2005).

36. Countries where dependency ratios are rising are a subset of the ones where relative cohort size is rising. They are Chad, Equatorial Guinea, Guinea-Bissau, Liberia, Niger, Republic of Congo, and Sierra Leone.

37. National Research Council and Institute of Medicine (2005) and UNICEF (2000).

38. The definitions of child labor have evolved over time to reflect refinement of norms and standards. In its current definition of child labor, the ILO includes all children under age 11 who are economically active, all 12- to 14-year-olds who are economically active for more than 14 hours per week, and all those age 17 and under who are engaged in hazardous activity and the worst forms of labor including trafficking, bonded labor, armed conflict, prostitution and pornography, and illicit work (National Research Council and Institute of Medicine (2005)).

39. For sources, see chapter 5.

40. National Research Council and Institute of Medicine (2005).

Spotlight on demographics

1. Unless otherwise stated, we use the UN World Population Prospects, (United Nations (2005)) for all demographic analysis. See http://www.un.org/esa/population/publications/WPP2004/wpp2004.htm for definitions, assumptions, and other details.

2. For this classification we assume that a country has reached its peak if the peak youth population occurs between 2000 and 2010 or the peak population occurs after 2010 but the growth rate between 2005 and 2015 is below 0.5 percent per year. See Lam (2006) for further details.

3. For this classification, we assume that a country has reached its peak if the peak youth population occurs between 2010 and 2030 and the growth rate between 2005 and 2015 is above 0.5 percent per year, or the peak youth population occurs after 2030 but the growth rate between 2025 and 2035 is below 0.5 percent per year.

Chapter 2

1. World Bank (2003f).

2. An exception is Moehling (2005) who studies the bargaining power of working children in the United States during the turn of the last century.

3. These ideas have been developed by several Nobel Laureates—George Akerlof, James Heckman, Daniel Kahneman, Michael Spence, and Joseph Stiglitz—among others.

4. For an extensive review, see chapter 7 of *World Development Report 2006* (World Bank (2005r)).

5. UNESCO (2004b), Summary, p. 35.

6. Kurz, Peplinsky, and Johnson-Welch (1994).

7. Strauss and Thomas (1995).

8. Perhaps best documented are the long-term effects of early childhood development programs in the United States. Analysis of the long-term effects of the national Head Start program indicates that it increases the probability of graduating from high school and attending college. Among African Americans the program also lowers the likelihood of having been charged or convicted of a crime (Garces, Thomas, and Currie (2000)).

9. Glewwe, Jacoby, and King (2001).

10. Kagitcibasi, Sunar, and Bekman (2001).

11. World Bank (2005f).

12. It is difficult to know how much this would cost, but a very rough order of magnitude can be inferred from a recent costing exercise by Binder (2005), who estimated the annual global cost of universalizing secondary education to be $28 billion annually over a 25-year horizon ($22 billion if efficiency gains from the experi-

ence of "best practice" countries are adopted universally). If lower secondary is about half as long as upper secondary, an annual tab of $11–14 billion may not be far from the mark. Cohen and Bloom (2005) conclude that these amounts are affordable.

13. World Bank (2003f).

14. Studies show that in most countries, the rate of human capital accumulation, measured by its effect on productivity and wages, is at its highest during youth and decreases by more than a third (half) by the age of 30 (40). See chapter 4.

15. UNESCO (2005) p. 174.

16. Lee and Rhee (1999).

17. McKenzie (2004).

18. Bloom and Canning (2005).

19. In Malaysia, labor force participation of 20- to 24-year-old women increased 23 percent between 1970 and 2000. Also see Joekes (1995).

20. Maloney and Nuñez Mendez (2004) and Montenegro and Pagés (2004).

21. Heckman and Pagés (2000).

22. UNDP (1995) estimates that two-thirds of women's work is unpaid and outside national accounts.

23. Computed from household survey "Enquete Niveau de Vies des Menages, Institut National de la Statistique, Republique de Côte d'Ivoire" (2002).

24. World Bank (2004e).

25. World Bank (2003f).

26. This definition of "agency" is used by Kabeer (1999). The concept has been popular among social scientists for some time, but it has been given great impetus by Sen (1985).

27. Arnett (2000). Social psychologists have distinguished two contexts. Broad socialization, characteristic of many Western industrial societies, is consistent with emphasizing independence, individualism, and self-expression. Narrow socialization emphasizes conformity to expectations (Shanahan and others (2005).

28. These findings are consistent with an earlier UNICEF (2001) survey of East Asian countries, not comparable with the one above.

29. Iversen (2002) p. 821.

30. UNESCO (2005).

31. Basu and Foster (1998).

32. Basu, Ku, and Zarghamee (2006).

33. Vietnam Ministry of Health and General Statistics Office, UNICEF, and WHO (2005).

34. World Bank (2006g).

35. O'Donoghue and Rabin (2001).

36. Knowles and Behrman (2005).

37. Dupas (2006).

38. Jensen (2006).

39. Vegas and Umansky (2005).

40. Akerlof and Kranton (2000).

41. See Shanahan and others (2005) for evidence from the United States.

42. Ali and others (2006) p. 11.

43. Billari, Philipov, and Baizán Munoz (2001).

44. De Ferranti and others (2003).

45. Jacoby and Skoufias (2002).

46. Mathur, Greene, and Jamhotra (2003). This kind of "entrapment" limits social mobility of young brides by forcing them to be apprentices for domestic labor.

47. Pitt and Khandker (1996).

48. Jimenez and Lockheed (1989).

49. O'Donoghue and Rabin (2001).

50. Gruber and Zinman (2001).

51. World Bank (2005p).

52. Bruns, Mingat, and Rakotomalala (2003).

53. Strauss and Thomas (1995).

54. Groce (2003).

55. Levitt and Lochner (2001).

56. Hahn and Leavitt (2003).

57. World Bank (2003f).

58. O'Donoghue and Rabin (2001).

59. National Youth Council of Ireland (2001).

60. Calculated from figures obtained from Economic Research and Consulting, Swiss Reinsurance Company, Zurich.

61. Knowles and Behrman (2003) pp. 39–40 show that a $1,000 investment in adult basic education and literacy could produce about 10.23 trainees They compare the benefits of this as equivalent to one year of primary schooling (lower bound) or four years of primary schooling (upper bound). If one were to use the unit cost of education in Bangladesh (about $31, seeWorld Bank, Unesco Institute for Statistics (UIS), and OECD (2006)), a similar investment would yield 32.3 primary school students. Thus, the bounds are roughly 0.8 to 3 times the cost, without opportunity costs.

62. See, for example, Goldscheider (2000).

63. Span Jr. (2000).

64. Hanushek and Wößmann (2005).

65. Philippine News online.

66. Filmer, Jimenez, and Richter (2006).

67. Jensen (2006).

Spotlight on gender

1. In Muslim societies restrictions take the form of *purdah,* in others early curfews or prohibitions against traveling alone. See World Bank (2004b) and World Bank (2005a).

2. Singh (1998).

3. WHO (2002b).

4. Buvinic and others (2006).

5. National Research Council and Institute of Medicine (2005).

6. Lloyd, Mensch, and Clark (2000).

7. Grown, Rao Gupta, and Kes (2005).

8. Ritchie, Lloyd, and Grant (2004).

9. Levison, Moe, and Knaul (2001).

10. Enrollment rates for primary school have decreased for boys in 24 countries: Azerbaijan, China, Gabon, Georgia, Indonesia, the Islamic Republic of Iran, Jamaica, Jordan, Latvia, Macedonia, Malaysia, Maldives, Mauritius, Mexico, Moldova, Myanmar, Namibia, Oman, Peru, the Slovak Republic, Sri Lanka, St. Lucia, West Bank and Gaza, and Zimbabwe. This trend is repeated for secondary school in 12 countries: Albania, Armenia, Belarus, Georgia, Kazakhstan, the Kyrgyz Republic, Moldova, Niger, Romania, Seychelles, Ukraine, and Uzbekistan. Calculations based on UNESCO Institute of Statistics database.

11. The percentages of idle girls in the other countries are 10 percent in Brazil, 23 percent in Cameroon, 27 percent in Turkey, and 28 percent in Guatemala.

12. Lavy (1996) and World Bank (2005a).

13. Amin and others (1998).

14. World Bank (2005a).

15. Buvinic (2005).

16. *Ministerio del Trabajo Peru (1998).*

Chapter 3

1. Carneiro and Heckman (2003) and Cunha and others (2005).

2. Knudsen (2004); Newport (2002); and Shonkoff and Phillips (2000).

3. Experimental evidence from the United States. Heckman, LaLonde, and Smith (1999).

4. Currie and Thomas (1995).

5. See Alderman, Hoddinott, and Kinsey (forthcoming); Paxson and Schady (forthcoming); and Carneiro and Heckman (2003) for reviews of the literature in developed and developing countries.

6. Paxson and Schady (forthcoming).

7. Experimental studies in India and Indonesia found large impacts on cognitive development and school performance of iron supplementation among anemic children (Soewondo, Husaini, and Pollitt (1989) and Seshadri and Gopaldas (1989)). For programs in Jamaica, Argentina, and the Philippines, see, respectively Walker and others (2005); Berlinsky, Galiani, and Gertler (2006); and Armecina and others (2006).

8. UIS-UNESCO data: http://stats.uis.unesco.org/.

9. Canals-Cerda and Ridao-Cano (2004). This effect works mainly by increasing the probability of working during primary and secondary school. The effect of grade repetition is only defined for secondary school completion.

10. These tests include the Anti-Social Behavior, Rosenberg Self-Esteem, and Rotter Locus of Control indexes.

11. Woessmann and Hanushek (forthcoming).

12. Compulsory school laws have been found to increase educational attainment (Lochner and Moretti (2004)), adult earnings (Patrinos and Sakellariou (2005)), and health and employment (Oreopoulos (2005)); and to lower crime (Lochner and Moretti (2004)) and teenage pregnancy (Black, Devereaux, and Salvanes (2004)).

13. Knight and Sabot (1990) and Mete (2004).

14. World Bank (2005r).

15. Filmer (forthcoming).

16. UNESCO Institute for Statistics (2005).

17. World Bank (2002a) and UNESCO Institute for Statistics (2005).

18. Most private schools in tertiary education are independent (91 percent) relative to government-dependent private schools, whereas in secondary education there is a fairly even split. UNESCO Institute for Statistics (2005).

19. http://www.onderwijsraad.nl/Doc/English/masterofmarket .pdf.

20. World Bank (2002a).

21. UNESCO Institute for Statistics (2005).

22. For example, the California higher education system combines selective admissions to centers of excellence with more open admissions to other two- and four-year teritiary institutions. See http://www.cpec.ca.gov/.

23. World Bank (2005f).

24. Benavot (2004).

25. World Bank (2002a) and World Bank (2005l).

26. Levy and Murnane (2004).

27. Lee and Wong (2005).

28. UNESCO (2004b).

29. After experimenting with other nontraditional teaching methods, England implemented a structured teaching model in the 1990s. In addition, some of the worst performing schools in the United States have implemented it with great success. The successful Balsakhi remedial education program in India also uses similar methods. For review see Gauthier and Dembélé (2004).

30. BRAC's Non-Formal Primary Education Schools in Bangladesh are one example of combining interactive pedagogy with routine assessments of student progress, teaching methods, and curricula that invite the input of students and teachers themselves (see box 3.11). An experiment in the Philippines that provided pedagogical materials and training to teachers improved learning outcomes. See Tan, Lane, and Lassibille (1999).

31. This can be achieved by reducing the time allocated to low priority subject areas or increasing instructional time. See UNESCO (2004b) for a detailed discussion of time use.

32. World Bank (2003b). Empirical studies in developed countries show strong wage premiums associated with computer use (Autor, Katz, and Krueger (1998)). Studies that control for unobserved heterogeneity find positive but smaller effects and show that what really matters is computer skills (Pabilonia and Zoghi (forthcoming)).

33. Kuku, Orazem, and Singh (2005) use data from nine transition economies to show that English proficiency is positively associated with computer use. Worker-firm matched data for Malaysia show that English language proficiency is the skill that workers feel they lack the most (48 percent), followed by information and technology skills. There is a labor market premium associated with languages of international commerce (Munshi and Rosensweig (2003)). See UNESCO (2004b) on literacy and local languages.

34. Evidence on these programs from the United States suggests that financial literacy education improves young people's financial knowledge and behaviors, by making money go further (Varcoe and others (2005)).

35. Cox (2004).

36. Kemple and Scott-Clayton (2004).

37. Johanson and Adams (2004).

38. Chen and Kenney (2005).

39. UNESCO (2004b).

40. For teacher absence, see Chaudhury and others (2006). Teacher shortages are particularly a problem in mathematics, science, and technology as well as in rural areas. World Bank (2005f).

41. See, for example, Jacob and Lefgren (2002).

42. For more on teacher training, see UNESCO (2004b) and World Bank (2005k).

43. See Vegas and Umansky (2005) for evidence in Latin American and Caribbean countries.

44. Banerjee and Duflo (2006) and Vegas and Umansky (2005). One of the challenges of implementing benficiary control programs with parents has been low demand for education, but involving young people in holding teachers accountable has yet to be tried (except at the tertiary level), and in some cases they may have a higher demand for education than their parents.

45. Lavy (2002).

46. "Basti" is Bangla for shantytown.

47. World Bank (2003b).

48. Pratham Resource Centre (2005).

49. World Bank (2005k). This project also included provision of textbooks and facilities improvements.

50. See, for example, Caldwell, Levacic, and Ross (1999).

51. Fuchs and Woessmann (2004).

52. World Bank (2006d) and Reinikka and Svensson (2002). However, the rule-based nature of formula funding does not make it immune to capture. Appropriate control and monitoring mechanisms need to be put in place. School grants need to include a fixed component to account for the fixed cost of running a school. Also, indivisible inputs, such as teachers, are better handled through other funding channels.

53. Bray (2004).

54. Woessmann (2003); Woessmann and Hanushek (forthcoming).

55. World Bank (2005b) and Patrinos (2005).

56. Angrist and Lavy (2002) and Angrist, Bettinger, and Kremer (forthcoming).

57. Filer and Münich (2002).

58. Patrinos (2005) and Barrera Osorio (2005)..

59. Behrman and others (2002).

60. De Walque (2005).

61. De Fraja, Oliveira, and Zanchi (2005).

62. Sacerdote (2001) and Kremer and Levy (2003). Establishing the causal effect of peer groups on the behavior of individuals has been a challenge, particularly because peer group formation is often endogenous.

63. See Lazear (2001) and Fertig (2003) for how optimal class size or composition can vary with heterogeneity. See Fryer and Torelli (2005) and Akerlof and Kranton (2005b) for the effects of student heterogeneity at the school level.

64. Ding and Lehrer (forthcoming).

65. Slavin (1996) cited in UNESCO (2004b).

66. Boisjoly and others (2004).

67. Slavin and Cooper (1999) and Steinberg and Cauffman (1996).

68. Kremer, Miguel, and Thornton (2004).

69. Akerlof and Kranton (2002).

70. OECD (2005b).

71. Blum and Libbey (2004).

72. Catalano and others (2004).

73. Kessler and others (1995).

74. de Jong and others (2001).

75. Blum and Libbey (2004).

76. See both UNESCO (2004a) and National Research Council and Institute of Medicine (2005) for extensive reviews.

77. See Hoff and Pandey (2004) and Dréze and Gazdar (1997) on caste in India; National Research Council and Institute of Medicine (2005) on girls in many countries; Akerlof and Kranton (2002) for several different groups in the United States.

78. Lloyd, Mensch, and Clark (2000). The study controls for a variety of factors that typically predict drop-out including parental characteristics and typical school quality variables such as parent-teacher ratios.

79. Hoff and Pandey (2004).

80. Davies, Williams, and Yamashita (2006). In one study from England, 12 schools with higher participation had higher outcomes than would be predicted by student characteristics (Hannam (2001)).

81. Davies, Williams, and Yamashita (2006).

82. Brett and Specht (2004).

83. Pro-Rector for Student Affairs at the Plekhanov Academy of Moscow, Professor Oleg Cherkov, March 13th, 2006 seminar.

84. Main portal: www.aimhigher.ac.uk, with a parallel site for those ages 14–16 called "Don't Stop" (http://www.aimhigher.ac.uk/dontstop/home/). The evaluation is based on one year exposure to it among 16-year-old individuals (Emmerson and others (2005)). A more comprehensive evaluation of the program is under way.

85. Carneiro and Ridao-Cano (2005). The same is being done for Mexico. Also see Aakvik, Salvanes, and Vaage (2003) for Norway. However, expected returns are just one factor in determining education attainment (see Carneiro and Lee (2005) for the United States and Fleisher and others (2004) for China.

86. This was a randomized experiment in urban areas (Jensen (2006)).

87. These costs can offset the effect of certainty on risk-averse individuals, which would tend to increase educational investments. There is robust experimental evidence showing that individuals from poor family backgrounds are more risk averse than those from better-off families (Dohmen and others (2005)). Thus, the poor would tend to underinvest in education as a result of greater uncertainty, higher risk aversion, lower aspirations, and greater liquidity constraints.

88. This is because repayment of income-contingent loans is contingent on the ex post realization of earnings. Income-contingent loans are covered later in this chapter.

89. Carneiro and Heckman (2002). However, credit constraints may be more important than suggested by the authors, for two reasons. Individuals may be credit constrained even when their families are not but are not willing to finance their education. Also, the result is conditional on a given policy environment: part of the reason for the small role of short-run credit constraints may be the success of policies to address them.

90. See, for example, Lillard and Willis (1994), who find an insignificant association between income and the transition to secondary and tertiary, and Behrman and Knowles (1999) who find strong income effects for children ages 6–17 in Vietnam. Behrman and Knowles (1999) summarize the findings of 42 studies in 21 countries. Estimates of the relationship between household income and schooling are significant but small in most cases.

91. See Jacoby and Skoufias (2002) for Mexico and Sawada and Lokshin (2001) for Pakistan.

92. The extent to which working children are able to combine work with school depends on household demand factors (poverty), job opportunities for children, and the institutional differences in education systems (length of the school day).

93. Levison, Moe, and Knaul (2001).

94. Beegle, Dehejia, and Gatti (2004).

95. Canals-Cerda and Ridao-Cano (2004).

96. Gunnarson, Orazem, and Sánchez (2006).

97. Greene and Merrick (2005); Singh (1998); and National Research Council and Institute of Medicine (2005).

98. Eloundou-Enyegue (2004).

99. Behrman and others (2006).

100. See Rawlings and Rubio (2005) and Morley and Coady (2003) for reviews.

101. Skoufias and Parker (2001); Schultz (2004); and Skoufias, Davis, and de la Vega (2001).

102. Todd and Wolpin (2003).

103. Coady (2000).

104. Sadoulet and de Janvry (2006) show that efficiency gains in the program could be achieved by selecting among the poor those children induced to go to school with the scholarship and calibrating the size of the transfer so that it is just sufficient to induce children to go to school.

105. Skoufias and Parker (2001). A similar program in Nicaragua was also found to decrease the incidence of work among 12- to 13-year-olds (Maluccio (forthcoming)). Ravallion and Wodon (2000) found that the Food for Education program in Bangladesh reduced child labor but the effect only accounted for 25 percent of the increase in the enrollment of boys. See de Janvry and others (2006) for shocks.

106. Yap, Sedlacek, and Orazem (2001).

107. Arends-Kuenning and Amin (2000).

108. Angrist and others (2002); Angrist, Bettinger, and Kremer (forthcoming).

109. The impact evaluation of the means-tested scholarship program in Indonesia (Sparrow (2004)) shows no impact on upper secondary school enrollment.

110. The program was discontinued, and it was not emulated when Bolsa Escola was adopted as a national program. Lavinas, Barbosa, and Tourinho (2001).

111. Carneiro and Heckman (2003).

112. This is partly due to the brain development process. Different skills have different critical stages in the learning process, and when these are missed later remedy is not possible.

113. Bray (2004).

114. Lavy and Schlosser (2005).

115. Banerjee and others (2005).

116. For a series of studies on emotional connections to school and dropout rates, see Blum and Libbey (2004); World Bank (2006d) for the Philippines; and CRECE (2005) for Colombia.

117. Abadzi (2003).

118. Heckman, LaLonde, and Smith (1999) and Betcherman, Olivas, and Dar (2004).

119. Heckman, Smith, and Clements (1997).

120. Betcherman, Olivas, and Dar (2004).

121. Reports on youth consultations conducted for the *World Development Report 2007*.

Spotlight on Vietnam

1. This spotlight is based on material in Asian Development Bank (2005); Nguyen Anh, Duong, and Hai Van (2005); Nguyen Anh (2005); Parliamentary Committee for Social Affairs (2005); Vietnam Ministry of Health and General Statistics Office, UNICEF, and WHO (2005); Lautrédou (2005); World Bank (2003e); and World Bank (2005q).

2. Vietnam Ministry of Health and General Statistics Office, UNICEF, and WHO (2005).

Chapter 4

1. National Research Council and Institute of Medicine (2005).

2. ILO (2006). In this chapter child labor and economically active children are used interchangeably. Economically active children are defined as those who performed at least one hour of work in the reference week during the regular school year. Work comprises paid and unpaid work in home-owned enterprises. The ILO has a pre-

cise definition of child labor that is a subset of economically active children, depending on age and hours-of-work thresholds.

3. Duryea and others (forthcoming).

4. Fares and Raju (2006).

5. Yap, Sedlacek, and Orazem (2001) and Emerson and Souza (2002).

6. Kaushik and Tzannatos (2003) and Betcherman and others (2001).

7. See Gunnarson, Orazem, and Sánchez (2006) for evidence on child labor and school performance in Latin America; Rosati and Rossi (2003) for Pakistan and Nicaragua; and Heady (2003) for Ghana.

8. Ilahi, Orazem, and Sedlacek (2005), Emerson and Souza (2006).

9. These estimates were obtained from a simple Mincer type earning model using data from 61 household surveys (Fares, Montenegro, and Orazem (2006b)).

10. Emerson and Souza (2003).

11. Kassouf, McKee, and Mossialos (2001).

12. Fares, Montenegro, and Orazem (2006a).

13. Borgarello and others (2005). The country sample includes Albania, Argentina, Georgia, Hungary, Poland, the Russian Federation, Ukraine, and República Bolivariana de Venezuela.

14. ILO (2004). The ILO produces global and regional estimates based on several national surveys and the ILO Global Employment Trends model.

15. Kabbani and Kothari (2005).

16. ILO (2005).

17. World Bank (2003d).

18. O'Higgins (2003).

19. Fares and Montenegro (2006).

20. Fares and Tiongson (2006).

21. Mroz and Savage (2001) and Card and Lemieux (2000b).

22. Freeman (2000) and Fougère, Kramarz, and Pouget (2006).

23. Hettige, Mayer, and Salih (2004).

24. Topel and Ward (1992).

25. Parent (2006).

26. Hemmer and Mannel (1989).

27. Borgarello and others (2005).

28. Audas, Berde, and Dolton (2005).

29. Guarcello, Mealli, and Rosati (2003) and Parent (2006).

30. O'Higgins (2003) and Korenman and Neumark (2000).

31. Fares and Montenegro (2006).

32. O'Higgins (2003). Also Korenman and Neumark (2000) for developed countries.

33. See Rosati (forthcoming).

34. National Research Council and Institute of Medicine (2005).

35. Mammen and Paxson (2000); Huffman and Orazem (2004); and Greenwood, Seshadri, and Vandenbroucke (2005).

36. The index includes measures of trade; fiscal, monetary, labor, and regulatory policies; state ownership; government intervention in finance and capital flows; property rights; and the importance of the gray economy.

37. World Bank (1995); World Bank (2004e); and World Bank (2005c).

38. See spotlight on baby booms following chapter 4 and Lazear (1983); Bentolila and Bertola (1990); and Bertola, Blau, and Kahn (2002).

39. Hopenhayn and Rogerson (1993).

40. Pagés and Montenegro (1999) and Montenegro and Pagés (2004).

41. Heckman and Pagés (2000). Jimeno and Rodríguez-Palenzuela (2002), using a panel of OECD countries, also found that institutional settings (including employment protection laws) that increase labor market rigidity tend to increase the youth unemployment rate.

42. Cunningham and Siga (2006) for Brazil; Montenegro and Pagés (2004) for Chile; and Neumark and Wascher (1999) for cross-country comparison for OECD.

43. Maloney and Nuñez Mendez (2004).

44. Boudarbat (2005).

45. World Bank (2003d).

46. Serneels (2004).

47. Gorpe, Fares, and Montenegro (2006).

48. Paniza (2000) shows that the public wage premium is positive for low-skilled and negative for high-skilled male workers, with the opposite trend for females. Filmer and Lindauer (2001) show that low-skilled workers in Indonesia have a higher public wage premium, but the differences were not statistically significant.

49. Tzannatos (1999).

50. Ragui and Arntz (2005).

51. O'Higgins (2003) for cross-country comparison; Fares and Montenegro (2006) for Brazil and Chile; Rosati (forthcoming).

52. All figures above come from authors' calculation using Investment Climate Surveys for Brazil, Indonesia, and Vietnam.

53. Noorkôiv and others (1998).

54. Sánchez-Páramo and Schady (2003) . Other results from East Asia and Sub-Saharan Africa also show these effects.

55. Japan Bank for International Cooperation (2006).

56. Gruben and McLeod (2006).

57. World Bank (2004e).

58. Kugler (2004).

59. Cahuc and Carcillo (2006) and Blanchard (2006).

60. World Bank (2004e).

61. Social Protection Note, World Bank, forthcoming, "More and better jobs in developing and emerging economies."

62. Neumark and Wascher (1999).

63. Gill, Montenegro, and Dömeland (2002).

64. OECD (2005a).

65. Kluve (2006).

66. Fretwell, Benus, and O'Leary (1999) and Kluve (2006).

67. Cockx and Göbel (2004).

68. Hazell and Haggblade (1993).

69. Huffman and Orazem (2004).

70. Haggblade, Hazell, and Reardon (forthcoming).

71. Köbrich and Dirven (2006).

72. Ferreira and Lanjouw (2001) and Kijima and Lanjouw (2004).

73. Haggblade, Hazell, and Reardon (forthcoming).

74. Otsuka (forthcoming).

75. Kijima and Lanjouw (2004), Ferreira and Lanjouw (2001).

76. Authors' calculation based on Probit models for employment, unemployment, and labor force participation. The models were estimated for those 15–24 years old. The specifications include education, gender indicator, and country-specific effects. The data were pooled from 29 country household surveys.

77. World Bank (2005n).

78. Au and Henderson (forthcoming).

79. The 2000 Census found that nearly 12 percent of the population did not have legal residency status.

80. State council policy paper, "Opinion of the state council on the issue of rural migrant workers." Beijing (2006).

81. Pritchett (2006).

82. Ryan (2001).

83. Johanson and Adams (2004).

84. van Eekelen, de Luca, and Ismail (2001).

85. Adams (2006).

86. Atchoarena and Delluc (2001).

87. Haan and Serriere (2002).

88. Johanson and Adams (2004).

89. Riley and Steel (1999).

90. Tan (2005).

91. Tan and Batra (1995).

92. Johanson and Adams (2004).

93. World Bank (2006e).

94. Johanson and Adams (2004) and Cinterfor/ILO (2001).

95. Llisterri and others (2006).

96. "Entrepreneurs by necessity or by opportunity" is a definition adopted by Global Entrepreneurship Monitor to differentiate the motives of people to become an entrepreneur (Reynolds and others (2002)). The same concepts are used here applied to those people that are already entrepreneurs while Global Entrepreneurship Monitor uses them to classify those who are engaged in creating a business.

97. The InterAmerican Development Bank database includes data from Argentina, Brazil, Chile, Costa Rica, El Salvador, Mexico, Peru, and Uruguay. A broad study comparing the emergence and development of dynamic ventures in Latin America, East Asia, and South Europe can be found in Llisterri and others (2006).

98. Kantis (2003).

99. Betcherman, Olivas, and Dar (2004).

100. Elway (1999).

101. Betcherman and others (2006). This inventory of existing interventions targeting youth in the labor market would provide needed future guidance on what works and what does not.

102. Ravallion and others (2005).

103. Galasso, Ravallion, and Salvia (2001).

104. Pound and Knight (2006). http://www.usnews.com/usnews/biztech/articles/060403/3worldbank.htm.

105. Galasso, Ravallion, and Salvia (2001).

106. UNICEF (2000), table 4.11.

107. See http://www.jobsnet.lk/.

108. Lasida and Rodríguez (2006).

109. Devia (2003) and Santiago Consultores Asociados (1999).

Spotlight on baby booms in OECD countries

1. Korenman and Neumark (2000).

2. Ryan (2001).

3. Burgess and others (2003).

4. Card and Lemieux (2000a).

5. Blanco and Kluve (2002).

6. Gould, Weinberg, and Mustard (1998); Grogger (1998); and Machin and Meghir (2004).

7. Fougère, Kramarz, and Pouget (2006).

8. Blanchard and Wolfers (2000); Nickell and Layard (1999); and Blau and Kahn (1999) provide comprehensive reviews of the literature on how labor market institutions affect the labor market.

9. Jimeno and Rodríguez-Palenzuela (2002).

10. Neumark and Wascher (1999) found that minimum wages had the most severe effects when imposed in combination with other employment protection rules.

11. Bertola, Blau, and Kahn (2002).

12. Ryan (2001).

13. Kluve (2006) and Martin and Grubb (2001).

Chapter 5

1. National Research Council and Institute of Medicine (2005).

2. WHO (2002a). The survival probabilities for girls are generally higher, but the cross-country comparisons are similar.

3. López and others (2006).

4. Lule and others (2005).

5. See Mullahy and Sindelar (1991), DeSimone (2002).

6. Rodríguez Ospina, Duque Ramirez, and Rodríguez García (1993).

7. World Bank (2005d).

8. Hibbell and others (2000) and Bloomfield and others (2003).

9. WHO and World Bank (2005).

10. Lundberg, Over, and Mujinja (2003) and Yamano and Jayne (2004).

11. Kalemli-Ozcan (2001); Kalemli-Ozcan (2005).

12. Witoelar, Rukumnuaykit, and Strauss (2005).

13. Ezzati and Lopez (2004).

14. Ebbeling, Pawlak, and Ludwig (2002) and Koplan, Liverman, and Kraak (2005).

15. Slaymaker and others (2004).

16. World Bank (1999c).

17. World Bank (1993b).

18. World Bank (1999b).

19. Russell (2000).

20. UNAIDS (2000).

21. World Bank (1999a).

22. Bateman (2001); Chandra, Jairam, and Jacob (2004); and Visinntini and others (1996).

23. Montoya Díaz (2002).

24. Singh and others (2000). Trend analysis based on MEASURE Demographic and Health Survey data from African countries where surveys were carried out between 2000 and 2004.

25. McCauley and Salter (1995).

26. Mensch, Singh, and Casterline (2006).

27. Demographic and Health Surveys.

28. Clark (2004).

29. Konde-Lule, Sewankambo, and Morris (1997).

30. National Research Council and Institute of Medicine (2005).

31. Family Health International (2005).

32. Dunkle and others (2004).

33. Jejeebhoy and Bott (2003). Note that researchers and young people may differ in their definition of transactional sex. Focus group discussions among young people in Durban, South Africa, found that gift-giving among same-age adolescents is common in sexual relationships. Adolescents view the exchange of cash for sex as prostitution but do not consider noncash gifts in the same way (Kaufman and Stavrou (2004)).

34. Luke (2003).

35. Human Rights Watch (2002b).

36. WHO (2004).

37. Hibbell and others (2000).

38. Singleton, Lee, and Meltzer (2001) and Institute of Alcohol Studies (2006).

39. Peden and others (2000).

40. World Bank (1999c).

41. Parry and others (2000).

42. Gajakashmi and others (2000).

43. Jha and Chaloupka (2000).

44. Witoelar, Rukumnuaykit, and Strauss (2005). Based on analysis of Indonesia Family Life Survey, 1993–2000.

45. National Research Council and Institute of Medicine (2005).

46. United Nations Economic and Social Council (2001).

47. UNICEF, UNAIDS, and WHO (2002).

48. Osmond and Barker (2000); Martorell and others (1998); Ramakrishnan (2004).

49. Gluckman and others (2005) and Sawaya and others (2003).

50. FAO (2006).

51. Popkin (1994); Popkin (2002); and Popkin and Gordon-Larsen (2004).

52. Fernald and others (2004).

53. Gertler and others (2006).

54. World Bank (1993b); Reddy (2002); Deparment of Health Services Sri Lanka (2002); and FAO (2006).

55. Hubley (2000) and Gatawa (1995).

56. Cohen (2004) and Gregson and others (2006).

57. Bloom (2005a) and Blum and Ireland (2004).

58. Kenkel (2000).

59. Lansdown and others (2002).

60. Cáceres and others (1994); Eggleston and others (2000); and Boyer and Shafer (1997).

61. Knowles and Behrman (2005).

62. James-Traore and others (2002).

63. Agha (2002).

64. Abaunza (2002).

65. See Muirhead, Kumaranayake, and Watts (2001).

66. Focus group discussion with youth in Ho Chi Minh City in January 2006, Vietnam Youth Association.

67. James-Traore and others (2002).

68. Cohen (2004).

69. Estimates of transmission probabilities per act vary from 0.0001 to 0.0014 in U.S. and European studies, 0.002 in Thailand, and 0.0001 to 0.004 in Uganda. Higher transmission probabilities (up to 0.10) have been reported among men who had contacts with prostitutes in Thailand and Kenya (Gray and others (2001)).

70. See Jha and Chaloupka (2000) for tobacco; Moore and Cook (1995) for alcohol; Aarts, Paulussen, and Schaalma (1997) for exercise; and Shafii and others (2004) for condom use.

71. Knowles and Behrman (2005).

72. James-Traore and others (2002).

73. Dupas (2006).

74. Kirby, Laris, and Rolleri (2005).

75. De Walque (2004).

76. Kirby (2001).

77. Brückner and Bearman (2005); Bearman and Brückner (2001); and Fortenberry (2005).

78. WHO (2003b).

79. Evidence of the impact of sport participation on empowerment and criminal or delinquent activity among youth is extremely weak Coakley (2002). See chapter 7 of this Report.

80. Brady (1998).

81. Smith, Bogin, and Bishai (2005).

82. Erulkar and others (2004).

83. Student Partnership Worldwide (2005) p. 2.

84. Cáceres and others (1994); Eggleston and others (2000); and Boyer and Shafer (1997).

85. Eggleston, Leitch, and Jackson (2000).

86. James-Traore and others (2002).

87. Alford, Cheetham, and Hauser (2005).

88. Mensch, Hewett, and Erulkar (2001); Erulkar and Mensch (1997); and James-Traore and others (2002).

89. Berer (2003).

90. Dupas (2006).

91. Gutierrez (2006).

92. World Bank (1999b).

93. Witoelar, Rukumnuaykit, and Strauss (2005).

94. Grossman (2005b).

95. World Bank (1999b).

96. See Townsend, Roderick, and Cooper (1994) for evidence from the United Kingdom.

97. Rehm (2003) and World Bank (1999b).

98. Nelson (2003) and Fichtenberg and Glantz (2002).

99. World Bank (1999b).

100. World Bank (1999b).

101. Jha and others (2005).

102. World Bank (1999b) and Fiore and others (2000).

103. World Bank (1999b).

104. UNDCP (2003).

105. Drucker and others (1998) and WHO (2005a).

106. Hurley, Jolley, and Kaldor (1997) and MacDonald and others (2003).

107. UNICEF, UNAIDS, and WHO (2002).

108. See, for example, Grosskurth and others (1995).

109. Okonofua and others (2003).

110. Stanback and Twum-Baah (2001).

111. Dickson-Tetteh, Pettifor, and Moleko (2001).

112. Temin and others (1999).

113. Knowles and Behrman (2005).

114. Thailand Ministry of Public Health and World Bank (2005).

115. Salomon and others (2005).

116. Over and others (2004).

117. Health and Treasury Task Team (2003).

118. Teixeira, Vitória, and Barcarolo (2003).

119. There is evidence that continuing drug use is a behavioral deterrent to ART adherence (Lucas and others (2001)).

120. UNAIDS and UNODCCP (2000).

121. Celentano and others (2001).

122. Shah and Ahman (2004a) and Shah and Ahman (2004b).

123. WHO (1998).

124. Ellertson and others (1995).

125. Aziken, Okonta, and Ande (2003).

126. World Bank (1993b).

127. Berer (2003).

128. Pauly (1968).

129. Population Council (2002).

130. Rowlands and others (2000).

131. See Over and others (2004) and the papers cited therein.

132. Marseille (2003).

133. Jha and others (2001).

134. Dupas (2006).

Spotlight on Brazil

1. All figures in bullets come from World Bank (2006i). The country's high levels of inequality, based on Gini coefficients, is second only to South Africa.

2. Bonelli and Veiga (2004).

3. World Bank (2006i).

4. Bourguignon, Ferreira, and Menendez (2005).

5. Verner, Blom, and Holm-Nielsen (2001).

6. Some states paid per child, others paid if all children went to school, to prevent parent's choosing between children. World Bank (2001a).

7. By merging cash-transfer programs that promoted schooling, health, food consumption, and compensation for adjustment, the government seeks to increase the efficiency and effectiveness of the many transfer programs.

8. World Bank (2006i).

9. The program has also dramatically reduced the rates of suicide, theft, drug use, sexual aggression, and armed robbery by students.

10. A program analysis conducted in 2002 compared schools under the Programa Abrindo Espaços and those that were not and found that schools that participated in the program had a lower violence index (sum of violent acts, weighted by their severity) than those that did not, by 16 percent in Rio and by 14 percent in Pernambuco (Waiselfisz and Maciel (2003)).

11. World Bank (2006a).

12. The target population is men 14- to 25-years-old and the mean age of participants in the three evaluation sites, Bangu, Maré, and Morro dos Macacos, was 17.

13. The scale is a composite of qualitative questions that reflect whether a respondent disagrees with "traditional" gender norms, such as, "there are times that a woman deserves to be beaten."

14. Barker (2003).

Chapter 6

1. National Research Council and Institute of Medicine (2005).

2. In this chapter, the term "marriage" captures actual marriages and consensual unions.

3. National Research Council and Institute of Medicine (2005). Calculations of first birth intervals for ever-married girls' (ages 20–24) using birth histories and age at marriage drawn from Demographic and Health Surveys conducted between 1998 and 2004. For these countries, the average first birth interval was 1.5 years.

4. Assaad and Zouari (2003).

5. Zabin and Kiragu (1998); Study Group on Female Genital Mutilation and Obstetric Outcome (2006).

6. Conde-Aguledo, Rosas-Bermúdez, and Kafury-Goeta (2006); Hediger and others (1997); Makinson (1985); Miller (1991); Scholl and others (1989); Scholl and others (1992); and Zabin and Kiragu (1998).

7. Gertler, Levine, and Martinez (2003).

8. Bhargava (2005).

9. National Research Council and Institute of Medicine (2005).

10. International Institute for Population Sciences (IIPS) and ORC Macro (2000).

11. Based on 2004 round of Demographic and Health Survey for Chad.

12. Jowett (2000) and Berman and Rose (1996).

13. Fafchamps and Quisumbing (2005).

14. Lundberg and Rose (2002).

15. Galloway and Anderson (1994).

16. Alderman and Behrman (2006).

17. Strauss and Thomas (1995) and Behrman and Deolalikar (1988).

18. Clark (2004).

19. Galloway and Anderson (1994).

20. Centers for Disease Control and Prevention (1998) and Yip and Dallman (1996).

21. Tests using Hemocue.

22. El-Zanaty and Way (2001).

23. International Nutritional Anemia Consultative Group (1989).

24. Li and others (1994).

25. Oyediran, Ishola, and Adewuyi (2002).

26. Mensch, Bruce, and Greene (1998).

27. See BPS-Statistics Indonesia and ORC Macro (2006) for a description of the 2002–03 Indonesia Young Adult Reproductive Health Survey.

28. Siddiqua and Kabir (2002).

29. Senderowitz (1995).

30. Akin and others (1984); Hodgkin (1996); Nanda (1999); and Wong and others (1987).

31. Khan (1998); Mumtaz and Salway (2005); and World Bank (2005a).

32. National Research Council and Institute of Medicine (2005).

33. Based on data from Measure DHS surveys in which questions were asked about components of antenatal care.

34. Calculated using data from the Kenya Demographic and Health Survey, 2003.

35. Senderowitz and Paxman (1985).

36. Senderowitz (1999).

37. World Bank (2005a).

38. Joshi and Schultz (2005).

39. World Bank (2005m).

40. See Rosen (2000).

41. See National Research Council and Institute of Medicine (2005).

42. Berer (2003).

43. See Caldwell and Caldwell (2002) and Askew and Maggwa (2002).

44. World Bank (2006f).

45. Knowles and Behrman (2003).

46. Delisle, Chandra-Mouli, and de Benoist (2000) and World Bank (2005m).

47. Partnership for Child Development (2006).

48. Delisle, Chandra-Mouli, and de Benoist (2000).

49. Gertler (2000) and Skoufias (2001).

50. Rawlings and Rubio (2005).

51. Behrman and others (2005b).

52. Lloyd and Grant (2004).

53. King (2005).

54. Dupas (2006).

55. Reported in Alford, Cheetham, and Hauser (2005).

56. FOCUS (1998) and Graft, Haberland, and Goldberg (2003).

57. Nanda, Switlick, and Lule (2005). The SIAGA Campaigns Indonesia Web site, http://www.comminit.com/experiences/pds62004/experiences-1983.html. JHPIEGO News Release (May 5, 2004) Indonesian mothers surviving childbirth more often with support from husbands, community, faith-based groups, http://www.jhpiego.org/media/releases/nr20040505.htm.

58. Delisle, Chandra-Mouli, and de Benoist (2000).

59. White (2005).

60. Loevinsohn (1990).

61. SCN News (2006).

62. Grantham-Mcgregor and others (1991) and Paxson and Schady (forthcoming).

63. Hallman and others (2005).

64. Ruel and others (2002).

65. Committee for Population and ORC Macro (2003).

66. Lokshin, Glinskaya, and Garcia (2004).

67. Nanda (1999).

68. Centre for Development and Population Activities (CEDPA) (2001).

69. Mathur, Mehta, and Malhotra (2004).

70. Institute for Health Management-Pachod (IHMP) and International Center for Research On Women (ICRW) (2003).

71. Arends-Kuenning and Amin (2000).

72. Amin and others (1998).

73. Singh and Darroch (2000).

74. Geronimus and Bound (1990); Geronimus and Korenman (1992); Hoffman (1998); and Klepinger, Lundberg, and Plotnick (1997).

75. Hofferth and Reid (2001).

76. Kaufman, de Wet, and Stadler (2001) and National Research Council and Institute of Medicine (2005).

77. Program description based on WHO (2003a).

78. WHO (2003c).

Chapter 7

1. Authors' interviews with student volunteers. For more information, see www.risepak.com.

2. Walzer (1989).

3. Marshall (1950).

4. Mamdani (1996).

5. Benhabib (2005) and Bauböck (2005).

6. Kymlicka (2001).

7. Harrington (2005).

8. Hooghe, Stolle, and Stouthuysen (2004).

9. Jennings and Stoker (2002).

10. Wattenberg (2006).

11. Norris (2005).

12. Miguel, Glennerster, and Whiteside (2006).

13. Schmitter and Treschel (2005).

14. Stolle and Hooghe (2004).

15. Macedo and others (2005) p. 48.

16. Gerber, Green, and Shachar (2003).

17. Plutzer (2002).

18. Firebaugh and Chen (1995).

19. Alwain and Krosnick (1991); Jennings and Stoker (2002); and McAdam (1988).

20. Chattopadhyay and Duflo (2003); Dhakal and Misbah (1997); and Pande (2005).

21. Stern, Dethier, and Rogers (2005).

22. Besley and others (2004); Jimenez and Sawada (1999); Narayan (1995); and Venkatraman and Falconer (1998).

23. Przeworski and others (2000).

24. Acemoglu, Johnson, and Robinson (2001).

25. Isham, Kaufmann, and Pritchett (1995); Lindert (2003); Rivera-Batiz (2002); and Sen (1999).

26. Arunatilake, Jayasuriya, and Kelegama (2001); Barrera and Ibáñez (2004); and Kutan and Drakos (2003).

27. *Ehtesaab* used by permission of Salman Ahmad. To learn more about Junoon, visit http://www.junoon.com.

28. Fearon and Laitin (2003) and Hegre (2003).

29. Steinberger (2001).

30. Stockard and O'Brien (2002) define relative cohort size as the ratio of the size of the younger generation (ages 15–29) to the size of the older generation (ages 30–65). A cohort effect is distinct from age or period effects in that it reflects influences unique to a particular group of people, such as those born between 1950 and 1954 or young men who came of age between 1940 and 1944.

31. A brief overview of the Easterlin hypothesis in Pampel and Peters (1995), pp. 164–169.

32. Stockard and O'Brien (2002) find that birth cohorts that are relatively less socially integrated and regulated have higher suicide rates. However, collective institutions such as those that support families and children can moderate the effect. Jacobson (2004) finds evidence that larger cohorts increase marijuana use by lowering the risk of a sales arrest and by generating informational economies. Jacobson (2004) and Levitt (1999) find little evidence of the effect of relative cohort size on murder, violent crime, and property crime rates. The effects of cohort size and educational and labor markets are analyzed elsewhere in this report.

33. See Cincotta, Engleman, and Anastasion (2003) on these demographic stress factors and how they interact. Mesquida and Wiener (1999) point out that while a high proportion of young males is a necessary condition for the emergence of violent conflict, it is not a sufficient one.

34. Cincotta, Engleman, and Anastasion (2003) p. 77.

35. For an exception, see Hudson and den Boer (2004) on China and India.

36. Mannheim (1972) p. 294, as cited in Cole (2004b).

37. Cole (2004a).

38. Acemoglu, Johnson, and Robinson (2001); Gauri and Lieberman (2004); Mamdani (1996); and Steinmo, Thelen, and Longstreth (1992).

39. Chiclet (2001).

40. La Cava and others (2006).

41. Diamond (2003), citing Freedom House data.

42. Rodríguez-Pose and Gill (2003).

43. For country-specific youth voter turnout rates, see Pintor and Gratschew (2002) and Franklin (2004).

44. Franklin (2004).

45. Wattenberg (2006).

46. Wintour (2006).

47. Franklin (2004).

48. Green and Gerber (2001).

49. Navarro and Hasan (2003).

50. Verba, Schlozman, and Brady (1995).

51. Zeldin and others (2000).

52. Matthews (2003).

53. Rajbhandary, Hart, and Khatiwada (2001).

54. In Thorup and Kinkade (2005) p. 77.

55. Edmunds, Forster, and Cottey (2002); Hirsch and Mehay (2003); and WDR 2007 InterMedia surveys.

56. Although national service is ostensibly universal in Scandinavian countries, budget cuts have meant that less than one-third of the eligible population actually serves.

57. Angrist (1990); Galiani, Rossi, and Schargrodsky (2006); Imbens and Van Der Klaauw (1995); Lokshin and Yemtsov (2005).

58. In a study of women who served in the U.S. military during the Vietnam era, 30 percent reported having been raped, and 35 percent reported being otherwise physically assaulted (Sadler, Booth, and Doebbeling (2005)). Another survey of more than 1,500 female veterans applying for posttraumatic stress disorder disability benefits found that 71 percent had experienced some form of sexual assault while in service (Murdoch and others (2004)).

59. Bedard and Deschênes (2006).

60. Abt Associates (2004); Gal and Eberly (2006); Obadare (2005); and Viva Rio (2005).

61. Personal communication with Susan E. Stroud, Executive Director, Innovations in Civic Participation, June 2006.

62. Erikson (1994) p. 245.

63. Akerlof and Kranton (2005a) pp. 10–11; Cole (2004b) p. 896; Pals and Tuma (2004); and Titma and Tuma (2005).

64. Erikson (1994); Roy (2004); and Sciolino, Wingfield, and Povoledo (2005) p. A8.

65. Neuhaus (2005).

66. Kriger (2005) and Moscow Human Rights Bureau (2005).

67. UNICEF (2005c).

68. Duryea, Olgiati, and Stone (2006).

69. Solinger (1999).

70. Balcells i Ventura (2005); Cogan, Morris, and Print (2002) p. 6; and Kymlicka (2001).

71. Torney-Purta and others (2001).

72. Hahn (2005) p. 835.

73. Finkel and Strumbas (2000).

74. Finkel and Strumbas (2000) p. 105.

75. Hahn, Dilworth, and Hughes (1998) in Gibson (2001) p. 7.

76. Billig (2006).

77. Dalrymple (2005).

78. Bay and Blekesaune (2002); Durham (forthcoming); Fougère, Kramarz, and Pouget (2006); and Reiss and Roth (1993).

79. National Research Council and Institute of Medicine (2005) p. 405.

80. Furlong and others (1997).

81. Hahn, Leavitt, and Aaron (1994).

82. Elliot and Tolan (2005).

83. The Office of Juvenile Justice and Delinquency Prevention (OJJDP) (1998).

84. Maclure and Sotelo (2004).

85. Levine (1999).

86. Thornberry (1998).

87. Rubio (2005).

88. Dowdney (2005).

89. Smith (2004).

90. Shaw (2001).

91. Decker and Van Winkle (1996).

92. Howell (1998); Thornberry (1998); and UNICEF (2005a).

93. Sherman and others (1998) and Rodgers (1999). For example, Krug and others (2002).

94. Authors' observations from the Ecuador Law and Justice for the Poor Program.

95. Mocan and Rees (1999).

96. Grogger (1998).

97. Krug and others (2002); Llorente and Rivas (2005); Sheley and Wright (1993); and Villaveces and others (2000).

98. Rashid (2000); Sageman (2004); and Taylor (1988).

99. Berrebi (2003); Post (1998); and Sageman (2004).

100. Berman and Laitin (2005); Bloom (2005b); Levine (1999) p. 342; Paxson (2002); Post (1998); Sageman (2004); Sprinzak (1998); and Stern (2004).

101. Erikson (1994) p. 196.

102. Human Rights Watch (1997a); Human Rights Watch (2003); and UNICEF (2005a), Innocenti Brief 3e.

103. Greenwood and others (1998).

104. Matthews, Griggs, and Caine (1999).

105. Human Rights Watch (2001a).

106. Akpokodje, Bowles, and Tigere (2002); Chen and Shapiro (2004); and Levitt (1998).

107. Bayer, Pintoff, and Pozen (2005) and Woolard and others (2005).

108. WHO (2005b).

109. Beyer (1997).

110. Department of Corrections (2003).

111. Petrosino, Turpin-Petrosino, and Buehler (2005).

112. Wilson, Mackenzie, and Mitchell (2005).

113. Van Ness (2005).

114. Miers (2001).

115. Latimer, Dowden, and Muise (2001); Akpokodje, Bowles, and Tigere (2002); and Roche (2006).

116. Brandt (2005).

117. AFP (2001); Arjona (2006); BBC (2001); Brown (1990); Coalition to Stop the Use of Child Soldiers (2000) in Singer (2005); Coalition to Stop the Use of Child Soldiers (2002); Coalition to Stop the Use of Child Soldiers (2003); Coalition to Stop the Use of Child Soldiers (2004); Human Rights Watch (2002a); Leopold (2001); McGirk (2001); Seyboldt (2000); and Singer (2005).

118. Arjona (2006); Humphreys and Richards (2005); Humphreys and Weinstein (2003); and Singer (2005).

119. Human Rights Watch (1997b); ILO (2003); World Bank (2005t).

120. Humphreys and Richards (2005).

121. Humphreys and Richards (2005).

122. Benus, Rude, and Patrabansh (2001).

123. Humphreys and Weinstein (2005) and Utas (2004).

124. Kofi Annan in a speech to the 1st World Conference of Ministers Responsible for Youth, Lisbon, Portugal, 1998.

Spotlight on Sierra Leone

1. Government of Sierra Leone (2005a). Government of Sierra Leone (2005b).

2. The Global Fund for AIDS (2005); and UNICEF (2005b).

3. Government of Sierra Leone (2002), p 1. Cited in Ginifer (2003). Based on Sierra Leone Integrated Household Survey, 2004.

4. Women's Commission for Refugee Women and Children (2002).

5. Based on Sierra Leone Integrated Household Survey, 2004

6. Glennerster, Imran, and Whiteside (2006).

7. World Bank (forthcoming) Education Sector Review.

8. Simon (2003).

9. ENCISS and World Bank (2006).

10. Goovaerts, Gasser, and Belman Inbal (2005).

11. Turniški (2004).

12. Miguel, Glennerster, and Whiteside (2006).

13. Richards, Bah, and Vincent (2004).

14. ENCISS and World Bank (2006).

15. Bellows and Miguel (2006).

16. Hart (2004).

17. Bannon, Holland, and Rahim (2005).

Chapter 8

1. Population Division of the Department of Economic and Social Affairs of the United Nations Secretariat, Trends in Total Migrant Stock: The 2005 Revision http://esa.un.org/migration, April 7, 2006.

2. World Bank staff calculations from Global Trade Analysis Project (GTAP) database of Parsons and others (2005).

3. The United Nations High Commissioner for Refugees (UNHCR (2005)) reports that 34 percent of refugees are ages 5 to 17 and 47 percent 18 to 59. In the United Kingdom, 15- to 24-year-olds make up 32 percent of female asylum seekers and 38 percent of male asylum seekers (Heath and Jeffries (2005)).

4. Sjaastad (1962).

5. World Bank staff calculations from the 2000 United States Census public use sample.

6. Massey and others (1998) p. 47.

7. See McKenzie, Gibson, and Stillman (2006) for recent evidence of how large the gain in income can be, based on a migration lottery.

8. See Dustmann (2001) for a review of these older studies and Reyes (1997) for Mexico.

9. World Bank (2005i).

10. World Bank (2005i).

11. Black (2003).

12. Hagopian and others (2005).

13. McKenzie (2006a).

14. Mattoo, Neagu, and Özden (2005).

15. Kleiner (2000).

16. Mishra (forthcoming).

17. World Bank Staff calculations from the Pacific Island–New Zealand Migration Survey 2005.

18. Yang (2004) for the Philippines and Cox Edwards and Ureta (2003) for El Salvador.

19. World Bank Staff calculations from OECD (2005c) and OECD (2003).

20. Davis (2003).

21. Lucas (2004).

22. Kandel and Kao (2001).

23. McKenzie and Rapoport (2006).

24. International Organization for Migration (IOM) (2005b); Simonet (2004); and Survelliance Unit of the NSACP, Sri Lanka.

Note that in these countries migrants are more likely to be tested for HIV/AIDS than nonmigrants, as part of the health tests needed for employment abroad. As a result, their share of diagnosed cases probably exceeds their share of all cases.

25. International Organization for Migration (IOM) (2005a).

26. Hildebrandt and McKenzie (2005).

27. Stepick, Stepick, and Kretsedemas (2001).

28. Martinez and Lee (2000).

29. Australia Immigration Visa Services (1998).

30. Fidrmuc and Doyle (2005) include measures of inequality and regional controls to try to isolate the political socialization effect of migration from the self-selection effect.

31. Donato and Patterson (2004).

32. See http://sandiego.indymedia.org/en/2005/10/111331.shtml and the database of deaths at the Arizona border provided by the Coalición de Derechos Humanos at http://www.derechoshumanosaz.net/deaths.php4 [both accessed November 19, 2005].

33. "Trafficking in persons" shall mean the recruitment, transportation, transfer, harbouring or receipt of persons, by means of the threat or use of force or other forms of coercion, of abduction, of fraud, of deception, of the abuse of power or of a position of vulnerability or of the giving or receiving of payments or benefits to achieve the consent of a person having control over another person, for the purpose of exploitation (United Nations, Palermo Protocol 2000)

34. U.S. Department of State (2005a).

35. Omelaniuk (2005) for the IOM data; Clert and others (2005) for the study in Southeastern Europe.

36. U.S.Department of State (2005b).

37. Holzmann (2005), table A.2., based on UN medium variant projections.

38. Hatton and Williamson (2005).

39. Hatton and Williamson (2003).

40. Longhi, Nijkamp, and Poot (2005).

41. Borjas (2003) finds a 0.3–0.4 reduction in wages from a 1 percent increase in immigration, while the more recent studies by Card (2005) and Dustmann, Fabbri, and Preston (2005) find less effect.

42. Angrist and Kugler (2003).

43. United Kingdom Home Office (2005).

44. Portes and French (2005).

45. However, in March 2006 the United Kingdom home office announced plans to eliminate these programs as part of the introduction of a points system.

46. Maclellan and Mares (2005) nicely summarize this program and the lessons for other countries.

47. Data calculated by Anna Paulson from the Survey of Income and Program Participation (SIPP) 1996–2000 for immigrants who came to the United States between 1990 and 1996.

48. See World Bank (2005i) for a thorough discussion and examples.

49. Gibson, McKenzie, and Rohorua (2006).

50. See Mesnard (2004) for Tunisia; Yang (2005) for the Philippines.

51. In Malaysia, a scheme targeting the 250,000 skilled workers overseas with tax exemptions and other incentives to return only led to the return of 104 expatriates in the first two years of operation; whereas South Korea and Taiwan (China) have seen more substantial return, helped in large part by their booming economies (International Organization for Migration (IOM) (2005b)).

52. El-Cherkeh, Stirbu, and Tolciu (2006). Romania does not have a mutually agreed convention with the United States or Germany as it does with several other countries, but students can have their diplomas recognized through a special office.

53. Narayan and Petesch (2006).

54. World Bank staff calculations from Spain 2001 Census public use sample.

55. McKenzie (2005) provides the analysis cited in this paragraph.

56. Average over 1993–2000 based on the Survey on Overseas Filipinos of the National Statistics Office of the Philippines. Data was kindly supplied by Dean Yang for this purpose.

57. Gebrekristos and others (2005).

58. Enlaces Centro de Educación y Tecnología (2005) and Halewood and Kenny (2006).

59. Mar Gadio (2001).

60. Internet World Statistics, http://www.internetworldstats.com/stats.htm, November 21, 2005, update [accessed December 5, 2005].

61. Dodds, Muhamad, and Watts (2003).

62. Halewood and Kenny (2006).

63. McKinsey Global Institute (2005).

64. Special tabulations for youth provided by Guo Liang. See Liang (2005) for full details of the survey.

65. Curtain (2001).

66. Samuel, Shah, and Hadingham (2005).

67. Mungai (2005).

68. ILO (2001).

69. http://www.digitaldividedata.com. [accessed December 3, 2005].

70. Instituto Nacional para la Evaluación de la Educación de Mexico (2005).

71. Perkinson (2005).

72. World Links Impact Evaluation Series (2002).

73. Halewood and Kenny (2006). The discretionary budget covers all costs apart from teacher salaries, including supplies, teaching equipment, utility bills, building maintenance, and other classroom needs.

74. Neto and others (2005).

75. Banerjee and others (2005).

76. Gough and Grezo (2005).

77. Online Computer Library Center (OCLC) (2005).

78. Geary and others (2005).

79. Mar Gadio (2001).

80. Chewning and others (1996).

81. Parham (2004).

82. See Jorgenson (forthcoming) for a recent review.

83. See World Bank (2006c) for an assessment of the growth impact.

84. Clarke and Wallsten (2004).

85. Jensen (2006).

86. Neto and others (2005).

87. Guermazi and Satola (2005).

88. Rao (1999).

89. http://www.wordtracker.com unfiltered list of top 500 search terms for December 6, 2005.

90. Note that although these point systems typically give *more* points to young migrants than to older migrants, the other skill

criteria needed to obtain points typically disadvantage youth. As a result, most developing country youth are not provided an opportunity to migrate under the existing points systems.

Spotlight on donors

1. The most significant international commitments for youth include the 1989 UN Convention on the Rights of the Child, the 1999 ILO Convention on Child Labor, and the 2000 UN Program of Action on Youth updated in 2005. In addition, there are regional commitments such as that of the Council of Europe and the Ibero-American Convention on Youth Rights.

2. In Timor Leste, in the first two years after conflict about half of government spending on education was financed by external sources, allowing many children and young teenagers to attend school. See World Bank (2004d).

Chapter 9

1. Instituto Mexicano de la Juventud (IMJ) and Organización Iberoamericana de la Juventud (OIJ) (2006).

2. Although the stage of the demographic transition is correlated with income, there is enormous diversity among both low- and middle-income countries. Chad and Tajikistan are at very similar levels of income per capita, but in Chad fertility is approximately 6.0 births per woman, while in Tajikistan it is 3.5.

3. The discussion in this paragraph is based on special surveys commissioned for this Report from InterMedia (WDR 2007 Inter-Media surveys). See methodological note at the beginning of the Report. Also, figure 2.4.

4. Washington (2006) demonstrates how having female children influences legislators' voting records on women's issues in the United States, making them significantly more in favor of women's rights.

5. German Technical Cooperation and German Technical Cooperation and International Council on National Youth Policy (2005).

6. World Bank (2003f).

7. In addition to this Report, see National Research Council and Institute of Medicine (2005), and Knowles and Behrman (2005) for a discussion of this point. There is a large developed-country literature; however, the very different circumstances of developed-country youth and differences in capacity for implementation limit the applicability of these studies.

8. See, for example, Vegas and Umansky (2005) on school management; Banerjee and others (2005) on remedial education; Miguel and Kremer (2004) on deworming; and Glewwe, Jacoby, and King (2001) on early childhood development.

9. German Technical Cooperation and German Technical Cooperation and International Council on National Youth Policy (2005).

10. It should be borne in mind that some youth movements may not articulate strong demand for policies supporting youth because it is a transitory phase. By the time such policies would be implemented, many of the leaders of these movements would no longer be young. This lack of a permanent interest group can weaken political support for youth-focused policy.

11. German Technical Cooperation and German Technical Cooperation and International Council on National Youth Policy (2005). This is not to detract from the fact that many regional organizations play an important role promoting dialogue across countries on issues of common regional concern, including issues with implications beyond a member country's immediate borders.

12. Instituto Mexicano de la Juventud (IMJ) and Organización Iberoamericana de la Juventud (OIJ) (2006).

13. German Technical Cooperation and German Technical Cooperation and International Council on National Youth Policy (2005). As mentioned previously, about two-thirds of countries with national youth councils do not give voice to youth NGOs.

14. Dulci (2005).

15. Clementino (2006).

16. World Bank (2006g).

17. For a list of all indicators on youth that are collected by the UN system, see http://www.un.org/esa/socdev/unyin/documents/youthindicatorsexist.pdf. Also, for the status of discussions on which indicators should be used as a part of a worldwide effort to monitor youth outcomes, see http://www.un.org/esa/socdev/unyin/documents/youthindicatorsreport.pdf.

18. For example, questions on the citizenship block could be obtained from more detailed criminal justice records, the inclusion of questions on legal identity and citizenship in household surveys and censuses, and the incorporation of modules on political and social participation and knowledge in existing surveys.

19. See, for example, Summers (1992); Summers (1994); and Van der Gaag and Tan (1998).

20. Knowles and Behrman (2005).

21. Discriminant analysis was used on census data in the initial stages to identify target communities and households within those communities. See Knowles and Behrman (2005).

Spotlight on youth action

1. Two such sources are "Youth and the Millennium Development Goals" (Ad Hoc Working Group for Youth and the MDGs (2005)) and Kinkade and Macy (2005).

2. Peters (2006).

3. Ogar (2005).

4. Ekehaug (2005).

References

The word "processed" describes informally reproduced works that may not be commonly available through libraries.

Aakvik, Arild, Kjell G. Salvanes, and Kjell Vaage. 2003. "Measuring Heterogeneity in the Returns to Education in Norway Using Education Reforms." Bonn: Institute for the Study of Labor (IZA), Discussion Paper Series 815.

Aarts, Henk, Theo Paulussen, and Herman Schaalma. 1997. "Physical Exercise Habit: On the Conceptualization and Formation of Habitual Health Behaviours." *Health Education Research* 12(3):363–74.

Abadzi, Helen. 2003. *Improving Adult Literacy Outcomes: Lessons from Cognitive Research for Developing Countries.* Washington, DC: World Bank.

Abaunza, Humberto. 2002. "Puntos de Encuentro: Communication for Development in Nicaragua." *Sexual Health Exchange* 2002(1):2–3.

Abeyratne, Sirimal. 2004. "Economic Roots of Political Conflict: The Case of Sri Lanka." *World Economy* 27(8):1295–314.

Abt Associates. 2004. *Serving Country and Community: A Longitudinal Study of Service in AmeriCorps.* Washington, DC: Corporation for National and Community Service.

Abu-Ghaida, Dina, and Marie Connolly. 2003. *Trends in Relative Demand for Workers with Secondary Education: A Look at Nine Countries in East Asia, Africa and MENA.* Washington, DC: Background Paper prepared for *Expanding Opportunities and Building Competencies for Young People: A New Agenda for Secondary Education*, World Bank.

Acemoglu, Daron. 2003. "Patterns of Skill Premia." *Review of Economic Studies* 70(2):199–230.

Acemoglu, Daron, Simon Johnson, and James A. Robinson. 2001. "The Colonial Origins of Comparative Development: An Empirical Investigation." *American Economic Review* 91(5):1369–401.

Ackerman, Susan. 1996. "Rebellion and Autonomy in Industrializing Penang: The Career History of a Young Malay Divorcee." *Southeast Asian Journal of Social Science* 24(1):52–63.

Ad Hoc Working Group for Youth and the MDGs. 2005. "Youth and the Millennium Development Goals: Challenges and Opportunities for Implementation." Final report. Available online at http://www.un.org/esa/socdev/unyin/documents/youthmdgs.pdf.

Adams, Arvil V. 2006. "The Role of Skills Development in the Transition to Work: A Global Review." Background paper for the WDR 2007.

Aedo, Cristián, and Sergio Nuñez. 2001. "The Impact of Training Policies in Latin America and the Caribbean: The Case of Programa Joven." ILADES - Georgetown University. Santiago de Chile. Processed.

Aedo, Cristián, and Marcelo Pizarro Valdivia. 2004. "Rentabilidad Económica del Programa de Capacitación Laboral de Jóvenes 'Chile Joven.'" INACAP and Mideplan. Santiago de Chile. Processed.

AFP. 2001. "Amman Conference to Seek Ban on Use of Child Soldiers in Region, World." *AFP*, April 7.

Agha, Sohail. 2002. "A Quasi-experimental Study to Assess the Impact of Four Adolescent Sexual Health Interventions in Sub-Saharan Africa." *International Family Planning Perspectives* 28(2):67-70-& 113-118.

Akerlof, George A., and Rachel E. Kranton. 2000. "Economics and Identity." *Quarterly Journal of Economics* 115(3):715–53.

———. 2002. "Identity and Schooling: Some Lessons for the Economics of Education." *Journal of Economic Literature* 40(4):1167–201.

———. 2005a. "Identity and the Economics of Organizations." *Journal of Economic Perspectives* 19(1):9–32.

———. 2005b. "Social Divisions within Schools: How School Policies Can Affect Students' Identities and Educational Choices." *In* Christopher B. Barrett, (eds.), *The Social Economics of Poverty: On Identities, Groups, Communities and Networks.* London: Routledge.

Akin, John S., Charles C. Griffen, David K. Guilkey, and Barry M. Popkin. 1984. *The Demand for Primary Health Services in the Third World.* Totowa, NJ: Littlefield Adams.

Akpokodje, Joseph, Roger Bowles, and Emmanuel Tigere. 2002. *Evidence-based Approaches to Crime Prevention in Developing Countries - A Scoping Review of the Literature.* York, United Kingdom: Centre for Criminal Justice Economics and Psychology.

Alderman, Harold, and Jere R. Behrman. 2006. "Reducing the Incidence of Low Birth Weight in Low-Income Countries Has Substantial Economic Benefits." *World Bank Research Observer* 21(1):25–48.

Alderman, Harold, John Hoddinott, and Bill Kinsey. Forthcoming. "Long Term Consequences of Early Childhood Malnutrition." *Oxford Economic Papers.*

Alford, Sue, Nicole Cheetham, and Debra Hauser. 2005. *Science & Success in Developing Countries: Holistic Programs That Work to Prevent Teen Pregnancy, HIV & Sexually Transmitted Infections.* Washington, DC: Advocates for Youth.

Ali, Tariq Omar, Nuzhat Imam, Raihana Karim, and Nasheeba Selim. 2006. *Voices of the Youth: Findings from Youth Consultations in Bangladesh.* Dhaka, Bangladesh: BRAC Research and Evaluation Division. Available online at http://www.bracresearch.org/reports/final_youth_report_revised.pdf.

Alwain, Duane F., and Jon A. Krosnick. 1991. "Aging, Cohorts, and the Stability of Sociopolitical Orientations Over the Life Span." *American Journal of Sociology* 97(1):169–95.

Amin, Sajeda, Ian Diamond, Ruchira T. Naved, and Margaret Newby. 1998. "Transition to Adulthood of Female Garment-factory Workers in Bangladesh." *Studies in Family Planning* 29(2):185–200.

Andersen, Susan L. 2003. "Trajectories of Brain Development: Point of Vulnerability or Window of Opportunity?" *Neuroscience and Biobehavioral Reviews* 27(1-2):3–19.

Angrist, Joshua, Eric Bettinger, Erik Bloom, Elizabeth King, and Michael Kremer. 2002. "Vouchers for Private Schooling in Colombia: Evidence from a Randomized Natural Experiment." *American Economic Review* 92(5):1535–58.

Angrist, Joshua, Eric Bettinger, and Michael Kremer. Forthcoming. "Long-term Consequences of Secondary School Vouchers: Evidence from Administrative Records in Colombia." *American Economic Review.*

Angrist, Joshua, and Victor Lavy. 2002. "New Evidence on Classroom Computers and Pupil Learning." *Economic Journal* 112(482):735–86.

Angrist, Joshua D. 1990. "Lifetime Earnings and the Vietnam Era Draft Lottery: Evidence from Social Security Administrative Records." *American Economic Review* 80(3):313–36.

Angrist, Joshua D., and Adriana D. Kugler. 2003. "Protective or Counter-productive? Labour Market Institutions and the Effect of Immigration on EU Natives." *Economic Journal* 113(488): F302–F331.

Annan, Jeannie, Christopher Blattman, and Roger Horton. 2006. *The State of Youth and Youth Protection in Northern Uganda: Findings from the Survey of War Affected Youth.* Uganda: UNICEF. Available online at www.sway-uganda.org.

Arends-Kuenning, Mary, and Sajeda Amin. 2000. "The Effects of Schooling Incentive Programs on Household Resource Allocation in Bangladesh." New York: Population Council Policy Research Division, Working Paper 133.

Arjona, Ana. 2006. "Understanding Recruitment in Civil Wars." Background paper for the WDR 2007.

Armecina, G., Jere R. Behrman, P. Duazo, S. Chumanc, S. Gultianoa, Elizabeth King, and N. Lee. 2006. "Early Childhood Development through Integrated Programs: Evidence from the Philippines." World Bank. Washington, DC. Processed.

Arnett, Jeffrey Jensen. 2000. "Emerging Adulthood: A Theory of Development from the Late Teens through the Twenties." *American Psychologist* 55(5):469–80.

Arunatilake, Nisha, Sisira Jayasuriya, and Saman Kelegama. 2001. "The Economic Cost of the War in Sri Lanka." *World Development* 29(9):1483–500.

Asian Development Bank. 2005. *HIV/AIDS Prevention among Youth.* Hanoi: Viet Nam Comission for Population, Family and Children.

Asian Development Bank, and World Bank. 2005. *Country Gender Assessment.* Manila and Washington, DC: Asian Development Bank and World Bank.

Askew, Ian, and Ndugga Baker Maggwa. 2002. "Integration of STI Prevention and Management with Family Planning and Antenatal Care in Sub-saharan Africa: What More Do We Need to Know?" *International Family Planning Perspectives* 28(2):77–86.

Assaad, R., and S. Zouari. 2003. "Estimating the Impact of Marriage and Fertility on the Female Labor Force Participation when Decisions are Inter related: Evidence from Urban Morocco." *Topics in Middle Eastern and North African Economics, Electronic Journal* 5, Middle East Economic Association and Loyola University Chicago.

Atchoarena, David, and Andre Marcel Delluc. 2001. "Revisiting Technical and Vocational Education in Sub-Saharan Africa: An Update on Trends, Innovations, and Challenges." Paris: International Institute for Educational Planning, IIEP/Prg.DA 1.320.

Au, Chun-Chung, and J. Vernon Henderson. Forthcoming. "How Migration Restrictions Limit Agglomeration and Productivity in China." *Journal of Development Economics.*

Audas, Rick, Eva Berde, and Peter Dolton. 2005. "Youth Unemployment and Labour Market Transitions in Hungary." *Education Economics* 13(1):1–25.

Australia Immigration Visa Services. 1998. *Immigration Laws: December 1998.* Sidney: Australia Immigration Visa Services. Available online at http://www.migrationint.com.au/news/malta/dec_1998-03mn.asp.

Autor, David H., Lawrence F. Katz, and Alan B. Krueger. 1998. "Computing Inequality: Have Computers Changed the Labor Market?" *Quarterly Journal of Economics* 113(4):1169–213.

Aziken, Michael E., Patrick I. Okonta, and Adedapo B. A. Ande. 2003. "Knowledge and Perception of Emergency Contraception among Female Nigerian Undergraduates." *International Family Planning Perspective* 29(2):84–7.

Balcells i Ventura, Laia. 2005. "Explaining Variation in the Salience of Catalan Nationalism Across the France/Spain Border." Paper presented at the 7th Annual Retreat of the Society for Comparative Research. March 6. Budapest.

Banerjee, Abhijit, Shawn Cole, Esther Duflo, and Leigh Linden. 2005. "Remedying Education: Evidence from Two Randomized Experiments in India." London, U.K.: BREAD Working Paper 109.

Banerjee, Abhijit, and Esther Duflo. 2006. "Addressing Absence." *Journal of Economics Perspectives* 20(1):117–32.

Bankole, Akinrinola, Susheela Singh, Vanessa Woog, and Deirdre Wulf. 2004. *Risk and Protection: Youth and HIV/AIDS in Sub-Saharan Africa.* New York: The Alan Guttmacher Institute.

Bannon, Ian, Peter Holland, and Aly Rahim. 2005. "Youth in Post-conflicts Settings." Washington, DC: World Bank, Youth Development Notes 1(1).

Barker, G. 2003. "How Do We Know If Men Have Changed? Promoting and Measuring Attitude Change with Young Men. Lessons from Program H in Latin America." Paper presented at the Expert Group Meeting on 'The Role of Men and Boys in Achieving Gender Equality'. November 21. Brasilia.

Barr, Nicholas. 2004. "Higher Education Funding." *Oxford Review of Economic Policy* 20(2):264–83.

Barrera Osorio, Felipe. 2005. "Impact of Private Provision of Public Education: Empirical Evidence from Bogotá's Concessions Schools." Paper presented at the Mobilizing the Private Sector for Public Education Conference. May 10. Harvard University, Boston, MA.

Barrera, Felipe, and Ana María Ibáñez. 2004. "Does Violence Reduce Investment in Education? A Theoretical and Empirical Approach." Universidad de Los Andes: Documentos CEDE 000582. Available online at http://economia.uniandes.edu.co/~economia/archivos/temporal/d2004-27.pdf.

Barro, Robert J. 1999. "Human Capital and Growth in Cross-Country Regression." *Swedish Economic Policy Review* 6(2):237–77.

Basu, Kaushik, and James E. Foster. 1998. "On Measuring Literacy." *Economic Journal* 108(451):1733–49.

Basu, Kaushik, Hyejin Ku, and Homa Zarghamee. 2006. "Determinants of Youth Behaviour and Outcomes: A Review of Theory, Evidence and Policy Implications." Background paper for the WDR 2007.

Bate, Peter. 2004. *The Story Behind Oportunidades.* Washington, DC: Inter-American Development Bank, Online Magazine: FOCUS. Available online at http://www.iadb.org/idbamerica/.

Bateman, C. 2001. "Doctor Burnout Silent and Fatal." *South African Medical Journal* 91(2):98–100.

Bauböck, Rainer. 2005. "Expansive Citizenship - Voting Beyond Territory and Membership." *Political Science & Politics* 38(4):683–87.

Bay, Ann-Helén, and Morten Blekesaune. 2002. "Youth, Unemployment and Political Marginalization." *International Journal of Social Welfare* 11(2):132–39.

Bayer, Patrick, Randi Pintoff, and David Pozen. 2005. "Building Criminal Capital Behind Bars: Peer Effects in Juvenile Corrections." New Haven, CT: Center for Economic Growth Working Paper, Yale University 864.

BBC. 2001. "U.N. Finds Congo Child Soldiers." *BBC News,* February 21.

Bearman, Peter, and Hannah Brückner. 2001. "Promising the Future: Virginity Pledges and First Intercourse." *American Journal of Sociology* 106(4):859–912.

Becker, Gary S. 1964. *Human Capital.* Chicago, IL: University of Chicago Press.

Becker, Gary S., and Kevin M. Murphy. 1988. "A Theory of Rational Addiction." *Journal of Political Economy* 96(4):675–700.

Bedard, Kelly, and Olivier Deschênes. 2006. "The Long-Term Impact of Military Service on Health: Evidence from World War II and Korean War Veterans." *American Economic Review* 96(1):176–94.

Beegle, Kathleen, Rajeev Dehejia, and Roberta Gatti. 2004. "Why Should We Care about Child Labor?" Washington, DC: World Bank Policy Research Division Working Paper Series 3479.

Behrman, Jere R., Nancy Birdsall, and Miguel Szekely. 2003. "Economic Policy and Wage Differentials in Latin America." Washington, DC: Center for Global Development Working Paper 29.

Behrman, Jere R., and Anil B. Deolalikar. 1988. "Health and Nutrition." *In* H. Chenery and T. N. Srinivasan, (eds.), *Handbook of Development Economics vol. 1.* Amsterdam: Elsevier.

Behrman, Jere R., M. R. Foster, Mark Rosenzweig, and P. Vashishtha. 2002. "Does Increasing Women's Schooling Raise the Schooling of the Next Generation?" *American Economic Review* 92(1):323–34.

Behrman, Jere R., John Hoddinott, John A. Maluccio, Erica Soler-Hampejsek, Emily Berhman, Reynaldo Martorell, Agnes Quisumbing, Manuel Ramirez, and Aryeh D. Stein. 2005a. "What Determines Post-school Skills? Impacts of Pre-School, School Years and Post School Experiences in Guatemala." University of Pennsylvania, International Food Policy Research Institute, Middleburry College, Emory University and INCAP-Guatemala. Philadelphia, PA. Processed.

Behrman, Jere R., and James C. Knowles. 1999. "Household Income and Child Schooling in Vietnam." *World Bank Economic Review* 13(2):211–56.

Behrman, Jere R., A. Murphy, Agnes Quisumbing, Usha Ramakrishna, and Kathyrn Young. 2005b. "What is the Real Impact of Schooling on Age of First Union and Age of First Parenting?

New Evidence from Guatemala." Emory University, University of Pennsylvania, and International Food Policy Research Institute. Philadelphia, and Washington, DC. Processed.

Behrman, Jere R., Alexis Murphy, Agnes Quisumbing, Usha Ramakrishna, and Kathyrn Young. 2006. "What is the Real Impact of Education on Age of First Parenthood and Family Formation?" Background paper for the WDR 2007.

Behrman, Jere R., Piyali Sengupta, and Petra Todd. 2001. *Progressing through PROGRESA: An Impact Assessment of a School Subsidy Experiment.* Washington, DC: International Food Policy Research Institute.

Bell, Clive, Ramona Bruhns, and Hans Gersbach. 2006. "Economic Growth, Education and Aids in Kenya Model: A Long-run Analysis." Background paper for the WDR 2007.

Bell, Clive, Shantayanan Devarajan, and Hans Gersbach. 2006. "The Long-run Economic Costs of AIDS: A Model with an Application to South Africa." *World Bank Economic Review* 20(1):55–89.

Bell, Clive, Hans Gersbach, Ramona Bruhns, and Dagmar Volker. 2004. "Economic Growth, Human Capital and Population in Kenya in the Time of AIDS: A Long-run Analysis in Historical Perspective." University of Heidelberg. Heidelberg. Processed.

Bellows, John, and Edward Miguel. 2006. "War and Institutions: New Evidence from Sierra Leone." *American Economic Review* 96(2):394–99.

Benavot, Aaron. 2004. *Comparative Analysis of Secondary Education Curricula.* Washington, DC: World Bank and International Bureau of Education.

Benhabib, Seyla. 2005. "Borders, Boundaries, and Citizenship." *Political Science & Politics* 38(4):673–77.

Bentolila, Samuel, and Giuseppe Bertola. 1990. "Firing Costs and Labour Demand: How Bad Is Eurosclerosis?" *Review of Economic Studies* 57(3):381–402.

Benus, Jacob, James Rude, and Satyendra Patrabansh. 2001. *Bosnia & Herzegovina: Impact of the Emergency Demobilization and Reintegration Project.* Washington, DC: US Department of Labor, Bureau of International Affairs, Office of Foreign Relations.

Bercovich, Alicia. 2004. *People with Disability in Brazil: A Look at the 2000 Census Results.* Rio de Janeiro: Instituto Brasilero de Geografía e Estatistica. Available online at http://iussp2005.princeton.edu/download.aspx?submissionId=52108.

Berer, Marge. 2003. "Integration of Sexual and Reproductive Health Services: A Health Sector Priority." *Reproductive Health Matters* 11(21):6–15.

Berlinsky, S., S. Galiani, and P. Gertler. 2006. "Public Pre-primary Schooling and Primary School Performance." University College, Universidad de San Andrés, and World Bank. London and Washington, DC. Processed.

Berman, Eli, and David D. Laitin. 2005. "Hard Targets: Theory and Evidence on Suicide Attacks." Cambridge, MA: National Bureau of Economic Research Working Paper Series 11740.

Berman, Eli, and Stephen Machin. 2000. "Skill-biased Technology Transfer Around the World." *Oxford Review of Economic Policy* 16(3):12–22.

Berman, Peter, and Laura Rose. 1996. "The Role of Private Providers in Maternal and Child Health and Family Planning Services in Developing Countries." *Health Policy and Planning* 11(2):142–55.

Bernasconi, Andrés, and Fernando Rojas. 2004. *Informe sobre la Educación Superior en Chile: 1980-2003.* Santiago, Chile: Editorial Universitaria.

Berrebi, Claude. 2003. "Evidence about the Link between Education, Poverty, and Terrorism Among Palestinians." Princeton, NJ: Princeton University Industrial Relations Section Working Paper 477.

Bertola, Giuseppe, Francine D. Blau, and Lawrence M. Kahn. 2002. "Labor Market Institutions and Demographic Employment Patterns." Cambridge, MA: National Bureau of Economic Research Working Paper Series 9043.

Bertrand, Marianne, Sendhil Mullanaithan, and Douglas Miller. 2003. "Public Policies and Extended Families: Evidence from Pensions in South Africa." *World Bank Economic Review* 17(1):27–50.

Besley, Timothy, Lawrence Haddad, John Hoddinott, and Michelle Adato. 2004. "Community Participation and the Performance of Public Works Programs in South Africa." Dalhousie University. Halifax, Nova Scotia. Processed.

Betcherman, Gordon, Jean Fares, Amy Luinstra, and Robert Prouty. 2001. "Child Labor, Education, and Children's Rights." *In* Philip Alston and Mary Robinson, (eds.), *Human Rights and Development: Toward Mutual Reinforcement.* New York: Oxford University Press.

Betcherman, Gordon, Martin Godfrey, Susana Puerto, Friederike Rother, and Antoneta Stavreska. 2006. "Supporting Young Workers: Results of the Global Inventory of Interventions." World Bank. Washington, DC. Processed.

Betcherman, Gordon, Karina Olivas, and Amit Dar. 2004. "Impacts of Active Labor Market Programs: New Evidence from Evaluations with Particular Attention to Developing and Transition Countries." Washington, DC: World Bank, Social Protection Discussion Paper Series 0402.

Beyer, Marty. 1997. "Experts for Juveniles at Risk of Adult Sentences." *In* Patricia Puritz, Alycia Capozello, and Wendy Shang, (eds.), *More Than Meets the Eye: Rethinking Assessment, Competency and Sentencing for a Harsher Era of Juvenile Justice.* Washington, DC: American Bar Association Juvenile Justice Center.

Bhargava, Alok. 2005. "AIDS Epidemic and the Psychological Well-being and School Participation of Ethiopian Orphans." *Psychology, Health and Medicine* 10(3):263–75.

Bhatnagar, Deepti, Ankita Dewan, Magüi Moreno Torres, and Parameeta Kanung. 2003. "The Bangladesh Female Secondary School Assistance Project." World Bank. Washington, DC. Processed.

Billari, Francesco C., Dimiter Philipov, and Pau Baizán Munoz. 2001. "Leaving Home in Europe: The Experience of Cohorts Born Around 1960." *International Journal of Population Geography* 7(5):339–56.

Billig, Shelley. 2006. "Service Learning." *In* Lonnie R. Sherrod, Constance A. Flanagan, Ron Kassimir, and Amy K. Bertelsen, (eds.), *Youth Activism: An International Encyclopedia.* Westport, CT: Greenwood Press.

Binder, Melissa. 2005. *The Cost of Providing Universal Secondary Education in Developing Countries.* Cambridge, MA: American Academy of Arts and Sciences. Available online at http://www.amacad.org/projects/ubase.aspx.

Black, Richard. 2003. *Soaring Remittances Raise New Issues.* Washington, DC: Migration Policy Institute. Available online at http://www.migrationinformation.org/about.cfm.

Black, Sandra E., Paul J. Devereaux, and Kjell G. Salvanes. 2004. "Fast Times at Ridgemont High? The Effect of Compulsory Schooling Laws on Teenage Births." Cambridge, MA: National Bureau of Economic Research Working Paper Series 10911.

Blanchard, Olivier. 2006. "Emploi: La Solution passe par le CUP (Contract Unique Progressif)." MIT. Cambridge, MA. Processed.

Blanchard, Olivier, and Justin Wolfers. 2000. "The Role of Shocks and Institutions in the Rise of European Unemployment: The Aggregate Evidence." *Economic Journal* 110(2000):C1–C33.

Blanchard, Olivier J., and Augustin Landier. 2001. "The Perverse Effects of Partial Labor Markets Reform: Fixed Duration Contracts in France." Cambridge, MA: MIT, Department of Economics, Working Paper Series 01-14.

Blanco, Almudena, and Jochen Kluve. 2002. "Why not Stay Home: Nest-leaving Behavior in Western Europe." University of California, Berkeley. Berkeley, CA. Processed.

Blau, Francine D., and Lawrence M. Kahn. 1999. "Institutions and Laws in Labor Markets." *In* Orley Ashenfelter and David Card, (eds.), *Handbook of Labor Economics. Vol. 3A.* Amsterdam: Elsevier.

Bloom, David E. 2005a. "Education and Public Health: Mutual Challenges Worldwide." *Comparative Education Review* 49:437–51.

Bloom, David E., and David Canning. 2005. "Global Demographic Change: Dimensions and Economic Significance." Cambridge, MA: Harvard Initiative for Global Health Working Paper No. 1. Available online at http://www.hsph.harvard.edu/pgda/working/working_paper1.pdf.

Bloom, David E., David Canning, and Pia Malaney. 2000. "Population Dynamics and Economic Growth in Asia." *Population and Development Review* 26(supplement 2000):257–90.

Bloom, David E., and Jeffrey D. Sachs. 1998. "Geography, Demography, and Economic Growth in Africa." *Brookings Papers on Economic Activity* 0(2):207–73.

Bloom, David E., and Jeffrey G. Williamson. 1998. "Demographic Transitions and Economic Miracles in Emerging Asia." *World Bank Economic Review* 12(3):419–55.

Bloom, Mia. 2005b. *Dying to Kill: The Allure of Suicide Terror.* New York, NY: Columbia University Press.

Bloomfield, Kim, Tim Stockwell, Gerhard Gmel, and Nina Rehn. 2003. "International Comparisons of Alcohol Consumption." *Alcohol Research & Health* 27(1):95–109.

Blum, R. W., and M. Ireland. 2004. "Reducing Risk, Increasing Protective Factors: Findings from the Caribbean Youth Health Survey." *Journal of Adolescence Health* 35(6):493–500.

Blum, Robert. 2006. "The Adolescent Brain." Background note for the WDR 2007.

Blum, Robert W., and Heather P. Libbey. 2004. "School Connectedness - Strengthening Health and Education Outcomes for Teenagers." *Journal of School Health* 74(7):231–34.

Blum, Robert W., and Kristin Nelson-Mmari. 2004. "The Health of Young People in a Global Context." *Journal of Adolescent Health* 35(5):402–18.

Boisjoly, Johanne, Greg J. Duncan, Michael Kremer, Dan M. Levy, and Jacque Eccles. 2004. "Empathy or Antipathy? The Impact of Diversity." Harvard University. Cambridge, MA. Processed.

Bonelli, Regis, and Alinne Veiga. 2004. "Determinants of Educational Exclusion in Five States of Brazil." *In* Maria-Valeria Pena and Maria Madalena, (eds.), *Children's and Youth Vulnerability: Poverty, Exclusion and Social Risk in Five Brazilian States.* Brasilia: World Bank.

Borgarello, Andrea, Susan Duryea, Olgiati Scarpetta, and Stefano Scarpetta. 2005. "Early Experiences of Youths in the Labor Market: Stepping Stones or Traps?" World Bank. Washington, DC. Processed.

Borjas, George J. 2003. "The Labor Demand Curve IS Downward Sloping: Reexamining the Impact of Immigration on the Labor Market." *Quarterly Journal of Economics* 118(4):1335–74.

Boudarbat, Brahim. 2005. "Job-search Strategies and the Unemployment of University Graduates in Morocco." Paper presented at the IZA-EBRD International Conference on Labor Market Dynamics. May 5. Bologna, Italy.

Bourguignon, Francois, Francisco Ferreira, and Marta Menendez. 2005. "Inequality of Opportunity in Brazil?" World Bank. Washington, DC. Processed.

Bowles, Samuel, and Howard Gintis. 1976. *Schooling in Capitalist America: Educational Reform and the Contradictions of Economic Life.* New York: Basic.

Boyer, Cherrie B., and Mary-Ann Shafer. 1997. "Evaluation of a Knowledge -and Cognitive- Behavioral Skills-Building Intervention to Prevent STDs and HIV Infection in High School Students." *Adolescence* 32(125):25–42.

Brady, Martha. 1998. "Laying the Foundation for Girls' Healthy Futures: Can Sports Play a Role?" *Studies in Family Planning* 29(1):79–82.

Brandt, Pamela Robin. 2005. "The Brotherhood." *American Way Magazine.* May 15, 2005.

Bray, Mark. 2004. "Sharing the Burden of Financing: Government and Household Partnerships for Basic Education." *Economic Affairs* 24(4):22–26.

Brett, Rachel, and Irma Specht. 2004. *Young Soldiers: Why They Choose to Fight.* Geneva: Lynne Rienner Publisher for the International Labour Organization.

Brown, Gillian, Laila Al-Hamad, and Carmen de Paz Nieves. 2005. *Gender Equality in East Asia: Progress, and the Challenges of Economic Growth and Political Change.* Washington, DC: World Bank, East Asia and Pacific Region, Social Development Team.

Brown, Ian. 1990. *Khomeini's Forgotten Sons: The Story of Iran's Boy Soldiers.* London, U.K.: Grey Seal.

Bruce, Judith, and Shelley Clark. 2004. *The Implications of Early Marriage for HIV/AIDS Policy. Brief based on background paper prepared for the WHO/UNFPA/Population Council Technical Consultation on Married Adolescents.* New York: Population Council.

Brückner, Hannah, and Peter Bearman. 2005. "After the Promise: The STD Consequences of Adolescent Virginity Pledges." *Journal of Adolescent Health* 36(4):271–8.

Bruns, Barbara, Alain Mingat, and Ramahatra Rakotomalala. 2003. *Achieving Universal Primary Education by 2015: A Chance for Every Child.* Washington, DC: World Bank.

Burgess, Simon, Carol Propper, Hedley Reeys, and Arran Shearer. 2003. "The Class of 1981: The Effects of Early Career Unemployment on Subsequent Unemployment Experiences." *Labor Economics* 10(3):291–309.

Buvinic, Mayra. 1998. "The Cost of Adolescent Childbearing: Evidence from Chile, Barbados, Guatemala and Mexico." *Studies in Family Planning* 29(2):201–9.

———. 2005. "Economic Opportunities for Women: Experiences from Latin America and the Caribbean." Paper presented at the High-Level Policy Forum on Enhancing Women Economic Participation and Opportunities. El Cairo, Egypt.

Buvinic, Mayra, Andre Medici, Elisa Fernandez, and Ana Cristina Torres. 2006. "Gender Differentials in Health." *In* Dean T. Jamison, Joel Breman, Anthony R. Measham, George Alleyne, Mariam Claeson, David B. Evans, Prabhat Jha, Anne Mills, and Philip R. Musgrove, (eds.), *Disease Control Priorities in Developing Countries.* New York: Oxford University Press.

Cáceres, Carlos F., Anna M. Rosasco, Jeffrey S. Mandel, and Norman Hearst. 1994. "Evaluating a School-based Intervention for STD/AIDS Prevention in Peru." *Journal of Adolescent Health* 15(7):582–91.

Cahuc, Pierre, and Stéphane Carcillo. 2006. *Que Peut-on Attendre des Contrats Nouvelle Embauche et Premiere Embauche?* Paris: Université de Paris. Available online at http://www.crest.fr/pageperso/cahuc/CNECahucCarcillo.pdf.

Caldwell, Brian J., Rosalind Levacic, and Kenneth N. Ross. 1999. "The Role of Formula Funding of Schools in Different Educational Policy Contexts." *In* Rosalind Levacic and Kenneth N. Ross, (eds.), *Needs-Based Resource Allocation in Education: Via Formula Funding of Schools.* Paris: UNESCO, International Institute for Educational Planning.

Caldwell, John C., and Pat Caldwell. 2002. "Is Integration the Answer for Africa?" *International Family Planning Perspective* 28(2):108–10.

Canals-Cerda, José, and Cristobal Ridao-Cano. 2004. "The Dynamics of School and Work in Rural Bangladesh." Washington, DC: World Bank Policy Research Working Paper Series 3330.

Card, David. 2005. "Is the New Immigration Really that Bad?" *Economic Journal* 115(507):F300–F323.

Card, David, and Thomas Lemieux. 2000a. "Adapting to Circumstances: The Evolution of Work, School and Living Arrangments among North American Youth." *In* Dabid G. Blanchflower and Richard B. Freeman, (eds.), *Youth Employment and Joblessness in Advanced Countries.* Chicago, IL: University of Chicago Press.

———. 2000b. "Dropout and Enrollment Trends in the Post-War Period: What Went Wrong in the 1970's?" Cambridge, MA: National Bureau of Economic Research Working Paper Series 7658.

Carneiro, Pedro, and James J. Heckman. 2002. "The Evidence on Credit Constraints in Post-Secondary Schooling." *Economic Journal* 112(482):705–34.

———. 2003. "Human Capital Policy." *In* James J. Heckman and Alan B. Krueger, (eds.), *Inequality in America: What Role for Human Capital Policies?* Cambridge, MA: MIT Press.

Carneiro, Pedro, and Sokbae Lee. 2005. "Ability, Sorting and Wage Inequality." University College London. London. Processed.

Carneiro, Pedro, and Cristobal Ridao-Cano. 2005. "Heterogeneity and Uncertainty in Returns to High School: The Case of Indonesia." Background paper for the WDR 2007.

Catalano, Richard F., Kevin P. Haggerty, Sabrina Oesterle, Charles B. Fleming, and J. David Hawkins. 2004. "The Importance of Bonding to School for Healthy Development: Findings from the Social Development Research Group." *Journal of School Health* 74(7):252–61.

Celentano, David D., Noya C. Galai, Ajay K. Sethi, Nina G. Shah, Steffanie A. Strathdee, David Vlahov, and Joel E. Gallant. 2001. "Time to Initiating Highly Active Antiretroviral Therapy among HIV-Infected Injection Drug Users." *AIDS* 15(13):1707–15.

Centers for Disease Control and Prevention. 1993. "Mortality Trends for Selected Smoking-Related Cancers and Breast Cancer — United States, 1950-1990." *Morbidity and Mortality Weekly Report* 42(44):857–863-6.

———. 1998. "Recommendations to Prevent and Control Iron Deficiency in the United States, Recommendations and Report." *Morbidity and Mortality Weekly Report* 47(RR-3):1–36.

Centre for Development and Population Activities (CEDPA). 2001. *Adolescent Girls in India Choose a Better Future: An Impact Assessment.* Washington, DC: Center for Development and Population Activities (CEDPA).

Chandra, Prabha S., K. R. Jairam, and Anila Jacob. 2004. "Factors Related to Staff Stress in HIV/AIDS Related Palliative Care." *Indian Journal of Palliative Care* 10(2):48–54.

Chapman, Bruce. Forthcoming. "Income Contingent Loans for Higher Education: An International Reform." In Eric A. Hanushek and Finis Welch (eds.) *Handbook of the Economics of Education.* Amsterdam: North-Holland.

Chattopadhyay, Raghabendra, and Esther Duflo. 2003. "Women as Policy Makers: Evidence from a India-Wide Randomized Policy Experiment." MIT. Cambridge, MA. Processed.

Chaudhuri, Saulma, and Pratima Paul-Majumder. 1995. *The Conditions of Garment Workers in Bangladesh: An Appraisal.* Dhaka: Bangladesh Institute of Development Studies.

Chaudhury, Nazmul, Jeffrey Hammer, Michael Kremer, Karthik Muralidharan, and F. Halsey Rogers. 2006. "Missing in Action: Teacher and Health Worker Absence in Developing Countries." *Journal of Economic Perspectives* 20(1):91–116.

Chen, Kun, and Martin Kenney. 2005. "Universities/Research Institutes and Regional Innovation Systems: The Case of Beijing and Shenzhen." Berkeley, CA: BRIE Working Paper 168. Available online at http://brie.berkeley.edu/publications/wp168revised.pdf.

Chen, M. Keith, and Jesse M. Shapiro. 2004. "Does Prison Harm Inmates? A Discontinuity-Based Approach." Harvard University. Cambridge, MA. Processed.

Chewning, Betty, Pat Mosena, Dale Wilson, Harold Erdman, Sandra Potthoff, Anita Murphy, and Kathleen Kennedy Kuhnen. 1996. "Evaluation of a Computerized Contraceptive Decision Aid for Adolescent Ppatients." *Patient Education and Counseling* 38(3):227–39.

Chiclet, Christophe. 2001. "Otpor: The Youth who Booted Milosevic." *UNESCO Courier.*

Cincotta, Richard P., Robert Engleman, and Daniele Anastasion. 2003. *The Security Demographic: Population and Civil Conflict after the Cold War.* Washington, DC: Population Action International.

Cinterfor/ILO. 2001. *Modernization in Vocational Education and Training in the Latin American and the Caribbean Region.* Montevideo: Cinteford - ILO.

Clark, Shelley. 2004. "Early Marriage and HIV Risks in Sub-Saharan Africa." *Studies in Family Planning* 35(3):149–60.

Clarke, George R. G., and Scott Wallsten. 2004. "Has the Internet Increased Trade? Evidence from Industrial and Developing Countries." Washington DC: World Bank Policy Research Working Paper Series 3215.

Clementino, Josbertini. 2006. Speech at Vozes Jovens Pernambuco (part of *WDR* consultations), Recife, Brazil, January 17.

Clert, Carine, Elizabeth Gomart, Ivana Aleksic, and Natalie Otel. 2005. "Human Trafficking in South Eastern Europe: Beyond Crime Control, an Agenda for Social Inclusion and Development." World Bank. Washington, DC. Processed.

Coady, David P. 2000. *The Application of Social Cost-benefit Analysis to the Evaluation of PROGRESA. Report Submitted to PROGRESA.* Washington, DC: International Food Policy Research Institute.

Coakley, Jay. 2002. "Using Sports to Control Deviance and Violence among Youths: Let's Be Critical and Cautious." *In* Margaret Gatz, Michael A. Messner, and Sandra J. Ball-Rokeach, (eds.),

Paradoxes of Youth and Sport. Albany: State University of New York Press.

Coale, Ansley J., and Edgar M. Hoover. 1958. *Population Growth and Economic Development in Low-Income Countries: A Case Study of India's Prospects.* Princeton, NJ: Princeton University Press.

Coalition to Stop the Use of Child Soldiers. 2000. "The Use of Children by OSCE Member States." Paper presented at the Human Dimension Seminar on Children and Armed Conflict. Warsaw, Poland.

———. 2002. "DRC Child Soldiers." London, UK: Child Soldiers Newsletter 3.

———. 2003. *The Use of Child Soldiers in the Americas: An Overview.* London, U.K.: Coalition to Stop the Use of Child Soldiers.

———. 2004. *Child Soldier Use 2003: A Briefing for the 4th UN Security Council Open Debate on Children and Armed Conflict.* London, U.K.: Coalition to Stop the Use of Child Soldiers.

Cockx, Bart, and Christian Göbel. 2004. "Subsidized Employment for Young Long-term Unemployed Workers – An Evaluation." Université Catholique de Louvain. Louvain. Available online at http://www.iza.org/en/webcontent/teaching/summerschool_html/7thsummer_school_files/ss2004_goebel.pdf. Processed.

Cogan, John J., Paul Morris, and Murray Print, eds. 2002. *Civic Education in the Asia-Pacific Region: Case Studies Across Six Societies.* Oxford, U.K.: Rutledge.

Cohen, Joel E., and David E. Bloom. 2005. "Cultivating Minds: Educating All Children is not only Urgent but also Feasible within the Next Few Years." *Finance and Development* 42(2):8–14.

Cohen, Susan A. 2004. "Beyond Slogans: Lessons From Uganda's Experience with ABC and HIV/AIDS." *Reproductive Health Matters* 12(23):132–35.

Cole, Jennifer. 2004a. "Fresh Contact in Tamatave, Madagascar: Sex, Money, and Intergenerational Transformation." *American Ethnologist* 31(4):573–88.

———. 2004b. "The Jaombilo of Tamatave (Madagascar), 1992-2004: Reflections on Youth and Globalization." *Journal of Social History* 38(4):891–914.

Committee for Population, Family and Children Vietnam, and ORC Macro. 2003. *Vietnam Demographic and Health Survey 2002.* Calverton, MD: Committee for Population, Family and Children (Vietnam), ORC Macro.

Conde-Agueledo, Agustín, Anyeli Rosas-Bermúdez, and Ana Cecilia Kafury-Goeta. 2006. "Birth Spacing and Risk of Adverse Perinatal Outcomes: A Meta-analysis." *Journal of the American Medical Association* 295(15):1809–23.

Cox Edwards, Alejandra, and Manuelita Ureta. 2003. "International Migration, Remittances and Schooling: Evidence from El Salvador." *Journal of Development Economics* 72(2):429–61.

Cox, Cristián. 2004. "Policy Formation and Implementation in Secondary Education Reform: The Case of Chile in the 1990s." Paper presented at the Second Regional Secondary Education in Africa Conference. June 6. Dakar.

CRECE. 2005. *Sistema de Aprendizaje Tutorial.* Columbia: CRECE.

Cunha, Flavio, James J. Heckman, Lance Lochner, and Dimitriy V. Masterov. 2005. "Interpreting the Evidence on Life Cycle Skill Formation." Cambridge, MA: National Bureau of Economic Research Working Paper Series 11331.

Cunningham, Wendy, and Lucas Siga. 2006. "Wage and Employment Effects of Minimum Wage on Vulnerable Groups in the Labor Market: Brazil and Mexico." World Bank. Washington, DC. Processed.

Currie, Janet, and Duncan Thomas. 1995. "Does Head Start Make a Difference?" *American Economic Review* 85(3):341–64.

Curtain, Richard. 2001. "Promoting Youth Employment through Information and Communication Technologies (ICT): Best Practice Examples in Asia and the Pacific." Paper presented at the ILO/Japan Tripartite Regional Meeting on Youth Employment in Asia and the Pacific. Bangkok.

———. 2005. *Case for Investing in Young People as Part of a National Poverty Reduction Strategy*. New York: UNFPA. Available online at http://www.unfpa.org/upload/lib_pub_file/424_filename_Investing.pdf.

Dalrymple, William. 2005. "Inside the Madrasas." *The New York Review of Books.*

Davies, Lynn, Christopher Williams, and HiromiMan-Hing Aubrey Ko Yamashita. 2006. *Inspiring Schools: Taking up the Challenge of Pupil Participation*. London, U.K.: Carnegie Trust.

Davis, Todd M. 2003. *Atlas of Student Migration*. New York: Institute of International Education.

de Cordoba, José. 2004. "As Venezuela Tilts Left, a Rum Mogul Reaches Out to the Poor." *Wall Street Journal*, November 10. Page: A1.

De Ferranti, David, Guillermo E. Perry, Indermit S. Gill, J. Luis Guasch, William F. Maloney, Carolina Sánchez-Páramo, and Norbert Schady. 2003. *Closing the Gap in Education and Technology*. Washington, DC: World Bank.

De Fraja, Gianni, Tania Oliveira, and Luisa Zanchi. 2005. "Must Try Harder. Evaluating the Role of Effort in Educational Attainment." London: Centre for Economic Policy Research Discussion Papers 5048.

de Janvry, Alain, Frederico Finan, Elisabeth Sadoulet, and Renos Vakis. 2006. "Can Conditionnal Cash Transfers Serve as Safety Nets in Keeping Children at School and from Working when Exposed to Shocks?" *Journal of Development Economics* 79(2):349–73.

de Jong, Joop T. V. M., Ivan H. Komproe, Mark Van Ommeren, Mustafa El Masri, Mesfin Araya, Noureddine Khaled, Willem van de Put, and Daya Somasundaram. 2001. "Lifetime Events and Posttraumatic Stress Disorder in 4 Postconflict Settings." *Journal of American Medical Association* 286(5):555–62.

de Moura Castro, Claudio. 1999. *Proyecto Joven: New Solutions and Some Surprises*. Washington, DC: Inter-American Development Bank. Available online at http://www.colombiajoven.gov.co/injuve/instit/bid/4_pjov.pdf.

De Walque, Damien. 2004. "How Does the Impact of an HIV/AIDS Information Campaign Vary with Educational Attainment? Evidence from Rural Uganda." Washington, DC: World Bank Policy Research Working Paper Series 3289.

———. 2005. "Parental Education and Children's Schooling Outcomes: Is the Effect Nature, Nurture, or Both? Evidence from Recomposed Families in Rwanda." Washington, DC: World Bank Policy Research Working Paper Series 3483.

Deaton, Angus S., and Christina H. Paxson. 1997. "The Effects of Economic and Population Growth in National Saving and Inequality." *Demography* 34(1):97–114.

Decker, Scott H., and Barrik Van Winkle. 1996. *Life in the Gang: Family, Friends and Violence*. New York, NY: Cambridge University Press.

Delisle, Hélène, Venkatraman Chandra-Mouli, and Bruno de Benoist. 2000. "Should Adolescents Be Specifically Targeted for Nutrition in Developing Countries? To Address Which Problems, and How?" World Health Organization. Geneva. Processed.

DeMaeyer, E. M. 1989. *Preventing and Controlling Iron Deficiency Anemia through Primary Health Care: A Guide for Health Administrators and Programme Managers*. Geneva: World Health Organization.

Deparment of Health Services Sri Lanka. 2002. *Annual Health Bulletin 2002*. Colombo, Sri Lanka: Sri Lanka, Department of Health Services.

Department of Corrections. 2003. *Draft White Paper On Corrections in South Africa*. Pretoria, South Africa: Department of Corrections.

DeSimone, Jeff. 2002. "Illegal Drug Use and Employment." *Journal of Labor Economics* 20(4):952–77.

Devia, Sergio. 2003. *Exito o Fracaso de las Políticas Públicas de Capacitación Laboral a Jóvenes? - Evaluación del Programa Testigo: 'Proyecto Joven' de Argentina (1993-2000)*. Geneva: International Labour Office. Available online at http://www.ilo.org/.

Dhakal, Raju Malla, and M. Sheikh Misbah. 1997. *Breaking Barriers Building Bridges: A Case Study of USAID/Nepal's SO3 Women's Empowerment Program*. Kathmandu, Nepal: USAID.

Diamond, Larry. 2003. "Universal Democracy." *Policy Review* 119(June & July):3–25.

Dickson-Tetteh, Kim, Audrey Pettifor, and Winnie Moleko. 2001. "Working with Public Sector Clinics to Provide Adolescent-Friendly Services in South Africa." *Reproductive Health Matters* 9(17):160–69.

Ding, Weili, and Stephen F. Lehrer. Forthcoming. "Do Peers Affect Student Achievement in China's Secondary Schools?" *Review of Economic and Statistics.*

Dodds, Peter S., Roby Muhamad, and Duncan J. Watts. 2003. "An Experimental Study of Search in Global Social Networks." *Science* 301(5634):827–29.

Dohmen, Thomas, Armin Falk, David Huffman, Uwe Sunde, Jürgen Schupp, and Gert Wagner. 2005. "Five Facts about Risk Attitudes: Evidence from a Large, Representative, Experimentally-Validated Survey." Institute for the Study of Labor (IZA). Bonn. Processed.

Donato, Katharine M., and Evelyn Patterson. 2004. "Women and Men on the Move: Undocumented Border Crossing." *In* Jorge Durand and Douglas S. Massey, (eds.), *Crossing the Border: Research from the Mexican Migration Project*. New York, NY: Russell Sage Foundation.

Dowdney, Luke. 2005. *Neither War nor Peace: International Comparisons of Children and Youth in Organized Violence*. Rio de Janeiro, Brazil: Children and Youth in Organized Armed Violence, Viva Rio, Instituto de Estudos da Religião.

Dréze, Jean, and Haris Gazdar. 1997. "Uttar Pradesh: The Burden of Inertia." *In* Jean Dréze and Amartya Sen, (eds.), *Indian Development: Selected Regional Perspectives*. New Delhi: Oxford University Press.

Drucker, Ernest, Peter Lurie, Alex Wodak, and Philip Alcabes. 1998. "Measuring Harm Reduction: The Effects of Needle and Syringe Exchange Programs and Methadone Maintenance on the Ecology of HIV." *AIDS* 12(Suppl A):217–30.

Duflo, Esther, Pascaline Dupas, Michael Kremer, and Samuel Simei. 2006. "Education and HIV/AIDS Prevention: Evidence from a Randomized Evaluation in Western Kenya." Background paper for the WDR 2007.

Dulci, Luiz. 2005. Speech at seminar "Young Voices—A View of Youth Organizations and Movements on 21st Century Brazil," Brasilia, Brazil, May 24.

Dunkle, Kristin L., Rachel K. Jewkes, Heather C. Brown, Glenda E. Gray, James A. McIntryre, and Siobán D. Harlow. 2004. "Transactional Sex among Women in Soweto, South Africa: Prevalence, Risk Factors and Association with HIV Infection." *Social Science & Medicine* 59(8):1581–92.

Dupas, Pascaline. 2006. "Relative Risks and the Market for Sex: Teenagers, Sugar Daddies and HIV in Kenya." EHESS-PSE. Paris. Processed.

Durham, Deborah. Forthcoming. "Empowering Youth: Making Youth Citizens in Botswana." *In* Jennifer Cole and Deborah Durham (eds.) *Generations and Globalization: Family, Youth and Age in the New World Economy.* Bloomington, I.N.: Indiana University Press.

Duryea, Susan, Jasper Hoek, David Lam, and Deborah Levison. Forthcoming. "Dynamics of Child Labor: Labor Force Entry and Exit in Urban Brazil." *In* Peter F. Orazem, Guilherme Sedlacek, and Zafiris Tzannatos (eds.) *Child Labor and Education in Latin-America.* Washington, DC: Inter-American Development Bank.

Duryea, Suzanne, Analia Olgiati, and Leslie Stone. 2006. "The Under-Registration of Births in Latin America." Washington, DC: Inter-American Development Bank Working Paper Series 551.

Dustmann, Christian. 2001. "Why Go Back? Return Motives of Migrant Workers." *In* Slobodan Djajic, (eds.), *International Migration: Trends, Policies and Economic Impacts.* Oxford: Routledge.

Dustmann, Christian, Francesca Fabbri, and Ian Preston. 2005. "The Impact of Immigration on the British Labor Market." *Economic Journal* 115(507):F324–341.

Ebbeling, Cara B., Dorota B. Pawlak, and David S. Ludwig. 2002. "Childhood Obesity: Public-health Crisis, Common Sense Cure." *The Lancet* 360(9331):473–482.

Edmunds, Timothy, Anthony Forster, and Andrew Cottey. 2002. "Armed Forces and Society: A Framework for Analysis." Bristol, U.K.: The Transformation of Civil-Military Relations in Central and Eastern Europe 1.13c.

Eggleston, Elizabeth, Jean Jackson, Wesley Rountree, and Zhiying Pan. 2000. "Evaluation of a Sexuality Education Program for Young Adolescents in Jamaica." *Revista Panamericana de la Salud Publica* 7(2):102–12.

Eggleston, Elizabeth, Joan Leitch, and Jean Jackson. 2000. "Consistency of Self-reports of Sexual Activity among Young Adolescents in Jamaica." *International Family Planning Perspectives* 26(2):79–84.

Ekehaug, Vidar. 2005. *African Youth at the UN World Summit!* World Wide Web: Panorama: A TakingITGlobal Online Publication. Available online at http://www.takingitglobal.org/express/panorama/article.html?ContentID=6543.

El-Cherkeh, Tanja, Elena Stirbu, and Andrea Tolciu. 2006. "Youth Migration to Europe: Potential Impact on the Labour Market of the Countries of Origin." Background paper for the WDR 2007.

El-Zanaty, Fatma, and Ann Way. 2001. *Egypt Demographic and Health Survey 2000.* Calverton, MD: Egypt Ministry of Health and Population, National Population Council and ORC Macro. Available online at http://www.measuredhs.com/.

Elias, Victor, F. Ruiz-Nuñez, R. Cossa, and D. Bravo. 2004. "An Econometric Cost-benefit Analysis of Argentina's Youth Training Program." Washington, DC: Inter-American Development Bank, Research Network Working Paper R-482.

Ellertson, Charlotte, Beverly Winikoff, Elizabeth Armstrong, Sharon Camp, and Pramilla Senanayake. 1995. "Expanding Access to Emergency Contraception in Developing Countries." *Studies in Family Planning* 26(5):251–63.

Elliot, Delbert S., and Patrick H. Tolan. 2005. "Youth Violence Prevention, Intervention, and Social Policy: An Overview." *In* Daniel J. Flanner and C. Ronald Huff, (eds.), *Youth Violence Prevention, Intervention, and Social Policy.* Washington, DC: American Psychiatric Press, Inc.

Eloundou-Enyegue, Parfait M. 2004. "Pregnancy Related Dropouts and Gender Inequality in Education: A Lifetable Approach and Application to Cameroon." *Demography* 41(3):509–28.

Eltigani, Eltigani E. 2000. "Changes in Family-Building Patterns in Egypt and Morocco: A Comparative Analysis." *International Family Planning Perspectives* 26(2):73–8.

Elway, Ann. 1999. "Poverty and Disability: A Review of the Literature." Washington, DC: World Bank, Social Protection Discussion Paper Series 9932.

Emerson, Patrick M., and André P. Souza. 2002. "The Effect of Adolescent Labor on Adult Earnings and Female Fertility in Brazil." University of Colorado. Denver, CO. Processed.

———. 2003. "Is There a Child Labor Trap? Inter-generational Persistence of Child Labor in Brazil." *Economic Development and Cultural Change* 51(2):375–98.

Emerson, Patrick M., and André Portela Souza. 2006. "Is Child Labor Harmful? The Impact of Working Earlier in Life on Adult Earnings." University of Colorado at Denver and Cornell University. Denver, CO and Cornell, NY. Processed.

Emmerson, Carl, Christine Frayne, Sandra McNally, and Olmo Silva. 2005. *Evaluation of Aimhigher: Excellence Challenge. The Early Impact of Aimhigher: Excellence Challenge on Pre-16 Outcomes: An Economic Evaluation.* London: British Department for Education and Skills. Available online at http://www.dfes.gov.uk/research/data/uploadfiles/RR652.pdf.

ENCISS, and World Bank. 2006. "Youth in Sierra Leone: Focus Group Discussions." World Bank. Washington, DC. Processed.

Enlaces Centro de Educación y Tecnología. 2005. *Estadisticas Nacionales Enlaces 2005.* Santiago de Chile: Chile, Ministerio de Educación. Available online at http://www.enlaces.cl/libro/estadisticas.pdf.

Erikson, Erik H. 1994. *Identity: Youth and Crisis.* New York, NY: W. W. Norton & Company, Inc.

Erulkar, Annabel S., Linus I. A. Ettyang, Charles Onoka, Frederik K. Nyagah, and Alex Muyonga. 2004. "Behavior Change Evaluation of a Culturally Consistent Reproductive Health Program for Young Kenyans." *International Family Planning Perspectives* 30(2):58–67.

Erulkar, Annabel S., and Barbara S. Mensch. 1997. *Youth Centers in Kenya: Evaluation of the Family Planning Association of Kenya Programme.* Nairobi, Kenya: Population Council.

Eusuf and Associates, and Center on Social Research and Human Development. 2002. *Non-formal Education Project-3: Mid-term Evaluation Report.* Dhaka: Eusuf Associates and Center on Social Research and Human Development for the Government of Bangladesh.

Ezzati, Majid, and Alan D. Lopez. 2004. "Smoking and Oral Tobacco use." *In* Majid Ezzati, Alan D. Lopez, Anthony Rodgers, and Christopher J. L. Murray, (eds.), *Comparative Quantification of Health Risks: Global and Regional Burden of Disease Attributable to Selected Major Risk Factors.* Geneva: WHO.

Fafchamps, Marcel, and Agnes R. Quisumbing. 2005. "Marriage, Bequest, and Assortative Matching in Rural Ethiopia." *Economic Development and Cultural Change* 53(2):347–80.

Family Health International. 2005.*Network* 23(4)

FAO. 2006. *Assessment of the Double Burden of Malnutrition in Six Case Study Countries.* Rome: Food and Agriculture Organization.

Fares, Jean, and Claudio E. Montenegro. 2006. "Youth Unemployment's Dynamics: Evidence from Brazil (1978-2002) and Chile (1957-2005)." Background paper for the WDR 2007.

Fares, Jean, Claudio E. Montenegro, and Peter F. Orazem. 2006a. "How are Youth Faring in the Labor Market? Evidence from Around the World." Background paper for the WDR 2007.

———. 2006b. "Variation in the Returns to Schooling Across and Within Developing Economies." Background paper for the WDR 2007.

Fares, Jean, and Dhushyanth Raju. 2006. "Child Labor across the Developing World: Patterns, Correlations and Determinants." Background paper for the WDR 2007.

Fares, Jean, and Erwin Tiongson. 2006. "Entering the Labor Market and Early Mobility of Youth: Evidence from Panel Estimates in Bosnia and Herzegovina." Background paper for the WDR 2007.

Fearon, James D., and David D. Laitin. 2003. "Ethnicity, Insurgency, and Civil War." *American Political Science Review* 97(1):75–90.

Fernald, Lia C., Juan Pablo Gutierrez, Lynnette M. Neufeld, Gustavo Olaiz, Stefano F. Bertozzi, Michelle Mietus-Snyder, and Paul J. Gertler. 2004. "High Prevalence of Obesity Among the Poor in Mexico." *Journal of the American Medical Association* 291(21):2544–5.

Ferreira, Francisco H. G., and Peter Lanjouw. 2001. "Rural Nonfarm Activities and Poverty in the Brazilian Northeast." *World Development* 29(3):509–28.

Fertig, Michael. 2003. "Education Production, Endogenous Peer Group Formation and Class Composition - Evidence from PISA 2002 Study." Bonn: Institute for the Study of Labor (IZA), Discussion Paper Series 714.

Fichtenberg, Caroline M., and Stanton A. Glantz. 2002. "Youth Access Interventions Do Not Sffect Youth Smoking." *Pediatrics* 109(6):1088–92.

Fidrmuc, Jan, and Orla Doyle. 2005. *Does Where You Live Affect How You Vote: An Analysis of Migrant Voting Behaviour.* Uxbridge: Brunel Business School.

Filer, Randall K., and Daniel Münich. 2002. "Responses of Private and Public Schools to Voucher Funding." The Center for Economic Research and Graduate Education - Economic Institute. Prague. Processed.

Filmer, Deon. Forthcoming. "School Availability and School Participation in 21 Developing Countries." *Journal of Development Studies.*

Filmer, Deon, Emmanuel Jimenez, and Annette Richter. 2006. "Simulating the Returns to Youth Opportunity Agency and Second Chances." Background note for the WDR 2007.

Filmer, Deon, and David L. Lindauer. 2001. "Does Indonesian Have a 'Low Pay' Civil Service?" *Bulletin of Indonesian Economic Studies* 37(2):189–205.

Finkel, Steve E, and Sheryl Strumbas. 2000. *Civic Education in South Africa: The Impact of Adult and School Programs on Democratic Attitudes and Participation.* Washington, DC: USAID. Available online at http://pdf.dec.org/pdf_docs/PNACH577.pdf.

Fiore, M. C., W. C. Bailey, S. J. Cohen, S. F. Dorfman, M. G. Goldstein, E. R. Gritz, R. B. Heyman, C. R. Jaen, T. E. Kottke, H. A. Lando, R. E. Mecklenburg, P. D. Mullen, L. M. Nett, L. Robinson, M. L. Stitzer, A. C. Tommasello, L. Villejo, and M. E. Wewers.

2000. "Treating Tobacco Use and Dependence: A Public Health Service Clinical Practice Guideline." Paper presented at the Press Briefing, HHS Auditorium. June 27. Washington, DC

Firebaugh, Glenn, and Kevin Chen. 1995. "Vote Turnout of Nineteenth Amendment Women: The Enduring Effect of Disenfranchisement." *American Journal of Sociology* 100(4):972–96.

Fitzgerald, A. M., B. F. Stanton, N. Terreri, H. Shipena, X. Li, J. Kahihuata, I. B. Ricardo, J. S. Galbraigth, and A. M. de Jaeger. 1999. "Use of Western-Based HIV Risk-Reduction Interventions Targeting Adolescents in an African Setting." *Journal of Adolescent Health* 25(1):52–61.

Fleisher, Belton M., Haizheng Li, Shi Li, and Xiaojun Wang. 2004. "Sorting, Selection, and Transformation of the Return to College Education in China." Bonn: Institute for the Study of Labor (IZA), Discussion Paper Series 1446.

FOCUS. 1998. *Reproductive Health Programs for Young Adults: Health Facility Programs.* Watertown, MA: FOCUS on Young Adults, Pathfinder International.

Fortenberry, J. Dennis. 2005. "The Limits of Abstinence-only in Preventing Sexually Transmitted Infections." *Journal of Adolescent Health* 36(4):269–70.

Fougère, Denis, Francis Kramarz, and Julien Pouget. 2006. "Youth Unemployment and Crime in France." Bonn, Germany: Discussion Paper Series of the Institute for the Study of Labor (IZA) 2009.

Franklin, Mark N. 2004. *Voter Turnout and the Dynamics of Electoral Competition in Established Democracies since 1945.* Cambridge, United Kingdom: Cambridge University Press.

Freedom House. 2006. *Freedom in the World 2005 : The Annual Survey of Political Rights and Civil Liberties.* Long Beach, CA: Rowman & Littlefield Publishers, Inc.

Freeman, Richard B. 2000. "Disadvantaged Young Men and Crime." In David G. Blanchflower and Richard B. Freeman, (eds.), *Youth Employment and Joblessness in Advanced Countries.* Chicago and London: University of Chicago Press for the National Bureau of Economic Research.

Fretwell, David H., Jacob Benus, and Christopher J. O'Leary. 1999. "Evaluating the Impact of Active Labour Market Programme: Results of Cross-Country Studies in Europe and Central Asia." Washington, DC: World Bank, Social Protection Discussion Paper 9915.

Fryer, Roland G., and Paul Torelli. 2005. "An Empirical Analysis of 'Acting White.'" Harvard University. Cambridge, MA. Processed.

Fuchs, Thomas, and Ludger Woessmann. 2004. "What Accounts for International Differences in Student Performance? A Re-Examination Using PISA Data." Munich, Germany: CESifo Working Paper Series 1235.

Furlong, Andy, Fred Cartmel, Janet Powney, and Stuart Hall. 1997. *Evaluating Youth Work with Vulnerable Young People.* Edinburgh: Scottish Council for Research in Education.

Fussell, Elizabeth. 2006. "Comparative Adolescences: The Transition to Adulthood in Brazil, Kenya, Mexico, the U.S., and Vietnam." University of Tennessee. Knoxville, TN. Processed.

Gajakashmi, C. K., P. Jha, K. Ranson, and S. Nguyen. 2000. "Global Patterns of Smoking and Smoking-Attributable Mortality." In Prabhat Jha and Frank J. Chaloupka, (eds.), *Tobacco Control in Developing Countries.* New York: Oxford University Press.

Gal, Reuven, and Donald Eberly. 2006. *Service Without Guns.* New Zealand: Lulu Press.

Galasso, Emanuela, Martin Ravallion, and Agustin Salvia. 2001. "Assisting the Transition from Workfare to Work: A Randomized Experiment." Washington, DC: World Bank Policy Research Working Paper Series 2738.

Galiani, Sebastian, Martin Rossi, and Ernesto Schargrodsky. 2006. "Conscription and Crime." Background paper for the WDR 2007.

Galloway, Rae, and Mary Ann Anderson. 1994. "Prepregnancy Nutritional Status and Its Impact on Birthweight." *SCN News* 1994(11):6–10.

Garces, Eliana, Duncan Thomas, and Janet Currie. 2000. "Longer Term Effects of Head Start." Cambridge, MA: National Bureau of Economic Research Working Paper Series 8054.

Gatawa, B. G. 1995. *Zimbabwe: AIDS Education for Schools.* Harare, Zimbabwe: UNICEF.

Gauri, Varun, and Evan S. Lieberman. 2004. "Institutions, Social Boundaries, and Epidemics: Explaining Government AIDS Policies in Brazil and South Africa." Paper presented at the Annual Meetings of the American Political Science Association. September 2. Chicago, IL.

Gauthier, Clermont, and Martial Dembélé. 2004. *Quality of Teaching and Quality of Education: A Review of Research Findings.* Paris: Background paper for the UNESCO Global Monitoring Report 2005. Available online at http://portal.unesco.org/.

Geary, Cindy W., Hally Mahler, William Finger, and Kathleen H. Shears. 2005. *Using Global Media to Reach Youth: The 2002 MTV Staying Alive Campaign.* Arlington, VA: Family Health International, YouthNet Program.

Gebrekristos, Hirut, Stephen Resch, Khangelani Zuma, and Mark Lurie. 2005. "Estimating the Impact of Establishing Family Housing on the Annual Risk of HIV Infection in the South African Mining Communities." *Sexually Transmitted Diseases* 32(6):333–40.

Gerber, Alan S., Donald P. Green, and Ron Shachar. 2003. "Voting May be Habit Forming: Evidence from a Randomized Field Experiment." *American Journal of Political Science* 47(3):540–50.

German Technical Cooperation, and International Council on National Youth Policy. 2005. *Comparative Analysis of National Youth Policy.* Eschborn, Germany: International Council on National Youth Policy (ICNYP). Available online at http://www.icnyp.net.

Geronimus, Arline T., and John Bound. 1990. "Black/white Differences in Women's Reproductive-Related Health Status: Evidence from Vital Statistics." *Demography* 27(3):457–66.

Geronimus, Arline T., and Sanders Korenman. 1992. "The Socioeconomic Consequences of Teen Childbearing Reconsidered." *Quarterly Journal of Economics* 107(4):1187–214.

Gertler, Paul J. 2000. *Final Report: The Impact of PROGRESA on Health.* Washington, DC: International Food Policy Research Institute.

Gertler, Paul J., Stefano F. Bertozzi, Juan Pablo Gutierrez, and J. Sturdy. 2006. "Preliminary Results from Analysis of Poverty and Adolescent Risk Behavior in Mexico." World Bank. Washington, DC. Processed.

Gertler, Paul J., David Levine, and Sebastian Martinez. 2003. "The Presence and Presents of Parents: Do Parents Matter for More than their Money?" University of California. Berkeley, CA Available online at http://faculty.haas.berkeley.edu/. Processed.

Gian, Cong, Doan Hong Quang, Nguyen Thi Lan Huong, and Remco H. Oostendorp. 2006. "Trade Liberalization, the Gender Wage Gap and Returns to Education in Vietnam." Tinbergen Institute, Amsterdam Institute for International Development. Amsterdam. Processed.

Gibson, Cynthia. 2001. "From Inspiration to Participation: A Review of Perspectives on Youth Civic Engagement." Paper presented at the Grantmaker Forum on Community and National Service. Berkeley, CA

Gibson, John, David J. McKenzie, and Halahingano Rohorua. 2006. "How Cost Elastic Are Remittances? Evidence from Tongan Migrants in New Zealand." *Pacific Economic Review* 21(1):112–38.

Gill, Indermit S., and Ih Chon-Sun. 2000. "Republic of Korea." *In* Indermit S. Gill, Fred Fluitman, and Amit Dar, (eds.), *Vocational Education and Training Reform: Matching Skills to Markets and Budgets.* New York: Oxford Univesity Press.

Gill, Indermit S., Claudio E. Montenegro, and Dörte Dömeland, eds. 2002. *Crafting Labor Policy: Techniques and Lessons from Latin America.* Washington, DC: Oxford University Press for the World Bank.

Ginifer, Jeremy. 2003. "Reintegration of Ex-Combatants." *In* Mark Malan, Sarah Meek, Thokozani Thusi, and Jeremy Ginifer, (eds.), *Sierra Leone: Building the Road to Recovery.* Pretoria, South Africa: Institute for Securities Studies.

Glennerster, Rachel, Shehla Imran, and Katherine Whiteside. 2006. "Baseline Report on the Quality of Primary Education in Sierra Leone: Teacher Absence, School Inputs, and School Supervision in District Education Committee and Government-Assisted Schools in Sierra Leone." Processed.

Glewwe, Paul, Hanan G. Jacoby, and Elizabeth M. King. 2001. "Early Childhood Nutrition and Academic Achievement: A Longitudinal Analysis." *Journal of Public Economics* 81(3):345–68.

Gluckman, Peter D., Mark A. Hanson, Susan M. B. Morton, and Catherine S. Pinal. 2005. "Life-Long Echoes - A Critical Analysis of the Developmental Origins of Adult Disease Model." *Biology of the Neonate* 87:127–39.

Goldscheider, Frances K. 2000. "Why Study Young Adult Living Arrangements? A View of the Second Demographic Transition." Brown University. Providence, RI. Processed.

Gonzalez, Rosa Amelia, and Patricia Marquez. 2005. *Ron Santa Teresa's Social Initiatives.* Washington, DC: Inter-American Development Bank, Social Enterprise Knowledge Network.

Goovaerts, Piet, Martin Gasser, and Alisa Belman Inbal. 2005. "Demand Driven Approaches to Livelihood Support in Post-War Contexts." Washington, DC: World Bank, Social Development Papers 29.

Gorpe, Mehmet Ziya, Jean Fares, and Claudio E. Montenegro. 2006. "Public Wage Premium Around the World." Background paper for the WDR 2007.

Gough, Neil, and Charlotte Grezo. 2005. "Africa: The Impact of Mobile Phones." Berkshire, England: Vodafone Policy Paper Series 2.

Gould, Eric D., Bruce A. Weinberg, and David B. Mustard. 1998. "Crime Rates and Local Labor Market Opportunities in the United States: 1979-1997." *Review of Economic and Statistics* 84(1):45–61.

Government of Sierra Leone. 2002. *Survey on Reinsertion & Reintegration Assistance to Ex-Combatants.* Freetown, Sierra Leone: Government of Sierra Leone, report submitted to National Center for the Dissemination of Disability Research.

———. 2005a. "National Population Based HIV Seroprevalence Survey of Sierra Leone". Freetown, Sierra Leone, Statistics Sierra Leone.

———. 2005b. *Poverty Reduction Strategy Paper: A National Programme for Food Security, Job Creation and Good Governance*

(2005-2007). Freetown, Sierra Leone: Government of Sierra Leone.

Graft, Auralice, Nicole Haberland, and Rachel Goldberg. 2003. "Married Adolescents: A Review of Programs." Paper presented at the WHO/UNFPA/Population Council Technical Consultation on Married Adolescents. Geneva.

Grantham-Mcgregor, S. M., C. A. Powell, S. P. Walker, and J. H. Himes. 1991. "Nutritional Supplementation, Psychosocial Stimulation, and Mental Development of Stunted Children: The Jamaica Study." *Lancet* 338(8758):1–5.

Gray, Ronald H., Maria J. Wawer, Ron Brookmeyer, Nelson K. Sewankambo, David Serwadda, Fred Wabwire-Mangen, Tom Lutalo, Xianbin Li, Thomas van Cott, Thomas C. Quinn, and Rekai Project Team. 2001. "Probability of HIV-1 Transmission per Coital Act in Monogamous, Heterosexual, HIV-1-discordant Couples in Rakai, Uganda." *Lancet* 357(9263):1149–53.

Green, Donald P., and Alan S. Gerber. 2001. *Getting out the Youth Vote: Results from Randomized Field Experiments*. Youth Vote Coalition: Pew Charitable Trusts.

Greene, Margaret E., and Thomas Merrick. 2005. "Poverty Reduction: Does Reproductive Health Matter?" Washington, DC: World Bank Health, Nutrition and Population Discussion Paper July 2005.

Greenwood, Jeremy, Ananth Seshadri, and Guillaume Vandenbroucke. 2005. "The Baby Boom and Baby Bust." *American Economic Review* 95(1):183–207.

Greenwood, Peter W., Karyn E. Model, C. Peter Rydell, and James Chiesa. 1998. *Diverting Children from a Life of Crime: Measuring Costs and Benefits*. Santa Monica, CA: RAND.

Gregson, Simon, Geoffrey P. Garnett, Constance A. Nyamukapa, Timothy B. Hallett, James J. C. Lewis, Peter R. Mason, Stephen K. Chandiwana, and Roy M. Anderson. 2006. "HIV Decline Associated with Behavior Change in Eastern Zimbabwe." *Science* 311(5761):664–66.

Groce, Nora Ellen. 2003. "Adolescents and Youth with Disability: Issues and Challenges." PhD thesis. Yale School of Public Health.

Grogger, Jeffrey. 1998. "Market Wages and Youth Crime." *Journal of Labor Economics* 16(4):756–91.

Grosskurth, Heiner, Frank Mosha, James Todd, Ezra Mwijarubi, Arnoud Klokke, Kesheni Senkoro, Philippe Mayaud, John Changalucha, Angus Nicoll, Gina ka Gina, James Newell, Kokugonza Mugeye, David Mabye, and Richard Hayes. 1995. "Impact of Improved Treatment of Sexually Transmitted Diseases on HIV Infection in Rural Tanzania: Randomised Controlled Trial." *Lancet* 346(8974):530–36.

Grossman, Michael. 2005a. "Education and Nonmarket Outcomes." Cambridge, MA: National Bureau of Economic Research Working Paper Series 11582.

———. 2005b. "Individual Behaviors and Substance Use: The Role of Price." *In* Björn Lindgren and Michael Grossman, (eds.), *Substance Use: Individual, Behavioral, Social Interactions, Markets, and Policies*. Amsterdam: Elsevier.

Grown, Caren, Geeta Rao Gupta, and Aslihan Kes. 2005. *Taking Action: Achieving Gender Equality and Empowering Women*. Sterling, VA: Earthscan.

Gruben, William C., and Darryl McLeod. 2006. "Apparel Exports and Education: How Developing Nations Encourage Women's Schooling." *Economic Letter - Federal Reserve Bank of Dallas* 1(3):1–8.

Gruber, Jonathan, eds. 2001. *Risky Behavior among Youths: An Economic Analysis*. Chicago: University of Chicago Press.

Gruber, Jonathan, and Jonathan Zinman. 2001. "Youth Smoking in the United States: Evidence and Implications." *In* Jonathan Gruber, (eds.), *Risk Behavior among Youths: an Economic Analysis*. Chicago: Chicago University Press.

Guarcello, Lorenzo, Fabrizia Mealli, and Furio Camillo Rosati. 2003. "Household Vulnerability and Child Labour: The Effects of Shocks, Credit Rationing and Insurance." Washington, DC: World Bank, Social Protection Unit, Human Development Network 0322.

Guermazi, Boutheina, and David Satola. 2005. "Creating the 'Right' Enabling Environment for ICT." *In* Robert Schware, (eds.), *E-development: from excitement to effectiveness*. Washington, DC: World Bank.

Gunnarson, Victoria, Peter F. Orazem, and Mario A. Sánchez. 2006. "Child Labor and School Achievement in Latin America." *World Bank Economic Review* 20(1):31–54.

Gutierrez, Juan Pablo. 2006. "*Oportunidades* for the Next Generation: Effects of a Conditional Cash Transfer on the Wellbeing of Mexican Youths." Background paper for the WDR 2007.

Haan, Hans Christiaan, and Nicholas Serriere. 2002. *Training for Work in the Informal Sector: Fresh Evidence from West and Central Africa*. Turin: International Training Centre of the International Labour Organization. Available online at http://siteresources.worldbank.org/INTLM/214578-1103217503703/20295542/TrainingforWorkWCA.pdf.

Haggblade, Steven, Peter B. R. Hazell, and Thomas Reardon. (eds.) Forthcoming. "*Transforming the Rural Nonfarm Economy*." Baltimore, MD: John Hopkins University Press.

Hagopian, Amy, Anthony Ofosu, Adesegun Fatusi, Richard Biritwum, Ama Essel, L. Gary Hart, and Carolyn Watts. 2005. "The Flight of Physicians from West Africa: Views of African Physicians and Implications for Policy." *Social Science & Medicine* 61(8):1750–60.

Hahn, Andrew. 1999. "Extending the Time of Learning." *In* Douglas J. Besharov, (eds.), *Americua's Disconnected Youth: Towards a Preventive Strategy*. Washington, DC: Child Welfare League of America Inc.

Hahn, Andrew, Susan Lanspery, and Tom Leavitt. 2005. *Documentation of Outcomes in the Philippines Make A Connection Program*. Baltimore, MD: International Youth Foundation and Nokia Corporation.

Hahn, Andrew, and Tom Leavitt. 2003. *Joined-Up Government. Coordination and Collaboration Opportunities to Strengthen Multi-Sectoral Youth Policy Implementation in Jamaica*. Washington, DC: World Bank.

Hahn, Andrew, Tom Leavitt, and Paul Aaron. 1994. *Evaluation of the Quantum Opportunities Program: Did the Program Work?* Waltham, MA: Brandeis University. Available online at http://eric.ed.gov/ERICDocs/data/ericdocs2/content_storage_01/0000000b/80/27/39/7a.pdf.

Hahn, Carole L, Paulette Patterson Dilworth, and Michael Hughes. 1998. *IEA Civic Education Project, Phase 1, The United States - A Review of Literature, Volume 1*. Washington, DC: International Association for the Evaluation of Educational Achievement.

Hahn, Carole L. 2005. "School Influences and Civic Engagement." *In* Lonnie R. Sherrod, Constance A. Flanagan, Ron Kassimir, and Amy K. Syvertsen, (eds.), *Youth Activism: An International Encyclopedia*. Westport, CT: Greenwood Publishing Group.

Halewood, Naomi, and Charles Kenny. 2006. "Young People and Communications Technologies." Background paper for the WDR 2007.

Hallman, Kelly, Agnes R. Quisumbing, Marie Ruel, and Bénédicte de la Briere. 2005. "Mothers' Work and Child Care: Findings from the Urban Slums of Guatemala City." *Economic Development and Cultural Change* 53(4):855–86.

Halpern-Felsher, Bonnie L., and Elizabeth Cauffman. 2001. "Costs and Benefits of a Decision: Decision-making Competence in Adolescents and Adults." *Journal of Applied Developmental Psychology* 22(3):257–73.

Hannam, Derry. 2001. *A Pilot Study to Evaluate the Impact of Student Participation Aspects of the Citizenship Order on Standards of Education in Secondary Schools*. London, U.K.: DFEE. Available online at http://www.csv.org.uk/csv/hannamreport.pdf.

Hanushek, Eric A., and Dennis D. Kimko. 2000. "Schooling, Labor Force Quality, and the Growth of Nations." *American Economic Review* 90(5):1184–208.

Hanushek, Eric A., and Ludger Wößmann. 2005. "Does Educational Tracking Affect Performance and Inequality? Differences-in-Differences Evidence Across Countries." Cambridge, MA: National Bureau of Economic Research Working Paper Series 11124.

Harrington, Julia. 2005. "Voiding Human Rights: Citizenship and Discrimination in Africa." *Justice Initiatives: Human Rights and Justice Sector Reform in Africa* February:23–28.

Hart, Jason. 2004. *Children's Participation in Humanitarian Action: Learning from Zones of Armed Conflict*. Oxford: Refugees Studies Center.

Hatton, Timothy J., and Jeffrey G. Williamson. 2003. "Demographic and Economic Pressure on Emigration out of Africa." *Scandinavian Journal of Economics* 105(3):465–486.

———. 2005. "What Fundamentals Drive World Migration?" *In* George J. Borjas and Jeff Crips, (eds.), *Poverty, International Migration and Asylum*. New York, NY: Palgrave MacMillan.

Hazell, Peter B. R., and Steven Haggblade. 1993. "Farm-Nonfarm Growth Linkages and the Welfare of the Poor." *In* Michael Lipton and Jacques Van der Gaag, (eds.), *Including the Poor*. Washington, DC: World Bank.

Heady, Christopher. 2003. "What is the Effect of Child Labour on Learning Achievement? Evidence from Ghana." Florence, Italy: Innocenti Working Papers inwopa00/7.

Health and Treasury Task Team. 2003. *Full Report of the Joint Health and Treasury Task Team Charged with Examining Treatment Options to Supplement Comprehensive Care for HIV/AIDS in the Public Health Sector*. South Africa: Ministry of Health & Ministry of Treasury.

Heckman, James J., Robert J. LaLonde, and Jeffrey A. Smith. 1999. "The Economics and Econometrics of Active Labor Market Programs." *In* Orley Ashenfelter and David Card, (eds.), *Handbook of Labor Economics, vol. 3A*. Amsterdam: North-Holland.

Heckman, James J., and Xuesong Li. 2004. "Selection Bias, Comparative Advantage and Heterogeneous Returns to Education: Evidence from China in 2000." *Pacific Economic Review* 9(3):155–71.

Heckman, James J., and Carmen Pagés. 2000. "Regulation and Deregulation: Lessons from Latin American Labor Markets." *Economía* 1(1):123–45.

Heckman, James J., Jeffrey A. Smith, and Nancy Clements. 1997. "Making the Most out of Social Experiments: The Intrinsic Uncertainty in Evidence from Randomized Trials with an Application to the National JTPA Experiment." *Review of Economic Studies* 64(4):487–535.

Heckman, James J., Jora Stixrud, and Sergio Urzua. 2006. "The Effects of Cognitive and Noncognitive Abilities on Labor Market Outcomes and Social Behavior." Cambridge, MA: National Bureau of Economic Research Working Paper Series 12006.

Hediger, M. L., T. O. Scholl, J. I. Schall, and P. M. Krueger. 1997. "Young Maternal Age and Preterm Labour." *Annals of Epidemiology* 7(6):400–6.

Hegre, Håvard. 2003. "Disentangling Democracy and Development as Determinants of Armed Conflict." Paper presented at the 44th Annual Convention of the International Studies Association. February 25. Portland, O.R.

Hemmer, Hans R., and C. Mannel. 1989. "On the Economic Analysis of the Urban Informal Sector." *World Development* 17(10):1543–52.

Hettige, S. T., Markus Mayer, and Maleeka Salih. 2004. "School-to-work Transition of Youth in Sri Lanka." Colombo: University of Colombo, Employment Policies Unit, Employment Strategy Department, Employment Strategy Paper 2004/19. Available online at http://www.ilo.org/public/english/employment/strat/download/esp19.pdf.

Hibbell, Björn, Barboro Anderson, Salme Ahlström, Olga Balakireva, Thoroddur Bjarnason, Anna Kokkevi, and Mark Morgan. 2000. *The 1999 ESPAD Report: Alcohol and Other Drug Use Among Students in 30 European Countries*. Stockholm: The Swedish Council for Information on Alcohol and Other Drugs (CAN) and the Pompidou Group at the Council of Europe.

Hildebrandt, Nicole, and David J. McKenzie. 2005. "The Effects of Migration on Child Health in Mexico." *Economia* 6(1):257–89.

Hirsch, Barry T., and Stephen L. Mehay. 2003. "Evaluating the Labor Market Performance of Veterans Using a Matched Comparison Group Design." *Journal of Human Resources* 38(3):673–700.

Hodgkin, Dominic. 1996. "Household Characteristics Affecting Where Mothers Deliver in Rural Kenya." *Health Economics* 5(4):333–40.

Hoff, Karla, and Priyanka Pandey. 2004. "Belief Systems and Durable Inequalities: An Experimental Investigation of Indian Caste." Washington, DC: World Bank Policy Research Working Paper Series 3351.

Hofferth, Sandra L., and Lori Reid. 2001. "The Effects of Early Childbearing on Schooling Over Time." *Family Planning Perspectives,* 33(6):259–67.

Hoffman, Saul D. 1998. "Teenage Childbearing Is Not So Bad After All. Or is it? A Review of the New Literature." *Family Planning Perspectives* 30(5):236–39.

Holzmann, Robert. 2005. "Demographic Alternatives for Aging Industrial Societies: Enhanced Immigration, Labor Force Participation, or Total Fertility." Washington, DC: World Bank, Social Protection Discussion Paper 0540.

Hooghe, Marc, Deitlind Stolle, and Patrick Stouthuysen. 2004. "Head Start in Politics: The Recruitment Function of Youth Organizations of Political Parties in Belgium (Flanders)." *Party Politics* 10(2):193–212.

Hopenhayn, Hugo, and Richard Rogerson. 1993. "Job Turnover and Policy Evaluation: A General Equilibrium Analysis." *Journal of Political Economy* 101(5):915–38.

Howell, James C. 1998. "Abolish the Juvenile Court? Nonsense!" *Juvenile Justice Update* 1:1–13.

Hubley, J. 2000. *Interventions Targeted at Youth Aimed at Influencing Sexual Behavior and AIDS/STDs*. Leeds, U.K.: Leeds Health Education Database.

Hubner, John. 2005. *Last Chance in Texas: The Redemption of Criminal Youth*. New York, NY: Random House.

Hudson, Valerie M., and Andrea M. den Boer. 2004. *Bare Branches: The Security Implications of Asia's Surplus Male Population*. Cambridge, MA: The MIT Press.

Huffman, W. E., and Peter F. Orazem. 2004. "Agriculture and Human Capital in Economic Growth: Farmers, Schooling and Health." Ames, Iowa: Iowa State University, Economics Working Papers 04016.

Human Rights Watch. 1997a. *Juvenile Justice: Police Abuse and Detention of Street Children in Kenya*. New York, NY: Human Rights Watch.

———. 1997b. *The Scars of Death: Children Abducted by the Lord's Resistance Army in Uganda*. New York, NY: Human Rights Watch.

———. 2001a. *Easy Targets: Violence Against Children Worldwide*. New York, NY: Human Rights Watch.

———. 2001b. *Scared at School: Sexual Violence against Girls in South African Schools*. New York, NY: Human Rigths Watch. Available online at http://www.hrw.org/reports/2001/safrica/.

———. 2002a. *My Gun was as Tall as Me*. New York, NY: Human Rights Watch.

———. 2002b. *Suffering in Silence: The Links Between Human Rights Abuses and HIV Transmission to Girls in Zambia*. New York, NY: Human Rights Watch.

———. 2003. *Charged with Being Children: Egyptian Police Abuse of Children in Need of Protection*. New York, NY: Human Rights Watch.

Humphreys, Macartan, and Paul Richards. 2005. "Prospects and Opportunities for Achieving the MDGs in Post-Conflict Countries: A Case Study of Sierra Leone and Liberia." NEPAD. New York, NY Available online at http://www.columbia.edu/~mh2245/papers1/HR.pdf. Processed.

Humphreys, Macartan, and Jeremy M. Weinstein. 2003. *What the Fighters Say: A Survey of Ex-Combatants in Sierra Leone June-August 2003*. Freetown, Sierra Leone: The Post-Conflict Reintegration Initiative for development and Empowerment (PRIDE).

———. 2005. "Disentangling the Determinants of Successful Disarmament, Demobilization, and Reintegration." Paper presented at the 101st Meeting of the American Political Science Association. September. Washington, DC

Hurley, Susan F., Damien J. Jolley, and John M. Kaldor. 1997. "Effectiveness of Needle Exchange Programmes for Prevention of HIV Infection." *Lancet* 349(9068):1797–800.

Ilahi, Nadeem, Peter F. Orazem, and Guilherme Sedlacek. 2005. "How Does Working as a Child Affect Wages, Income and Poverty as an Adult?" Washington, DC: World Bank, Social Protection Discussion Paper Series 0514.

ILO. 2001. *World Employment Report 2001: Life at Work in the Information Economy*. Geneva: International Labour Office.

———. 2003. *Wounded Childhood: The Use of Children in Armed Conflict in Central Africa*. Geneva: International Labour Office.

———. 2004. *Global Employment Trends for Youth*. Geneva: International Labour Office.

———. 2005. *Global Youth Employment Trends*. Geneva: International Labour Office.

———. 2006. *The End of Child Labour: Within Reach*. Geneva: International Labour Office. Available online at http://www.ilo.org/public/english/standards/relm/ilc/ilc95/pdf/rep-i-b.pdf.

Imbens, Guido, and Wilbert Van Der Klaauw. 1995. "Evaluating the Cost of Conscription in The Netherlands." *Journal of Business and Economic Statistics* 13(2):207–215.

Inglehart, Ronald, Miguel Basáñez, Jaime Díez-Medrano, Loek Halman, and Ruud Luijkx, eds. 2004. *Human Beliefs and Values: A Cross-cultural Sourcebook based on the 1999-2002 Values Surveys*. Mexico, D.F.: Siglo Veinteiuno.

Institute for Health Management-Pachod (IHMP), and International Center for Research On Women (ICRW). 2003. *Increasing Low Age at Marriage in Rural Maharashtra, India*. Maharashtra, India: Institute for Health Management. Available online at http://www2.phishare.org/files/1046_IHMP_marriagebrief_Dec2003.pdf.

Institute of Alcohol Studies. 2006. *Adolescents and Alcohol*. St. Ives: Institute of Alcohol Studies.

Instituto Mexicano de la Juventud (IMJ), and Organización Iberoamericana de la Juventud (OIJ). 2006. *Institucionalidad y Políticas Públicas de Juventud*. Mexico City: Instituto Mexicano de la Juventud por encargo y con la colaboración de la Organización Iberoamericana de la Juventud.

Instituto Nacional para la Evaluación de la Educación de Mexico. 2005. "Las Telesecundarias Mexicanas: Un Recorrido sin Atajos." *Online Magazine*.

Inter-American Development Bank. 2005. *Ex-post Evaluation of Training Programs 'Youth Labor Training Program' (PROJOVEN) in PERU. Ex-Post Project Report. Preliminary version*. Washington, DC: Inter-American Development Bank. Available online at http://www.iadb.org/ove/Documents/uploads/cache/498982.pdf.

Interagency Gender Working Group. 2005. *An Education in Making Schools Safe*. Washington, DC: Interagency Gender Working Group. Available online at http://www.igwg.org/articles/safe-schools.htm.

International Center for Prison Studies. 2003. "World Prison Brief". London, UK, King's College London, University of London. Available online at http://www.kcl.ac.uk/depsta/rel/icps/worldbrief/world_brief.html.

International Council on National Youth Policy. 2005. *ICNYP Profiles on Country Actions to Promote Implementation of National Youth Policies*. Vienna: International Council on National Youth Policy (ICNYP). Available online at http://www.icnyp.net.

International Institute for Population Sciences (IIPS), and ORC Macro. 2000. *National Family Health Survey (NFHS-2), 1998-99, India*. Mumbai: IIPS.

International Nutritional Anemia Consultative Group. 1979. *Iron Deficiency in Infancy and Childhood*. Geneva: World Health Organization.

———. 1989. *Iron Deficiency in Women*. Geneva: World Health Organization.

International Organization for Migration (IOM). 2005a. *HIV/AIDS, Population Mobility and Migration in Southern Africa: Defining a Research and Policy Agenda*. South Africa: IOM South Africa Office. Available online at http://www.iom.org.za/Reports/PopulationMobilityReport.pdf.

———. 2005b. *World Migration 2005: Costs and Benefits of International Migration*. Geneva: International Organization for Migration.

International Telecommunication Union (ITU). 2005. *The African Virtual University*. Geneva: International Telecommunication Union. Available online at http://www.itu.int/osg/spu/wsis-themes/ict_stories/Themes/Case_studies/AVU.html .

Internet Safety Group. 2005. *New Survey Illustrate the Profound Impact of Mobile Phones on Many New Zealand Youth.* Auckland, New Zealand: Internet Safety Group. Available online at http://www.netsafe.org.nz/isgnews/text_generation.aspx.

Isham, Jonathan, Daniel Kaufmann, and Lant Pritchett. 1995. "Governance and Project Performance." Washington, DC: World Bank Policy Research Working Paper Series 1550.

Iversen, Vegard. 2002. "Autonomy of Child Labor Migrants." *World Development* 30(5):817–34.

Jacob, Brian A., and Lars Lefgren. 2002. "The Impact of Teacher Training on Student Achievement: Quasi-Experimental Evidence from School Reform Efforts in Chicago." Cambridge, MA: National Bureau of Economic Research Working Paper Series 8916.

Jacobson, Mireille. 2004. "Baby Booms and Drug Busts: Trends in Youth Drug Use in the United States: 1975-2000." *Quarterly Journal of Economics* 119(4):1481–512.

Jacoby, Hanan G., and Emannuel Skoufias. 2002. "Financial Constraints on Higher Education: Evidence from Mexico." World Bank and IFPRI. Washington, DC. Processed.

James-Traore, Tijuana, Robert Magnani, Nancy Murray, Judith Senderowitz, Ilene Speizer, and Lindsay Steward. 2002. "Intervention Strategies that Work for Youth: Summary of the FOCUS on Young Adults End of Program Report." Arlington, VA: Family Health International, YouthNet Program, Youth Issues Paper 1. Available online at http://www.fhi.org/.

Japan Bank for International Cooperation. 2006. "Meeting the Increasing and Changing Demand for Quality Labor in FDI-led Growth: From Adaptability to Creativity." Japan Bank for International Cooperation (JBIC). Tokyo. Processed.

Javate de Dios, Aurora. 2002. "From the Margins to the Mainstream: Making Government Work for Gender Equality." Paper presented at the ASEAN-World Bank High Level Conference on Social Development in the National Development. January 16. Jakarta.

Jejeebhoy, Shireen J., and Sarah Bott. 2003. "Non-consensual Sexual Experiences of Young People: A Review of the Evidence from Developing Countries." New Delhi: Populaiton Council South & East Asia Regional Working Papers 16.

Jennings, Kent M, and Laura Stoker. 2002. "Generational Change, Life Cycle Processes, and Social Capital." Paper presented at the Workshop on "Citizenship on Trial: Interdisciplinary Perspectives on the Political Socialization of Adolescents". June 20. Montreal, Canada.

Jensen, Robert. 2006. "Do the Perceived Returns to Education Affect Schooling Decisions? Evidence from a Randomized Experiment." John F. Kennedy School of Government, Harvard University. Cambridge, MA. Processed.

Jensen, Robert, and Rebecca Thornton. 2003. "Early Female Marriage in the Developing World." *Gender and Development* 11(2):9–19.

Jha, Prabhat, and Frank Chaloupka, eds. 2000. *Tobacco Control in Developing Countries.* New York: Oxford University Press.

Jha, Prabhat, Frank J. Chaloupka, James Moore, Vendhan Gajalakshmi, Prakash C. Gupta, Richard Peck, Samira Asma, and Witold Zatonski. 2005. "Tobacco Addiction." *In* Dean T. Jamision, David B. Evans, George Alleyne, Prabhat Jha, Joel G. Breman, Anthony R. Measham, Mariam Claeson, Anne Mills, and Philip R. Musgrove, (eds.), *Disease Control Priorities in Developing Countries.* Bethesda, MD: Disease Control Priorities Project.

Jha, Prabhat, Lara M. E. Vaz, Francis A. Plummer, Nico J. D. Nagelkerke, Bridget Willbond, Elizabeth N. Ngugi, Stephen

Moses, Grace John, Ruth Nduati, Kelly MacDonald, and Seth Berkley. 2001. "The Evidence Base for Interventions to Prevent HIV Infection in Low and Middle-Income Countries." Geneva: Commission on Macroeconomics and Health Working Paper Series WG 5 Paper 2.

Jimenez, Emmanuel. 1995. "Human and Physical Infrastructure: Public Investment and Pricing Policies in Developing Countries." *In* J. R. Behrman and T. N. Srinivasan, (eds.), *Handbook of Development Economics vol. 3.* Amsterdarm: Elsevier.

Jimenez, Emmanuel, and Marlaine E. Lockheed. 1989. "Enhanching Girls' Learning Through Single-Sex Education: Evidence and a Policy Conundrum." *Educational Evaluation and Policy Analysis* 11(2):117–42.

Jimenez, Emmanuel, and Yasuyuki Sawada. 1999. "Do Community-Managed Schools Work? An Evaluation of El Salvador's EDUCO Program." *World Bank Economic Review* 13(3):415–41.

Jimeno, Juan F., and Diego Rodríguez-Palenzuela. 2002. "Youth Unemployment in the OECD: Demographic Shifts, Labour Market Institutions, and Macroeconomic Shocks." Frankfurt: European Central Bank, Working Paper Series 155.

Joekes, Susan. 1995. "Trade- Related Employment for Women in Industry and Services in Developing Countries." New York, NY: United Nations Development Program, Occasional Paper 5. Available online at http://www.unrisd.org/.

Johanson, Richard K., and Arvil V. Adams. 2004. *Skills Development in Sub-Saharan Africa.* Washington, DC: World Bank.

Johnson, Amy W. 1996. "An Evaluation of the Long-Term Impacts of the Sponsor-A-Scholar Program on Student Performance." Mathematica Policy Research, Inc. Princeton, NJ. Processed.

Johnson, D. Gale. 2000. "Population, Food, and Knowledge." *American Economic Review* 90(1):1–14.

Jorgenson, Dale W. Forthcoming. "Accounting for Growth in the Information Age." *In* Philippe Aghion and Steven Durlauf (eds.) *Handbook of Economic Growth.* Amsterdam: North-Holland.

Joshi, Shareen, and Paul Schultz. 2005. "Family Planning as an Investment in Female Human Capital: Evaluating the Long Term Consequences in Matlab, Bangladesh." Yale University. New Haven, CT. Processed.

Jowett, Matthew. 2000. "Safe Motherhood Interventions in Low-income Countries: An Economic Justification and Evidence of Cost Effectiveness." *Health Policy* 53(3):201–28.

Kabbani, Nader, and Ekta Kothari. 2005. "Youth Employment in the MENA Region: A Situational Assessment." Washington, DC: World Bank SP Discussion Paper 0534.

Kabeer, Naila. 1999. "Resources, Agency, Achievements: Reflections on the Measurement of Women's Empowerment." *Development and Change* 30(3):435–64.

Kagitcibasi, Cigdem, Diane Sunar, and Sevda Bekman. 2001. "Long-term Effects of Early Intervention: Turkish Low-Income Mothers and Children." *Applied Developmental Pshychology* 22:333–61.

Kalemli-Ozcan, Sebnem. 2001. "The Effect of Mortality on Fertility and Human Capital Investment: What Do We Learn from AIDS?" University of Houston. Houston. Processed.

———. 2005. "AIDS, Reversal of the Demographic Transition and Economic Development: Evidence from Africa." University of Houston and NBER. Houston. Processed.

Kandel, William, and Grace Kao. 2001. "The Impact of Temporary Labor Migration on Mexican Children's Educational Aspirations and Performance." *International Migration Review* 35(4):1205–1231.

Kantis, H., eds. 2003. *Estudios de Desarrollo Empresarial en Argentina: La Creación de Empresas y su Entorno Institucional.* Buenos Aires: JICA.

Kassouf, Ana Lucia, Martin McKee, and Elias Mossialos. 2001. "Early Entrance to the Job Market and its Effect on Adult Health: Evidence from Brazil." *Health Policy and Planning* 16(1):21–28.

Kaufman, C. E., T. de Wet, and J. Stadler. 2001. "Adolescent Pregnancy and Parenthood in South Africa." *Studies in Family Planning* 32(2):147–60.

Kaufman, Carol E., and Stavros E. Stavrou. 2004. "Bus Fare, Please: The Economics of Sex and Gifts Among Adolescents in Urban South Africa." *Culture, Health and Sexuality* 6(5):377–91.

Kaushik, Basu, and Zafiris Tzannatos. 2003. "The Global Child Labor Problem: What Do We Know and What Can We Do?" *World Bank Economic Review* 17(2):147–73.

Kemple, James J., and Judith Scott-Clayton. 2004. *Career Academies: Impacts on Labor Market Outcomes and Educational Attainment.* New York: Manpower Demonstration Research Corporation (MDRC).

Kenkel, Donald S. 2000. "Prevention." *In* Anthony J. Culyer and Joseph P. Newhouse, (eds.), *Handbook of Health Economics.* Amsterdam: Elsevier.

Kessler, Ronald C., Cindy L. Foster, William B. Saunders, and Paul E. Stang. 1995. "Social Consequences of Psychiatric Disorders I: Educational Attainment." *American Journal of Psychiatry* 152(7):1026–32.

Khan, Ayesha. 1998. *Female Mobility and Social Barriers to Accessing Health and Family Planning Services: A Qualitative Research Study in Three Punjabi Villages.* Islamabad: Ministry for Population Welfare.

Khandker, Shahidur R. 2005. "Microfinance and Poverty: Evidence Using Panel Data from Bangladesh." *World Bank Economic Review* 19(2):263–86.

Khandker, Shahidur R., Mark M. Pitt, and Nobuhiko Fuwa. 2003. "Subsidy to Promote Girls' Secondary Education: The Female Stipend Program in Bangladesh." World Bank. Washington, DC. Processed.

Kibria, Nazli. 1995. "Culture, Social Class, and Income Control in the Lives of Women Garment Workers in Bangladesh." *Gender and Society* 9(3):289–309.

Kijima, Yoko, and Peter Lanjouw. 2004. "Non-farm Employment, Agricultural Wage, and Poverty Trends in Rural India." World Bank. Washington, DC. Processed.

Kim, Gwang-Jo. 2002. "Education Policies and Reform in South Korea." *In* World Bank, (eds.), *Secondary Education in Africa: Strategies for Renewal.* Washington, DC: World Bank.

King, Elizabeth M. 2005. "Schemes to Acknowledge the Value of Daughters in India." World Bank. Washington, DC. Processed.

Kinkade, Sheila, and Christina Macy. 2005. *Our Time is Now: Young People Changing the World.* New York, NY: Pearson Foundation.

Kirby, Douglas. 2001. *Emerging Answers: Research Findings on Programs to Reduce Teen Pregnancy.* Washington, DC: National Campaign to Prevent Teen Pregnancy.

Kirby, Douglas, B. A. Laris, and Lori Rolleri. 2005. "Impact of Sex and HIV Education Programs on Sexual Behaviors of Youth in Developing and Developed Countries." Research Triangle Park, N.C.: Family Health International, Youth Research Working Paper 2.

Kirby, Douglas, Gina Lepore, and Jennifer Ryan. 2005. *A Matrix of Risk and Protective Factors Affecting Teen Sexual Behavior, Pregnancy, Childbearing and Sexually Transmitted Diseases.* Washington, DC: National Campaign to Prevent Teen Pregnancy. Available online at http://www.etr.org/recapp/theories/RiskProtectiveFactors/Matrix_Kirby.pdf.

Kleiner, Morris M. 2000. "Occupational Licensing." *Journal of Economics Perspectives* 14(4):189–202.

Klepinger, Daniel, Shelly Lundberg, and Robert Plotnick. 1997. "How Does Adolescent Fertility Affect the Human Capital and Wages of Young Women?" Madison, Wisconsin: Institute for Research on Poverty, University of Wisconsin, Discussion Paper 1145-97.

Kluve, Jochen. 2006. "The Effectiveness of European Active Labor Market Policy." Bonn: Institute for Labor Policies (IZA), Discussion Paper 2018.

Knight, John B., and Richard H. Sabot. 1990. *Education, Productivity, and Inequality: The East African Natural Experiment.* Washington, DC: World Bank.

Knowles, James, and Jere R. Behrman. 2003. *Assessing the Economic Returns to Investing in Youth in Developing Countries.* Washington, DC: World Bank, HNP Discussion Paper.

Knowles, James C., and Jere R. Behrman. 2005. "The Economic Returns to Investing in Youth in Developing Countries: A Review of the Literature." Washington, DC: World Bank: Health, Nutrition, and Population Discussion Paper January 2005.

Knudsen, Eric I. 2004. "Sensitive Periods in the Development of the Brain and Behavior." *Journal of Cognitive Neuroscience* 16(8):1412–25.

Köbrich, Claus, and Martine Dirven. 2006. "Características del Empleo Rural no Agrícola en America Latina con Enfasis en los Servicios." ECLAC. Santiago de Chile. Processed.

Kohlberg, Lawrence. 1973. "The Claim to Moral Adequacy of a Highest Stage of Moral Judgment." *Journal of Philosophy* 70(18):630–46.

Konde-Lule, J. K., N. Sewankambo, and M. Morris. 1997. "Adolescent Sexual Networking and HIV Transmission in Rural Uganda." *Health Transition Review* 7(Suppl):89–100.

Koplan, Jeffrey P., Catharyn T. Liverman, and Vivica I. Kraak, eds. 2005. *Preventing Childhood Obesity: Health in the Balance.* Washington, DC: The National Academies Press. Available online at http://www.nap.edu/catalog/11015.html.

Korenman, Sanders, and David Neumark. 2000. "Cohort Crowding and Youth Labor Markets: A Cross-National Analysis." *In* David G. Blanchflower and Richard B. Freeman, (eds.), *Youth Employment and Joblessness in Advanced Countries.* Chicago and London: University of Chicago Press for the National Bureau of Economic Research.

Kremer, Michael, and Dan M. Levy. 2003. "Peer Effects and Alcohol Use Among College Students." Cambridge, MA: National Bureau of Economic Research Working Paper Series 9876.

Kremer, Michael, Edward Miguel, and Rebecca Thornton. 2004. "Sensitive Periods in the Development of the Brain and Behavior." Cambridge, MA: National Bureau of Economic Research Working Paper Series 10971.

Kriger, Norma. 2005. "ZANU(PF) Strategies in General Elections, 1980-2000: Discourse and Coercion." *African Affairs* 104(414):1–34.

Krug, Etienne G., Linda L. Dahlberg, James A. Mercy, Anthony B. Zwi, and Rafael Lozano. 2002. *World Report on Violence and Health.* Geneva, Switzerland: World Health Organization.

Kugler, Adriana D. 2004. "The Effect of Job Security Regulations on Labor Market Flexibility: Evidence from the Colombian Labor Market Reform." *In* James J. Heckman and Carmen Pagés, (eds.), *Law and Employment: Lessons from Latin America and the Caribbean.* Chicago and London: The University of Chicago Press.

Kugler, Adriana D., Juan F. Jimeno, and Virginia Hernanz. 2003. "Employment Consequences of Restrictive Permanent Contracts." London: Centre for Economic Policy Research Discussion Paper 3724.

Kuku, Yemisi, Peter F. Orazem, and Rajesh Singh. 2005. "Computer Adoption and Returns in Transition." Ames, Iowa: Iowa State University Economics Working Paper 04021.

Kurz, Kathleen M., Nancy L. Peplinsky, and Charlotte Johnson-Welch. 1994. *Investing in the Future: Six Principles for Promoting the Nutritional Status of Adolescent Girls in Developing Countries.* Washington, DC: International Center for Research on Women.

Kutan, Ali M., and Kostas Drakos. 2003. "Regional Effects of Terrorism on Tourism." *Journal of Conflict Resolution* 47(5):621–641.

Kymlicka, Will. 2001. *Politics in the Vernacular: Nationalism, Multiculturalism, and Citizenship.* New York, NY: Oxford University Press.

La Cava, Gloria, Zeynep Ozbil, Sarah Michael, Elena Galliano, Minna Mattero, and Mio Takada. 2006. "Youth and the Transition to Citizenship: The Role of the State in Promoting Positive Youth Religious and Ethnic Identities and Young People's Role in Peace-Building and Social Change." Background paper for the WDR 2007.

Lam, David. 2006. "The Demography of Youth in Developing Countries and its Economic Implications." Background paper for the WDR 2007.

Lanjouw, Peter, and Nicholas Stern. 2006. *Economic Development in Palanpur Over Five Decades.* New York: Oxford University Press.

Lansdown, R., A. Ledward, A. Hall, W. Issae, E. Yona, J. Matulu, M. Mweta, C. Kihamia, U. Nyandindi, and D. Bundy. 2002. "Schistosomiasis, Helminth Infection and Health Education in Tanzania: Achieving Behavior Change in Primary Schools." *Health Education Research* 17(4):425–33.

Lasida, Javier, and Ernesto Rodríguez. 2006. "Entrando al Mundo de Trabajo: Resultados de Seis Proyectos Entra 21." Baltimore, MD: International Youth Foundation, Serie de Aprendizaje 2.

Latimer, Jeff, Craig Dowden, and Danielle Muise. 2001. *The Effectiveness of Restorative Justice Practices: A Meta-Analysis.* Canada: Research and Statistics Division, Department of Justice.

Lautrédou, Gérard. 2005. "Viet Nam: A Tale of Two Cities." *The Magazine of the International Red Cross and Red Crescent Movement.*

Lavinas, Lena, Maria Lígia Barbosa, and Octávio Tourinho. 2001. *Assessing Local Minimum Income Programmes in Brazil: ILO-World Bank Agreement.* Geneva: International Labour Office. Available online at http://www-ilo-mirror.cornell.edu/public/english/protection/ses/download/docs/2brazil.pdf.

Lavy, V., and A. Schlosser. 2005. "Targeted Remedial Education for Underperforming Teenagers: Costs and Benefits." *Journal of Labor Economics* 23(4):839–74.

Lavy, Victor. 1996. "School Supply Constraints and Children's Educational Outcomes in Rural Ghana." *Journal of Development Economics* 51(2):291–314.

———. 2002. "Evaluating the Effect of Teachers' Group Performance Incentives on Pupil Achievement." *Journal of Political Economy* 110(6):1286–317.

Lazear, Edward. 2001. "Educational Production." *Quarterly Journal of Economics* 116(3):777–803.

Lazear, Edward P. 1983. "A Competitive Theory of Monopoly Unionism." *American Economic Review* 73(4):631–43.

Lee, Jong-Wha, and Changyong Rhee. 1999. "Social Impacts of the Asian Crisis: Policy Challenges and Lessons." New York: UNDP Occasional Paper 33.

Lee, Lena, and Poh Kam Wong. 2005. "Entrepreneurship Education - A Compendium of Related Issues." Singapore: SSRN Electronic Paper Collection Available online at http://ssrn.com/abstract=856227.

Leff, Nathaniel H. 1969. "Dependency Rates and Saving Rates." *American Economic Review* 59(5):886–96.

Leopold, Evelyn. 2001. "Congolese Kids Face Horrific Conditions." *Reuters*, June 17.

Lesthaeghe, R., and G. Moors. 2000. "Recent Trends in Fertility and Household Formation in the Industrialized World." *Review of Population and Social Policy* 9:121–70.

Levine, Saul. 1999. "Youth in Terrorist Groups, Gangs, and Cults: The Allure, the Animus, and the Alienation." *Psychiatric Annals* 29(6):342–49.

Levison, Deborah, Karine S. Moe, and Felicia M. Knaul. 2001. "Youth Education and Work in Mexico." *World Development* 29(1):167–88.

Levitt, Steven D. 1998. "Juvenile Crime and Punishment." *Journal of Political Economy* 106(6):1156–1187.

———. 1999. "The Limited Role of Changing Age Structure in Explaining Aggregate Crime Rates." *Criminology* 37(3):581–98.

Levitt, Steven D., and Lance Lochner. 2001. "The Determinants of Juvenile Crime." *In* Jonathan Gruber, (eds.), *Risky Behavior among Youths: An Economic Analysis.* Chicago, IL: University of Chicago Press for the National Bureau of Economic Research.

Levy, Frank, and Richard Murnane. 2004. *The New Division of Labor: How Computers Are Creating the Next Job Market.* Princeton, NJ: Princeton University Press.

Levy, Santiago, and Evelyne Rodríguez. 2004. *Economic Crisis, Political Transition and Poverty Policy Reform.* Washington, DC: Inter-American Development Bank, Regional Operations Department II. Policy Dialogue Series.

Li, R., X. Chen, Yan.H., P. Deurenberg, L. Garby, and J. G. Hautvast. 1994. "Functional Consequences of Iron Supplementation in Iron-deficient Female Cotton Mill Workers in Beijing, China." *American Journal of Clinical Nutrition* 59(4):908–13.

Liang, Gui. 2005. *The CASS Internet Survey Report 2005: Surveying Internet Use and Impact in 5 Chinese Cities.* Beijing: Chinese Academy of Social Sciences. Available online at http://www.worldinternetproject.net/publishedarchive/China%20Report%202005.pdf.

Lillard, Lee A., and Robert J. Willis. 1994. "Intergenerational Educational Mobility: Effects of Family and State in Malaysia." *Journal of Human Resources* 29(4):1126–66.

Lindert, Peter H. 2003. "Voice and Growth: Was Churchill Right." *Journal of Economic History* 63(2):315–50.

Llisterri, J., H. Kantis, P. Angelelli, and L. Tejerina. 2006. "Youth Entrepreneurship in Latin America, Inter-American Development Bank Forthcoming." Background paper for the WDR 2007.

Llorente, María Victoria, and Angela Rivas. 2005. "Case Study: Reduction of Crime in Bogota: A Decade of Citizen's Security Policies." Washington, DC: World Bank Working Paper Series 35128.

Lloyd, Cynthia B. 2003. "The Impact of Educational Quality on School Exit in Egypt." *Comparative Education Review* 47(4):444–67.

Lloyd, Cynthia B., and Monica J. Grant. 2004. "Growing Up in Pakistan: The Separate Experiences of Males and Females." New York: Population Council, Policy Research Division, Working Paper Series 188.

Lloyd, Cynthia B., Barbara S. Mensch, and Wesley H. Clark. 2000. "The Effects of Primary School Quality on School Dropout Among Kenyan Girls and Boys." *Comparative Education Review* 44(2):113–47.

Lochner, Lance, and Enrico Moretti. 2004. "The Effect of Education on Crime: Evidence from Prison Inmates, Arrests, and Self-Reports." *American Economic Review* 94(1):155–89.

Loevinsohn, Benjamin P. 1990. "Health Education Intervention in Developing Countries: A Methodological Review of Published Articles." *International Journal of Epidemiology* 19(4):788–94.

Lokshin, Michael, Elena Glinskaya, and Marito Garcia. 2004. "The Effect of Early Childhood Development Programs on Women's Labor Force Participation and Older Children's Schooling in Kenya." *Journal of African Economies* 13(2):240–76.

Lokshin, Michael, and Ruslan Yemtsov. 2005. "Who Bears the Cost of Russia's Military Draft?" Washington, DC: World Bank Policy Research Working Paper 3547.

Longhi, Simonetta, Peter Nijkamp, and Jacques Poot. 2005. "A Meta-analytic Assessment of the Effect of Immigration on Wages." *Journal of Economic Surveys* 19(3):451–77.

López, Alan D., Colin D. Mathers, Majad Ezzati, Dean T. Jamison, and Christopher J. L. Murray, eds. 2006. *Global Burden of Disease and Risk Factors.* Washington, DC: World Bank and Oxford University Press.

Lucas, Gregory M., Laura W. Cheever, Richard E. Chaisson, and Richard D. Moore. 2001. "Detrimental Effects of Continued Illicit Drug Use on the Treatment of HIV-1 Infection." *Journal of Acquired Immune Deficiency Syndromes* 27(3):251–9.

Lucas, Robert E. B. 2004. *International Migration Regimes and Economic Development.* Boston: Boston University, Department of Economics.

Luke, Nancy. 2003. "Age and Economic Asymmetries in the Sexual Relationships of Adolescent Girls in Sub-Saharan Africa." *Studies in Family Planning* 34(2):67–86.

Lule, Elizabeth, James E. Rosen, Susheela Singh, James C. Knowles, and Jere R. Behrman. 2005. "Adolescent Health Programs." *In* Dean T. Jamison, David B. Evans, George Alleyne, Prabhat Jha, Joel G. Breman, Anthony R. Measham, Mariam Claeson, Anne Mills, and Philip R. Musgrove, (eds.), *Disease Control Priorities in Developing Countries.* Bethesda, MD: Disease Control Priorities Project.

Lundberg, Mattias K. A., Mead Over, and Phare Mujinja. 2003. "Do Savings Predict Death? Precautionary Savings During an Epidemic." UNAIDS. Geneva. Processed.

Lundberg, Shelly, and Elaina Rose. 2002. "The Effects of Sons and Daughters On Men's Labor Supply and Wages." *Review of Economics and Statistics* 84(2):251–68.

MacDonald, Margaret, Matthew Law, John Kaldor, Jim Hales, and Gregory J. Dore. 2003. "Effectiveness of Needle and Syringe Programmes for Preventing HIV Transmission." *International Journal of Drug Policy* 14(5-6):353–57.

Macedo, Stephen, Yvette Alex-Assensoh, Jeffrey M. Berry, Michael Brintnall, David E. Campbell, Luis Ricardo Fraga, Archon Fung, William A Galston, Christopher F. Karpowitz, Margaret Levi, Meira Levinson, Keena Lipsitz, Richard G. Niemi, Robert D. Putnam, Wendy M. Rahn, Rob Reich, Robert R. Rodgers, Todd Swanstrom, and Katherine Cramer Walsh. 2005. *Democracy at Risk: How Political Choices Undermine Citizen Participation, and*

What We Can Do About It. Washington, DC: Brookings Institution Press.

Machin, Stephen, and Costas Meghir. 2004. "Crime and Economic Incentives." *Journal of Human Resources* 39(4):958–79.

Maclellan, Nic, and Peter Mares. 2005. "Labour Mobility in the Pacific: Creating Seasonal Work Programs in Australia." Paper presented at the Globalisation, Governance and the Pacific Islands. State, Society and Governance in Melanesia Project (SSGM) Australian National University, Canberra, 25 - 27 October 2005.

Maclure, Richard, and Melvin Sotelo. 2004. "Youth Gangs in Nicaragua: Gang Membership as Structured Individualization." *Journal of Youth Studies* 7(4):417–32.

Makinson, Carolyn. 1985. "The Health Consequences of Teenage Fertility." *Family Planning Perspectives* 17(3):132–39.

Maloney, William F., and Jairo Nuñez Mendez. 2004. "Measuring the Impact of Minimum Wages: Evidence from Latin America." *In* James Heckman and Carmen Pagés, (eds.), *Law and Employment: Lessons from Latin America and the Caribbean.* Chicago: University of Chicago Press.

Maluccio, John A. Forthcoming. "Education and Child Labor: Experimental Evidence from a Nicaraguan Conditional Cash Transfer Program." *In* Peter F. Orazem, Guilherme Sedlacek, and Zafiris Tzannatos (eds.) *Eradicating Child Labor in Latin America in the 90s: The Promise of Demand Side Interventions.* Washington, DC: World Bank and Inter-American Development Bank.

Mamdani, Mahmood. 1996. *Citizen and Subject: Contemporary Africa and the Legacy of Late Colonialism.* Princeton, NJ: Princeton University Press.

Mammen, Kristin, and Christina Paxson. 2000. "Women's Work and Economic Development." *Journal of Economic Perspectives* 14(4):141–64.

Mangiaterra, Viviana, and Gerold Vollmer. 2006. "Youth Consultations for the WDR 2007: Synthesis Report of Country and Grassroots Consultations." Background paper for the WDR 2007.

Mannheim, Karl. 1972. "The Problem of Generations." *In* P Altbach and R Laufer, (eds.), *The New Pilgrims: Youth Protest in Transition.* New York, NY: David McKay and Company.

Mar Gadio, Coumba. 2001. *Exploring the Gender Impacts of World Links in some Selected Participating African Countries: A Qualitative Approach.* Washington, DC: World Links. Available online at http://www.world-links. org/modules/Downloads/fileuploads/gender_study_v2.pdf.

Marseille, Elliot. 2003. *The External Effects of HAART. A Background Paper for HIV/AIDS Treatment and Prevention in India.* Washington, DC: World Bank.

Marshall, T. H. 1950. *Citizenship and Social Class and Other Essays.* Cambridge, U.K.: Cambridge University Press.

Martin, John P., and David Grubb. 2001. "What Works and for Whom: A Review of OECD Countries' Experiences with Active Labour Market Policies." *Swedish Economic Policy Review* 8(2):9–56.

Martinez, Ramiro Jr., and Matthew T. Lee. 2000. "On Immigration and Crime." *In* U.S.Department of Justice Office of Justice Programs, (eds.), *Criminal Justice 2000.* Washington, DC: National Institute of Justice.

Martorell, R., U. Ramakrishnan, D. G. Schroeder, P. Melgar, and L. Neufeld. 1998. "Intrauterine Growth Retardation, Body Size, Body Composition and Physical Performance in Adolescence." *European Journal of Clinical Nutrition* 52(Supplement):S43–53.

Mason, Andrew, eds. 2001. *Population Change and Economic Development in East Asia: Challenges Met, Opportunities Seized.* Stanford, CA: Stanford University Press.

Massey, Douglas S., Joaquín Arango, Graeme Hugo, Ali Kouaouchi, Adela Pellegrino, and Edward Taylor. 1998. *Worlds in Motion: Understanding International Migration at the End of the Millennium.* Oxford: Oxford University Press.

Mathur, Sanyukta, Margaret Greene, and Anju Jamhotra. 2003. *Too Young to Wed: The Lives, Rights and Health of Young Married Girls.* Washington, DC: International Center for Research on Women.

Mathur, Sanyukta, Manisha Mehta, and Anju Malhotra. 2004. *Youth Reproductive Health in Nepal: Is Participation the Answer?* Washington, DC: International Center for Research On Women. Available online at http://www.icrw.org/docs/nepal_0104.pdf.

Mattero, Minna. 2006. "Youth Policies and the Institutional Framework." Background paper for the WDR 2007.

Matthews, Iole, Richard Griggs, and Glenda Caine. 1999. *The Experience Review of Interventions and Programmes Dealing with Youth Violence in Urban Schools in South Africa.* Durban, South Africa: Independent Projects Trust.

Matthews, Limb H. 2003. "Another White Elephant? Youth Councils as Democratic Structures." *Space Polity* 7(2):172–92.

Mattoo, Aaditya, IIeana Cristina Neagu, and Caglar Özden. 2005. "Brain Waste? Educated Immigrants in the U.S. Labor Market." Washington, DC: World Bank Policy Research Working Paper No. 3581.

McAdam, Doug. 1988. *Freedom Summer.* New York, NY: Oxford University Press.

McCauley, A. P., and C. Salter. 1995. "Meeting the Needs of Young Adults." Baltimore, MD: Johns Hopkins School of Public Health, Population Information Program Series J, No. 43.

McGirk, Jan. 2001. "Brutality of Child Army Shocks Colombia." *The Independent*, May 2.

McKenzie, David J. 2004. "Aggregate Shocks and Urban Labor Market Responses: Evidence from Argentina's Financial Crisis." *Economic Development and Cultural Change* 52(4):719–58.

———. 2005. "Paper Walls are Easier to Tear Down: Passport Costs and Legal Barriers to Emigration." Washington, DC: World Bank Policy Research Working Paper 3783.

———. 2006a. "A Profile of the World's Young Developing Country Migrants." Background paper for the WDR 2007.

———. 2006b. "Remittances in the Pacific." Paper presented at the Werner-Sichel lecture. February 15b. University of Western Michigan.

McKenzie, David J., John Gibson, and Steven Stillman. 2006. "How Important is Selection? Experimental vs Non-experimental Measures of the Income Gains from Migration." Washington, DC: World Bank Policy Research Working Paper Series 3906.

McKenzie, David J., and Hillel Rapoport. 2006. "Can Migration Reduce Education? Depressing Evidence from Mexico." World Bank. Washington, DC. Processed.

McKinsey Global Institute. 2005. *The Emerging Global Labor Market: Part I - The Demand for Offshore Talent in Services.* Washington, DC: McKinsey Global Institute. Available online at http://www.mckinsey.com/mgi/publications/emergingglobal-labormarket/Part1/Index.asp.

Meager, Nigel, and Ceri Evans. 1998. "The Evaluation of Active Labour Market Measures for the Long-term Unemployed." Geneva: International Labour Office, International Migration Paper Series 16.

Mensch, Barbara S., Judith Bruce, and Margaret E. Greene. 1998. *The Uncharted Passage: Girls' Adolescence in the Developing World.* New York: Population Council.

Mensch, Barbara S., Paul C. Hewett, and Annabel S. Erulkar. 2001. "The Reporting of Sensitive Behavior Amons Adolescents: A Methodological Experiment in Kenya." *Demography* 40(2):247–68.

Mensch, Barbara S., Susheela Singh, and John B. Casterline. 2006. "Trends in the Timing of First Marriage Among Men and Women in the Developing World." *In* Cynthia B. Lloyd, Jere R. Behrman, Nelly P. Stromquist, and Barney Cohen, (eds.), *The Changing Transitions to Adulthood in Developing Countries: Selected Studies.* Washington, DC: The National Academies Press.

Mesnard, Alice. 2004. "Temporary Migration and Capital Market Imperfections." *Oxford Economic Papers* 56(2):242–262.

Mesquida, Christian G., and Neil I Wiener. 1999. "Male Age Composition and Severity of Conflicts." *Political and Life Sciences* 18(2):181–9.

Mete, Cem. 2004. "The Inequality Implications of Highly Selective Promotion Practices." *Economics of Education Review* 23(3):301–14.

Miers, David. 2001. "An International Review of Restorative Justice." London, U.K.: Crime Reduction Research Series 10.

Miguel, Edward, Rachel Glennerster, and Kate Whiteside. 2006. "Civil Conflict and Local Collective Action in Sierra Leone." Paper presented at the Annual Meeting Allied Social Science Associations. Boston, MA.

Miguel, Edward, and Michael Kremer. 2004. "Worms: Identifying Impacts on Education and Health in the Presence of Treatment Externalities." *Econometrica* 72(1):159–217.

Miller, J. E. 1991. "Birth Intervals and Perinatal Health: An Investigation of Three Hypotheses." *Family Planning Perspectives* 23(2):62–70.

Ministerio del Trabajo Peru. 1998. *La Evaluacion de Impacto del Programa de Capacitación Laboral Juvenil Projoven.* Lima, Peru: Ministerio del Trabajo de Peru.

Mishra, Prachi. Forthcoming. "Emigration and Wages in Source Countries: Evidence from Mexico." *Journal of Development Economics.*

Mocan, H. Naci, and Daniel I. Rees. 1999. "Economic Conditions, Deterrence, and Juvenile Crime: Evidence From Micro Data." Cambridge, MA: National Bureau of Economic Research Working Paper Series 7405.

Moehling, Carolyn M. 2005. "She Has Suddenly Become Powerful: Youth Employment and Household Decision-Making in the Early Twentieth Century." *Journal of Economic History* 65(2):414–38.

Montenegro, Claudio E., and Carmen Pagés. 2004. "Who Benefits from Labor Market Regulations?" *In* James Heckman and Carmen Pagés, (eds.), *Law and Employment: Lessons from Latin America and the Caribbean.* Chicago: University of Chicago Press. Reprinted in Jorge Enrique Restrepo and Andrea Tokman R. (eds.) *"Labor Markets and Institutions,"* (2005), Santiago de Chile: Banco Central de Chile.

Montoya Díaz, M. Dolores. 2002. "Socio-economic Health Inequalities in Brazil: Gender and Age Effects." *Health Economics* 11:141–54.

Moore, Michael J., and Philip J. Cook. 1995. "Habit and Heterogeneity in the Youthful Demand for Alcohol." Cambridge, MA: National Bureau of Economic Research Working Paper Series 5152.

Morley, Samuel, and David Coady. 2003. *From Social Assistance to Social Development: Targeted Education Subsidies in Developing Countries*. Washington, DC: Institute for International Economics.

Moscow Human Rights Bureau. 2005. *Racism, Xenophobia, Anti-Semitism and Ethnic Discrimination in Russia, January-June 2005*. Moscow, Russia: Moscow Human Rights Bureau.

Mroz, Thomas A., and Timothy H. Savage. 2001. *The Long-Term Effects of Youth Unemployment*. Chapel Hill, N.C.: University of North Carolina at Chapel Hill and Welch Consulting Economists. Available online at http://www.epionline.org/studies/mroz_10-2001.pdf.

Muirhead, Debbie., Lilani Kumaranayake, and Charlotte Watts. 2001. *Economically Evaluating the 4th Soul City Series: Costs and Impact onHIV/AIDS and Violence Against Women*. Johannesburg; London: Institute for Health and Development Communication, and the London School of Hygiene and Tropical Medicine.

Mullahy, John, and Jody L. Sindelar. 1991. "Gender Differences in Labor Market Effects of Alcoholism." *American Economic Review: Papers and Proceedings* 81(2):161–65.

Mumtaz, Z., and S. Salway. 2005. "I Never Go Anywhere: Extricating the Links between Women's Mobility and Uptake of Reproductive Health Services in Pakistan." *Social Science and Medicine* 60(8):1751–65.

Mungai, Wainaina. 2005. "Using ICTs for Poverty Reduction and Environmental Protection in Kenya: The "M-vironment" Approach." *In* Maja Andejelkovic, (eds.), *A Developing Connection: Bridging the Policy Gap between the Information Society and Sustainable Development*. Winnipeg, Canada: IISD.

Munshi, Kaivan, and Mark Rosensweig. 2003. "Traditional Institutions Meet the Modern World: Caste, Gender and Schooling Choice in a Globalizing Economy." Cambridge, MA: Bureau for Research in Economic Analysis of Development(BREAD) Working Paper Series 038. Available online at http://www.cid.harvard.edu/bread/papers/working/038.pdf.

Murdoch, Maureen, Melissa A. Polusny, James Hodges, and Nancy O'Brien. 2004. "Prevalence of in-service and Post-service Assault among Combat and Non-combat Veterans Applying for Department of Veterans Affairs Posttraumatic Stress Disorder Disability Benefits." *Military Medicine* 169(5):392–5.

Murray, Sarah. 2004. "Investing in Young People: A Force with a Huge Potential." *Financial Times*, January 23.

Myers, David, and Allen Schirm. 1999. "The Impacts of Upward Bound: Final Report for Phase I of the National Evaluation Analysis and Highlights." Mathematica Policy Research, Inc. Washington, DC. Processed.

Nanda, Geeta, Kimberly Switlick, and Elizabeth Lule. 2005. "Accelerating Progress towards Achieving the MDG to improve Maternal Health, Health Nutrition and Population." Washington, DC: World Bank, Health Nutrition and Population Discussion Paper 31969.

Nanda, Priya. 1999. "Women's Participation in Rural Credit Programmes in Bangladesh and their Demand for Formal Health Care: Is there a Positive Impact?" *Health Economics and Econometrics* 8:415–28.

Narayan, Deepa. 1995. *The Contribution of People's Participation: Evidence from 121 Rural Water Supply Projects*. Washington, DC: World Bank.

Narayan, Deepa, and Patti Petesch. 2006. "Moving out of Poverty: Some Preliminary Results." World Bank, PRMPR. Washington, DC. Processed.

National Assessment and Examination Center. 2005. *Unified National University Entry Examinations*. Tiblisi: Ministry of Education and Science, Government of Georgia.

National Research Council and Institute of Medicine. 2005. *Growing Up Global: The Changing Transitions to Adulthood in Developing Countries*. Panel on Transitions to Adulthood in Developing Countries. Cynthia B. Lloyd, ed. Committee on Population and Board on Children, Youth, and Families. Division of Behavioral and Social Sciences and Education. Washington, DC: The National Academies Press.

National Youth Council of Ireland. 2001. *The Plunder Years: A Report on Young Drivers and Motor Insurance in Ireland*. Dublin: National Youth Council of Ireland.

Navarro, Napoleon, and Amer Hasan, eds. 2003. *Good Practices in Asia and the Pacific: Expanding Choices, Empowering People*. New York, NY: UNDP. Available online at http://www.undp.org/rbap/BestPrac/BGD_Elections.pdf.

Nelson, Jon P. 2003. "Youth Smoking Prevalence in Developing Countries: Effect of Advertising Bans." *Applied Economic Letters* 10(13):805–11.

Neto, Isabel, Charles Kenny, Subramaniam Janakiram, and Charles Watt. 2005. "Look Before you Leap: The Bumpy Road to E-development." *In* Robert Schware, (eds.), *E-development: From Excitement to Effectiveness*. Washington, DC: World Bank.

Neuhaus, Tom. 2005. "No Nazi: Youth Rebels of the Third Reich." *History Today* 55(11):52–7.

Neumark, David, and William Wascher. 1999. "A Cross-National Analysis of the Effects of Minimum Wages on Youth Employment." Cambridge, MA: National Bureau of Economic Research Working Paper Series 7299.

Newport, Elissa L. 2002. "Critical Periods in Language Development." *In* Lynn Nadel, (eds.), *Encyclopedia of Cognitive Science*. London: Macmillan Publishers Ltd./Nature Publishing Group.

Nguyen Anh, Dang. 2005. "Viet Nam Internal Migration: Opportunities and Challenges for Development." Paper presented at the Regional Conference on Migration and Development in Asia. Lanwhou, China.

Nguyen Anh, Dang, Le Bach Duong, and Nguyen Hai Van. 2005. "Youth Employment in Viet Nam: Characteristics, Determinants and Policy Responses." Geneva: ILO Employment Strategy Papers 2005/9. Available online at http://www.ilo.org/public/english/employment/strat/download/esp2005-9.pdf.

Nickell, Stephen, and Richard Layard. 1999. "Labor Market Institutions and Economic Performance." *In* Orley Ashenfelter and David Card, (eds.), *Handbook of Labor Economics. Vol. 3C*. Amsterdam: Elsevier.

Noorkôiv, Rivo, Peter F. Orazem, Allan Puur, and Milan Vodopivec. 1998. "Employment and Wage Dynamics in the Estonia Transition, 1989-1995." *Economics of Transition* 6(2):481–503.

Norris, Pippa. 2005. *Democratic Phoenix: Reinventing Political Activism*. Cambridge, U.K.: Cambridge University Press.

O'Donoghue, Ted, and Matthew Rabin. 2001. "Risky Behavior Among Youths: Some Issues from Behavioral Economics." *In* Jonathan Gruber, (eds.), *Risky Behavior among Youths: An Economic Analysis*. Chicago, IL: University of Chicago Press for the National Bureau of Economic Research.

O'Higgins, Niall. 2003. "Trends in the Youth Labor Market in Developing and Transition Countries." Washington, DC: World Bank, Social Protection Discussion Paper Series 0321.

Obadare, Ebenezer. 2005. *Statism, Youth and the Civic Imagination: A Critical Study of the National Youth Service Corps*

(NYSC) Programme in Nigeria. Missouri: Global Service Institute, Washington University.

OECD. 2003. *Trends in International Migration: SOPEMI 2002 Edition.* Paris: Organization for Economic Co-operation and Development.

———. 2004. *OECD Employment Outlook 2004.* Paris: Organization for Economic Co-operation and Development.

———. 2005a. *OECD Employment Outlook 2005.* Paris: Organization for Economic Co-operation and Development.

———. 2005b. *School Factors Related to Quality and Equity: Results from PISA 2000.* Paris: Organization for Economic Co-operation and Development.

———. 2005c. *Trends in International Migration: SOPEMI 2004 Edition.* Paris: Organization for Economic Co-operation and Development.

Ogar, Joel. 2005. *A Friend's Slap.* World Wide Web: Panorama: A TakingITGlobal Online Publication. Available online at http://www.takingitglobal.org/express/panorama/article.html?ContentID=6505.

Okonofua, F. E., P. Coplan, S. Collins, F. Oronsaye, D. Ogunsakin, J. T. Ogonor, J. A. Kaufman, and K. Heggenhougen. 2003. "Impact of an Intervention to Improve Treatment-seeking Behavior and Prevent Sexually Transmitted Diseases among Nigerian Youths." *International Journal of Infectious Diseases* 7(1):61–73.

Omelaniuk, Irena. 2005. "Trafficking in Human Beings." World Bank. Washington, DC. Processed.

Ong, Aihwa. 1987. *Spirits of Resistance and Capitalist Discipline: Factory Women in Malaysia.* Albany: State University of New York Press.

Online Computer Library Center (OCLC). 2005. *Country and Language Statistics.* Dublin, O.H.: Online Computer Library Center (OCLC). Available online at http://www.oclc.org/research/projects/archive/wcp/stats/intnl.htm.

ORC Macro. 2006. "The Demographic and Health Surveys STAT Compiler". www.measuredhs.com, ORC Macro.

Oreopoulos, Philip. 2005. "Do Dropouts Drop Out Too Soon? International Evidence From Changes in School-Leaving Laws." Cambridge, MA: National Bureau of Economic Research Working Paper Series 10155.

Osmond, C., and D. J. Barker. 2000. "Fetal, Infant, and Childhood Growth are Predictors of Coronary Heart Disease, Diabetes, and Hypertension in Adult Men and Women." *Environmental Health Perspectives* 108(Supp. 3):545–53.

Otsuka, Keijiro. Forthcoming. "The Rural Industrial Transition in East Asia: Influences and Implications." *In* Steven Haggblade, Peter B. R. Hazell, and Thomas Reardon (eds.) *Transforming the Rural Nonfarm Economy.* Baltimore, MD: John Hopkins University Press.

Over, Mead, Peter Heywood, Julian Gold, Indrani Gupta, Subhash Hira, and Elliot Marseille. 2004. *HIV/AIDS Treatment and Prevention in India: Modeling the Costs and Consequences.* Washington, DC: World Bank; Health, Nutrition, and Population Series.

Oyediran, Kola A., Gbenga P. Ishola, and Alfred A. Adewuyi. 2002. "Knowledge of Possible Pregnancy at First Coitus: A Study of In-school Adolescents in Ibadan, Nigeria." *Journal of Biosocial Science* 34(2):233–48.

Pabilonia, Sabrina W., and Cindy Zoghi. Forthcoming. "Returning to the Returns to Computer Use." *American Economic Review.*

Pagés, Carmen, and Claudio E. Montenegro. 1999. "Job Security and the Age Composition of Employment: Evidence from Chile." Washington, DC: Inter-American Development Bank, Office of the Chief Economist Working Paper Series 398.

Pals, Heili, and Nancy Brandon Tuma. 2004. "Entrepreneurial Activities in Post-Soviet Societies: Impacts of Social Psychological Characteristics." *International Journal of Sociology* 34(2):11–38.

Pampel, Fred C., and H. Elizabeth Peters. 1995. "The Easterlin Effect." *Annual Review of Sociology* 21:163–94.

Pande, Rohini. 2005. "Can Mandated Political Representation Increase Policy Influence for Disadvantaged Minorities? Theory and Evidence from India." *American Economic Review* 93(4):1132–51.

Paniza, Hugo. 2000. "The Public Sector Premium and the Gender Gap in Latin America: Evidence from the 1980s and 1990s." Washington, DC: Inter-American Development Bank, Research Department, Working Paper 431.

Parent, Daniel. 2006. "Youth Labor Markets in Burkina Faso: Recent Trends and Analysis." McGill University. Montreal. Processed.

Parham, Angel Adams. 2004. "Diaspora, Community and Communication: Internet Use in Transnational Haiti." *Global Networks* 4(2):199–217.

Parker, Susan. 2003. "Evaluación de Impacto de *Oportunidades* sobre la Inscripción Escolar: Primaria, Secundaria y Media Superior." Mexico, D.F.: Secretaria de Desarrollo Social, Documento de Investigación 6.

Parliamentary Committee for Social Affairs. 2005. *Assessment on Urban Migration Policy.* Hanoi: UNFPA.

Parry, C. D. H., A. Louw, E. Vardas, and A. Plüddemann. 2000. *Medical Research Council and Institute for Security Studies: 3-Metros Arrestee Study (Phase 1).* Parow: Medical Research Council.

Parsons, Christopher R., Ronald Skeldon, Terrie L. Walmsley, and L. Alan Winters. 2005. *Quantifying the International Bilateral Movements of Migrants.* Sussex University: The World Bank and the Development Research Centre on Migration, Globalisation and Poverty at Sussex University.

Partnership for Child Development, Working Group on the Nutrition of the School Age Child. 2006. *Survey of School Health and Nutrition Programs for the UN Subcommittee on Nutrition.* New York: United Nations.

Patrinos, Harry A. 2005. "Education Contracting: Scope of Future Research." World Bank. Washington, DC. Processed.

Patrinos, Harry A., and Chris Sakellariou. 2005. "Schooling and Labor Market Impacts of a Natural Policy Experiment." *Labour* 19(4):705–19.

Paul-Majumder, Pratima, and Anwara Begum. 2000. "The Gender Imbalances in the Export Oriented Garment Industry in Bangladesh: Measures for Eliminating Gender Imbalances in Export-oriented Garment Industries." Washington, DC: World Bank, Policy Research Report on Gender and Development Working Paper Series 12.

Pauly, Mark V. 1968. "The Economics of Moral Hazard." *American Economic Review* 58(3):531–7.

Paxson, Christina H. 2002. "Comment on Alan Krueger and Jitka Maleckova, "Education, Poverty and Terrorism: Is There a Causal Connection?"" Princeton, NJ: Princeton University Research Program in Development Studies Working Paper 207.

Paxson, Christina H., and Norbert Schady. Forthcoming. "Cognitive Development among Young Children in Ecuador: The Roles of Wealth, Health and Parenting." *Journal of Human Resources.*

———. Forthcoming. "Early Childhood Development in Latin America and the Caribbean." *Journal of Human Resources.*

Peden, M., H. Donson, M. Maziko, and P. Smith. 2000. "Substance Abuse Trends Among Trauma Patients: The South African Experience." Paper presented at the 5th World Injury Prevention and Control Congress. New Delhi.

Perkinson, Ron. 2005. "Beyond Secondary Education: The Promise of ICT for Higher Education and Lifelong Learning." *In* Robert Schware, (eds.), *E-development: From Excitement to Effectiveness.* Washington, DC: World Bank.

Perlman, Janice E. 2005. "Policy Roundtable on the Policy Implications of Rio Favela Re-Study." Paper presented at the World Bank Policy Roundtable on the Policy Implications of Rio Favela Re-Study. June 9. Washington, DC

Perlman, Janice E., and Sarah E. Anthony. 2006. "Citizenship and Youth in the Favelas of Rio de Janeiro." Background paper for the WDR 2007.

Peters, Krijn. 2006. "Footpaths to Reintegration: Armed Conflict, Youth and the Rural Crisis in Sierra Leone." PhD thesis. Wageningen University.

Petrosino, Anthony, Carolyn Turpin-Petrosino, and John Buehler. 2005. "Scared Straight and Other Juvenile Awareness Programs for Preventing Juvenile Delinquency". Chichester, U.K., John Wiley & Sons, Ltd.

Pintor, Rafael López, and Maria Gratschew. 2002. *Voter Turnout Since 1945.* Stockholm, Sweden: International Institute for Democracy and Electoral Assistance (International IDEA).

Pitt, Mark, and Shahidur Khandker. 1996. "Household and Intrahousehold Impact of the Grameen Bank and Similar Targeted Credit Programs in Bangladesh." Washington, DC: World Bank Discussion Paper 320.

Pitt, Mark M., Shahidur R. Khandker, Signe-Mary Mckernan, and M. Abdul Latif. 1999. "Credit Programs for the Poor and Reproductive Behavior in Low Income Countries: Are the Reported Causal Relationships the Result of Heterogeneity Bias?" *Demography* 36(1):1–21.

Plutzer, Eric. 2002. "Becoming a Habitual Voter: Inertia, Resources, and Growth in Young Adulthood." *American Political Science Review* 96(1):41–56.

Popkin, Barry M. 1994. "The Nutrition Transition in Low-income Countries: An Emerging Crisis." *Nutrition Reviews* 52(9):285–98.

———. 2002. "An Overview on the Nutrition Transition and Its Health Implications: The Bellagio Meeting." *Public Health Nutrition* 5(1A):93–103.

Popkin, Barry M., and P. Gordon-Larsen. 2004. "The Nutrition Transition: Worldwide Obesity Dynamics and Their Determinants." *International Journal of Obesity* 28(Supp. 3):2–9.

Population Council. 2002. "Does Easy Accessibility of Emergency Contraception Increase Sexual Risk-Taking?" *Momentum*, October.

Portes, Jonathan, and Simon French. 2005. "The Impact of Free Movement of Workers from Central and Eastern Europe on the UK Labour Market: Early Evidence." London: United Kingdom Department of Work and Pensions Working Paper 18.

Post, Jerrold M. 1998. "Terror Psycho-Logic: Terrorist Behavior as a Product of Psychological Forces." *In* Walter Reich, (eds.), *Origins of Terrorism: Psychologies, Ideologies, Theologies, States of Mind.* Washington, DC: Woodrow Wilson Center Press.

Pound, Edward T., and Danielle Knight. 2006. "Cleaning Up the World Bank." *U.S.News and World Report*, April 3.

Prakesh, Siddhartha. 2003. "The African Virtual University and Growth in Africa: A Knowledge and Learning Challenge." Washington, DC: World Bank, Human Development Findings 223. Available online at http://www.worldbank.org/afr/findings/english/find223.pdf.

Pratham Resource Centre. 2005. *Annual Status of Education Report: Aser 2005.* Mumbai: Pratham Resource Centre. Available online at http://www.pratham.org/aserrep.php.

Pritchett, Lant. 2001. "Where Has All the Education Gone?" *World Bank Economic Review* 15(3):367–91.

———. 2006. "Boom Towns and Ghost Countries: Geography, Agglomeration and Population Mobility." Harvard University. Cambridge, MA. Processed.

Przeworski, Adam, Michael E. Alavarez, Jose Antonio Cheibub, and Fernando Limongi. 2000. *Democracy and Development: Political Institutions and Well-Being in the World, 1950-1990.* Cambridge, U.K.: Cambridge University Press.

Ragui, Assaad, and Melanie Arntz. 2005. "Constrained Geographic Mobility and Gendered Labor Market Outcomes under Structural Adjustment." *World Development* 33(3):431–54.

Rahman, Rushidan Islam. 1995. "Formal Sector Emplyoment Among Women in Bangladesh and Gender Composition of Industrial Workers." World Bank, Background paper for the 1995 World Development Report. Washington, DC. Processed.

Rajbhandary, Jasmine, Roger Hart, and Chandrika Khatiwada. 2001. *Extracts from The Children's Clubs of Nepal: A Democratic Experiment.* London, U.K.: International Institute for Environment and Development. Available online at http://www.iied.org/NR/agbioliv/pla_notes/documents/plan_04205.pdf.

Ramakrishnan, Usha. 2004. "Nutrition and Low Birth Weight: From Research to Practice." *American Journal of Clinical Nutrition* 9(1):17–21.

Rao, Madanmohan. 1999. *Internet Content in India: Local Challenges, Global Aspirations.* The Hague: International Institute for Communication and Development (IICD).

Rashid, Ahmed. 2000. *Taliban: Militant Islam, Oil and Fundamentalism in Central Asia.* New Haven, CT: Yale University Press.

Ravallion, Martin, Gaurav Datt, and Dominique van de Walle. 1991. "Quantifying Absolute Poverty in the Developing World." *Review of Income and Wealth* 37 (4): 345–61.

Ravallion, Martin, Emanuela Galasso, Teodoro Lazo, and Ernesto Philipp. 2005. "What Can Ex-participants Reveal about a Program's Impact?" *Journal of Human Resources* 40(1):208–30.

Ravallion, Martin, and Quentin Wodon. 2000. "Does Child Labour Displace Schooling? Evidence on Behavioural Responses to an Enrollment Subsidy." *Economic Journal* 110(462):C158–C175.

Rawlings, Laura B., and Gloria M. Rubio. 2005. "Evaluating the Impact of Conditional Cash Transfer Programs." *World Bank Research Observer* 20(1):29–55.

Reddy, K. Srinath. 2002. "Cardiovascular Diseases in the Developing Countries: Dimensions, Determinants, Dynamics and Directions for Public Health Action." *Public Health Nutrition* 5(1a):231–7.

Refaat, A. 2004. "Practice and Awareness of Health Risk Behaviour among Egyptian University Students." *Eastern Mediterranean Health Journal* 10(1/2):72–81.

Rehm, Jürgen. 2003. "Alcohol, Addiction and Public Health." Washington, DC: Disease Control Priorities Project, Working Paper 33. Available online at http://www.dcp2.org/file/47/wp33.pdf.

Reinikka, Ritva, and Jacob Svensson. 2002. "Assessing Frontline Service Delivery." World Bank. Washington, DC. Processed.

Reiss, Albert J. Jr, and Jeffrey A Roth, eds. 1993. *Understanding and Preventing Violence*. Washington, DC: National Academies Press.

Reynolds, Paul D., William D. Bygrave, Erkko Autio, Larry W. Cox, and Michael Hay. 2002. *Global Entrepreneurship Monitor. Executive Report 2002*. London: Babson College, London School of Business and Ewing Marion Kauffman Foundation. Available online at http://www.kauffman.org/pdf/GEM2002.pdf.

Richards, Paul, Khadija Bah, and James Vincent. 2004. "Social Capital and the Survival: Prospects for Community-Driven Development in Post-Conflict Sierra Leone." Washington, DC: World Bank, Social Development Papers 12.

Riley, Thira, and William Steel. 1999. "Kenya Voucher Program for Training and Business Development Services." World Bank. Washington, DC. Processed.

Ritchie, Amanda, Cynthia B. Lloyd, and Monica Grant. 2004. "Gender Differences in Time Use among Adolescents in Developing Countries: The Implications of Rising School Enrollment Rates." Washington, DC: Population Council Working Paper 193. Available online at http://www.popcouncil.org/pdfs/wp/193.pdf.

Rivera-Batiz, Francisco L. 2002. "Democracy, Governance and Economic Growth: Theory and Evidence." New York, NY: Columbia University Department of Economics Discussion Paper Series 0102-57. Available online at http://www.columbia.edu/cu/economics/discpapr/DP0102-57.pdf.

Roche, Declan. 2006. "Dimensions of Restorative Justice." *Journal of Social Issues* 62(2):217–38.

Rodgers, A., T. Corbett, D. Bramley, T. Riddell, M. Willis, R-B. Lin, and M. Jones. 2005. "Do U Smoke after Text? Results of a Randomized Trial of Smoking Cessation Using Mobile Phone Text Messaging." *Tobacco Control* 2005(14):255–61.

Rodgers, Dennis. 1999. "Youth Gangs in Latin America and the Caribbean: A Literature Survey." Washington, DC: Latin America and the Caribbean Sustainable Development Working Paper, Urban Peace Program Series 4.

Rodríguez Ospina, Edgar, Luis Fernando Duque Ramirez, and Jesús Rodríguez García. 1993. "National Household Survey on Drug Abuse". Bogota, Colombia, Escuela Colombiana de Medicina y Fundación Santa Fé de Bogota.

Rodríguez-Pose, Andrés, and Nicholas Gill. 2003. "The Global Trend Towards Devolution and its Implications." *Environment and Planning C: Government and Policy* 21(3):333–51.

Rosati, Furio. Forthcoming. "Child Labour and Youth Employment: Ethiopia Country Study." *In* World Bank (eds.) *Youth in Africa's Labor Market*. Washington, DC: World Bank.

Rosati, Furio Camillo, and Mariacristina Rossi. 2003. "Children's Working Hours and School Enrollment: Evidence From Pakistan and Nicaragua." *World Bank Economic Review* 17(2):283–95.

Rosen, James E. 2000. "Contracting for Reproductive Health Care: A Guide." Washington, DC: World Bank, Health Nutriton and Population Discussion Paper 28900.

Rowlands, S., H. Devalia, R. Lawrenson, J. Logie, and B. Ineichen. 2000. "Repeated Use of Hormonal Emergency Contraception by Younger Women in the UK." *Journal of Family Planning and Reproductive Health Care* 26(3):138–43.

Roy, Olivier. 2004. *Globalised Islam: The Search for a New Ummah*. London, U.K.: C. Hurst & Co. Ltd.

Rubio, Mauricio. 2005. "La Mara, Trucha y Voraz." Inter-American Development Bank. Washington, DC. Processed.

Ruel, Marie T., Bénédicte de la Briere, Kelly Hallman, Agnes Quisumbing, and Nora Coj. 2002. "Does Subsidized Childcare Help Poor Working Women in Urban Areas? Evaluation of a Government-Sponsored Program in Guatemala City." Washington, DC: IFPRI, FCND Discussion Paper 131.

Ruoen, Ren, and Chen Kai. 1995. "China's GDP in U.S. Dollars Based on Purchasing Power Parity." Washington, DC: World Bank Policy Research Working Paper Series 1415.

Russell, Michele. 2000. "Community Based Care and Support Services in South Africa." Paper presented at the The 13th International AIDS Conference. July 7. Durban, South Africa.

Ryan, Paul. 2001. "The School-to-Work Transition: A Cross-National Perspective." *Journal of Economic Literature* 39(1):34–92.

Sacerdote, Bruce. 2001. "Peer Effects with Random Assignment: Results for Dartmouth Roommates." *Quarterly Journal of Economics* 116(2):681–704.

Sadler, Anne G., Brenda M. Booth, and Bradley N. Doebbeling. 2005. "Gang and Multiple Rapes During Military Service: Health Consequences and Health Care." *Journal of American Medical Women's Association* 60(1):33–41.

Sadoulet, Elisabeth, and Alain de Janvry. 2006. "Making Conditionnal Cash Transfers More Efficient: Designing for Maximum Effect of the Conditionality." *World Bank Economic Review* 20(1):1–29.

Sageman, Marc. 2004. *Understanding Terror Networks*. Philadelphia, PA: University of Pennsylvania Press.

Salomon, Joshua A., Daniel R. Hogan, John Stover, Karen A. Stanecki, Neff Walker, Peter D. Ghys, and Bernhard Schwartländer. 2005. "Integrating HIV Prevention and Treatment: From Slogans to Impact." *PLOS Medicine* 2(1):50–56.

Samuel, Jonathan, Niraj Shah, and Wenona Hadingham. 2005. "Mobile Communications in South Africa, Tanzania and Egypt: Results from Community and Business Surveys." Newbury, Berkshire, U.K.: Vodafone Policy Paper Series 2.

Sánchez-Páramo, Carolina, and Norbert Schady. 2003. "Off and Running? Technology, Trade, and the Rising Demand for Skilled Workers in Latin America." Washington, DC: World Bank Policy Research Working Paper Series 3015.

Santiago Consultores Asociados. 1999. *Evaluación Ex-Post Chile Joven Fase II*. Santiago de Chile: Santiago Consultores Asociados. Available online at http://www.cinterfor.org.uy/public/spanish/region/ampro/cinterfor/temas/youth/doc/not/libro225/libro225.pdf.

Sathar, Zeba A., Minhaj ul Haque, Azeema Faizunnissa, Munawar Sultana, Cynthia B. Lloyd, Judith A. Diers, and Monica Grant. 2002. *Adolescents and Youth in Pakistan 2001-2002: A Nationally Representative Survey*. Islamabad: UNICEF.

Sawada, Yasuyuki, and Mikhail Lokshin. 2001. "Household Schooling Decisions in Rural Pakistan." Washington, DC: World Bank Policy Research Working Paper Series 2541.

Sawaya, A. L., P. Martins, D. Hoffman, and S. B. Roberts. 2003. "The Link Between Childhood Undernutrition and Risk of Chronic Diseases in Adulthood: A Case Study of Brazil." *Nutrition Reviews* 61(5):168–75.

Schmitter, Philippe C., and Alexander H. Treschel. 2005. *Green Paper on the Future of Democracy in Europe for The Council of Europe*. Paris: Council of Europe. Available online at http://www.coe.int/t/e/integrated_projects/democracy/05_Key_texts/02_Green_Paper/default.asp.

Scholl, T. O., M. L. Hediger, J. Huang, F. E. Johnson, W. Smith, and I. G. Ances. 1992. "Young Maternal Age and Parity. Influences on Pregnancy Outcome." *Annals of Epidemiology* 2:565–75.

Scholl, T. O., R. W. Hediger, D. H. Salmon, H. Belsky, and I G. Ances. 1989. "Association Between Low Gynaecological Age and Preterm Birth." *Paediatric and Perinatal Epidemiology* 3:357–66.

Schultz, T. Paul. 2000. *Final Report: The Impact of PROGRESA on School Enrollments.* Washington, DC: International Food Policy and Research Institute.

———. 2002. "Why Governments Should Invest More to Educate Girls." *World Development* 30(2):207–25.

———. 2003. "Evidence of Return to Schooling in Africa from Household Surveys: Monitoring and Restructuring the Market for Education." New Haven, CT: Yale University, Economic Growth Center Discussion Paper No. 875. Available online at http://www.econ.yale.edu/growth_pdf/cdp875.pdf.

———. 2004. "School Subsidies for the Poor: Evaluating the Mexican Progresa Poverty Program." *Journal of Development Economics* 74(1):199–250.

Schweinhart, Lawrence J., Helen V. Barnes, and David P. Weikart. 1993. *Significant Benefits: The High-Scope Perry Pre-school Study through Age 27.* Ypsilanti, MI: High Scope Press.

Sciolino, Elaine, Brian Wingfield, and Elisabetta Povoledo. 2005. "From Tapes, a Chilling Voice of Islamic Radicalism in Europe." *The New York Times*, November 18. Page: 1.

SCN News. 2006. "Adolescence." *U.N.Standing Committee on Nutrition* 31

Sen, Amartya. 1985. "Well-being, Agency and Freedom, The Dewey Lectures 1984." *Journal of Philosophy* 82(4):169–221.

———. 1999. *Development as Freedom.* New York, NY: Random House, Inc.

Senderowitz, Judith. 1995. "Adolescent Health: Reassessing the Passage to Adulthood." Washington, DC: World Bank Discussion Paper 272.

———. 1999. *Making Reproductive Health Services Youth Friendly.* Washington, DC: Focus on Young Adults: Research Program and Policy Series.

Senderowitz, Judith, and John Paxman. 1985. "Adolescent Fertility: Worldwide Concerns." *Population Bulletin* 40(2):3–51.

Serneels, Pieter. 2004. "The Nature of Unemployment in Urban Ethiopia." Oxford, U.K.: CSAE (Oxford) Working Paper 2004-18.

Seshadri, S., and T. Gopaldas. 1989. "Impact of Iron Supplementation on Cognitive Functions in Preschool and School-aged Children: The Indian Experience." *American Journal of Clinical Nutrition* 50(3):675S–84S.

Seyboldt, Taylor, eds. 2000. *SIPRI Yearbook 2000: Armaments, Disarmament and International Security.* Oxford, U.K.: Oxford University Press.

Shafii, Taraneh, Katherine Stovel, Robert Davis, and King Holmes. 2004. "Is Condom Use Habit Forming? Condom Use at Sexual Debut and Subsequent Condom Use." *Sexually Transmitted Diseases* 31(6):366–72.

Shah, I., and E. Ahman. 2004a. "Age Patterns of Unsafe Abortion in Developing Country Regions." *Reproductive Health Matters,* 12(24 (Abortion law, policy and practice supplement)):9–17.

———, eds. 2004b. *Unsafe Abortion: Global and Regional Estimates of the Incidence of Unsafe Abortion and Associated Mortality in 2000, 4th ed.* Geneva: World Health Organization.

Shanahan, Michael J., Erik J. Porfeli, Jeylan T. Mortimer, and Lance D. Erickson. 2005. "Subjective Age Identity and the Transition to Adulthood: When Do Adolescents Become Adults?" *In* Richard A. Settersten Jr., Frank F. Furstenberg Jr., and Rubén G. Rumbaut, (eds.), *On the Frontier of Adulthood: Theory, Research, and Public Policy.* Chicago, IL: University of Chicago Press.

Shaw, Margaret. 2001. *Investing in Youth: International Approaches to Preventing Crime and Victimization.* Montreal, Quebec, Canada: International Center for the Prevention of Crime.

Sheley, Joseph F., and James D. Wright. 1993. *Gun Acquisition and Possession in Selected Juvenile Samples.* Washington, DC: US Department of Justice, National Institute of Justice.

Sherman, Lawrence W., Denise C. Gottfreddson, Doris L. Mackenzie, Joun Eck, Peter Reuter, and Shawn D. Bushway. 1998. *Preventing Crime: What Works, What Doesn't, What's Promising: A Report to the U.S. Congress.* Washington DC: National Institute of Justice.

Shonkoff, Jack, and Deborah Phillips, eds. 2000. *From Neurons to Neighborhoods: The Science of Early Childhood Development.* Washington, DC: National Academy Press.

Siddiqua, Yasmin, and M. Kabir. 2002. "Adolescent Reproductive Health: What Are the Lessons Learned from the Intervention Projects." *Asia-Pacific Population Journal* 17(3):79–100.

Simon, Arthy. 2003. *Ex Combatant Reintegration: Key Issues for Policy Makers and Practitioners, Based on Lessons from Sierra Leone, Phase 3 evaluation.* London: DFID.

Simonet, Daniel. 2004. "The AIDS Epidemic and Migrants in South Asia and South-East Asia." *International Migration* 42(5):35–67.

Singer, Peter Warren. 2005. *Children at War.* New York, NY: Pantheon Books.

Singh, Susheela. 1998. "Adolescent Childbearing in Developing Countries: A Global Review." *Studies in Family Planning* 29(2):117–36.

Singh, Susheela, and Jacqueline E. Darroch. 2000. "Adolescent Pregnancy and Childbearing: Levels and Trends in Developed Countries." *Family Planning Perspectives* 32(1):14–23.

Singh, Susheela, and Renee Samara. 1996. "Early Marriage Among Women in Developing Countries." *International Family Planning Perspectives* 22(4):148–75.

Singh, Susheela, Deirdre Wulf, Renee Samara, and Yvette P. Cuca. 2000. "Gender Differences in the Timing of First Intercourse: Data from 14 Countries." *International Family Planning Perspectives* 26(1):21–9.

Singleton, Nicola, Alison Lee, and Howard Meltzer. 2001. *Psychiatric Morbidity among Adults Living in Private Households 2000: Technical Report.* London: HMSO Office for National Statistics.

Sjaastad, Larry A. 1962. "The Costs and Returns of Human Migration." *Journal of Political Economy* 70(5):80–93.

Skoufias, Emmanuel. 2001. *Progressa and Its Impact on the Human Capital and Welfare of Household in Rural Mexico: A Synthesis of the Results of an Evaluation by IFPRI.* Washington, DC: International Food Policy Research Institute (IFPRI).

Skoufias, Emmanuel, Benjamin Davis, and Sergio de la Vega. 2001. "Targeting the Poor: An Evaluation of the Selection of Households into PROGRESA." *World Development* 29(10):1769–84.

Skoufias, Emmanuel, and Susan W. Parker. 2001. "Conditional Cash Transfers and Their Impact on Child Work and Schooling:

Evidence from the PROGRESA Program in Mexico." *Economia* 2(1):45–86.

Slavin, R. E. 1996. *Success or Fall.* Lisse, The Netherlands: Swets & Zeitlinger.

Slavin, R. E., and R. Cooper. 1999. "Improving Intergroup Relations: Lessons Learned from Cooperative Learning Programs." *Journal of Social Issues* 55(4):647–64.

Slaymaker, Emma, N. Walker, B. Zaba, and M. Collumbien. 2004. "Comparative Risk Assessment: Unsafe Sex." *In* M. Ezzati, A. Lopez, A. Rodgers, and C. Murray, (eds.), *Comparative Quantification of Health Risks: Global and Regional Burden of Disease due to Selected Major Risk Factors.* Geneva: World Health Organization.

Smith, Daniel Jordan. 2004. "The Bakassi Boys: Vigilantism, Violence, and Political Imagination in Nigeria." *Cultural Anthropology* 19(3):429–55.

Smith, P. K., B. Bogin, and D. Bishai. 2005. "Are Time Preference and Body Mass Index Associated? Evidence from the National Longitudinal Survey of Youth." *Economics & Human Biology* 3(2):259–70.

Soewondo, S., M. Husaini, and E. Pollitt. 1989. "Effects of Iron Deficiency on Attention and Learning Processes of Preschool Children." *American Journal of Clinical Nutrition* 50(3):667–74.

Solinger, Dorothy. 1999. *Contesting Citizenship in Urban China: Peasant Migrants, the State, and the Logic of Market.* Berkeley, CA: University of California Press.

Span Jr., Milton G. 2000. *Remediation: A Must for the 21st Century Learning Society.* Denver, CO: Education Commission of the States.

Sparrow, Robert. 2004. "Protecting Education for the Poor in Times of Crisis: An Evaluation of the Scholarships Program in Indonesia." Jakarta, Indonesia: East Asian Bureau of Economic Research, Development Economics Working Papers 96.

Sprinzak, Ehud. 1998. "The Psychopolitical Formation of Extreme Left Terrorism in a Democracy: The Case of the Weathermen." *In* Walter Reich, (eds.), *Origins of Terrorism: Psychologies, Ideologies, Theologies, States of Mind.* Washington, DC: Woodrow Wilson Center Press.

Stanback, John, and K. A. Twum-Baah. 2001. "Why Do Family Planning Providers Restrict Access to Services? An Examination in Ghana." *International Family Planning Perspectives* 27(1):37–41.

Stanton, Bonita F., Xiaoming Li, Joshua Kahihuata, Ann M. Fitzgerald, Simeone Neumbo, Geraldus Kanduuombe, Izabel B. Ricardo, Jennifer S. Galbraith, Nancy Terreri, Irene Guevara, Hannu Shipena, Johan Strijdom, Rebecca Clemens, and R. F. Zimba. 1999. "Increased Protected Sex and Abstinence among Namibian Youth Following a HIV Risk-Reduction Intervention: a Randomized, Longitudinal Study." *AIDS* 12(18):2473–80.

Stapleton, David C., and Rirchard V. Burkhauser, eds. 2003. *Decline in Employment of People with Disabilities: A Policy Puzzle.* Kalamazoo, MI: W.E. Upjohn Institute for Employment Research.

Steinberg, Laurence, and Elizabeth Cauffman. 1996. "Maturity of Judgement in Adolescence: Psychosocial Factors in Adolescent Decision Making." *Law and Human Behavior* 20(3):249–72.

Steinberger, Michael. 2001. "So, Are Civilizations at War?" *The Observer*, October 21.Available online at http://observer.guardian.co.uk/islam/story/0,1442,577982,00.html.

Steinmo, Sven, Kathleen Thelen, and Frank Longstreth, eds. 1992. *Structuring Politics: Historical Institutionalism in Comparative Analysis.* New York, NY: Cambridge University Press.

Stepick, Alex, Carol Dutton Stepick, and Philip Kretsedemas. 2001. *Civic Engagement of Haitian Immigrants and Haitian Americans In Miami-Dade County.* Miami, Florida: Haitian American Foundation, Human Services Coalition of Dade County and Kellog Foundation.

Stern, Jessica. 2004. *Terror in the Name of God: Why Religious Militants Kill.* New York, NY: HarperCollins Publishers Inc.

Stern, Nicholas, Jean-Jacques Dethier, and F. Halsey Rogers. 2005. *Growth and Empowerment: Making Development Happen.* Cambridge, MA: MIT Press.

Sternberg, Robert. 1985. *Beyond IQ: A Triarchic Theory of Human Intelligence.* Cambridge: Cambridge University Press.

Stockard, Jean, and Robert M. O'Brien. 2002. "Cohort Effects on Suicide Rates: International Variations." *American Sociological Review* 67(6):854–72.

Stohl, Rachel. 2001. *Global Report on Child Soldiers Released.* Washington, DC: Center for Defense Information.

Stolle, Deitlind, and Marc Hooghe. 2004. "Review Article: Inaccurate, Exceptional, One-Sided or Irrelevant? The Debate about the Alleged Decline of Social Capital and Civic Engagement in Western Societies." *British Journal of Political Science* 35(1):149–67.

Strauss, John, and Duncan Thomas. 1995. "Human Resources: Empirical Modeling of Household and Family Decisions." *In* Jere R. Behrman and T. N. Srinivasan, (eds.), *Handbook of Development Economics Volume 3A.* Amsterdam: Elsevier.

Student Partnership Worldwide. 2005. *The Regai Dzive Shiri Programme: 2002-2007.* London: Student Partnership Worldwide. Available online at http://www.spw.org/.

Study Group on Female Genital Mutilation and Obstetric Outcome. 2006. "Female Genital Mutilation and Obstetric Outcome: WHO Collaborative Prospective Study in Six African Countries." *Lancet* 367:1835–41.

Summers, Lawrence H. 1992. "Investing in All the People." *Pakistan Development Review* 31(4):367–93.

———. 1994. "Investing in All the People: Educating Women in Developing Countries." Washington, DC: World Bank, Economic Development Institute Seminar Paper 45.

Swedish International Development Agency (SIDA). 2005. *Cedeca-Ceara Project.* Stockholm: Swedish International Development Agency (SIDA).

Tan, Hong W. 2005. "In-service Skills Upgrading and Training Policy: Global and Regional Perspectives." Paper presented at the MNA Job Creation and Skills Development Conference. Cairo.

Tan, Hong W., and Geeta Batra. 1995. "Enterprise Training in Developing Countries: Incidence, Productivity Effects, and Policy Implications." Washington, DC: World Bank, Private Sector Development Department Working Paper 15373.

Tan, J. P., J. Lane, and G. Lassibille. 1999. "Outcomes in Philippine Elementary Schools: An Evaluation of Four Experiments." *World Bank Economic Review* 13(3):493–508.

Taylor, Maxwell. 1988. *The Terrorist.* London, U.K.: Brassey's.

Teixeira, Paulo R., Marco Antônio Vitória, and Jhoney Barcarolo. 2003. "The Brazilian Experience in Providing Universal Access to Antiretroviral Therapy." *In* Dumoulin J. P. Moatti, B. Coriat, Y. Souteyrand, T. Barnett, and Y. A. Flori, (eds.), *Economics of AIDS and Access to HIV/AIDS Care in Developing Countries, Issues and Challenges.* Paris: Agence Nationale de Recherches sur le Sida.

Temin, Miriam J., Friday E. Okonofua, Francesca O. Omorodion, Elisha P. Renne, Paul Coplan, H. Kris Heggenhougen, and Joan Kaufman. 1999. "Perceptions of Sexual Behavior and Knowledge

About Sexually Transmitted Diseases Among Adolescents in Benin City, Nigeria." *International Family Planning Perspectives* 25(4):186–190.

Thailand Ministry of Public Health, and World Bank. 2005. *Expanding Access to Antiretroviral Treatment in Thailand: Achieving Treatment Benefits while Promoting Effective Prevention.* Bangkok and Washington, DC: Thailand Ministry of Public Health and World Bank.

The Global Fund for AIDS, TB and Malaria. 2005. *Development of a Comprehensive National Response to HIV/AIDS that Includes Adequate Prevention, Treatment, Care and Support for Those Affected.* Freetown: The Global Fund for AIDS, TB and Malaria.

The Office of Juvenile Justice and Delinquency Prevention (OJJDP). 1998. *Juvenile Justice Bulletin.* Washington, DC: U.S. Department of Justice, Office of Justice Programs, Office of Juvenile Justice and Delinquency Prevention.

Thorn, Kristian, Lauritz Holm-Nielsen, and Samuel Jeppesen. 2004. "Approaches to Results-Based Funding in Tertiary Education: Identifying Finance Reform Options for Chile." Washington, DC: World Bank Policy Research Working Paper Series 3436.

Thornberry, Terence P. 1998. "Membership in Youth Gangs and Involvement in Serious and Violent Offending." *In* Rolf Loeber and David P. Farrington, (eds.), *Serious and Violent Offenders: Risk Factors and Successful Interventions.* Thousand Oaks, CA: Sage Publications, Inc.

Thorup, Cathryn L., and Sheila Kinkade. 2005. *What Works in Youth Engagement in the Balkans.* Baltimore, MD: International Youth Foundation. Available online at http://www.iyfnet.org/section.cfm/31/223.

Titma, Mikk, and Nancy Brandon Tuma. 2005. "Human Agency in the Transition from Communism." *In* K. Warner Schaie and Glen Elder, (eds.), *Historical Influences on Lives and Aging.* New York, NY: Springer Publishing Company.

Todd, Petra, and Kenneth I. Wolpin. 2003. "Using a Social Experiment to Validate a Dynamic Behavioral Model of Child Schooling and Fertility: Assessing the Impact of a School Subsidy Program in Mexico." University of Pennsylvania. Philadelphia. Processed.

Topel, Robert H., and Michael P. Ward. 1992. "Job Mobility and the Careers of Young Men." *Quarterly Journal of Economics* 107(2):439–79.

Torney-Purta, Judith, Rainer Lehmann, Hans Oswald, and Wolfram Schulz. 2001. *Citizenship and Education in Twenty-Eight Countries: Civic Knowledge and Engagement at Age Fourteen.* Amsterdam, Netherlands: International Association for the Evaluation of Educational Achievement (IEA). Available online at http://www.wam.umd.edu/~jtpurta/interreport.htm.

Townsend, J., P. Roderick, and J. Cooper. 1994. "Cigarette Smoking by Socio-Economic Group, Sex and Age: Effects of Price, Income and Health Publicity." *British Medical Journal* 309:923–26.

Tudawe, Indra. 2001. "Chronic Poverty and Development Policy in Sri Lanka: Overview Study." Manchester, U.K.: CPRC Working Paper 9. Available online at http://www.chronicpoverty.org/pdfs/09Tudawe.pdf.

Turniški, Maja. 2004. *The Place of Participation in the Recovery of Identity in Adolescents and Young Adults Affected by War and Displacement in Croatia.* New York, NY: The Graduate Center, City University of New York.

Tzannatos, Zafiris. 1999. "Women and Labor Market Changes in the Global Economy." *World Development* 27(3):551–69.

U.S.Department of State. 2005a. *Trafficking in Persons Report 2005.* Washington, DC: U. S. Department of State, Office of the Under Secretary for Global Affairs.

———. 2005b. *Visa Bulletin for October 2005.* Washington, DC: United States, Department of State. Available online at http://travel.state.gov/visa/frvi/bulletin/bulletin_2631.html.

UNAIDS. 2000. *Report on the Global HIV/AIDS Epidemic 2000.* Geneva: UNAIDS.

UNAIDS, and UNODCCP. 2000. *Drug Use and HIV Vulnerability: Policy Research Study in Asia.* Bangkok, Thailand: UNAIDS.

UNDCP. 2003. *Investing in Drug Abuse Treatment: A Discussion Paper for Policy Makers.* New York: UNDCP.

UNDP. 1995. *The World's Women 1995: Trends & Statistics.* New York: United Nations, Department of Economic and Social Affairs Statistics Division.

UNESCO. 2004a. *Gender and Education for All Global Monitoring Report 2003/4: The Leap to Equality.* Paris: UNESCO.

———. 2004b. *Global Monitoring Report 2005. Education for All: The Quality Imperative.* Paris: UNESCO.

———. 2005. *World Education Indicators 2005.* Paris: UNESCO, Institute for Statistics.

UNESCO Institute for Statistics. 2005. *Global Education Digest: Comparing Education Statistics Across the World.* Montreal: UNESCO Institute for Statistics.

UNICEF. 2000. "Young People in Changing Societies." Florence: UNICEF Innocenti Research Center Report 7. Available online at http://www.unicef-icdc.org.

———. 2005a. *Innocenti Digest: Juvenile Justice.* Florence, Italy: Innocenti Research Center.

———. 2005b. *The Impact of Conflict on Women and Girls in West and Central Africa and the UNICEF Response.* Paris: UNICEF.

———. 2005c. *The State of the World's Children 2006.* New York, NY: UNICEF.

UNICEF, UNAIDS, and WHO. 2002. *Young People and HIV/AIDS: Opportunity in Crisis.* New York: UNICEF. Available online at http://www.unicef.org/publications/files/pub_youngpeople_hivaids_en.pdf.

United Kingdom Home Office. 2005. *Accession Monitoring Report.* London: United Kingdom Home Office. Available online at http://www.workingintheuk.gov.uk/ind/en/home/0/reports/accession_monitoring.Maincontent.0018.file.tmp/Accession_Monitoring_ReportNW2%5B1%5D.2doc.pdf.

United Nations. 2003. *World Youth Report 2003: Global Situation of Young People.* New York: United Nations, Department of Economic and Social Affairs.

———. 2005. *World Population Prospects: The 2004 Revision (CD-ROM).* New York: United Nations Population Division, Department of Economic and Social Affairs.

United Nations Economic and Social Council. 2001. *World Situation with Regard to Drug Abuse, with Particular Reference to Children and Youth.* Vienna: United Nations.

United Nations Office on Drugs and Crime. 2004. *Solvent Abuse Among Street Children in Pakistan.* Islamabad: United Nations System in Pakistan.

UNODCCP. 2002. *Street Children of Cairo and Alexandria: Drug Abuse Trends, Consequences and Response.* El Cairo: UNODCCP Regional Office in El Cairo.

Upchurch, Dawn M., Lee A. Lillard, and Constantijn W. A. Panis. 2002. "Nonmarital Childbearing: Influences of Education, Marriage, and Fertility." *Demography* 39(2):311–29.

Urdal, Henrik. 2004. "The Devil in the Demographics: The Effect of Youth Bulges on Domestic Armed Conflicts, 1950-2000." Washington, DC: World Bank, Social Development Papers, Conflict Prevention and Reconstruction 14.

Utas, Mats. 2004. "Building the Future: The Reintegration and Marginalisation of Ex-combatant Youth in Liberia." *In* Paul Richards, (eds.), *No Peace, No War: An Anthropology of Contemporary Armed Conflicts.* Oxford, U.K.: James Currey.

Van der Gaag, Jacques, and Jee-Peng Tan. 1998. *The Benefits of Early Child Development Programs, An Economic Analysis.* Washington, DC: World Bank, Human Development Network.

van Eekelen, Willem, Loetta de Luca, and Nagwa Ismail. 2001. "Youth Employment in Egypt. InFocus Programme on Skills, Knowledge, and Employability Skills." Geneve: International Labour Office, Skills Working Paper 2. Available online at http://www.ilo.org/public/english/employment/skills/youth/download/skillswp2.pdf.

Van Ness, Daniel W. 2005. "An Overview of Restorative Justice Around the World." Paper presented at the 11th United Nations Congress on Crime Prevention, and Criminal Justice. Bangkok, Thailand.

Varcoe, Karen P., Allen Martin, Zana Devitto, and Charles Go. 2005. "Using A Financial Education Curriculum For Teens." *Journal of Financial Counseling and Planning* 16(1):63–71.

Vegas, Emiliana, and Ilana Umansky. 2005. *Improving Teaching and Learning through Effective Incentives: What Can We Learn from Education Reforms in Latin America?* Washington, DC: World Bank.

Venkatraman, Arjunamurthy, and Julie Falconer. 1998. *Rejuvenating India's Decimated Forests through Joint Action: Lessons from Andhra Pradesh.* Washington, DC: World Bank.

Verba, Sidney, Kay Lehman Schlozman, and Henry E. Brady. 1995. *Voice and Equality.* Cambridge, U.K.: Cambridge University Press.

Verner, Dorte, Andreas Blom, and Lauritz Holm-Nielsen. 2001. "Education, Earnings, and Inequality in Brazil 1982-1998." Washington, DC: World Bank Policy Research Working Paper Series 2686.

Vietnam Ministry of Health and General Statistics Office, UNICEF, and WHO. 2005. *Survey Assessment of Vietnamese Youth.* Hanoi: Government of Vietnam.

Villaveces, Andrés, Peter Cummings, Victoria E. Espitia, Thomas D. Koepsell, Barbara McKnight, and Arthur L. Kellermann. 2000. "Effect of a Ban on Carrying Firearms on Homicide Rates in 2 Colombian Cities." *Journal of American Medical Association* 283:1205–9.

Visinntini, R., E. Campanini, A. Fossati, M. Bagnato, L. Novella, and C. Maffei. 1996. "Psychological Stress in Nurses' Relationships with HIV-infected Patients: The Risk of Burnout Syndrome." *AIDS Care* 8(2):183–94.

Viva Rio. 2005. *Youth Service: A Policy for Preventing and Providing Alternatives to Youth Involvement in Urban Violence in Brazil.* Rio de Janeiro, Brazil: Viva Rio.

Vodopivec, Matija. 2005. "Wage and Productivity Differentials during Slovenia's Transition: Matched Employer-Employee Evidence." Senior Honors thesis. Macalester College.

Waiselfisz, Julio Jacobo, and Maria Maciel. 2003. *Revertendo Violências, Semeando Futuros: Avaliação de Impacto do Programa Abrindo Espaços no Rio de Janeiro e em Pernambuco.* Brasilia: UNESCO Office Brasilia.

Walker, S. P., S. M. Grantham-Mcgregor, C. A. Powell, and S. M. Chang. 2005. "Effects of Early Childhood Psychosocial Stimulation and Nutritional Supplementation on Cognition and Education in Growth-stunted Jamaican Children: Prospective Cohort Study." *Lancet* 366(9499):1804–7.

Walzer, Michael. 1989. "Citizenship." *In* Terrence Ball, James Farr, and Russell L Hanson, (eds.), *Political Innovation and Conceptual Change.* New York, NY: Cambridge University Press.

Washington, Ebonya. 2006. "Female Socialization: How Daughters Affect their Legislators Father's Voting on Women's Issues." Cambridge, MA: National Bureau of Economic Research Working Paper Series 11924.

Wattenberg, Martin P. 2006. *Is Voting for Young People?* New York, NY: Longman.

Watts, Anthony G., and David H. Fretwell. 2004. "Public Strategies for Designing Career Information and Guidance Systems in Middle-Income and Transition Economies." World Bank. Washington, DC. Processed.

White, Howard. 2005. *Maintaining Momentum towards the MDGs: An Impact Evaluation of Interventions to Improve Maternal and Child Health and Nutrition Outcomes in Bangladesh.* Washington, DC: World Bank, Operation Evaluation Division.

Whiteside, Katherine, John Bellows, Mame Fatou Diagne, Benn Eifert, Rachel Glennerster, Edward Miguel, David Zimmer, and Yongmei Zhou. 2006. "Baseline Measures of Social Capital in GoBifo Communities: Report for IRCBP." Processed.

WHO. 1998. *The Second Decade: Improving Adolescent Health and Development.* Geneva: World Health Organization. Available online at http://www.who.int/reproductive-health/docs/adolescenthealth.html.

———. 1999. *Volatile Solvent Abuse: A Global Overview.* Geneva: World Health Organization.

———. 2002a. *The World Health Report 2002: Reducing Risks, Promoting Healthy Life.* Geneva: World Health Organization.

———. 2002b. *World Report on Violence and Health: Summary.* Geneva: World Health Organization.

———. 2003a. *Adolescent Pregnancy: Unmet Needs and Undone Deeds. A Review of the Literature and Programs.* Geneva: World Health Organization.

———. 2003b. *Health and Development through Physical Activity and Sport.* Geneva: World Health Organization.

———. 2003c. *Pregnancy, Childbirth, Postpartum and Newborn Care: A Guide for Essential Practice.* Geneva: World Health Organization.

———. 2004. *Global Status Report on Alcohol.* Geneva: World Health Organization.

———. 2005a. *Effectiveness of Drug Dependence Treatment in Preventing HIV among Injecting Drug Users.* Geneva: World Health Organization.

WHO, and World Bank, eds. 2005. *World Report on Road Traffic Injury Prevention.* Geneva and Washington, DC: World Health Organization and World Bank.

WHO, Regional Office for Europe. 2005b. "Status Paper on Prisons, Drugs and Harm Reduction." Copenhagen: World Health Organization Regional Office for Europe EUR/05/5049062.

Willis, Robert J., and John G. Haaga. 1996. "Economic Approaches to Understanding Nonmarital Fertility." *Population and Development Review* 22(Supp.):67–86.

Wilson, David B., Doris L. Mackenzie, and Fawn Ngo Mitchell. 2005. *Effects of Correctional Boot Camps on Offending.* Canberra,

Australia: Campbell Collaboration's Crime & Justice Coordinating Group, Australian Institute of Criminology.

Wintour, Patrick. 2006. "Brown Backs Votes at 16 in Radical Shakeup of Politics." *The Guardian*, February 27. Available online at http://politics.guardian.co.uk/apathy/story/0,,1718744,00 .html.

Witoelar, Finman, Pungpond Rukumnuaykit, and John Strauss. 2005. "Smoking Behavior Among Youth in a Developing Country: Case of Indonesia." Princeton University. Princeton, NJ. Available online at http://paa2006.princeton.edu/download. aspx?submissionId=60756. Processed.

Woessmann, Ludger. 2003. "Schooling Resources, Educational Institutions, and Student Performance: The International Evidence." *Oxford Bulletin of Economics and Statistics* 65(2):117–70.

Woessmann, Ludger, and Eric A. Hanushek. Forthcoming. "Does Educational Tracking Affect Performance and Inequality? Differences-in-Differences Evidence across Countries." *Economic Journal.*

Women´s Commission for Refugee Women and Children. 2002. *Precious Resources Adolescents in the Reconstruction of Sierra Leone, Participatory Research Study with Adolescents and Youth in Sierra Leone.* New York: Women´s Commission for Refugee Women and Children. Available online at http://www.reliefweb. int/library/documents/2002/wcrwc-sie-31oct.pdf.

Wong, Emelita L., Barry M. Popkin, David K. Guiley, and John S. Akin. 1987. "Accessibility, Quality of Care and Prenatal Care in the Philippines." *Social Science & Medicine* 24(11):927–44.

Woolard, Jennifer L., Candice Odgers, Lonn Lanza-Kaduce, and Hayley Daglis. 2005. "Juveniles within Adult Correctional Settings: Legal Pathways and Developmental Considerations." *International Journal of Forensic Mental Health* 4(1):1–18.

World Bank. 1990. *World Development Report 1990: Poverty.* New York: Oxford University Press.

———. 1993a. *World Bank Policy Research Report 1993. The East Asian Miracle: Economic Growth and Public Policy.* New York: Oxford University Press.

———. 1993b. *World Development Report 1993: Investing in Health.* New York: Oxford University Press.

———. 1995. *World Development Report 1995: Workers in an Integrating World.* New York: Oxford University Press.

———. 1999a. *Confronting AIDS: Public Priorities in a Global Epidemic.* New York: Oxford University Press.

———. 1999b. *Curbing the Epidemic: Governments and the Economics of Tobacco Control.* Washington, DC: World Bank.

———. 1999c. *Proposed Learning and Innovation Loan in the Amount of $4.75 Million to the Argentine Republic for an Integrated Drug Prevention Pilot Project.* Washington, DC: World Bank.

———. 2000. *World Development Report 1999/2000: Entering the 21st Century.* New York: Oxford University Press.

———. 2001a. *An Assessment of the Bolsa Escola Programs Report No. 20208-BR.* Washington, DC: World Bank.

———. 2001b. *Caribbean Youth Development, A World Bank Country Study.* Washington, DC: World Bank.

———. 2001c. *World Bank Policy Research Report 2001: Engendering Development Through Gender Equality In Rights, Resources And Voice.* New York: Oxford University Press.

———. 2001d. *World Development Report 2000/01: Attacking Poverty.* New York: Oxford University Press.

———. 2002a. *Constructing Knowledge Societies: New Challenges for Tertiary Education.* Washington, DC: World Bank.

———. 2002b. *Russian Economic Report # 3.* Washington, DC: World Bank.

———. 2003a. "Caribbean Youth Report: Issues and Policy Directions." World Bank. Washington, DC. Processed.

———. 2003b. *Closing the Gap in Education and Technology.* Washington, DC: World Bank.

———. 2003c. *Project Performance Assessment Report, Bangladesh Female Secondary School Assistance Project (Credit 2469).* Washington, DC: World Bank, Operations Evaluation Department.

———. 2003d. *Republic of Tunisia: Employment Strategy. Report # 25456-TUN.* Washington, DC: World Bank.

———. 2003e. *Vietnam Development Report 2004: Poverty. Report No. 27130-VN.* World Bank: Washington, DC

———. 2003f. *World Development Report 2004: Making Services Work for Poor People.* New York: Oxford University Press.

———. 2004a. *Addressing HIV/AIDS in East Asia and the Pacific.* Washington, DC: World Bank.

———. 2004b. *Gender and Development in the Middle East and North Africa: Women in the Public Sphere.* Washington, DC: World Bank.

———. 2004c. *Serbia and Montenegro: Poverty Reduction Strategy Paper and Joint IDA-IMF Staff Assessment of the PRSP, 9.* Washington, DC: World Bank.

———. 2004d. *Timor-Leste Education Since Independence From Reconstruction to Sustainable Improvement.* Washington, DC: World Bank, Human Development Sector Report EAP.

———. 2004e. *World Development Report 2005: A Better Investment Climate for Everyone.* New York: Oxford University Press.

———. 2005a. *Bridging the Gender Gap: Opportunities and Challenges, Pakistan Country Gender Assessment.* Washington, DC: World Bank.

———. 2005b. *Colombia: Contracting Education Services.* Washington, DC: World Bank.

———. 2005c. *Doing Business in 2005: Removing Obstacles to Growth.* Washington, DC: World Bank, International Finance Corporation and Oxford University Press.

———. 2005d. *Dying Too Young: Addressing Premature Mortality and Ill Health Due to Non-Communicable Diseases and Injuries in the Russian Federation.* Washington, DC: World Bank.

———. 2005e. *Economic Growth in the 1990s: Learning from a Decade of Reform.* Washington, DC: World Bank.

———. 2005f. *Expanding Opportunities and Building Competencies for Young People: A New Agenda for Secondary Education.* Washington, DC: World Bank.

———. 2005g. "Gender Assessment in Vietnam." World Bank. Washington, DC. Processed.

———. 2005h. "Gender Mainstreaming Process in the Lao PDR." World Bank. Washington, DC. Processed.

———. 2005i. *Global Economic Prospects 2006: Economic Implications of Remittances and Migration.* Washington DC: World Bank.

———. 2005j. *Global Monitoring Report.* Washington, DC: World Bank.

———. 2005k. *Implementation Completion Report on a Credit to the Republic of Guyana for the Secondary School Reform Project.* Washington, DC: World Bank.

———. 2005l. *Malaysia: Firm Competitiveness, Investment Climate, and Growth. Report N0. 26841-MA.* Washington, DC: World Bank.

———. 2005m. "Pakistan Country Gender Report (Gray Cover)." World Bank. Washington, DC. Processed.

———. 2005n. *Policy Note on Employment of Migrants in China.* Washington, DC: World Bank.

———. 2005o. *Republic of Uruguay. Policy Notes. Report No. 31338-UY.* Washington, DC: World Bank.

———. 2005p. *Tobacco Use in Indonesia.* Washington, DC: World Bank.

———. 2005q. *Vietnam Business: Vietnam Development Report 2006. Report No. 34474-VN.* World Bank: Washington, DC

———. 2005r. *World Development Report 2006: Equity and Development.* New York: Oxford University Press.

———. 2005s. "Youth Development in Kenya." World Bank. Washington, DC. Processed.

———. 2005t. "Youth in Post-Conflict Settings." Washington, DC: Youth Development Notes Volume 1, Number 1.

———. 2006a. "Crime, Violence, and Economic Development in Brazil: Elements for Effective Public Policy." World Bank. Washington, DC. Processed.

———. 2006b. *Global Monitoring Report 2006.* Washington, DC: World Bank.

———. 2006c. *Information and Communications for Development: Global Trends and Policies.* Washington, DC: World Bank.

———. 2006d. *Mobilizing Resources for Secondary Education in EAP and LAC.* Washington, DC: World Bank.

———. 2006e. *Public Training Reform Issues in Colombia: The Case of SENA. Report # 27752.* Washington, DC: World Bank.

———. 2006f. *Repositioning Nutrition as Central to Development: A Strategy for Large Scale Action.* Washington, DC: World Bank.

———. 2006g. "School-to-Work Transition and Youth Inclusion in Southern Russia." World Bank. Washington, DC. Processed.

———. 2006h. *World Development Indicators.* Washington, DC: World Bank.

———. 2006i. *Youth at Risk in Brazil, Report No. 32310-BR.* Washington, DC: World Bank.

World Bank, Unesco Institute for Statistics (UIS), and OECD. 2006. *Education Statistics (EDSTATS).* Washington, DC:

World Bank. Available online at http://www1.worldbank. org/education/edstats/.

World Links Impact Evaluation Series. 2002. *Uganda Tracer Study: An Impact Assessment of Information and Communications Technologies on World Links Participating Students.* Washington DC: World Links.

Yamano, Takashi, and T. S. Jayne. 2004. "Measuring the Impacts of Working-Age Adult Mortality on Small-Scale Farm Households in Kenya." *World Development* 32(1):91–119.

Yang, Dean. 2004. "International Migration, Human Capital, and Entrepreneurship: Evidence from Philippine Migrants' Exchange Rate Shock." Washington D.C: World Bank policy research working paper 3578.

———. 2005. "Why Do Inmigrants Return to Poor Countries? Evidence from Philippines Migrant's Responses to Exchange Rate Shocks." University of Michigan. Ann Arbor. Processed.

Yap, Yoon-Tien, Guilherme Sedlacek, and Peter F. Orazem. 2001. "Limiting Child Labor Through Behavior-Based Income Transfers: An Experimental Evaluation of the PETI Program in Rural Brazil." World Bank. Washington, DC. Processed.

Yip, R. 1994. "Iron Deficiency: Contemporary Scientific Issues and International Programmatic Approaches." *Journal of Nutrition* 124(8):1479S–1490S.

Yip, R., and P. R. Dallman. 1996. "Iron." *In* E. E. Ziegler and L. J. Jr. Filer, (eds.), *Present Knowledge of Nutrition. 7th ed.* Washington, DC: International Life Sciences Institute Press.

Zabin, Laurie Schwab, and Karungari Kiragu. 1998. "The Health Consequences of Adolescent Sexual and Fertility Behavior in Sub-Saharan Africa." *Studies in Family Planning* 29(2):210–32.

Zeldin, Shepherd, Annette Kusgen McDaniel, Dimitri Topitzes, and Matt Calvert. 2000. *Youth in Decision-Making: A Study on the Impacts of Youth on Adults and Organizations.* Madison, W.I.: Innovation Center for Community and Youth Development, University of Wisconsin-Madison. Available online at http://www.theinnovationcenter.org/pdfs/Youth_in_Decision_Making_Brochure.pdf.

Zins, J. E., R. P. Weissberg, M. C. Wang, and H. J. Walberg, eds. 2004. *Building Academic Success on Social and Emotional Llearning: What Does the Research Say?* New York: Teachers College Press.

Selected indicators

Selected world development indicators

Table A1. Learning

	Survey year	Total ages 12-14	Total ages 15-17	Total ages 18-24	Male ages 12-14	Male ages 15-17	Male ages 18-24	Female ages 12-14	Female ages 15-17	Female ages 18-24	Grade 9 completion rate[a] Total	Grade 9 completion rate[a] Male	Grade 9 completion rate[a] Female
Afghanistan	2003	36	25	11	54	42	18	19	8	3	20	31	6
Albania	2002	89	46	11	90	47	9	88	45	13	35	36	34
Angola	1999	55	45	18	56	48	20	53	41	16	10	11	10
Argentina	2001	97	86	46	97	84	43	98	87	48	78	76	81
Armenia	1999	98	73	19	98	68	13	99	77	25	..	..	..
Azerbaijan	2002	100	81	17	100	79	17	100	83	17	..	..	..
Bangladesh	2000	67	46	17	62	40	24	72	54	11	40	38	41
Benin	2003	65	49	23	72	56	34	56	41	14	48	55	39
Bhutan	2003	67	52	22	71	61	29	63	44	16	46	53	40
Bolivia	2002	54	51	34	54	52	35	55	49	32	31	31	31
Bosnia and Herzegovina	2001	98	90	28	98	93	22	99	87	34	..	..	..
Brazil	2001	95	81	34	95	82	34	95	80	34	57	57	57
Bulgaria	1995	92	77	24	92	80	22	93	74	25	53	56	50
Burkina Faso	2003	32	20	9	36	21	12	28	18	7	18	19	16
Burundi	1998	52	36	19	59	39	21	47	34	17	26	30	22
Cambodia	2004	88	61	15	89	66	21	86	55	11	38	43	34
Cameroon	2001	83	63	28	86	71	34	80	55	22	55	61	49
Cape Verde	2000	91	63	21	91	62	20	91	64	22	59	58	60
Chile	2003	98	91	40	98	91	41	99	91	38	79	80	79
Colombia	2000	85	66	27	84	64	28	86	68	26	50	49	51
Costa Rica	2001	87	66	37	88	64	36	87	68	38	60	58	62
Côte d'Ivoire	2002	61	39	17	69	50	23	51	29	12	36	46	26
Dominican Republic	2004	96	83	40	96	81	37	96	84	42	75	76	75
Ecuador	2004	85	68	33	85	66	32	85	69	35	62	61	63
Egypt, Arab Rep.	1998	84	69	26	88	73	29	81	65	23	64	68	61
El Salvador	2002	87	66	25	86	68	26	87	65	24	50	50	49
Estonia	2000	99	93	42	100	92	43	99	95	41	81	80	82
Fiji	1996	92	68	14	91	65	15	93	71	13	61	60	63
Ghana	1998	85	67	22	88	72	28	81	61	16	..	..	..
Guatemala	2002	71	46	20	79	52	26	63	40	15	35	41	29
Guinea	1994	36	29	13	44	37	22	26	19	6	34	44	24
Guyana	2000	94	64	0	92	62	0	95	66	0	45	42	47
Honduras	2003	77	48	23	77	45	21	78	52	25	47	45	50
Hungary	2002	100	98	50	100	98	50	100	97	51	..	..	..
India	2000	71	51	16	77	57	21	65	43	11	..	..	..
Indonesia	2002	88	62	16	87	62	18	88	61	15	43	44	43
Jamaica	2002	98	74	9	97	70	7	99	78	10	46	42	50
Jordan	2002	87	85	31	86	84	30	87	86	32	69	67	72
Kenya	1997	92	77	22	92	80	28	92	73	17	45	51	38
Kiribati	2000	89	58	9	87	52	8	91	65	9	..	..	..
Kyrgyz Republic	2002	96	90	30	96	89	24	96	90	35	..	..	..
Lesotho	2002	86	60	19	80	58	21	91	61	16	38	40	38
Malawi	1997	90	80	33	91	85	47	88	74	22	..	..	..
Maldives	1998	92	72	21	93	73	19	92	71	24	44	43	45
Marshall Islands	1999	86	70	29	85	69	32	87	70	27	55	55	56
Mauritania	2000	53	39	20	56	43	22	51	36	19	32	31	33
Mexico	2002	90	61	26	90	61	28	89	61	25	47	48	45
Micronesia, Fed. Sts.	2000	86	68	21	84	64	20	88	71	21	49	47	52
Moldova	2002	98	74	24	99	69	23	98	78	25	..	..	..
Mozambique	1996	58	37	10	64	44	17	52	28	4	10	13	8
Namibia	1993	94	84	40	94	83	43	94	84	37	..	..	..
Nepal	1995	61	43	14	71	51	18	51	36	9	0	0	0
Nicaragua	2001	82	59	27	79	54	25	86	63	29	48	42	53
Niger	2002	69	43	25	70	43	27	68	43	22	44	44	44
Nigeria	2003	64	58	36	64	59	42	65	58	30	44	44	43
Pakistan	2001	53	37	10	63	46	13	43	27	7	24	30	18
Palau	2000	96	88	31	95	86	30	96	91	31	76	75	78
Panama	2003	92	76	35	92	73	33	92	79	38	64	61	68
Paraguay	2001	87	64	28	87	61	28	87	67	29	55	53	58
Peru	2002	94	73	29	95	75	29	93	71	29	56	56	56
Poland	2002	100	99	54	100	98	52	100	99	57	..	..	..
Romania	1994	95	80	21	95	80	19	95	81	24	0	0	0
Rwanda	1997	77	40	14	77	42	15	78	39	13	23	23	23
São Tomé and Principe	2000	76	48	14	75	50	15	76	45	14	35	36	34
Senegal	1995	68	38	23	79	42	28	59	34	19	38	43	35
Sierra Leone	2003	77	61	31	81	68	43	72	52	21	51	59	43
Solomon Islands	1999	74	58	19	76	63	24	73	53	15	33	36	29
South Africa	2000	96	90	43	96	91	45	96	90	42	75	77	74
Swaziland	2000	90	76	25	89	78	34	91	75	18	60	64	57
Tajikistan	1999	91	63	10	94	72	15	88	54	6	..	..	..
Tanzania	2000	78	49	9	79	52	11	77	46	6	10	9	11
Thailand	2002	94	77	29	93	71	29	95	82	30	67	62	72
Tonga	1996	95	77	24	94	74	24	96	81	24	70	67	73
Trinidad and Tobago	1992	90	68	19	87	64	17	93	72	21	..	..	..
Turkey	2002	85	49	11	91	59	16	78	40	7	..	..	..
Uganda	2002	92	72	20	93	74	30	92	70	13	46	51	42
Uruguay	2003	96	81	44	95	78	41	96	84	48	72	69	76
Venezuela, RB	2004	93	76	26	92	74	23	95	78	28	59	57	62
Vietnam	2001	88	63	25	89	66	26	87	60	24	56	58	54
Zambia	2002	84	69	24	84	75	30	84	64	19	44	48	42

a. The statistic is computed using the information from nationally representative household surveys on last grade completed and current school participation of individuals ages 10-19 at the time of the survey. Estimates are are based on Kaplan-Meier method which takes into account whether the individual is still in school.

Table A2. Program for International Student Assessment

	Literacy, age 15, 2003			Math, age 15, 2003			Problem solving scale, age 15, 2003		
	Total	Male	Female	Total	Male	Female	Total	Male	Female
Australia	526	506	545	524	527	522	530	527	533
Austria	491	467	514	506	509	502	506	505	508
Belgium	508	489	526	529	533	525	525	522	527
Brazil	402	384	419	357	365	348	371	374	368
Canada	530	514	546	535	541	530	529	533	532
Czech Republic	489	473	504	516	524	509	516	520	513
Denmark	492	479	505	514	523	506	517	519	514
Finland	543	521	565	544	548	541	548	543	553
France	495	476	514	511	515	507	519	519	520
Germany	492	471	513	503	508	499	513	511	517
Greece	472	453	490	445	455	436	448	450	448
Hong Kong, China	510	494	525	550	552	548	548	545	550
Hungary	483	467	498	490	494	486	501	499	503
Iceland	493	464	522	515	508	523	505	490	520
Indonesia	382	370	394	360	362	359	361	358	365
Ireland	516	501	530	503	510	495	498	499	498
Italy	475	455	495	466	475	457	469	467	471
Japan	498	487	509	534	539	530	547	546	548
Korea, Dem. Rep.	536	526	547	540	552	528	550	554	546
Latvia	490	470	509	483	485	482	483	481	484
Mexico	399	389	410	385	391	380	384	387	382
Netherlands	513	503	524	538	540	535	520	522	518
New Zealand	522	508	535	524	531	516	533	531	534
Norway	500	475	525	495	498	492	490	486	494
Poland	497	477	516	490	493	488	487	486	487
Portugal	477	459	495	466	472	460	470	470	470
Russian Federation	442	428	456	468	474	463	479	480	477
Serbia and Montenegro	412	390	433	437	438	436	420	416	424
Slovak Republic	470	453	486	498	507	489	492	495	488
Spain	480	461	500	485	490	481	482	479	485
Sweden	514	496	533	509	512	506	509	504	514
Switzerland	500	482	518	526	535	518	521	520	523
Thailand	418	396	439	417	415	419	425	418	431
Tunisia	374	362	387	359	365	353	345	346	343
Turkey	443	426	459	423	430	415	408	408	406
United States	495	479	511	483	486	480	477	477	478
Uruguay	434	414	453	422	428	416	411	412	409

Table A3. Going to work

| | | Labor force participation rate, ages 15–24 | | | Unemployment rate | | | | | | Not in the labor force and not in school, ages 15–24 | | |
| | | | | | by age group | | by gender, ages 15–24 | | by urban/rural, ages 15–24 | | | | |
		Total	Male	Female	Young, ages 15–24 total	Adult, ages 25–49 total	Male	Female	Urban	Rural	Total	Male	Female
Afghanistan	2003	39.9	60.8	17.3	7.5	3.9	6.0	12.8	..	..	46.1	18.0	77.1
Albania	2002	42.5	42.0	43.0	14.2	9.6	16.3	12.1	45.2	4.6	36.2	37.7	34.6
Angola	1999	46.4	48.1	44.9	8.0	3.8	10.5	5.6	9.3	0.4	30.7	26.9	34.1
Argentina	2001	38.6	47.4	29.9	28.8	12.0	27.4	31.1	28.8	..	13.1	6.8	19.4
Azerbaijan	2002	35.9	41.6	30.3	..	..	..	..	..	..	25.6	19.2	31.9
Bangladesh	2000	33.9	58.9	7.3	4.1	1.1	3.2	11.6	6.8	3.3	39.9	11.8	69.9
Belarus	2002	30.4	30.5	30.3	21.8	6.3	22.9	20.7	21.9	21.3	..	..	..
Benin	2003	53.9	46.3	61.8	5.9	3.0	6.0	5.9	8.8	4.5	14.5	12.4	16.5
Bhutan	2003	55.8	51.8	59.3	1.4	0.5	1.1	1.5	5.1	0.8	11.6	7.2	15.4
Bolivia	2002	58.9	66.9	51.3	13.7	7.0	9.9	18.4	20.0	5.5	9.0	7.7	10.4
Bosnia and Herzegovina	2004	46.0	..	..	43.0	19.9	42.5	43.6	..	..	..	..	..
Brazil	2001	61.8	72.7	51.2	17.9	7.2	14.6	22.4	20.5	5.2	13.5	5.8	21.0
Bulgaria	1995	39.7	40.9	38.4	38.6	12.7	37.2	40.1	37.4	40.7	19.0	17.6	20.4
Burkina Faso	2003	79.1	82.4	76.2	3.8	1.8	3.9	3.6	22.1	0.7	8.7	3.1	13.7
Burundi	1998	70.7	67.8	73.1	0.4	0.5	0.6	0.3	25.3	..	3.9	3.8	3.9
Cambodia	2004	77.9	79.3	76.5	1.4	0.5	1.5	1.2	4.2	0.8	9.8	6.3	13.2
Cameroon	2001	48.7	51.0	46.7	12.6	5.8	14.7	10.6	29.5	4.5	17.0	8.4	24.8
Cape Verde	2000	50.8	58.7	43.1	26.1	8.7	24.5	28.3	30.5	21.1	15.1	8.2	21.8
Chile	2003	36.1	41.7	30.3	21.2	8.3	17.8	26.1	22.3	14.0	14.4	7.8	21.1
Colombia	2000	57.1	66.1	48.6	30.2	13.6	23.1	39.3	36.0	20.1	14.2	5.6	22.4
Costa Rica	2001	51.4	64.8	37.0	13.4	4.0	11.9	16.4	14.0	12.7	16.5	5.7	28.1
Côte d'Ivoire	2002	48.4	53.0	44.3	5.0	3.9	6.0	3.8	12.9	1.3	28.4	16.5	39.0
Croatia	2004	34.7	37.6	31.5	36.0	13.5	32.2	41.1	36.7	35.5	7.1	7.8	6.2
Dominican Republic	2004	51.3	67.5	35.0	20.6	8.8	16.6	28.2	22.0	17.6	48.7	32.5	65.0
Ecuador	2004	50.8	62.9	38.3	12.2	4.7	10.1	15.6	17.5	3.8	16.6	6.7	26.9
Egypt, Arab Rep.	1998	42.3	44.8	39.5	23.7	5.2	22.1	25.7	32.5	19.6	18.7	12.2	25.8
El Salvador	2002	45.7	60.8	31.4	11.5	4.9	13.1	8.4	11.7	11.1	22.5	7.8	36.6
Estonia	2000	38.8	44.3	32.7	21.2	11.5	24.2	16.9	19.1	25.6	9.1	4.2	14.6
Ethiopia	2000	62.0	75.0	50.1	3.9	1.8	2.8	5.3	27.9	0.6	..	..	..
Fiji	1996	35.7	49.7	21.2	16.2	4.3	12.9	24.2	18.1	14.9	30.9	17.6	44.7
Gambia, The	1998	36.4	32.4	40.2	9.2	3.4	12.9	6.4	26.6	2.9	34.6	30.7	38.4
Ghana	1998	49.1	47.5	50.8	15.7	3.4	16.1	15.2	26.0	11.5	22.6	20.4	24.9
Guinea	1994	71.1	67.9	74.2	2.1	2.2	2.5	1.6	7.4	0.2	10.5	5.1	15.8
Haiti	2001	39.0	42.9	35.2	54.6	22.5	48.8	61.7	70.6	39.5	..	..	..
Honduras	2003	52.2	73.5	31.5	7.9	4.7	6.1	12.1	12.0	4.2	31.6	8.5	56.6
Hungary	2002	33.6	34.6	32.5	11.5	7.6	12.6	10.2	9.7	14.6	4.4	3.9	5.1
India	2000	44.3	63.0	24.1	8.1	1.6	8.4	7.0	15.6	5.9	29.2	5.1	55.3
Indonesia	2002	49.7	60.1	39.4	22.0	3.3	20.6	24.1	28.1	16.8	21.0	9.2	32.6
Jamaica	2002	30.0	37.2	22.6	18.9	6.6	14.5	26.3	17.8	18.7	40.1	35.7	44.6
Jordan	2002	33.6	51.2	15.1	42.2	17.0	37.6	58.8	40.4	48.7	18.9	3.0	35.6
Kazakhstan	2002	43.3	48.3	37.9	20.8	7.3	19.0	23.4	17.6	24.3	..	..	..
Kenya	1997	39.7	43.1	36.5	20.7	6.3	22.1	19.1	31.5	17.4	24.7	15.9	33.0
Kiribati	2000	76.1	77.7	74.4	2.0	1.3	2.0	2.0	..	..	4.2	4.3	4.2
Kyrgyz Republic	2002	35.1	39.3	30.9	16.7	3.9	18.4	14.5	37.8	10.5	14.5	13.6	15.4
Latvia	2004	30.6	36.0	24.9	21.7	11.4	22.0	21.2	..	..	7.0	6.7	7.3
Lesotho	2002	47.7	48.7	46.8	52.4	32.4	46.7	58.0	42.2	56.3	21.2	18.5	23.8
Lithuania	2000	..	..	..	9.2	10.5	11.1	7.2	9.6	8.2	..	..	..

		Labor force participation rate, ages 15–24			Unemployment rate						Not in the labor force and not in school, ages 15–24		
					by age group		by gender, ages 15–24		by urban/rural, ages 15–24				
		Total	Male	Female	Young, ages 15–24 total	Adult, ages 25–49 total	Male	Female	Urban	Rural	Total	Male	Female
Madagascar	2001	59.9	64.6	55.3	4.1	3.3	3.9	4.2	9.3	2.7	..	..	..
Malawi	1997	..	..	..	7.9	2.1	10.6	4.9	21.0	5.5	31.3	17.4	44.2
Marshall Islands	1999	..	..	..	21.2	5.7	16.4	28.9	24.2	16.9	44.0	39.4	48.6
Mauritania	2000	26.1	33.6	19.2	10.8	7.9	11.2	10.1	26.9	3.2	46.5	36.1	56.0
Mexico	2002	49.0	64.8	33.6	6.7	1.9	7.6	4.9	7.2	5.3	20.3	5.3	35.2
Micronesia, Fed. Sts.	2000	38.9	43.5	34.0	30.7	14.3	27.4	35.3	..	..	28.3	25.2	31.6
Moldova	2002	66.8	66.1	67.6	5.7	4.4	5.8	5.6	12.5	0.7	11.9	13.0	10.9
Mozambique	1996	64.2	59.2	68.8	1.1	0.6	2.4	0.2	7.2	0.3	16.9	13.8	19.6
Namibia	1993	35.3	37.8	33.1	35.1	18.2	32.6	37.7	49.0	22.8	14.7	9.9	19.1
Nepal	1995	62.3	59.6	65.0	..	..	..	..	..	..	23.0	22.4	23.7
Netherlands	1999	53.6	49.7	57.8	3.8	2.0	3.7	3.9	..	..	1.9	1.5	2.3
Nicaragua	2001	50.2	70.2	30.1	5.2	3.3	4.4	7.0	7.3	2.6	24.0	9.6	38.5
Niger	2002	36.6	48.6	26.8	20.8	8.7	21.0	20.4	..	..	35.3	22.6	45.7
Nigeria	2003	..	..	..	5.6	1.1	5.9	5.3	10.2	3.5	35.4	30.9	40.1
Pakistan	2001	44.7	65.1	24.9	10.4	4.4	8.0	16.5	14.9	8.6	37.9	13.1	62.1
Palau	2000	27.5	29.0	25.8	9.9	3.4	9.5	10.4	..	..	25.2	24.6	25.9
Panama	2003	46.1	60.2	31.5	21.4	7.8	18.4	27.4	27.3	11.3	15.9	5.4	26.8
Paraguay	2001	61.1	75.7	45.8	13.8	5.6	11.7	17.3	18.4	7.7	16.3	6.2	26.9
Peru	2002	57.4	64.3	50.3	13.5	6.9	13.0	14.2	..	..	13.3	7.4	19.4
Poland	2002	55.6	56.4	54.8	19.4	15.3	19.9	18.8	22.1	16.2	10.2	10.2	10.2
Romania	2002	63.3	63.6	63.1	24.2	11.8	24.0	24.4	26.3	22.4	..	..	..
Russian Federation	2002	37.8	38.5	37.0	25.7	11.5	24.2	27.4	21.7	35.4	..	..	..
Rwanda	1997	72.9	71.5	74.1	9.6	9.1	10.1	9.2	27.6	8.0	5.9	5.6	6.1
São Tomé and Principe	2000	35.2	50.3	20.0	8.5	1.4	7.1	11.6	7.2	10.1	40.5	24.2	57.0
Senegal	1995	37.5	53.1	24.2	10.1	9.0	12.3	6.0	..	..	33.6	12.6	51.0
Serbia and Montenegro	2005	36.6	41.1	31.9	61.0	26.0	64.3	56.5	..	..	..	..	..
Sierra Leone	2003	40.3	34.2	46.0	1.8	3.0	2.2	1.5	3.6	1.0	19.2	14.7	23.5
Slovak Republic	1992	41.7	47.2	36.2	19.6	7.3	20.5	18.4	15.3	19.8	15.5	7.9	22.9
Slovenia	1999	38.4	43.4	32.8	30.3	10.9	27.4	34.6	..	..	0.6	0.7	0.5
Solomon Islands	1999	54.8	57.3	52.2	11.5	4.8	12.7	10.1	..	..	20.7	14.5	27.0
South Africa	2000	27.8	29.5	26.1	54.1	25.4	49.6	59.1	53.8	54.9	16.2	13.4	18.9
Sri Lanka	2002	50.0	59.5	40.6	45.2	10.3	39.9	52.9	47.3	44.9	..	..	..
Swaziland	2000	34.6	37.2	32.1	13.8	5.8	16.6	10.6	10.2	15.4	22.8	14.3	30.9
Sweden	2000	55.8	57.9	53.6	32.0	6.1	33.3	30.4	29.6	34.4	1.2	1.1	1.2
Tajikistan	1999	48.9	54.5	43.6	25.8	12.9	27.9	23.4	23.8	26.3	28.1	18.5	37.2
Tanzania	2000	66.9	69.1	65.2	2.8	0.8	4.6	1.4	10.9	1.1	12.7	6.8	17.5
Thailand	2002	51.8	57.8	46.0	9.2	1.1	10.4	7.8	12.8	7.4	5.9	2.6	9.0
Tonga	1996	42.1	53.9	29.7	30.2	8.7	31.9	27.0	..	..	16.4	6.2	27.1
Trinidad and Tobago	1992	38.9	50.9	26.8	19.6	12.9	18.2	22.4	21.2	18.5	29.8	21.4	38.2
Turkey	2002	45.3	58.8	34.1	18.2	5.5	21.5	13.6	12.5	23.7	31.9	11.8	48.7
Uganda	2002	55.0	49.1	60.1	6.0	1.8	4.2	7.2	23.2	2.5	8.6	5.5	11.3
Ukraine	2003	32.4	36.8	27.6	39.1	18.2	37.8	40.9	33.3	51.4	..	..	..
Uruguay	2003	52.6	59.8	45.3	38.0	13.4	33.5	44.0	..	..	10.0	5.7	14.4
Venezuela, RB	2004	46.5	59.3	33.2	19.3	11.1	17.9	21.9	..	..	20.2	10.7	30.1
Vietnam	2001	63.9	63.7	64.0	5.4	1.1	5.8	5.0	14.6	3.6	5.0	3.7	6.3
Yemen, Rep.	1998	26.3	37.4	14.9	14.5	5.3	17.9	5.7	34.7	10.9	..	..	..
Zambia	2002	34.8	33.8	35.8	25.0	6.1	28.4	21.8	46.2	4.2	26.2	21.0	31.2

Table A4. Child labor

		Economically active children				
		% of children ages 7–14			% of children ages 7–14	
	Survey year	Total	Male	Female	Work only	Work and study
Albania	2000	36.6	41.1	31.8	43.1	56.9
Angola	1995	5.2	4.9	5.6	77.6	22.4
Argentina	1997	20.7	25.4	16.0	8.6	91.4
Azerbaijan	2000	9.7	12.0	7.3	4.2	95.8
Bangladesh	2003	17.5	20.9	13.9	63.3	36.7
Bolivia	2000	19.2	20.4	18.0	19.7	80.3
Bosnia and Herzegovina	2000	20.2	22.8	17.6	4.0	96.0
Brazil	2003	7.1	9.5	4.6	5.8	94.2
Burkina Faso[a]	1998	66.5	65.4	67.7	95.9	4.1
Burundi	2000	37.0	38.4	35.7	48.3	51.7
Cambodia	2001	52.3	52.4	52.1	16.5	83.5
Cameroon[a]	2001	15.9	14.5	17.4	52.5	47.5
Central African Republic	2000	67.0	66.5	67.6	54.9	45.1
Chad	2000	69.9	73.5	66.5	44.6	55.4
Chile	2003	8.8	10.5	6.9	4.0	96.0
Colombia	2001	12.2	16.6	7.7	23.0	77.0
Congo, Dem. Rep.	2000	39.8	39.9	39.8	35.7	64.3
Costa Rica	2002	6.7	9.7	3.5	20.8	79.2
Côte d'Ivoire	2000	40.7	40.9	40.5	46.4	53.6
Dominican Republic	2000	12.5	16.7	8.1	7.2	92.8
Ecuador	2001	17.9	22.1	13.6	25.1	75.0
Egypt, Arab Rep.	1998	6.4	4.0	8.9	60.9	39.1
El Salvador	2003	12.7	17.1	8.1	19.5	80.5
Ethiopia	2001	57.1	67.9	45.9	63.5	36.5
Gambia, The	2000	25.3	25.4	25.3	41.6	58.4
Ghana	2000	28.5	28.5	28.4	36.4	63.6
Guatemala	2000	20.1	25.9	13.9	38.5	61.5
Guinea	1994	48.3	47.2	49.5	98.6	1.4
Guinea-Bissau	2000	67.5	67.4	67.5	63.7	36.3
Honduras	2002	11.4	16.5	6.1	41.9	58.1
India	2000	5.2	5.3	5.1	89.8	10.2
Iraq	2000	13.7	17.4	9.7	51.7	48.3
Kazakhstan	1996	29.7	30.3	29.1	4.4	95.6
Kenya	1999	6.7	6.9	6.4	44.8	55.2
Kyrgyz Republic	1998	8.6	9.7	7.6	7.0	93.0
Lesotho	2000	30.8	34.2	27.5	17.6	82.4
Madagascar	2001	25.6	26.1	25.1	85.1	14.9
Malawi	2000	10.6	9.4	11.6	17.1	82.9
Mali	2001	25.3	32.3	18.6	68.7	31.3
Mexico[b]	1996	14.7	20.0	9.5	45.6	54.4
Moldova	2000	33.5	34.1	32.8	3.8	96.2
Mongolia	2000	22.0	23.5	20.6	28.2	71.8
Morocco	1998/99	13.2	13.5	12.8	93.2	6.8
Namibia	1999	15.4	16.2	14.7	9.5	90.5
Nepal	1999	47.2	42.2	52.4	35.6	64.4
Nicaragua	2001	12.1	17.5	6.5	33.3	66.7
Panama	2000	4.0	6.4	1.4	37.5	62.5
Paraguay	1999	8.1	11.7	4.4	24.2	75.7
Peru	1994	17.7	20.4	15.2	7.3	92.7
Philippines	2001	13.3	16.3	10.0	14.8	85.2
Portugal	2001	3.6	4.6	2.6	3.6	96.4
Rwanda	2000	33.1	36.1	30.3	27.5	72.5
Senegal	2000	35.4	43.2	27.7	56.2	43.8
Sierra Leone	2000	74.0	24.7	72.7	53.8	46.2
South Africa	1999	27.7	29.0	26.4	5.1	94.9
Sudan	2000	19.1	21.5	16.8	55.9	44.1
Swaziland	2000	11.2	11.4	10.9	14.0	86.0
Tanzania	2001	40.4	41.5	39.2	40.0	60.0
Togo	2000	72.5	73.4	71.6	28.4	71.6
Trinidad and Tobago	2000	3.9	5.2	2.8	12.8	87.2
Turkey	1999	4.5	5.2	3.8	66.8	33.2
Uganda	2002/03	13.1	15.0	11.3	18.3	81.7
Uzbekistan	2000	18.1	22.0	14.0	4.1	95.9
Venezuela, RB	2003	9.1	11.4	6.6	17.6	82.4
Yemen, Rep.	1999	13.1	12.4	14.0	64.3	35.7
Zambia	1999	14.4	15.0	13.9	72.8	27.2

a. Data are for children ages 10–14. b. Data are for children ages 12–14.

Table A5. Staying healthy

| | Tobacco use in adolescents | | | Probability that a 15-year-old will die before the age of 60, 2003 | |
| | | Female | Male | per 1,000 | |
	Survey year	% ages 13–15	% ages 13–15	Female	Male
Afghanistan				448	510
Albania	2006	9	16	92	167
Algeria		..	..	125	155
Andorra				41	107
Angola		..	..	488	584
Antigua and Barbuda	2000	11	16	122	193
Argentina	2000	34	31	90	176
Armenia		..	..	108	240
Australia		..	..	51	89
Austria		..	..	59	115
Azerbaijan		..	..	120	220
Bahamas, The	2000	14	23	146	257
Bahrain	2001	12	34	81	117
Barbados	2002	13	16	106	189
Belize	2003	14	24	153	257
Bangladesh		..	..	258	251
Belarus		..	..	130	370
Belgium		..	..	66	125
Benin	2003	10	24	332	393
Bhutan		..	..	202	261
Bolivia	2000	24	35	180	247
Bosnia and Herzegovina	2003	12	19	89	190
Botswana	2001	12	17	839	850
Brazil	2002	18	21	129	240
Brunei		..	..	86	114
Bulgaria	2002	42	33	91	216
Burkina Faso	2001	7	18	462	533
Burundi		..	..	525	654
Cambodia	2003	3	11	285	441
Cameroon		..	..	461	503
Canada		..	..	57	93
Cape Verde		..	..	129	213
Central African Republic		..	..	590	641
Chad		..	..	444	513
Chile	2000	42	33	66	133
China	2003	6	14	103	164
Colombia	2001	29	30	97	231
Comoros		..	..	182	254
Congo, Dem. Rep.		..	..	452	578
Congo, Rep.		..	..	381	434
Costa Rica	2002	19	20	76	129
Côte d'Ivoire		..	..	450	558
Croatia	2002	15	19	70	173
Cuba	2001	18	17	87	137
Cyprus		..	..	47	99
Czech Republic	2002	33	36	74	166
Denmark		..	..	73	121
Djibouti		..	..	311	376
Dominica	2000	16	24	118	210
Dominican Republic		..	..	147	250
Ecuador	2001	17	21	127	212
Egypt, Arab Rep.	2001	16	23	157	242
El Salvador	2003	15	25	138	248
Eritrea		..	..	301	359
Estonia	2002	30	35	114	319
Ethiopia	2003	6	12	386	450
Fiji	1999	13	24	173	275
Finland		..	..	57	134
France		..	..	59	132
Gambia, The		..	..	262	332
Gabon		..	..	323	397
Georgia	2002	13	34	76	195
Germany		..	..	59	115
Ghana	2000	19	20	295	352
Grenada	2000	14	18	220	258
Greece		..	..	48	118
Guatemala	2002	12	18	165	289
Guinea		..	..	342	403
Guyana	2004	5	15	255	290
Guinea-Bissau		..	..	405	479
Haiti	2001	18	18	385	450
Honduras	2003	19	27	181	248
Hungary	2002	33	34	111	257
Iceland		..	..	53	81
India	2001	20	29	213	283
Indonesia	2000	5	37	204	241
Iran, Islamic Rep.	2003	5	14	125	201
Iraq		..	..	205	466
Ireland		..	..	60	100
Israel		..	..	51	92

Table A5. Staying healthy *(continued)*

| | Tobacco use in adolescents | | | Probability that a 15-year-old will die before the age of 60, 2003 per 1,000 | |
	Survey year	Female % ages 13–15	Male % ages 13–15	Female	Male
Italy		..	..	47	93
Jamaica	2001	15	24	123	165
Japan		..	..	45	96
Jordan	2004	12	28	120	189
Kazakhstan		..	..	187	419
Kenya	2003	14	21	521	495
Kiribati		..	..	191	304
Korea, Dem. Rep.		..	..	168	231
Korea, Rep.		..	..	61	155
Kuwait	2001	18	33	53	73
Kyrgyz Republic		..	..	160	339
Lao PDR	2003	4	18	303	335
Latvia	2002	33	41	120	306
Lebanon	2001	40	46	138	199
Lesotho	2002	20	32	781	912
Liberia		..	..	484	590
Libya	2003	9	19	101	172
Lithuania	2001	32	40	106	302
Luxembourg		..	..	63	115
Macedonia, FYR	2002	8	12	86	202
Madagascar		..	..	260	337
Malawi	2001	15	20	615	652
Malaysia		..	..	108	195
Mali	2001	13	45	427	486
Malta		..	..	49	84
Marshall Islands		..	..	280	333
Mauritania	2001	23	34	312	408
Mauritius		..	..	115	218
Mexico	2002	20	24	95	166
Micronesia, Fed. Sts.		..	..	172	206
Monaco		..	..	47	110
Moldova		..	..	152	303
Mongolia		..	..	179	310
Morocco	2001	9	17	103	159
Mozambique	2002	10	11	543	621
Myanmar	2001	5	37	222	337
Namibia		..	..	529	619
Nauru		..	..	303	448
Nepal	2001	6	15	284	290
Netherlands		..	..	66	93
New Zealand		..	..	65	98
Nicaragua		..	..	138	209
Niger	2001	14	27	477	508
Nigeria	2001	17	24	470	511
Norway		..	..	58	96
Oman	2003	9	27	91	163
Pakistan		..	..	199	225
Palau	2001	62	55	205	226
Panama	2002	16	19	84	146
Papua New Guinea		..	..	246	309
Paraguay	2003	23	24	119	171
Peru	2001	16	24	133	193
Philippines	2003	8	21	149	271
Poland	1999	24	33	81	202
Portugal		..	..	63	150
Qatar		..	..	76	93
Romania	2006	20	27	107	239
Russian Federation	2001	29	41	182	480
Rwanda		..	..	455	541
St. Kitts and Nevis	2002	16	20	145	200
St. Lucia	2001	10	19	131	224
St. Vincent and the Grenadines	2001	20	27	192	233
Samoa		..	..	203	235
San Marino		..	..	32	73
São Tomé and Principe		..	..	244	295
Saudi Arabia	2006	..	5[a]	119	196
Senegal	2002	6	25	280	350
Serbia and Montenegro	2003	17	16	99	186
Seychelles	2002	25	36	92	235
Sierra Leone		..	..	517	597
Singapore	2006	8	11	51	87
Slovak Republic	2002	23	27	77	204
Slovenia	2003	29	27	69	165
South Africa	2003	27	38	579	642
Spain		..	..	46	116
Sri Lanka	2006	1	3	120	235
Sudan	2001	13	20	248	348
Swaziland	2001	10	21	790	894
Sweden		..	..	50	79
Switzerland		..	..	50	90

Table A5. Staying healthy *(continued)*

| | | Tobacco use in adolescents | | Probability that a 15-year-old will die before the age of 60, 2003 | |
| | | Female | Male | per 1,000 | |
	Survey year	% ages 13–15	% ages 13–15	Female	Male
Syrian Arab Republic	2002	15	24	126	188
Tajikistan		..	..	169	225
Tanzania		..	..	550	587
Thailand		..	..	153	267
Togo	2002	10	20	377	448
Trinidad and Tobago	2000	12	20	155	249
Tunisia	2001	7	29	113	167
Turkey		..	..	111	176
Turkmenistan		..	..	171	352
Uganda	2002	16	22	459	533
Ukraine	1999	35	46	142	384
United Arab Emirates	2002	13	30	121	168
United Kingdom		..	..	64	103
United States	2000	20	26	82	139
Uruguay	2001	26	22	87	180
Uzbekistan		..	..	142	226
Venezuela, RB	2003	12	15	97	181
Vietnam	2003	2	10	129	205
Yemen, Rep.	2002	14	21	227	298
Zambia	2002	24	25	685	719
Zimbabwe	2001	14	19	819	830

a. Data refer to capital cities only.

Table A6. Staying healthy

| | Condom use among sexually active youth | | | | | Knowledge of HIV prevention methods | |
| | Female | | Male | | | Female | Male |
	Survey year	% ages 15–19	% ages 20–24	% ages 15–19	% ages 20–24	Survey year	% ages 15–24	% ages 15–24
Albania		..	..	..	..	2000	39	..
Armenia	2000	0.2	4.0	..	..	2000	37	52
Azerbaijan		..	..	..	..	2000	9	..
Benin	2001	3.6	4.5	16.8	27.0	2001	40	45
Bolivia	2003	1.2	4.3	..	..	2000	52	..
Botswana		..	..	..	..	2000	71	..
Burkina Faso	2003	6.3	8.9	11.2	36.7	2003	45	54
Cambodia	2000	0.1	0.6	..	..	2000	59	..
Cameroon	2004	11.3	16.0	..	..	2004	64	73
Chad	2004	0.4	0.9	4.6	11.0		..	..
Colombia	2005	6.2	9.4	..	..		..	..
Congo, Dem. Rep.		..	..	..	..	2000	42	..
Côte d'Ivoire	1998/99	6.0	7.7	21.6	30.8	2000	46	..
Dominican Republic	2002	1.3	2.9	..	..	2002	80	78
Eritrea	2002	0.4	0.4	..	..	2002	58	..
Ethiopia	2000	0.3	0.7	1.6	3.4		..	..
Gambia, The		..	..	..	..	2000	45	..
Gabon	2000	10.9	13.0	40.8	48.4		..	..
Ghana	2003	5.2	7.7	..	..	2003	72	75
Guatemala	1998/99	0.8	1.1	..	..		..	..
Guinea	1999	2.3	2.7	14.4	27.8		..	..
Guyana		..	..	..	..	2000	60	..
Guinea-Bissau		..	..	..	..	2000	24	..
Haiti	2000	2.0	4.9	..	..	2000	44	69
Indonesia		..	..	..	..	2002/03	21[a]	32[a]
Kazakhstan	1999	2.2	5.1	20.7	35.1		..	..
Kenya	2003	1.8	1.6	..	..	2003	55	65
Lesotho		..	..	..	..	2000	47	..
Madagascar	2003/04	1.1	1.7	5.4	6.4	2000	32	..
Malawi	2000	2.8	2.9	..	..	2000	57	65
Mali	2001	1.0	1.1	5.0	17.6	2001	33	43
Mauritania	2000/01	0.0	0.4	1.2	3.4		..	..
Moldova		..	..	..	..	2000	47	..
Mongolia		..	..	..	..	2000	71[b]	..
Morocco	2003/04	0.0	0.4	..	..	2003/04	36	..
Mozambique	2003	9.2	5.8	..	..	2003	47	63
Namibia	2000	10.8	11.0	..	..	2000	65	81
Nepal		..	..	..	..	2001	38[c]	75[c]
Nicaragua	2001	1.0	2.6	..	..		..	..
Niger	1998	0.0	0.2	2.6	8.9	2000	28	..
Nigeria	2003	2.6	6.0	..	..	2003	40	58
Peru	2000	0.9	3.3	..	..		..	..
Philippines	2003	0.1	1.0	..	..	2000	46	..
Rwanda	2000	0.3	0.8	..	..	2000	52	63
São Tomé and Principe		..	..	..	..	2000	20	..
Senegal		..	..	..	..	2000	46	..
Sierra Leone		..	..	..	..	2000	27	..
South Africa	1998	2.0	3.5	..	..	1998	74	..
Tajikistan		..	..	..	..	2000	4[d]	..
Tanzania	1999	3.7	6.0	10.6	20.9	2003/04	61	65
Togo	1998	6.9	6.7	12.8	30.4	2000	58	..
Trinidad and Tobago		..	..	..	..	2000	48	..
Turkey	1998	0.9	5.2	0.0	3.0		..	..
Turkmenistan	2000	0.1	0.4	..	..	2000	15	..
Uganda	2000/01	5.7	4.9	..	..	2000/01	66	77
Uzbekistan		..	..	..	..	2002	25	40
Vietnam		..	..	..	..	1997	52	..
Zambia	2001/02	4.0	5.2	..	..		..	..
Zimbabwe	1999	1.8	2.8	9.4	27.7	1999	64	69

a. Sample included ever married women and currently married men. b. Self weighting sample. c. Sample included ever married women and men. d. Sample was not random.

Table A7. Forming families

	Fertility rate per 1,000 women		Women who gave birth before age 18	
	Survey year	ages 15–24	Survey year	women ages 15–24 %
Armenia	2000	199	2000	8.0
Azerbaijan	..	..	2006	7.0
Bangladesh	2004	328	2004	45.5
Benin	2001	370	2001	23.8
Bolivia	2003	267	2003	19.0
Burkina Faso	2003	384	2003	27.1
Cambodia	2000	222	2000	12.1
Cameroon	2004	374	2004	33.0
Cape Verde	..	..	2006	24.0
Chad	..	..	2004	48.0
Colombia	2000	227	2005	19.5
Côte d'Ivoire	..	..	2006	
Djibouti	..	..	2006	4.0
Dominican Republic	2002	306	2002	25.0
Ecuador	..	..	2006	18.0
Egypt, Arab Rep.	2000	247	2000	9.5
El Salvador	..	..	2006	24.0
Eritrea	2002	262	2002	25.4
Ethiopia	2000	335	2000	24.2
Gabon	2000	338	2000	35.4
Georgia	..	..	2006	11.0
Ghana	2003	250	2003	14.9
Guatemala	1998/99	393	2006	24.0
Guinea	1999	406	2006	47.0
Haiti	2000	269	2000	15.2
Honduras	..	..	2006	28.0
India	1998/99	317	2006	28.0
Indonesia	2002/03	182	2002/03	11.9
Jordan	2002	178	2002	5.0
Kazakhstan	1999	207	2006	6.0
Kenya	2003	357	2003	22.7
Madagascar	2003/04	395	2003/04	31.3
Malawi	2000	477	2000	30.3
Mali	2001	475	2001	45.0
Mauritania	2000/01	246	2006	25.0
Morocco	2003/04	136	2003/04	7.5
Mozambique	2003	424.2	2006	42.0
Namibia	2000	254	2000	20.5
Nepal	2001	358	2001	26.0
Nicaragua	2001	297	2001	28.1
Niger	..	..	2006	47.0
Nigeria	2003	355	2003	28.0
Paraguay	..	..	2006	13.0
Peru	2000	206	2000	14.2
Philippines	2003	231	2003	6.9
Romania	..	..	2006	5.0
Rwanda	2000	292	2000	9.2
Senegal	..	..	2006	27.0
South Africa	..	..	2006	20.0
Syrian Arab Republic	..	..	..	..
Tanzania	1999	406	2006	26.0
Togo	..	..	2006	19.0
Turkey	..	..	2006	8.0
Turkmenistan	2000	214	2000	1.8
Uganda	2000/01	509	2000/01	42.0
Uzbekistan	..	..	2006	4.0
Vietnam	2002	163	2002	3.9
Yemen, Rep.	..	..	..	..
Zambia	2001/02	426	2001/02	34.6
Zimbabwe	1999	311	2006	20.0

Table A8. Forming families

	Pregnant women			
	not receiving prenatal care[a] ages 15–24		not informed of the complications[b] ages 15–24	
	Survey year	%	Survey year	%
Armenia	2000	7.0	2000	50.4
Bangladesh	2004	38.1	2004	50.1
Benin	2001	9.3	2001	17.3
Bolivia	2003	16.5	2003	62.9
Burkina Faso	2003	23.7	2003	15.1
Cameroon	2004	16.8	2004	36.5
Chad	2004	52.0	2004	14.1
Colombia	2000	10.1	2000	80.8
Côte d'Ivoire	1998	10.4		..
Dominican Republic	2002	1.0	2002	60.2
Egypt, Arab Rep.		..	2000	41.1
Ethiopia	2000	74.7	2000	20.4
Gabon	2000	3.1		..
Ghana	2003	5.1	2003	57.3
Guatemala	1998/99	11.7		..
Guinea	1999	18.8		..
Haiti	2000	18.6	2000	29.0
India	1998/99	30.3		..
Indonesia	2002/03	7.5	2002/03	28.6
Kazakhstan	1999	4.5		..
Kenya	2003	8.9	2003	34.2
Malawi	2002	4.1	2002	69.5
Mali	2001	40.5	2001	23.6
Morocco	2003/04	35.2	2003/04	37.3
Mozambique	2003	12.0	2003	51.6
Namibia	2000	5.0	2000	46.5
Nepal	2001	42.1	2001	52.0
Nicaragua	2001	11.6	2001	76.1
Peru	2004	5.0	2004	81.2
Philippines	2003	5.3	2003	46.9
Rwanda	2000	7.1	2000	5.7
Turkey	1998	28.0		..
Uganda	2001	4.8	2001	15.8
Vietnam	2002	20.2		..
Zambia	1001	4.2		..
Zimbabwe	1999	7.2	1999	43.8

a. Restricted to most recent births in the three years previous to the survey date.

b. Restricted to those who used antenatal care for the latest infants during three years previous to the survey date.

Technical notes

Table A1. Learning

Enrollment rates by age group are based on nationally-representative household surveys. They measure the proportion of people in a given age range reported to be attending school at the time of the household survey.

Grade 9 completion rates are computed using the information from nationally representative household surveys on last grade completed and current school participation of individuals ages 10-19 at the time of the survey. Estimates are based on Kaplan-Meier method which takes into account whether the individual is still in school.

Table A2. Program for International Student Assessment

The **Program for International Student Assessment (PISA)** assesses the performance of 15-year-olds in reading, mathematical, and scientific literacy as well as problem solving in terms of mastery of the school curriculum and the use of knowledge for everyday tasks and challenges.

Table A3. Going to work

Labor force participation rate is the share of the youth population, either employed or unemployed, that is, economically active.

Unemployment rate is the share of the labor force that is unemployed. To be considered unemployed, an individual must be not employed but actively seeking work.

Not in the labor force and not in school is the youth population that is neither in the labor force nor in school.

Table A4. Child labor

The data in the table refer to children's economic activity, a broader concept than child labor. According to a gradually emerging consensus, child labor is a subset of children's economic activity or children's work that is injurious and therefore targeted for elimination.

In line with the international definition of employment, a child who spends at least one hour on economic activity during the reference week is classified as economically active. Economic activity is as defined by the 1993 United Nations System of National Accounts (revision 3) and corresponds to the international definition of employment adopted by the Thirteenth International Conference of Labor Statisticians in 1982. Economic activity covers all market production and certain types of nonmarket production, including production of goods for own use. It excludes household chores performed by children in their own household. Some forms of economic activity are not captured by household surveys and so are not reflected in the estimates. These include unconditional forms of child labor, such as child commercial sexual exploitation and child slavery, which require different data collection methodologies.

The data used to develop the indicators are from household surveys conducted by the International Labour Organization (ILO), the United Nations Children's Fund (UNICEF), the World Bank, and national statistical offices. These surveys yield a variety of data in education, employment, health, expenditure, and consumption that relate to child work; they do not provide information on unconditional forms of children's work.

Household survey data generally include information on work type—for example, whether a child is working for pay in cash or in kind or is involved in unpaid work, whether a child is working for someone who is not a member of the household, whether a child is involved in any type of family work (on a farm or in a business), and the like. The ages used in country surveys to define child labor range from 5 to 14 years old. The data in the table have been recalculated to present statistics for children ages 7–14.

Although efforts are made to harmonize the definition of employment and the questions on employment used in survey questionnaires, some differences remain among the survey instruments used to collect the information on working children. Differences exist not only among different household surveys in the same country, but also within the same type of survey carried out in different countries.

Because of the differences in the underlying survey instruments and in survey dates, estimates of the economically active child population are not fully comparable across countries. Caution should be exercised in drawing conclusions concerning relative levels of child economic activity across countries or regions based on the published estimates.

Economically active children refer to children involved in economic activity for at least one hour in the reference week of the survey. **Work only** refers to children involved in economic activity and not attending school. **Work and study** refers to children attending school in combination with economic activity.

Table A5. Staying healthy (1)

Tobacco use in adolescents is the percent of youth ages 13–15 who currently use tobacco. Data is based on World Health Organization (WHO) and Centers for Disease Control and Prevention's *Global Youth Tobacco Survey* and augmented by Population Reference Bureau's *World's Youth 2006 Data Sheet*.

Probability that a 15-year old will die before the age of 60 is the probability of dying per 1,000 population ages 15–60. Based on figures computed by the WHO (*The World Health Report 2005*), which may differ from official statistics that may use other rigorous methods.

Table A6. Staying healthy (2)

Condom use among sexually active youth is the percent of currently married or sexually active unmarried men and women ages 15–19 and 20–24 using condoms. Data based on ORC Macro, 2006, MEASURE DHS STAT compiler.

Knowledge of HIV prevention methods is the percent of respondents who, in response to a prompted question, say that people can protect themselves from contracting HIV by using condoms or having sex only with one faithful, uninfected partner. Numerator is the number of respondents who, in response to a prompted question, correctly identify using condoms or having sex only with one faithful, uninfected partner as means of protection against HIV infection. Denominator is the total number of respondents. Data based on ORC Macro, 2006, MEASURE DHS STAT compiler.

Table A7. Forming families (1)

Fertility rate per 1,000 women ages 15–24 are age-specific fertility rates (women ages 15–24) for the three years preceding the survey. Based on ORC Macro, 2006, MEASURE DHS STAT compiler.

Women who gave birth before age 18 is the percentage of all women ages 15–24 who gave birth by age 18. Based on ORC Macro, 2006, MEASURE DHS STAT compiler and Population Reference Bureau *World's Youth Survey 2006 Data Sheet.*

Symbols

..
means that data are not available.

0 or 0.0
means zero or less than half the unit shown.

/
in dates, as in 1990/91, means that the period of time, usually 12 months, straddles two calendar years and refers to a survey year, an academic year, or a fiscal year.

A blank means not applicable.

Table A8. Forming families (2)

Pregnant women not receiving antenatal care ages 15–24 is the percentage of mothers aged 15–24 who used antenatal care for the latest infants born within the three years previous to the survey date. Based on Demographic and Health Surveys.

Pregnant women not informed of the complications ages 15–24 is the percentage of mothers aged 15–24 who used antenatal care for the latest infants born within the three years previous to the survey date but were not informed of pregnancy complications. Based on Demographic and Health Surveys.

Selected world development indicators

In this year's edition of the Selected World Development Indicators, development data are presented in six tables presenting comparative socioeconomic data for more than 130 economies for the most recent year for which data are available and, for some indicators, for an earlier year. An additional table presents basic indicators for 75 economies with sparse data or with populations of less than 2 million.

The indicators presented here are a selection from more than 800 included in *World Development Indicators 2006*. Published annually, *World Development Indicators* reflects a comprehensive view of the development process. Its opening chapter reports on the Millennium Development Goals, which grew out of agreements and resolutions of world conferences in the 1990s, and were formally recognized by the United Nations General Assembly after member states unanimously adopted the Millennium Declaration at the Millennium Summit in September 2000. In September 2005, the United Nations World Summit reaffirmed the principles in the 2000 Millennium Declaration and recognized the need for ambitious national development strategies backed by increased international support. The other five main sections recognize the contribution of a wide range of factors: human capital development, environmental sustainability, macroeconomic performance, private sector development and the investment climate, and the global links that influence the external environment for development. *World Development Indicators* is complemented by a separately published database that gives access to over 1,000 data tables and 800 time-series indicators for 222 economies and regions. This database is available through an electronic subscription (*WDI Online*) or as a CD-ROM.

Data sources and methodology

Socioeconomic and environmental data presented here are drawn from several sources: primary data collected by the World Bank, member country statistical publications, research institutes, and international organizations such as the United Nations and its specialized agencies, the International Monetary Fund (IMF), and the Organisation for Economic Co-operation and Development (OECD) (see the *Data sources* following the *Technical notes* for a complete listing). Although international standards of coverage, definition, and classification apply to most statistics reported by countries and international agencies, there are inevitably differences in timeliness and reliability arising from differences in the capabilities and resources devoted to basic data collection and compilation. For some topics, competing sources of data require review by World Bank staff to ensure that the most reliable data available are presented. In some instances, where available data are deemed too weak to provide reliable measures of levels and trends or do not adequately adhere to international standards, the data are not shown.

The data presented are generally consistent with those in *World Development Indicators 2006*. However, data have been revised and updated wherever new information has become available. Differences may also reflect revisions to historical series and changes in methodology. Thus data of different vintages may be published in different editions of World Bank publications. Readers are advised not to compile data series from different publications or different editions of the same publication. Consistent time-series data are available on *World Development Indicators 2006* CD-ROM and through *WDI Online*.

All dollar figures are in current U.S. dollars unless otherwise stated. The various methods used to convert from national currency figures are described in the *Technical notes*.

Because the World Bank's primary business is providing lending and policy advice to its low- and middle-income members, the issues covered in these tables focus mainly on these economies. Where available, information on the high-income economies is also provided for comparison. Readers may wish to refer to national statistical publications and publications of the OECD and the European Union for more information on the high-income economies.

Classification of economies and summary measures

The summary measures at the bottom of each table include economies classified by income per capita and by region. GNI per capita is used to determine the following income classifications: low-income, $875 or less in 2005; middle-income, $876 to $10,725; and high-income, $10,726 and above. A further division at GNI per capita $3,465 is made between lower-middle-income and upper-middle-income economies. See the table on classification of economies at the end of this volume for a list of economies in each group (including those with populations of less than 2 million).

Summary measures are either totals (indicated by **t** if the aggregates include estimates for missing data and nonreporting countries, or by **s** for simple sums of the data available), weighted averages (**w**), or median values (**m**) calculated for groups of economies. Data for the countries excluded from the main tables (those presented in table 5) have been included in the summary measures, where data are available, or by assuming that they follow the trend of reporting countries. This gives a more consistent aggregated measure by standardizing country coverage for each period shown. Where missing information accounts for a third or more of the overall estimate, however, the group measure is reported as not available. The *Statistical methods* section in the *Technical notes* provides further information on aggregation methods. Weights used to construct the aggregates are listed in the technical notes for each table.

From time to time an economy's classification is revised because of changes in the above cutoff values or in the economy's measured level of GNI per capita. When such changes occur, aggregates based on those classifications are recalculated for the past period so that a consistent time series is maintained.

Terminology and country coverage

The term *country* does not imply political independence but may refer to any territory for which authorities report separate social or economic statistics. Data are shown for economies as they were constituted in 2004, and historical data are revised to reflect current political arrangements. Throughout the tables, exceptions are noted. Unless otherwise noted, data for China do not include data for Hong Kong, China; Macao, China; or Taiwan, China. Data for Indonesia include Timor-Leste through 1999 unless otherwise noted.

Symbols

..
means that data are not available or that aggregates cannot be calculated because of missing data in the years shown.

0 or 0.0
means zero or less than half the unit shown.

/
in dates, as in 1990/91, means that the period of time, usually 12 months, straddles two calendar years and refers to a survey year, an academic year, or a fiscal year.

$
means current U.S. dollars unless otherwise noted.

>
means more than.

<
means less than.

A blank means not applicable or, for an aggregate, not analytically meaningful.

Technical notes

Because data quality and intercountry comparisons are often problematic, readers are encouraged to consult the *Technical notes*, the table on Classification of Economies by Region and Income, and the footnotes to the tables. For more extensive documentation see *World Development Indicators 2006*.

Readers may find more information on the WDI 2006, and orders can be made online, by phone, or fax as follows:

For more information and to order on line: **http://www.worldbank.org/data/wdi2006/index.htm**.

To order by phone or fax: phone 1-800-645-7247 or 1-703-661-1580; fax 1-703-661-1501

To order by mail: The World Bank, P.O. Box 960, Herndon, VA 20172-0960, U.S.A.

Classification of economies by region and income, FY2007

East Asia and the Pacific		Latin America and the Caribbean		South Asia		High income OECD
American Samoa	UMC	Argentina	UMC	Afghanistan	LIC	Australia
Cambodia	LIC	Barbados	UMC	Bangladesh	LIC	Austria
China	LMC	Belize	UMC	Bhutan	LIC	Belgium
Fiji	LMC	Bolivia	LMC	India	LIC	Canada
Indonesia	LMC	Brazil	LMC	Maldives	LMC	Denmark
Kiribati	LMC	Chile	UMC	Nepal	LIC	Finland
Korea, Dem. Rep.	LIC	Colombia	LMC	Pakistan	LIC	France
Lao PDR	LIC	Costa Rica	UMC	Sri Lanka	LMC	Germany
Malaysia	UMC	Cuba	LMC			Greece
Marshall Islands	LMC	Dominica	UMC	**Sub-Saharan Africa**		Iceland
Micronesia, Fed. Sts.	LMC	Dominican Republic	LMC	Angola	LMC	Ireland
Mongolia	LIC	Ecuador	LMC	Benin	LIC	Italy
Myanmar	LIC	El Salvador	LMC	Botswana	UMC	Japan
Northern Mariana Islands	UMC	Grenada	UMC	Burkina Faso	LIC	Korea, Rep.
Palau	UMC	Guatemala	LMC	Burundi	LIC	Luxembourg
Papua New Guinea	LIC	Guyana	LMC	Cameroon	LMC	Netherlands
Philippines	LMC	Haiti	LIC	Cape Verde	LMC	New Zealand
Samoa	LMC	Honduras	LMC	Central African Republic	LIC	Norway
Solomon Islands	LIC	Jamaica	LMC	Chad	LIC	Portugal
Thailand	LMC	Mexico	UMC	Comoros	LIC	Spain
Timor-Leste	LIC	Nicaragua	LMC	Congo, Dem. Rep.	LIC	Sweden
Tonga	LMC	Panama	UMC	Congo, Rep.	LMC	Switzerland
Vanuatu	LMC	Paraguay	LMC	Côte d'Ivoire	LIC	United Kingdom
Vietnam	LIC	Peru	LMC	Equatorial Guinea	UMC	United States
		St. Kitts and Nevis	UMC	Eritrea	LIC	
Europe and Central Asia		St. Lucia	UMC	Ethiopia	LIC	**Other high income**
Albania	LMC	St. Vincent and the Grenadines	UMC	Gabon	UMC	Andorra
Armenia	LMC	Suriname	LMC	Gambia, The	LIC	Antigua and Barbuda
Azerbaijan	LMC	Trinidad and Tobago	LMC	Ghana	LIC	Aruba
Belarus	LMC	Uruguay	UMC	Guinea	LIC	Bahamas, The
Bosnia and Herzegovina	LMC	Venezuela, RB	UMC	Guinea-Bissau	LIC	Bahrain
Bulgaria	LMC			Kenya	LIC	Bermuda
Croatia	UMC	**Middle East and North Africa**		Lesotho	LMC	Brunei Darussalam
Czech Republic	UMC	Algeria	LMC	Liberia	LIC	Cayman Islands
Estonia	UMC	Djibouti	LMC	Madagascar	LIC	Channel Islands
Georgia	LMC	Egypt, Arab Rep.	LMC	Malawi	LIC	Cyprus
Hungary	UMC	Iran, Islamic Rep.	LMC	Mali	LIC	Faeroe Islands
Kazakhstan	LMC	Iraq	LMC	Mauritania	LIC	French Polynesia
Kyrgyz Republic	LIC	Jordan	LMC	Mauritius	UMC	Greenland
Latvia	UMC	Lebanon	UMC	Mayotte	UMC	Guam
Lithuania	UMC	Libya	UMC	Mozambique	LIC	Hong Kong, China
Macedonia, FYR	LMC	Morocco	LMC	Namibia	LMC	Isle of Man
Moldova	LMC	Oman	UMC	Niger	LIC	Israel
Poland	UMC	Syrian Arab Republic	LMC	Nigeria	LIC	Kuwait
Romania	UMC	Tunisia	LMC	Rwanda	LIC	Liechtenstein
Russian Federation	UMC	West Bank and Gaza	LMC	São Tomé and Principe	LIC	Macao, China
Serbia and Montenegro	LMC	Yemen, Rep.	LIC	Senegal	LIC	Malta
Slovak Republic	UMC			Seychelles	UMC	Monaco
Tajikistan	LIC			Sierra Leone	LIC	Netherlands Antilles
Turkey	UMC			Somalia	LIC	New Caledonia
Turkmenistan	LMC			South Africa	UMC	Puerto Rico
Ukraine	LMC			Sudan	LIC	Qatar
Uzbekistan	LIC			Swaziland	LMC	San Marino
				Tanzania	LIC	Saudi Arabia
				Togo	LIC	Singapore
				Uganda	LIC	Slovenia
				Zambia	LIC	Taiwan, China
				Zimbabwe	LIC	United Arab Emirates
						Virgin Islands (U.S.)

Source: World Bank data.

Note: This table classifies all World Bank member economies, and all other economies with populations of more than 30,000. Economies are divided among income groups according to 2005 GNI per capita, calculated using the World Bank Atlas method. The groups are: low income (LIC), $875 or less; lower middle income (LMC), $876–3,465; upper middle income (UMC), $3,466–10,725; and high income, $10,726 or more.

Table 1. Key indicators of development

	Population			Population age composition	Gross national income (GNI)[a]		PPP gross national income (GNI)[b]		Gross domestic product per capita % growth	Life expectancy at birth		Adult Literacy rate	Carbon dioxide emissions
	Millions 2005	Average annual % growth 2000–05	density people per sq. km 2005	% Ages 0–14 2005	$ billions 2005	$ per capita 2005	$ billions 2005	$ per capita 2005	% growth 2004–05	Male Years 2004	Female Years 2004	% ages 15 and older 2000–04	per capita metric tons 2002
Albania	3	0.5	114	27	8.1	2,580	17	5,420	4.9	71	77	99	0.8
Algeria	33	1.5	14	30	89.6	2,730	222[c]	6,770[c]	3.7	70	73	70	2.9
Angola	16	2.9	13	46	21.5	1,350	35[c]	2,210[c]	11.5	40	43	67	0.5
Argentina	39	1.0	14	26	173.0	4,470	539	13,920	8.2	71	79	97	3.5
Armenia	3	−0.4	107	21	4.4	1,470	15	5,060	14.4	68	75	99	1.0
Australia	20	1.2	3	20	654.6	32,220	622	30,610	1.5	77	83	..	18.1
Austria	8	0.5	100	16	303.6	36,980	272	33,140	1.4	76	82	..	7.9
Azerbaijan	8	0.8	102	26	10.4	1,240	41	4,890	25.0	70	75	99	3.4
Bangladesh	142	1.9	1,090	35	66.2	470	296	2,090	3.5	63	64	..	0.3
Belarus	10	−0.5	47	15	27.0	2,760	77	7,890	9.8	63	74	100	6.0
Belgium	10	0.4	319	17	373.8	35,700	342	32,640	0.7	76	82	..	8.9
Benin	8	3.2	76	44	4.3	510	9	1,110	0.7	54	55	35	0.3
Bolivia	9	2.0	9	38	9.3	1,010	25	2,740	2.1	62	67	87	1.2
Bosnia and Herzegovina	4	0.2	76	17	9.5	2,440	30	7,790	5.4	72	77	97	4.7
Brazil	186	1.4	22	28	644.1	3,460	1,534	8,230	0.9	67	75	89	1.8
Bulgaria	8	−0.8	70	14	26.7	3,450	67	8,630	5.8	69	76	98	5.3
Burkina Faso	13	3.2	48	47	5.2	400	16[c]	1,220[c]	1.6	47	49	22	0.1
Burundi	8	3.1	294	45	0.7	100	5[c]	640[c]	−2.6	43	45	59	0.0
Cambodia	14	2.0	80	37	5.3	380	35[c]	2,490[c]	5.0	53	60	74	0.0
Cameroon	16	1.9	35	41	16.5	1,010	35	2,150	0.8	45	47	68	0.2
Canada	32	1.0	4	18	1,051.9	32,600	1,040	32,220	2.0	77	83	..	16.5
Central African Republic	4	1.3	7	43	1.4	350	5[c]	1,140[c]	0.9	39	40	49	0.1
Chad	10	3.5	8	47	3.9	400	14	1,470	2.3	43	45	26	0.0
Chile	16	1.1	22	25	*95.7*	5,870	187	11,470	5.2	75	81	96	3.6
China	1,305	0.6	140	21	2,263.8	1,740	8,610[d]	6,600[d]	9.2	70	73	91	2.7
Hong Kong, China	7	0.8	..	14	192.1	27,670	241	34,670	6.3	79	85	..	5.2
Colombia	46	1.6	44	31	104.5	2,290	338[c]	7,420[c]	3.6	70	76	93	1.3
Congo, Dem. Rep.	58	2.8	25	47	6.9	120	41[c]	720[c]	3.5	43	45	67	0.0
Congo, Rep.	4	3.1	12	47	3.8	950	3	810	6.0	51	54	..	0.6
Costa Rica	4	1.9	85	28	19.9	4,590	42[c]	9,680[c]	2.3	76	81	95	1.4
Cote d'Ivoire	18	1.6	57	42	15.3	840	27	1,490	−1.9	45	47	49	0.4
Croatia	4	0.2	80	16	35.8	8,060	57	12,750	4.2	72	79	98	4.7
Czech Republic	10	−0.1	132	15	109.2	10,710	205	20,140	6.2	73	79	..	11.2
Denmark	5	0.3	128	19	256.8	47,390	182	33,570	2.8	75	80	..	8.8
Dominican Republic	9	1.5	184	33	21.1	2,370	64[c]	7,150[c]	3.0	64	71	87	2.5
Ecuador	13	1.5	48	32	34.8	2,630	54	4,070	2.5	72	78	91	2.0
Egypt, Arab Rep.	74	1.9	74	34	92.9	1,250	329	4,440	2.9	68	73	71	2.1
El Salvador	7	1.8	332	34	16.8	2,450	35[c]	5,120[c]	1.0	68	74	..	1.0
Eritrea	4	4.4	44	45	1.0	220	4[c]	1,010[c]	0.8	53	56	..	0.2
Ethiopia	71	2.1	71	45	11.1	160	71[c]	1,000[c]	6.8	42	43	..	0.1
Finland	5	0.3	17	17	196.5	37,460	163	31,170	1.8	75	82	..	12.0
France	61	0.6	110	18	2,177.7[e]	34,810[e]	1,855	30,540	0.9	77	84	..	6.2
Georgia	4	−1.1	64	19	6.0	1,350	15[c]	3,270[c]	10.4	67	75	..	0.7
Germany	82	0.1	236	14	2,852.3	34,580	2,409	29,210	0.9	76	81	..	10.3
Ghana	22	2.2	97	39	10.0	450	52[c]	2,370[c]	3.7	57	58	58	0.4
Greece	11	0.3	86	14	218.1	19,670	262	23,620	3.4	77	81	96	8.5
Guatemala	13	2.4	116	43	30.3	2,400	56[c]	4,410[c]	0.8	64	71	69	0.9
Guinea	9	2.2	38	44	3.5	370	21	2,240	0.8	54	54	29	0.1
Haiti	9	1.4	309	37	3.9	450	16[c]	1,840[c]	0.5	51	53	..	0.2
Honduras	7	2.3	64	39	8.6	1,190	21[c]	2,900[c]	2.3	66	70	80	0.9
Hungary	10	−0.2	110	16	101.2	10,030	171	16,940	4.3	69	77	..	5.6
India	1,095	1.5	368	32	793.0	720	3,787[c]	3,460[c]	7.1	63	64	61	1.2
Indonesia	221	1.3	122	28	282.2	1,280	820	3,720	4.2	66	69	90	1.4
Iran, Islamic Rep.	68	1.2	41	29	187.4	2,770	545	8,050	4.9	69	72	77	5.5
Ireland	4	1.7	60	20	166.6	40,150	144	34,720	2.6	76	81	..	11.0
Israel	7	1.9	318	28	128.7	18,620	175	25,280	3.5	77	81	97	10.6
Italy	57	−0.1	195	14	1,724.9	30,010	1,657	28,840	0.2	77	83	98	7.5
Jamaica	3	0.5	245	31	9.0	3,400	11	4,110	1.3	69	73	80	4.1
Japan	128	0.2	351	14	4,988.2	38,980	4,019	31,410	2.6	78	85	..	9.4
Jordan	5	2.6	61	37	13.5	2,500	29	5,280	4.5	70	73	90	3.3
Kazakhstan	15	0.3	6	23	44.4	2,930	117	7,730	8.4	60	71	100	9.9
Kenya	34	2.2	60	43	18.0	530	40	1,170	0.4	49	48	74	0.2
Korea, Rep.	48	0.5	489	19	764.7	15,830	1,055	21,850	3.5	74	81	..	9.4
Kuwait	3	2.9	142	24	59.1	24,040	59[c]	24,010[c]	5.3	75	80	93	25.6
Kyrgyz Republic	5	0.9	27	31	2.3	440	10	1,870	−1.8	64	72	99	1.0
Lao PDR	6	2.3	26	41	2.6	440	12	2,020	4.6	54	57	69	0.2
Latvia	2	−0.6	37	15	15.5	6,760	31	13,480	10.8	66	78	100	2.7
Lebanon	4	1.0	350	29	22.1	6,180	21	5,740	−0.0	70	75	..	4.7
Lithuania	3	−0.5	55	17	24.1	7,050	49	14,220	8.0	66	78	100	3.6
Macedonia, FYR	2	0.2	80	20	5.8	2,830	14	7,080	3.8	71	76	96	5.1
Madagascar	19	2.8	32	44	5.4	290	16	880	1.8	54	57	71	0.1
Malawi	13	2.3	137	47	2.1	160	8	650	0.4	40	40	64	0.1
Malaysia	25	2.0	77	32	125.8	4,960	262	10,320	3.4	71	76	89	6.3
Mali	14	3.0	11	48	5.1	380	14	1,000	2.3	48	49	19	0.0
Mauritania	3	3.0	3	43	1.7	560	7[c]	2,150[c]	2.3	52	55	51	1.1

Note: For data comparability and coverage, see the technical notes. Figures in italics are for years other than those specified.

Table 1. Key indicators of development *(continued)*

	Population			Population age composition	Gross national income (GNI)[a]		PPP gross national income (GNI)[b]		Gross domestic product per capita	Life expectancy at birth		Adult Literacy rate	Carbon dioxide emissions
	Millions 2005	Average annual % growth 2000–05	density people per sq. km 2005	% Ages 0–14 2005	$ billions 2005	$ per capita 2005	$ billions 2005	$ per capita 2005	% growth 2004–05	Male Years 2004	Female Years 2004	% ages 15 and older 2000–04	per capita metric tons 2002
Mexico	103	1.0	54	31	753.4	7,310	1,034	10,030	1.9	73	78	91	3.8
Moldova	4	–0.3	128	18	3.2[f]	880[f]	9	2,150	7.3	65	72	98	1.6
Mongolia	3	1.3	2	30	1.8	690	6	2,190	4.6	62	68	98	3.4
Morocco	30	1.7	68	31	52.3	1,730	132	4,360	0.4	68	72	52	1.5
Mozambique	20	2.0	25	44	6.1	310	25[c]	1,270[c]	5.7	41	42	..	0.1
Namibia	2	1.4	3	42	6.1	2,990	16[c]	7,910[c]	2.4	47	48	85	1.1
Nepal	27	2.1	190	39	7.3	270	42	1,530	0.3	62	63	49	0.2
Netherlands	16	0.5	482	18	598.0	36,620	530	32,480	0.8	76	81	..	9.3
New Zealand	4	1.4	15	21	106.7	25,960	95	23,030	0.7	77	82	..	8.6
Nicaragua	5	2.0	45	39	5.0	910	20	3,650	1.9	68	73	77	0.7
Niger	14	3.4	11	49	3.3	240	11[c]	800[c]	1.1	45	45	29	0.1
Nigeria	132	2.3	144	44	74.2	560	137[c]	1,040[c]	4.7	43	44	..	0.4
Norway	5	0.6	15	20	275.2	59,590	187	40,420	1.7	78	82	..	13.9
Oman	3	1.0	8	35	23.0	9,070	37	14,680	..	73	76	81	12.1
Pakistan	156	2.4	202	38	107.3	690	366	2,350	5.2	64	66	50	0.7
Panama	3	1.8	43	30	15.0	4,630	24[c]	7,310[c]	4.5	73	78	92	2.0
Papua New Guinea	6	2.1	13	40	3.9	660	14[c]	2,370[c]	1.0	55	57	57	0.4
Paraguay	6	2.4	16	38	7.9	1,280	31[c]	4,970[c]	0.4	69	74	..	0.7
Peru	28	1.5	22	32	73.0	2,610	163	5,830	5.1	68	73	88	1.0
Philippines	83	1.9	279	35	108.3	1,300	440	5,300	3.3	69	73	93	0.9
Poland	38	–0.2	125	16	271.4	7,110	515	13,490	3.3	70	79	..	7.7
Portugal	11	0.6	115	16	170.7	16,170	208	19,730	–0.2	74	81	..	6.0
Romania	22	–0.7	94	15	82.9	3,830	193	8,940	4.4	68	75	97	4.0
Russian Federation	143	–0.4	9	15	639.1	4,460	1,523	10,640	6.9	59	72	99	9.8
Rwanda	9	2.3	366	43	2.1	230	12[c]	1,320[c]	3.2	42	46	65	0.1
Saudi Arabia	25	2.7	11	37	289.2	11,770	362[c]	14,740[c]	3.9	70	74	79	15.0
Senegal	12	2.4	61	43	8.2	710	21[c]	1,770[c]	3.7	55	57	39	0.4
Serbia and Montenegro	8	0.1	80	18	26.8[g]	3,280[g]	..	..	5.7	71	76	96	..
Sierra Leone	6	4.2	77	43	1.2	220	4	780	3.8	40	43	35	0.1
Singapore	4	1.4	6,495	20	119.6	27,490	130	29,780	3.7	77	81	93	13.7
Slovak Republic	5	0.0	112	17	42.8	7,950	85	15,760	5.9	70	78	100	6.8
Slovenia	2	0.1	99	14	34.7	17,350	44	22,160	3.8	73	81	..	7.7
South Africa	45	0.5	37	33	224.1	4,960	548[c]	12,120[c]	5.6	44	45	82	7.6
Spain	43	1.4	87	14	1,100.1	25,360	1,120	25,820	1.7	77	84	..	7.4
Sri Lanka	20	0.5	303	24	22.8	1,160	89	4,520	4.4	72	77	91	0.5
Sudan	36	1.9	15	39	23.3	640	72	2,000	5.9	55	58	61	0.3
Sweden	9	0.4	22	17	370.5	41,060	284	31,420	2.3	78	83	..	5.8
Switzerland	7	0.7	186	16	408.7	54,930	276	37,080	1.2	79	84	..	5.6
Syrian Arab Republic	19	2.5	104	37	26.3	1,380	71	3,740	1.7	72	75	80	2.8
Tajikistan	7	1.1	47	39	2.2	330	8	1,260	6.2	61	67	99	0.7
Tanzania	38	2.0	43	43	12.7[h]	340[h]	28	730	5.0	46	47	69	0.1
Thailand	64	0.9	126	24	176.9	2,750	542	8,440	3.6	67	74	93	3.7
Togo	6	2.7	113	43	2.2	350	10[c]	1,550[c]	0.2	53	57	53	0.3
Tunisia	10	0.9	65	26	29.0	2,890	79	7,900	3.3	71	75	74	2.3
Turkey	73	1.5	94	29	342.2	4,710	612	8,420	6.0	69	71	87	3.0
Turkmenistan	5	1.4	10	32	..	..[i]	..	..	..	59	67	99	9.1
Uganda	29	3.5	146	50	7.9	280	43[c]	1,500[c]	1.9	48	50	67	0.1
Ukraine	47	–0.9	81	15	71.4	1,520	317	6,720	3.3	63	74	99	6.4
United Kingdom	60	0.2	249	18	2,263.7	37,600	1,968	32,690	1.2	76	81	..	9.2
United States	296	1.0	32	21	12,969.6	43,740	12,438	41,950	2.5	75	80	..	20.2
Uruguay	3	0.7	20	24	15.1	4,360	34	9,810	5.8	72	79	..	1.2
Uzbekistan	27	1.5	63	33	13.5	510	54	2,020	5.5	64	70	..	4.8
Venezuela, RB	27	1.8	30	31	127.8	4,810	171	6,440	7.5	71	77	93	4.3
Vietnam	83	1.1	255	30	51.7	620	250	3,010	7.4	68	73	90	0.8
West Bank and Gaza	4	4.1	..	45	3.8	1,120	..	..	..	71	75	92	..
Yemen, Rep.	21	3.2	40	46	12.7	600	19	920	1.0	60	63	..	0.7
Zambia	12	1.7	16	46	5.7	490	11	950	3.4	39	38	68	0.2
Zimbabwe	13	0.6	34	40	4.5	340	25	1,940	–7.6	38	37	..	1.0
World	6,438s	1.2w	50w	28w	44,983.3t	6,987w	60,644t	9,420w	2.4w	65w	69w	80w	3.9w
Low income	2,353	1.9	83	36	1,363.9	580	5,849	2,486	5.6	58	60	62	0.8
Middle income	3,073	0.9	45	26	8,113.1	2,640	22,115	7,195	5.4	68	73	90	3.3
Lower middle income	2,475	1.0	63	25	4,746.5	1,918	15,622	6,313	5.9	68	73	89	2.6
Upper middle income	599	0.6	21	24	3,367.9	5,625	6,541	10,924	5.0	66	73	94	6.2
Low & middle income	5,426	1.3	56	30	9,476.8	1,746	27,954	5,151	5.2	63	67	80	2.2
East Asia & Pacific	1,885	0.9	119	24	3,067.4	1,627	11,149	5,914	7.8	68	72	91	2.4
Europe & Central Asia	473	0.0	20	20	1,945.0	4,113	4,324	9,142	5.9	64	73	97	6.7
Latin America & Caribbean	551	1.4	28	30	2,209.7	4,008	4,472	8,111	3.1	69	75	90	2.4
Middle East & North Africa	305	1.9	34	33	684.6	2,241	1,856	6,076	2.8	68	71	72	3.2
South Asia	1,470	1.7	308	33	1,005.3	684	4,618	3,142	6.4	63	64	60	1.0
Sub-Saharan Africa	741	2.3	31	44	552.2	745	1,469	1,981	3.1	46	47	..	0.7
High income	1,011	0.7	31	18	35,528.8	35,131	32,893	32,524	2.1	76	82	..	12.8

a. Calculated using the World Bank Atlas method. b. PPP is purchasing power parity; see Definitions. c. The estimate is based on regression; others are extrapolated from the latest International Comparison Programme benchmark estimates. d. Based on a 1986 bilateral comparison of China and the United States (Ruoen and Kai 1995), employing a different methodology than that used for other countries. This interim methodology will be revised in the next few years. e. GNI and GNI per capita estimates include the French overseas departments of French Guiana, Guadeloupe, Martinique, and Reunion. f. Excludes data for Transnistria. g. Excludes data for Kosovo. h. Data refers to mainland Tanzania only. i. Estimated to be lower middle income ($876–$3,465).

Table 2. Poverty

	National poverty line								International poverty line				
	Population below the poverty line				Population below the poverty line					Population below $1 a day %	Poverty gap at $1 a day %	Population below $2 a day %	Poverty gap at $2 a day %
	Survey year	Rural %	Urban %	National %	Survey year	Rural %	Urban %	National %	Survey year				
Albania	2002	29.6	19.8	25.4		..	..	..	2002[a]	<2	<0.5	11.8	2.0
Algeria	1988	16.6	7.3	12.2	1995	30.3	14.7	22.6	1995[a]	<2	<0.5	15.1	3.8
Argentina	1995	..	28.4	..	1998	..	29.9	..	2003[b]	7.0	2.0	23.0	8.4
Armenia	1998–99	50.8	58.3	55.1	2001	48.7	51.9	50.9	2003[a]	<2	<0.5	31.1	7.1
Azerbaijan	1995	..	..	68.1	2001	42.0	55.0	49.0	2001[a]	3.7	0.6	33.4	9.1
Bangladesh	1995–96	55.2	29.4	51.0	2000	53.0	36.6	49.8	2000[a]	36.0	8.1	82.8	36.3
Belarus	2000	..	..	41.9		..	..	..	2002[a]	<2	<0.5	<2	<0.5
Benin	1995	25.2	28.5	26.5	1999	33.0	23.3	29.0	2003[a]	30.9	8.2	73.7	31.7
Bolivia	1997	77.3	53.8	63.2	1999	81.7	50.6	62.7	2002[b]	23.2	13.6	42.2	23.2
Bosnia and Herzegovina	2001–02	19.9	13.8	19.5		..	..	..					
Botswana		..	..	..		..	..	..	1993[a]	23.5	7.7	50.1	22.8
Brazil	1996	54.0	15.4	23.9	1998	51.4	14.7	22.0	2003[b]	7.5	3.4	21.2	8.5
Bulgaria	1997	..	..	36.0	2001	..	..	12.8	2003[a]	<2	<0.5	6.1	1.5
Burkina Faso	1998	61.1	22.4	54.6	2003	52.4	19.2	46.4	2003[a]	27.2	7.3	71.8	30.4
Burundi	1990	36.0	43.0	36.4		..	..	..	1998[a]	54.6	22.7	87.6	48.9
Cambodia	1997	40.1	21.1	36.1	1999	40.1	13.9	35.9	1997[a]	34.1	9.7	77.7	34.5
Cameroon	1996	59.6	41.4	53.3	2001	49.9	22.1	40.2	2001[a]	17.1	4.1	50.6	19.3
Central African Republic		..	..	..		..	..	..	1993[a]	66.6	38.1	84.0	58.4
Chad	1995–96	67.0	63.0	64.0		..	..	..		..	..	..	..
Chile	1996	..	..	19.9	1998	..	..	17.0	2000[b]	<2	<0.5	9.6	2.5
China	1996	7.9	<2	6.0	1998	4.6	<2	4.6	2001[a]	16.6	3.9	46.7	18.4
Colombia	1995	79.0	48.0	60.0	1999	79.0	55.0	64.0	2003[b]	7.0	3.1	17.8	7.7
Costa Rica	1992	25.5	19.2	22.0		..	..	..	2001[b]	2.2	0.8	7.5	2.8
Côte d'Ivoire		..	..	..		..	..	..	2002[a]	14.8	4.1	48.8	18.4
Croatia		..	..	..		..	..	..	2001[a]	<2	<0.5	<2	<0.5
Czech Republic		..	..	..		..	..	..	1996[b]	<2	<0.5	<2	<0.5
Dominican Republic	1992	49.0	19.3	33.9	1998	42.1	20.5	28.6	2003[b]	2.5	0.8	11.0	3.6
Ecuador	1995	56.0	19.0	34.0	1998	69.0	30.0	46.0	1998[b]	15.8	6.3	37.2	15.8
Egypt, Arab Rep.	1995–96	23.3	22.5	22.9	1999–00	..	..	16.7	1999–00[a]	3.1	<0.5	43.9	11.3
El Salvador	1992	55.7	43.1	48.3		..	..	..	2002[b]	19.0	9.3	40.5	17.7
Eritrea	1993–94	..	..	53.0		..	..	..		..	..	..	..
Estonia	1995	14.7	6.8	8.9		..	..	..	2003[a]	<2	<0.5	7.5	1.9
Ethiopia	1995–96	47.0	33.3	45.5	1999–00	45.0	37.0	44.2	1999–00[a]	23.0	4.8	77.8	29.6
Gambia, The	1992	..	..	64.0	1998	61.0	48.0	57.6	1998[a]	26.5	8.8	54.3	25.2
Georgia	2002	55.4	48.5	52.1	2003	52.7	56.2	54.5	2003[a]	6.5	2.1	25.3	8.6
Ghana	1992	..	..	50.0	1998–99	49.9	18.6	39.5	1998–99[a]	44.8	17.3	78.5	40.8
Guatemala	1989	71.9	33.7	57.9	2000	74.5	27.1	56.2	2002[b]	13.5	5.5	31.9	13.8
Guinea	1994	..	..	40.0		..	..	..					
Haiti	1987	..	..	65.0	1995	66.0	..	..	2001[b]	53.9	26.6	78.0	47.4
Honduras	1997	58.0	35.0	47.0	1999	58.0	37.0	48.0	1999[b]	20.7	7.5	44.0	20.2
Hungary	1993	..	..	14.5	1997	..	..	17.3	2002[a]	<2	<0.5	<2	<0.5
India	1993–94	37.3	32.4	36.0	1999–00	30.2	24.7	28.6	1999–00[a]	34.7	8.2	79.9	35.3
Indonesia	1996	..	..	15.7	1999	34.4	16.1	27.1	2002[a]	7.5	0.9	52.4	15.7
Iran, Islamic Rep.		..	..	..		..	..	..	1998[a]	<2	<0.5	7.3	1.5
Jamaica	1995	37.0	18.7	27.5	2000	25.1	12.8	18.7	2000[a]	<2	<0.5	13.3	2.7
Jordan	1991	..	..	15.0	1997	..	..	11.7	2002–03[a]	<2	<0.5	7.0	1.5
Kazakhstan	1996	39.0	30.0	34.6		..	..	..	2003[a]	<2	<0.5	16.0	3.8
Kenya	1994	47.0	29.0	40.0	1997	53.0	49.0	52.0	1997[a]	22.8	5.9	58.3	23.9
Korea, Rep.		..	..	..		..	..	..	1998[b]	<2	<0.5	<2	<0.5
Kyrgyz Republic	2000	56.4	43.9	52.0	2001	51.0	41.2	47.6	2003[a]	<2	<0.5	21.4	4.4
Lao PDR	1993	48.7	33.1	45.0	1997–98	41.0	26.9	38.6	2002[a]	27.0	6.1	74.1	30.2
Latvia		..	..	..		..	..	..	2003[a]	<2	<0.5	4.7	1.2
Lesotho		..	..	..		..	..	..	1995[a]	36.4	19.0	56.1	33.1
Lithuania		..	..	..		..	..	..	2003[a]	<2	<0.5	7.8	1.8
Macedonia, FYR		..	..	..		..	..	..	2003[a]	<2	<0.5	<2	<0.5

Note: For data comparability and coverage, see the technical notes. Figures in italics are for years other than those specified.

Table 2. Poverty *(continued)*

	National poverty line								International poverty line				
	Population below the poverty line				Population below the poverty line					Population below $1 a day %	Poverty gap at $1 a day %	Population below $2 a day %	Poverty gap at $2 a day %
	Survey year	Rural %	Urban %	National %	Survey year	Rural %	Urban %	National %	Survey year				
Madagascar	1997	76.0	63.2	73.3	1999	76.7	52.1	71.3	2001[a]	61.0	27.9	85.1	51.8
Malawi	1990–91	..	..	54.0	1997–98	66.5	54.9	65.3	1997–98[a]	41.7	14.8	76.1	38.3
Malaysia	1989	..	..	15.5		..	..	..	1997[b]	<2	<0.5	9.3	2.0
Mali	1998	75.9	30.1	63.8		..	..	..	1994[a]	72.3	37.4	90.6	60.5
Mauritania	1996	65.5	30.1	50.0	2000	61.2	25.4	46.3	2000[a]	25.9	7.6	63.1	26.8
Mexico	1996	52.4	26.5	37.1	2002	34.8	11.4	20.3	2002[a]	4.5	1.2	20.4	6.5
Moldova	2001	64.1	58.0	62.4	2002	67.2	42.6	48.5	2001[a]	22.0	5.8	63.7	25.1
Mongolia	1995	33.1	38.5	36.3	1998	32.6	39.4	35.6	1998[a]	27.0	8.1	74.9	30.6
Morocco	1990–91	18.0	7.6	13.1	1998–99	27.2	12.0	19.0	1999[a]	<2	<0.5	14.3	3.1
Mozambique	1996–97	71.3	62.0	69.4		..	..	..	1996[a]	37.9	12.0	78.4	36.8
Namibia		..	..	..		..	..	..	1993[b]	34.9	14.0	55.8	30.4
Nepal	1995–96	43.3	21.6	41.8	2003–04	34.6	9.6	30.9	2003–04[a]	24.1	5.4	68.5	26.8
Nicaragua	1993	76.1	31.9	50.3	1998	68.5	30.5	47.9	2001[a]	45.1	16.7	79.9	41.2
Niger	1989–93	66.0	52.0	63.0		..	..	..	1995[a]	60.6	34.0	85.8	54.6
Nigeria	1985	49.5	31.7	43.0	1992–93	36.4	30.4	34.1	2003[a]	70.8	34.5	92.4	59.5
Pakistan	1993	33.4	17.2	28.6	1998–99	35.9	24.2	32.6	2002[a]	17.0	3.1	73.6	26.1
Panama	1997	64.9	15.3	37.3		..	..	..	2002[b]	6.5	2.3	17.1	6.9
Papua New Guinea	1996	41.3	16.1	37.5		..	..	..		..	..	..	..
Paraguay	1991	28.5	19.7	21.8		..	..	..	2002[b]	16.4	7.4	33.2	16.2
Peru	1994	67.0	46.1	53.5	1997	64.7	40.4	49.0	2002[b]	12.5	4.4	31.8	13.4
Philippines	1994	53.1	28.0	40.6	1997	50.7	21.5	36.8	2000[a]	15.5	3.0	47.5	17.8
Poland	1993	..	..	23.8		..	..	..	2002[a]	<2	<0.5	<2	<0.5
Portugal		..	..	..		..	..	..	1994[b]	<2	<0.5	<2	<0.5
Romania	1994	27.9	20.4	21.5		..	..	..	2003[a]	<2	0.5	12.9	3.0
Russian Federation	1994	..	..	30.9		..	..	..	2002[a]	<2	<0.5	12.1	3.1
Rwanda	1993	..	..	51.2	1999–00	65.7	14.3	60.3	1999–00[a]	51.7	20.0	83.7	45.5
Senegal	1992	40.4	23.7	33.4		..	..	..	1995[a]	22.3	5.7	63.0	25.2
Sierra Leone	1989	..	..	82.8	2003–04	79.0	56.4	70.2	1989[a]	57.0	39.5	74.5	51.8
Slovak Republic		..	..	..		..	..	..	1996[b]	<2	<0.5	2.9	0.8
Slovenia		..	..	..		..	..	..	1998[a]	<2	<0.5	<2	<0.5
South Africa		..	..	..		..	..	..	2000[a]	10.7	1.7	34.1	12.6
Sri Lanka	1990–91	22.0	15.0	20.0	1995–96	27.0	15.0	25.0	2002[a]	5.6	0.8	41.6	11.9
Tajikistan		..	..	..		..	..	..	2003[a]	7.4	1.3	42.8	13.0
Tanzania	1991	40.8	31.2	38.6	2000–01	38.7	29.5	35.7	2000–01[a]	57.8	20.7	89.9	49.3
Thailand	1990	..	..	18.0	1992	15.5	10.2	13.1	2002[a]	<2	<0.5	25.1	6.2
Togo	1987–89	..	..	32.3		..	..	..		..	..	..	..
Trinidad and Tobago	1992	20.0	24.0	21.0		..	..	..	1992[b]	4.0	1.0	20.0	6.3
Tunisia	1990	13.1	3.5	7.4	1995	13.9	3.6	7.6	2000[a]	<2	<0.5	6.6	1.3
Turkey	1994	..	..	28.3	2002	34.5	21.9	27.0	2003[a]	3.4	0.8	18.7	5.7
Uganda	1999–00	37.4	9.6	33.8	2002–03	41.7	12.2	37.7		..	..	..	..
Ukraine	2000	34.9		31.5	2003	28.4		19.5	2003[b]	<2	<0.5	4.9	0.9
Uruguay	1994	..	20.2		1998	..	24.7	..	2003[b]	<2	<0.5	5.7	1.6
Uzbekistan	2000	30.5	22.5	27.5		..	..	..	2000[b]				
Venezuela, RB	1989	..	..	31.3		..	..	..		8.3	2.8	27.6	10.2
Vietnam	1998	45.5	9.2	37.4	2002	35.6	6.6	28.9		..	..	..	..
Yemen, Rep.	1998	45.0	30.8	41.8		..	..	..	1998[a]	10.2	2.3	45.2	15.0
Zambia	1996	82.8	46.0	69.2	1998	83.1	56.0	72.9	2002–03[a]	75.8	36.4	94.1	62.2
Zimbabwe	1990–91	35.8	3.4	25.8	1995–96	48.0	7.9	34.9	1995–96[a]	56.1	24.2	83.0	48.2

a. Expenditure base. b. Income base.

Table 3. Millennium Development Goals: eradicating poverty and improving lives

	Survey year	Percentage share of poorest quintile in national consumption or income	Eradicate extreme poverty and hunger — Prevalence of child malnutrition % of children under 5		Achieve universal primary education — Primary completion rate (%)		Promote gender equality — Gender parity ratio in primary and secondary school		Reduce child mortality — Under-five mortality rate per 1,000		Improve maternal health — Maternal mortality ratio per 100,000 live births Modeled estimates	Births attended by skilled health staff % of total		Combat HIV/AIDS and other diseases — HIV prevalence % of population ages 15–49
			1989–94a	2000–04a	1991	2004	1991	2004	1990	2004	2000	1990–94a	2000–04a	2005
Albania	2002^b	9.1	..	14	..	*99*	96	*97*	45	19	55	..	98	
Algeria	1995^b	7.0	9	10	79	94	83	99	69	40	140	77	96	0.1
Angola		..	20	31	35	..	..	..	260	260	1,700	..	45	3.7
Argentina	2003^c,d	3.2	2	..	..	*100*	..	*103*	29	18	82	96	99	0.6
Armenia	2003^b	8.5	..	3	..	107	..	103	60	32	55	..	97	0.1
Australia	1994^d	5.9	..	..	..	98	101	98	10	6	8	100	..	0.1
Austria	2000^d	8.6	..	..	..	..	95	96	10	5	4	100	..	0.3
Azerbaijan	2002^b	12.2	..	7	..	96	100	97	105	90	94	..	84	0.1
Bangladesh	2000^b	9.0	68	48	..	76	..	*106*	149	77	380	10	13	<0.1
Belarus	2002^b	8.5	..	..	95	101	..	100	17	11	35	..	100	0.3
Belgium	2000^d	8.5	..	..	79	..	101	98	10	5	10	..	..	0.3
Benin	2003^b	7.4	..	23	21	49	50	71	185	152	850	..	66	1.8
Bolivia	2002^b	1.5	15	8	..	100	..	98	125	69	420	47	67	0.1
Bosnia and Herzegovina	2001^b	9.5	..	4	..	..	..	..	22	15	31	97	100	<0.1
Brazil	2003^d	2.6	7	..	..	*109*	..	*103*	60	34	260	72	96	0.5
Bulgaria	2003^b	8.7	..	..	85	98	99	96	19	15	32	..	99	<0.1
Burkina Faso	2003^b	6.9	33	38	21	29	62	76	210	192	1,000	42	38	2.0
Burundi	1998^b	5.1	..	45	46	33	82	82	190	190	1,000	..	25	3.3
Cambodia	1997^b	6.9	..	45	..	82	73	87	115	141	450	..	32	1.6
Cameroon	2001^b	5.6	15	18	56	63	83	81	139	149	730	58	62	5.4
Canada	2000^d	7.2	..	..	..	..	99	*100*	8	6	6	..	98	0.3
Central African Republic	1993^b	2.0	..	24	27	..	60	..	168	193	1,100	..	44	10.7
Chad		..	..	37	18	29	41	58	203	200	1,100	..	14	3.5
Chile	2000^d	3.3	1	1	..	95	100	98	21	8	31	100	100	0.3
China	2001^b	4.7	17	8	103	..	87	100	49	31	56	..	96	0.1
Hong Kong, China	1996^b	5.3	..	..	102	111	103	95	..	..	..	..	..	..
Colombia	2003^d	2.5	10	7	70	94	108	104	36	21	130	82	86	0.6
Congo, Dem. Rep.		..	..	31	46	..	..	..	205	205	990	..	61	3.2
Congo, Rep.		..	..	..	54	66	85	90	110	108	510	..	..	5.3
Costa Rica	2001^d	3.9	2	..	79	92	101	*102*	18	13	43	98	98	0.3
Côte d'Ivoire	2002^b	5.2	24	17	43	*43*	65	*68*	157	194	690	45	68	7.1
Croatia	2001^b	8.3	1	..	..	*91*	102	*101*	12	7	8	..	100	<0.1
Czech Republic	1996^d	10.3	1	..	..	104	98	100	13	4	9	..	100	0.1
Denmark	1997^d	8.3	..	..	98	99	101	102	9	5	5	..	..	0.2
Dominican Republic	2003^d	3.9	10	5	..	91	..	105	65	32	150	93	98	1.1
Ecuador	1998^b	3.3	..	12	..	101	..	100	57	26	130	..	..	0.3
Egypt, Arab Rep.	1999–2000^b	8.6	10	9	..	95	81	95	104	36	84	41	69	<0.1
El Salvador	2002^d	2.7	11	10	41	86	102	98	60	28	150	51	92	0.9
Eritrea		..	41	40	..	43	..	71	147	82	630	..	28	2.4
Ethiopia	1999–2000^b	9.1	48	47	..	55	68	73	204	166	850	..	6	..
Finland	2000^d	9.6	..	..	97	100	109	102	7	4	6	100	100	0.1
France	1995^d	7.2	..	..	104	*99*	102	100	9	5	17	99	..	0.4
Georgia	2003^b	5.6	..	..	..	91	98	99	47	45	32	..	..	0.2
Germany	2000^d	8.5	..	..	..	96	..	99	9	5	8	..	..	0.1
Ghana	1998–99^b	5.6	27	22	63	72	79	91	122	112	540	44	47	2.3
Greece	2000^d	6.7	..	..	..	99	99	100	11	5	9	..	..	0.2
Guatemala	2002^d	2.9	..	23	..	70	..	91	82	45	240	..	41	0.9
Guinea	1994^b	6.4	27	33	17	49	46	72	240	155	740	31	56	1.5
Haiti	2001^d	2.4	27	17	27	..	95	..	150	117	680	23	24	3.8
Honduras	2003^d	3.4	18	17	65	79	108	107	59	41	110	45	56	1.5
Hungary	2002^b	9.5	..	..	93	95	100	99	17	8	16	..	100	0.1
India	1999–2000^b	8.9	53	..	..	89	70	88	123	85	540	34	43	0.9
Indonesia	2002^b	8.4	..	28	91	101	93	99	91	38	230	37	72	0.1
Iran, Islamic Rep.	1998^b	5.1	..	..	91	95	85	100	72	38	76	..	90	0.2
Ireland	2000^d	7.4	..	..	..	101	104	102	9	6	5	..	100	0.2
Israel	2001^d	5.7	..	..	..	104	105	100	12	6	17	..	..	..
Italy	2000^d	6.5	..	..	104	101	100	99	9	5	5	..	..	0.5
Jamaica	2000^b	6.7	5	4	90	84	102	101	20	20	87	79	97	1.5
Japan	1993^d	10.6	..	..	101	..	101	100	6	4	10	100	..	<0.1
Jordan	2002–03^b	6.7	6	4	73	97	101	101	40	27	41	87	100	..
Kazakhstan	2003^b	7.4	..	..	..	110	102	98	63	73	210	..	..	0.1
Kenya	1997^b	6.0	23	20	..	91	94	94	97	120	1,000	45	42	6.1
Korea, Rep.	1998^d	7.9	..	..	98	105	99	100	9	6	20	98	..	<0.1
Kuwait		..	..	..	..	91	97	104	16	12	5	..	..	..
Kyrgyz Republic	2003^b	8.9	..	7	..	93	..	101	80	68	110	..	99	0.1
Lao PDR	2002^b	8.1	40	40	..	74	75	84	163	83	650	..	19	0.1
Latvia	2003^b	6.6	..	..	..	92	100	99	18	12	42	..	..	0.8
Lebanon		..	..	..	..	94	..	102	37	31	150	..	..	0.1
Lithuania	2003^b	6.8	..	..	..	98	..	99	13	8	13	..	100	0.2
Macedonia, FYR	2003^b	6.1	..	..	..	96	99	99	38	14	23	..	99	<0.1
Madagascar	2001^b	4.9	45	42	33	45	98	..	168	123	550	57	51	0.5
Malawi	1997^b	4.9	28	22	28	59	81	99	241	175	1,800	55	61	14.1
Malaysia	1997^d	4.4	22	11	91	*91*	101	*106*	22	12	41	..	97	0.5
Mali	1994^b	4.6	..	33	11	44	59	74	250	219	1,200	..	41	1.7
Mauritania	2000^b	6.2	48	32	33	43	67	96	133	125	1,000	40	57	0.7

Note: For data comparability and coverage, see the technical notes. Figures in italics are for years other than those specified.

Table 3. Millennium Development Goals: eradicating poverty and improving lives *(continued)*

			Eradicate extreme poverty and hunger		Achieve universal primary education		Promote gender equality		Reduce child mortality		Improve maternal health	Improve maternal health		Combat HIV/AIDS and other diseases
	Survey year	Percentage share of poorest quintile in national consumption or income	Prevalence of child malnutrition % of children under 5 1989–94a	2000–04a	Primary completion rate (%) 1991	2004	Gender parity ratio in primary and secondary school 1991	2004	Under-five mortality rate per 1,000 1990	2004	Maternal mortality ratio per 100,000 live births Modeled estimates 2000	Births attended by skilled health staff % of total 1990–94a	2000–04a	HIV prevalence % of population ages 15–49 2005
Mexico	2002b	4.3	17	..	86	99	98	102	46	28	83	..	95	0.3
Moldova	2003b	7.8	..	..	..	91	105	102	40	28	36	..	..	1.1
Mongolia	1998b	5.6	12	13	..	96	109	108	108	52	110	..	99	<0.1
Morocco	1998–99b	6.5	10	10	47	75	70	88	89	43	220	31	63	0.1
Mozambique	1996–97b	6.5	..	24	..	30	72	82	235	152	1,000	..	48	16.1
Namibia	1993d	1.4	26	24	..	81	108	104	86	63	300	68	76	19.6
Nepal	2003–04b	6.0	..	48	..	75	59	85	145	76	740	7	15	0.5
Netherlands	1999d	7.6	..	..	..	100	97	98	9	6	16	..	..	0.2
New Zealand	1997d	6.4	..	..	100	..	101	105	11	7	7	95	..	0.1
Nicaragua	2001b	5.6	11	10	44	73	109	103	68	38	230	..	67	0.2
Niger	1995b	2.6	43	40	17	25	57	71	320	259	1,600	15	16	1.1
Nigeria	2003b	5.1	39	29	..	75	79	84	230	197	800	31	35	3.9
Norway	2000d	9.6	..	..	100	101	102	101	9	4	16	..	..	0.1
Oman		..	24	..	..	91	89	98	32	13	87	..	95	..
Pakistan	2002b	9.3	40	38	..	..	..	73	130	101	500	19	23	0.1
Panama	2002d	2.5	6	..	..	97	..	101	34	24	160	86	93	0.9
Papua New Guinea	1996b	4.5	..	..	47	54	80	87	101	93	300	..	41	1.8
Paraguay	2002d	2.2	4	5	71	91	99	98	41	24	170	67	77	0.4
Peru	2002d	3.2	11	7	..	100	96	100	80	29	410	..	59	0.6
Philippines	2000b	5.4	30	28	..	97	100	102	62	34	200	53	60	<0.1
Poland	2002b	7.5	..	..	98	100	101	100	18	8	13	..	100	0.1
Portugal	1997d	5.8	..	..	95	..	103	102	14	5	5	98	100	0.4
Romania	2003b	8.1	6	3	..	93	99	100	31	20	49	99	99	<0.1
Russian Federation	2002b	6.1	4	6	..	..	104	99	29	21	67	..	99	1.1
Rwanda	1983–85b	..	29	24	33	37	96	100	173	203	1,400	26	31	3.1
Saudi Arabia		..	15	..	56	62	84	92	44	27	23	..	..	..
Senegal	1995b	6.4	22	23	..	45	69	90	148	137	690	47	58	0.9
Serbia and Montenegro		..	..	2	..	96	..	101	28	15	11	..	93	0.2
Sierra Leone	1989b	..	29	27	..	..	67	74	302	283	2,000	..	42	1.6
Singapore	1998d	5.0	..	3	..	..	95	..	8	3	30	..	..	0.3
Slovak Republic	1996d	8.8	..	..	..	99	..	101	14	9	3	..	99	<0.1
Slovenia	1998–99d	9.1	..	..	..	114	..	100	10	4	17	100	100	<0.1
South Africa	2000b	3.5	..	..	75	96	104	101	60	67	230	..	..	18.8
Spain	2000d	7.0	..	..	..	..	104	102	9	5	4	..	..	0.6
Sri Lanka	1999–2000b	8.3	38	30	97	..	102	102	32	14	92	94	96	<0.1
Sudan		..	34	41	41	49	78	88	120	91	590	86	87	1.6
Sweden	2000d	9.1	..	..	96	..	102	102	7	4	2	..	..	0.2
Switzerland	2000d	7.6	..	..	53	97	97	96	9	5	7	..	..	0.4
Syrian Arab Republic		..	12	7	89	107	85	94	44	16	160	77	..	..
Tajikistan	2003b	7.9	..	..	..	92	..	89	119	93	100	..	71	0.1
Tanzania	2000–01b	7.3	29	..	61	54	97	..	161	126	1,500	44	46	6.5
Thailand	2002b	6.3	19	..	..	..	95	98	37	21	44	..	99	1.4
Togo		..	..	..	35	66	59	73	152	140	570	..	61	3.2
Tunisia	2000b	6.0	..	4	74	97	86	102	52	25	120	..	90	0.1
Turkey	2003b	5.3	10	4	90	88	81	86	82	32	70	76	83	..
Turkmenistan	1998b	6.1	..	12	..	..	..	..	97	103	31	..	97	<0.1
Uganda	1999b	5.9	23	23	..	57	82	97	160	138	880	38	39	6.7
Ukraine	2003b	9.2	..	1	92	100	..	99	26	18	35	..	100	1.4
United Kingdom	1999d	6.1	..	..	..	..	98	102	10	6	13	..	..	0.6
United States	2000d	5.4	1	2	..	..	100	99	11	8	17	99	..	0.6
Uruguay	2003c,d	5.0	4	..	94	91	..	106	25	17	27	..	..	0.5
Uzbekistan	2000b	9.2	..	8	..	97	94	98	79	69	24	..	96	0.2
Venezuela, RB	2000d	4.7	5	4	43	89	105	103	27	19	96	..	94	0.7
Vietnam	2002b	7.5	45	28	..	101	..	94	53	23	130	..	90	0.5
West Bank and Gaza		..	..	..	..	98	..	103	..	..	..	..	97	..
Yemen, Rep.	1998b	7.4	39	46	..	62	..	63	142	111	570	16	27	..
Zambia	2002–03b	6.1	25	23	..	66	..	93	180	182	750	51	43	17.0
Zimbabwe	1995b	4.6	16	..	99	80	92	96	80	129	1,100	69	..	20.1
World		..	..w	25w,e	..w	..w	86w	93w	95w	79w	410w	43w	62w	1.0w
Low income		..		39e	64f	78g	73	85	147	122	684	32	41	1.7
Middle income		..		11e	91f	96g	91	99	58	39	150	..	87	0.6
Lower middle income		..		12e	93f	97g	89	99	62	42	163	..	86	0.3
Upper middle income		..		7e	87f	95g	98	98	41	28	91	..	95	2.2
Low & middle income		..		26e	80f	87g	84	92	103	86	450	40	60	1.1
East Asia & Pacific		19		15e	97f	98g	89	99	59	37	117	..	86	0.2
Europe & Central Asia		..		5e	92f	94g	97	96	49	34	58	..	94	0.7
Latin America & Carib.		..		7e	84f	96g	..	102	54	31	194	77	88	0.6
Middle East & N. Africa		..		13e	75f	88g	82	92	81	55	183	46	72	0.1
South Asia		53		45e	73f	87g	70	85	129	92	564	30	37	0.7
Sub-Saharan Africa		..		29e	51f	61g	80	83	185	168	921	43	42	6.2
High income		..		3e	..	..	100	99	11	7	14	..	99	0.4

a. Data are for the most recent year available. b. Refers to expenditure shares by percentiles of population, ranked by per capita expenditure. c. Urban data. d. Refers to income shares by percentiles of population, ranked by per capita income. e. Data are for 1995–2004. f. Data are for 1989–94. g. Data are for 2000–05.

Table 4. Economic activity

	Gross domestic product		Agricultural productivity		Value added as % of GDP			Household final cons. expenditure	General gov't final cons. expenditure	Gross capital formation	External balance of goods and services	GDP implicit deflator
	Millions of dollars	Avg. annual % growth	Agricultural value added per worker 2000 $		Agriculture	Industry	Services	% of GDP	% of GDP	% of GDP	% of GDP	Avg. annual % growth
	2005	2000–05	1992–94	2002–04	2005	2005	2005	2005	2005	2005	2005	2000–05
Albania	8,379	5.3	916	1,469	25	20	55	88	9	25	−23	4.0
Algeria	102,257	5.1	1,743	1,983	8	62	29	39	7	32	22	7.8
Angola	28,038	9.1	99	168	8	66	26	73	..ᵃ	13	15	80.0
Argentina	183,309	2.2	7,335	9,311	10	36	54	63	11	19	7	12.5
Armenia	4,903	12.3	1,464	2,722	21	44	35	73	11	30	−13	4.2
Australia	700,672	3.3	20,693	27,058	3	26	71	60	18	25	−3	3.2
Austria	304,527	1.3	12,881	21,083	2	31	67	56	18	22	5	1.7
Azerbaijan	12,561	12.7	922	1,061	12	55	32	59	11	53	−24	6.0
Bangladesh	59,958	5.3	251	309	21	28	52	77	6	24	−7	4.3
Belarus	29,566	7.6	1,964	2,612	10	41	49	50	20	30	1	35.8
Belgium	364,735	1.5	27,442	41,536	1	25	73	54	23	20	3	2.0
Benin	4,287	4.0	391	591	32	13	54	78	15	20	−13	2.9
Bolivia	9,334	3.0	678	749	16	31	53	69	15	12	4	4.8
Bosnia and Herzegovina	9,369	5.1	3,028	5,709	12	28	61	85	23	21	−29	3.5
Brazil	794,098	2.2	1,839	3,111	10	38	52	58	15	19	8	10.1
Bulgaria	26,648	5.0	2,152	6,635	9	30	60	72	17	28	−17	4.0
Burkina Faso	5,171	5.1	157	166	31	20	50	83	13	19	−15	2.7
Burundi	800	2.2	104	79	35	20	45	87	28	12	−28	8.3
Cambodia	5,391	6.6	276	289	33	29	38	80	5	26	−11	2.7
Cameroon	16,985	3.8	720	1,111	41	14	45	70	10	20	−0	2.2
Canada	1,115,192	2.6	29,378	38,509	..	..	..	56	20	20	4	2.3
Central African Republic	1,369	−1.4	292	415	54	21	25	..	..	..	..	2.0
Chad	5,469	14.5	191	225	23	51	26	58	5	17	20	7.6
Chile	115,250	3.0	4,235	3,222	6	47	48	57	12	23	8	5.3
China	2,228,862	9.6	273	373	13	46	41	49	10	39	3	3.2
Hong Kong, China	177,722	4.3	..	..	0	10	90	59	9	21	12	−3.6
Colombia	122,309	3.5	3,208	2,971	13	34	53	61	19	19	0	6.6
Congo, Dem. Rep.	6,974	4.4	183	153	46	25	29	87	7	14	−8	43.7
Congo, Rep.	5,091	3.9	295	337	6	46	48	34	14	24	28	−0.6
Costa Rica	19,432	4.0	3,364	4,285	8	29	63	77	5	21	−3	9.5
Cote d'Ivoire	16,055	−0.5	608	757	22	21	57	71	8	10	10	2.9
Croatia	37,412	4.4	5,189	9,237	8	28	64	57	19	28	−5	3.3
Czech Republic	122,345	3.5	3,531	4,543	3	39	58	50	22	28	0	2.8
Denmark	254,401	1.5	22,271	37,443	2	25	73	48	27	20	5	1.9
Dominican Republic	28,303	2.1	2,482	4,169	13	27	60	76	7	19	−2	20.4
Ecuador	36,244	5.0	1,027	1,478	6	28	66	68	8	26	−2	11.7
Egypt, Arab Rep.	89,336	3.7	1,575	2,007	14	39	47	70	13	17	−0	5.6
El Salvador	16,974	2.2	1,639	1,618	11	30	60	92	11	15	−18	2.9
Eritrea	986	3.6	91	56	23	23	55	82	45	20	−48	15.1
Ethiopia	11,174	4.2	147	144	48	13	39	82	14	26	−23	4.2
Finland	193,176	2.4	17,815	31,339	3	31	66	53	22	19	6	1.1
France	2,110,185	1.5	24,724	40,521	2	22	76	56	24	20	0	1.7
Georgia	6,395	7.4	2,127	1,442	17	27	56	65	18	27	−10	6.0
Germany	2,781,900	0.7	13,908	23,616	1	29	70	59	19	17	5	0.9
Ghana	10,695	5.1	301	341	39	25	37	74	15	30	−19	22.6
Greece	213,698	4.2	8,315	9,303	7	23	70	66	17	26	−9	3.1
Guatemala	31,683	2.5	2,178	2,275	23	19	58	89	6	18	−13	7.2
Guinea	2,689	2.9	175	229	26	38	37	85	6	12	−3	9.4
Haiti	4,245	−0.5	672	421	28	17	55	91	8	30	−29	18.0
Honduras	7,976	3.6	992	1,163	13	31	56	72	14	29	−15	7.3
Hungary	109,154	4.0	2,825	3,986	4	31	65	68	10	23	−1	6.3
India	785,468	6.9	353	382	19	28	54	61	11	30	−2	3.8
Indonesia	287,217	4.7	498	564	14	41	45	64	8	23	5	8.2
Iran, Islamic Rep.	196,343	5.8	2,042	2,438	10	44	46	51	14	32	5	18.8
Ireland	196,388	5.0	..	..	3	41	56	44	15	25	16	3.5
Israel	123,434	1.9	..	..	..	..	..	59	28	19	−5	1.3
Italy	1,723,044	0.7	13,672	21,553	3	28	70	60	19	20	1	2.8
Jamaica	9,696	1.5	2,162	1,916	5	33	62	72	14	31	−17	10.7
Japan	4,505,912	1.3	19,958	26,557	1	31	68	57	18	24	2	−1.8
Jordan	12,861	5.9	1,810	1,192	2	29	69	91	16	27	−34	2.6
Kazakhstan	56,088	10.1	1,585	1,420	7	40	54	52	11	28	9	11.7
Kenya	17,977	2.8	301	317	27	18	55	70	11	25	−6	4.3
Korea, Rep.	787,624	4.6	6,257	9,996	4	41	55	52	13	30	4	2.4
Kuwait	74,658	7.3	..	13,898	0	53	47	38	21	14	27	6.4
Kyrgyz Republic	2,441	4.0	625	942	34	21	45	82	18	20	−20	4.7
Lao PDR	2,855	6.2	376	461	46	28	26	..	..	17	−4	11.0
Latvia	15,771	7.9	1,624	2,505	4	23	73	64	17	27	−8	4.8
Lebanon	22,210	4.1	..	..	7	21	72	87	15	20	−22	2.5
Lithuania	25,495	7.8	..	4,363	6	31	63	62	17	25	−5	1.1
Macedonia, FYR	5,762	1.7	2,104	3,034	12	29	59	77	20	21	−18	2.1
Madagascar	5,040	2.0	183	174	28	16	56	84	8	22	−15	11.0
Malawi	2,072	3.4	73	131	35	19	46	95	17	15	−26	14.7
Malaysia	130,143	4.8	3,918	4,690	9	50	40	43	13	23	21	3.4
Mali	5,098	5.8	205	229	36	24	40	79	10	24	−13	3.5
Mauritania	1,888	5.0	283	282	17	32	51	..	..	..	..	8.5

Note: For data comparability and coverage, see the technical notes. Figures in italics are for years other than those specified.

Table 4. Economic activity *(continued)*

	Gross domestic product		Agricultural productivity		Value added as % of GDP			Household final cons. expenditure	General gov't final cons. expenditure	Gross capital formation	External balance of goods and services	GDP implicit deflator
	Millions of dollars	Avg. annual % growth	Agricultural value added per worker 2000 $		Agriculture	Industry	Services	% of GDP	% of GDP	% of GDP	% of GDP	Avg. annual % growth
	2005	2000–05	1992–94	2002–04	2005	2005	2005	2005	2005	2005	2005	2000–05
Mexico	768,438	1.9	2,295	2,727	4	26	70	68	12	22	−2	7.1
Moldova	2,906	7.0	902	732	21	24	55	97	15	20	−32	10.6
Mongolia	1,880	5.8	811	661	22	27	51	57	17	37	−11	11.5
Morocco	51,745	4.2	1,275	1,582	13	31	56	63	20	26	−9	1.0
Mozambique	6,630	8.6	98	142	23	30	47	77	11	22	−10	11.4
Namibia	6,126	4.6	845	1,097	10	32	58	50	23	26	1	5.3
Nepal	7,346	2.6	191	208	40	21	38	76	11	26	−13	4.1
Netherlands	594,755	0.6	27,857	39,358	2	26	72	49	25	20	5	2.7
New Zealand	109,041	3.8	20,319	27,660	..	..	..	60	18	23	0	2.4
Nicaragua	4,911	3.0	1,221	1,916	19	30	52	88	11	29	−28	6.9
Niger	3,405	3.7	165	172	40	17	43	79	12	19	−9	2.4
Nigeria	98,951	5.9	610	863	24	56	20	41	21	21	18	17.4
Norway	283,920	1.7	23,252	32,779	2	39	59	45	22	19	14	2.4
Oman	24,284	3.0	1,000	1,128	2	56	42	45	23	18	14	1.8
Pakistan	110,732	4.8	603	688	22	25	53	80	8	17	−5	6.0
Panama	15,467	4.3	2,450	3,570	8	18	75	69	13	20	−2	1.6
Papua New Guinea	4,731	1.3	451	482	26	45	30	..	..	..	..	9.4
Paraguay	8,152	1.8	2,165	2,453	27	24	49	72	7	24	−3	12.3
Peru	78,431	4.2	1,169	1,764	9	33	58	66	10	19	5	2.7
Philippines	98,306	4.5	901	1,021	14	33	53	75	10	16	−1	5.1
Poland	299,151	3.1	1,510	2,003	5	31	65	63	19	19	−0	2.3
Portugal	173,085	0.3	4,414	5,735	4	27	70	63	21	23	−8	3.3
Romania	98,559	5.8	2,312	3,519	10	35	55	74	12	24	−10	21.8
Russian Federation	763,720	6.2	1,746	2,297	6	38	56	50	16	21	14	16.8
Rwanda	2,131	4.9	183	229	42	20	38	88	13	21	−22	5.9
Saudi Arabia	309,778	4.2	8,905	14,284	4	59	37	26	23	16	34	6.3
Senegal	8,318	4.9	236	235	17	20	63	76	13	23	−14	2.0
Serbia and Montenegro	27,059	5.3	..	1,446	16	32	52	88	18	17	−22	25.3
Sierra Leone	1,193	13.7	..	..	46	24	30	90	13	15	−19	6.8
Singapore	116,764	4.2	28,729	32,267	0	34	66	41	11	19	30	0.5
Slovak Republic	46,412	4.9	..	..	3	29	67	56	20	29	−4	4.1
Slovenia	34,030	3.4	12,339	34,447	3	35	62	55	20	25	−0	5.4
South Africa	240,152	3.7	1,764	2,463	3	31	66	59	20	18	4	6.6
Spain	1,123,691	3.1	12,611	19,132	3	29	67	58	18	28	−4	4.2
Sri Lanka	23,479	4.2	713	743	17	26	57	77	9	26	−12	8.7
Sudan	27,699	6.1	384	728	34	30	37	65	17	22	−4	9.8
Sweden	354,115	2.2	21,654	31,716	2	29	69	48	28	16	8	1.6
Switzerland	365,937	0.9	21,565	22,190	..	..	..	61	12	20	7	0.9
Syrian Arab Republic	26,320	4.0	2,356	2,977	21	26	53	65	13	20	1	4.7
Tajikistan	2,326	9.7	367	401	22	36	42	95	9	14	−19	21.3
Tanzania[b]	12,111	6.9	242	287	45	18	38	77	14	19	−9	6.3
Thailand	176,602	5.4	481	599	10	47	44	61	10	31	−2	2.3
Togo	2,203	2.7	360	409	42	23	35	86	10	18	−13	1.2
Tunisia	28,683	4.5	2,365	2,415	13	28	59	63	14	25	−3	2.3
Turkey	363,300	5.2	1,772	1,793	12	24	65	69	13	25	−7	25.5
Turkmenistan	6,774	..	1,179	..	21	45	34	52	14	25	9	..
Uganda	8,712	5.4	192	231	34	21	46	77	14	23	−13	5.1
Ukraine	81,664	8.0	1,235	1,442	11	34	55	55	18	19	8	10.7
United Kingdom	2,192,553	2.3	23,089	26,897	1	26	73	65	21	17	−3	2.7
United States	12,455,068	2.8	22,868	36,863	1	22	77	71	16	18	−5	2.2
Uruguay	16,792	1.0	6,213	7,102	11	29	60	74	11	13	2	11.4
Uzbekistan	13,667	5.3	1,263	1,567	28	29	43	51	16	25	8	29.0
Venezuela, RB	138,857	1.3	4,781	5,899	5	52	44	50	13	21	16	28.6
Vietnam	52,408	7.5	225	294	22	40	38	65	6	36	−7	5.9
West Bank and Gaza	3,454	−13.3	..	..	6	12	82	84	53	3	−39	10.9
Yemen, Rep.	14,452	5.9	383	511	13	35	52	80	13	17	−10	6.9
Zambia	7,257	4.7	160	206	19	25	56	70	13	26	−9	20.4
Zimbabwe	3,364	−6.1	238	242	22	28	50	68	29	38	−35	223.4
World	44,384,871t	2.8w	772w	863w	4w	28w	68w	62w	17w	21w	0w	
Low income	1,391,362	6.0	327	364	22	28	50	65	11	27	−2	
Middle income	8,535,129	5.1	581	726	10	37	53	58	14	26	2	
Lower middle income	4,869,491	6.3	451	587	13	41	46	56	13	29	2	
Upper middle income	3,665,404	3.5	2,279	2,733	7	32	62	63	14	22	1	
Low & middle income	9,926,393	5.3	477	567	12	36	52	59	13	26	2	
East Asia & Pacific	3,032,573	8.3	..	..	13	45	42	52	10	34	3	
Europe & Central Asia	2,190,933	5.4	1,652	1,971	8	32	60	61	16	23	1	
Latin America & Caribbean	2,455,621	2.3	2,233	2,831	8	32	60	64	13	20	3	
Middle East & North Africa	632,570	4.1	1,589	1,978	11	41	48	60	13	26	1	
South Asia	995,809	6.4	357	394	19	27	54	64	10	28	−2	
Sub-Saharan Africa	615,216	4.2	293	334	17	32	51	63	17	20	0	
High income	34,466,198	2.2	..	..	2	26	72	62	18	20	0	

a. Data on general government final consumption expenditure are not available separately; they are included in household final consumption expenditure.
b. Data refer to mainland Tanzania only.

Table 5. Trade, aid, and finance

	Merchandise trade							External debt			
	exports	imports	Manufactured exports	High technology exports	Current account balance	Foreign direct investment	Official development assistance or official aid[a]	Total	Present value	Domestic credit provided by banking sector	Net migration
	$ millions 2005	$ millions 2005	% of total merchandise exports 2004	% of manufactured exports 2004	$ millions 2005	$ millions 2004	$ per capita 2004	$ millions 2004	% of GNI 2004	% of GDP 2005	thousands 2000–05
Albania	654	2,650	82	1	−572	426	117	1,549	17	10	−100
Algeria	44,390	20,040	2	1	..	882	10	21,987	32	11.0	−100
Angola	23,120	8,150	..	..	686	1,444	74	9,521	69	5.4	145
Argentina	40,044	28,692	29	8	3,281	4,084	2	169,247	159	45.4	−100
Armenia	950	1,768	62	1	−204	219	84	1,224	50	7.2	−100
Australia	105,825	125,280	25	14	−42,084	42,469		..	..	102.4	500
Austria	123,317	124,749	84	12	3,848	4,022		..	..	105.6	100
Azerbaijan	4,346	4,202	11	2	167	3,556	21	1,986	23	9.7	−100
Bangladesh	9,190	13,868	90	0	−279	449	10	20,344	26	30.1	−350
Belarus	15,992	16,699	60	3	469	169	5	3,717	20	13.9	−10
Belgium	329,650	320,363	81	8[b]	6,563	40,080		..	..	73.1	67
Benin	620	960	9	2	−331	60	46	1,916	24[c]	14.6	99
Bolivia	2,671	2,200	14	9	285	117	85	6,096	38[c]	52.5	−100
Bosnia and Herzegovina	2,440	7,199	..	..	−2,087	613	172	3,202	34	43.6	40
Brazil	118,308	77,576	54	12	14,199	18,166	2	222,026	47	81.0	−130
Bulgaria	11,725	18,181	62	4	−3,133	2,005	80	15,661	83	36.8	−50
Burkina Faso	440	1,230	8	10	..	35	48	1,967	23[c]	14.9	100
Burundi	110	280	5	6	−25	3	48	1,385	15	40.5	192
Cambodia	3,100	3,700	97	0	−217	131	35	3,377	68	9.3	−10
Cameroon	2,500	2,450	5	1	..	0	48	9,496	20[c]	9.1	13
Canada	359,578	320,105	60	14	25,268	6,284		..	..	97.0	1,050
Central African Republic	140	165	37	0	..	−13	26	1,078	75	7.2	−45
Chad	3,230	850	..	..	..	478	34	1,701	33[c]	3.2	271
Chile	39,536	32,542	13	5	703	7,603	3	44,058	57	62.5	30
China	761,999	660,118	91	30	68,659	54,937	1	248,934	15	120.1	−1,950
Hong Kong, China	292,328[d]	300,635	97[d]	32	19,706	34,035	1	..	..	147.6	300
Colombia	21,187	21,204	38	6	−1,930	3,052	11	37,732	49	34.4	−200
Congo, Dem. Rep.	2,190	2,270	..	..	..	0	33	11,841	36	1.5	−322
Congo, Rep.	5,000	1,980	..	..	−3	0	30	5,829	331	3.2	−14
Costa Rica	7,039	9,798	63	37	−832	620	3	5,700	36	32.3	84
Côte d'Ivoire	7,180	4,690	20	8	303	175	9	11,739	90	14.4	−371
Croatia	8,809	18,547	73	13	−2,541	1,243	27	31,548	110	57.5	100
Czech Republic	78,474	76,863	90	13	−5,595	4,454	27	45,561	51	33.2	50
Denmark	85,708	76,539	66	20	5,941	−8,804		..	..	160.3	61
Dominican Republic	5,854	9,210	..	..	1,399	645	10	6,965	39	36.7	−140
Ecuador	9,821	9,609	9	7	−157	1,160	12	16,868	70	22.0	−250
Egypt, Arab Rep.	10,344	16,552	31	1	3,922	1,253	20	30,292	32	110.8	−450
El Salvador	3,383	6,712	60	4	−612	466	31	7,250	54	41.9	−38
Eritrea	9	495	..	..	..	30	61	681	53	32.7	280
Ethiopia	860	4,160	11	0	−668	545	26	6,574	30[c]	48.9	−150
Finland	65,998	58,737	83	21	9,698	3,075		..	..	68.7	41
France	459,246	495,796	83	19	−38,781	24,521		..	..	90.8	300
Georgia	867	2,491	37	38	−689	499	70	2,082	37	9.8	−248
Germany	970,688	774,069	84	17	115,519	−34,903		..	..	112.3	1,100
Ghana	2,520	5,090	14	4	−236	139	63	7,035	32[c]	13.1	12
Greece	17,192	54,031	59	11	−17,879	1,355		..	..	78.6	179
Guatemala	3,477	8,810	42	7	−1,188	155	18	5,532	23	15.2	−300
Guinea	910	845	25	0	−162	100	30	3,538	45	3.7	−299
Haiti	473	1,471	..	..	−13	7	29	1,225	29	14.9	−105
Honduras	1,694	4,484	27	2	−413	293	91	6,332	38	37.4	−30
Hungary	62,194	65,711	88	29	−7,962	4,608	30	63,159	76	46.4	50
India	89,843	131,648	73	5	6,853	5,335	1	122,723	18	36.9	−1,400
Indonesia	86,285	68,736	56	16	3,108	1,023	0	140,649	61	24.0	−1,000
Iran, Islamic Rep.	58,400	41,561	9	2	..	500	3	13,622	9	38.6	−1,379
Ireland	109,525	66,356	86	34	−3,946	11,040		..	..	136.9	194
Israel	42,588	46,910	94	19	2,385	1,664	70	..	..	92.2	158
Italy	366,797	379,696	88	8	−26,814	16,772		..	..	87.7	600
Jamaica	1,487	4,560	65	0	−509	602	29	6,399	89	28.3	−100
Japan	595,750	516,075	93	24	165,783	7,805		..	..	99.5	270
Jordan	4,284	10,455	72	5	−18	620	110	8,175	73	74.0	100
Kazakhstan	27,849	17,353	16	2	−486	4,104	18	32,310	101	26.7	−600
Kenya	3,450	6,360	21	3	−379	46	19	6,826	34	40.2	−212
Korea, Rep.	284,742	261,028	92	33	27,613	8,189	−1	..	..	98.2	−80
Kuwait	44,016	17,422	..	..	18,884	−20	1	..	..	71.6	240
Kyrgyz Republic	672	1,108	43	2	−75	77	51	2,100	82	7.1	−75
Lao PDR	435	605	..	..	..	17	47	2,056	76	6.3	−7
Latvia	5,122	8,625	61	5	−1,959	699	71	12,661	110	44.3	−12
Lebanon	1,880	9,340	68	2	−4,805	288	75	22,177	121	75.6	−35
Lithuania	11,815	15,453	58	5	−1,771	773	73	9,475	54	25.7	−20
Macedonia, FYR	2,041	3,228	77	1	−415	157	122	2,044	39	23.2	−10
Madagascar	750	1,550	23	1	−309	45	68	3,462	38[c]	10.0	0
Malawi	460	1,035	16	2	..	16	38	3,418	60[c]	22.1	−20
Malaysia	140,948	114,607	76	55	14,872	4,624	12	52,145	53	133.7	150
Mali	1,150	1,500	..	..	−271	180	43	3,316	33[c]	20.0	−134
Mauritania	410	740	..	..	..	300	60	2,297	57[c]	25.9	30

Note: For data comparability and coverage, see the technical notes. Figures in italics are for years other than those specified.

Table 5. Trade, aid, and finance *(continued)*

	Merchandise trade		Manufactured exports	High technology exports	Current account balance	Foreign direct investment	Official development assistance or official aid[a]	External debt		Domestic credit provided by banking sector	Net migration
	exports	imports						Total	Present value		
	$ millions 2005	$ millions 2005	% of total merchandise exports 2004	% of manufactured exports 2004	$ millions 2005	$ millions 2004	$ per capita 2004	$ millions 2004	% of GNI 2004	% of GDP 2005	thousands 2000–05
Mexico	213,711	231,670	80	21	−5,708	17,377	1	138,689	24	34.6	−2,000
Moldova	1,091	2,312	36	4	−286	81	28	1,868	75	21.3	−40
Mongolia	1,045	1,145	38	0	63	93	104	1,517	86	32.0	−50
Morocco	10,463	20,124	69	10	970	769	24	17,672	39	56.7	−400
Mozambique	1,790	2,420	3	9	−607	245	63	4,651	17[c]	2.1	−20
Namibia	1,990	2,450	41	3	634	..	89	..	..	53.2	−6
Nepal	830	1,860	74	0	197	0	16	3,354	37	..	−100
Netherlands	401,333	357,869	70	29	40,187	377		..	..	166.3	150
New Zealand	21,731	26,224	31	14	−6,456	2,271		..	..	121.1	79
Nicaragua	858	2,595	11	6	−772	250	229	5,145	35	85.6	−100
Niger	410	920	8	3	−219	0	40	1,950	26[c]	6.3	−10
Nigeria	43,500	15,200	2	2	12,264	1,875	5	35,890	71	15.6	−170
Norway	103,256	54,907	19	18	49,488	502		..	..	11.1	58
Oman	17,119	9,000	12	1	443	−17	22	3,872	18	34.9	−160
Pakistan	15,942	25,335	85	1	−817	1,118	9	35,687	35	29.3	−1,810
Panama	1,080	4,180	10	2	−818	1,012	12	9,469	94	88.2	8
Papua New Guinea	3,070	1,710	6	39	..	25	46	2,149	66	10.1	0
Paraguay	1,495	2,880	13	7	20	93	0	3,433	52	17.9	−25
Peru	17,206	12,502	20	2	1,030	1,816	18	31,296	57	17.4	−300
Philippines	41,224	46,257	55	64	2,080	469	6	60,550	73	34.3	−900
Poland	88,940	100,487	81	3	−4,364	12,613	40	99,190	45	26.6	−80
Portugal	37,858	60,175	85	9	−17,007	825		..	..	150.3	250
Romania	27,730	40,463	82	3	−6,382	5,440	42	30,034	51	9.7	−150
Russian Federation	245,255	125,123	21	9	84,249	12,479	9	197,335	46	24.2	400
Rwanda	120	410	10	25	−6	8	53	1,656	15[c]	10.7	45
Saudi Arabia	178,755	56,092	12	2	87,132	..	1	..	..	56.0	250
Senegal	1,600	3,330	39	7	−437	70	92	3,938	22[c]	21.2	−100
Serbia and Montenegro	5,142	11,558	57	..	..	966	144	15,882	77	..	−100
Sierra Leone	150	350	7	31	−74	26	67	1,723	37[c]	4.7	438
Singapore	229,620[d]	200,030	84[d]	59	27,897	16,032	2	..	..	106.2	200
Slovak Republic	31,973	35,301	86	5	−282	1,122	44	22,068	67	31.2	5
Slovenia	18,698	20,141	90	6	−362	827	31	..	..	45.9	10
South Africa	51,874	66,500	58[e]	6	−10,079	585	14	28,500	17	156.4	50
Spain	186,099	277,597	77	7	−83,136	16,594		..	..	125.4	2,025
Sri Lanka	6,275	8,985	74	2	−648	233	27	10,887	50	31.5	−160
Sudan	5,150	6,100	2	0	−2,768	1,511	25	19,332	151	7.6	−519
Sweden	129,922	110,645	81	17	27,485	−588		..	..	105.9	157
Switzerland	125,898	121,156	93	22	49,710	−797		..	..	161.2	40
Syrian Arab Republic	6,001	7,754	11	1	210	275	6	21,521	101	11.8	−30
Tajikistan	909	1,330	..	..	−19	272	38	896	41	17.4	−345
Tanzania	1,482	2,659	20	2	−437	249	46	7,800	22[c,f]	8.6	−345
Thailand	110,110	118,191	75	30	−3,719	1,412	−0	51,307	35	103.7	−50
Togo	755	1,050	47	0	−162	60	10	1,812	83	16.0	−4
Tunisia	10,494	13,177	78	5	−555	593	33	18,700	79	71.1	−20
Turkey	73,275	116,352	85	2	−15,543	2,733	4	161,595	70	54.6	−250
Turkmenistan	4,935	3,588	..	..	..	..	8	..	..	..	−10
Uganda	870	1,810	15	13	−267	222	42	4,822	33[c]	6.8	−15
Ukraine	34,287	36,141	67	5	2,531	1,715	8	21,652	42	25.0	−700
United Kingdom	377,856	501,223	77	24	−57,616	72,561		..	..	156.3	686
United States	904,289	1,732,706	82	32	−804,961	106,831		..	..	269.4	5,800
Uruguay	3,422	3,425	32	2	−103	311	6	12,376	108	30.4	−10
Uzbekistan	4,706	3,640	..	..	..	140	9	5,007	46	..	−300
Venezuela, RB	56,200	24,933	12	3	25,359	1,518	2	35,570	45	10.8	40
Vietnam	32,233	36,881	53	6	−926	1,610	22	17,825	39	58.9	−200
West Bank and Gaza	..	..	..	..	..	..	324	..	..	..	−40
Yemen, Rep.	4,883	4,328	3	13	1,215	144	12	5,488	37	7.7	−100
Zambia	1,720	2,750	10	1	..	334	94	7,279	36	8.0	−65
Zimbabwe	1,490	2,220	29	1	..	60	14	4,798	33	49.6	−50
World	10,392,567t	10,652,542t	77w	20w		664,877s	14w	..s		145.5w	..w[g]
Low income	256,309	310,841	51	4		16,576	15	426,945		32.0	−4,000
Middle income	2,785,199	2,551,288	64	20		194,808	11	2,328,780		68.4	−11,987
Lower middle income	1,512,592	1,375,639	68	23		106,037	10	1,140,272		84.8	−10,086
Upper middle income	1,272,607	1,175,649	61	16		88,771	12	1,188,508		47.0	−1,901
Low & middle income	3,041,588	2,862,091	64	19		211,385	16	2,755,725		63.3	−15,987
East Asia & Pacific	1,185,932	1,059,945	80	34		64,563	4	588,888		105.7	−3,939
Europe & Central Asia	759,841	746,370	57	9		62,212	25	794,943		32.0	−2,665
Latin America & Carib.	561,873	517,073	56	13		60,843	13	778,970		48.9	−4,012
Middle East & N. Africa	221,252	182,440	20	3		5,340	35	163,935		47.3	−2,374
South Asia	123,050	186,039	76	4		7,151	5	193,933		35.5	−1,680
Sub-Saharan Africa	189,636	170,236	31	4		11,276	36	235,056		74.4	−1,318
High income	7,351,037	7,790,420	81	20		453,492	..			166.6	15,970

a. Regional aggregates include data for economies that are not specified elsewhere. World and income group totals include aid not allocated by country or region. b. Includes Luxembourg. c. Data are from debt sustainability analysis undertaken as part of the Heavily Indebted Poor Countries (HIPC) initiative. d. Includes re-exports. e. Data on total exports and imports refer to South Africa only. Data on export commodity shares refer to the South African Customs Union (Botswana, Lesotho, Namibia, and South Africa). f. GNI refers to mainland Tanzania only. g. World total computed by the UN sums to zero, but because the aggregates shown here refer to World Bank definitions, regional and income group totals do not equal zero.

Table 6. Key indicators for other economies

	Population			Population age composition	Gross national income (GNI)[a]		PPP gross national income (GNI)[b]		Gross domestic product	Life expectancy at birth		Adult Literacy rate	Carbon dioxide emissions
	Thousands 2005	Avg. annual % growth 2000–2005	density people per sq. km 2005	% Ages 0–14 2005	Millions of dollars 2005[b]	per capita dollars 2005	Millions of dollars 2005	per capita dollars 2005	per capita % growth 2004–2005	Male Years 2004	Female Years 2004	% ages 15 and older 2000–2004	per capita metric tons 2002
Afghanistan	..	..	..	..	6,957	..[d]	..	..	..	..	..	28	..
American Samoa	58	1.1[c]	292	..	..	..[e]	..	..	..	..	..	..	..
Andorra	66	0.2[c]	141	..	..	..[f]	..	..	..	..	..	..	..
Antigua and Barbuda	81	1.0	184	..	885	10,920	948	11,700	2.6	..	..	..	4.7
Aruba	101	0.8[c]	529	..	..	..[f]	..	..	..	..	..	97	..
Bahamas, The	323	1.4	32	28	..	..[f]	..	..	..	67	74	..	6.7
Bahrain	727	1.6	1,023	27	10,288	14,370	15,470	21,290	5.3	73	76	87	30.6
Barbados	270	0.3	627	19	..	..[e]	..	..	..	73	78	..	4.6
Belize	292	3.1	13	37	1,021	3,500	1,967	6,740	-0.2	69	74	..	3.0
Bermuda	65	0.2	1,293	..	..	..[f]	..	..	..	..	..	..	7.7
Bhutan	918	2.6	20	38	799	870	..	..	3.3	62	65	..	0.5
Botswana	1,765	0.1	3	38	9,145	5,180	18,090	10,250	4.0	36	35	81	2.3
Brunei	374	2.3[c]	71	30	..	..[f]	..	..	..	75	79	93	17.7
Cape Verde	507	2.4	126	40	947	1,870	3,041[g]	6,000[g]	3.0	67	74	..	0.3
Cayman Islands	45	2.3[c]	173	..	..	..[f]	..	..	..	..	..	..	..
Channel Islands	149	0.4	745	16	..	..[f]	..	..	..	76	83	..	..
Comoros	600	2.1	269	42	387	640	1,201[g]	2,000[g]	0.7	61	65	..	0.1
Cuba	11,269	0.3	103	19	..	..[h]	..	..	..	75	79	100	2.1
Cyprus	835	1.2	90	20	13,633	16,510	18,360[g]	22,230[g]	..	77	81	97	8.3
Djibouti	793	2.1	34	42	807	1,020	1,776[g]	2,240[g]	1.4	52	54	..	0.5
Dominica	72	0.2[c]	96	..	273	3,790	400	5,560	2.3	..	..	..	1.7
Equatorial Guinea	504	2.3	18	44	..	..[e]	3,737[g]	7,580[g]	..	42	43	87	0.4
Estonia	1,345	-0.4	32	15	12,244	9,100	20,740	15,420	10.1	66	77	100	11.7
Faeroe Islands	48	0.2[c]	34	..	..	..[f]	..	..	..	..	..	..	..
Fiji	848	0.9	46	32	2,784	3,280	5,052	5,960	0.9	66	70	..	1.6
French Polynesia	257	1.7	70	28	..	..[f]	..	..	..	71	76	..	2.9
Gabon	1,384	1.7	5	40	6,930	5,010	8,151	5,890	0.6	54	55	..	2.6
Gambia, The	1,517	2.8	152	40	442	290	2,913[g]	1,920[g]	2.2	55	58	..	0.2
Greenland	57	0.3	0	..	..	..[f]	..	..	..	..	..	..	10.0
Grenada	107	1.0	313	..	418	3,920	773	7,260	0.2	..	..	..	2.2
Guam	170	1.8	308	30	..	..[f]	..	..	..	73	77	..	25.4
Guinea-Bissau	1,586	3.0	56	48	283	180	1,110	700	0.5	44	46	..	0.2
Guyana	751	0.2	4	29	759	1,010	3,178[g]	4,230[g]	-2.9	61	67	..	2.2
Iceland	295	1.0	3	22	13,671	46,320	10,258	34,760	4.5	78	82	..	7.7
Iraq	..	..	..	..	..	..[h]	..	..	..	..	..	74	..
Isle of Man	77	0.3	135	..	2,138	27,770	..	..	..	..	..	..	..
Kiribati	99	1.8	136	..	137	1,390	..	..	-0.9	..	..	..	0.3
Korea, Dem. Rep.	22,488	0.6	187	25	..	..[d]	..	..	..	61	67	..	6.5
Lesotho	1,795	0.1	59	39	1,718	960	6,120	3,410	1.4	35	37	82	..
Liberia	3,283	1.4	34	47	436	130	..	..	3.9	42	43	..	0.1
Libya	5,854	2.0	3	30	32,354	5,530	..	..	1.5	72	77	..	9.1
Liechtenstein	34	0.6[c]	215	..	..	..[f]	..	..	..	..	..	..	..
Luxembourg	457	0.8	174	19	29,976	65,630	29,841	65,340	3.2	75	81	..	21.3
Macao, China	460	0.7	..	16	..	..[f]	..	..	..	78	82	91	4.0
Maldives	329	2.5	1,097	41	787	2,390	..	..	-6.0	68	67	96	3.4
Malta	404	0.7	1,263	18	5,491	13,590	7,662	18,960	1.8	77	81	88	7.4
Marshall Islands	63	3.6	352	..	185	2,930	..	..	0.2	..	..	..	..
Mauritius	1,248	1.0	615	25	6,560	5,260	15,538	12,450	3.4	69	76	84	2.6
Mayotte	180	4.0[c]	430	..	..	..[e]	..	..	..	..	..	..	..
Micronesia, Fed. Sts.	111	0.6	158	39	254	2,300	..	..	-0.4	67	69	..	..
Monaco	33	0.6[c]	159	..	..	..[f]	..	..	..	..	..	..	..
Myanmar	50,519	1.1	77	29	..	..[d]	..	..	..	58	64	90	0.2
Northern Mariana Islands	79	1.5[c]	161	..	..	..[e]	..	..	..	..	..	..	..
Netherlands Antilles	183	0.8	228	23	..	..[f]	..	..	..	73	79	96	27.8
New Caledonia	234	1.9	13	28	..	..[f]	..	..	..	72	78	..	8.2
Palau	20	1.3[c]	43	..	154	7,630	..	..	4.5	..	..	..	3.5
Puerto Rico	3,911	0.5	441	22	..	..[f]	..	..	..	74	82	..	3.5
Qatar	813	6.2	74	22	..	..[f]	..	..	..	72	76	89	53.0
Samoa	185	0.8	65	41	387	2,090	1,199[g]	6,480[g]	4.8	67	73	..	0.8
San Marino	28	0.7[c]	473	..	..	..[f]	..	..	..	..	..	..	..
Sao Tome and Principe	157	2.3	163	39	60	390	..	..	0.7	62	64	..	0.6
Seychelles	84	0.8	184	..	701	8,290	1,347[g]	15,940[g]	-3.3	..	..	92	6.4
Solomon Islands	478	2.6	17	41	282	590	898	1,880	1.8	62	63	..	0.4
Somalia	8,228	3.2	13	44	..	..[f]	..	..	..	46	48	..	..
St. Kitts and Nevis	48	1.6	133	..	394	8,210	600	12,500	2.7	..	..	..	2.4
St. Lucia	166	1.2	271	29	794	4,800	990	5,980	3.9	72	75	..	2.4
St. Vincent and the Grenadines	119	0.5	305	29	427	3,590	769	6,460	4.4	69	74	..	1.6
Suriname	449	0.7	3	30	1,140	2,540	..	..	4.5	66	73	90	5.1
Swaziland	1,131	1.6	66	41	2,579	2,280	5,870	5,190	0.8	43	42	80	0.9
Timor-Leste	976	4.4	66	41	729	750	..	..	-3.5	..	..	..	..
Tonga	102	0.4	142	36	224	2,190	823[g]	8,040[g]	2.0	71	74	99	1.0
Trinidad and Tobago	1,305	0.3	254	22	13,632	10,440	17,190	13,170	6.4	67	73	..	31.8
United Arab Emirates	4,533	6.7	54	22	102,693	23,770	104,069	24,090	..	77	81	..	25.0
Vanuatu	211	2.0	17	40	338	1,600	670[g]	3,170[g]	4.8	67	71	74	0.4
Virgin Islands (U.S.)	115	1.1	329	24	..	..[f]	..	..	..	76	81	..	92.8

a. Calculated using the World Bank Atlas method. b. PPP is purchasing power parity; see Definitions. c. Data are for 2003–2005. d. Estimated to be low income ($875 or less). e. Estimated to be upper middle ($3,466–$10,725). f. Estimated to be high income ($10,726 or more). g. The estimate is based on regression; others are extrapolated from the latest International Comparison Program benchmark estimates. h. Estimated to be lower middle income ($876–3,465).

Technical notes

These technical notes discuss the sources and methods used to compile the indicators included in this edition of Selected World Development Indicators. The notes follow the order in which the indicators appear in the tables. The Selected World Development Indicators uses terminology in line with the 1993 System of National Accounts (SNA).

Sources

The data published in the Selected World Development Indicators are taken from *World Development Indicators 2006*. Where possible, however, revisions reported since the closing date of that edition have been incorporated. In addition, newly released estimates of population and gross national income (GNI) per capita for 2005 are included in table 1 and table 6.

The World Bank draws on a variety of sources for the statistics published in *World Development Indicators*. Data on external debt for developing countries are reported directly to the World Bank by developing member countries through the Debtor Reporting System. Other data are drawn mainly from the United Nations and its specialized agencies, from the IMF, and from country reports to the World Bank. Bank staff estimates are also used to improve currentcy or consistency. For most countries, national accounts estimates are obtained from member governments through World Bank economic missions. In some instances these are adjusted by staff to ensure conformity with international definitions and concepts. Most social data from national sources are drawn from regular administrative files, special surveys, or periodic censuses.

For more detailed notes about the data, please refer to the World Bank's *World Development Indicators 2006*.

Data consistency and reliability

Considerable effort has been made to standardize the data, but full comparability cannot be assured, and care must be taken in interpreting the indicators. Many factors affect data availability, comparability, and reliability: statistical systems in many developing economies are still weak; statistical methods, coverage, practices, and definitions differ widely; and cross-country and intertemporal comparisons involve complex technical and conceptual problems that cannot be unequivocally resolved. Data coverage may not be complete because of special circumstances or for economies experiencing problems (such as those stemming from conflicts) affecting the collection and reporting of data. For these reasons, although the data are drawn from the sources thought to be most authoritative, they should be construed only as indicating trends and characterizing major differences among economies rather than offering precise quantitative measures of those differences. Discrepancies in data presented in different editions reflect updates by countries as well as revisions to historical series and changes in methodology. Thus readers are advised not to compare data series between editions or between different editions of World Bank publications. Consistent time series are available from *World Development Indicators 2006* CD-ROM and in *WDI Online*.

Ratios and growth rates

For ease of reference, the tables usually show ratios and rates of growth rather than the simple underlying values. Values in their original form are available from *World Development Indicators 2006* CD-ROM. Unless otherwise noted, growth rates are computed using the least-squares regression method (see the *Statistical methods* section below). Because this method takes into account all available observations during a period, the resulting growth rates reflect general trends that are not unduly influenced by exceptional values. To exclude the effects of inflation, constant price economic indicators are used in calculating growth rates. Data in italics are for a year or period other than that specified in the column heading—up to two years before or after for economic indicators and up to three years for social indicators, because the latter tend to be collected less regularly and change less dramatically over short periods.

Constant price series

An economy's growth is measured by the increase in value added produced by the individuals and enterprises operating in that economy. Thus, measuring real growth requires estimates of GDP and its components valued in constant prices. The World Bank collects constant price national accounts series in national currencies and recorded in the country's original base year. To obtain comparable series of constant price data, it rescales GDP and value added by industrial origin to a common reference year, 2000 in the current version of *World Development Indicators*. This process gives rise to a discrepancy between the rescaled GDP and the sum of the rescaled components. Because allocating the discrepancy would give rise to distortions in the growth rate, it is left unallocated.

Summary measures

The summary measures for regions and income groups, presented at the end of most tables, are calculated by simple addition when they are expressed in levels. Aggregate growth rates and ratios are usually computed as weighted averages. The summary measures for social indicators are weighted by population or subgroups of population, except for infant mortality, which is weighted by the number of births. See the notes on specific indicators for more information.

For summary measures that cover many years, calculations are based on a uniform group of economies so that the composition of the aggregate does not change over time. Group measures are compiled only if the data available for a given year account for at least two-thirds of the full group, as defined for the 2000 benchmark year. As long as this criterion is met, economies for which data are missing are assumed to behave like those that provide estimates. Readers should keep in mind that the summary measures are estimates of representative aggregates for each topic and that nothing meaningful can be deduced about behavior at the country level by working back from group indicators. In addition, the estimation process may result in discrepancies between subgroup and overall totals.

Table 1. Key indicators of development

Population is based on the de facto definition, which counts all residents, regardless of legal status or citizenship, except for refugees not permanently settled in the country of asylum, who are generally considered part of the population of the country of origin.

Average annual population growth rate is the exponential rate of change for the period (see the *Statistical methods* section below).

Population density is midyear population divided by land area. Land area is a country's total area excluding areas under inland bodies of water and coastal waterways. Density is calculated using the most recently available data on land area.

Population age composition, ages 0–14 refers to the percentage of the total population that is ages 0–14.

Gross national income (GNI) is the broadest measure of national income, measures total value added from domestic and foreign sources claimed by residents. GNI comprises gross domestic product (GDP) plus net receipts of primary income from foreign sources. Data are converted from national currency to current U.S. dollars using the World Bank Atlas method. This involves using a three-year average of exchange rates to smooth the effects of transitory exchange rate fluctuations. (See the section on statistical methods below for further discussion of the Atlas method.)

GNI per capita is GNI divided by midyear population. It is converted into current U.S. dollars by the Atlas method. The World Bank uses GNI per capita in U.S dollars to classify economies for analytical purposes and to determine borrowing eligibility.

PPP gross national income, which is GNI converted into international dollars using purchasing power parity (PPP) conversion factors, is included because nominal exchange rates do not always reflect international differences in relative prices. At the PPP rate, one international dollar has the same purchasing power over domestic GNI that the U.S. dollar has over U.S. GNI. PPP rates allow a standard comparison of real price levels between countries, just as conventional price indexes allow comparison of real values over time. The PPP conversion factors used here are derived from price surveys covering 118 countries conducted by the International Comparison Program. Data for OECD countries data come from the most recent round of surveys, completed in 1999; data for other countries are from either the 1996 survey or the 1993 or earlier round (extrapolated to the 1996 benchmark). Estimates for countries not included in the surveys are derived from statistical models using available data.

PPP GNI per capita is PPP GNI divided by midyear population.

Gross domestic product (GDP) per capita growth is based on GDP measured in constant prices. Growth in GDP is considered a broad measure of the growth of an economy. GDP in constant prices can be estimated by measuring the total quantity of goods and services produced in a period, valuing them at an agreed set of base year prices, and subtracting the cost of intermediate inputs, also in constant prices. See the section on statistical methods for details of the least-squares growth rate.

Life expectancy at birth is the number of years a newborn infant would live if patterns of mortality prevailing at its birth were to stay the same throughout its life. Data are presented for males and females separately.

Adult literacy rate is the percentage of persons ages 15 and above who can, with understanding, read and write a short, simple statement about everyday life. In practice, literacy is difficult to measure. To estimate literacy using such a definition requires census or survey measurements under controlled conditions. Many countries estimate the number of literate people from self-reported data. Some use educational attainment data as a proxy but apply different lengths of school attendance or level of completion. Because definition and methodologies of data collection differ across countries, data need to be used with caution.

Carbon dioxide emissions (CO_2) measures those emissions stemming from the burning of fossil fuels and the manufacture of cement. These include carbon dioxide produced during consumption of solid, liquid, and gas fuels and from gas flaring. Carbon dioxide per capita is CO_2 divided by the mid-year population.

The Carbon Dioxide Information Analysis Center (CDIAC), sponsored by the U.S. Department of Energy, calculates annual anthropogenic emissions of CO_2. These calculations are derived from data on fossil fuel consumption, based on the World Energy Data Set maintained by the UNSD, and from data on world cement manufacturing, based on the Cement Manufacturing Data Set maintained by the U.S. Bureau of Mines. Each year the CDIAC recalculates the entire time series from 1950 to the present, incorporating its most recent findings and the latest corrections to its database. Estimates exclude fuels supplied to ships and aircraft engaged in international transportation because of the difficulty of apportioning these fuels among the countries benefiting from that transport.

Table 2. Poverty

The World Bank produced its first global poverty estimates for developing countries for the *World Development Report 1990* using household survey data for 22 countries (Ravallion, Datt, and van de Walle 1991). Incorporating survey data collected during the last 15 years, the database has expanded considerably and now includes 440 surveys representing almost 100 developing countries. Some 1.1 million randomly sampled households were interviewed in these surveys, representing 93 percent of the population of developing countries. The surveys asked detailed questions on sources of income and how it was spent and on other household characteristics such as the number of people sharing that income. Most interviews were conducted by staff of government statistics offices. Along with improvements in data coverage and quality, the underlying methodology has also improved, resulting in better and more comprehensive estimates.

Data availability

Since 1979 there has been considerable expansion in the number of countries that field such surveys, the frequency of the surveys, and the quality of their data. The number of data sets rose dramatically from a mere 13 between 1979 and 1981 to 100 between 1997 and 1999. The drop to 41 available surveys after 1999 reflects the lag between the time data are collected and the time they become available for analysis, not a reduction in data collection. Data coverage is improving in all regions, but Sub-Saharan Africa continues to lag, with only 28 of 48 countries having at least one data set available. A complete overview of data availability by year and country can be obtained at http://iresearch.worldbank.org/povcalnet/.

Data quality

The problems of estimating poverty and comparing poverty rates do not end with data availability. Several other issues, some related to data quality, also arise in measuring household living standards from survey data. One relates to the choice of income or consumption as a welfare indicator. Income is generally more difficult to measure accurately, and consumption comes closer to the notion of standard of living. And income can vary over time even if the standard of living does not. But consumption data are not always available. Another issue is that household surveys can differ widely, for example, in the number of consumer goods they identify. And even similar surveys may not be strictly comparable because of differences in timing or the quality and training of survey enumerators.

Comparisons of countries at different levels of development also pose a potential problem because of differences in the relative importance of consumption of nonmarket goods. The local market value of all consumption in kind (including own production, particularly important in underdeveloped rural economies) should be included in total consumption expenditure. Similarly, imputed profit from the production of nonmarket goods should be included in income. This is not always done, though such omissions were a far bigger problem in surveys before the 1980s. Most survey data now include valuations for consumption or income from own production. Nonetheless, valuation methods vary. For example, some surveys use the price in the nearest market, while others use the average farmgate selling price.

Whenever possible, the table uses consumption data for deciding who is poor and income surveys only when consumption data are unavailable. In recent editions of *World Development Indicators*, there has been a change in how income surveys are used. In the past, average household income was adjusted to accord with consumption and income data from national accounts. But in testing this approach using data for some 20 countries for which income and consumption expenditure data were available from the same surveys, income was found to yield not only a higher mean than consumption but also higher inequality. When poverty measures based on consumption and income were compared, these two effects roughly cancelled each other out: statistically, there was no significant difference. Recent editions of *World Development Indicators* use income data to estimate poverty directly, without adjusting average income measures.

International poverty lines

International comparisons of poverty estimates entail both conceptual and practical problems. Countries have different definitions of poverty, and consistent comparisons across countries can be difficult. Local poverty lines tend to have higher purchasing power in rich countries, where more generous standards are used, than in poor countries. Is it reasonable to treat two people with the same standard of living—in terms of their command over commodities—differently because one happens to live in a better-off country?

Poverty measures based on an international poverty line attempt to hold the real value of the poverty line constant across countries, as is done when making comparisons over time. The commonly used $1 a day standard, measured in 1985 international prices and adjusted to local currency using purchasing power parities (PPPs), was chosen for the World Bank's *World Development Report 1990* because it is typical of the poverty lines in low-income countries. PPP exchange rates, such as those from the Penn World Tables or the World Bank, are used because they take into account the local prices of goods and services not traded internationally. But PPP rates were designed for comparing aggregates from national accounts, not for making international poverty comparisons. As a result, there is no certainty that an international poverty line measures the same degree of need or deprivation across countries.

Early editions of *World Development Indicators* used PPPs from the Penn World Tables. Recent editions use 1993 consumption PPP estimates produced by the World Bank. Recalculated in 1993 PPP terms, the original international poverty line of $1 a day in 1985 PPP terms is now about $1.08 a day. Any revisions in the PPP of a country to incorporate better price indexes can produce dramatically different poverty lines in local currency.

Issues also arise when comparing poverty measures within countries. For example, the cost of living is typically higher in urban than in rural areas. One reason is that food staples tend to be more expensive in urban areas. So the urban monetary poverty line should be higher than the rural poverty line. But it is not always clear that the difference

between urban and rural poverty lines found in practice reflects only differences in the cost of living. In some countries the urban poverty line in common use has a higher real value—meaning that it allows the purchase of more commodities for consumption—than does the rural poverty line. Sometimes the difference has been so large as to imply that the incidence of poverty is greater in urban than in rural areas, even though the reverse is found when adjustments are made only for differences in the cost of living. As with international comparisons, when the real value of the poverty line varies it is not clear how meaningful such urban-rural comparisons are.

By combining all this information, a team in the World Bank's Development Research Group calculates the number of people living below various international poverty lines, as well as other poverty and inequality measures that are published in *World Development Indicators*. The database is updated annually as new survey data become available, and a major reassessment of progress against poverty is made about every three years.

Do it yourself: PovcalNet

Recently, this research team developed *PovcalNet*, an interactive Web-based computational tool that allows users to replicate the calculations by the World Bank's researchers in estimating the extent of absolute poverty in the world. *PovcalNet* is self-contained and powered by reliable built-in software that performs the relevant calculations from a primary database. The underlying software can also be downloaded from the site and used with distributional data of various formats. The *PovcalNet* primary database consists of distributional data calculated directly from household survey data. Detailed information for each of these is also available from the site.

Estimation from distributional data requires an interpolation method. The method chosen was Lorenz curves with flexible functional forms, which have proved reliable in past work. The Lorenz curve can be graphed as the cumulative percentages of total consumption or income against the cumulative number of people, starting with the poorest individual. The empirical Lorenz curves estimated by *PovcalNet* are weighted by household size, so they are based on percentiles of population, not households.

PovcalNet also allows users to calculate poverty measures under different assumptions. For example, instead of $1 a day, users can specify a different poverty line, say $1.50 or $3. Users can also specify different PPP rates and aggregate the estimates using alternative country groupings (for example, UN country groupings or groupings based on average incomes) or a selected set of individual countries. *PovcalNet* is available online at http://iresearch.worldbank.org/povcalnet/.

Notes on the 2002 estimates

Survey year is the year in which the underlying data were collected.

Rural poverty rate is the percentage of the rural population living below the national rural poverty line.

Urban poverty rate is the percentage of the urban population living below the national urban poverty line.

National poverty rate is the percentage of the population living below the national poverty line. National estimates are based on population-weighted subgroup estimates from household surveys.

Population below $1 a day and **population below $2 a day** are the percentages of the population living on less than $1.08 a day and $2.15 a day at 1993 international prices. As a result of revisions in PPP exchange rates, poverty rates for individual countries cannot be compared with poverty rates reported in earlier editions of *World Development Indicators.*

Poverty gap is the mean shortfall from the poverty line (counting the nonpoor as having zero shortfall), expressed as a percentage of the poverty line. This measure reflects the depth of poverty as well as its incidence.

Table 3. Millennium Development Goals: eradicating poverty and improving lives

Percentage share of the poorest quintile in national consumption or income is the share of total consumption or income that accrues to the lowest 20 percent of the population.

Prevalence of child malnutrition is the percentage of children under five whose weight for age is less than minus two standard deviations from the median for the international reference population ages 0–59 months. The reference population, adopted by the World Health Organization in 1983, is based on children from the United States, who are assumed to be well nourished. Estimates of child malnutrition are from national survey data. The proportion of children who are underweight is the most common indicator of malnutrition. Being underweight, even mildly, increases the risk of death and inhibits cognitive development in children. Moreover, it perpetuates the problem from one generation to the next, as malnourished women are more likely to have low-birth-weight babies.

Primary completion rate is the percentage of students completing the last year of primary school. It is calculated by taking the total number of students in the last grade of primary school, minus the number of repeaters in that grade, divided by the total number of children of official graduation age. The primary completion rate reflects the primary cycle as defined by the International Standard Classification of Education (ISCED), ranging from three or four years of primary education (in a very small number of countries) to five or six years (in most countries) and seven (in a small number of countries). Because curricula and standards for school completion vary across countries, a high rate of primary completion does not necessarily mean high levels of student learning.

Gender parity ratio in primary and secondary school is the ratio of the female gross enrollment rate in primary and secondary school to the male gross enrollment rate.

Eliminating gender disparities in education would help to increase the status and capabilities of women. This indicator is an imperfect measure of the relative accessibility of schooling for girls. With a target date of 2005, this is the first of the targets to fall due. School enrollment data are reported to the UNESCO Institute for Statistics by national education authorities. Primary education provides children with basic reading, writing, and mathematics skills along with an elementary understanding of such subjects as history, geography, natural science, social science, art, and music. Secondary education completes the provision of basic education that began at the primary level, and aims at laying foundations for lifelong learning and human development, by offering more subject- or skill-oriented instruction using more specialized teachers.

Under-five mortality rate is the probability that a newborn baby will die before reaching age five if subject to current age-specific mortality rates. The probability is expressed as a rate per 1,000. The main sources of mortality date are vital registration systems and direct or indirect estimates based on sample surveys or censuses. To produce harmonized estimates of under-five mortality rates that make use of all available information in a transparent way, a methodology that fits a regression line to the relationship between mortality rates and their reference dates using weighted least squares was developed and adopted by both UNICEF and the World Bank.

Maternal mortality ratio is the number of women who die from pregnancy-related causes during pregnancy and childbirth per 100,000 live births. The values are modeled estimates based on an exercise carried out by the WHO and UNICEF. In this exercise, maternal mortality was estimated with a regression model using information on fertility, birth attendants, and HIV prevalence. This cannot be assumed to provide an accurate estimate of maternal mortality in any country in the table.

Births attended by skilled health staff are the percentage of deliveries attended by personnel trained to give the necessary supervision, care, and advice to women during pregnancy, labor, and the postpartum period; to conduct deliveries on their own; and to care for newborns. The share of births attended by skilled health staff is an indicator of a health system's ability to provide adequate care for pregnant women. Good antenatal and postnatal care improves maternal health and reduces maternal and infant mortality. But data may not reflect such improvements because health information systems are often weak, material deaths are underreported, and rates of maternal mortality are difficult to measure.

Prevalence of HIV is the percentage of people ages 15–49 who are infected with HIV. Adult HIV prevalence rates reflect the rate of HIV infection in each country's population. Low national prevalence rates can be very misleading, however. They often disguise serious epidemics that are initially concentrated in certain localities or among specific population groups and threaten to spill over into the wider population. In many parts of the developing world most new infections occur in young adults, with young women especially vulnerable. The estimates of HIV prevalence are based on extrapolations from data collected through surveys and from surveillance of small, nonrepresentative groups.

Table 4. Economic activity

Gross domestic product is gross value added, at purchasers' prices, by all resident producers in the economy plus any taxes and minus any subsidies not included in the value of the products. It is calculated without deducting for depreciation of fabricated assets or for depletion or degradation of natural resources. Value added is the net output of an industry after adding up all outputs and subtracting intermediate inputs. The industrial origin of value added is determined by the ISIC revision 3. The World Bank conventionally measures GDP in U.S. dollars and applies the average official exchange rate reported by the IMF for the year shown. An alternative conversion factor is applied if the official exchange rate is judged to diverge by an exceptionally large margin from the rate effectively applied to transactions in foreign currencies and traded products.

Gross domestic product average annual growth rate is calculated from constant price GDP data in local currency.

Agricultural productivity refers to the ratio of agricultural value added, measured in constant 2000 U.S. dollars, to the number of workers in agriculture.

Value added is the net output of an industry after adding up all out-puts and subtracting intermediate inputs. The industrial origin of value added is determined by the ISIC revision 3.

Agriculture value added corresponds to ISIC divisions 1–5 and includes forestry and fishing.

Industry value added comprises mining, manufacturing, construction, electricity, water, and gas (ISIC divisions 10–45).

Services value added correspond to ISIC divisions 50–99.

Household final consumption expenditure is the market value of all goods and services, including durable products (such as cars, washing machines, and home computers) purchased by households. It excludes purchases of dwellings but includes imputed rent for owner-occupied dwellings. It also includes payments and fees to governments to obtain permits and licenses. Here, household consumption expenditure includes the expenditures of nonprofit institutions serving households, even when reported separately by the country. In practice, household consumption expenditure may include any statistical discrepancy in the use of resources relative to the supply of resources.

General government final consumption expenditure includes all government current expenditures for purchases of goods and services (including compensation of employees). It also includes most expenditures on national defense and security, but excludes government military expenditures that are part of government capital formation.

Gross capital formation consists of outlays on additions to the fixed assets of the economy plus net changes in the level of inventories and valuables. Fixed assets include land improvements (fences, ditches, drains, etc.); plant, machinery, and equipment purchases; and the construction of buildings, roads, railways, and the like, including commercial and industrial buildings, offices, schools, hospitals, and private dwellings. Inventories are stocks of goods held by firms to meet temporary or unexpected fluctuations in production or sales, along with "work in progress." According to the 1993 SNA, net acquisitions of valuables are also considered capital formation.

External balance of goods and services is exports of goods and services less imports of goods and services. Trade in goods and services comprise all transactions between residents of a country and the rest of the world involving a change in ownership of general merchandise, goods sent for processing and repairs, nonmonetary gold, and services.

The **GDP implicit deflator** reflects changes in prices for all final demand categories, such as government consumption, capital formation, and international trade, as well as the main component, private final consumption. It is derived as the ratio of current to constant price GDP. The GDP deflator may also be calculated explicitly as a Paasche price index in which the weights are the current period quantities of output.

National accounts indicators for most developing countries are collected from national statistical organizations and central banks by visiting and resident World Bank missions. Data for high-income economies are from the OECD.

Table 5. Trade, aid, and finance

Merchandise exports show the free on board (FOB) value of goods provided to the rest of the world, valued in U.S. dollars.

Merchandise imports show the CIF value of goods (the cost of the goods including insurance and freight) purchased from the rest of the world valued in U.S. dollars. Data on merchandise trade come from the World Trade Organization (WTO) in its annual report.

Manufactured exports comprise the commodities in Standard Industrial Trade Classification (SITC) sections 5 (chemicals), 6 (basic manufactures), 7 (machinery and transport equipment), and 8 (miscellaneous manufactured goods), excluding division 68.

High technology exports are products with high R&D intensity. They include high-technology products such as in aerospace, computers, pharmaceuticals, scientific instruments, and electrical machinery.

Current account balance is the sum of net exports of goods and services, net income, and net current transfers.

Foreign direct investment is net inflows of investment to acquire a lasting management interest (10 percent or more of voting stock) in an enterprise operating in an economy other than that of the investor. It is the sum of equity capital, reinvestment of earnings, other long-term capital, and short-term capital, as shown in the balance of payments. Data on the current account balance, private capital flows, and foreign direct investment are drawn from the IMF's *Balance of Payments Statistics Yearbook* and *International Financial Statistics*.

Official development assistance or official aid from the high-income members of the OECD are the main source of official external finance for developing countries, but official development assistance (ODA) is also disbursed by some important donor countries that are not members of OECD's Development Assistance Committee (DAC). DAC has three criteria for ODA: it is undertaken by the official sector; it promotes economic development or welfare as a main objective; and it is provided on concessional terms, with a grant element of at least 25 percent on loans.

Official development assistance comprises grants and loans, net of repayments, that meet the DAC definition of ODA and are made to countries and territories in part I of the DAC list of aid recipients. Official aid comprises grants and ODA-like loans, net of repayments, to countries and territories in part II of the DAC list of aid recipients. Bilateral grants are transfers in money or in kind for which no repayment is required. Bilateral loans are loans extended by governments or official agencies that have a grant element of at least 25 percent and for which repayment is required in convertible currencies or in kind.

Total external debt is debt owed to nonresidents repayable in foreign currency, goods, or services. It is the sum of public, publicly guaranteed, and private nonguaranteed long-term debt, use of IMF credit, and short-term debt. Short-term debt includes all debt having an original maturity of one year or less and interest in arrears on long-term debt.

Present value of debt is the sum of short-term external debt plus the discounted sum of total debt service payments due on public, publicly guaranteed, and private nonguaranteed long-term external debt over the life of existing loans.

The main sources of external debt information are reports to the World Bank through its Debtor Reporting System from member countries that have received World Bank loans. Additional information has been drawn from the files of the World Bank and the IMF. Summary tables of the external debt of developing countries are published annually in the World Bank's *Global Development Finance*.

Domestic credit provided by banking sector includes all credit to various sectors on a gross basis, with the exception of credit to the central government, which is net. The banking sector includes monetary authorities, deposit money banks, and other banking institutions for which data are available (including institutions that do not accept transferable deposits but do incur liabilities such as time and savings deposits). Examples of other banking institutions include savings and mortgage loan institutions and building and loan associations. Data are from the IMF's *International Financial Statistics.*

Net migration is the net average annual number of migrants during the period, that is, the annual number of immigrants less the annual number of emigrants, including both citizens and noncitizens. Data shown in the table are five-year estimates. Data are from the United Nations Population Division's *World Population Prospects: The 2004 Revision.*

Table 6. Key indicators for other economies

See technical notes for table 1, Key indicators of development.

Statistical methods

This section describes the calculation of the least-squares growth rate, the exponential (endpoint) growth rate, and the World Bank's Atlas method for calculating the conversion factor used to estimate GNI and GNI per capita in U.S. dollars.

Least-squares growth rate

Least-squares growth rates are used wherever there is a sufficiently long time series to permit a reliable calculation. No growth rate is calculated if more than half the observations in a period are missing.

The least-squares growth rate, r, is estimated by fitting a linear regression trendline to the logarithmic annual values of the variable in the relevant period. The regression equation takes the form

$$\ln X_t = a + bt,$$

which is equivalent to the logarithmic transformation of the compound growth equation,

$$X_t = X_o (1 + r)t.$$

In this equation, X is the variable, t is time, and $a = \log X_o$ and $b = ln (1 + r)$ are the parameters to be estimated. If b^* is the least-squares estimate of b, the average annual growth rate, r, is obtained as $[\exp(b^*)-1]$ and is multiplied by 100 to express it as a percentage.

The calculated growth rate is an average rate that is representative of the available observations over the entire period. It does not necessarily match the actual growth rate between any two periods.

Exponential growth rate

The growth rate between two points in time for certain demographic data, notably labor force and population, is calculated from the equation

$$r = \ln (p_n /p_1)/n,$$

where p_n and p_1 are the last and first observations in the period, n is the number of years in the period, and ln is the natural logarithm operator. This growth rate is based on a model of continuous, exponential growth between two points in time. It does not take into account the intermediate values of the series. Note also that the exponential growth rate does not correspond to the annual rate of change measured at a one-year interval, which is given by

$$(p_n - p_{n-1})/p_{n-1}.$$

World Bank Atlas method

In calculating GNI and GNI per capita in U.S. dollars for certain operational purposes, the World Bank uses the Atlas conversion factor. The purpose of the Atlas conversion factor is to reduce the impact of exchange rate fluctuations in the cross-country comparison of national incomes. The Atlas conversion factor for any year is the average of a country's exchange rate (or alternative conversion factor) for that year and its exchange rates for the two preceding years, adjusted for the difference between the rate of inflation in the country and that in Japan, the United Kingdom, the United States, and the Euro Zone. A country's inflation rate is measured by the change in its GDP deflator. The inflation rate for Japan, the United Kingdom, the United States, and the Euro Area, representing international inflation, is measured by the change in the SDR deflator. (Special drawing rights, or SDRs, are the IMF's unit of account.) The SDR deflator is calculated as a weighted average of these countries' GDP deflators in SDR terms, the weights being the amount of each country's currency in one SDR unit. Weights vary over time because both the composition of the SDR and the relative exchange rates for each currency change. The SDR deflator is calculated in SDR terms first and then converted to U.S. dollars using the SDR to dollar Atlas conversion factor. The Atlas conversion factor is then applied to a country's GNI. The resulting GNI in U.S. dollars is divided by the midyear population to derive GNI per capita.

When official exchange rates are deemed to be unreliable or unrepresentative of the effective exchange rate during a period, an alternative estimate of the exchange rate is used in the Atlas formula (see below).

The following formulas describe the calculation of the Atlas conversion factor for year t:

$$e_t^* = \frac{1}{3}[e_{t-2}\left(\frac{p_t}{p_{t-2}}/\frac{p_t^{s\$}}{p_{t-2}^{s\$}}\right) + e_{t-1}\left(\frac{p_t}{p_{t-1}}/\frac{p_t^{s\$}}{p_{t-1}^{s\$}}\right) + e_t]$$

and the calculation of GNI per capita in U.S. dollars for year t:

$$Y_t^\$ = (Y_t/N_t)/e_t^*,$$

where e_t^* is the Atlas conversion factor (national currency to the U.S. dollar) for year t, e_t is the average annual exchange rate (national currency to the U.S. dollar) for year t, p_t is the GDP deflator for year t, $p_t^{s\$}$ is the SDR deflator in U.S. dollar terms for year t, $Y_t^\$$ is the Atlas GNI per capita in U.S. dollars in year t, Y_t is current GNI (local currency) for year t, and N_t is the midyear population for year t.

Alternative conversion factors

The World Bank systematically assesses the appropriateness of official exchange rates as conversion factors. An alternative conversion factor is used when the official exchange rate is judged to diverge by an exceptionally large margin from the rate effectively applied to domestic transactions of foreign currencies and traded products. This applies to only a small number of countries, as shown in the primary data documentation table in *World Development Indicators 2006.* Alternative conversion factors are used in the Atlas methodology and elsewhere in the Selected World Development Indicators as single-year conversion factors.

Index

In the index, *b* refers to box, *f* refers to figure, and *t* refers to table.